REMEMBERING THE DEAD

MEMORIA AND REMEMBRANCE PRACTICES

VOLUME 5

Series Editors
Arnoud-Jan Bijsterveld, *The Netherlands*
Sanne Frequin, *The Netherlands*
Tillmann Lohse, *Germany*
Meta Niederkorn, *Austria*
Corine Schleif, *U.S.A.*
Annemarie Stauffer, *Germany*
Anne-Laure Van Bruaene, *Belgium*
Philipp Winterhager, *Germany*

Remembering the Dead

Collective Memory and Commemoration in Late Medieval Livonia

GUSTAVS STRENGA

BREPOLS

Published with the support of the Association for the Advancement of Baltic Studies (Book Publication Subvention)
We acknowledge support for the open access publication from the University of Greifswald

Cover illustration: The Reval *Totentanz* by Bernt Notke (around 1468). Tallinn, Art Museum of Estonia, EKM j 18761

© 2023, Brepols Publishers n.v., Turnhout, Belgium.

This is an open access publication made available under a CC BY-NC 4.0 International License: https://creativecommons.org/licenses/by-nc/4.0/. Some rights reserved. No part of this publication may be reproduced, stored in a retrieval system, or transmitted, in any form or by any means, for commercial purposes, without the prior permission of the publisher, or as expressly permitted by law, by license or under terms agreed with the appropriate reprographics rights organization.

D/2023/0095/199
ISBN 978-2-503-59119-3
eISBN 978-2-503-59120-9
DOI 10.1484/M.MEMO-EB.5.121329
ISSN 2565-8565
eISSN 2565-9804

Printed in the EU on acid-free paper.

To my parents

Contents

List of illustrations   11

Preface   13

List of Abbreviations   15

Introduction   17
   Memory, *Memoria*, and Livonia   19
   Collective Remembering: Cultural Memory, Realms of Memory, and the Present   20
   Medieval Memory and the Research of *Memoria*   23
   Livonia   35

Chapter 1. Remembering Origins   43
   Space and Memory: the Church of Riga Remembering its Beginnings   43
   Teutonic Order in Livonia and Memory of the Origins   53
   Memoria of the Brethren Fallen in Livonia by the Houses of the Western European Bailiwicks   56
   Memoria of the Anonymous Brethren   61
   The Battle at Durbe (1260) as a Site of Memory   63
   Historical Writing and *Memoria*: The Livonian Rhymed Chronicle   67
   Conclusion   72

Chapter 2. Commemoration of a Group and its Leaders   75
   Commemoration of the Brethren in the Teutonic Order   75
   Memoria for a Master: A Leader's Remembrance   79
   Individual Remembrance of the Master: Heidenreich Vincke von Overberg   82
   The Master as Patron of the Remembrance   85
   Commemoration of the Livonian Masters. An Urban Perspective   92
   Heaven, Purgatory, and Hell according to Dietrich Nagel. *Memoria* of the Cathedral Canons in the Late Fifteenth Century   95
   Conclusion   101

Chapter 3. Networks of Memory – Livonia and Beyond   103
   Cistercian Nuns and Dominican Friars as Commemorators in the City   104

Cistercian Networks of Memory   112
Memorial Networks of the Cistercian Nuns in Livonia   115
Annales Dunamundenses: Bonding of the Historical Traditions between the Cistercians and the Teutonic Order   120
Conclusion   130

Chapter 4. Conflict and Memory   133
Memory and the Struggle between the Teutonic Order and the Church of Riga   134
The Residence as a Commemorative Space   141
New Friends and Old Enemies: The Conquest of Memorial Space by the Teutonic Order   144
Conclusion   149

Chapter 5. *Memoria* and Urban Elites   151
Memoria in the Merchant Guilds of Riga and Reval   155
Merchant Table Guilds in Riga and Reval: Between Poor Relief, *Memoria*, and Social Capital   160
The Remembrance of Rich Men: The Botherhoods of the Black Heads in Riga and Reval   171
Ratsmemoria: The Commemoration of the Political Elites   186
Conclusion   197

Chapter 6. *Memoria* and the Non–elites   199
Non–elites in Late Medieval Riga and the Transport Workers' Guilds   201
Commemoration within the Non–elites in Late Medieval Riga   208
Practices of Commemoration: The Fine Book of the Porters Guild (1450–1459)   217
Entfengen in unse broderschop: Elite Members in the Brotherhoods of the Beer Carters and Porters   221
City Councillors and Clergymen as Patrons of *Memoria* in the Non–elite Guilds   227
Elites and the Commemorational Spaces of the Non–elites   233
Conclusion   236

Chapter 7. Reformation and *Memoria*   239
Reformation and *Ratsmemoria*   243
Reformation and *Memoria* of the Elite Guilds in Riga and Reval   244
Reformation and *Memoria* of Non–elite Guilds in Riga   247
Conclusion   252

Conclusion   255

Place Name Equivalents   267

Bibliography 269

Index 311

List of illustrations

Figures

Figure 1:	Map of medieval Livonia (after 1346). Designed by Una Grants	37
Figure 2:	Map of medieval Riga. Designed by Una Grants	39
Figure 3:	Map of medieval Reval. Designed by Una Grants	40
Figure 4:	The chancel of Riga Cathedral and the 19th century replica of the tomb of Bishop Meinhard (on the left side). Photo: Christofer Herrmann, 2016.	48
Figure 5:	Bishop Meinhard's tomb before its partial destruction in 1786. Drawing of J. Ch. Brotze (1742–1823). *Sammlung versebiedner Liefländischen Monumente, Prospecte, Munzen, Wapen etc.* vol. 1, p. 93. LUAB Ms. Photo: University of Latvia Academic Library	49
Figure 6:	Drawing of Meinhard's grave slab by Julius Döring based on an 1883 photograph. *Sitzungsberichte der kurländischen Gesellschaft für Literatur und Kunst, 1886* (Mitau: J.F. Steffenhagen und Sohn, 1887), Taf. I.	51
Figure 7:	Grave slab of Andreas von Steinberg found in the ruins of Ascheraden medieval church. Photo: National History Museum of Latvia, Neg. Nr. 41922	91
Figure 8:	Dünamunde annals. Tallinn, TLA f. 230, n. 1, Cm 8, fol. 29^v. Photo: Tallinn City Archives	124
Figure 9:	The plan of Riga cathedral and placement of the altar of Holy Cross (1). Designed by Una Grants, based on Prānis, *Missale Rigense Livonijas garīgajā kultūrā*, p. 135.	138
Figure 10:	The record commemorating archbishop Silvester Stodewescher in the calendar of Riga Missal. *Missale Rigense*, Rīga, LUAB, R, Ms. 1. Photo: University of Latvia Academic Library	140
Figure 11:	The Reval *Totentanz* by Bernt Notke (around 1468). Tallinn, EKM j 18761. Photo: Art Museum of Estonia, Niguliste Museum	152
Figure 12:	Altarpiece of the Virgin Mary of the brotherhood of the Black Heads in Reval in a half-opened position. Tallinn, EKM j 18760. Photo: Art Museum of Estonia, Niguliste Museum	180
Figure 13:	Altarpiece of the Virgin Mary, a fragment. Photo: Art Museum of Estonia, Niguliste Museum	181
Figure 14:	The plan of St Peter's church in Riga and position of the Porters guild's altar. Designed by Una Grants	235

Preface

Why should we deal with the past and memories? During my studies I consciously tried to avoid the history of the twentieth–century and the conflicting pasts it has produced. Yet my background and cultural experiences in my native Latvia have constantly reminded me that the history and memories about the traumatic experiences of the past are permanently present. Furthermore, it made me aware that memories of the past have an impact on the actions of individuals and groups in the present. As a medievalist, I was driven by a curiosity about that how groups and societies in the pre–modern past have dealt with their memories of different kinds of experiences and why they commemorated certain people and events. Livonia (modern–day Latvia and Estonia) was an intriguing case study for such processes.

This book is based on the doctoral dissertation *Remembering the Dead: Collective Memoria in Late Medieval Livonia*, which I defended at Queen Mary University of London in 2013. Thus, I am grateful to my supervisor Miri Rubin who guided me around the cliffs and treacherous sandbanks in my attempt to navigate the high seas of doctoral research. Her supervision has been instrumental for this book and in my career. I have been incredibly lucky to have met numerous friendly and generous and yet demanding supervisors and academic mentors. At the University of Latvia, Aleksandrs Gavriļins and Ilgvars Misāns fostered my interest in medieval history. Gerhard Jaritz at the Central European University and a fruitful year spent in Budapest set me on the path of further research into medieval *memoria* culture. Birgit Studt at the University of Freiburg, offered invaluable feedback and much–needed intellectual guidance during my Freiburg years.

I owe a great debt to my academic colleagues for supporting me during this lengthy path. The long conversations and intensive collaboration with Sharon Adams, Andris Levāns, Jānis Krēsliņš Jr. have resulted in better–formulated thoughts, numerous research questions and ideas integrated in this book. I am grateful to David D'Avray and Matthias Thumser for sharing their time and thoughts on medieval *memoria* and Livonia. Academic comradery and friendship with fellow medievalists Kati Ihnat and Erik Niblaeus influenced my research during my PhD studies. Colleagues Pauls Daija, Cordelia Heß, and Marek Tamm have provided encouragement and support for the continuation of my scholarly work. Una Bergmane, who led by a good example, persuaded me to finally publish this book. I want to thank Emily Thelen and Una Grants for making this book better.

This book would not have been possible without the financial support of the Deutsche Forschungsgemeinschaft (DFG) and the PhD research group 'Friends, Patrons, Clients' (GRK 1288) at the University of Freiburg. The Herder Institute in Marburg kindly financed a necessary two-month research stay in Marburg. I am also grateful to many other people and organisations who have supported my studies financially, among them the Latvian Welfare Fund in the United Kingdom and late Andrejs V. Ozolins. My heartfelt thanks also go out to Māris Gailis and to Sarmīte Ēlerte. Finally, the Association for the Advancement of Baltic Studies (AABS) provided much-needed financial support for the publication of this book.

Many archivists, librarians, and historians have offered their help and advice during the course of my research. Juhan Kreem and Tiina Kala in the Tallinn City Archives never hesitated to answer even the most difficult question. Aija Taimiņa from the University of Latvia Academic Library shared her knowledge of late medieval manuscripts with me, and Kārlis Zvirgzdiņš led me through the labyrinths that are the Latvian State Historical Archives. Architecture historians Agnese Bergholde and Christofer Herrmann provided me with several essential images, while colleagues Johannes Götz and Gregory Leighton helped to locate the Teutonic Order's sources in the archives. Rūta Brusbārde shared her research and knowledge of Riga's urban sources. The staff members of the British Library, Freiburg University library, the National Library of Latvia, Hamburg City Archives, and the National Archives of Estonia also supported me during the research.

My friends accompanied me during the long process of creating this book, and I am deeply grateful to them. Last but not least, I am thankful to my parents for the constant support that they have offered me.

Finally, the Association for the Advancement of Baltic Studies (AABS) and the University of Greifswald provided much-needed financial support for the publication of this book.

List of Abbreviations

DOZA	Wien, Deutschordenszentralarchiv
DSHI	Marburg, Dokumentensammlung des Herder–Instituts
EAA	Tartu, Rahvusarhiiv (National Archives of Estonia, former Eesti Ajalooarhiiv),
EKM	Tallinn, Eesti Kunstimuuseum (Art Museum of Estonia)
GStA PK	Berlin, Geheimen Staatsarchiv Preußischer Kulturbesitz
LGU	Livländische Güterurkunden
LMAVB	Vilnius, Lietuvos mokslų akademijos Vrublevskių biblioteka (The Wroblewski Library of the Lithuanian Academy of Sciences)
LSL	Linköping, Linköping Stifts– och Landsbiblioteket (Linköping Diocesan and Regional Library)
LUAB	Rīga, Latvijas Universitātes Akadēmiskā Bibliotēka (University of Latvia Academic Library)
LUB	Liv–, est– und kurländisches Urkundenbuch
LVVA	Rīga, Latvijas Nacionālais arhīvs, Latvijas Valsts vēstures arhīvs (Latvian National Archive, Latvian State Historical Archives)
StAH	Hamburg, Staatsarchiv der Freien und Hansestadt Hamburg
StAL	Ludwigsburg, Stadtarchiv Ludwigsburg
TLA	Tallinn, Tallinna Linnaarhiiv (Tallinn City Archives)
UUB	Uppsala, Uppsala universitetsbibliotek (Uppsala University Library)

Introduction

> Obliuion the cancard enemie to Fame and renounce the suckyng serpent of aunciente memory, the dedly darte to the glory of princes, and the defacer of all conquestes and notable actes (…) How muche therfore are princes, gouernoures and noble menne bounde to theim whiche haue so liuely set furth the liues and actes of their parentes, that all though thei bee ded by mortall death, yet thei by writyng and Fame liue and bee contiunally present. (…) Thus, writyng is the keye to enduce vertue, and represse vice. Thus memorie maketh menne ded many a thousande yere still to liue as though thei were present.[1]
>
> Edward Hall (c. 1498–1547)

> *Memoria (ist) die Überwindung des Todes und des Vergessens durch Gedächtnis und Erinnerung (…)*[2]
>
> Memoria is the overcoming of death and oblivion by means of memory and remembrance (…)
>
> Otto Gerhard Oexle (1939–2016)

Mourning and commemoration of the dead are fundamental parts of the human experience and can be found in every society and culture.[3] As Aleida Assmann has argued, commemoration of the dead, has been a basic form of collective memory throughout human history.[4] In ancient Egypt, for example, the commemoration of the dead was one of the cores of long lasting collective

---

1 Edward Hall, *The Vnion of the Two Noble and Illustre Famelies of Lancastre [and] Yorke*, [..] (London: Richard Grafton, 1550), p. 1.
2 Otto Gerhard Oexle, 'Memoria in der Gesellschaft und Kultur des Mittelalters', in *Modernes Mittelalter. Neue Bilder einer populären Epoche*, ed. by Joachim Heinzle (Frankfurt am Main: Insel-Verlag, 1994), pp. 297–323, 297.
3 On the universality of death and relationships of the living and the dead in different cultures, see Nigel Barley, *Dancing on the Grave: Encounters with Death* (London: John Murray, 1995).
4 Aleida Assmann, *Cultural Memory and Western Civilization: Functions, Media, Archives* (Cambridge: Cambridge University Press, 2011), p. 23, the German edition: Aleida Assmann, *Erinnerungsräume: Formen und Wandlungen des kulturellen Gedächtnisses* (München: Beck, 2006), p. 33.

memory.⁵ *Memoria* – commemoration of the dead – played an essential role in medieval and early modern European society. It was not just a religious phenomenon, an attempt through prayers to lessen the suffering of the souls in purgatory. *Memoria*, as a form of collective memory and social practice, created groups, shaped their identities, helped to remember the past, and created relationships between individuals and groups.

Memory studies are interdisciplinary, touching on fields in the humanities and social sciences and ranging over cultures and periods. The increase in the study of collective memory in the humanities and social sciences over the past several decades has created a certain 'memory boom'. There is abundance of inspiring, innovative, and mediocre research; as Jeffrey Olick has rightly pointed out, the texts produced annually on the topic in their entirety cannot be bought by an individual nor read.⁶ Despite the abundance of studies on collective memory, historical research on how societies in the past remembered has yet to reveal the ways and strategies by which they formed their identities and perceived themselves. This book aims to bring together the two – medieval commemoration and collective memory – using the tools and theoretical concepts developed by those who have researched memory in different time periods and cultures.

Medieval commemoration of course has a strong religious component. Most scholars have worked on medieval *memoria* as a religious phenomenon.⁷ This book approaches late medieval *memoria* as both a form of collective memory in which the past was recollected and a social practice that shaped the present and the future. The particular emphasis here is put on the role of *memoria* in creating and sustaining medieval groups, their identities, and relationships in a specific European region – Livonia (modern day Latvia and Estonia) – revealing the memorial practices of a range of social groups who lived side by side. Moreover, the study of memory sheds light on different aspects of the political, social, and cultural life of groups and societies in a particular European region.

---

5 Jan Assmann, *Cultural Memory and Early Civilization: Writing, Remembrance, and Political Imagination* (Cambridge: Cambridge University Press, 2011), p. 45; the German edition: Jan Assmann, *Das kulturelle Gedächtnis: Schrift, Erinnerung und politische Identität in frühen Hochkulturen* (München: Beck, 1992), pp. 60–63; Jan Assmann, *Der Tod als Thema der Kulturtheorie: Todesbilder und Totenriten im Alten Ägypten* (Frankfurt am Main.: Suhrkamp, 2000).

6 On the development of studies of collective memory, see Jeffrey K. Olick and Joyce Robbins, 'Social Memory Studies. From "Collective Memory" to the Historical Sociology of Mnemonic Practices', *Annual Review of Sociology*, 24 (1998), 105–40; Jeffrey K. Olick, '"Collective Memory": A Memoir and Prospect', *Memory Studies*, 1 (2008), 23–30; for more general overview see, *Cultural Memory Studies: An International and Interdisciplinary Handbook*, ed. by Astrid Erll and Ansgar Nünning (Berlin: de Gruyter, 2008); *A Cultural History of Memory in the Early Modern Age*, ed. by Marek Tamm and Alessandro Arcangeli (London: Bloomsbury, 2020).

7 The research of *memoria* is discussed below.

Memory, *Memoria*, and Livonia

This study focuses not only on the practice of remembering but also on the impact of *memoria* on groups and relationships within groups. Why focus on group *memoria*? *Memoria* is used here as a tool to study memorial practices and social history. In my view, *memoria* both constitutes and reflects social relations. Moreover, in commemoration individual practices become collective. *Memoria* reveals individuality, but this is cast in a collective framework. *Memoria* is a group phenomenon, a cyclical process that creates groups, as groups create *memoria*. The repetition of names, rituals, and regular invocation of events contributed to a collective memory. The practices of commemoration can also be signs of affiliation with a group. *Memoria* creates and sustains relationships between individuals and groups. The regularity of practice and repetition that commemoration builds reinforces and renews the coherence and sense of identity in groups, while involvement in memorial activities further reinforces the individual participant's sense of self, of belonging.

This book approaches the analysis of group remembrance with a number of questions in mind. Some of these are generic to the study of remembrance in late medieval European society, while others are more directly linked to the socio-political particularities of Livonia. How did political elites use *memoria* and memories of their groups' origins for self-legitimation and the maintenance of power? What impact did *memoria* have on the relationships between the groups that exercised power in Livonia, particularly during periods of conflict? In what ways did *memoria* operate to form groups and shape the dynamics of the relationship between individuals and groups and between groups? How did groups use their past to maintain their identities in the present? How did participation in joint memorial practices influence the relationships between the German urban elites and the indigenous non-elites folk? How was *memoria* of various groups dissolved during the Reformation, and what impact did the dissolution have on them? The guiding principle of this book is that the study of *memoria* should not be limited to liturgical manifestations but that it be considered – as Otto Gerhard Oexle has put it – as a 'total social phenomenon' that had impact on all spheres of human activities.

This book takes the form of a series of case studies, which illustrate specific phenomena of memory and commemoration within Livonian social groups and institutions. The chapters are divided according to the phenomena of commemoration and remembering: the myths and stories of beginnings (Chapter 1); the commemoration of leaders (Chapter 2); the networks of memory (Chapter 3); conflict and memory (Chapter 4); the role of *memoria* for the urban power and elite groups (Chapter 5); the remembrance of the poor (Chapter 6); and the Reformation and *memoria* (Chapter 7).

The book focuses on numerous groups active in medieval Livonia: the urban elites in Riga and Reval; urban non-elite groups in Riga; the Teutonic Order in Livonia; and the Livonian clergy (particularly the archbishops of Riga and their chapter) and religious communities. The selection of the case studies has been influenced by the strengths and weaknesses of surviving documentation and by the specific characteristics of the region. Although this book does not focus solely on elite *memoria*, peasants and urban artisan groups cannot be extensively considered due to the lack of source material. The Livonian cities did not have well-developed urban history writing and communal memory like towns in German-speaking Western Europe.[8] The memorial practices of the nobility are also not examined in detail, since Livonia did not have courts with memorial culture, such as existed elsewhere in Europe.[9] Despite these obvious weaknesses of the regional source material, the unique landscape of memorial practices can be studied over a long period through contrasting social groups and the role that memory played in their conflicts and crises.

The timeframe of this study is late medieval, focusing on case studies from the early fifteenth to the early sixteenth centuries, but it also uses evidence from the earlier period where available and from across the Reformation in the mid-1520s. From the early fifteenth century onwards, source material is continuous and rich, and it allows us to conduct the analysis of group *memoria*. Although *memoria* also continued to exist after the Reformation in the Protestant environments, this study focuses on it medieval forms and their dissolution during the religious reform in the 1520s.

Collective Remembering: Cultural Memory, Realms of Memory, and the Present

Since the concept of collective memory and the ones deriving from it are essential for this book, I would like to present them here briefly. Though disputed and challenged, Maurice Halbwachs's concept of collective memory has fundamentally shaped the way we look at how premodern groups and societies remembered the past. In his book *Social Frameworks of Memory* (*Les Cadres sociaux de la mémoire*) published in 1925, Halbwachs reminds us that collective memory is shaped by individual memories, which influence on collective memory differently.[10] In his view, 'it is individuals as group members

---

8 *Städtische Geschichtsschreibung in Spätmittelalter und Früher Neuzeit – Standortbestimmung und Perspektiven eines Forschungsfelds*, ed. by Pia Eckhart and Marco Tomaszewski (Göttingen: V&R unipress, 2019).

9 Only a dozen noble testaments and few foundation charters survive from medieval Livonia, and thus detailed group analysis is not possible. For testaments of the Livonian noblemen, see 'Testamente Adeliger aus dem fünfzehnten und sechzehnten Jahrunderte', in *Archiv für die Geschichte Liv–, Est– und Kurlands* 4 (1845), 209–24; *Livländische Güterurkunden*, vols. 1–2, ed. by Hermann von Bruiningk and Nikolaus Busch (Riga: Jonck & Poliewsky, Gulbis, 1908–1923), [hereafter LGU] 1, nos. 142, 147; LGU 2, no. 80, 193.

10 Maurice Halbwachs, *Les cadres sociaux de la mémoire* (Paris: Félix Alcan, 1925); for English translation of this work, see Maurice Halbwachs, *On Collective Memory*, trans. by Lewis A. Coser (Chicago: University of Chicago Press, 1992).

who remember. While these remembrances are mutually supportive of each other and common to all, individual members still vary in the intensity with which they experience them'.[11] However, Halbwachs also argues that memories of individuals are socially mediated, exposed to the collective memory of groups, and this enables individuals to 'remember' events they have never experienced.[12] According to Halbwachs, even our most intimate memories – which are not shared – are bound to collective memory.[13] Thus, on the one hand, collective memory is created by individual memories, while on the other, the 'social frame' influences individual memories, even those that are not held collectively. Halbwachs also notes that the collective memory does not exceed the boundaries of the group.[14] Already shortly after publishing his first book on collective memory, Halbwachs was criticised, for example, by historian Marc Bloch for collectivisation of individual psychological phenomena.[15]

The concept of cultural memory developed by German Egyptologist Jan Assmann is beneficial to every work on premodern collective memory.[16] Assmann studied ancient Egyptian, Babylonian, Greek, and Jewish cultures through their means of preserving the past. In Assmann's view, collective memory consists of several components that include communicative memory sustained by language and communication and cultural memory, which uses written and visual carriers of information.[17] Communicative memory is based on everyday communications: it is not organized, refers to recent events, and lasts for three to four generations, a century at most.[18] Because eyewitnesses die, communicative memory has to be transformed into cultural memory to survive longer than forty to eighty years after an event.[19] Cultural memory is set apart from the everyday; it is codified and organized, refers to the more

---

11 Maurice Halbwachs, *The Collective Memory*, trans. by Francis J. Ditter, jr. and Vida Yazdi Ditter (New York: Harper & Row, 1980), p. 48.
12 Halbwachs demonstrates these shared memories and experiences using the example of the family, see Halbwachs, *On Collective Memory*, pp. 52–83; Jeffrey K. Olick, 'Collective Memory. The Two Cultures', *Sociological Theory*, 17, 3 (1999), 333–48 (335).
13 Halbwachs, *On Collective Memory*, p. 53.
14 Halbwachs, *The Collective Memory*, p. 80; Olick, 'Collective Memory', p. 334.
15 Halbwachs wrote two additional books on the collective memory: one was published during his lifetime, the other posthumously, see Maurice Halbwachs, *La topographie légendaire des Évangiles en Terre Sainte: étude de mémoire collective* (Paris: Presses universitaires de France, 1941); Maurice Halbwachs, *La mémoire collective* (Paris: Presses universitaires de France, 1950), English translation Halbwachs, *The Collective Memory*; for Bloch's criticism, see Marc Bloch, *Mémoire collective, tradition et coutume. À propos d'un livre récent.* (Paris: La renaissance du livre, 1925); English translation, Marc Bloch, 'From "Mémoire Collective, Tradition et Coutume: À Propos d'un Livre Récent"', in *The Collective Memory Reader*, ed. by Jeffrey K. Olick, Vered Vinitzky-Seroussi, and Daniel Levy (Oxford: Oxford University Press, 2011), pp. 150–55; Astrid Erll, *Memory in Culture*, trans. by Sara B. Young (Basingstoke: Palgrave Macmillan, 2011), p. 14.
16 Assmann, *Cultural Memory and Early Civilization*, pp. 21–33.
17 Assmann, *Cultural Memory and Early Civilization*, pp. 5–6.
18 Assmann, *Cultural Memory and Early Civilization*, pp. 36–37; Jan Assmann, 'Collective Memory and Cultural Identity', *New German Critique*, 65 (1995), 125–34 (126–27).
19 Assmann, *Cultural Memory and Early Civilization*, p. 41; Assmann, 'Collective Memory and Cultural Identity', p. 128.

distant past, and is transformed into myth.[20] Cultural memory is constructed and maintained by a wide range of media: texts, monuments, images, rituals, and feasts.[21] Although Assmann's analysis is based on ancient cultures, he emphasises the universality of communicative and cultural memory. In his view, 'the concept of cultural memory comprises that body of reusable texts, images, and rituals specific to each society in each epoch, whose "cultivation" serves to stabilise and convey that society's self–image.'[22]

Jan Assmann's thoughts have proven to be influential in the field of memory studies, and scholars working far beyond Ancient cultures have applied his concept of cultural memory.[23] Aleida Assmann has been one of the prime examples of the application of this concept to the studies of early modern literature and commemorative culture in twentieth–century Germany.[24] Cultural and communicative memory as concepts are beneficial for the research of the commemoration of the dead because they demonstrate the variety of carriers used for the remembrance: written and engraved belonging to cultural memory, and ephemeral ones, such as memories of eyewitnesses, that belong to the realm of communicative memory.

The concept of realms of memory helps to convey the importance of memories for the identities of groups and nations. French historian Pierre Nora has formulated two concepts: *lieux de mémoire* – sites (realms) of memory – and *milieux de mémoire* – environments of memory.[25] *Lieux de mémoire* directly refer to the ancient mnemotechnics and *loci memoriae*, which are not real spaces but imaginary ones, which 'exist because *milieux de mémoire* have disappeared and are essentially fictional, mediated and relative'.[26] Etienne François and Hagen Schulze, being influenced by Nora's work, have defined the realms of memory as places of remembrance that are 'long–lasting, generational focal points of collective memory and identity that are embedded in social, cultural, and political practices and that change as their modes of perception, appropriation, application, and transmission change'.[27] Describing French sites of memory, Nora and his colleagues in the monumental work *Realms of Memory*

---

20 Assmann, *Cultural Memory and Early Civilization*, pp. 37–38.
21 Assmann, *Cultural Memory and Early Civilization*, pp. 41–44.; Assmann, 'Collective Memory and Cultural Identity', p. 129.
22 Assmann, 'Collective Memory', p. 132.
23 Erll, *Memory in Culture*, pp 27–37.
24 Aleida Assmann, *Erinnerungsräume: Formen und Wandlungen des kulturellen Gedächtnisses* (München: Beck, 2006); Aleida Assmann, 'Canon and Archive', in *Cultural Memory Studies: An International and Interdisciplinary Handbook*, pp. 97–108; Aleida Assmann, 'Theories of Cultural Memory and the Concept of "Afterlife"', in *Afterlife of Events: Perspectives on Mnemohistory*, ed. by Marek Tamm (Basingstoke: Palgrave Macmillan, 2015), pp. 79–94; Aleida Assmann, *Der lange Schatten der Vergangenheit: Erinnerungskultur und Geschichtspolitik* (München: Beck, 2006).
25 Pierre Nora, 'Between Memory and History. Les Lieux de Mémoire', *Representations*, 26 (1989), 7–24.
26 Devesh Soneji, *Unfinished Gestures: Devadāsīs, Memory, and Modernity in South India* (Chicago: University of Chicago Press, 2012), p. 17.
27 *Deutsche Erinnerungsorte*, vol. 1, ed. by Etienne François and Hagen Schulze (München: Beck, 2001), p. 18.

have defined numerous events, institutions, spaces, notions, and processes as the sites of memory, for example, Joan of Arc, the Eiffel Tower, the Vichy regime, *La Marseillaise* and others.²⁸ Although the notions of *lieux de mémoire* and *milieux de mémoire* have been predominantly studied in modern nation states, they can also be fruitfully applied to medieval societies.²⁹

Collective memory can be broadly defined as 'the means by which information is transmitted among individuals and groups and from one generation to another'.³⁰ Collective memory is not just the flow of information about the past, it 'involves sets of practices like commemoration and monument building and general forms like tradition, myth, or identity.'³¹ It is definitely not the 'truth' about the past. Medievalist Chris Wickham and social anthropologist James Fentress have stated that 'social memory is, in fact, often selective, distorted, and inaccurate.'³² As historian Wulf Kansteiner argues, the memory 'can take hold of historically and socially remote events but it often privileges the interests of the contemporary.'³³ Sociologist Barry Schwartz has similarly observed that 'collective memory reflects reality by interpreting the past in terms of images appropriate and relevant to the present; it shapes reality by providing people with a program in terms of which their present lines of conduct can be formulated and enacted.'³⁴ Thus, collective memory not only reflects the past but also reflects and, moreover, shapes the present moment when memories are recalled. In my opinion, the study of collective memory illustrates practices of remembering the past but equally demonstrates how societies and groups in certain points of time perceive the past, perform, and enact it, as well as how they structure the information they wish to pass on to succeeding generations.

Medieval Memory and the Research of *Memoria*

The 'memory boom' has also influenced medieval studies. The early scholarship on memory in the Middle Ages was led by Frances Yates and Mary

---

28 *Realms of Memory: The Construction of the French Past*, 3 vols, ed. by Pierre Nora and Lawrence D. Kritzman, trans. by Arthur Goldhammer (New York: Columbia University Press, 1996–1998).
29 Jean-Marie Moeglin, 'Hat das Mittelalter europäische Lieux de Mémoire erzeugt?', *Jahrbuch für Europäische Geschichte*, 3 (2002), 17–38; Bernd Schneidmüller, 'Europäische Erinnerungsorte im Mittelalter', *Jahrbuch für Europäische Geschichte*, 3 (2002), 39–58.
30 Carole L. Crumley, 'Exploring Venues of Social Memory', in *Social Memory and History: Anthropological Perspectives*, ed. by Jacob Climo and Maria G. Cattell (Walnut Creek: AltaMira Press, 2002), pp. 39–52, p. 39.
31 Olick and Robbins, 'Social Memory Studies', p. 106.
32 James Fentress and Chris Wickham, *Social Memory* (Oxford: Blackwell, 1992), p. xi.
33 Wulf Kansteiner, 'Finding Meaning in Memory. A Methodological Critique of Collective Memory Studies', *History and Theory*, 41.2 (2002), 179–97 (180).
34 Barry Schwartz, *Abraham Lincoln and the Forge of National Memory* (Chicago: University of Chicago Press, 2000), p. 18.

Carruthers.³⁵ These studies, however, focus on the 'art of memory' (*ars memorativa/ars memoriae*) and the techniques of remembering as part of medieval intellectual culture.³⁶ This book follows a different path. Though, as Gadi Algazi has pointed out, *memoria* as mnemotechnics and *memoria* as the commemoration of the dead are linked, here we will discuss *memoria* as commemoration and collective remembering.³⁷

Collective memory has come to the attention of medieval historians too. Yet, most medievalists have – intentionally or unintentionally – avoided using the term 'collective memory'.³⁸ This may be due to the fact that the sources they work with do not easily lend themselves to that kind of approach, or perhaps they have made only limited use of concepts developed primarily for other periods.³⁹ Nonetheless, some forms of collective memory have been studied in depth and benefit from a strong research tradition. Since the late 1960s, German medievalists have worked on the remembrance of the dead in the Middle Ages, known as *memoria*. *Memoriaforschung* (also *Memoria-Forschung, Memorialforschung*), which started as a positivistic prosopographic analysis of lists of names found in confraternity books (*libri vitae* and *libri memoriales*) of the early medieval monastic communities.⁴⁰ The subject has developed over the last five decades into a diverse and rich research topic for medievalists and early modernists.⁴¹ During this period of dynamic development, scholars of *memoria* have formulated not only new approaches and methodologies, but also important theoretical concepts, which now can be

---

35 Mary J. Carruthers, *The Book of Memory: A Study of Memory in Medieval Culture* (Cambridge: Cambridge University Press, 1990); Frances A. Yates, *The Art of Memory* (Chicago: University of Chicago Press, 1966), pp. 55–128.
36 For the recent research of medieval memory see, *Creative Selection between Emending and Forming Medieval Memory*, ed. by Gerald Schwedler and Sebastian Scholz (Berlin: de Gruyter, 2022); *A Cultural History of Memory in the Middle Ages*, vol. 2, ed. by Gerald Schwedler (London: Bloomsbury Academic, 2020); *The Making of Memory in the Middle Ages*, ed. by Lucie Doležalová (Leiden: Brill, 2010).
37 Gadi Algazi, 'Forget Memory: Some Critical Remarks on Memory, Forgetting and History', in *Damnatio in Memoria: Deformation und Gegenkonstruktionen von Geschichte*, ed. by Sebastian Scholz, Gerald Schwedler, and Kai-Michael Sprenger (Köln: Böhlau, 2014), pp. 25–34, p. 26.
38 For example, Wickham and Fentress intentionally avoid using the term 'collective memory'. See Fentress and Wickham, *Social Memory*, p. ix.
39 Because Jan Assmann's work has great influence on German medievalists, they have recently begun using the term *Errinerungskulturen* to describe cultures of remembering in different social groups, for example, within the nobility. See *Adelige und bürgerliche Erinnerungskulturen des Spätmittelalters und der Frühen Neuzeit*, ed. by Werner Rösener (Göttingen: Vandenhoeck und Ruprecht, 2001).
40 Karl Schmid, 'Personenforschung und Namenforschung am Beispiel der Klostergemeinschaft von Fulda', *Frühmittelalterliche Studien*, 5 (1971), 235–67; Karl Schmid and Joachim Wollasch, 'Societas et Fraternitas. Begründung eines kommentierten Quellenwerkes zur Erforschung der Personen und Personengruppen des Mittelalters', *Frühmittelalterliche Studien*, 9 (1975), 1–48.
41 On the development of *Memoriaforschung*, see Dieter Geuenich, 'Von der Adelsforschung zur Memoriaforschung', in *Pro remedio et salute anime peragemus: Totengedenken am Frauenstift Essen im Mittelalter*, ed. by Thomas Schilp (Essen: Klartext, 2008), pp. 9–18; Michael Borgolte, 'Memoria. Zwischenbilanz eines Mittelaltersprojekts', *Zeitschrift für Geschichtswissenschaft*, 46 (1998), 197–211; Michael Borgolte, 'Zur Lage der deutschen Memoria-Forschung', in *Memoria. Ricordare e dimenticare nella cultura del medioevo: Trento, 4–6 aprile 2002*, ed. by Michael Borgolte, Cosimo Damiano Fonseca, and Hubert Houben (Bologna: Il mulino, 2005), pp. 21–28.

described as 'classical'.⁴² Joachim Wollasch and Karl Schmid led with their work on memorial sources, and commemorational and charitable practices in the early medieval monasteries provided an initial research framework.⁴³ Otto Gerhard Oexle, however, brought a new vibrancy and has laid down theoretical foundations of *Memoriaforschung* since the 1970s.

Memoria is a form, a manifestation of collective memory. Oexle has defined *memoria* as 'the overcoming of death and oblivion by means of memory and remembrance'.⁴⁴ According to Assmann, the commemoration of the dead stands between communicative and cultural memory, because it utilises both.⁴⁵ *Memoria* is 'communicative' in its 'human form' of everyday secular and religious practices of mourning and remembering, and 'cultural' in its forms of transmission, e.g. texts and images, monuments and rituals, historical and literary writings, and institutions.⁴⁶ Medieval *memoria* was not just memory of the past but also a social practice that bound together the living and the dead; it created a community.⁴⁷ In Oexle's view *memoria* combines ways of thinking and practice and involves both individuals and groups.⁴⁸ *Memoria* has to be seen as a form of memory that was also cultural practice, arising from remembering the past.

This book builds on several key concepts developed by Oexle and his colleagues: the presence of the dead in the present, *memoria's* socially constitutive character, *memoria* as a 'total social phenomenon', and *memoria* as gift exchange. One of Oexle's key contentions is that through commemorating the person by name, the physically absent living and dead were made present (*Vergegenwärtigung*) during the liturgy and other commemorative events.⁴⁹ Oexle further claims that the dead are invoked as individuals in the act of

---

42 Borgolte, 'Zur Lage der deutschen Memoria-Forschung', p. 21.
43 Karl Schmid and Joachim Wollasch, 'Die Gemeinschaft der Lebenden und Verstorbenen in Zeugnissen des Mittelalters', *Frühmittelalterliche Studien*, 1 (1967), 365–405; Karl Schmid, 'Das liturgische Gebetsgedenken in seiner historischen Relevanz am Beispiel der Verbrüderungsbewegung des Frühen Mittelalters', in *Gebetsgedenken und adliges Selbstverständnis im Mittelalter: Ausgewählte Beiträge : Festgabe Zu Seinem Sechzigsten Geburtstag*, by Karl Schmid, ed. by Gerd Althoff and Dieter Geuenich (Sigmaringen: J. Thorbecke, 1983), pp. 620–44; Schmid and Wollasch, 'Societas et Fraternitas', pp. 1–48; *Memoria: der geschichtliche Zeugniswert des liturgischen Gedenkens im Mittelalter*, ed. by Karl Schmid and Joachim Wollasch (München: Fink, 1984); *Gedächtnis, das Gemeinschaft stiftet*, ed. by Karl Schmid and Joachim Wollasch (München: Schnell und Steiner, 1985); Joachim Wollasch, 'Toten- und Armensorge', in *Gedächtnis, das Gemeinschaft stiftet*, pp. 9–38.
44 Oexle, 'Memoria in der Gesellschaft', p. 297.
45 Assmann, *Das kulturelle Gedächtnis*, p. 61.
46 Assmann, *Das kulturelle Gedächtnis*, p. 61; Oexle, 'Memoria in der Gesellschaft', p. 297.
47 Otto Gerhard Oexle, 'Die Gegenwart der Toten', in *Death in the Middle Ages*, ed. by Herman Braet and Werner Verbeke (Leuven: Leuven University Press, 1983), pp. 19–77, p. 29; Schmid and Wollasch, 'Gemeinschaft der Lebenden und Verstorbenen', pp. 365–405.
48 Oexle, 'Memoria in der Gesellschaft', p. 297.
49 Oexle, 'Gegenwart der Toten', p. 22, 25; Otto Gerhard Oexle, 'Memoria und Memorialbild', in *Memoria. Der geschichtliche Zeugniswert*, pp. 384–440, p. 385; Otto Gerhard Oexle, 'Memoria und Memoriaüberlieferung im frühen Mittelalter', in *Frühmittelalterliche Studien* 10 (1976), 70–95 (79–80).

speaking their names aloud (*Namensnennung*).[50] This adds to his argument that the dead in the Middle Ages retained their legal rights and continued to be subjects of social relationships.[51] Thanks to commemoration, the dead never left the community and *memoria* could be defined as 'the creation of community by making the absent present in a non-physical way.'[52]

Making the dead present during the liturgy was a focal point of *memoria*, but it was not the only way in which the presence of the dead was realised.[53] Liturgical remembrance was just one of the forms of *memoria*.[54] Oexle recognises historical and social *memoria* alongside liturgical *memoria*.[55] *Memoria* has also frequently been divided into liturgical and non-liturgical remembrance. Non-liturgical forms of *memoria*, like commemoration of the dead during communal meals, however, have received less attention from scholars working on *memoria*.

Oexle makes use of Mauss' concept of a gift when he claims that *memoria* was a 'total social phenomenon'.[56] According to this interpretation *memoria* influenced all spheres of life: religion, economy, everyday life, philosophy, law, art, literature, historiography, social relationships, social behaviours, and social practices.[57] Yet, this claim of 'totality' cannot be perceived as the reduction of every medieval phenomenon to the remembering of the dead.[58] The 'totality' of *memoria* was linked to a variety of practices and manifestations of *memoria*.

Memoria's 'totality' meant that it was manifested through a wide range of media. *Memoria* was created by and reflected in written texts: necrologies, last wills, foundation charters, legal documents, account books of different institutions, liturgical manuscripts, and historiographical, hagiographical, and

---

50 Oexle, 'Gegenwart der Toten', p. 31. Halbwachs also refers to the speaking of names as an important element of remembering, see Halbwachs, *On Collective Memory*, p. 71.
51 Oexle, 'Gegenwart der Toten', p. 22.
52 David L. D'Avray, *Medieval religious rationalities: a Weberian analysis* (Cambridge: Cambridge University Press, 2010), p. 35.
53 Lusiardi, 'Die Lebenden und Toten', p. 674.
54 Thomas Schilp, 'Totengedenken des Mittelalters und kulturelles Gedächtnis. Überlegungen zur Perspektive der Memorialforschung für das Frauenstift Essen', in *Pro remedio et salute anime peragemus: Totengedenken am Frauenstift Essen im Mittelalter*, ed. by Thomas Schilp (Essen: Klartext, 2008), pp. 19–38, p. 29.
55 Otto Gerhard Oexle, 'Die Gegenwart der Lebenden und der Toten. Gedanken über Memoria', in *Gedächtnis das Gemeinschaft stiftet*, pp. 74–107, pp. 74–75; Oexle, 'Memoria und Memoriaüberlieferung', p. 84.
56 Marcel Mauss, *The Gift : The Form and Reason for Exchange in Archaic Societies*, trans. W.D. Halls (London: Routledge, 1990), p. 3; Oexle, 'Memoria in der Gesellschaft', p. 301; Borgolte, 'Memoria. Zwischenbalanz', p. 207.
57 Oexle, 'Memoria in der Gesellschaft', p. 301; Otto Gerhard Oexle, 'Die mittelalterlichen Gilden. Ihre Selbstdeutung und ihr Beitrag zur Formung sozialer Strukturen', in *Soziale Ordnungen im Selbstverständnis des Mittelalters*, ed. by Albert Zimmermann (Berlin: de Gruyter, 1979), pp. 203–26, p. 206; on *memoria* and literature see Friedrich Ohly, 'Bemerkungen eines Philologen zur Memoria', in *Memoria. Der geschichtliche Zeugniswert des liturgischen Gedenkens im Mittelalter*, pp. 9–68.
58 Schilp, 'Totengedenken des Mittelalters', pp. 21–22.

literary works as well.⁵⁹ Likewise, objects played a crucial role in the creation of *memoria*. Grave slabs, altars and altarpieces, statues, murals, liturgical vessels, church buildings, and chapels enhanced memorial practice and served as media of *memoria*.⁶⁰

Memoria was a socially constitutive phenomenon, which helped create and maintain medieval groups, and shaped their identities.⁶¹ The scholars of *Memoriaforschung* have formulated remembrance of the dead as 'memory that creates a community' (*Gedächtnis das Gemeinschaft stiftet*) that united the living and also the living with the dead.⁶² In Oexle's view, remembrance of the dead was particularly important for the existence of noble families and kin groups: 'without *memoria* there exists no "nobility" (*Adel*) and therefore also no legitimation for noble power'.⁶³ *Memoria* demonstrated not only the longevity of the bloodline and the line of succession but also its origins. As Jan Assmann famously expressed it, 'power requires origin'.⁶⁴

The concept of *memoria* as a socially constitutive phenomenon is equally applicable to groups other than nobility. Oexle demonstrates *memoria's* constitutive character with the example of medieval urban guilds and brotherhoods, for whom *memoria* was essential, because it provided a feeling of security for its members and thus assurance of the guild's abilities to provide not only social but also spiritual support.⁶⁵ *Memoria* also created a sense of the group's continuity and an awareness of its history; by remembering dead individuals, groups remembered their pasts.⁶⁶ Therefore, memorial sources reflect not only

---

59 On historical writing and *memoria*, see Oexle, 'Gegenwart der Toten', pp. 27; Hans-Werner Goetz, *Geschichtsschreibung und Geschichtsbewußtsein im hohen Mittelalter* (Berlin: Akademie-Verlag, 1999), pp. 297–300; on hagiography and *memoria*, see Franz Neiske, 'Vision und Totengedenken', *Frühmittelalterliche Studien* 20 (1986): 137–85; on necrologies and memoria, see Franz Neiske, 'Die Ordnung der Memoria. Formen necrologischer Tradition im mittelalterlichen Klosterverband', in *Institution und Charisma: Festschrift für Gert Melville zum 65. Geburtstag*, ed. by Franz J. Felten, Annette Kehnel, and Stefan Weinfurter (Cologne: Böhlau, 2009), pp. 127–37.

60 Oexle, 'Memoria und Memorialbild', pp. 384–440, p. 384–90; Oexle, 'Gegenwart der Lebenden', pp. 74–107, pp. 85–99; for the memorial character of grave slabs, see Andreas Zajic, 'Jahrtag und Grabdenkmal. Spätmittelalterliche Stiftungen und die Realien der Memoria', in *Freund Hein? Tod und Ritual in der Geschichte*, ed. by Wolfgang Hameter, Meta Niederkorn-Bruck, and Martin Scheutz (Innsbruck: Studien-Verlag, 2007), pp. 82–99; Michael Borgolte, 'Das Grab in der Topographie der Erinnerung. Vom sozialen Gefüge des Totengedenkens im Christentum vor der Moderne', *Zeitschrift für Kirchengeschichte* 111 (2000): pp. 291–312; *Memory and the Medieval Tomb*, ed. by Elizabeth Valdez del Alamo and Carol Stamatis Pendergast (Aldershot: Ashgate, 2000).

61 Otto Gerhard Oexle, 'Memoria als Kultur', in *Memoria als Kultur*, ed. by Otto Gerhard Oexle (Göttingen: Vandenhoeck & Ruprecht, 1995), pp. 9–78, p. 37; Oexle, 'Gegenwart der Lebenden', p. 75.

62 *Gedächtnis das Gemeinschaft stiftet*, pp. 7–8; Otto Gerhard Oexle, 'Liturgische Memoria und historische Erinnerung. Zur Frage nach dem Gruppenbewußtsein und dem Wissen der eigenen Geschichte in den mittelalterlichen Gilden', in *Tradition als historische Kraft: interdisziplinäre Forschungen zur Geschichte des früheren Mittelalters*, ed. by Norbert Kamp and Joachim Wollasch (Berlin: de Gruyter, 1982), pp. 323–40, p. 333; Assmann, *Cultural Memory and Early Civilization*, p. 16.

63 Oexle, 'Memoria als Kultur', p. 38.

64 Assmann, *Cultural Memory and Early Civilization*, p. 54.

65 Oexle, 'Liturgische Memoria', p. 335.

66 Oexle, 'Gegenwart der Toten', p. 34; Oexle, 'Liturgische Memoria', p. 333; Otto Gerhard Oexle, 'Soziale Gruppen in der Ständegesellschaft. Lebensformen des Mittelalters und ihre historischen Wirkungen', in

religious or social practices but also the historical self-consciousness.[67] For medieval groups it was important to remember their dead founders, because as part of the founding myth (*Ursprungsmythos*) also known as foundational memory, they shaped group identities in the present.[68]

Memoria created groups, but it also created and reflected social relationships.[69] Most frequently these were relationships between founders or donors, who made material contributions, and commemorators, who prayed for these benefactors. This relationship can be described as a spiritual 'gift economy'.[70] Motivated by *memoria*, material gifts in the form of real property, money, and valuables were exchanged for immaterial goods, such as prayers, as a counter-gift.[71] This gift exchange 'created and preserved the memory of the dead,' and during the early Middle Ages involved the nobility and monastic communities as partners in exchange for spiritual goods.[72] Thus, the foundation, a material bequest directed for a specific purpose, was one of the elements that created *memoria*, granted it financial resources, and ensured its longevity.[73] Equally, charity was a practice of *memoria*, in which the rich exchanged their alms – food and clothing – for the prayers of the poor.[74] Food and drink were part of medieval *memoria* because monastic communities and urban associations commemorated their deceased members during festive communal meals.[75]

Although Oexle's perception of *memoria* is widely accepted, some scholars have challenged it and have emphasized the limited temporal nature of

---

Die Repräsentation der Gruppen: Texte – Bilder – Objekte, ed. by Otto Gerhard Oexle and Andrea von Hülsen-Esch (Göttingen: Vandenhoeck und Ruprecht, 1998), pp. 9–44, p. 31.

67 Gerd Althoff, 'Geschichtsbewußtsein durch Memorialüberlieferung', in *Hochmittelalterliches Geschichtsbewußtsein im Spiegel nichthistoriographischer Quellen*, ed. by Hans-Werner Goetz (Berlin: Akademie-Verlag, 1998), pp. 85–100, p. 87.

68 Assmann, *Das kulturelle Gedächtnis*, p. 76; Althoff, 'Geschichtsbewusstsein', p. 86.

69 Oexle, 'Memoria und Memorialüberliefung', p. 95.

70 D'Avray, *Medieval Religious Rationalities*, p. 31.

71 Michael Borgolte, 'Totale Geschichte' des Mittelalters? Das Beispiel der Stiftungen. Antrittsvorlesung, 2. Juni 1992. (Berlin: Präsidentin der Humboldt-Universität, 1993), p. 13; Oexle, 'Memoria und Memoriaüberlieferung', p. 87; Arnoud-Jan Bijsterveld, *Do ut Des: Gift Giving, Memoria, and Conflict Management in the Medieval Low Countries* (Hilversum: Verloren, 2007); Arnoud-Jan Bijsterveld, 'The Medieval Gift as Agent of Social Bonding and Political Power: A Comparative Approach', in *Medieval Transformations. Texts, Power, and Gifts in Context*, ed. by Esther Cohen and Mayke De Jong (Leiden: Brill, 2001), pp. 124–56, pp. 133–40.

72 Patrick J. Geary, *Phantoms of Remembrance: Memory and Oblivion at the End of the First Millennium* (Princeton: Princeton University Press, 1994), p. 77.

73 Borgolte, 'Totale Geschichte', pp. 3–18; Michael Borgolte, 'Stiftungen des Mittelalters im Spannungsfeld von Herrschaft und Genossenschaft', in *Memoria in der Gesellschaft des Mittelalters*, ed. by Dieter Geuenich and Otto Gerhard Oexle (Göttingen: Vandenhoeck & Ruprecht, 1994), pp. 267–85, pp. 267–85; Karl Schmid, 'Stiftungen für das Seelenheil', in *Gedächtnis das Gemeinschaft stiftet*, pp. 51–73; Christine Sauer, *Fundatio und memoria: Stifter und Klostergründer im Bild: 1100 bis 1350* (Göttingen: Vandenhoeck & Ruprecht, 1993), p. 16.

74 Wollasch, 'Toten- und Armensorge', pp. 9–38; Joachim Wollasch, 'Gemeinschaftsbewußtsein und soziale Leistung im Mittelalter', *Frühmittelalterliche Studien*, 9 (1975), 268–86.

75 Otto Gerhard Oexle, 'Mahl und Spende im mittelalterlichen Totenkult', *Frühmittelalterliche Studien*, 18 (1984), 401–20; Oexle, 'Gegenwart der Lebenden', p. 81; Oexle, 'Gegenwart der Toten', pp. 48–57; Oexle, 'Mittelalterlichen Gilden', p. 214; Wollasch, 'Gemeinschaftsbewußtsein', pp. 271–75.

memoria. French historian Jean-Claude Schmitt controversially argues that *memoria* 'as a form of collective memory was a social technique of forgetting'.[76] Schmitt claims that the function of *memoria* 'was to "cool off" the memory under the guise of maintaining it, to soothe the painful memory of the deceased until their memory became indistinct.' In Schmitt's view *memoria* served to shorten the stay of the dead 'in purgatorial punishment (or in purgatory), and finally, to enable the living to forget the deceased.'

This understanding of *memoria* clashes with the tradition of *Memoriaforschung*. Ralf Lusiardi counters Schmitt, describing *memoria* rather as 'a social technique of mourning', which helped individuals to deal with the deaths of those who meant a great deal to them.[77] *Memoria* had no temporal boundaries, medieval people wanted to be commemorated in perpetuity, but *memoria* could fade if it was not properly maintained, as could any other form of collective memory.

Belief in the existence of purgatory and fear of purgatorial punishment were essential motivations for late medieval remembrance, but *memoria* was not dependent on them. Practices of *memoria* predated the ideas of purgation after death and the high Middle Ages, when according to Jacques Le Goff purgatory 'was born'.[78] By the eighth and ninth centuries, monastic communities were commemorating dead members and sustained the *memoria* of their secular founders.[79] The relationship between *memoria* and purgatory can be explicitly seen during the Reformation. Liturgical remembrance and the theological justification for it were abolished, but *memoria* continued to exist in Protestant culture, albeit in a changed form.[80] According to Oexle, the real period of change was the eighteenth century when social and legal attitudes towards the dead changed radically.[81]

Medieval remembrance of the dead embodied at one and the same time religious aspirations for a future in the uncertain afterlife and the collective memory of the dead that shaped identities and created communities, uniting

---

76 Jean-Claude Schmitt, *Ghosts in the Middle Ages: The Living and the Dead in Medieval Society*, trans. by Teresa Lavender Fagan (Chicago: University of Chicago Press, 1998), pp. 5–6.

77 Ralf Lusiardi, 'Die Lebenden und die Toten. Spätmittelalterliche Memoria zwischen Vergegenwärtigung und Vergessen', *Annali Dell'Istituto Storico Italo-Germanico in Trento*, 27 (2001), 671–90 (687).

78 D'Avray, *Medieval Religious Rationalities*, p. 35; Jacques Le Goff, *La Naissance Du Purgatoire* (Paris: Gallimard, 1981).

79 Oexle, 'Gegenwart der Toten', p. 28; Schmid and Wollasch, 'Gemeinschaft der Lebenden und Verstorbenen', pp. 370–89; Schmid, 'Liturgische Gebetsgedenken', pp. 620–44.

80 For *memoria* after the Reformation, see Otto Gerhard Oexle, 'Die Memoria der Reformation', in *Die Wirklichkeit und das Wissen: Mittelalterforschung – Historische Kulturwissenschaft – Geschichte und Theorie der historischen Erkenntnis*, ed. by Bernhard Jussen, Andrea von Hülsen-Esch, and Frank Rexroth (Göttingen: Vandenhoeck & Ruprecht, 2011), pp. 187–242, pp. 199–215; Oexle, 'Memoria als Kultur', pp. 53–57; Craig Koslofsky, *The Reformation of the Dead: Death and Ritual in Early Modern Germany, 1450–1700* (Basingstoke: Macmillan Press, 2000); Craig Koslofsky, 'From Presence to Remembrance. The Transformation of Memory in the German Reformation', in *The Work of Memory: New Directions in the Study of German Society and Culture*, ed. by Alon Confino and Peter Fritzsche (Chicago: University of Illinois Press, 2002), pp. 25–38.

81 Oexle, 'Gegenwart der Toten', pp. 21, 71–72.

individuals across the past, present, and future.[82] Here religious beliefs and collective memory combined. Memorial prayers and masses offered spiritual benefits but were also a ritualized form of remembering that bonded groups together.

Memoria has been extensively researched by several generations of scholars. As mentioned, during the initial stages of the *Memoriaforschung*, researchers focused on the remembrance of early medieval monastic communities and aristocratic families.[83] During this early stage, *memoria* was approached from theological and liturgical perspectives.[84] From the mid-1980s on, the approach broadened and became more interdisciplinary.[85] In addition to the study of the textual memorial sources, *memoria* scholarship now embraces the artistic and architectural manifestations of remembrance.[86] Also musicologists have been involved in the research of *memoria*.[87] The geographical scope of *memoria* studies expanded as well, and *memoria* in southern Europe and in Orthodox Rus' has been studied alongside research on commemoration in northern and western Europe.[88]

Until the 1990s, the study of medieval commemoration was dominated by German scholarship but since then has become an international field of research. Patrick Geary significantly opened up the field with his two books

---

82 Schilp, 'Totengedenken des Mittelalters', p. 24.

83 Joachim Wollasch, 'Die mittelalterlicher Lebensform der Verbrüderung', in *Memoria. Der geschichtliche Zeugniswert*, pp. 215–32; Gerd Althoff was active in the research into the Ludophian and Ottonian *memoria* from the 1970s, see his Gerd Althoff, *Adels- und Königsfamilien im Spiegel ihrer Memorialüberlieferung: Studien zum Totengedenken der Billunger und Ottonen: Bestandteil des Quellenwerkes, Societas et Fraternitas* (München: W. Fink, 1984); Gerd Althoff, *Amicitiae und pacta: Bündnis, Einung, Politik und Gebetsgedenken im beginnenden 10. Jahrhundert* (Hannover: Hahn, 1992).

84 Arnold Angenendt, 'Theologie und Liturgie der mittelalterliche Toten-Memoria', in *Memoria. Der geschichtliche Zeugniswert*, pp. 79–199; Arnold Angenendt, 'Buße und liturgisches Gedenken', in *Gedächtnis das Gemeinschaft stiftet*, pp. 39–50.

85 Truus van Bueren, Kim Ragetli, and Arnoud-Jan Bijsterveld, 'Researching Medieval Memoria: Prospects and Possibilities. With an Introduction to Medieval Memoria Online (MeMO)', *Jaarboek voor Middeleeuwse Geschiedenis*, 14 (2011), 183–234.

86 A selected bibliography on *memoria* and art: Renate Kroos, 'Grabbräuche–Grabbilder', in *Memoria. Der geschichtliche Zeugniswert*, pp. 285–353; Oexle, 'Memoria und Memorialbild', pp. 387–94; Alarich Rooch, *Stifterbilder in Flandern und Brabant: Stadtbürgerliche Selbstdarstellung in der Sakralen Malerei des 15. Jahrhunderts* (Essen: Die Blaue Eule, 1988); *Grabmäler: Tendenzen der Forschung an Beispielen aus Mittelalter und früher Neuzeit*, ed. by Wilhelm Maier, Wolfang Schmid, and Michael Viktor Schwarz (Berlin: Gebrüder Mann, 2000); Caroline Horch, *Der Memorialgedanke und das Spektrum seiner Funktionen in der bildenden Kunst des Mittelalters* (Königstein im Taunus: Langewiesche, 2001); *Grab, Kult, Memoria: Studien zur gesellschaftlichen Funktion von Erinnerung*, ed. by Carolin Behrmann, Horst Bredekamp, and Philipp Zitzlsperger (Köln: Böhlau, 2007); Antje Fehrmann, 'Grabmal und Totengedächtnis im westlichen Mittelalter', in *Sterben, Tod und Trauer in den Religionen und Kulturen der Welt*, ed. by Christoph Elsas (Hamburg: EB-Verlag, 2007), pp. 281–98.

87 van Bueren, Ragetli, and Bijsterveld, 'Researching Medieval Memoria: Prospects and Possibilities', p. 198.

88 On *memoria* in Italy, see Thomas Frank, *Studien zu italienischen Memorialzeugnissen des XI. und XII. Jahrhunderts* (Berlin: de Gruyter, 1991); Thomas Frank, 'Bruderschaften, Memoria und Recht im spätmittelalterlichen Italien', in *Memoria. Ricordare*, pp. 327–46; on the late medieval and early modern Russian Orthodox *memoria*, see Ludwig Steindorff, *Memoria in Altrussland: Untersuchungen zu den Formen christlicher Totensorge* (Stuttgart: Steiner, 1994).

on early medieval remembering and forgetting and the relationship between the living and the dead.[89] In the *Phantoms of Remembrance* Geary puts the commemoration of the dead in the social and political setting of northern France, the Rhine region, and Bavaria, thus demonstrating how rulers and aristocracy used memory for the creation of their identities and the fostering of power. Geary's work demonstrates *memoria* in action, showing the memory's mnemotechnical aspect – sustaining knowledge –, its historiographical aspect in creating narratives about the past, and also its gender aspect – what role women played in remembering.

In recent few decades, the remembrance of the dead in the Middle Ages has been researched by the scholars whose methodological approaches have not been based on the *Memoriaforschung* research tradition. Their studies of commemoration in the medieval European cities and commemorative cultures of European aristocracies have contributed greatly on our knowledge about medieval commemoration.[90]

Though the preponderance of studies of medieval commemoration has decreased, the role of memory and commemoration in medieval culture still attracts scholarly attention.[91] During the last three decades, numerous digital projects have emerged, and the book series *Memoria and Remembrance practices*, in which this monograph is published, has been established.[92] The

---

89 Geary, *Phantoms of Remembrance*; Patrick J. Geary, *Living with the Dead in the Middle Ages* (Ithaca: Cornell University Press, 1994).

90 Jacques Chiffoleau, *La Comptabilité de l'au–Delà: Les Hommes, La Mort et La Religion Dans La Région d'Avignon à La Fin Du Moyen Âge (Vers 1320 – Vers 1480)* (Rome: École française de Rome, 1980); Megan McLaughlin, *Consorting with Saints: Prayer for the Dead in Early Medieval France* (Ithaca: Cornell University Press, 1994); *The Place of the Dead: Death and Remembrance in Late Medieval and Early Modern Europe*, ed. by Bruce Gordon and Peter Marshall (Cambridge: Cambridge University Press, 2000); Christopher Daniell, *Death and Burial in Medieval England, 1066–1550* (London: Routledge, 1997); Steven R. Bassett, *Death in Towns: Urban Responses to the Dying and the Dead, 100–1600* (Leicester: Leicester University Press, 1992); *Memory and Commemoration in Medieval England: Proceedings of the 2008 Harlaxton Symposium*, ed. by Caroline M. Barron and Clive Burgess (Donington: Tyas, 2010); Nigel Saul, *Death, Art, and Memory in Medieval England: The Cobham Family and Their Monuments, 1300–1500* (Oxford: Oxford University Press, 2001); Charlotte A. Stanford, *Commemorating the Dead in Late Medieval Strasbourg: The Cathedral's Book of Donors and Its Use (1320–1521)* (Farnham: Ashgate, 2011).

91 *Memory and Commemoration in Medieval Culture*, ed. by Elma Brenner, Mary Franklin–Brown, and Meredith Cohen (London: Routledge, 2016).

92 *Care for the Here and the Hereafter: Memoria, Art and Ritual in the Middle Ages*, ed. by Truus van Bueren and Andrea van Leerdam (Turnhout: Brepols, 2005); Truus van Bueren and Wilhelmina C. M. Wüstefeld, *Leven Na de Dood: Gedenken in de Late Middeleeuwen* (Turnhout: Brepols, 1999); MeMO database on memoria in the Netherlands at http://memo.hum.uu.nl/ (accessed: 01.03.2022); *Reformations and Their Impact on the Culture of Memoria*, ed. by Truus van Bueren and others (Turnhout: Brepols, 2016); *Memoria, Erinnerungskultur, Historismus: zum Gedenken an Otto Gerhard Oexle (28. August 1939 – 16. Mai 2016)*, ed. by Thomas Schilp and Caroline Horch (Turnhout: Brepols, 2019); Thomas Schilp, *Stadtgesellschaft und Memoria: die Ausrichtung auf das Jenseits und ihre sozialen Implikationen*, ed. by Arnoud–Jan Bijsterveld, Meta Niederkorn–Bruck and Annemarie Staufer (Turnhout: Brepols, 2023).

relationship between *memoria* and forgetting has also been researched.⁹³ Commemoration in northern Europe has recently received attention as well.⁹⁴ Somewhat surprisingly, the region that is the focus of this book – medieval Livonia – has been featured in numerous studies, allowing Livonian *memoria* to be put in a European context. *Memoria* of the urban groups including guilds, brotherhoods, religious communities, and merchant families in the Livonian cities have been researched.⁹⁵ The scholars have studied the culture of memory in Livonian historiography, described commemoration of the Livonian clergymen, and the memorial culture of the Livonian branch of the Teutonic Order.⁹⁶

---

93 See volume *Damnatio in Memoria: Deformation und Gegenkonstruktionen von Geschichte* and Gerald Schwedler, *Vergessen, Verändern, Verschweigen und damnatio memoriae im frühen Mittelalter* (Köln: Böhlau, 2020).

94 Mads Vedel Heilskov, 'The Commemoration of the Lay Elite in the Late Medieval Danish Realm, c. 1340–1536: Rituals, Community and Social Order' (unpublished PhD thesis, University of Aberdeen, 2018); Anna-Stina Hägglund features commemoration in her thesis *Birgittine Landscapes: Three Monasteries in Their Local and Regional Environment across the Baltic Sea Region c. 1410–1530* (Åbo: Åbo Akademis förlag, 2022); Piotr Kołodziejczak, 'Pious Gifts in Late Medieval Stockholm in the Context of Baltic Towns' (unpublished PhD Thesis, Uniwersytet Mikołaja Kopernika w Toruniu, 2023).

95 Anu Mänd, 'Church Art, Commemoration of the Dead and the Saints' Cult. Constructing Individual and Corporate Memoria in Late Medieval Tallinn', *Acta Historica Tallinnensia*, 16 (2011), 3–30; Anu Mänd, 'Frauen, Memoria und Sakralräume im spätmittelalterlichen Livland', *Forschungen zur baltischen Geschichte*, 8 (2013), 11–39; Kadri-Rutt Allik, 'Revaler Testamente aus dem 15. Jahrhundert. Das Testament des Revaler Bürgers Gerd Satzem (1491)', in *Zeitschrift für Ostmitteleuropaforschung 46/2* (1997), pp. 178–204; Kadri-Rutt Hahn, *Revaler Testamente im 15. und 16. Jahrhundert* (Berlin: LIT, 2015); Anu Mänd, 'Memoria and Sacral Art in Late Medieval Livonia: The Gender Perspective', in *Images and Objects in Ritual Practices in Medieval and Early Modern Northern and Central Europe*, ed. by Krista Kodres and Anu Mänd (Newcastle upon Tyne: Cambridge Scholars, 2013), pp. 239–73; Gustavs Strenga, '"Bidden vor myner sele". The Dominicans as Intercessors Between Townspeople and God in Late Medieval Reval', in *Annual of Medieval studies at CEU* 13 (2007), 111–32; Gustavs Strenga, 'Cistercian Networks of Memory: Commemoration as a Form of Institutional Bonding in Livonia and beyond during the Late Middle Ages', in *Making Livonia : Actors and Networks in the Medieval and Early Modern Baltic Sea Region*, ed. by Anu Mänd and Marek Tamm (London: Routledge, 2020), pp. 212–31; Gustavs Strenga, 'Donations, Discipline and Commemoration. Creating Group Identity in the Transport Workers Guilds of Mid Fifteenth-Century Riga', *Journal of Medieval History*, 48, 1 (2022), 103–28.

96 Linda Kaljundi, *The Baltic Crusades and the Culture of Memory: Studies on Historical Representation, Rituals, and Recollection of the Past* (Helsinki: University of Helsinki, 2016); Andris Levāns, 'Die lebendigen Toten. Memoria in der Kanzlei der Erzbischöfe von Riga im Spätmittelalter', in *Kollektivität und Individualität: der Mensch im östlichen Europa: Festschrift für Prof. Dr. Norbert Angermann zum 65. Geburtstag*, ed. by Karsten Brüggemann, Thomas M. Bohn, and Konrad Maier (Hamburg: Kovač, 2001), pp. 3–35; Anu Mänd, 'Church Art, Commemoration of the Dead and the Saints' Cult', pp. 3–30; Anu Mänd, 'Vicarius, Canonicus et Episcopus: Three Late Medieval Grave Slabs from Tartu and Tallinn', *Baltic Journal of Art History*, 7 (2014), 11–30; Gustavs Strenga, 'Remembering the common past: Livonia as a lieu de mémoire of the Teutonic Order in the Empire', in *Livland – eine Region am Ende der Welt? Forschungen zum Verhältnis zwischen Zentrum und Peripherie im späten Mittelalter = Livonia – a region at the end of the world? Studies on the relations between centre and periphery in the later Middle Ages*, ed. by Anti Selart and Matthias Thumser (Köln: Böhlau, 2017), pp. 347–70; Gustavs Strenga, 'Distorted Memories and Power: Patrons of the Teutonic Order in the Fifteenth Century Prayer of the Livonian Branch', *Journal of Baltic Studies*, 50, 2 (2019), 143–61; Anu Mänd, 'Visuelle Memoria: die Grabplatten der livländischen Ordensmeister und Gebietiger', *Forschungen zur baltischen Geschichte*, 15 (2020), 59–92; Anu Mänd, 'Rome, Rostock and a Remote Region: Art Commissions and Networks of

Research has focused not only on the liturgical dimension of *memoria* but also on its social aspects, including for example, the relationship between gift giving and *memoria*.[97] The memorial cultures of the late medieval aristocracy have also attracted the attention of historians.[98] Likewise the gender aspects of the aristocratic and urban commemoration have received detailed study.[99] Urban commemoration in late medieval northern European cities has, however, dominated the field, in particular the memorial aspects of testamentary bequests through the analysis of wills.[100] Studies of wills have enabled analyses of the memorial practices and collective identities of specific urban groups such as political elites.[101] The commemorational practices of a single European

---

Livonian Bishops', in *Networking in Late Medieval Central Europe : Friends, Families, Foes*, ed. by Beata Możejko, Leslie Carr–Riegel, and Anna Paulina Orłowska (London: Routledge, 2023), pp. 107–24.

97 Bijsterveld, *Do ut des*; Bijsterveld, 'The Medieval Gift as Agent of Social Bonding', pp. 133–40; Patrick Geary, 'Exchange and Interaction between the Living and the Dead in Early Medieval Society', in *Living with the Dead*, pp. 77–92; Gabriela Signori, '"Family Traditions". Moral Economy and Memorial "Gift Exchange" in the Urban World of the Late Fifteenth-Century', in *Negotiating the Gift. Pre–Modern Figuration of Exchange.*, ed. by Gadi Algazi, Valentin Groebner, and Bernhard Jussen (Göttingen: Vandenhoeck & Ruprecht, 2003), pp. 285–318.

98 Cornell Babendererde, *Sterben, Tod, Begräbnis und liturgisches Gedächtnis bei weltlichen Reichsfürsten des Spätmittelalters* (Ostfildern: Thorbecke, 2006); Karl–Heinz Spieß, 'Liturgische Memoria und Herrschaftsrepräsentation im nichtfürstlichen Hochadel des Spätmittelalters', in *Adelige und bürgerliche Erinnerungskulturen*, pp. 97–123; *Mittelalterliche Fürstenhöfe und ihre Erinnerungskulturen*, ed. by Carola Fey (Göttingen: V und R Unipress, 2007); Klaus Graf, 'Fürstliche Erinnerungskultur. Eine Skizze zum neuen Modell des Gedenkens in Deutschland im 15. und 16. Jahrhundert', in *Les princes et l'histoire du XIVe au XVIIIe siècle: actes du colloque organisé par l'Université de Versailles – Saint-Quentin et l'Institut Historique Allemand, Paris/Versailles, 13–16 mars 1996*, ed. by Chantal Grell, Werner Paravicini, and Jürgen Voss (Bonn: Bouvier, 1998), pp. 1–11.

99 Mathias Herweg, 'Weibliches Mäzenatentum zwischen dynastischer Bestimmung, politischem Kalkül und höfischer Memoria', *Zeitschrift für Literaturwissenschaft und Linguistik*, 40.3 (2010), 9–34; Grzegorz Pac, 'Frauen und Memoria in der Dynastie der Piasten im 11. und 12. Jahrhundert. Drei Beispiele', *Zeitschrift für Ostmitteleuropa-Forschung*, 60.2 (2011), 163–85; Mänd, 'Frauen, Memoria und Sakralräume im spätmittelalterlichen Livland'; Anu Mänd, 'Women Shaping Sacred Space: Case Studies from Early 16th Century Lübeck and Tallinn', in *Hansische Identitäten*, ed. by Kerstin Petermann, Anja Rasche, and Gerhard Weilandt (Petersberg: Michael Imhof Verlag, 2018), pp. 83–91.

100 A selection of publications on memorial bequests in wills: Birgit Noodt, *Religion und Familie in der Hansestadt Lübeck anhand der Bürgertestamente des 14. Jahrhunderts* (Lübeck: Schmidt–Römhild, 2000); *Seelenheil und irdischer Besitz: Testamente als Quellen für den Umgang mit den 'letzten Dingen'*, ed. by Markwart Herzog and Cecilie Hollberg (Konstanz: UVK Verlagsgesellschaft, 2007); Olivier Richard, '"Fromme Klauseln" – "profane Klauseln". Eine sinnvolle Unterscheidung?', in *Seelenheil und irdischer Besitz*, pp. 69–78; Kerstin Seidel, *Freunde und Verwandte: Soziale Beziehungen in einer spätmittelalterlichen Stadt* (Frankfurt am Main: Campus Verlag, 2009), pp. 56–83; Marianne Riethmüller, *to troste miner sele: Aspekte spätmittelalterlicher Frömmigkeit im Spiegel Hamburger Testamente (1310–1400)* (Hamburg: Verein für Hamburgische Geschichte, 1994); Brigitte Klosterberg, *Zur Ehre Gottes und zum Wohl der Familie: Kölner Testamente von Laien und Klerikern im Spätmittelalter* (Köln: Janus, 1995); Regina Rößner, 'Zur Memoria Lübecker Kaufleute im Mittelalter', in *Beiträge zur Sozialgeschichte Lübecker Oberschichten im Spätmittelalter*, ed. by Harm von Seggern and Gerhard Fouquet (Kiel: Selbstverlag des Historischen Seminars, Kiel, 2005), pp. 75–84; on the urban memoria, see Dietrich W. Poeck, 'Biddet gott vor enne. Zum Totengedenken in Soest', in *Soest. Die Welt der Bürger, Politik, Gesellschaft und Kultur im spätmittelalterlichen Soest*, vol. 2, ed. by Heinz–Dieter Heimann (Soest: Westfälische Verlag Buchhandlung Mocker und Jahn, 1996), pp. 915–36.

101 Olivier Richard has analysed wills of the urban patriciate in late medieval Regensburg, see his Olivier Richard, *Mémoires bourgeoises: 'memoria' et identité urbaine à Ratisbonne à la fin du Moyen Age* (Rennes:

merchant family, the Fuggers, have been evaluated thanks to a vast deposit of documentation.[102] These studies have not been restricted to the *memoria* of elite groups but have included commemoration within artisan brotherhoods and the poor.[103]

The commemoration of the dead in the Hanseatic space has been studied extensively. Numerous studies of the political elites in the Hanseatic cities show how important *memoria* was for legitimation of political power and self-representation of elite groups.[104] In addition, attention has been paid to *memoria* of the elite brotherhoods and merchant families in the largest Hanseatic cities, as well as of memorial foundations in smaller Hanseatic cities.[105] *Memoria* of Hanseatic merchants has been considered not only within the Hanse itself but also outside it, in the territories and cities where Hanse merchants were active.[106] The funerary monuments in the Hanseatic space

---

Presses universitaires de Rennes, 2009); Christian Speer has studied piety and *memoria* of the town's elites in Görlitz, see his *Frömmigkeit und Politik: städtische Eliten in Görlitz zwischen 1300 und 1550* (Berlin: Akademie–Verlag, 2011).

102 Benjamin Scheller, *Memoria an der Zeitenwende: die Stiftungen Jakob Fuggers des Reichen vor und während der Reformation (c. 1505–1555)* (Berlin: Akademie–Verlag, 2004); Otto Gerhard Oexle, 'Adel, Memoria und kulturelles Gedächtnis. Bemerkungen zur Memorial-Kapelle der Fugger in Augsburg', in *Les princes et l'histoire*, pp. 339–57.

103 Patrick Schmidt, *Wandelbare Traditionen – Tradierter Wandel: Zünftische Erinnerungskulturen in Der Frühen Neuzeit*, 36 (Köln: Böhlau, 2009); on *memoria* and the poor, see Frank Rexroth, 'Armut und Memoria im spätmittelalterlichen London', in *Memoria in der Gesellschaft des Mittelalters*, pp. 336–60; Hermann Queckenstedt, *Die Armen und die Toten: Sozialfürsorge und Totengedenken im spätmittelalterlich-frühneuzeitlichen Osnabrück* (Osnabrück: Universitätsverlag Rasch, 1997).

104 Dietrich Poeck has contributed greatly to our understanding of Hanseatic *memoria*. See his, 'Totengedenken in Hansestädten', in *Vinculum societatis: Joachim Wollasch zum 60. Geburtstag*, ed. by Franz Neiske, Dietrich Poeck, and Mechthild Sandmann (Sigmaringendorf: Regio-Verlag Glock und Lutz, 1991), pp. 175–232; Dietrich W. Poeck, 'Rat und Memoria', in *Memoria in der Gesellschaft des Mittelalters*, pp. 286–335; Dietrich W. Poeck, 'Sühne durch Gedenken. Das Recht der Opfer', in *Die Legitimität der Erinnerung und die Geschichtswissenschaft*, ed. by Clemens Wischermann (Stuttgart: Steiner, 1996), pp. 113–36; Dietrich W. Poeck, '"…bidde vor uns". Zu Fürbitte und Totengedenken im mittelalterlichen Bremen', *Bremisches Jahrbuch*, 72 (1993), 16–33; Stefanie Rüther also has worked on the elite *memoria*, see her 'Strategien der Erinnerung. Zur Repräsentation der Lübecker Ratsherren', in *Gemeinschaft und Geschichtsbilder*, pp. 101–23; Stefanie Rüther, *Prestige und Herrschaft: zur Repräsentation der Lübecker Ratsherren in Mittelalter und Früher Neuzeit* (Köln: Böhlau, 2003); Stefanie Rüther, 'Wo die Schwestern, die Armen und die Waisen wohnen. Zur Konstruktion einer sakralen Topographie Lübecks im 15. und 16. Jahrhundert', in *Topographien des Sakralen: Religion und Raumordnung in der Vormoderne*, ed. by Susanne Rau and Gerd Schwerhoff (München: Dölling und Galitz, 2008), pp. 330–47.

105 Sonja Dünnebeil, *Die Lübecker Zirkel–Gesellschaft: Formen der Selbstdarstellung einer städtischen Oberschicht* (Lübeck: Archiv der Hansestadt Lübeck, 1996), pp. 51–55, 64–67, 72–75; Frauke Plate, 'Biddet vor dat geslecht. Memoria und Repräsentation im mittelalterlichen Hamburg', in *Gemeinschaft und Geschichtsbilder im Hanseraum*, ed. by Thomas Hill and Dietrich W. Poeck (Frankfurt am Main: Lang, 2000), pp. 61–100; Ralf Lusiardi, *Stiftung und städtische Gesellschaft: religiöse und soziale Aspekte des Stiftungsverhaltens im spätmittelalterlichen Stralsund* (Berlin: Akademie–Verlag, 2000).

106 Renée Rössner, 'Hansische Geschichtsbilder. Das Brügger Kontor', in *Gemeinschaft und Geschichtsbilder im Hanseraum*, ed. by Thomas Hill and Dietrich W. Poeck (Frankfurt am Main: Lang, 2000), pp. 27–44; Renée Rössner, *Hansische Memoria in Flandern: Alltagsleben und Totengedenken der Osterlinge in Brügge und Antwerpen (13. bis 16. Jahrhundert)* (Frankfurt am Main: Lang, 2001); Carsten Jahnke, 'Hansische Kaufleute und deren Religiosität außerhalb ihrer Heimat', *Zapiski historyczne*, 84 (2019), 7–41; Gustavs

have also been studied though the lens of *memoria's* artistic representations and still provide numerous artefacts for case studies.[107]

With this intensive research into medieval *memoria* in recent decades, it may seem as if that new perspectives and approaches would be hard to find. Yet thus far the main focus has been on individuals or particular groups, with few studies of collective commemoration in groups and regional studies of *memoria* in its many forms.

Livonia

Livonia (Ger. Livland, Latv. Livonija, Est. Liivimaa) (see Figure 1) was at the periphery of Europe, and yet numerous influences converged there.[108] Until the late twelfth century, Livonia was a pagan domain, inhabited by the Baltic Semigallians, Couronians, and Latgalians (later Latvians), Finno–Ugric Livonians (Livs), and Estonians. In the 1180s, a peaceful Christian mission from northern Germany arrived in the region led by Augustinian canon Meinhard, who in 1186 became the first Livonian bishop.[109] The missionaries baptised pagan Livonians in the lower stretches of the river Düna (Daugava) and established a missionary centre in Üxküll (Ikšķile) (from 1186 to 1201 seat of a bishop). By the end of the century, after Meinhard's death, the mission turned violent. The Baltic crusades began in 1198, attracting knights, and drawing attention and resources from many European regions; this area was soon

---

Strenga, 'Distance, Presence, Absence and Memoria: Commemoration of Deceased Livonian Merchants Outside Their Native Cities during the Late Middle Ages', *Hansische Geschichtsblätter*, 136 (2018), 63–92.

107 Ursula Wolkewitz, *Die gravierten Messinggrabplatten des 13. und 14.Jahrhunderts im Bereich der norddeutschen Hanse – ihre Herkunft und ihre Bedeutung: Erinnern – Mahnen – Belehren* (Kassel: kassel university press, 2015); for the art historical studies of *memoria* in the Hanseatic space, see Mänd, 'Church Art, Commemoration of the Dead and the Saints' Cult'; Mänd, 'Vicarius, Canonicus et Episcopus'; Mänd, 'Memoria and Sacral Art in Late Medieval Livonia'.

108 On Livonia, see Andrejs Plakans, *A Concise History of the Baltic States* (Cambridge: Cambridge University Press, 2011), pp. 33–47, 54–62, 67–76; Indriķis Šterns, *Latvijas Vēsture: 1290–1500* (Riga: Daugava, 1997); *Eesti ajalugu II. Eesti keskaeg*, ed. by Anti Selart (Tartu: Tartu Ülikool, 2012), the English edition will be published by Brepols as a History of Livonia; Marek Tamm, 'Inventing Livonia. The Name and Fame of a New Christian Colony on the Medieval Baltic Frontier', *Zeitschrift für Ostmitteleuropa-Forschung*, 60 (2011), 186–209; *Making Livonia : Actors and Networks in the Medieval and Early Modern Baltic Sea Region*, ed. by Anu Mänd and Marek Tamm (London: Routledge, 2020); Matthias Thumser, 'Medieval Livonia: Structures of a European Historical Region', in *Das mittelalterliche Livland und sein historisches Erbe = Medieval Livonia and Its Historical Legacy*, ed. by Ilgvars Misāns, Andris Levāns, and Gustavs Strenga (Marburg: Verlag Herder-Institut, 2022), pp. 11–23.

109 On the early Livonian mission, see Carsten Selch Jensen, 'The Nature of the Early Missionary Activities and Crusades in Livonia, 1185–1201', in *Medieval Spirituality in Scandinavia and Europe: A Collection of Essays in Honour of Tore Nyberg*, ed. by Lars Bisgaard (Odense: Odense University Press, 2001), pp. 121–37.

joined by the military orders.[110] The two main historiographic texts telling the story of the Christianisation are the Chronicle of Henry of Livonia (*c.* 1227) and the Livonian Rhymed Chronicle (*c.* 1290).[111] Alongside missionaries and crusaders from northern Germany, the Baltic mission also involved Danes, who controlled the north of Livonia. The crusades lasted for almost a century until, after numerous setbacks, the Christian forces, led by the Teutonic Order, finally defeated the resistance of the Semigallians in 1290.[112]

The immigration that accompanied the process of Christianisation caused long-term spatial and social transformations in Livonia. Most of the political, ecclesiastical, and economic elites, together with their related social and political structures, were brought to Livonia from western Europe. From the thirteenth century, Livonia experienced intensive immigration from northern German cities, the Rhineland, Westphalia, Frisia, other territories of the Holy German Empire, and Scandinavia.[113] The ranks of the clergy, urban elites, and military orders were dominated by immigrants, who spoke Middle Low German. This created a certain antagonism between the locals and immigrants because the locals were partially marginalized and excluded from the political and economic elites.[114] Despite this political and social dominance, immigrants

---

110 On the Baltic crusades, see *Crusade and Conversion on the Baltic Frontier, 1150–1500*, ed. by Alan V. Murray (Aldershot: Ashgate, 2001); Alan V. Murray, 'The Structure, Genre and Intended Audience of the Livonian Rhymed Chronicle', in *Crusade and Conversion*, pp. 235–51.

111 The Chronicle of Henry of Livonia: *Heinrichs Livländische Chronik*, ed. by Leonid Arbusow jun. and Albert Bauer (Hannover: Hahn, 1955), the English translation: *The Chronicle of Henry of Livonia*, trans. by James A. Brundage (New York: Columbia University Press, 2003); the Livonian Ryhmed Chronicle: *Atskaņu hronika. Livländische Reimchronik*, ed. by Ēvalds Mugurēvičs, trans. by Valdis Bisenieks (Rīga: Zinātne, 1998), the English translation: *The Livonian Rhymed Chronicle*, ed. by Jerry Christopher Smith and William L. Urban (Chicago: Lithuanian Research and Studies Center, 2001); for information on the both chronicles, see *Crusading and Chronicle Writing on the Medieval Baltic Frontier: A Companion to the Chronicle of Henry of Livonia*, ed. by Marek Tamm, Linda Kaljundi, and Carsten Selch Jensen (Farnham: Ashgate, 2011), especially the contribution of James A. Brundage, 'Introduction: Henry of Livonia, The Writer and His Chronicle', pp. 1–22; Murray, 'Structure, Genre and Intended Audience', pp. 235–51.

112 William L. Urban, *The Baltic Crusade* (Chicago: Lithuanian Research and Studies Center, 1994); Indriķis Šterns, *Latvijas vēsture: 1180–1290. Krustakari* [History of Latvia. 1180–1290. Crusades] (Rīga: Latvijas Vēstures institūta apgāds, 2002); *Baltic Crusades and Societal Innovation in Medieval Livonia, 1200–1350*, ed. by Anti Selart (Leiden: Brill, 2022).

113 Friedrich Benninghoven, *Rigas Entstehung und der frühhansische Kaufmann* (Hamburg: Velmede, 1961), p. 105; Heinz von zur Mühlen, 'Das Stadtbürgertum', in *Sozialgeschichte der baltischen Deutschen*, ed. by Wilfried Schlau (Köln: Wissenschaft und Politik, 2000), pp. 63–108, p. 75; Inna Põltsam-Jürjo, 'Die Städte: Alltag, soziale Schichten, Handel und Gewerbe', in *Das Baltikum: Geschichte einer europäischen Region. Band 1. Von der Vor- und Frühgeschichte bis zum Ende des Mittelalters*, ed. by Karsten Brüggemann and others (Stuttgart: Hiersemann Verlag, 2018), pp. 296–340.

114 A selected bibliography on the non-Germans in Livonia, see Leonid Arbusow jun., 'Studien zur Geschichte der Lettischen Bevölkerung Rigas im Mittelalter und 16. Jahrhundert', *Latvijas Augstskolas Raksti. Acta Universitatis Latviensis*, 1 (1921), 76–100; Vilho Niitemaa, *Die Undeutsche Frage in der Politik der livländischen Städte im Mittelalter* (Helsinki: Uudenmaan Kirjapaino Osakeyhtio, 1949); Paul Johansen and Heinz von zur Mühlen, *Deutsch und Undeutsch im mittelalterlichen und frühneuzeitlichen Reval* (Köln: Böhlau, 1973); Tiina Kala, 'Gab es eine "Nationale Frage" in mittelalterlichen Reval?', *Forschungen zur baltischen Geschichte*, 7 (2012), 11–34; Anti Selart, 'Non-German Literacy in Medieval Livonia', in *Uses of the Written Word in Medieval Towns*, ed. by Marco Mostert and Anna Adamska (Turnhout: Brepols, 2014), pp. 37–63; Inna Põltsam-Jürjo, 'Die autochthone Bevölkerung', in *Das*

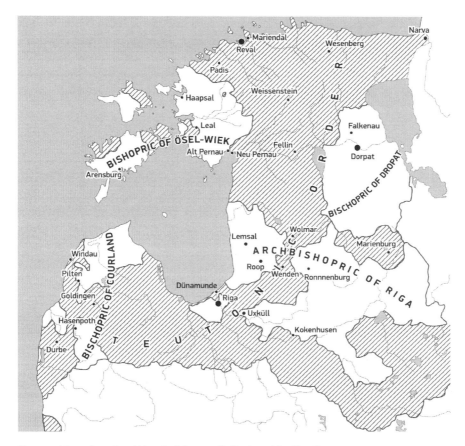

Figure 1: Map of medieval Livonia (after 1346). Designed by Una Grants

always remained a small minority of the entire Livonian population, possibly 5–10 per cent.

Livonia's political system differed from that of many other European regions.[115] It consisted of territories ruled by ecclesiastical overlords with the exception of northern Livonia (Estonia), which was held by the kings of Denmark until 1346. Livonia was divided into five bishoprics, and four of its

---

Baltikum: Geschichte einer europäischen Region. Band 1. Von der Vor- und Frühgeschichte bis zum Ende des Mittelalters, ed. by Karsten Brüggemann and others (Stuttgart: Hiersemann Verlag, 2018), pp. 341–75; Gustavs Strenga, 'Die Formierung der Letten als Ethnische Gemeinschaft zur Zeit der Reformation in Riga', in *Reformation und Ethnizität. Sorben, Letten und Esten im 16. und 17. Jahrhundert*, ed. by Madlena Mahling, Susanne Hose, and Friedrich Pollack (Bautzen: Domowina-Verlag, 2019), pp. 77–97; Gustavs Strenga, 'Turning Transport Workers into Latvians? The Ethnicity and Transport Workers' Guilds in Riga before and after the Reformation', *Journal of Baltic Studies*, 52, 1 (2021), 61–83; Ilgvars Misāns, 'The Western Model and the Autochthons: The Livs and Would-Be Latvians in Medieval Livonia', in *Das Mittelalterliche Livland und sein historisches Erbe*, pp. 83–104.

115 On the political model of Livonia, see Andris Levāns, 'Politiskās organizācijas modeļi viduslaiku Livonijā, 13.–16. gadsimts: manifestācijas un leģitimācijas formas', in *Latvieši un Latvija: Valstiskums*

bishops also held secular power.[116] The largest and most politically influential was the archbishopric of Riga (founded in 1201, promoted to archbishopric in 1253).[117] Alongside the bishoprics, extensive territories were held by the military orders. The Order of the Sword Brethren (*Fratres militiae Christi Livoniae*), founded in 1202, was initially the main military power in Livonia, but after its defeat at the battle of Saule (1236) by the Lithuanians and Semigallians, the remnants of the Sword Brethren were incorporated into the Teutonic Order in 1237 (*Ordo fratrum domus Sanctae Mariae Teutonicorum Ierosolimitanorum*).[118] The Teutonic Order established its Livonian branch, an autonomous structure with its own Master.[119] It inherited the territories of the Sword Brethren and further added to them by subsequent conquests, becoming the largest territorial power in Livonia. The Teutonic Knights arrived when the political structures were already in place and were consequentially under the authority of the bishop and later the archbishop of Riga. The Order's aspirations for political hegemony, similar to that which they held in neighbouring Prussia, caused constant tensions between them and other parties, especially the archbishops of Riga.[120] These tensions on numerous occasions erupted in physical violence. During the early fourteenth century (1297–1330), the Order fought a war against its opponents, the city of Riga, the archbishop, and the bishops of Dorpat and Ösel–Wiek, in which Knight Brethren prevailed.[121] In 1428 the brethren of the Teutonic Order drowned in a lake sixteen envoys sent to Rome by the Livonian bishops.[122] On other occasions when the Order tried to destroy one of its main enemies – the church of Riga – by incorporating it in the Order, the Knight Brethren sought to use diplomacy and resources

---

Latvijā un Latvijas valsts – izcīnītā un zaudētā, ed. by Tālavs Jundzis and Guntis Zemītis (Rīga: Latvijas Zinātņu akadēmija, 2013), pp. 52–76.

116 Livonia had bishoprics of Riga, Courland, Dorpat, Ösel–Wiek, and Reval. The bishop of Reval, however, had no political power because the bishopric was owned by the Danish king and later the Teutonic Order.

117 The Rigan archdiocese united all Livonian and Prussian dioceses except Reval, which belonged to the archdiocese Lund. Bernhart Jähnig, 'Erzbistum Riga', in *Die Bistümer des Heiligen Römischen Reiches von ihren Anfängen bis zur Säkularisation*, ed. by Erwin Gatz (Freiburg im Breisgau: Herder, 2003), pp. 623–30; for the biographies of the archbishops, see *Die Bischöfe des Heiligen Römischen Reiches 1198 bis 1448: Ein biographisches Lexikon*, ed. by Erwin Gatz and Clemens Brodkorb (Berlin: Duncker & Humblot, 2001), pp. 643–57.

118 Friedrich Benninghoven, *Der Orden der Schwertbrüder: Fratres milicie Christi de Livonia* (Köln: Böhlau, 1965).

119 On the Livonian branch of the Teutonic Order, see Bernhart Jähnig, *Verfassung und Verwaltung des Deutschen Ordens und seiner Herrschaft in Livland* (Berlin: LIT, 2011).

120 Eva Eihmane, *Rīgas arhibīskapa un Vācu ordeņa cīņas par varu viduslaiku Livonijā* (Rīga: LU Akadēmiskais Apgāds, 2012).

121 Manfred Hellmann, 'Der Deutsche Orden und die Stadt Riga', in *Stadt und Orden. Das Verhältnis des Deutschen Ordens zu den Städten in Livland, Preußen und im Deutschen Reich*, ed. by Udo Arnold (Marburg: Elwert, 1993), pp. 1–33; Šterns, *Latvijas Vēsture. 1290–1500*, pp. 350–86; Māra Caune, 'Rīgas pilsētas un Livonijas ordeņa karš 1297.–1330. gadā', *Latvijas PSR Zinātņu Akadēmijas Vēstis*, 12 (1973), 63–74; Eihmane, *Rīgas arhibīskapa un Vācu ordeņa cīņas par varu*, pp. 16–25.

122 Eva Eihmane, 'Livonijas bīskapu delegācijas slepkavība 1428. gadā: zināmais un nezināmais', *Latvijas Vēstures Institūta Žurnāls*, 1 (2013), 29–59.

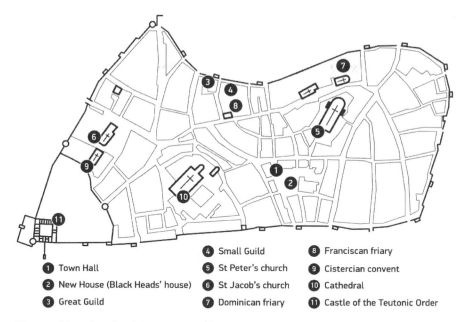

① Town Hall	④ Small Guild	⑧ Franciscan friary
② New House (Black Heads' house)	⑤ St Peter's church	⑨ Cistercian convent
③ Great Guild	⑥ St Jacob's church	⑩ Cathedral
	⑦ Dominican friary	⑪ Castle of the Teutonic Order

Figure 2: Map of medieval Riga. Designed by Una Grants

at their disposal to outplay its Livonian opponents in the papal curia.[123] The political struggle between the Order and its adversaries continued until the late fifteenth century.

Its strategic location was one of the key reasons why the Christianisation of Livonia was attempted from the start. Essential trading routes ran through the Eastern Baltic, connecting western European markets with Russia and Lithuania; German merchants had been using these routes since the twelfth century. Commercial settlements were established after the beginning of the mission, which later developed into strong 'colonial towns'.[124] In 1201, bishop Albert founded Riga on the banks of Düna, near where it meets the sea, and it became the largest Livonian city and an important political actor; decades later Reval (Tallinn) (see Map 3) and Dorpat (Tartu) were established.[125] In these cities, Rhenish wine met Russian furs, Flemish cloths met Lithuanian flax and wax. Riga, Reval, and Dorpat experienced rapid growth and their success

---

123 William Urban, 'The Diplomacy of the Teutonic Knights at the Curia', *Journal of Baltic Studies*, 9.2 (1978), 116–28.

124 On Riga as a 'colonial town', see Robert Bartlett, *The Making of Europe: Conquest, Colonization, and Cultural Change, 950–1350* (London: Allen Lane, 1993). pp. 194–96.

125 Benninghoven, *Rigas Entstehung*; *Riga und der Ostseeraum: von der Gründung 1201 bis in die frühe Neuzeit*, ed. by Ilgvars Misāns and Horst Wernicke (Marburg: Verlag Herder-Institut, 2005); Johansen and von zur Mühlen, *Deutsch und Undeutsch*; Kevin C. O'Connor, *The House of Hemp and Butter: A History of Old Riga* (Ithaca: Cornell University Press, 2019).

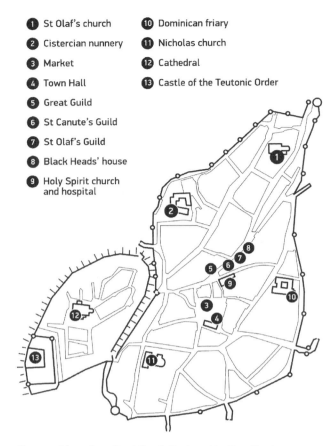

Figure 3: Map of medieval Reval. Designed by Una Grants

was enhanced by their participation in the Hanse.[126] The Hanse was not solely a merchant network but also a cultural framework that influenced the lives of its member cities. The seaports, Riga and Reval, were two large cities, with approximately eight and six thousand inhabitants respectively during the later Middle Ages.[127] These cities were governed by German merchant elites, but between a half and a third of their population was composed of local non–Germans (Latvians, Livs, and Estonians), Russians, Swedes, and Finns.[128]

---

[126] Paul Johansen, 'Die Bedeutung der Hanse für Livland', *Hansische Geschichtsblätter*, 65/66 (1940), 1–55; *Die Hanse: Lebenswirklichkeit und Mythos. Textband zur Hamburger Hanse-Ausstellung von 1989*, ed. by Jörgen Bracker, Volker Henn, and Reiner Postel (Lübeck: Schmidt-Römhild, 1998).

[127] Ahasver von Brandt, 'Die gesellschaftliche Struktur des spätmittelalterlichen Lübeck', in *Lübeck, Hanse, Nordeuropa: Gedächtnisschrift für Ahasver von Brandt*, ed. by Klaus Friedland and Rolf Sprandel (Köln: Böhlau, 1979), pp. 209–32, p. 213; Johansen and von zur Mühlen, *Deutsch und Undeutsch*, p. 92.

[128] Johansen and von zur Mühlen, *Deutsch und Undeutsch*, p. 124; Benninghoven, *Rigas Entstehung*, pp. 98–99.

Livonia was a set of political territories established during the crusading period of the thirteenth century with a common aim of Christian mission, and later was kept together by these bonds.[129] Livonia had a territorial but not a common political identity. Livonian political actors frequently shared common interests but had different political aims, and so conflicts were unavoidable. Livonia ceased to exist as a territorial entity after the Reformation (in the mid-1520s), in 1561, when the Livonian branch of the Teutonic Order was dissolved.

The turbulent post-medieval history of Livonia's territory has shaped the landscape of surviving sources. Livonian sources from the Middle Ages are scarce in comparison with other parts of Europe. Most sacred art and liturgical artefacts – altarpieces, altars, murals, statues, and grave slabs – were destroyed during the Reformation or in the numerous wars of later centuries.[130] Only a small number of documents have survived from the former archives of the archbishopric of Riga and the Livonian branch of the Teutonic Order, the remnants of which were taken to Poland and Sweden respectively during the seventeenth century.[131] Likewise, the medieval city archive of Dorpat, the third largest Livonian city, was completely destroyed during the sixteenth century.

The evidence on which this book is based is drawn primarily from the city archives of Riga and Reval. The city archives of Reval (Tallinn) hold one of the largest surviving collections of medieval sources in northern Europe, including more than one hundred testaments, while the former city archives of Riga have experienced significant losses in the post-medieval period.[132] For the urban groups, the most frequently used sources are testaments, account books, and ledgers of the urban governments and brotherhoods, confraternity members' lists, and foundation charters, as well as some visual sources in the case of the elite brotherhoods. For the clergy and the Teutonic Order in Livonia, sources are scarce, yet more diverse: chronicles and other historiographical texts, statutes, liturgical manuscripts, charters, legal documents, political treaties,

---

129 Although Livonia is frequently described as the 'confederation', it is not the right term. See Thumser, 'Medieval Livonia', p. 19.
130 On the Livonian iconoclasm, see Leonid Arbusow jun., *Die Einführung der Reformation in Liv-, Est- und Kurland* (Leipzig: M.Heinsius, 1921), pp. 291–326; Sergiusz Michalski, 'Bildersturm im Ostseeraum', in *Macht und Ohnmacht der Bilder: reformatorischer Bildersturm im Kontext der europäischen Geschichte*, ed. by Peter Blickle and others (München: Oldenbourg, 2002), pp. 223–38; Sergiusz Michalski, '"Hölzer wurden zu Menschen" Die reformatorischen Bilderstürme in den baltischen Landen zwischen 1524 und 1526', in *Die baltischen Lande im Zeitalter der Reformation und Konfessionalisierung. Teil 4.*, ed. by Matthias Asche, Werner Buchholz, and Anton Schindling (Münster: Aschendorff, 2012), pp. 147–63.
131 On the archiepiscopal and the Teutonic Order's archives, see Arnold Feuereisen, 'Über das baltische Archivwesen', in *Arbeiten des ersten Baltischen Historikertages zu Riga 1908*, ed. by Bernhard A. Hollander (Riga: Löffler, 1909), pp. 249–73; Juhan Kreem, 'The Archives of the Teutonic Order in Livonia: Past and Present', in *Entre Deus e o Rei. O Mundo Das Ordens Militares*, ed. by Isabel Cristina Ferreira Fernandes (Município de Palmela: GEsOS, 2018), p. 57–65.
132 on the Tallinn city archives, see Urmas Oolup, 'Über das Stadtarchiv Tallinn (Reval) in Estland und seine Bestände', *Archivalische Zeitschrift*, 87.1 (2005), 165–84; on the history of the medieval archive of the Riga city council, see Madlena Mahling, *Ad rem publicam et ad ignem: das mittelalterliche Schriftgut des Rigaer Rats und sein Fortbestand in der Neuzeit* (Marburg: Verlag Herder-Institut, 2015).

grave slabs, and for the Teutonic Order, necrologies from outside Livonia. The scarcity of sources has shaped my research, but it has also motivated me to link them through comparative study based on wide-ranging reading and also to focus on symbolic manifestations of commemoration.

CHAPTER 1

Remembering Origins

Remembering the origins is the main aim of cultural memory. According to Jan Assmann, foundational memory refers to origin stories with the help of various media including rituals, dances, myths, patterns, dress, jewellery, tattoos, paintings, landscapes etc. to support the memory and identity of the groups.[1] The commemoration keeps 'the foundational past alive in the present'.[2] Commemorating and recalling the origins for those who remember helps to understand where they are placed in space and time and can help to provide an answer to the question of who they are as a group. The stories of origin are a cultural capital of immense value, and as you will see in this chapter, they were essential in the medieval context for claiming rights and privileges in the present. Moreover, they can save communities in moments of crisis and strengthen their identities.

This chapter focuses on the origin stories of the two most relevant political groups of medieval Livonia: the Church of Riga (archbishops and the cathedral chapter) and the Livonian branch of the Teutonic Order. For both groups the aim was the same – to commemorate how these groups came to Livonia during the late twelfth and early thirteenth centuries and their experiences in spreading Christianity in the Eastern Baltic. As the chapter will demonstrate, the origin stories could be remembered in the spaces where the founders were buried, thus physically present, and also within the environments created by narratives, thousands of kilometres away from the places where the events commemorated took place. Likewise, the origin stories represented here transcend the boundaries of medieval Livonia, showing the important place of the struggle with the Livonian pagans in the cultural memory of the Teutonic Order, which serves as an example of international cooperation.

Space and Memory: the Church of Riga Remembering its Beginnings

The late medieval *memoria* of the Church of Riga also went back to its roots in the late twelfth and early thirteenth centuries and remembered its founders. Legal documents drafted by Archbishop Silvester Stodewescher and

---

1 Assmann, *Cultural Memory and Early Civilization*, p. 37.
2 Assmann, *Cultural Memory and Early Civilization*, p. 38.

his associates between 1450 and 1452 show that memories about the founding bishops were essential for sustaining the archbishop's and cathedral chapter's identities during periods of crisis and conflict.³ For generations the archbishops and cathedral canons had shaped not only the liturgical and historiographical memory of their church but the cathedral itself as a space of memory.⁴ Riga Cathedral was home to the tombs of many bishops, archbishops, and lesser clergymen, though only some of their grave slabs have survived.⁵ Thus, the physical space of the cathedral itself helped the Riga clergy to commemorate its bishops, supplementing the remembrance, which was imprinted in the liturgy as well as in historical texts. Here 'the architecture as a medium of memory was itself a memorial message', constantly reminding the viewers about the past and their predecessors.⁶

The construction of the cathedral in Riga began in 1211.⁷ The third Livonian bishop, Albert Buxthoeven (e. 1199–1229), had moved the bishop's seat from the first Livonian cathedral in Üxküll to the newly founded city of Riga in 1201 together with the cathedral chapter of twelve canons led by a provost.⁸ The cathedral's buildings belonging to the chapter's jurisdiction were separated from the rest of the city within the cathedral close.⁹

Riga Cathedral as a commemorational site was shaped by the resting places of the founding bishops of the diocese of Üxküll/Riga: Meinhard (e. 1186–1196), Berthold Schulte (e. 1196–1198), and Albert, who had led the Christian mission.¹⁰ The three founding bishops were never canonised and their role as

---

3 Levāns, 'Die lebendigen Toten', pp. 3–35.
4 Dietrich W. Poeck, 'Der Dom als Ort der Erinnerung', in *Der Dom als Anfang: 1225 Jahre Bistum und Stadt Osnabrück*, ed. by Hermann Queckenstedt and Franz-Josef Bode (Osnabrück: Dom–Buchhanlung Osnabrück, 2005), pp. 301–26.
5 Heinz Löffler, *Die Grabsteine, Grabmäler und Epitaphien in den Kirchen Alt–Livlands vom 13.–18. Jahrhundert* (Riga: Löffler, 1929), pp. 18, 22, 23.
6 The quotation is from Klaus Lange, who had interpreted Marshall McLuhan's theory of 'medium as the message'. See his, 'Sakralarchitektur und Memoria. Das Essener Münster als Ort der Erinnerung', in *Pro remedio et salute anime peragemus*, pp. 59–78, p. 62; Marshall McLuhan, *Understanding Media: The Extensions of Man* (New York: Routledge, 2008), pp. 7–23.
7 Andris Caune and Ieva Ose, *Latvijas viduslaiku mūra baznīcas* (Rīga: Latvijas vēstures institūta apgāds, 2010), p. 252; Agnese Bergholde, *Rīgas Doma viduslaiku arhitektūra un būvplastika eiropeisko analoģiju kontekstā: disertācija = Mittelalterliche Architektur und Bauplastik des Doms zu Riga im europäischen Vergleich* (Rīga: LMA Mākslas Vēstures Institūts, 2015).
8 The cathedral chapter was led by the provost (*prepositus, provest*), and his deputy was a dean (*decanus, dekenn*). Each canon had his own office, for example, of cantor, scholastic, treasurer, and others. See Šterns, *Latvijas Vēsture. 1290–1500*, p. 31; Mario Glauert, 'Die Bindung des Domkapitels von Riga an die Regel des Deutschen Ordens', in *Die Domkapitel des Deutschen Ordens in Preußen und Livland*, ed. by Radosław Biskup and Mario Glauert (Münster: Aschendorff, 2004), pp. 269–316, pp. 272–73;
9 Benninghoven, *Rigas Entstehung*, pp. 72–73.
10 Manfred Hellmann, 'Meinhard von Riga', in *Neue Deutsche Biographie*, vol. 16, ed. by Fritz Wagner (Berlin: Duncker & Humblot, 1990), p. 655; Paul Ludwig Feser, 'Bischof Berthold von Livland (1196–1198)', *Freiburger Geschichtsblätter*, 52 (1963), 101–28; Bernhart Jähnig, 'Bertholt Schulte', in *Die Bischöfe des Heiligen Römischen Reiches 1198 bis 1448*, pp. 644–45, p. 644; Bernhart Jähnig, 'Albert von Bekeshovede (Buxhöveden)', in *Die Bischöfe des Heiligen Römischen Reiches 1198 bis 1448*, pp. 645–47; Bernd Ulrich Hucker, 'Die Anfänge Christlicher Mission in Den Baltischen Ländern', in *Studien über die Anfänge der Mission in Livland*, ed. by Manfred Hellmann (Sigmaringen: Thorbecke, 1989), pp. 39–64.;

possible local saints is still being discussed in the scholarship.[11] Their tombs reflected the narrative of beginnings the Chronicle of Henry of Livonia also told, as the story of three first Livonian (Üxküll/Riga) bishops.[12] As Linda Kaljundi has rightly pointed out, Henry's chronicle as a frontier chronicle shows 'a remarkable concern for the commemoration of the past, as well as for the remediation and repetition of the events, heroes, and figures of this sacred past in textual as well as performative media'.[13] The tombs as places for commemorative performance combined with historiography created the central narrative for the collective memory of the Church of Riga. The memory was real and present in the space of the cathedral.

The first bishops of Üxküll, Meinhard and Berthold, were the key figures to whom the Livonian church referred even centuries after their deaths. Meinhard, a priest from the community of Augustinian canons regular at Segeberg (Holstein), arrived in Livonia as the first Christian missionary in 1184, became bishop of Üxküll in 1186, died peacefully in 1196, and was buried in the church of Üxküll.[14] Two years later, on 24 July 1198, his successor Berthold, a former abbot of the Cistercian abbey in Loccum, was killed in battle with the pagan Livs in 'the place of Riga' (*ad locum Rige*), and was also buried in Üxküll.[15] When bishop Albert moved the centre of the Livonian church to Riga in 1201, the tombs of the two bishops remained in Üxküll. According to Henry of Livonia, the papal legate William of Modena (also known as William of Sabina) (c. 1180–1251) visited Meinhard's and Bertold's tombs (*tumbe episcoporum*) in 1225, and celebrated the memory of 'the first holy bishops' (*primorum sanctorum episcoporum memoriam commemorans*).[16]

Henry's account shows that at the time of writing (1225–1227), the Livonian church perceived Meinhard and Berthold as holy men.[17] He emphasized

---

Manfred Hellmann, 'Die Anfänge christlicher Mission in den baltischen Ländern', in *Studien über die Anfänge der Mission in Livland*, pp. 7–38, pp. 19–38.

11 Anu Mänd and Anti Selart, 'Livonia – a Region without Local Saints?', in *Symbolic Identity and the Cultural Memory of Saints*, ed. by Nils Holger Petersen, Anu Mänd, Sebastián Salvadó, and Tracey R. Sands (Newcastle upon Tyne: Cambridge Scholars Publishing, 2018), p. 91–122.

12 For the description of Meinhard's, Berthold's and Albert's deeds in the Chronicle of Henry of Livonia, see *Heinrichs Livländische Chronik*, pp. 1–222.

13 Kaljundi, *The Baltic Crusades and the Culture of Memory*, p. 110.

14 'Horum corpora in Ykescolensi quiescent ecclesia atque apposite sunt tumbe episcoporum Meynardi et Bertoldi, quorum primus confessor, secundus martyr, ut supra dictum est, ab eisdem Lyvonibus occisus occubuit'. *Heinrici Chronicon*, p. 7, 36, 212; Levāns, 'Lebendigen Toten', p. 19; Loeffler, *Grabsteine*, pp. 41–42; Hellmann, 'Anfänge', pp. 19–20; Mänd and Selart, 'Livonia – a Region without Local Saints?', p. 103.

15 *Heinrici Chronicon*, p. 10; Jähnig, 'Bertholt Schulte', p. 644; Hucker, 'Bertold', pp. 39–53, p. 51.

16 *Heinrici Chronicon*, p. 212; Hermann Bruiningk, 'Die Frage der Verehrung der ersten livländischen Bischöfe als Heilige', in *Sitzungsberichten der Gesellschaft für Geschichte und Alterthumskunde der Ostseeprovinzen Russlands für das Jahr 1902* (Riga: W. F. Häcker, 1903), pp. 3–35, pp. 10–11; Hucker, 'Bertold', p. 52; Gustav Adolf Donner, *Kardinal Wilhelm von Sabina, Bischof von Modena 1222–1234: Päpstlicher Legat in den nordischen Ländern (+ 1251)* (Helsingfors: Tilgmann, 1929).

17 Norbert Angermann, 'Die mittelalterliche Chronistik', in *Geschichte der deutschbaltischen Geschichtsschreibung*, ed. by Georg von Rauch (Köln: Böhlau, 1986), pp. 3–20, p. 7.

their sanctity elsewhere in the chronicle too, by naming Meinhard a confessor and Berthold a martyr.[18] The fame of Berthold's martyrdom reached further west. In his *Chronica Slavorum* (*c.* 1210), Arnold of Lübeck presented a miracle: Berthold's body was found on the day after the battle and despite the heat, had not decayed like the other corpses.[19] However, the bishops' veneration most likely was local, as they were never canonized.[20]

The bodies of the two holy bishops were precious to the Riga Cathedral and its community as relics that attracted devotion and shaped a sacred space.[21] They were also an essential part of local collective memory.[22] The remains of Meinhard and Berthold were translated from Üxküll – which lost its status after 1201 – to Riga, the centre of the Livonian church and later the seat of the archbishop. The translation of saints, even though they were not yet canonized by the papal curia, was a festive event that emphasized their saintly status and nonetheless conveyed their importance in local veneration.[23]

If, as Bernd Ulrich Hucker claims, the translation took place in 1229 or 1230, then it was precipitated by the death and burial of the third Livonian bishop, Albert, who died on 17 January 1229.[24] However, the translation of Meinhard's and Berthold's remains from Üxküll may have taken place during the last decades of the fourteenth century when his decorated tomb was constructed.[25] According to a sixteenth-century chronicle (*Kleine Meisterchronik*), Albert was buried in the cathedral chancel 'under the third grave slab, under

---

18 *Heinrici Chronicon*, p. 36.
19 Bruiningk, 'Die Frage der Verehrung', pp. 15–16; Anu Mänd, ''Saints' Cults in Medieval Livonia', in *The Clash of Cultures on the Medieval Baltic Frontier*, ed. by Alan V. Murray (Farnham: Ashgate, 2009), pp. 191–223, p. 220; Mänd and Selart, 'Livonia – a Region without Local Saints?', p. 104; Anti Selart, 'Meinhard, Berthold, Bernhard – kein Heiliger für Livland', in *Credo – Christianisierung Europas im Mittelalter*, ed. by Hanne Lovise Aannestad and others (Petersberg: Michael Imhof Verlag, 2013), pp. 434–40, p. 436; Marek Tamm, 'How to Justify a Crusade? The Conquest of Livonia and New Crusade Rhetoric in the Early Thirteenth Century', *Journal of Medieval History*, 39.4 (2013), 431–55 (448).
20 Bruiningk, 'Die Frage der Verehrung', pp. 3–4; as the Cistercian, Berthold was remembered not only in Riga, but also in his former abbey – Loccum – in whose necrology his name was recorded on 25 July, see Hucker, 'Bertold', p. 51.
21 On the relics, see Arnold Angenendt, *Heilige und Reliquien: die Geschichte ihres Kultes vom frühen Christentum bis zur Gegenwart* (München: Beck, 1997), pp. 167–72; for Riga as a pilgrim destination, see Andris Levāns, 'War Riga eine "heilige" Stadt im Mittelalter. Religiosität, Pilger und der urbane Raum. Riga in der Wahrnehmung des europäischen Stadtbürgertums', in *Starptautiska konference Hanza vakar – Hanza rīt, Rīga, 1998. g. 8.–13. jūnijs = International conference Hansa yesterday – Hansa tomorrow, Riga, June 8–13, 1998*, ed. by Ojārs Spārītis (Riga: Izdevniecība Vārds, 2001), pp. 53–81.
22 Olaf B. Rader, 'Legitimationsgenerator Grab. Zur politischen Instrumentalisierung von Begräbnislagen', in *Grab – Kult – Memoria: Studien zur gesellschaftlichen Funktion von Erinnerung*, ed. by Carolin Behrmann and Horst Bredekamp (Köln: Böhlau, 2007), pp. 7–20, p. 9.
23 This was the case with St Wenceslas, see František Graus, *Lebendige Vergangenheit. Überlieferung im Mittelalter und in den Vorstellungen vom Mittelalter* (Köln: Böhlau, 1975), pp. 161–62.
24 Mänd, 'Saints' Cults', pp. 220–21; Levāns, 'Lebendigen Toten', p. 19; Jähnig, 'Bertholt Schulte', p. 644; according to Hucker the processional transfer took place on 11 October, when Meinhard's bones were taken to Riga and ten days later, on 20 or 21 October Berthold's remains arrived there see Hucker, 'Bertold', p. 52.
25 Mänd and Selart, 'Livonia – a Region without Local Saints?', p. 105.

the Paschal candlestick'.[26] The cathedral was incomplete as a memorial site with Albert's sole tomb; the translation created a clear line of succession and a continuous history.

The importance of the two bishops was reflected in the locations of their tombs within the cathedral. Meinhard was reburied in a central location, in the chancel in front of the Holy Blood altar, not far away from the high altar.[27] During the late fourteenth century a richly decorated niche tomb was built into the north wall of the chancel, where Meinhard's bones – in an oak casket – were placed and on which a small tombstone with an image of a bishop was erected.[28] The contemporary inscription states: 'In this grave lie the bones of the bishop Meinhard' (*Hac sunt in fossa Meijnhardi presulis ossa*).[29] Although according to tradition Meinhard died on 14 August, the date 11 (12) October (*IV (V) idus mensis octobris*) was inscribed on the tombstone, probably the date of his reburial and liturgical commemoration.[30] The Gothic decoration of the tomb was destroyed during the late eighteenth century, yet reconstructions show that it was influenced by the tomb of the saintly pope Urban V (1310–1370) in the abbey of St Victor in Marseilles.[31] This elaboration of Meinhard's tomb was undertaken with the aim of emphasizing his holiness visually. The construction of the tomb revived Meinhard's *memoria* two centuries after his death. Such erection of tombs centuries after the death of their occupants was practiced in cases when a group needed to refer to its founders in order to reconfirm its present identity.[32] As with the tombs of holy bishops in other cathedrals, Meinhard's tomb became the heart of the cathedral's life, where pilgrims and believers came to pray.[33]

---

26 'Cronica episcoporum Rigensium', in *Archiv für die Geschichte Liv-, Est- und Kurlands*, 5 (1846), 174–80, (174); Antje Thumser, 'Livländische Amtsträgerreihen des Mittelalters. Kleine Meisterchronik – Rigaer Bischofschronik – Series episcoporum Curoniae', in *Geschichtsschreibung im mittelalterlichen Livland*, ed. by Matthias Thumser (Berlin: LIT, 2011), pp. 201–54, p. 220.

27 Bruiningk, 'Die Frage der Verehrung', p. 6; Hermann von Bruiningk, *Messe und kanonisches Stundengebet nach dem Brauche der Rigaschen Kirche im späteren Mittelalter* (Riga: N. Kymmel, 1904), pp. 320, 590; Mänd, 'Saints' Cults', pp. 220–21; Mänd and Selart, 'Livonia – a Region without Local Saints?', p. 106.

28 Paul Campe, 'Ein neuaufgefundenes Fragment der im Jahre 1786 zerstörten Umrahmung des Grabmals Bischof Meinhards im St. Marien–Dom zu Riga', *Latvijas Universitātes Raksti. Arhitektūras Fakultātes Sērija*, 1.5 (1932), 305–26 (305–07, 309–10); Loeffler, *Grabsteine*, pp. 41–57; Bruiningk, 'Die Frage der Verehrung', p. 10.

29 The whole inscription was 'Hac sunt in fossa Meijnhardi presulis ossa. (Nobis) primo fidem dedit annis quator idem. (actis) millenis, centenis nonaque genis + (annis cum) senis, hic ab his it ad ethera p(oenis) (IV idu)s mensis octobris +'. Campe, 'Fragment', p. 305; *Heinrici Chronicon*, p. 7.

30 Bruiningk, 'Die Frage der Verehrung', p. 9; *Heinrici Chronicon*, p. 7.

31 Julian Gardner, *The Tomb and the Tiara: Curial Tomb Sculpture in Rome and Avignon in the Later Middle Ages* (Oxford: Oxford University Press, 1992), pp. 151–53; Loeffler, *Grabsteine*, pp. 45–47; Campe, 'Fragment', pp. 307, 309–10; Bruiningk, 'Die Frage der Verehrung', p. 10.

32 Rader, 'Legitimationsgenerator Grab', p. 11.

33 In Meissen, for example, the tomb of the holy Bishop Benno was in centre of the cathedral. See Matthias Donath, 'Der Meißner Dom als Grablege', in *Die Grabmonumente im Dom zu Meißen*, ed. by Matthias Donath (Leipzig: Leipziger Universitäts Verlag, 2004), pp. 11–24, p. 15.

Figure 4: The chancel of Riga Cathedral and the 19th century replica of the tomb of Bishop Meinhard (on the left side). Photo: Christofer Herrmann, 2016.

Figure 5: Bishop Meinhard's tomb before its partial destruction in 1786. Drawing of J. Ch. Brotze (1742–1823). *Sammlung versebiedner Liefländischen Monumente, Prospecte, Munzen, Wapen etc.* vol. 1, p. 93. LUAB Ms. Photo: University of Latvia Academic Library

Berthold's grave slab has not survived. According to a sixteenth-century chronicle, his tomb was also placed in a prestigious location, in front of the Holy Cross altar, next to the chancel.[34] Like Meinhard, Berthold – at least in the post-medieval Cistercian tradition – was commemorated on 20/21 October, the day of his translation to Riga.[35]

Meinhard and Berthold maintained their role in the memory of the Church of Riga for two centuries after their reburial in the cathedral. In Archbishop Silvester Stodewescher's complaint against the city of Riga in 1452, the founding bishops (*unser ersten vorfarn*) were portrayed as martyrs, who had 'bought' with their own blood the whole of Livonia, even the land on which the city of Riga was later built.[36] In their arguments for their right to lordship over Riga, the archbishop and chapter both referred to the three bishops: Meinhard, Berthold, and Albert.[37]

These early bishops were not only remembered but may have been venerated locally as 'quasi-saints' in the later Middle Ages.[38] According to Hermann Bruiningk, Meinhard and Berthold were perceived in Livonia as holy bishops until the Reformation and even beyond.[39] Albert – also buried in the chancel – played a less important role in the *memoria* of the Livonian church despite his thirty-year-long episcopate and his role in the Christianization of Livonia. Bruiningk concludes that Albert was not venerated as a saint since his name is absent from the surviving liturgical manuscripts, and no altar was erected next to his tomb.[40]

The tombs of the first Livonian bishops shaped the cathedral as an environment of memory (*milieu de mémoire*) where the whole history of the Church of Riga was remembered.[41] Thus the cathedral building was itself a memory. Most episcopal tombs were located in the chancel, next to the high altar. Since only Meinhard's funeral monument in some form has survived, we rely completely on the narrative of the sixteenth-century *Cronica episcoporum Rigensium* for information about other bishops' burials. According to the chronicle, the following bishops were buried in the chancel alongside Meinhard and Albert: Bishop Nicholas (e.1229–1253) (*unnter dem grossen pulte*), Archbishops Albert Suerbeer (e. 1253–1272/73) (*under dem anderenn Steine vor dem hoen Altare*), Johannes von Vechta (e. 1286–1294) (*vor dem hohen Altar*), Johannes Ambundi (e. 1418–1424) (*vor dem hohenn altahre*),

---

34 'Cronica episcoporum', p. 174; Bruiningk, *Messe und kanonisches Stundengebet*, p. 314, 590; Thumser, 'Livländische Amtsträgerreihen', p. 220.
35 Bruiningk, 'Die Frage der Verehrung', p. 14, 27–34; Hucker, 'Bertold', p. 51.
36 Levāns, 'Lebendigen Toten', p. 29; *Akten und Rezesse der livländischen Ständetage: (1304–1460)*, vol. 1, ed. by Oskar Stavenhagen and Leonid Arbusow (Riga: Deubner, 1907), no. 549, p. 533.
37 Levāns, 'Lebendigen Toten', pp. 12–21.
38 Mänd and Selart, 'Livonia – a Region without Local Saints?', p. 103.
39 Bruiningk, 'Die Frage der Verehrung', pp. 17–19.
40 Albert appears as a saint in the post-medieval tradition and was commemorated on 1 June. Bruiningk, *Messe und kanonisches Stundengebet*, pp. 353–54; Bruiningk, 'Die Frage der Verehrung', p. 20.
41 Nora, 'Between Memory and History', pp. 7–24.

Figure 6: Drawing of Meinhard's grave slab by Julius Döring based on an 1883 photograph. *Sitzungsberichte der kurländischen Gesellschaft für Literatur und Kunst, 1886* (Mitau: J.F. Steffenhagen und Sohn, 1887), Taf. I.

Silvester Stodewescher (e. 1448–1479) (*vor dem hohen altare, als man zu opper gehet*), Stefan Grube (e. 1479–1483) (*leit begrabenn beniedden Siluester*), and Jasper Linde (e.1509–1524) under a brass grave slab (*im kor unnder das Messingsteine*).[42] The tombs of archbishops Johannes von Lune (e.1273–1284) (*vor Sannth Katharinenn Altar*), and Henning Scharpenberg (e.1424–1448) were also located in the cathedral, but not in the chancel.[43] Michael Hildebrand's (e.1484–1509) tomb was exceptional among the archbishops' tombs: it was a brick-laid tomb, placed not in the chancel but outside the cathedral in the cloister garden (*in Kreutzhoue bey dem Umgange nach der Schule in ein gemeurten grabe*).[44] It remains unknown why Hildebrand was buried outside the cathedral.

Only bishops and archbishops of Riga were buried in the chancel; thus it was the place where the history of Christianity in Livonia and the diocese of Riga was constantly present in the form of the bishops' grave slabs. The comparison can be made with the way in which the chapel of St Wenceslaus (*c.* 907–35) in St Vitus cathedral in Prague – the burial place of the royal saint himself – functioned as the centre of medieval Bohemian monarchy.[45] In a similar fashion, the chancel of Riga Cathedral, with tombs of its founder bishops, was the centre of the whole Livonian church. The sepulchres of Meinhard, Berthold, and Albert provided a link to the group's origins, but the grave slabs of their successors were a reminder of the more recent past. The episcopal burials demonstrated the power of the episcopal institution over the territory of the archbishopric and its control over the cathedral, as well as the archbishop's sovereignty. This was why the Teutonic Order, which from the late thirteenth century attempted to gain control over the bishopric, tried to enter the memorial site of the archbishops by burying their own leaders there. In 1451 the Livonian Master of the Teutonic Order, Johann von Mengede (†1469), was promised burial in Riga Cathedral's chancel, in an attempt to convert the chancel into the Order's memorial site and establish control of the

---

42 'Cronica episcoporum', pp. 174–78; Wilhelm Neumann, *Der Dom zu St. Marien in Riga: Baugeschichte und Baubeschreibung* (Riga: Löffler, 1912), p. 32.
43 'Cronica episcoporum', pp. 175; Bernhart Jähnig, 'Henning Scharpenberg', in *Bischöfe des Reiches*, p. 657.
44 Andris Celmiņš, 'Rīgas arhibīskapa Mihaela Hildebranda apbedījums Doma pagalmā', in *Senā Rīga: pētījumi pilsētas arheoloģijā un vēsturē*, vol. 4, ed. by Andris Caune, Ieva Ose, and Andris Celmiņš (Rīga: Latvijas vēstures institūts, 2003), pp. 92–104; 'Cronica episcoporum', p. 178.
45 Michael Viktor Schwarz, 'Kathedralen verstehen. St. Veit in Prag als räumlich organisiertes Medienensemble', in *Virtuelle Räume: Raumwahrnehmung und Raumvorstellung im Mittelalter*, ed. by Elisabeth Vavra (Berlin: Akademie-Verlag, 2005), pp. 47–68, p. 51; Franz Machilek, 'Böhmens Landespatrone im Mittelalter', in *Wenzel: Protagonist der böhmischen Erinnerungskultur*, ed. by Stefan Samerski (Paderborn: Schöningh, 2018), pp. 27–98.

Order over the archbishop and the cathedral chapter.[46] Although von Mengede was buried in the chancel, the Order's plan to take over the cathedral as a memorial site failed (see chapter 4).[47]

Teutonic Order in Livonia and Memory of the Origins

The Teutonic Order was established during the siege of Acre in the Holy Land in 1190 by merchants from Lübeck and Bremen as a hospital for the German crusaders.[48] The Order's main aim was to fight against the pagans and nonbelievers. However, the Teutonic Order was not just an army with purely military objectives. Its network of houses and territories stretched from the Holy Land in the East (until 1291), to Sicily in the South, Spain in the West, and Livonia in the North. In all of these locations, the Order was involved in social, political, religious, cultural, charitable, and economic activities.[49]

The Order arrived in Livonia to subjugate the Livonian pagans by military force four decades after the beginning of the crusading in the Eastern Baltic. In 1237 the Livonian Order of the Sword Brethren (*Fratres militiae Christi Livoniae*), founded in 1202, was incorporated into the Teutonic Order after being defeated in the battle of Saule (1236).[50] In its struggle with the Livonian pagans and closest neighbours, the Order suffered setbacks. It was defeated by the Novgorodians and their allies in 1242 at Lake Peipus during the later mythologised Battle on the Ice and by the Lithuanians and Curonians at the battle of Durbe in 1260. The Order also experienced other major defeats in 1262, 1270, 1279, and 1287 but finally managed to regain military and political

---

46 See Chapter 4.
47 *Akten und Rezesse*, no. 537, § 14; Klaus Neitmann, 'Riga und Wenden als Residenzen des livländischen Landmeisters im 15. Jahrhundert', in *Stadt und Orden. Das Verhältnis des Deutschen Ordens zu den Städten in Livland, Preußen und im Deutschen Reich*, ed. by Udo Arnold (Marburg: Elwert, 1993), pp. 59–93, p. 78.
48 On the origins of the Teutonic Order, see Hartmut Boockmann, *Der Deutsche Orden: zwölf Kapitel aus seiner Geschichte* (München: Beck, 1994), pp. 28–37; Klaus Militzer, *Von Akkon zur Marienburg: Verfassung, Verwaltung und Sozialstruktur des Deutschen Ordens 1190–1309* (Marburg: Elwert, 1999), pp. 10–12; William L. Urban, *The Teutonic Knights: A Military History* (London: Greenhill Books, 2003), pp. 11–13; Nicholas Morton, *The Teutonic Knights in the Holy Land, 1190–1291* (Woodbridge: Boydell & Brewer, 2009), pp. 9–30; on the involvement of the Bremenians in the foundation, see Holger Stefan Brünjes, *Die Deutschordenskomturei in Bremen: ein Beitrag zur Geschichte des Ordens in Livland* (Marburg: Elwert, 1997), pp. 210–14.
49 The recent studies of Kristjan Toomaspoeg in particular show the close ties of the Teutonic Order in Sicily with the surrounding environment. See his '"Confratres, Procuratores, Negociorum Gestores et Factores Eorum". Storia Dei "Familiares" Dei Cavalieri Teutonici in Sicilia (1197–1492)', *Sacra Militia*, 1 (2001), 151–65; Kristjan Toomaspoeg, 'Der Deutsche Orden als Grund- und Kirchenherr in Italien', in *Die Ritterorden als Träger der Herrschaft: Territorien, Grundbesitz und Kirche*, ed. by Roman Czaja and Jürgen Sarnowsky (Toruń: UMK, 2007), pp. 187–201.
50 Benninghoven, *Der Orden der Schwertbrüder*, pp. 321–53.

strength. It concluded the crusade in Livonia in 1290 by conquering the last pagan stronghold: Semigallia.[51]

Despite the fact that the hospital out of which the Order had developed was founded by the burghers of Lübeck and Bremen, the Teutonic Order remained the exclusive preserve of the nobility throughout the Middle Ages.[52] The majority of the brethren in the Teutonic Order came from the lower nobility; it was frequently referred to by contemporaries as 'a hospice of poor German noblemen' (*Spital des Armen Adels deutscher Nation*).[53] Noble descent was one of the preconditions for admission to the Order, and the majority of the brethren were German, although other ethnic groups were to be found among the brethren.[54] The Order offered a refuge to members of the lower nobility of the Empire, and in this realm they could establish a considerable political influence, becoming high–ranking officials and even Masters.[55] The higher nobility did not have special privileges and opportunities in this Order.[56]

The Livonian branch recruited the majority of its brethren from the Order's bailiwicks in the Empire. Noblemen from Westphalia and Rhineland dominated the Livonian branch for the whole period of its existence between 1237 and 1561.[57] They were recruited and admitted into the Order while in the Empire and then left for Livonia, never returning to their bailiwick of origin, as was common in the later Middle Ages.[58] In the Livonian branch, only a few brethren of local descent can be identified.[59] Most of the brethren retained a 'foreign' element, whose social networks and customs reached back to their native regions. In addition, the Livonian branch was internally divided between the factions of the Westphalians and Rhinelanders; the Westphalians made up more than half, and the Rhinelanders were around 40 per cent of all the brethren.[60] The two groups within the Livonian branch were in conflict with

---

51 Klaus Militzer, *Die Geschichte des Deutschen Ordens* (Stuttgart: Kohlhammer, 2012), p. 80; Jähnig, *Verfassung und Verwaltung*, pp. 40–41; Eric Christiansen, *The Northern Crusades: The Baltic and the Catholic Frontier 1100–1525* (London: Macmillan, 1980), p. 99.
52 Johannes A. Mol, 'The "Hospice of the German Nobility". Changes in the Admission Policy of the Teutonic Knights in the Fifteenth Century', in *Mendicants, Military Orders, and Regionalism in Medieval Europe*, ed. by Jürgen Sarnowsky (Aldershot: Ashgate, 1999), pp. 115–30, p. 124.
53 Mol, 'Hospice', p. 124; Klaus Militzer, 'Recruitment of Brethren for the Teutonic Order in Livonia, 1237–1562', in *The Military Orders. Fighting for the Faith and Caring for the Sick*, ed. by Malcolm Barber (Aldershot: Variorum, 1994), pp. 270–77, p. 276.
54 Mol, 'Hospice', p. 123.
55 Manfred Hellmann, 'Bemerkungen zur sozialgeschichtlichen Erforschung des Deutschen Ordens', *Historisches Jahrbuch*, 80 (1961), 126–42, (130).
56 Militzer, 'Recruitment of Brethren', p. 276.
57 *Ritterbrüder im livländischen Zweig des Deutschen Ordens*, ed. by Lutz Fenske and Klaus Militzer (Köln: Böhlau, 1993), pp. 32, 37, 40, 44, 47; Klaus Militzer, 'Rheinländer im mittelalterlichen Livland', *Rheinische Vierteljahrsblätter*, 61 (1997), 79–95, (82–83).
58 Sonja Neitmann, *Von der Grafschaft Mark nach Livland: Ritterbrüder aus Westfalen im livländischen Deutschen Orden* (Köln: Böhlau, 1993), p. 49; Mol, 'Hospice', p. 121.
59 *Ritterbrüder*, p. 24.
60 Militzer, 'Recruitment of Brethren', p. 275.

each other.⁶¹ The recruitment was not centralised and also depended on the family networks of the branch's leaders in the Empire.⁶² Due to the brethren's origins, the Livonian branch was bound together with the institutions of the Order in the Empire.

Memoria promoted the self-awareness of groups and served as a source for knowledge about its own history.⁶³ Social groups created, recorded, and sustained their own memories with the aid of *memoria*, while groups and their identities were also constructed by memories.⁶⁴ Shared memories created the feeling of a common bond and thus constituted a group itself.⁶⁵ In this context, research into the Teutonic Order's *memoria* is particularly important; historians have not yet appreciated the influence of *memoria* on group construction and identity in the military orders. The brethren of the Teutonic Order, as Helen Nicholson has put it, 'were concerned to establish its historical origins and chronicle its deeds, perhaps to make clear to both brothers and patrons how and why the Order had expanded its activities outside the Holy Land'.⁶⁶ A study of the Livonian branch's memory, especially that of its own beginnings, can help us to understand how this corporation not only created its identities but also sustained them for the long term.

The *memoria* of the Livonian branch reflected all the historical, social, and political contexts presented above. Care for the burial and remembrance of its members was not only a religious practice for the Teutonic Order but also an element that ensured the continued existence of the group itself. As a community of men bonded together and living in celibacy, the inheritance of rights, privileges, power, and obligations did not derive from family but from the traditions handed over by their predecessors in office. The legitimacy was required through the remembrance of deceased brethren and of the historical events they had experienced. With the help of the rituals, the recruits were inducted in the community of the Teutonic Order and the knowledge about its past was shared.⁶⁷ The Order's liturgical practices played important role in

---

61 Johannes A. Mol, 'The Knight Brothers from the Low Countries in the Conflict between the Westphalians and the Rhinelanders in the Livonian Branch of the Teutonic Order', *Ordines Militares Colloquia Torunensia Historica. Yearbook for the Study of the Military Orders*, 20 (2015), 123–44.
62 Juhan Kreem, 'Mobility of the Livonian Teutonic Knights', in *Making Livonia: Actors and Networks in the Medieval and Early Modern Baltic Sea Region*, ed. by Anu Mänd and Marek Tamm (London: Routledge, 2020), pp. 158–69, p. 161.
63 Oexle, 'Gegenwart der Toten', p. 34.
64 Oexle, 'Gegenwart der Lebenden', p. 75.
65 Althoff, 'Geschichtsbewusstsein', p. 89.
66 Helen J. Nicholson, 'Memory and the Military Orders: An Overview', in *Entre Deus e o Rei. O Mundo das Ordens Militares. Between God and the King. The World of the Military Orders*, ed. by Isabel Cristina Ferreira Fernandes (Palmela: Municipio de Palmela/GEsOS, 2018), pp. 17–28, p. 23.
67 Nicholas W. Youmans, 'Between Commemoration and Living Memory: Symbolic Acts of the Teutonic Knights in Light of Cultural Theory', *Ordines Militares Colloquia Torunensia Historica. Yearbook for the Study of the Military Orders*, 26 (2021), 285–313 (297–98).

remembering the dead brethren and the corporation's past.[68] The continuity of the group depended on *memoria*.

The Teutonic Order also referred to their origin stories. The Order as 'a community of men who live and fight together' also commemorated their martyrs and heroes who had fallen in the struggle against the pagans and non-believers. The commemoration as role models of the brethren fallen during the crusading period was essential for the Teutonic Order's identity and was still practised in the late Middle Ages, even though the struggle against the pagans had ended. The continued commemoration maintained the brethren's identity as warriors of Christ and even helped to legitimise the Order's existence after the decline of crusading.

Memoria of the Brethren Fallen in Livonia by the Houses of the Western European Bailiwicks

Like all military orders, the Teutonic Order faced the challenges of long-distance communication.[69] The Livonian branch of the Teutonic Order, far to the east, was geographically disadvantaged in communicating with the rest of the Order. Yet, a constant flow of recruits and information from the west to the east linked the branches in Livonia and Prussia with the Empire.[70] Though recruits usually stayed in Livonia for the remainder of their careers, there were also brothers in the late Middle Ages who returned from Livonia to the Order's structures in the Empire or Prussia.[71] Until the fifteenth century, the communication between different regions of the Order involved not only the exchange of personnel, goods, and information but also of historical narratives and practices of remembrance.[72] Despite its distant location on the periphery of Europe, Livonia played a unique role in the Order's *memoria*, as the names

---

68 Anette Löffler, 'Die Rolle der Liturgie im Leben der Ordensbrüder: Norm und Wirklichkeit', in *Das Leben im Ordenshaus: Vorträge der Tagung der Internationalen Historischen Kommission zur Erforschung des Deutschen Ordens in Tallinn 2014*, ed. by Juhan Kreem (Ilmtal-Weinstraße: VDG, 2019), pp. 1–20, pp. 16-17.

69 This subchapter has been partially published in: Strenga, 'Remembering the common past', pp. 347–70; for the communication of the Teutonic Order, see Hartmut Boockmann, 'Der Deutsche Orden in der Kommunikation zwischen Nord und Süd', in *Kommunikation und Mobilität im Mittelalter: Begegnungen zwischen dem Süden und der Mitte Europas (11.–14. Jahrhundert)*, ed. by Siegfried de Rachewiltz and Josef Riedmann (Sigmaringen: Thorbecke, 1995), pp. 179–89, p. 179.

70 Boockmann, 'Der Deutsche Orden in der Kommunikation zwischen Nord und Süd', p. 181.

71 Kreem, 'Mobility of the Livonian Teutonic Knights', pp. 164–65; Juhan Kreem, 'Livland als Endstation? Mobilität nach Livland, in Livland und aus Livland', in *Akkon – Venedig – Marienburg: Mobilität und Immobilität im Deutschen Orden*, ed. by Hubert Houben (Ilmtal-Weinstraße: VDG, 2022), pp. 159–70, pp. 168–70.

72 On mobility in the Teutonic Order, see Klaus van Eickels, 'Secure Base and Constraints of Mobility. The Rheno–Flemish Bailiwick of the Teutonic Knights between Regional Bonds and Service to the Grand Master in the Later Middle Ages', in *International Mobility in the Military Orders (Twelfth to Fifteenth Centuries): Travelling on Christ's Business*, ed. by Helen J. Nicholson and Jochen Burgtorf (Cardiff: University of Wales Press, 2006), pp. 167–72; Kreem, 'Mobility of the Livonian Teutonic Knights'; see

of the dead were communicated to the western European bailiwicks.[73] Moreover, Livonia was a *lieu de mémoire* of the Teutonic Order, embedded within the Order's commemorational culture (*Erinnerungskultur*), and stories about the Order's experiences in Livonia became part of the whole organization's foundation memory.

Livonia was a battleground for clashes between Christian and pagan forces from the early thirteenth century. After the arrival of the Teutonic Order in 1237, this struggle became part of the Order's history, which was remembered long after crusading had come to an end and far beyond Livonia itself.[74] The memory of a violent past, heroic deeds, and martyrdom of brethren was represented in different media, which used various techniques to sustain memories of the Livonian crusades in the collective awareness of the Order. The remembrance of these events and of the fallen brethren shaped identity not only in the Livonian branch but also throughout the Order. Although the Order's territorial units – branches and bailiwicks – spread all over Europe had distinct experiences and memorial cultures, they also shared memories, which constituted the Teutonic Order as the group.[75] Thus the *memoria* of the Livonian branch became the experience of the whole Order.[76]

The main sources with references to brethren fallen in Livonia are necrologies and chronicles of the Order used in the western European bailiwicks of the Teutonic Order. The *memoria* of the brethren of the Livonian branch appear in four of the dozen surviving necrologies of the Order: that of Alden Biesen (bailiwick Biesen, c. 1350–1600s),[77] of Mergentheim (bailiwick Franconia, c. 1350–c. 1450),[78] of Hitzkirch (bailiwick of Alsace–Burgundy, 1423),[79] and

---

the contributions in the volume *Akkon – Venedig – Marienburg* particularly Juhan Kreem, 'Livland als Endstation?'.

73 Bailiwicks were territorial structures of the Order in western Europe, which united numerous commanderies and houses.

74 On crusades in Livonia, see, Christiansen, *Northern Crusades*, pp. 89–100; on arrival of the Teutonic Order in Livonia, see Benninghoven, *Der Orden der Schwertbrüder*, pp. 354–69.

75 Udo Arnold, 'Deutschordenshistoriographie im Deutschen Reich', in *Die Rolle der Ritterorden in der mittelalterlichen Kultur*, ed. by Zenon Hubert Nowak (Toruń: UMK, 1985), pp. 65–87, p. 66.

76 Oexle, 'Gegenwart der Lebenden', p. 75.

77 The Necrology of Alden Biesen: Wien, Deutschordenszentralarchiv (DOZA), Hs. 427c; Max Perlbach, 'Deutsch–Ordens Necrologe', *Forschungen zur deutschen Geschichte*, 17 (1877), 357–71; on history of the Alden Biesen necrology, see Udo Arnold, 'Edmund von Werth, priester van de Duitse Orde en bisschop van Koerland', in *Leden van de Duitse Orde in de Balije Biesen* (Bilzen: Historisch Studiecentrum Alden Biesen, 1994), pp. 189–213, p. 209; Udo Arnold, 'Die Deutschordensnekrologien von Alden Biesen und Mergentheim', in *Quellen kirchlicher Provenienz: neue Editionsvorhaben und aktuelle EDV–Projekte*, ed. by Helmut Flachenecker (Toruń: TNT, 2011), pp. 145–59.

78 I have used an unpublished transcription of the Mergentheim necrology made by Alois Seiler. Stadtarchiv Ludwigsburg (StAL) B 280 U 1; *800 Jahre Deutscher Orden: Ausstellung des Germanischen Nationalmuseums Nürnberg in Zusammenarbeit mit der Internationalen Historischen Kommission zur Erforschung des Deutschen Ordens*, ed. by Udo Arnold (Gütersloh: Bertelsmann Lexikon–Verlag, 1990), p. 405; Arnold, 'Deutschordensnekrologien', pp. 152–56.

79 *Das Jahrzeitbuch der Deutschordenskommende Hitzkirch: aus dem Jahre 1432/33, mit dem Fragment A von 1399*, ed. by Gottfried Boesch (Stans: Josef von Matt, 1970), p. 144.

of Bern (Alsace–Burgundy) (fourteenth century).[80] The *memoria* included in these necrologies was performed annually at liturgical services celebrated in the Order's houses from the late fourteenth until the late fifteenth centuries and even beyond in the case of the Alden Biesen. Historical texts, like the Livonian Rhymed Chronicle of the late thirteenth and early fourteenth centuries, also constitute part of the memorial culture of the Teutonic Order and can be considered alongside the necrologies.[81]

The brethren killed in Livonia were mentioned in many memorial narratives of the Teutonic Order but not in every single necrology. For example, the necrologies of the bailiwick Hessen (Marburg) and the house of Ulm (bailiwick Franconia), which date from the fifteenth century, mainly commemorated local brethren, local benefactors, and Masters of the German branch.[82] The focus on remembrance of local brethren and benefactors in the fifteenth century differs from the mid–fourteenth-century necrologies, which had numerous references to brethren from other houses and branches. It seems that as time passed, necrologies were less universal in reach.

The Order's necrologies focused on the remembrance of officials and particularly the Masters of the Livonian branch. The commemorative choices are very clear. The historical narratives and necrologies of the Teutonic Order commemorated only those thirteenth-century Livonian Masters who had died as martyrs. The Livonian Rhymed Chronicle, which describes the conquest of Livonia by the Order, omits the nonviolent deaths of those Livonian Masters, who between 1237 and 1290, had left Livonia to assume the offices of the Grand Master or Prussian Master. The only exception was Hermann von Balk, first Master of the Livonian branch, who died a natural death in 1239 as the Livonian and Prussian Master; the Livonian Rhymed Chronicle praised his outstanding deeds and peaceful death.[83]

Although Livonia was a conflict zone, only six of the twenty Masters of the Livonian branch who held office between 1237 and 1290 were killed on the battlefield: Burkhard von Hornhausen (†1260),[84] Otto von Lauterberg

---

80 Perlbach, 'Deutsch–Ordens Necrologe', pp. 361–62; Rainer Hugener, *Buchführung für die Ewigkeit. Totengedenken, Verschriftlichung und Traditionsbildung im Spätmittelalter* (Zürich: Chronos Verlag, 2014), p. 174.

81 *Atskaņu hronika. Livländische Reimchronik*; on *memoria* and the Livonian Rhymed Chronicle, see, Hartmut Kugler, 'Über die "Livländische Reimchronik". Text, Gedächtnis und Topographie', *Jahrbuch der Brüder Grimm-Gesellschaft*, 2 (1992), 85–104; Hartmut Kugler, 'Die "Livländische Reimchronik" des 13. Jahrhunderts', *Latvijas Zinātņu Akadēmijas Vēsti*, 9 (1993), 22–29; Gustavs Strenga, 'Stāsts par Livoniju ārpus Livonijas? Vecākā Livonijas Atskaņu hronika kā Vācu ordeņa vēsturiskais teksts', in *Grāmata Latvijai ārpus Latvijas: kolektīvā monogrāfija*, ed. by Viesturs Zanders (Rīga: Latvijas Nacionālā bibliotēka, 2021), pp. 27–54.

82 *Hessisches Urkundenbuch*, sect. 1, vol. 3, ed. by Arthur Wyss (Leipzig: Hirzel, 1899), no. 1290; Karl H. Lampe, 'Ein Anniversarienkalender des Deutschen Hauses zu Ulm', *Ulm und Oberschwaben*, 37 (1964), 154–81 (154–55).

83 *Livländische Reimchronik*, vers. 2291–2298; *Ritterbrüder*, no. 46.

84 *Ritterbrüder*, no. 440.

(Lutterberg, †1270),[85] Andreas Westfalen (†1270),[86] Ernest von Ratzenburg (†1279),[87] Gerhard von Katzenelnbogen (†1280),[88] and Wilhelm (Willekin) von Nindorf (†1287).[89] Three of them were commemorated regionally and had their place in the *memoria* of the Order's western European bailiwicks.

The necrology of Alden Biesen preserves the record of an anniversary (25 March) for 'forty three brethren and many others' killed in 1287 in a battle against the pagan Semigallians in Livonia, which took place just before the end of the crusading period.[90] The necrology names Wilhelm von Staden alias Willekin von Nindorf (1282–1287) as the Master of the Livonian branch who had fallen in this battle. Wilhelm/Willekin was also mentioned in the two chronicles of the Livonian branch.[91] The Livonian Rhymed Chronicle even urged the brethren to pray for the souls of these fallen brothers by petitioning the Virgin Mary.

Master Ernst von Ratzeburg, killed in 1279, was commemorated in a similar manner. The necrology of Mergentheim contains his anniversary on 5 March, and with him 70 fallen brethren are also mentioned.[92] The Livonian Rhymed Chronicle also reports Ernst's death, its immediate communication to the Empire, and the impact on the whole Teutonic Order.[93] According to the Chronicle, the Grand Master and all the commanders were informed about von Ratzeburg's death and summoned to Marburg for a meeting about the situation in Livonia. The fourteenth-century Livonian chronicle of Hermann of Wartberge also mentioned Ernst's death together with seventy-one other brethren near Ascheraden.[94]

The brethren who died in Livonia after 1290 no longer appeared in these necrologies because of the loosening of ties between the Livonian branch and the Order's western and southern imperial bailiwicks over the course of the fourteenth century. The bailiwicks of Alden Biesen, Franconia (Mergentheim), and Alsace–Burgundy (Bern and Hitzkirch) produced few brethren for the

---

85 *Ritterbrüder*, no. 537; Otto von Lauterberg was killed during the battle of Karusen with the Lithuanians and Semigallians and was most likely buried in the church of Karusen. Mänd, 'Visuelle Memoria', p. 60.
86 Andreas von Westfalen was a substitute of the Master. *Ritterbrüder*, no. 959.
87 *Ritterbrüder*, no. 695.
88 Gerhard von Katzenelnbogen was a substitute of the Master. *Ritterbrüder*, no. 483.
89 *Ritterbrüder*, no. 624.
90 '8. Kal. Apr. (25. März) Hac die occissus est frater Wilhelmus de Staden magister Lyvonie et cum eo XLIII fratres et multi alii'. Wien, DOZA, Hs. 427c, fol. 12^b; Perlbach, 'Deutsch-Ordens Necrologe', p. 363; *Vartberges Hermaņa Livonijas hronika. Hermanni de Wartberge Chronicon Livoniae*, ed. & trans. by Ēvalds Mugurēvičs (Rīga: Latvijas Vēstures institūta apgāds, 2005), p. 60.
91 *Ritterbrüder*, no. 624; *Livländische Reimchronik*, vers. 10675–10586; *Vartberges Hermaņa Livonijas hronika*, p. 60.
92 'Hic agitur anniversarium fratris Ernst magistri Livonie, qui occisus fuit cum LXX fratribus'. Ludwigsburg, StAL, B 280 U 1, fol. 15; *Ritterbrüder*, no. 695.
93 *Livländische Reimchronik*, vers. 8511–8536.
94 *Vartberges Hermaņa Livonijas hronika*, p. 58.

Livonian branch in the fourteenth century.⁹⁵ Furthermore, in the thirteenth century brethren had habitually returned to the bailiwicks in the west, but from the fourteenth century onwards, brethren who entered Livonian and Prussian branches remained there.⁹⁶ The gradual weakening of communication clearly diminished the exchange of *memoria* between Livonia and the Order in the Empire.

The remembrance of the brethren killed in Livonia is particularly prominent in the necrology of Alden Biesen, with eight records of brethren killed during the Order's struggle against the pagans.⁹⁷ Why then were the Livonian brethren so frequently represented in the necrology of Alden Biesen?

One possible explanation is the role of Bishop Edmund von Werth in the history of the commandery Alden Biesen.⁹⁸ Edmund von Werth, a priest of the Teutonic Order, later the bishop of Courland (1263–1292) in Livonia, died during his stay at the commandery of Alden Biesen.⁹⁹ In the necrology he was commemorated as 'venerabilis dominus Edmundus Curioniensis ecclesie episcopus'.¹⁰⁰ An additional record later noted that the bishop was buried in the chapel of Alden Biesen, where his grave slab stands today.¹⁰¹ For the community of Alden Biesen, Edmund was not an abstract person whose name was recorded in the necrology; the bishop in his tomb was present in the midst of the brethren during every liturgical service held in their chapel.

Edmund von Werth's burial and commemoration at Alden Biesen may have raised awareness of the Livonian branch and its dead. Most of the Livonian Masters and brethren mentioned in the necrology of Alden Biesen were killed during Edmund's episcopate (1263–1292) or shortly before in battles in Courland itself or in bordering Semigallia. Thus the remembrance of the Livonian brethren was the *memoria* of Edmund von Werth's contemporaries. All this

---

95 Militzer, 'Recruitment of Brethren', p. 275; Johannes A. Mol, 'Nederlandse Ridderbroeders van de Duitse Orde in Lijfland. Herkomst, afkomst en carrieres', *Bijdragen en Mededelingen betreffende de Geschiedenis der Nederlanden*, 111 (1999), 1–29 (11).

96 Klaus Militzer, 'Die Einbindung des Deutschen Ordens in die süddeutsche Adelswelt', in *Ritterorden und Region – politische, soziale und wirtschaftliche Verbindungen im Mittelalter*, ed. by Zenon Hubert Nowak (Toruń: UMK, 1995), pp. 141–60, pp. 146–47, 154; Mol, 'The Admission', p. 121.

97 Wien, DOZA, Hs. 427c; Perlbach, 'Deutsch–Ordens Necrologe', pp. 363, 365, 367.

98 Arnold, 'Edmund von Werth', pp. 189–213; Jan–Erik Beuttel, 'Edmund von Werth', in *Die Bischöfe des Heiligen Römischen Reiches 1198 bis 1448*, pp. 313–14.

99 Beuttel, 'Edmund von Werth', pp. 313–14.

100 '19. Kal. Jan. (14. Dec.) obiit venerabilis dominus Emundus Churoniensis ecclesie episcopus frater existens ordinis Theutonicorum'. Wien, DOZA, Hs. 427c, fol. 47ᵃ; Perlbach, 'Deutsch–Ordens Necrologe', p. 367.

101 Arnold, 'Edmund von Werth', p. 209; Clemens Guido de Dijn, 'Altenbiesen vom mittelalterlichen Wallfahrtsort zur Residenz (1220–1794)', in *Alden Biesen: Acht Jahrhunderte einer Deutschordens–Landkommende im Rhein–Maas–Gebiet*, ed. by Johan Fleerackers, Udo Arnold, and Paul Rock (Marburg: Elwert, 1988), pp. 45–82, p. 59, 60; on the history of the bailiwick Alden Biesen see Udo Arnold, 'Die Entwicklung von Balleistrukturen des Deutschen Ordens zwischen Mittelrhein und Nordsee – Biesen, Koblenz and Utrecht', in *Adel, ridderorde en erfgoed in het land van Maas en Rijn: opstellen und Aufsätze zu Ehren von Udo Arnold*, by Arnold, Udo, ed. by Jozef Mertens (Bilzen: Historisch Studiecentrum Alden Biesen, 2012), pp. 25–44.

combined to create a memorial narrative that commemorated the Order's struggle against the pagans and the remembrance of the deceased bishop, while referring to the Christian mission in the Eastern Baltic.

Memoria of the Anonymous Brethren

While the Livonian Masters and other officials were key figures in the necrologies and historical texts, most of the ordinary brethren killed while crusading in the Livonian forests and marshes remained anonymous.[102] The necrology of Alden Biesen contains numerous records in which anonymous Livonian brethren are commemorated. It mentions seven anonymous brethren killed on 25 July in the castle of Warthe, Courland in 1260.[103] On 1 August, the same necrology commemorated thirty-three anonymous brethren killed in Livonia, without specifying the time and circumstances in which they fell.[104] Similarly, the seven unnamed brethren killed in Livonia on 3 February and the seventeen unnamed brethren killed near Memel on 7 January were mentioned in the necrology of Alden Biesen.[105] The absence of the names of the brethren killed, or even those of their fallen leaders, can be observed in other necrologies. The Mergentheim necrology mentions only the number of the brethren killed in the battle of Durbe in 1260, though other necrologies name their fallen leaders: Master Burkhard and *junkher* Karl (Ulfsson).[106] As the last example shows, the absence of names from a specific necrology does not mean that these names were not present in the memorial or historical traditions of the Order.

In medieval necrologies in general, and in those of the Teutonic Order in particular, anonymity was the exception because it contradicted the aim of *memoria* – to sustain the presence of the dead by evocation of their names.[107] The name was the main medium of *memoria* and its inclusion in the necrology was itself of spiritual benefit.[108] Thus, in the surviving necrologies of the Order, commemorated brethren were always named, with the exception of the

---

102 This subchapter has been partially published in: Strenga, 'Remembering the common past', pp. 347–70.
103 'Item occisi fratres septem in Wartha'. Wien, DOZA, Hs. 427c, fol. 28ᵇ; Perlbach, 'Deutsch–Ordens Necrologe', p. 366.
104 'Occisi sunt in Lyvonia XXXIII fratres'. Wien, DOZA, Hs. 427c, fol. 29ᵇ; Perlbach, 'Deutsch–Ordens Necrologe', p. 366.
105 '3. Non. Febr. (3. Febr.) occisi sunt VIII fratres in Lyvonia'. This battle is mentioned in the chronicle of Wartberge and it had taken place at Lenewarden, where the Knight Brethren fought with the Lithuanians in 1261. Wien, DOZA, Hs. 427c, fol. 6ᵃ; Perlbach, 'Deutsch–Ordens Necrologe', p. 363; *Vartberges Hermaņa Livonijas hronika*, p. 42; '7. Id. Jan. (7. Jan.) Occisi sunt in Memela XVII fratres'. Wien, DOZA, Hs. 427c, fol. 3ᵇ; Perlbach, 'Deutsch–Ordens Necrologe', p. 363; most probably this is reference to the battle near Memel that took place between the forces of Master Burkhard von Hornhausen (1257–1260) and the Samogitians. *Livländische Reimchronik*, vers. 4489–4515.
106 'Obierunt C et XXX fratres, qui in Livonia interfecti sunt'. Ludwigsburg, StAL, B 280 U 1, fol. 48.
107 Oexle, 'Memoria und Memoriaüberlieferung', p. 84; Oexle, 'Liturgische Memoria', p. 332.
108 Franz Neiske, 'Funktion und Praxis der Schriftlichkeit im klösterlichen Totengedenken', in *Viva vox und ratio scripta: mündliche und schriftliche Kommunikationsformen im Mönchtum des Mittelalters*, ed. by Clemens M. Kasper and Klaus Schreiner (Münster: LIT, 1997), pp. 97–118, pp. 97–118, p. 117.

previously mentioned Livonian records and the ones that memorialized the battle of Tannenberg (1410) and its hundreds of dead.[109] Even in the case of Tannenberg, the names of the fallen leaders appeared in these commemorational records. The anonymous remembrance of the brethren fallen in Livonia and Prussia may be explained by the difficulties of communication of tens and hundreds of names.

The Order was aware that not all names of the brethren killed were recorded and remembered. The mid–fifteenth century Livonian prayer in the Order's statutes instructed the brethren: 'pray for all the brethren, who have been killed (*geslagen*) or died (*vorstorven*) in this Order since the time the Order has been founded; God knows all their names well'.[110] This prayer indicates that the brethren should be commemorated despite the absence of a specific name. It implies that the *memoria* of long dead and unnamed brethren was as important as the remembrance of those brethren whose names were known.[111] With the help of such remembrance, anonymous brethren were included in the community of the Order's living and dead. Despite the obscurity of their names, they were continuously commemorated.

Although the majority of simple brethren killed in Livonia remained unnamed, there were some who earned a place in the Order's *memoria*. Ludwig von Dietenhofen, killed in Livonia in 1253, was commemorated on 25 July in the necrology of Alden Biesen,[112] and the same necrology commemorated on 10 July two brethren, Wolfram and Friedrich, killed in Livonia some time during the thirteenth or fourteenth century.[113] These three men cannot be traced in any other memorial or historiographical texts of the Teutonic Order, and the reason why their names were recorded remains unknown.

In other circumstances, this anonymity would have meant oblivion, but in the case of the Teutonic Order, the slain brethren were namelessly remembered. It appears that the Order was capable of remembering and recording only a limited number of names of their deceased brethren and most likely accepted anonymity as part of its collective *memoria*. Presumably the names of the brethren were forgotten in cases when a large number of them was killed on the battlefield, but if they died a solitary martyr death, it was more likely that they would be remembered by their names. Yet, as the case of the battle of Durbe shows, anonymity could create different versions of how many brethren were killed during a battle.

---

109 Wien, DOZA, Hs. 427c, fol. 27^a; Perlbach, 'Deutsch–Ordens Necrologe', p. 365; Ludwigsburg, StAL, B 280 U 1, fol. 48.

110 Linköping, Stifts– och Landsbiblioteket [hereafter LSL] manuskript H 33, 2v; *Die Statuten des Deutschen Ordens. Nach den ältesten Handschriften*, ed. by Max Perlbach (Halle: Niemeyer, 1890), no. 10, p. 132; Strenga, 'Distorted Memories and Power', p. 145.

111 Statuten des Deutschen Ordens, no. 10, p. 132.

112 '8. Kal. Aug. (25 Juli) [..] Frater Ludewicus de Dydenhove occisus in Lyvonia'. Wien, DOZA, Hs. 427c, fol. 28^b; Perlbach, 'Deutsch–Ordens Necrologe', p. 365; *Ritterbrüder*, no. 163.

113 '6. Id. Jul. (10. Juli) […] Wolvelramus, Fridericus fratres occisi in Lyvonia'. Wien, DOZA, Hs. 427c, fol. 26^b; Perlbach, 'Deutsch–Ordens Necrologe', p. 365; *Ritterbrüder*, no. 983, 255.

The Battle at Durbe (1260) as a Site of Memory

In the necrologies analysed here, the citing of Livonia or one of its battlefields was the only indication of some kind of context and acted as an agent of memory.[114] Used in this way, the name of Livonia was a 'memory figure' (*Erinnerungsfigur*) that symbolized the experiences of the Order in that region.[115] Within the *memoria* of the Order, Livonia was a land where tens and hundreds of the brethren had suffered martyrdom in the struggle against pagans. Together with the memorialisation of slain Masters and some of the individual fallen brethren, the concentrated remembrance of Livonians within the necrology of Alden Biesen formed Livonia as a site of memory.[116]

One particularly prominent event in the necrologies can be described as the Teutonic Order's *lieu de mémoire*. The site of memory shared by numerous institutions of the Order is the battle of Durbe (Ger. Durben), in Courland, which took place on 13 July 1260. In this battle the Livonian branch, together with Swedish and Danish allied forces, took part in a raid and suffered defeat against pagan Lithuanians, Samogitians, and Curonians.[117] This defeat was one of the darkest chapters in the Teutonic Order's history, comparable with the defeats at Lake Peipus in 1242 and at Tannenberg/Grunwald in 1410.[118] The Livonian branch lost between one hundred thirty and two hundred men at Durbe.[119] For a group only some two hundred strong, this was a devastating result with political repercussions for the Order's policies.[120] This was the only event in the history of the Livonian branch that had so great an influence on the memorial culture of the Teutonic Order outside Livonia, and after the battle of Tannenberg, was the Order's *lieu de mémoire* that served for the remembrance of its defeats.[121]

---

114 This subchapter has been partially published in: Strenga, 'Remembering the common past', pp. 347–70.
115 Assmann, *Cultural Memory and Early Civilization*, pp. 23–24; Assmann, 'Collective memory', p. 129.
116 Nora, 'Between Memory and History', pp. 7–24; on the sites of memory see, Moeglin, 'Hat das Mittelalter europäische lieux de mémoire erzeugt?', pp. 17–38; Schneidmüller, 'Europäische Erinnerungsorte', pp. 39–58.
117 The Curonians changed sides during the battle. Carl August Lückerath, 'Durben', in *Lexikon des Mittelalters*, vol. 3 (München: LexMA-Verlag, 1986), cols. 1471–72; *1260 Metų Durbės mūšis: šaltiniai ir istoriniai tyrimai = The Battle of Durbe, 1260: Sources and Historical Research*, ed. by Vacys Vaivada (Klaipėda: Klaipėdos Universiteto Baltijos regiono istorijos ir archeologijos institutas, 2011).
118 On the battle of Tannenberg, see *Tannenberg – Grunwald – Žalgiris 1410 : Krieg und Frieden im Späten Mittelalter*, ed. by Werner Paravicini, Rimvydas Petrauskas, and Grischa Vercamer (Wiesbaden: Harrassowitz, 2012); Marian Tumler, *Der Deutsche Orden im Werden, Wachsen und Wirken bis 1400* (Wien: Panorama, 1955), p. 293.
119 *Livländische Reimchronik*, vers. 5657; Perlbach, 'Deutsch-Ordens Necrologe', p. 365, Ludwigsburg, StAL, B 280 U 1, fol. 48; *Vartberges Hermaņa Livonijas hronika*, p. 33.
120 The political consequences of the battle were the Lithuanian apostasy and the Curonian and Prussian insurrections. Militzer, 'Recruitment of Brethren', p. 272; Reinhard Wittram, *Baltische Geschichte: Die Ostseelande Livland, Estland, Kurland 1180–1918* (Darmstadt: Wissenschaftliche Buchgesellschaft, 1973), p. 24; Christiansen, *Northern Crusades*, p. 99.
121 On the commemoration of the medieval battles, see *Militärische Erinnerungskulturen vom 14. bis zum 19. Jahrhundert: Träger – Medien – Deutungskonkurrenzen*, ed. by Horst Carl and Ute Planert (Göttingen: V & R Unipress, 2012).

The commemoration of defeats was no less attractive than that of victories. As Aleida Assmann has pointed out, memories of military defeats in modern times did not destroy group self–image (*Selbstbild*) but could even strengthen it.[122] Reinhard Koselleck argues that in contrast to victors, those defeated can profit in the long term from reflection on their defeat, since the trauma of defeat stimulates fruitful self–examination.[123] This is true not only for modern nations but also for medieval societies and groups, which equally commemorated defeats in the long run.[124] For the Teutonic Order, defeat on the battlefield was not only a historical event but also a religious experience to be remembered.[125] *Memoria* of defeats enabled the Teutonic Order to remember its martyrs, shape the identity of the group, and value its aims. Memories of the catastrophes experienced at Durbe and Tannenberg were thus part of the Teutonic Order's cultural memory.

In contrast to commemoration of the late medieval battles, the remembrance of Durbe focused not on the event itself but on the liturgical remembrance of the fallen brethren.[126] Liturgical remembrance of the fallen was normally only one element of the communal programme of commemoration of late medieval battles. After the battle of Tannenberg, both sides founded commemorative chapels, churches, or monasteries close to the battlefield.[127] Durbe, however, remained a commemorative space rooted only in the memorial and historiographical tradition of the Teutonic Order.

The battle at Durbe qualifies as a *lieu de mémoire* because of its wide representation in the Teutonic Order's memorial texts and historiography. The battle and the brethren who fell during it are commemorated in the two oldest surviving necrologies of Alden Biesen[128] and Mergentheim,[129] as

---

122 Assmann, *Lange Schatten der Vergangenheit*, p. 65.

123 Reinhart Koselleck, 'Erfahrungswandel und Methodenwechsel. Eine historisch–anthropologische Skizze', in *Zeitschichten: Studien zur Historik*, by Reinhart Koselleck (Frankfurt am Main: Suhrkamp, 2000), pp. 27–77, p. 52.

124 For example, in Silesia the defeat at the battle of Liegnitz in 1241 was commemorated by the local monastic communities throughout the Middle Ages. Michał Kaczmarek, 'Die schlesischen Klöster und ihr Beitrag zur Memorialkultur', in *Schlesische Erinnerungsorte: Gedächtnis und Identität einer mitteleuropäischen Region*, ed. by Marek Czapliński, Hans–Joachim Hahn, and Tobias Weger (Görlitz: Neisse Verlag, 2005), pp. 29–58, pp. 55–56.

125 On the defeats and the commemorative practices of the Teutonic Order, see Stefan Kwiatkowski, 'Verlorene Schlachten und Gefallene in der geistigen Tradition des Deutschen Ordens', *Ordines Militares Colloquia Torunensia Historica. Yearbook for the Study of the Military Orders*, 16 (2011), 141–57 (146).

126 Klaus Graf, 'Schlachtgedenken im Spätmittelalter. Riten und Medien der Präsentation kollektiver Identität', in *Feste und Feiern im Mittelalter: Paderborner Symposion des Mediävistenverbandes*, ed. by Detlef Altenburg (Sigmaringen: Thorbecke, 1991), pp. 63–70, p. 65.

127 Sven Ekdahl, 'The Battle of Tannenberg–Grunwald–Žalgiris (1410) as Reflected in Twentieth–Century Monuments', in *The Military Orders. History and Heritage*, ed. by Victor Mallia–Milanes and Malcolm Barber (Aldershot: Ashgate, 2008), pp. 175–94 pp. 175–76; Sven Ekdahl, *Die Schlacht bei Tannenberg 1410. Einführung und Quellen*, vol. 1 (Berlin: Duncker & Humblot, 1982), pp. 134–36; Kwiatkowski, 'Verlorene Schlachten', pp. 151–54.

128 Wien, DOZA, Hs. 427c; Perlbach, 'Deutsch–Ordens Necrologe', pp. 363–67.

129 Ludwigsburg, StAL, B 280 U 1, fol. 48.

well as in the necrologies of Bern[130] and Hitzkirch.[131] It was also described in the Order's chronicles, the Livonian Rhymed Chronicle, and the chronicle of Wartberge,[132] as well as in the Cistercian annals of Dünamünde.[133] The necrology of Alden Biesen named the fallen leaders of the crusading forces and explained the reasons why they had sacrificed their lives. It stated that on 13 July, Master Burkhard von Hornhausen with 136 brethren and a Swedish Junker (*junckher*), Karl (Ulfsson), with 'his whole household' had fallen during 'a Christian conflict in the name of Jesus Christ'.[134] Burkhard's name is not represented in the other memorial records that commemorated the battle, such as the necrology of Mergentheim, which commemorated 130 fallen brethren but omitted the slaughtered leaders.[135] Similarly, the names of the Master and his companions were omitted from the two other necrologies of the Teutonic Order that refer to the battle in Livonia as well as the late fourteenth-century chronicle of Wartberge, and the Annals of Dünamünde.[136]

Although omitted in numerous necrologies and historical narratives, Master Burkhard played an important role in this site of memory. Burkhard's death and *memoria* are reflected in the Livonian Rhymed Chronicle.[137] Master Burkhard and other brethren killed at Durbe were celebrated as heroes (*helt*) and their death was depicted as martyrdom (*martir*).[138] Burkhard himself was described as an honourable (*degen*) and chaste (*erkorn*) man, who had been Master for three and a half years.[139] Although Burkhard's participation in the battle was only mentioned in a few lines, the chronicler, in Hartmut Kugler's opinion, by describing the battle and its aftermath, was not as interested in the political circumstances of the event so much as he was focused on the person of Master Burkhard himself.[140] The mention of Master Burkhard in the battle concluded the long description of his good and courageous deeds; thus it was a part of a literary programme that established Burkhard's fame

---

130 Perlbach, 'Deutsch-Ordens Necrologe', pp. 361–63.
131 *Jahrzeitbuch der Deutschordenskommende Hitzkirch*, p. 144.
132 *Vartberges Hermaņa Livonijas hronika*, p. 33.
133 Wolfgang Schmidt, 'Die Zisterzienser im Baltikum und in Finnland', *Finska Kyrkohistoriska Samfundets Årsskrift*, 29/30, (1939/1940), 1–286 (284–86); Konstantin Höhlbaum, 'Die Annalen von Dünamünde', *Neues Archiv der Gesellschaft für ältere Deutsche Geschichtskunde*, 8 (1883), 612–15.
134 '3. Id. (13. Juli) eodem die fuit occisus magister Lyfonie frater Borgardus de Horenhusen cum eo centum et XXXVI fratres, et Dominus Karolus dux de Sweden cum tota familia sua et multi alii obierunt in conflictu christianorum in nomine Jhesu Christi'. Wien, DOZA, Hs. 427c, fol. 27ª; Perlbach, 'Necrologe', p. 365; *Ritterbrüder*, No. 440; Birgitta Eimer, *Gotland unter dem Deutschen Orden und die Komturei Schweden zu Årsta* (Innsbruck: Universitätsverlag Wagner, 1966), pp. 56–57.
135 'Obierunt C et XXX fratres, qui in Livonia interfecti sunt'. Ludwigsburg, StAL, B 280 U 1, fol. 48.
136 *Jahrzeitbuch der Deutschordenskommende Hitzkirch*, p. 144; Perlbach, 'Deutsch-Ordens Necrologe', p. 362; *Wartberge*, p. 54, 56; 'Anno domini 1260 dimicatum est in Durben in die beate Margarete virginis'. Schmidt, 'Zisterzienser', p. 285.
137 *Livländische Reimchronik*, vers. 5677–5686.
138 *Livländische Reimchronik*, vers. 5646–5649.
139 *Livländische Reimchronik*, vers. 5680, 5685.
140 Kugler, 'Livländische Reimchronik', p. 26.

(*fama*).¹⁴¹ Kugler suggests that the chronicle's brief reference to Burkhard's death at Durbe was one of the building stones for the Master's *memoria*.¹⁴²

The Livonian Rhymed Chronicle not only created and sustained the *memoria* of this Master, but also referred to the battle itself. Kugler states that in the text, Burkhard's name was paired with the place of the battle, namely, Durbe. This pairing was used for mnemonic purposes as a combination of personal names and place names, similar to a pairing of *loci* and *imagines* in the classical art of memory (*ars memorativa*).¹⁴³ The combination helped sustain the memories of the battle at Durbe and the deceased Master Burkhard. According to this argument, the chronicle constructed both the *memoria* of Master Burkhard and the defeat at Durbe as the memory of the Teutonic Order.

The commemoration of the battle at Durbe existed not only within the communicative memory of the Teutonic Order but also as part of its cultural memory. The oldest memorial and historical texts commemorating the battle are from the mid–fourteenth or fifteenth century, forty to ninety years after the event.¹⁴⁴ During that time the communicative memory, supported by oral history and eyewitness accounts, had to be transformed into the cultural memory, fixed and recorded.¹⁴⁵ In the case of the battle at Durbe, it is evident that the surviving fourteenth–century necrologies and chronicles mentioning the battle based their narratives on earlier written sources, written down by contemporaries.¹⁴⁶

In this long chain of transmission through numerous media, the *memoria* of the defeat apparently lost its original context in some cases and was thus altered but did not completely lose its original meaning. Two necrologies from the bailiwick Alsace–Burgundy contain references to the battle of 1260. The fourteenth–century necrology of Bern commemorated 150 brethren killed in Prussia on 14 July, incorrectly dating the battle of 13 July in Livonia.¹⁴⁷ Similar inaccuracy can be found in the necrology of Hitzkirch in which the fifteenth–century scribe, while copying the record, had apparently misspelt Livonia as *Linphonia*.¹⁴⁸ These two mistaken records show that the *memoria* of the battle was spread through memorial texts in the Empire, though writers

---

141 *Livländische Reimchronik*, vers. 4405–5595.
142 Kugler, 'Livländische Reimchronik', p. 26.
143 On *imagines* and *loci* in the classical *ars memorativa*, see, Yates, *Art of Memory*, pp. 21–30; on *imagines* and *loci* in the Livonian Rhymed Chronicle, see, Kugler, 'Über die Livländische Reimchronik', pp. 98–102.
144 The necrologies of Alden Biesen and Mergentheim were composed around 1350, and the Livonian Rhymed Chronicle was written in the late thirteenth or early fourteenth century. *800 Jahre Deutscher Orden*, p. 405; Angermann, 'Die mittelalterliche Chronistik', p. 10.
145 Assmann, *Das kulturelle Gedächtnis*, pp. 50–51.
146 On the Livonian Rhymed Chronicle and the usage of written sources and oral tradition, see, Angermann, 'Mittelalterliche Chronistik', pp. 10–11; Kugler, 'Livländische Reimchronik', p. 22.
147 '2. Id. Jul. (14 Juli) obierunt centum XL fratres, qui occisi sunt in Brussia'. Perlbach, 'Necrologe', p. 362.
148 '13. Juli. Anniversarium centum LXX fratrum ordinis nostri, qui occisi sunt apud Linphoniam'. *Jahrzeitbuch der Deutschordenskommende Hitzkirch*, p. 144.

often lacked sufficient knowledge of it. To those using the necrologies of Bern and Hitzkirch for liturgical commemoration, it would have seemed that the martyrs were killed in a distant, even mythical territory.

In summary, the numerous references in necrologies and historical narratives used outside Livonia show that the defeat of the Livonian branch at Durbe on 13 July 1260 became rooted in the memorial culture of the whole Order. This defeat was a site of memory that helped form the identity of the Teutonic Order, like the battle at Tannenberg. It was commemorated as the martyrdom of the Order's brethren and helped maintain memories about both named and anonymous dead, thus forming the identity of the Order as a group that was fighting for the Christian faith. In the late fourteenth and fifteenth centuries this event was still commemorated in the western European bailiwicks of the Order, although it had lost its spatial context. The battle at Durbe was deeply rooted in the cultural memory of the whole Teutonic Order.

Historical Writing and *Memoria*: The Livonian Rhymed Chronicle

Commemoration of the dead brethren involved communication between the Teutonic Order's houses, bailiwicks, and branches, and the recording of their names in the necrologies.[149] As the example of the Order's necrologies shows, *memoria* from Livonia was transferred to the Order's institutions elsewhere in the Empire. This took place not only through social contacts but also by the exchange of written memorial traditions. We know very little about how this took place in the Teutonic Order, but we know more about how it operated in early medieval monastic communities.

Since the early Middle Ages, monastic houses exchanged the names of their dead with other monastic communities for reciprocal commemoration. Communication took place by exchanging letters and a mutual recording of the names of the deceased in the necrologies.[150] The Teutonic Order likewise internally communicated names of the dead brethren and officials, which meant communication over vast distances and between the Order's units. There is no general study of the Teutonic Order's necrologies to date, so it is difficult to estimate the frequency of such interaction. Yet, this interaction was active in the thirteenth century and diminished in the fourteenth century, when all types of contacts gradually decreased in regularity.

Historical writing played an important role in the transmission of memorial information over large distances and its distribution among numerous communities. Histories and necrologies had mutual sources and exchanges of information. As Franz Neiske argues, historical and hagiographical writings

---

149 This subchapter has been partially published in: Strenga, 'Remembering the common past', pp. 347–70.
150 *Jahrzeitbuch der Deutschordenskommende Hitzkirch*, pp. 97–98, 102.

served as sources for necrologies.[151] Such exchange of names between the historiographical texts and the necrologies may have also taken place in the Teutonic Order. One source for the Order's necrologies of non-Livonian houses was the Livonian Rhymed Chronicle, composed in Livonia by a member of the Teutonic Order soon after the end of the crusades.[152] Moreover, with the help of history and *memoria*, the chronicle transmitted to western Europe information about the Order's past in the Eastern Baltic which was important for the Order's identity.

The Livonian Rhymed Chronicle depicts the origins of the Christian faith and the Order in Livonia, describing the events that took place between 1180 and 1290; it was the Teutonic Order's oldest chronicle, written in Middle High German around 1300.[153] Some scholars argue that since the chronicle was written in Middle High German, it was intended for use in the Order's houses outside Livonia because Middle Low German dominated in the Livonian branch.[154] Hartmut Kugler suggests that the Livonian Rhymed Chronicle instructed seasonal guest crusaders (*pilgerine*) and brethren, who had come to Livonia from the regions in the Empire where Middle High German was spoken.[155] Alan Murray adds that the Livonian Rhymed Chronicle 'could have been used to mobilize support in Germany for the permanent crusade'.[156] It must, however, be remembered that the Chronicle was used long after crusades had come to an end in Livonia and was read not only within the western European bailiwicks but in Prussia too.[157]

The Livonian Rhymed Chronicle was thus intended for readers and listeners outside Livonia, that is for the brethren in the Empire where Middle High German was spoken. These are the very regions from which surviving necrologies commemorating Livonians originate. The Order's communities in Alden Biesen, Mergentheim, Hitzkirch, and Bern must have been exposed

---

151 Franz Neiske, 'Gebetsgedenken und päpstlicher Ablaß. Zur liturgischen Memoria französischer Könige und Grafen im Spätmittelalter', in *Memoria in der Gesellschaft des Mittelalters*, ed. by Dieter Geuenich and Otto Gerhard Oexle (Göttingen: Vandenhoeck & Ruprecht, 1994), pp. 178–206, p. 201.

152 Udo Arnold, 'Livländische Reimchronik', in *Die deutsche Literatur des Mittelalters – Verfasserlexikon*, vol. 5, ed. by Kurt Ruh (Berlin: de Gruyter, 1985), cols. 855–62; Angermann, 'Mittelalterliche Chronistik', pp. 9–11.

153 Edith Feistner, Michael Neecke, and Gisela Vollmann-Profe, *Krieg im Visier: Bibelepik und Chronistik im Deutschen Orden als Modell korporativer Identitätsbildung* (Tübingen: Niemeyer, 2007), pp. 79–80; Murray, 'The Structure, Genre and Intended Audience', pp. 235–51, p. 235; Michael Neecke, *Literarische Strategien narrativer Identitätsbildung: eine Untersuchung der frühen Chroniken des Deutschen Ordens* (Frankfurt: Lang, 2008), p. 21; Arnold, 'Livländische Reimchronik', col. 855–62; Wilhelm Brauns, 'Livländische Reimchronik', in *Die deutsche Literatur des Mittelalters – Verfasserlexikon*, vol. 5, ed. by Wolfgang Stammler and others (Berlin: de Gruyter, 1955), cols. 956–67.

154 Murray, 'Structure, Genre and Intended Audience', p. 237; Feistner, Neecke, and Vollmann-Profe, *Krieg im Visier*, p. 100.

155 Kugler, 'Livländische Reimchronik', p. 25.

156 Murray, 'Structure, Genre and Intended Audience', p. 249.

157 Ralf G. Päsler, *Deutschsprachige Sachliteratur im Preußenland bis 1500: Untersuchungen zu ihrer Überlieferung* (Köln: Böhlau, 2003), pp. 157–58.

to its historical and memorial tradition.[158] The text propagated *memoria* of the same dead Masters remembered in the necrologies. Masters Burkhard von Hornhausen, Ernest von Ratzeburg and Wilhelm von Nindorf, whose names appeared in the necrologies of Mergentheim and Alden Biesen, were elaborately described and celebrated as fallen heroes in the Livonian Rhymed Chronicle.[159]

The Livonian Rhymed Chronicle transmitted *memoria* over large distances, but it was also strongly influenced by memorial texts. In addition to charters, other historical narratives, and oral sources, the author used necrologies and other memorial manuscripts, a practice that was followed by other chroniclers of the Order.[160] Furthermore, these chronicles were not only based on memorial sources, but became memorial narratives in themselves.

As a form of historical memory, historical writing was part of the collective or cultural memory that dealt not only with the historical facts, but was also intended to remember the past.[161] Medieval historical writing had various forms and it was used for many purposes. According to Franz–Josef Schmale, all forms of history writing had one primary function: to sustain the relationship between living and future individuals with the dead through remembering of the past.[162] Schmale's definition certainly does not imply that the whole of medieval historiography was effectively a *memoria*, but that close bonds between *memoria* and historical memory existed. Like *memoria*, medieval historical texts commemorated founders of monasteries and created dynastic lines of bishops and abbots, thus sustaining identities of groups.[163]

The Livonian Rhymed Chronicle delineated the succession of the Masters of the Livonian branch by describing the tenure of each Master and celebrating those brethren whose deeds and deaths were particularly important to the history of the branch. The chronicle also had other mnemonic aims. It was a narrative without a clear literary aim: it monotonously described battle after battle, the construction of numerous fortifications, and also shaped the reader's knowledge of the mental geography of Livonia.[164] Hartmut Kugler states that the author used this mental mapping to attempt to create Livonia, namely

---

158 Alden Biesen though has to be considered as an exception, because in that region the Flemish language dominated.
159 *Livländische Reimchronik*, vers. 4405–5595, 8158–8616, 9735–11247; Ludwigsburg, StAL, B 280 U 1, fol. 15; Perlbach, 'Deutsch–Ordens Necrologe', pp. 363–65.
160 Angermann, 'Mittelalterliche Chronistik', pp. 10–11; Kugler, 'Livländische Reimchronik', p. 22; Mary Fischer, *Di Himels Rote: The Idea of Christian Chivalry in the Chronicles of the Teutonic Order* (Göppingen: Kümmerle Verlag, 1991), p. 173; Udo Arnold, 'Livländische Reimchronik', col. 859; Hartmut Boockmann, 'Die Geschichtsschreibung des Deutschen Ordens. Gattungsfragen und "Gebrauchssituationen"', in *Geschichtsschreibung und Geschichtsbewusstsein im späten Mittelalter*, ed. by Hans Patze (Sigmaringen: Thorbecke, 1987), pp. 447–69, p. 450.
161 Goetz, *Geschichtsschreibung*, p. 13, 297.
162 Franz–Josef Schmale, *Funktion und Formen mittelalterlicher Geschichtsschreibung: eine Einführung* (Darmstadt: Wissenschaftliche Buchgesellschaft Darmstadt, 1985), p. 144.
163 Goetz, *Geschichtsschreibung*, pp. 284, 298.
164 Kugler, 'Über die Livländische Reimchronik', p. 88.

Nieflant, as a memorial landscape (*Gedächtnislandschaft*) in the historical self-consciousness of the Order's brethren.[165] The chronicle applied a variety of mnemonic techniques to create and sustain memory of the Order's struggle against pagans.[166] By reflecting the Order's beginnings in Livonia, the chronicle contributed to the group's founding myth, which was essential for its identity.[167]

Because the evocation of names is an essential element of the medieval *memoria*, the Livonian Rhymed Chronicle would not have fulfilled any memorial functions if it had not been performed.[168] In fact, medieval chronicles were written to be performed, read, and heard. It is not known exactly how and on which occasions the Livonian Rhymed Chronicle was used. Some scholars have suggested that the Livonian Rhymed Chronicle was read as a *Tischbuch* during meals in the Order's houses.[169] The Order's statutes instructed the reading of the word of God (*Godes worte*) during mealtimes, and usually adapted biblical texts and saints' lives were read.[170] It has been assumed that the Chronicle was in circulation for these purposes in the Livonian houses of the Teutonic Order. Kugler has pointed out that, as a text read during the mealtimes, the Livonian Rhymed Chronicle had a function of 'social *memoria*'.[171] In his opinion, such reading was not done for didactic purposes – to inform the brethren about the group's history – but primarily 'to attain presence among the living of those not present or dead', namely the presence of the deceased brethren.[172] Kugler's suggestions allow us to understand this chronicle as a socially formative text that formed part of the Order's life in the fourteenth and fifteenth centuries.

The suggestion that the chronicle was used as a *Tischbuch*, however, has been contested recently, challenging the idea that it would have qualified as a religious text.[173] Yet evidence from late fourteenth-century Prussia shows that a close connection existed between the Order's chronicles and liturgical

---

165 Kugler, 'Über die Livländische Reimchronik', p. 98.
166 Kugler, 'Über die Livländische Reimchronik', p. 102.
167 Assmann, *Das kulturelle Gedächtnis*, p. 76
168 Oexle, 'Liturgische Memoria', pp. 332–33.
169 Brauns, 'Livländische Reimchronik', col. 963; Angermann, 'Mittelalterliche Chronistik', p. 11; Fischer, *Di Himels Rote*, p. 173.
170 *Statuten des Deutschen Ordens*, p. 41; Robert Mohr, 'Die Tischlesung im Deutschen Orden. Eine Institutionsspezifische Lehrform', *Das Mittelalter*, 17, 1 (2012), 76–84; Murray, 'Structure, Genre and Intended Audience', pp. 241–42; Jürgen Sarnowsky, 'Buchbesitz, Bibliotheken und Schriftkultur im mittelalterlichen Preußen', in *Mittelalterliche Kultur und Literatur im Deutschordensstaat in Preussen: Leben und Nachleben*, ed. by Jarosław Wenta, Sieglinde Hartmann, and Gisela Vollmann-Profe (Toruń: UMK, 2008), pp. 291–308, p. 306; for the newest take on *Tischlesung* in the Teutonic Order, see Arno Mentzel-Reuters, 'Leseprogramme und individuelle Lektüre im Deutschen Orden', in *Neue Studien zur Literatur im Deutschen Orden*, ed. by Bernhart Jähnig and Arno Mentzel-Reuters (Stuttgart: Hirzel, 2014), pp. 9–58, p. 37.
171 Kugler, 'Über die Livländische Reimchronik', pp. 103–04.
172 Oexle, 'Gegenwart der Lebenden', p. 81; Kugler, 'Über die Livländische Reimchronik', pp. 103–04.
173 Murray, 'Structure, Genre and Intended Audience', pp. 241–42; see also, Feistner, Neecke, and Vollmann-Profe, *Krieg im Visier*, pp. 99–100.

and theological texts. Records of the *Marienburger Ämterbuch* show that a copy of the Livonian Rhymed Chronicle was kept in the sacristy of St Mary's Church in the Grand Master's residence, Marienburg, alongside approximately fifty other liturgical and theological texts: bibles, patristic works, and liturgical manuscripts.[174] In the records from 1394 and 1398, the Livonian Rhymed Chronicle, referred to as the *Cronike von Lyeflande*, was recorded as one of twelve German texts; it was bound together with another text that was part of the Teutonic Order's repertoire – the rhymed *Apokalypse* of Heinrich von Hesler.[175] Besides the Livonian chronicle, the book collection kept in the sacristy of the Marienburg castle's main church also contained a manuscript of the Prussian chronicle, most likely the one written by Nikolaus of Jeroschin that was bound together with other texts.[176] These two, along with the Legend of Barlaam and the Song of Roland, were the only books that had no visible liturgical or theological character.[177] Another Prussian copy of the *Lieflandische cronica* can be found in the inventory of the castle church in Thorn in 1418 and 1446, where it was similarly part of a collection of liturgical and theological books.[178]

Although the chronicles were not liturgical or religious texts in *sensu stricto*, this does not mean that they had no influence on the Order's liturgical practices and liturgical *memoria*. The Livonian Rhymed Chronicle was as much a historical text as it was a memorial one; it provided the Order's brethren with information about their predecessors who had died in the struggle with pagans in Livonia. The presence of two chronicles of the Order that described events linked to the Order's early history on the eastern shore of the Baltic, found in the sacristy of the Grand Master's residence, suggests they may have been used for liturgical purposes or as sources for sermons.[179] As a residence of the Grand Master, Marienburg was the centre of the Teutonic Order and equally that of the Order's *memoria*, where its history was remembered. The crypt of St

---

174 *Das Marienburger Ämterbuch*, ed. by Walther Ziesemer (Danzig: A. W. Kafemann, 1916), pp. 124, 125; Arno Mentzel-Reuters, *Arma spiritualia: Bibliotheken, Bücher und Bildung im Deutschen Orden* (Wiesbaden: Harrassowitz, 2003), p. 249.

175 Päsler, *Deutschsprachige Sachliteratur*, p. 353; Susanne Ehrich, *Die 'Apokalypse' Heinrichs von Hesler in Text und Bild: Traditionen und Themen volkssprachlicher Bibeldichtung und ihre Rezeption im Deutschen Orden* (Berlin: Erich Schmidt, 2010); Arno Mentzel-Reuters, 'Heinrich von Hesler – von Thüringen nach Preußen. Facetten deutschsprachiger Bibeldichtung 1250–1350', in *Der Deutsche Orden und Thüringen: Aspekte einer 800-jährigen Geschichte*, ed. by Thomas T. Müller (Petersberg: Imhof, 2014), pp. 43–74.

176 Mentzel-Reuters, *Arma Spiritualia*, p. 249.

177 *Marienburger Ämterbuch*, pp. 124, 125.

178 *Das grosse Ämterbuch des deutschen Ordens*, ed. by Walther Ziesemer (Danzig: Kafemann, 1921), pp. 436, 458. It has been noted that at least theoretically these entries of *Lieflandische cronica* refer to *Jüngere Livländische Reimchronik*, but it seems unlikely. See Päsler, *Deutschsprachige Sachliteratur*, p. 272.

179 Mentzel-Reuters, 'Leseprogramme und individuelle Lektüre im Deutschen Orden', p. 34

Mary's Church, the chapel of St Anne, was after all where the Grand Masters were buried.[180]

All this shows that in the Teutonic Order, historical writing had a close relationship with *memoria* and was used to support remembrance. The Livonian Rhymed Chronicle served as a medium of *memoria* that not only transmitted information about the Order's history but also invoked the fallen in its performance. This Chronicle was one of the key elements that sustained collective memory of the Teutonic Order and was essential for the Order's *memoria*.

Conclusion

The space played a central role in the origin story of the church of Riga. Though in the scholarship the Chronicle of Henry of Livonia has been seen as the main media for the narrative of the early stages of the Christian mission, the cathedral of Riga and burials of the first Livonian bishops in its chancel (and its direct proximity) were essential for the group's past and identity. Bodies of Meinhard and Berthold most likely were transferred from Üxkull to the cathedral in the late 1220s, thus accompanying the grave of bishop Albert and making the narrative of the origin complete. These founding bishops in the Middle Ages were never canonised, yet they were most likely seen as saintly figures and their remembrance was the cornerstone of the collective memory of the church of Riga. Their successors (bishops and archbishops of Riga), who died in Livonia, were buried next to them, thus strengthening the legitimacy of the office. Chapter 4 shows the importance of the cathedral chancel as an environment of memory and its memorial and political significance when the Teutonic Order tried to take control over it in the late fifteenth century.

The collective memory of the Teutonic Order shaped the reality in which the knight brethren lived. This memory of the Order's experiences in Livonia, which was manifested through chronicles, necrologies, grave slabs, and other memorial media, told the story and provided justification for the Order's presence in the Eastern Baltic. These memories, through their transmission to other regional bodies, were used to shape the identity of the whole Order, emphasizing the group's crusading past. The commemoration of the fallen brethren in Livonia created a framework within which the identities of the Order were formed.

Despite the lack of serial sources for the *memoria* of the Teutonic Order in Livonia, it is possible to reconstruct numerous structures of memory, which existed in the Livonian branch and the whole Order. The events of the crusading period also dominated the collective memory of the Teutonic Order in later centuries. The battle of Durbe (1260) was a site of memory,

---

180 Sławomir Jóźwiak and Janusz Trupinda, *Organizacja życia na zamku krzyżackim w Malborku w czasach Wielkich Mistrzów: (1309–1457)* (Malbork: Muzeum Zamkowe, 2011), pp. 119, 479.

and the fallen brethren were commemorated far beyond Livonia. The battle and slain brethren were commemorated in the Order's necrologies in the western European houses. It was also described in the Order's chronicles. The commemoration of this defeat strengthened the identity not only of the Livonian branch but of the whole Order. Moreover, the brethren killed in other Livonian battles during the thirteenth century were also commemorated in the houses of the Teutonic Order outside Livonia. When the name of Livonia appeared in the necrologies and historical narratives of the Teutonic Order, Livonia was operating as a memorial device symbolising the Order's experiences in that region. This exchange of memories between the Order's branch in Livonia and its western European bailiwicks stopped soon after the end of the crusading in the Eastern Baltic. Yet like the case of the commandery in Alden Biesen, the brethren in the Empire continued to commemorate the brothers killed in Livonia. The reason for such continuity may have been the presence of the tomb of Edmund von Werth, a thirteenth-century bishop from Livonia in the chapel of Alden Biesen.

Memoria of the Teutonic Order focused on commemorating its high ranked officials. In the case of the Livonian branch, only the names of the Masters killed during the thirteenth-century crusades were transmitted to the Empire and recorded in the necrologies of the Order's western European houses. Likewise they were mentioned in the Order's Livonian chronicles. It is likely that those Masters who died non-violent deaths were commemorated regionally but did not arouse the interest of the Order's institutions outside Livonia. *Memoria* of the Masters who died as martyrs was recorded in the historical narratives of the Order and became part of the Order's collective memory.

The historiography of the Teutonic Order was part of its memorial culture. The Livonian Rhymed Chronicle, written in Middle High German around 1300, was not only a historical text but also reflected the memorial practices of the Order and served to create *memoria* of individuals mentioned in it. The chronicle itself was a medium of *memoria*. As the evidence from late fourteenth-century Prussia shows, the Livonian Rhymed Chronicle was kept together with liturgical and theological texts in the sacristies of at least two Prussian castles. Thus it may have been used as a source of information for the commemoration of the Order's past during liturgical services.

The Livonian branch of the Teutonic Order had a rich collective memory and memorial culture, which referred both to the experiences of the branch and its deceased brethren. This memory was used both to sustain corporate identity and to legitimize the Order's political aims. The Order focused on the remembrance of its leaders, but by commemorating them and nurturing their individual *memoria*, the Order was sustaining its identity and its own mission.

CHAPTER 2

Commemoration of a Group and its Leaders

The commemoration of leaders was important for the collective memory of medieval religious communities. The commemoration of bishops, abbots, priors, abbesses, Masters, provosts, and deans shaped the identity of a group because a group demonstrated its continuity and legitimacy by remembering a leadership. The leaders were not just representing themselves. In their office, they represented a group, their predecessors, and future successors as well as the group's resources, all of which were important to commemorate. They themselves were also part of different networks – kinship and social relationships – and thus the leaders could try to integrate commemoration of their family or friends in their own *memoria*.

This chapter explores how a leader's commemoration reflects the collective memory of a whole group and how a leader's *memoria* was used to foster the collective memory of a group. To demonstrate how the *memoria* of individuals was integrated within the commemoration of these groups, this chapter will focus on the commemoration of the Livonian Masters and the leaders of the Riga cathedral chapter.[1] This chapter also briefly sketches the individual remembrance of the ordinary brethren from the Teutonic Order.

Commemoration of the Brethren in the Teutonic Order

During the crusading years, the members of the military orders were constantly exposed to the risks of a violent death. As shown in the first part of this book, fallen brethren were commemorated as martyrs. In the late Middle Ages, the military orders, and the Teutonic Order in particular, were less frequently involved in military confrontations.[2] Most brethren died a natural death and were not venerated in necrologies of numerous Orders' houses across Europe. Individual brethren were commemorated by the house to

---

1 In the chapter the focus is on *memoria* of the Riga cathedral chapter, yet recently remembrance (surviving grave slabs) of the canons in other Livonian cathedral chapters has been studied. See Mänd, 'Vicarius, Canonicus et Episcopus', pp. 11–30.
2 After the end of the crusading, the Livonian branch fought the pagan Lithuanians and then the Russian schismatics. See Norbert Angermann, 'Livländisch–rußische Beziehungen im Mittelalter', in *Wolter von Plettenberg und das mittelalterliche Livland*, ed. by Norbert Angermann and Ilgvars Misāns (Lüneburg: Verlag Nordostdt. Kulturwerk, 2001), pp. 129–44.

which they belonged, but the range and force of the remembrance depended on their status, i.e. the Order's highest officials were granted more elaborate *memoria* than ordinary brethren.[3]

Military orders provided not only proper Christian burial and remembrance of their brethren for the salvation of their souls but also *memoria* of individual members, which was essential to the group history.[4] *Memoria* encompassed each Order as a group, and remembrance of individuals was an important part of this process.[5] Medieval *memoria* was closely bound to an individual, and *memoria* of a group always referred to an individual.[6] As already pointed out, *memoria* of individuals contributed to the memory of a group, shaping its self–consciousness and identity.[7]

Although *memoria* of individuals was important for collective memory in the Teutonic Order and its Livonian branch, little is known about such *memoria* of ordinary brethren. Within the Teutonic Order, the death of a brother was first communicated to the branch's or the bailiwick's main house – the residence of the Master or commander – and then to other houses. In the Prussian branch, the news of a brother's death was circulated in a letter known as a *Todenbrief*.[8] The *Todenbrief* had to be sent to the Grand Master's or Master's residence similar to the manner in which the death of the Livonian lay confraternity members had to be announced, by sending a letter to the Master's 'main chapel'.[9] The letter's circulation marked the beginning of the commemoration with a mass and prayers in other houses.[10]

The Teutonic Order granted burial and remembrance to its members, but the statutes and their legislative supplements hardly regulated how individual *memoria* of ordinary brethren was to be organized and performed.[11] The statutes briefly described the Masters' *memoria* but that of the brethren is mentioned in the discussion of vigils.[12] Vigils had to be celebrated for the remembrance of 'the lay confraternity members and the benefactors of the house in an anniversary, and when a brother dies'.[13]

Despite the absence of detailed regulation of the brethren's *memoria*, it was performed in every Order's house. The mid–fifteenth century prayer, which was included in a copy of the statute manuscript from an unnamed

---

3 Nicholson, 'Memory and the Military Orders: An Overview', p. 18.
4 For the Templar practices of commemoration in their houses, see Michael J. Peixoto, 'Maintaining the Past, Securing the Future in the Obituary of the Temple of Reims', *Viator*, 45.3 (2014), 211–35.
5 Oexle, 'Gegenwart der Toten', p. 34.
6 Oexle, 'Memoria als Kultur', pp. 49–50.
7 Oexle, 'Liturgische Memoria', p. 333.
8 Michael Burleigh, *Prussian Society and the German Order: An Aristocratic Corporation in Crisis c. 1410–1466*, (Cambridge: Cambridge University Press, 1984), p. 67.
9 LUB 2/1 No. 379.
10 Burleigh, *Prussian Society*, p. 67.
11 For the remembrance of the Hospitallers, see Lutrell, 'Spiritual Life', pp. 75–96.
12 *Statuten des Deutschen Ordens*, p. 90.
13 *Statuten des Deutschen Ordens*, p. 119.

house of the Livonian branch, shows the community's preoccupation with remembrance of its deceased members.[14] The prayer instructed living brethren to pray for all the dead brethren of the Order and mentions in particular 'the brethren from this house who have died this year'.[15] The prayer text left an empty space for the naming of the deceased brethren, marked by two capital letters 'N.N.'. As the practice of the Order's communities in the Empire and Prussia shows, every Order's house recorded names of the deceased brethren, and the necrologies served as sources of information for the commemorative prayers.[16] We may assume that every house of the Livonian branch also had its own necrology in which names of deceased brethren were recorded.[17]

If the Teutonic Order guaranteed only very basic commemoration – a funeral, one vigil, and an evocation during liturgical services – other military orders provided more elaborate remembrance even for their ordinary brethren. The Hospitallers, for example, celebrated thirty masses after burial of a brother and an annual anniversary office, while also recording the name of each deceased brother in his house's necrology.[18] While the Teutonic Order did not provide much beyond basic commemorational services, ordinary brethren could have supported their *memoria* individually.

Most of the brethren could not invest large sums of money or real properties in their future remembrance since they were bound by vows of poverty.[19] Yet during their lifetime they were allowed to keep some possessions. Some brethren belonging to old, rich, and influential noble families managed to retain considerable resources and thus were able to make memorial endowments or donations during their lifetime.[20] After death, however, all of these possessions became the Order's property.[21] Most of the brethren in the Teutonic Order died without making written testaments, and the making of memorial endowments depended on the permission of the Master; without it the Order could reclaim the resources invested and abolish the *memoria* they supported.[22]

---

14 *Statuten des Deutschen Ordens*, pp. XXVII–XXVIII, 132, no. 10; LSL H 33, 2v.
15 *Statuten des Deutschen Ordens*, p. 132, no. 10.
16 There are numerous surviving necrologies of the Teutonic Order that belonged to the houses in the Empire and Prussia, and they hold names of the ordinary deceased brethren as well. See Perlbach, 'Deutsch–Ordens Necrologe', pp. 357–71; Lampe, 'Anniversarienkalender', pp. 154–55; *Jahrzeitbuch der Deutschordenskommende Hitzkirch*.
17 The only Livonian necrology about which there is some information is a sixteenth–century Polish copy of the so–called necrology of Ronneburg in which the Knight Brethren were also present. 'Die Annalen und das Necrologium von Ronneburg', in *Hermanni de Wartberge Chronicon Livoniae*, ed. by Ernst Gottfried Wilhelm Strehlke (Leipzig: Hirzel, 1863), pp. 142–48, pp. 134–40.
18 Lutrell, 'Spiritual Life', p. 82.
19 *Statuten des Deutschen Ordens*, p. 21, Regel 1.
20 Sarnowsky, 'Vermächtnis', p. 637.
21 Sarnowsky, 'Vermächtnis', p. 636.
22 Burleigh, *Prussian Society*, pp. 67–68.

In contrast to other military orders, almost no wills or foundational charters of individual brethren have survived from the brethren of the Teutonic Order.[23]

The Teutonic Order's ordinary brethren were not buried in churches or chapels but in cemeteries, usually located in the outer ward of a castle, such as the castle of Marienburg in Prussia, where the cemetery was located next to the St Anne chapel where the Grand Masters rested. The ordinary brethren usually did not have inscribed grave slabs placed on their tombs.[24] The precise motivation for the absence of the inscribed grave slabs remains unknown, but presumably this was an aspect of their monastic poverty that necessitated a very simple burial. Additionally, the erection of elaborate tombs would have been financially unsustainable for the Order.[25] Only one surviving grave slab for an ordinary brother in the Danzig (Prussia) castle cemetery is engraved with a large cross, but this sole survival does not allow us to conclude that such stones were placed on the graves of all the ordinary brethren.[26] Remembrance without inscribed grave slabs was difficult to sustain in the long term because *memoria* needed a place – the grave – where the main commemorative services could take place.[27] *Memoria* of individual brethren was only mediated by the liturgical texts of the house to which they belonged next to their grave. Despite the limited extent of an individual brother's commemoration, the Teutonic Order offered *memoria* as one of the main elements of religious and political bonding to their lay associates (called *familiares*) and allies.[28]

To sum up, ordinary brethren had few opportunities to create memorial foundations or otherwise to stipulate their individual *memoria*. Their *memoria* depended on the willingness of their fellow brethren and their successors to commemorate them. In such circumstances, the *memoria* of the brethren could fade rapidly. The *memoria* of ordinary brethren in the later Middle Ages remained within the house to which they belonged during their lifetime and rarely travelled much beyond it.

---

23 *The Templars: Selected Sources*, ed. by Malcolm Barber and Keith Bate (Manchester: Manchester University Press, 2002), pp. 134–60.

24 Bernhart Jähnig, 'Organisation und Sachkultur der Deutschordensresidenz Marienburg', in *Vorträge und Forschungen zur Residenzenfrage: Hans Patze zum 70. Geburtstag*, ed. by Peter Johanek (Sigmaringen: Thorbecke, 1990), pp. 45–75, p. 52; Nicholson, 'Memory and the Military Orders: An Overview', p. 18; Jóźwiak and Trupinda, *Organizacja życia*, p. 481; Sławomir Jóźwiak and Janusz Trupinda, 'Pogrzeby, pochówki i sposoby upamiętnienia braci Zakonu Niemieckiego w średniowiecznych Prusach. Kilka uwag w kontekście funkcjonowania kaplicy św. Anny', in *Kaplica św. Anny na Zamku Wysokim w Malborku: dzieje, wystrój, konserwacja*, ed. by Janusz Hochleitner and Mariusz Mierzwiński (Malbork: Muzeum Zamkowe, 2016), pp. 27–36, p. 29.

25 *Statuten des Deutschen Ordens*, p. 21, Regel 1.

26 *800 Jahre Deutscher Orden*, p. 108.

27 Zajic, 'Jahrtag und Grabdenkmal', p. 85.

28 Gustavs Strenga, 'Bonding with "Friends" and Allies. The Teutonic Order's Confraternity and Networking Strategies of the Livonian Master Wolter von Plettenberg', *Letonica*, 36 (2017), 136–60.

Memoria for a Master: A Leader's Remembrance

The variety of memorial acts performed to commemorate medieval political leaders was not only a religious practice intended to obtain eternal life for their souls. *Memoria* was also an essential political tool. By remembering the dead, *memoria* legitimated rule in the present.[29] The legitimising nature of *memoria* was particularly important at the point when leaders changed or when there was a transfer of power between generations, as power and authority were founded on the memory and remembrance of previous generations.[30] Conversely, with its sense of continuity, *memoria* also looked to the future, linking rulers not just with their predecessors but also with their successors.[31]

Although leadership in the military orders was not hereditary, *memoria* had the same legitimising power as it did within dynastic polities. *Memoria* of the deceased leaders was also used for these purposes of self-representation and self-legitimation of the groups. The *memoria* of the Masters as the political leaders of the orders played a central role within the memorial cultures of these groups and attracted the greatest pomp.[32] Their remembrance was carefully nurtured, and the deceased Masters were buried in solemn ceremonies, their names recorded in the necrologies of the orders' houses and grave slabs erected.[33] Within the Teutonic Order, every branch focused on remembrance of its own Masters.

Here, however, a contradiction between a Master's real political role and his central role in the Order's *memoria* arose. Although the Masters of the Teutonic Order in Prussia and Livonia were also secular lords, as the leaders of the Order, they were not fully independent in their policies.[34] Within the Order they were considered as *primus inter pares* and not as princely lords.[35] In the Livonian branch, all the late medieval Masters originated from the lower nobility with limited political authority of their own.[36] They depended on high-standing officials, called *Gebietiger*, who occasionally had greater influence than

---

29 Oexle, 'Adel, Memoria und kulturelles Gedächtnis', p. 340.
30 Oexle, 'Memoria als Kultur', p. 38; Oexle, 'Adel, Memoria und kulturelles Gedächtnis', p. 340.
31 Oexle, 'Fama und Memoria', p. 62.
32 Malcolm Barber, *The New Knighthood: A History of the Order of the Temple* (Cambridge: Cambridge University Press, 1994), p. 185.
33 On the remembrance of the Templar Masters, see *The Templars: Selected Sources*; on *memoria* of the Hospitallers' Masters, see Sarnowsky, 'Tod des Großmeisters', pp. 205–16; Lutrell, 'Spiritual Life', pp. 75–96, pp. 81–82; on *memoria* of the Masters in the latter two and the Teutonic Order, see Sarnowsky, 'Vermächtnis', pp. 641–43; on the grave slabs of the leaders of the Teutonic Order's Livonian branch, see Anu Mänd, 'Visuelle Memoria', 59–92.
34 Militzer, *Von Akkon zur Marienburg*, pp. 140–41; Boockmann, *Deutsche Orden*, pp. 186–88; on the functions of the Order's Masters in different branches, see Klaus Militzer, 'Unterschiede in der Herrschaftsauffassung und Herrschaft und Verwaltung in den Zweigen des Deutschen Ordens', in *Herrschaft, Netzwerke, Brüder des Deutschen Ordens in Mittelalter und Neuzeit*, ed. by Klaus Militzer (Weimar: VDG, 2012), pp. 1–23.
35 Sarnowsky, 'Das Vermächtnis', p. 635.
36 Militzer, 'Recruitment of Brethren', p. 276.

the Masters themselves, and the Masters had to consult a group of advisors in their decision making.[37] The Livonian Masters depended not only on inner factions of brethren originating from Westphalia and the Rhineland but also on its external commitments. Until 1410 the Livonian Masters were elected in Marienburg; from the fifteenth century on, they became more independent, and the Grand Master now only confirmed a candidate elected within the Livonian branch.[38]

The Masters were leaders of the branch, and the scope of their leadership reached far beyond their lifetime because the office of the Master ensured continuity within the Order.[39] Individuals holding this position were transmitting the legitimacy of the office; therefore their remembrance was a practice that guaranteed political and institutional continuity. The Masters were the only brethren of the Teutonic Order to whom long-term *memoria* was granted by the statutes.[40] Their bodies were laid to rest in prestigious burial places, which became important for the Order's self-representation. The remembrance of deceased Masters embodied *memoria* of all the dead brethren of the Order, and when the Masters were commemorated, all other anonymous brethren were usually also included.

The death of a Master was a moment of a potential political instability. Therefore, the Order's statutes gave detailed instructions on the transmission of power. Remembrance played an important role in this process. Before the election of a new Master, the deceased Master had to be buried and commemorated.[41] Apparently it was the custom to only hold elections after forty days of mourning, as was the case in Livonia after the death of the Master Heidenreich Vincke von Overberg (1438–1450) in 1450.[42] After his death, a Master's name had to be recorded in the necrologies (*des meisters iartith zal men schriven*) 'to commemorate him there,' where he was buried.[43] The Livonian version of the statutes instructed that Masters were to be commemorated on their anniversaries with a vigil in all of the Order's (branch's) houses with a sung mass celebrated where they were buried.[44] Unfortunately, there are no documentary or liturgical sources describing the exact performance of the funerals and commemorations of the Livonian Masters.

Yet there are some descriptions of how Grand Masters were buried and commemorated. The funeral followed quickly after a Grand Master's death. Konrad von Erlichshausen (1441–1449) died in his chamber in the Grand Master's apartments in the castle of Marienburg on Friday, 7 November 1449,

---

37 Militzer, *Von Akkon zur Marienburg*, p. 143–44; *Statuten des Deutschen Ordens*, pp. 96, no. 7.
38 Jähnig, *Verfassung und Verwaltung*, pp. 142–43.
39 Militzer, *Von Akkon zur Marienburg*, p. 143.
40 *Statuten des Deutschen Ordens*, p. 90.
41 Militzer, *Von Akkon zur Marienburg*, p. 138.
42 LUB 11, no. 51; on the elections in the Order, see Urban, *The Teutonic Knights*, pp. 15–16.
43 *Statuten des Deutschen Ordens*, p. 90; Arnold, 'Deutschordensnekrologien', p. 147.
44 *Statuten des Deutschen Ordens*, p. 119.

and was buried three days later on Monday, 10 November, after Mass in the chapel of St Anne.[45] During a Grand Master's funeral, many candles were burnt; at the funeral of Grand Master Konrad von Jungingen in 1407 in Marienburg, the castle's officials paid for two stones (twelve kilograms) of wax.[46]

The statutes stipulated that after the death of a Master, all his clothing had to be distributed to the poor, and one needy man was to be fed for a year.[47] In Prussia, Grand Masters were commemorated with almsgiving to local and distant poor; in Marienburg, after the death of the Grand Master Konrad von Jungingen in 1407, the castle's officials distributed two marks to the poor for the Master's remembrance.[48] A donation of ten marks was given to the 'poor house' in Danzig in his memory.[49] The Order distributed numerous donations to Prussian monasteries and nunneries in remembrance of Konrad von Jungingen and paid six marks to a priest for masses celebrated over a year for the Grand Master's soul.[50]

Although the medieval sources on the *memoria* of the Livonian Masters are scarce, numerous mid- and late-sixteenth century historical narratives mirror the rich memorial tradition of the Livonian branch. For example, *Kleine Meisterchronik*, a narrative describing lives and deeds of all Livonian Masters produced after the Reformation (1535–1544) was apparently influenced not only by earlier historical texts, but also by memorial portraits of the Masters' lives.[51] These early modern historical narratives were based on medieval memorial texts aimed at creating perpetual fame and remembrance of the Masters.

Despite the fact that the executive power of the Masters was restricted, they were celebrated in remembrance as sole leaders of the Order and its branches. The funeral, mourning, and remembrance of the Masters were important elements in the transmission and legitimation of power. The scant source material does not allow us to establish the pattern of the Masters' *memoria*, but the statutes make it clear that *memoria* granted by the Order was focused around their burial place within the Master's residence, where regular liturgical anniversaries were celebrated.

---

45 Jóźwiak and Trupinda, *Organizacja życia*, p. 479; Sarnowsky, 'Der Tod des Großmeisters', p. 206.
46 *Das Marienburger Tresslerbuch der Jahre 1399–1409*, ed. by Erich Joachim (Bremerhaven-Mitte: Kniess, 1973), p. 425; Jóźwiak and Trupinda, *Organizacja życia*, p. 479.
47 *Statuten des Deutschen Ordens*, p. 90.
48 *Marienburger Tresslerbuch*, p. 474; on almsgiving practices in Marienbrug castle between 1399–1409, see Marek Radoch, 'Wspieranie ubogich przez wielkich mistrzów krzyżackich w latach 1399–1409 (w świetle księgi podskarbiego malborskiego)', *Komunikaty Mazursko-Warmińskie*, 243 (2004), 69–86.
49 *Das Marienburger Tresslerbuch*, p. 423.
50 *Das Marienburger Tresslerbuch*, p. 423, 435; Sarnowsky, 'Das Vermächtnis des Meisters', p. 642.
51 Antje Thumser, 'Livländische Amtsträgerreihen des Mittelalters. Kleine Meisterchronik – Rigaer Bischofschronik – Series episcoporum Curoniae', in *Geschichtsschreibung im mittelalterlichen Livland*, ed. by Matthias Thumser (Berlin: LIT, 2011), pp. 201–54, at p. 209.

Individual Remembrance of the Master: Heidenreich Vincke von Overberg

The individual *memoria* granted to the Masters by the statutes was very basic, and it included only remembrance performed within the structures of the Teutonic Order.[52] In order to foster their remembrance by involving other individuals and communities, the Masters had to possess their own resources and to lay out their memorial requests in a written form.

Medieval rulers used wills to define 'two different futures: [...] their own future [...] of their body's burial and their soul's welfare, and secondly, [...] the future of their family and the family estate'.[53] These two futures – private and political– were interdependent and influenced each other. Within the last wills of rulers, the private future – *memoria* – was created by help of the donations and endowments for *ad pias causas*: almsgiving, chantry foundations, and other kind of donations.[54] Such testaments named a burial place and expressed wishes for future commemoration.[55]

In the case of the Teutonic Order, it is evident that *memoria* of the group always referred to *memoria* of individuals, and likewise *memoria* of an individual referred to the remembrance of a group.[56] In *memoria* a Master represented not only himself but all the previous and future Masters and the whole branch and the Order: all the living and the dead brethren. As the foundation of the Livonian Master's physician (*artzte*) Johann Kerssenbrugge alias Osenbrugge (*Osnabrück*) (†1451) created in 1445 shows, the *memoria* of one Master almost automatically involved remembrance of all the Livonian Masters.[57] Kerssenbrugge wanted the Cistercian nuns in Riga to commemorate the living Master Heidenreich Vincke von Overberg and his family, two early fifteenth-century Masters, Konrad von Vietinghof (1401–1413) and Siegfried Lander von Spanheim (1415–1424), and all the other Livonian Masters as well.[58]

Only one charter of a memorial foundation created by a Livonian Master survives. On 20 June 1447, Heidenreich Vincke von Overberg leased a mill near Riga (*bruder Bartholdes mölen*) and the lands surrounding it to the

---

52 *Statuten des Deutschen Ordens*, p. 90.
53 John Gillingham, 'At the Deathbeds of the Kings of England, 1066–1216', in *Herrscher- und Fürstentestamente im westeuropäischen Mittelalter*, ed. by Brigitte Kasten (Köln: Böhlau, 2008), pp. 509–29, p. 509.
54 Babendererde, *Sterben*, pp. 27–59.
55 On the last wills of the medieval rulers, see *Herrscher- und Fürstentestamente im westeuropäischen Mittelalter*; for the memorial programs laid out in the royal testaments, see Jörg Rogge, 'Testament, Will and Intent. Bestimmungen und Verfügungen der englische Könige Heinrich IV., Heinrich V. und Heinrich VI. über die Nachfolge auf dem Thron, die Weitergabe und Verwendung ihres Besitzes sowie zur Sicherung ihres Seelenheils und der Memoria', pp. 545–71, pp. 554–66.
56 Oexle, 'Memoria als Kultur', pp. 49–50.
57 LUB 10, no. 150, 151, 179; Rīga, Latvijas Universitātes Akadēmiskā bibliotēka (University of Latvia Academic Library) (LUAB), R, Ms. 61, fols. 48^a, 57^a–57^b.
58 LUB 10 No. 150; *Ritterbrüder*, no. 121, 530;

Cistercian convent of St Mary Magdalene in Riga, requesting a remembrance in return.[59] Vincke's foundation was not intended to be an independent memorial chantry, and the *memoria* of the living Master was started soon after the lease of the mill.[60]

In contrast to other memorial foundations, Heidenreich Vincke's effort was rooted in the present, and its aims were to be accomplished during the founder's lifetime. Although the foundation aimed to commemorate 'all living and deceased brethren', the main focus of this *memoria* was the remembrance of Heidenreich Vincke himself and the future Livonian Masters.[61] In addition to the convent's prayers, one virtuous and educated nun had to be chosen in order to read 'a psalter' to commemorate the Masters' souls.[62]

In the charter 'we and our successors' – present and future Livonian Masters – were named twice as the main individuals to be commemorated. So the *memoria* founded by Heidenreich von Vincke was 'prospective' and not 'retrospective' *memoria*.[63] It was directed towards remembrance of the future Masters, alongside the current one, but was not meant to commemorate the Masters before Vincke von Overberg. The *memoria* of the present and future living was based on the liturgical concept of the two *memento* performed during the Mass, which meant that not only the dead (*defuncti*) but also the living (*viventes*) were liturgically remembered.[64] Consequently, the separate remembrance of *viventes* was predestined to turn into *memoria* of *defuncti*.

The aims of 'prospective' *memoria* were far-reaching. It enabled founders to communicate with their successors and future living, sending them a message of continuity.[65] This message strengthened the legitimacy and positions of their successors.[66] A medium of the message was the secular posthumous fame (*fama*), which emerged as a result of *memoria*.[67] The prospective *memoria* of

---

59 LUB 10, no. 351; Schmidt, 'Zisterzienser', pp. 165–67.
60 LUB 10, no. 150, 351.
61 LUB 10, no. 351.
62 A reading of a psalm was the usual commemorative prayer for the dead in the Order. LUB 10, no. 351; Kwiatkowski, 'Verlorene Schlachten', p. 147.
63 Oexle, 'Adel, Memoria und kulturelles Gedächtnis', p. 343; Assmann, *Das kulturelle Gedächtnis*, p. 61.
64 On liturgy and remembrance of the living, see Schmid, 'Liturgische Gebetsgedenken', pp. 640–41; on remembrance of the living rulers, see Carola Fey, 'Spätmittelalterliche Adelsbegräbnisse im Zeichen von Individualisierung und Insitutionalisierung', in *Tradition und Erinnerung in Adelsherrschaft und bäuerlicher Gesellschaft*, ed. by Werner Rösener (Göttingen: Vandenhoeck & Ruprecht, 2003), pp. 81–106, p. 90; Ralf Lusiardi, 'Familie und Stiftung im Mittelalter. Einige komparative Bemerkungen zum christlich-abendländischen Kulturkreis', in *Gestiftete Zukunft im mittelalterlichen Europa: Festschrift für Michael Borgolte zum 60. Geburtstag*, ed. by Wolfgang Huschner and Frank Rexroth (Berlin: Akademie-Verlag, 2008), pp. 353–73, p. 366.
65 Graf, 'Fürstliche Erinnerungskultur', p. 6.
66 Oexle, 'Adel, Memoria und kulturelles Gedächtnis', p. 343.
67 Oexle, 'Fama und Memoria', p. 62; Oexle, 'Adel, Memoria und kulturelles Gedächtnis', p. 340; Oexle, 'Memoria als Kultur', p. 48; on late medieval *fama*, see Klaus Graf, 'Nachruhm– Überlegungen zur fürstlichen Erinnerungskultur im deutschen Spätmittelalter', in *Principes: Dynastien und Höfe im späten Mittelalter*, ed. by Cordula Nolte, Ralf-Gunnar Werlich, and Karl-Heinz Spiess (Stuttgart: Thorbecke, 2002), pp. 315–36.

Heidenreich Vincke equally aimed to create the Master's fame even during his lifetime.

Although the *memoria* of the Masters created by this foundation was clearly 'prospective', the 'prospective' and the 'retrospective' *memoria* co–existed in the remembrance of all the brethren. The Master requested that the Cistercian nuns pray for 'all the living brethren of our order' 'four times a year' and that they commit to commemorating 'all the deceased Order's brethren' 'with sung vigils and Requiem Masses' for 'the eternal times'.[68]

Among the other aims of this foundation was spiritual support for the Order's military activities in the present. In the foundation charter, Heidenreich Vincke requested that the nuns pray for the Masters and the Order during the Order's wars and military campaigns against 'nonbelievers' (*ungelovigen*) by singing masses, 'attentive prayer', and other 'noble deeds'. During the military campaigns, one nun was to read a psalter and to pray for the Masters, 'us and our successors', and the Order. The prayers said during the military campaigns were part of *memoria* delivered for the living brethren of the Order and could have been transformed into the remembrance of the dead if the brethren were killed during the struggle against the *ungelovigen*.

Collective aims combined with individual ones in Vincke's foundation. The Master used collective resources to foster his own *memoria* by leasing the Order's mill to the Cistercian nuns.[69] Yet the Cistercian nuns were entrusted with sustaining *memoria* of the individual Livonian Masters – present and future – and care for the collective remembrance of the whole Livonian branch. This investment into the *memoria* of the future Masters had a clear political dimension.

Heidenreich Vincke von Overberg died on 29 June 1450, and four weeks later the city council of Reval organized his commemoration.[70] On 12 August the Livonian officers (*Gebietiger*) informed the Grand Master that the deceased Master was mourned with great grief and that they had completed the mourning forty days after Vincke von Overberg's death.[71] It remains unknown how the Cistercian nuns in Riga commemorated Master Vincke after his death and how long the *memoria* of the Livonian Masters was maintained by the nuns, yet the charter of the foundation had survived until the late sixteenth century when the Jesuits copied all remaining privileges and documents of the St Mary Magdalene convent.[72]

---

68 LUB 10, no. 351.
69 LUB 10, no. 351.
70 *Kämmereibuch der Stadt Reval: 1432–1463*, ed. by Reinhard Vogelsang (Köln: Böhlau, 1976), no. 828; LUB 11 no. 51; Philipp Schwartz, *Chronologie der Ordensmeister über Livland, der Erzbischöfe von Riga und der Bischöfe von Leal, Oesel-Wiek, Reval und Dorpat* (Riga: Deubner, 1879), p. 76; *Ritterbrüder*, no. 912.
71 LUB 11 no. 51.
72 Rīga, LUAB, R, Ms. 61.

Although not much is known about the remembrance of the Livonian Masters, the foundation made by Master Vincke von Overberg reveals how the Masters created individual *memoria* during their lifetime. Where Vincke's physician Kerssenbrugge fostered *memoria* of the living Master and his dead predecessors, the foundational charter issued by Vincke shows him to be exceptionally preoccupied with his own remembrance and with that of the future Masters. Vincke's foundation did not reflect on the group's past but focused on the prayers delivered in the future. Strict boundaries between the private and political or individual and collective *memoria* cannot be drawn, for the remembrance of a prominent individual meant the commemoration of the whole group and of the office of the Master itself.

The Master as Patron of the Remembrance

Although the Order lavished great care on the Masters' *memoria*, it sought to attract resources in support of commemoration from external sources too. This need developed because brethren of the Order were restricted in amounts of resources they could spend for *memoria*.[73] The Livonian branch used external resources to foster *memoria* of Masters, as well as some brethren, in external religious institutions. The memorial foundation created by Johann Kerssenbrugge allows us to analyse a liturgical remembrance of the Teutonic Order's Livonian branch, its Masters and the brethren, and the contexts that were important in creating this *memoria*.[74]

On 8 July 1445 Johann Kerssenbrugge founded a chantry in the Cistercian convent's church in Riga, dedicated to the Holy Virgin, St Procopius, St Matthew, and all the saints of God.[75] Kerssenbrugge's endowment and establishment of a memorial chantry were sanctioned not only by the Master Heidenrich Vincke von Overberg but also by the archbishop of Riga, Henning Scharpenberg (1424–1448).[76] His main aim was to create *memoria* of Johannnes Kerssenbrugge himself, his family, and also of the Order's brethren.

This is a unique case of the Order's *memoria*. Although Kerssenbrugge was collaborating closely with the Teutonic Order, his status in the Order is not clear. It is known that Kerssenbrugge had a degree of a master (*meister, magister*), and a licentiate in medicine; he is believed to have been a priest of Osnabrück diocese.[77] Yet, neither in his own foundational charter, nor in

---

73 Sarnowsky, 'Vermächtnis', p. 245.
74 The foundational charter created by Kerssenbrugge and the charters of the confirmation have survived in a form of late sixteenth–century copies recorded in a cartulary, which holds copies of the charters of the Cistercian convent in Riga. Riga, LUAB, R, Ms. 61, fols. 48ª, 49ª–51ª, 57ª.
75 LUB 10 No. 150.
76 LUB 10 no. 151; LUB 10 no. 179; Riga, LUAB, R, Ms. 61, fols. 48ª, 57ª–57ᵇ.
77 Isidorus Brennsohn, *Die Aerzte Livlands von den ältesten Zeiten bis zur Gegenwart : Ein Biographisches Lexikon nebst einer historischen Einleitung über das Medizinalwesen Livlands* (Riga: Bruhns, 1905), p. 233;

the charters of the archbishop and the Master, is it specified whether Kerssenbrugge was a brother of the Order or was a priest, who practiced as a physician as well.[78]

Although his affiliation with the Livonian branch is not clear, Kerssenbrugge was present in the entourage of consecutive Livonian Masters for several decades during the first half of the fifteenth century. He was a physician to the Livonian Master in 1426 (*des erwerdigen heren mesters van Lifflande arste*) and was in Livonia in the 1440s as a doctor and scribe of the Livonian branch.[79] The nineteenth-century Baltic German historians attributed to him the role of cathedral canon in Riga too, but this cannot be substantiated.[80]

Even if Kerssenbrugge was not a member of the Order, he had a close relationship with its Masters. Heidenreich Vincke von Overberg confirmed Kerssenbrugge's chantry, describing Johann as 'our doctor', who is 'very dear to me'.[81] It is evident from numerous sources that Kerssenbrugge accompanied Vincke von Overberg on his trips. During the latter stages of the Master's life, when he was ill, Kerssenbrugge was close at hand.[82]

The *memoria* created by Johannn Kerssenbrugge reflected his close relationship with the Teutonic Order. But it was Johannn Kerssenbrugge and not the Order or its officials who created this chantry, including 'one perpetual Mass' (*eine ewige misse*), to be celebrated after his death in the Cistercian convent at the altar of St Margareth.[83]

Johann Kerssenbrugge requested commemoration in the form of memorial Masses in which a chantry priest and an additional priest had to commemorate and to pray for his soul, souls of his parents (*miner olderen*), and all his friends (*leffhoveden*).[84] The name of the still living Master Heidenreich Vincke von Overberg is mentioned next. Remarkably, Kerssenbrugge implied that not only the Master himself had to be memorialized at the altar of St Margaret but also his parents and 'friends' as well.[85] In addition to Vincke and his family, Kerssenbrugge also requested *memoria* for two early fifteenth-century Livonian Masters, Konrad von Vietinghof (1401–1413) and Siegfried Lander von

---

Livlands Geistlichkeit vom Ende des 12. bis ins 16. Jahrhundert, ed. by Leonid Arbusow sen. (Mitau: J. F. Steffenhagen und Sohn, 1913), p. 155.

78 Rīga, LUAB, R, Ms. 61, fols. 48^a–49^b, 57^a–57^b.
79 LUB 7, no. 812; LUB 9, no. 832; LUB 10, no. 100; Brennsohn, *Ärzte Livlands*, p. 233; Rīga, LUAB, R, Ms. 61, fol. 57b.
80 Brennsohn, *Ärzte Livlands*, p. 233; *Livlands Geistlichkeit*, p. 81.
81 Rīga, LUAB, R, Ms. 61, fol. 48^a.
82 On Vincke von Overberg's illness, see, LUB 11 no. 14, 23, 25; *Kämmereibuch der Stadt Reval. 1432–1463*, no. 788.
83 LUB 10 No. 150; about the altar St Margrethen in the Cistercian convent, see Bruiningk, *Messe und kanonisches Stundengebet*, p. 472.
84 *Lefhovede* has at least two meanings: a close relative and a 'once-loved' person. In my opinion, *lefhovede* here is applied to all individuals with whom the person during the lifetime had close relationships and not only those who were his kin. LUB 10 No. 150.
85 LUB 10 No. 150.

Spanheim (1415–1424).[86] Finally, the souls of all the other Masters, *Gebietiger*, and the brethren of the Teutonic Order (evidently of the branch) were to be commemorated in perpetuity.[87]

It is clear why Kerssenbrugge created *memoria* for himself, his parents, and his friends but why would he request *memoria* for the living Master Heidenreich Vincke and his family and friends? Furthermore, why did Kerssenbrugge so actively foster *memoria* of this knightly corporation and its Masters? Was the chantry an act of appreciation of the Master, his patron?

Patronage is defined as 'the action of a patron in supporting, encouraging, or countenancing a person, institution, work, art, etc.'.[88] The Master as patron supported Kerssenbrugge's career and offered not only his own, but also an institutional support to this memorial foundation and the client. In return, Kerssenbrugge stipulated the remembrance of his patron and his patron's family. This apparently was both a social patronage and also a memorial patronage that served as a kind of insurance for the longevity of the *memoria*.

The Master's patronage and his own commemorative aims are demonstrated within the charter confirming Kerssenbrugge's foundation issued by Heidenreich Vincke on 15 December 1445.[89] In this charter, Vincke von Overberg implied that the chantry priests should commemorate all individuals mentioned in Kerssenbrugge's foundational charter.[90] Remarkably, in the list of persons who had to be commemorated by this chantry, the Master placed himself, his successors, and the whole Order before Kerssenbrugge, his parents, and family members. This placing of names manifests the Master's own memorial program that aimed first of all to foster *memoria* of himself, his predecessors, and the Teutonic Order and only then to provide remembrance for the founder and his kin.

Another detail shows the Master's wish to influence the performance of remembrance in Kerssenbrugge's chantry. In his charter the Master requested that the deceased brethren Johann Spee (*Speden*), once bailiff of Wenden, be remembered as well.[91] Johann Spee is not mentioned either in the foundational charter of Kerssebrugge or in the archbishop's charter.[92] Apparently this was a conscious decision of the Master to make Johann Spee also a part of *memoria* at Kerssenbrugge's chantry. Spee's name follows the two deceased Masters: Lander von Spanheim and von Vietinghof.

---

86 *Ritterbrüder*, no. 121, no. 530; LUB 10 No. 150.
87 LUB 10 No. 150.
88 Werner Gundersheimer, 'Patronage in the Renaissance. An Exploratory Approach', in *Patronage in the Renaissance*, ed. by Stephen Orgel and Guy Lytle (Princeton: Princeton University Press, 1982), pp. 3–23, at p. 3.
89 Rīga, LUAB, R, Ms. 61, fols. 48^a–48^b; LUB 10, no. 179.
90 Rīga, LUAB, R, Ms. 61, fol. 48^a.
91 Rīga, LUAB, R, Ms. 61, fol. 48^a; *Ritterbrüder*, no. 825, p. 781.
92 Rīga, LUAB, R, Ms. 61, fols. 57^a–57^b.

The reason for the Master's decision to include Johann Spee in the chantry of Kerssenbrugge lies in his career. Vincke himself had been bailiff of Wenden before heading the Livonian branch in 1438, and Johann Spee was his predecessor in the bailiff's office.[93] Even if Johann Spee was not a close associate of Vincke von Overberg[94] and had died before the future Master claimed the bailiff's office in Wenden, this fostering of his remembrance appears as a tribute to his predecessor. By commemorating his predecessor, Vincke von Overberg created a genealogy of the Order's offices. The Master used the foundation by his physician to commemorate his own associates, predecessors, and friends.

The example of Spee's integration within *memoria* performed at Kerssenbrugge's chantry shows the influence exerted by Master Vincke on this memorial foundation. Were all the choices of Kerssenbrugge's foundation, except those of himself and his family, part of the Master's and the Order's memorial program?

Kerssenbrugge had a long career as the Masters' physician, which had begun in the 1420s, and close relationships with numerous consecutive Masters followed.[95] Kerssenbrugge stated that his motivation in making this memorial foundation was not only for the sake of his own soul, but also for the sake of souls of 'his dear lords', the Livonian Masters.[96] The appearance of the two Livonian Masters, Konrad von Vietinghof (1401–1413) and Siegfried Lander von Spanheim (1415–1424), among the commemorated is noteworthy; Kerssenbrugge was first mentioned in Livonia only in 1426, after the two Masters had passed away.[97] It remains unclear why the Masters Lander von Spanheim and von Vietinghof and not, for example, Kerssenbrugge's contemporary Cisse von dem Rutenberg (1424–1433), were explicitly named in the charter.

Kerssenbrugge's foundation was supported by the Order and its Master, but it did not receive the Order's financial support. He had enough resources to finance *memoria* on his own. In the charter, Kerssenbrugge founded the chantry using as he says, 'my possessions' (*mynem gude*) 'earned with hard work during my service'.[98] The annuity rent mentioned in the charter was 25 old Rigan marks, but later, in the *Kämmereiregister*, the amount of 40 marks is recorded for payment to the priests.

After Kerssenbrugge's death in 1451, the chantry continued to function, as Riga's *Kämmereiregister* shows. Between 1451 and 1474, 40 Rigan marks were paid annually for Kerssenbrugge's chantry to the Cistercian convent in

---

93 *Ritterbrüder*, no. 912.
94 For example, a *lefhovede* was mentioned in the charter of foundation. LUB 10, no. 150.
95 LUB 7, no. 812; LUB 9, no. 832; LUB 10, no. 100; Brennsohn, *Ärzte Livlands*, p. 233.
96 LUB 10, No. 150.
97 LUB 7, no. 812.
98 '[…] datt ick mitt schwarem arbeide in minem denste vorworven hebbe […]'. LUB 10, no. 150.

Riga.⁹⁹ This rent was paid in two annual payments of 20 marks directly to two chantry priests. However, at least in the periods between 1451–1455 and 1463–1471, and despite Kerssenbrugge's wish to have two priests celebrating the memorial masses, only one chantry priest seems to have been active.¹⁰⁰ During this twenty-year period, the chantry employed altogether six priests, and one of them, Johannn Meyer, who is also mentioned in the foundation charter, celebrated memorial masses for sixteen years.¹⁰¹

This foundation benefited the *memoria* of the Livonian branch in general and its Masters in particular. Johann Kerssenbrugge not only invested his own resources in order to foster the remembrance of this corporation but also gained from the Order's commemoration. The strong presence of the Order's and its Masters' *memoria* in remembrance performed at the chantry altar meant that the Order would support the existence of the chantry and the performance of *memoria* long after Kerssenbrugge's death. The inclusion of future Masters ensured the long-term existence and continuity of this memorial foundation.

Grave Slab and Text: Memoria *of Andreas von Steinberg (†1375)*

High status officials of the Teutonic Order were commemorated in numerous ways: in liturgical remembrance, in records of their deeds in the Order's historical narratives, and through the burial of their physical remains and erection of grave slabs. Taken together, these forms of commemoration constructed a memorial image of a deceased person.¹⁰²

In 1939, during archaeological excavations in the ruins of a small, rural church in Ascheraden, the well-preserved grave slab of Andreas von Steinberg (†1375) was found.¹⁰³ Andreas von Steinberg was no ordinary brother of the Teutonic Order but a long-standing commander of the branch's military forces (*Landmarschall*) active for more than twenty years (1354–1375).¹⁰⁴ Therefore it is not surprising that after his death in an accident, a grave slab was placed on his grave and his *memoria* was continually integrated in the Order's collective memory. Yet, it remains unclear why Andreas von Steinberg was buried in the church of Ascheraden; Anu Mänd points out that Andreas should

---

99 *Kämmerei-Register der Stadt Riga 1348–1361 und 1405–1474*, ed. by August von Bulmerincq (Leipzig: Duncker & Humblot, 1909), pp. 249, 252, 255, 256, 259, 261, 264, 265, 268, 269, 272, 274, 275, 278, 281, 282, 285, 286, 289, 293, 296, 299, 300, 303, 304, 306, 307, 310, 311, 314, 318, 319, 323, 324, 327, 328, 331.
100 *Kämmerei-Register der Stadt Riga 1348–1361 und 1405–1474*, pp. 249, 252, 255, 256, 259, 261, 264.
101 Jurgen Daseberge (1451–1453); Hinrik Peynen (1453–1455), Georg Holland (1455–1463); Johannn Meyer (1455–1471); Johann Matczson (1471–1474); her Achylles (1472).
102 Oexle, 'Memoria und Memorialbilder', p. 387, 391.
103 *Latvijas viduslaiku mūra baznīcas*, p. 72; Pēteris Stepiņš, 'Senā Aizkraukles baznīca', *Senatne un Māksla*, 2 (1940), 30–40; Jähnig, *Verfassung und Verwaltung*, p. 144.
104 *Ritterbrüder*, no. 837; Andreas von Steinberg already during his lifetime was mentioned in the chronicle of Hoeneke, see *Die jüngere livländische Reimchronik des Bartholomäus Hoeneke 1315–1348*, ed. by Konstantin Höhlbaum (Leipzig: Duncker & Humblot, 1872), p. 22.

have been buried in the residence of Segewold.[105] It can be assumed that he had died not far away from Ascheraden, and the transportation of his body to Segewold was not possible.

Von Steinberg's grave slab was located in the centre of this rural church, right in front of the altar, and provides a key to understanding of his *memoria*.[106] This grave slab was the only surviving decorated grave slab in the church, having a coat of arms and an inscription. The inscription praised von Steinberg as 'a vigorous warrior of Christ' (*miles Christi strenuus*), who had died during a military campaign (*in expedicione*), 'under a falling tree' (*de casu unius arboris*).[107] Remarkably, this description corresponds with the textual tradition of the Teutonic Order. According to the chronicle of Wartberge, which reported the commander's death during the campaign against the pagan Lithuanians, *Landmarschall* was killed by 'a tree that fell over'.[108] Also a fourteenth-century Order's text originating from Prussia refers to the fallen tree as the cause of the *Lanmarschall's* death.[109] The inscription on the grave slab called for all those who could read it to 'pray for him' (*orate pro eo*).[110] Though the Order's texts and the grave slab mention the accidental death of Andreas von Steinberg, he still was seen as a courageous man, a hero.

The message of these commemorative media are similar in tone and intent, suggesting that they belong to the same memorial and historical tradition. The chronicler may have been present in Livonia at the time, seen the grave slab, and then used the information in his chronicle.[111] But it is more likely that Wartberge drew upon an oral tradition or texts circulating in the Teutonic Order.

In this case, both the grave slab and the chronicle acted as triggers of memory, assisted by the Order's texts, helping the memory to transform in the cultural memory, creating a unified memorial image of von Steinberg. It is plausible that the inscription on the grave slab and the description in the chronicle referred to existing memorial texts, an entry in necrology or annals, for example; in turn, these two media were augmented by liturgical commemoration in the church of Ascheraden and in the Order's churches. Both media had different audiences: those who are present in the place of the burial and those who are at a distance to it; yet the message was identical.

---

105 Mänd, 'Visuelle Memoria', p. 69.
106 Stepiņš, 'Senā Aizkraukles baznīca', pp. 35–36; Mänd, 'Visuelle Memoria', pp. 67–69.
107 'Anno Domini Mccclxxv frater Andreas Stenberg lantmarscalcus obiit de casu unius arboris in expedicione – miles Christi Strenuus. Orate pro eo'. Caune and Ose, *Latvijas viduslaiku mūra baznīcas*, p. 72.
108 'Frater Andreas de Stenberg lantmarsalcus (…) a ruina arboris, qui in exitu hoc imporvise super eum corruit, occubuit' *Vartberges Hermaņa Livonijas hronika*, pp. 134–35.
109 I am grateful to Gregory Leighton for providing a reference to the text. Berlin, Geheimes Staatsarchiv Preußischer Kulturbesitz (GStA PK) XX. HA, OF 281, fol. 115.
110 Caune and Ose, *Latvijas viduslaiku mūra baznīcas*, pp. 67, 72.
111 *Die jüngere livländische Reimchronik*, p. XLIII.

Figure 7: Grave slab of Andreas von Steinberg found in the ruins of Ascheraden medieval church. Photo: National History Museum of Latvia, Neg. Nr. 41922

Commemoration of the Livonian Masters. An Urban Perspective

The death of a medieval ruler influenced not only the ruling family or group but also the ruler's subjects.[112] In the period between the death of a ruler and the investiture or election of a new one, the subjects mourned and commemorated the deceased ruler. Such commemoration occurred not only where the burial took place but also in more distant regions; it made a ruler present in those places where remembrance was performed.[113] Commemoration of a deceased ruler was important for the transfer of the power and also reinforced ties of allegiance between a lord and subjects.

Livonia was not a secular domain but a collection of ecclesiastical estates and the territories of the Teutonic Order. The bishops and the Masters of the Livonian branch functioned as feudal lords as well as religious leaders. In total, eleven Livonian cities were the subjects of the Order and the Masters.[114] As a lord, each Master developed relationships with these cities, issuing privileges and legal acts. This relationship was also confirmed by his personal presence. The Livonian material provides rich evidence of the Master's visits to the cities subject to him, of his lordly entry (*adventus*), ceremony of homage, swearing of oaths, exchange of gifts, and communal meals.[115] This relationship governed by symbolic and material exchange between the lords and their subjects was not limited to the lifetimes of the Livonian Masters, but was also continued after their death. The extent of remembrance of the Masters depended on the specific political and historical circumstances in each city.

Relations between the two largest Livonian cities, Riga and Reval, and the Livonian Masters were somewhat complicated. The relationship between Riga and the Order was one of constant tension, which from the early fourteenth century regularly erupted into diplomatic or military conflicts.[116] Reval's relationship with the Teutonic Order developed differently. The Order established its power over Reval only in 1346 and co-operation rather than dissent char-

---

112 Peter Schmid, 'Sterben – Tod – Leichenbegängnis König Maximilians I', in *Der Tod des Mächtigen: Kult und Kultur des Todes spätmittelalterlicher Herrscher*, ed. by Lothar Kolmer (Paderborn: Schöningh, 1997), pp. 185–215, p. 185.

113 Friedrich Edelmayer, 'Die Leichenfeiern für Ferdinand den Katholischen in den Niederlanden (1516)', in *Der Tod des Mächtigen*, pp. 229–45, pp. 239–40; Oexle, 'Gegenwart der Lebenden', p. 74.

114 Roman Czaja, 'Der Deutsche Orden als Stadtherr im Reich, in Preußen und in Livland', in *Die Ritterorden als Träger der Herrschaft: Territorien, Grundbesitz und Kirche*, ed. by Roman Czaja and Jürgen Sarnowsky (Toruń: UMK, 2007), pp. 127–39, at p. 131.

115 Anu Mänd, 'Signs of Power and Signs of Hospitality. The Festive Entries of the Ordensmeister into Late Medieval Reval', in *The Man of Many Devices, Who Wandered Full Many Ways: Festschrift in Honor of János M. Bak*, ed. by Balázs Nagy (Budapest: Central European University Press, 1999), pp. 281–93; Juhan Kreem, *The Town and Its Lord: Reval and the Teutonic Order (in the Fifteenth Century)* (Tallinn: Kirjastus Ilo, 2002), pp. 42–52.

116 See, Hellmann, 'Deutsche Orden und die Stadt Riga', pp. 1–33.

acterised the relationship between the city and its lord.[117] These different historical and political contexts affected the role of the Livonian Master as lords of the cities. Relations between the Masters and the two largest cities were to a certain extent formed by the oath of fealty.[118] The relationship created by the oath of allegiance also influenced the *memoria* of the lord. In Riga, this oath was given to the Livonian Master and the Teutonic Order after 1452.[119] In Reval, however, the question of an oath of allegiance generated much uncertainty.

Although Reval was part of the Order's possessions in Livonia, when the Order purchased northern Estonia from the Danish king in 1346, it became a dominion of the Grand Master not of the Livonian Master; a relationship of dependency between the Grand Master and Reval persisted until the Reformation.[120] Even though Grand Master Ludwig von Erlichshausen (1450–1467) surrendered northern Estonia to the Livonian Master in 1452, this surrender was not final.[121] It is still unclear whether during the late fifteenth and early sixteenth century the Livonian Master received the oath as the Grand Master's representative or as the Livonian Master in his own right.[122] The city paid homage to both Masters and reconfirmed it every time the Grand or Livonian Master changed. Until 1525, however, the Grand Master remained the city's overlord.[123]

Reval was directly involved in a relationship with individual Masters.[124] In Reval the oath was sworn not to the Order but explicitly to the (Grand) Master (*mineme heren deme meistere*).[125] This personal bond between the Grand/Livonian Masters and the city (Reval), resembles the relationship between king and subjects, and also influenced communal *memoria*.

Both the Grand Masters and the Livonian Masters were commemorated in fifteenth-century Reval with liturgical services after their burial. The remembrance of the Grand Masters is less frequently recorded in the rich Revalian medieval source material than that of the Livonian Masters. The town books

---

117 For Reval's and the Teutonic Order's relations, see Kreem, *Town and its Lord*; Reinhard Vogelsang, 'Reval und der Deutsche Orden. Zwischen städtischer Autonomie und landesherrlicher Gewalt', in *Stadt und Orden*, pp. 34–58.

118 On the oath of fealty, see Magnus Ryan, 'The Oath of Fealty and the Lawyers', in *Political Thought and the Realities of Power in the Middle Ages = Politisches Denken und die Wirklichkeit der Macht im Mittelalter*, ed. by Joseph Canning and Otto Gerhard Oexle (Göttingen: Vandenhoeck & Ruprecht, 1998), pp. 211–28.

119 For the text of the oath given by Riga's city councillors, see *Akten und Rezesse der livländischen Ständetage*, vol. 1, ed. by Oskar Stavenhagen and Leonid Arbusow (Riga: Deubner, 1907), no. 554; Riga's city councillors swore an oath of fealty to the Master Wolter von Plettenberg in 1495, see LUB 2/1, no. 158.

120 Kreem, *Town and its Lord*, p. 29; LUB 2, no. 879.

121 Kreem, *Town and its Lord*, p. 33; LUB 8, no. 823.

122 Kreem, *Town and its Lord*, pp. 33–34, 42–47.

123 When the Teutonic Order in Prussia was secularized in 1525, the Livonian Master Wolter von Plettenberg took over the rights to receive the homage. Kreem, *Town and its Lord*, pp. 43–45; Ritscher, *Reval an der Schwelle*, p. 67.

124 Kreem, *Town and its Lord*, p. 44.

125 *Akten und Rezesse* 1, no. 554; Kreem, *Town and its Lord*, p. 44.

record only one case of the commemoration of a Grand Master. On 11 January 1450, the city council of Reval paid 5 marks and 3 schillings for the funeral service of a *homester*, the deceased Konrad von Erlichshausen (1441–1449), who had died on 7 November 1449.[126]

In contrast to the *memoria* of the Grand Masters, numerous Livonian Masters were remembered in Reval during the fifteenth century.[127] As the council's ledger shows, all of the Livonian Masters who died in office in the period between 1432 and the Reformation received such *memoria*. The first Livonian Master whose remembrance was recorded in the *Kämmereibuch* is Heinrich von Böckenförde, known as Schüngel (1435–1437).[128] The Master died at the end of 1437, between Karkus and Riga, and on 7 January 1438 the city council paid 18 Riga marks for his commemoration.[129] The Revalians also commemorated Schüngel's successor Heidenreich Vincke von Overberg (†1450); on 8 August 1450, the city council of Reval paid 17 marks for the Master's commemoration.[130] Although the exact programme of these funeral services is not known, it seems that the city council, by spending almost the same sum for remembrance, followed a certain routine in commemoration.

A few weeks after the death of Master Johann von Mengede Osthof on 15 August 1469, the city council of Reval celebrated a commemorative service with less expenditure than for Heidenreich Vincke and Schüngel, just 4 ½ Riga marks.[131] The Master's *memoria* took numerous forms. The commemoration took place at three altars, in the Dominican church of St Catherine, in the church of Holy Spirit, and elsewhere. The wife of a burgomaster donated candles for these altars to support the remembrance. In addition, the Master was commemorated liturgically with a vigil and a requiem mass in the Holy Spirit church, where the council's altar was situated. The city council also invited some 'women to pray' for the soul of the Master. Bells were rung 'in all churches' in his remembrance, a common feature provided for in the remembrance of Masters in Reval. When the Livonian Master Johannn Freitag von Loringhoven died in 1494, the churchwardens of St Nicholas received 5 marks as *ludegelt*, that is bell–ringing money.[132] Bell ringing organized by city councils was also an important part of the commemoration of the deceased rulers in the Imperial cities of Germany.[133]

The remembrance of Masters manifested the allegiance and loyalty of the cities towards their deceased lord. In this way, Reval appears to have developed

---

126 *Kämmereibuch der Stadt Reval 1432–1463*, no. 812; *Die Hochmeister des Deutschen Ordens 1190–1994*, ed. by Udo Arnold (Marburg: Elwert, 1998), pp. 128–30.
127 Mänd, 'Visuelle Memoria', pp. 60–64.
128 *Ritterbrüder*, no. 83.
129 *Kämmereibuch der Stadt Reval 1432–1463*, no. 296;
130 *Kämmereibuch der Stadt Reval 1432–1463*, no. 828, 827.
131 *Kämmereibuch der Stadt Reval: 1463–1507*, ed. by Reinhard Vogelsang (Köln: Böhlau, 1983), no. 1382.
132 Tallinn, TLA, f. 31, n. 1, s. 216. fol. 80.
133 Franz Fuchs, 'Der Tod Kaiser Friedrichs III. und die Reichsstadt Nürnberg', in *Der Tod des Mächtigen*, pp. 333–48, at p. 345.

a special relationship with the Masters and Grand Masters of the Teutonic Order, commemorating them soon after their deaths. The *memoria* of both the Grand and Livonian Masters in Reval were organized, and expenses were covered by the city council, just as it organized the *adventus* or solemn entrance of the lord into the city. The commemoration of the Master symbolically concluded the relationship with the deceased Master, and thus the city was ready to await entrance of a new Master and pay homage to him. From the surviving sources, it seems that Reval commemorated the Grand Masters, who were officially its overlords, less frequently than the Livonian Masters, and it shows that the city had a closer relationship with the latter.

Heaven, Purgatory, and Hell according to Dietrich Nagel. *Memoria* of the Cathedral Canons in the Late Fifteenth Century

On Candlemas (2 February) 1447, five individuals – cathedral provost Dietrich Nagel, laymen Andreas Seppelbeke and Hinrik Harnisch, a priest Georg Dazeberg, and a noblewoman Anna van Aalen – founded a memorial chantry in the Riga Cathedral.[134] The foundation charter is remarkable in that it not only explains the founders' memorial preferences but also proclaims their views on death, the afterlife, and *memoria*. In the introduction, the author describes what happens to all people after death and how they should be remembered. He begins by stating that 'all humans are mortal, and blessed are those who have died well in the Lord Christ, but the death of a sinner is terrible, dreadful, and very bad because they stay perpetually separated from God with the prince of darkness damned in hell, in perpetual death, and no memory stays with those dead'.[135] The author goes on to make a strong statement: those in hell 'are erased from the book of the living,' and 'we also forget them and do not commemorate them'. Hell was a place of eternal damnation where the dead were obliterated from the memory of the living. After this description of sinners in hell, the author described those lucky folk who had died in the grace of the Lord, saints whose righteousness 'will never be forgotten' (*nummer wert vorgheten*) by God and men. Saints do not need the prayers of the living, but the living praised and venerated them, and prayed to them for intercession.

---

134 LUB 10, no. 297; Arbusow, *Einführung*, p. 108.
135 'Nademe dat alle mynschen sterflik syn unde salich dejennen syn, de in Cristo deme heren wol vorstorven syn, de doet edder des sunders vorveerlik, greslik unde alto quaed is, wente van Gode ewichliken gescheden blivet se mit deme vorsten der dusternisse vordomet an der helle yn ewigem dode, der der nyne dechtnisse blivet mit den salighen, wente se vordelget syn uthe deme boke der levendighen unde mit den ghuden se nicht werden geschreven. Hirumme wy erer ok vorgheten unde to dessem male nicht mer ghedenken'. LUB 10, no. 297, p. 201.

According to the text, remembering and praying were closely bound. There was a third group of individuals, to which the founders themselves belonged, which were to be intensively remembered with prayers for their souls. These people, although they had died in grace (*yn gnaden*), were exposed to 'great suffering' (*swaren pynen entholden syn*) for a period of time (*tor tyd*).[136] The place of this suffering – purgatory – is not specifically named in the text, but the instruments of their salvation are clearly indicated. The living could help these souls by praying, giving alms, and celebrating the Eucharist at the altar.[137] This meant that these dead should be remembered, and their names had to be evoked.[138]

With an emotive description, the author explained why the living should remember those suffering souls, for they 'are calling the living unceasingly by begging: have mercy on us, have mercy on us, our dear friends'.[139] He also encouraged those praying for the dead with the words of Jesus quoting scripture: 'whatever you did for one of the least of these brothers and sisters of mine, you did for me.'[140] Prayers for the dead are acts of mercy and good deeds that would also benefit the living after their own deaths. After explaining and justifying prayers for the dead, the charter laid out in detail how the *memoria* of the five founders should be established and maintained.[141]

With its vivid descriptions of hell, heaven, and purgatory, the charter was most likely written by Dietrich Nagel, provost of the cathedral chapter, whose name appears first among the founders. Nagel had been a key figure in the Livonian church for forty years, a long-time leader of the central ecclesiastical institution in Livonia – the cathedral chapter of Riga. Born around 1400 in Münder, near Hanover, he studied in Leipzig and Rostock and was a notary as well as a priest.[142] Nagel was first mentioned in Riga in 1425, at which time he was a schoolmaster of St Peter's Church.[143] In 1429 he was appointed a canon of the cathedral, and he subsequently represented the archbishop in Rome (1429–1432); he later became the provost of the cathedral chapter in 1439/42, an office that he held until his death in 1469.[144] Nagel was a highly respected clergyman not only in Livonia but also in the highest circles of the Church. He represented the Church of Riga at the Council of Basel (in attendance 1437–

---

136 LUB 10, no. 297, p. 201; on the purgatory, see Le Goff, *La Naissance du Purgatoire*.
137 LUB 10, no. 297, p. 201.
138 Oexle, 'Gegenwart der Toten', p. 31.
139 'Desse alle ropen ane underlaet to uns yn beghere: Vorbarmet yw unser, vorbarmet yw unser, unse leven vrunde'. LUB 10, no. 297, p. 201.
140 'Wat gy den mynsten don van den mynen, dat do gy my sulven'. LUB 10, no. 297, p. 201; Matthew 25:40.
141 LUB 10, no. 297, p. 202.
142 Brigide Schwarz, 'Prälaten aus Hannover im spätmittelalterlichen Livland: Dietrich Nagel, Dompropst von Riga († ende 1468/anfang 1469), und Ludolf Nagel, Domdekan von Ösel, Verweser von Reval († nach 1477)', *Zeitschrift für Ostmitteleuropa-Forschung*, 49 (2000), 495–532 (500–02); Levāns, 'Lebendigen Toten', p. 11.
143 Schwarz, 'Prälaten', pp. 501–02; *Livlands Geistlichkeit*, pp. 146–47.
144 Schwarz, 'Prälaten', p. 503, 505; *Livlands Geistlichkeit*, pp. 146–47; Levāns, 'Lebendigen Toten', p. 10.

1440), where Enea Silvio Piccolomini, the future Pope Pius II (p. 1458–1464), described him as a man known for his righteousness (*probitate cognitus*); the representatives of the Teutonic Order at the council saw Nagel as a great threat to their interest.[145]

Back in Riga, Nagel was an intellectual and political leader of the local ecclesiastical community. He was an energetic individual who possessed great historical knowledge about the Church of Riga, so essential for defending the interests of the chapter and the archbishop. He wrote a chronicle in Latin on the history of the Riga bishops and archbishops, and during the 1450s, drafted the Archbishop Silvester Stodewescher's (1448–1479) legal documents on the history of the Livonian church as evidence of the struggle with the Teutonic Order.[146] Nagel was highly conscious of the significance of the cathedral of Riga as a memorial site. Both as a notary and as a canon, he had worked with the thirteenth-century chronicles and charters, which referred to the origins of the church in Livonia and Bishops Meinhard, Berthold, and Albert, all of whom were buried in the cathedral.[147]

By the time the foundation charter was issued in 1447, Dietrich Nagel had already proven himself as a leader. When archbishop Henning Scharpenberg was still alive, Nagel was sent to Rome in 1447 on a mission to defend the archbishop's rights over the city of Riga and to promote the Teutonic Order's opponent, Ludolf Grove (1438–1458), as bishop of Ösel.[148] However, a year after the foundation of the chantry, Archbishop Henning Scharpenberg died, and the Grand Master's favourite Silvester Stodewescher was appointed in his place.[149] The foundation charter was issued when Nagel was at the peak of his power; Archbishop Scharpenberg was already old, and his closest collaborators must have assumed that his death was imminent. Furthermore, this expectation may have motivated Nagel to invest in his own self-image because the current Archbishop Henning Scharpenberg had also been the chapter's provost before his election.[150] By 1448, Nagel was also the administrator of

---

145 Schwarz, 'Prälaten', p. 511; Levāns, 'Lebendigen Toten', p. 11.
146 Nagel's chronicle has been lost. Brück, 'Konflikt und Rechtfertigung', pp. 87–88; Levāns, 'Lebendigen Toten', pp. 9–11; Leonid Arbusow, 'Die handschriftliche Überlieferung des "Chronicon Livoniae" Heinrichs von Lettland', *Latvijas Universitātes Raksti. Acta Universitatis Latviensis*, 15 (1926), 189–341 (294–96); Angermann, 'Mittelalterliche Chronistik', p. 17; Mäesalu, 'Historical Memory', pp. 1016–17, 1019, 1021, 1027–29.
147 Levāns, 'Lebendigen Toten', p. 11; Mäesalu, 'Historical Memory', pp. 1016–17.
148 Schwarz, 'Prälaten', p. 513; Bernhart Jähnig, 'Ludolf Grove', in *Bischöfe des Reiches*, pp. 500–01; Brigide Schwarz, 'Eine „Seilschaft" von Klerikern aus Hannover im Spätmittelalter', *Quellen und Forschungen aus italienischen Archiven und Bibliotheken*, 81 (2001), 256–77 (261).
149 Hartmut Boockmann, 'Der Einzug des Erzbischofs Sylvester Stodewescher von Riga in sein Erzbistum im Jahre 1449', *Zeitschrift für Ostforschung*, 35 (1986), 1–17; Gustavs Strenga, 'Gifts and Conflicts: Objects given during the Entry of Archbishop Silvester Stodewescher in the Riga Cathedral (1449)', in *Gift-Giving and Materiality in Europe, 1300–1600: Gifts as Objects*, ed. by Lars Kjær and Gustavs Strenga (London: Bloomsbury Academic, 2022), pp. 77–102.
150 Bernhart Jähnig, 'Henning Scharpenberg', in *Die Bischöfe des Heiligen Römischen Reiches 1198 bis 1448*, p. 657.

the diocese. Nevertheless, the cathedral chapter first elected Nikolaus Sachow (*c.* 1385–1449), the bishop of Lübeck, as the archbishop, and then the Order succeeded in appointing its own man as archbishop and not the eminently suitable Nagel or Sachow.[151]

The aim of this collective foundation was to create a perpetual memorial mass (*eyne ewighe selemissen*) for the founders in Riga Cathedral and to erect an altar dedicated to St Joseph at which it was to be celebrated.[152] The memorial mass was scheduled to follow the morning Marian Mass in the chapel (*na unser leven vrowen missen*).[153] During these services, a pall had to be laid over a bier, and two lights were to be placed beside it, imitating a funeral and imparting a real presence of those commemorated.[154] The chantry employed four or as many priests as it could afford with its annual income of ten new Riga marks, an income granted by the *rentbreve* of the city council.[155] In addition to the memorial masses, these priests for memorial purposes had to sing the canonical hours (*officium*) seven times annually.[156] They were additionally expected to recite the *Requiem eternam* for all Christian souls on other appropriate occasions.[157] The services planned were a busy schedule of commemoration in perpetuity, supported by a sizeable endowment.

Nagel paid careful attention to funding the *memoria* and perhaps joined with others for that very reason. Some of Nagel's predecessors had died in debt, endangering their long-term *memoria*, and thus it was more secure to create it with other individuals and to attract resources from different sources.[158]

As provost, Dietrich Nagel inhabited a privileged position. Like leaders of cathedral chapters elsewhere in the medieval Europe, he controlled the creation of memorial foundations within the cathedral by the chapter's canons.[159] Nagel was a privileged founder of an impressive memorial chantry; he funded the creation of individual *memoria* by the resources of the cathedral chapter. With the consent of the chapter, he endowed the chantry with 50 Riga marks from the chapter income and with 30 marks from the inheritance of the intes-

---

151 Glauert, 'Bindung des Domkapitels', pp. 306–10; Schwarz, 'Prälaten', pp. 513–14; Strenga, 'Gifts and Conflicts', p. 81.
152 LUB 10, no. 297, p. 202; Bruiningk, *Messe und kanonisches Stundengebet*, pp. 454–55.
153 LUB 10, no. 297, p. 203.
154 LUB 10, no. 297, p. 203; Oexle, 'Memoria der Reformation', p. 188.
155 LUB 10, no. 297, p. 202, 203.
156 The Office had to be said on: Christmas day, Easter, three days after Easter, the second Sunday of Easter, Ascension, Pentecost, Corpus Christi, the Assumption of Mary, and Trinity Sunday. LUB 10, no. 297, p. 202, 203.
157 LUB 10, no. 297.
158 Schwarz, 'Prälaten', p. 505.
159 Stijn Bossuyt, 'Founding a Memory. The Legitimation of "Memoria". Foundations in Flanders, *c.* 1100–1350 (Lille, Saint-Omer, and Bruges)', in *Negotiating Heritage: Memories of the Middle Ages*, ed. by Mette Birkedal Bruun and Stephanie Glaser (Turnhout: Brepols, 2008), pp. 125–48, pp. 136–37.

tate priest Nikolaus Falkenberg.[160] Other founders invested lesser amounts; Andreas Sepelbeke endowed 75 marks, Hinrik Harnsch and Georg Dazeberg 36 ½ marks each, and Anna van Aalen only 25 new Riga marks.[161] Altogether 250 Riga marks provided an annual income of 10 Riga marks, which were paid to the chantry priests. Nagel was both founder and patron of this foundation, able to grant resources and space by virtue of his office and to attract powerful chantry wardens.

Although the founders of chantries always aimed for perpetual provision, even minor crises could halt the flow of prayer. In order to ensure continuity, the five founders involved both ecclesiastical and urban authorities as chantry wardens. They required the provost of the cathedral chapter to act as the chantry's patron. In this way, Nagel obliged his successors to take care of these services and with the chantry wardens to oversee the celebration of masses and prayers. Johan Meyer, a cathedral vicar, was also chosen to be a chantry warden alongside the provost.[162] Alongside those two clergymen, two powerful laymen were chosen as wardens: the Riga burgomasters Hinrik Eppinghusen and Gerwen Gendena.[163] In the event of a warden's death, the surviving three chose a successor.[164] The wardens were also entitled to transfer these memorial services to another church if they could not be continued in the cathedral of Riga.

This foundation charter is particularly interesting since it strictly regulates not only the commemoration but also the long–term existence of the foundation. Two copies were made; one to be kept by the city council, the other, together with the account book, money, and precious liturgical objects, in the hands of the wardens.[165] By appointing influential wardens and entrusting them with numerous functions, the founders formed the memorial chantry as a robust institution.

Nagel and his co–founders had clearly given much thought to the issue of remembering. They instructed that those who made donations and endowments be recorded in the inventory (*inventarium*), their names alongside their gifts (*se alle by namen mit erer gifte*), so that they would not be forgotten (*nicht vorgheten werden*).[166] Once a year, when the priests were paid their salaries, these names had to be read out so that the priests would know 'from whom they [were to] receive their alms and for whom they were obliged to pray.'[167] After receiving the annual stipend, each one of them had to celebrate

---

160 Falkenberg was a priest in Riga in the 1430s and 1440s. LUB 10, no. 297, p. 203; *Livlands Geistlichkeit*, p. 51.
161 LUB 10, no. 297, p. 203.
162 *Livlands Geistlichkeit*, p. 137.
163 LUB 10, no. 297, p. 204; Böthführ, *Rathslinie*, no. 312, 323.
164 LUB 10, no. 297, p. 205.
165 LUB 10, no. 297, p. 205.
166 LUB 10, no. 297, pp. 203–04.
167 LUB 10, no. 297, pp. 203–04.

a vigil and a memorial mass. The founders perceived the commemoration as a counter–gift and wished that they and their gifts would be known to the recipients, the commemorators.[168] This was a ritual by which the benefactors were introduced to their commemorators; it created a bond between the dead and the living.

Nagel was acting in a tradition laid down by provosts before him. In 1463 Dietrich Nagel issued a charter regarding his predecessor Arnold von Brinke, who had endowed 1000 Riga marks for the chantry of the Three Kings in the cathedral.[169] Nagel and his successors were responsible for the maintenance of the chantry and thus for von Brinke's *memoria*.

The foundation charter of 1447 reveals a clear sense of the purpose and structure of the proposed *memoria*, which were manifested once again in the confirmation charter issued by Archbishop Silvester in 1464.[170] The archbishop praises his cathedral provost and restates the beneficiaries of the chantry: the soul of Dietrich himself, the souls of his predecessors and successors, the souls of Nagel's parents, and the souls of the living and dead peasants of the cathedral chapter (*pro agricolis et rusticis prepositure Rigensi*).[171] Silvester fostered Nagel's chantry by ensuring episcopal protection and financially by endowing it with 500 old Riga marks.[172] The endowment had to deliver an annual payment for the chantry even during Nagel's lifetime. After Nagel's death, the provost and his predecessors were to be commemorated on his obit by the cathedral's canons and the chantry priests.[173] Money was also distributed to the priests on this anniversary, following the practice laid down in the foundation charter of 1447.[174]

Though their relationship was full of mistrust at the beginning, Silvester Stodewescher's endowment seems to be a sign of his allegiance to the cathedral chapter and to Nagel personally, following their close collaboration during the preparation of the treaty of Kircholm (1452).[175] In addition to supporting the individual remembrance of Nagel, Silvester also invested 500 marks in the institutional *memoria* of the cathedral chapter, particularly that of its provosts. The charter claims that many of Nagel's predecessors had died and were buried outside Livonia (*extra patriam*) and that the endowment therefore secured their *memoria* in Riga.[176] The fact that the cathedral chapter's living and deceased peasants were also included for commemoration further reinforces the institutional character of the chantry that was already integral

---

168 On the gift and remembrance see Bijsterveld, *Do ut des*, pp. 17–27, 25.
169 LGU 1, no. 407; *Livlands Geistlichkeit*, p. 33.
170 LUB 12, no. 255.
171 LUB 12, no. 255, p. 146; Schwarz, 'Prälaten', p. 515.
172 LUB 12, no. 255.
173 LUB 12, no. 255.
174 LUB 10, no. 297, p. 205; LUB 12, no. 255, p. 146.
175 Levāns, 'Lebendigen Toten', pp. 9–10; Strenga, 'Gifts and Conflicts', p. 84.
176 The provost Andreas Patkull died in Rome in 1429. Schwarz, 'Prälaten', p. 505, 515; LUB 12, no. 255, p. 146; *Livlands Geistlichkeit*, p. 158.

to the foundation charter in 1447.[177] Stodewescher's charter and endowment shaped this chantry to commemorate all members of the cathedral chapter of Riga, thus creating a community of clerics and laymen, living and dead. Here, as in other case studies discussed in this book, individual remembrance was intertwined with *memoria* of an institution and community, past and future; the *memoria* of Nagel and his family became part of the institutional remembrance of the cathedral chapter.

Conclusion

The collective memory of a group was represented by the commemoration its leaders. The Teutonic Order in Livonia focused its collective *memoria* of the group on the commemoration of the branch's leader, the Livonian Master. If the *memoria* of the brethren was limited in their resources, and grave slabs in most occasions were not placed on their graves, the *memoria* of the Master of the Order as well as the resources of individuals affiliated to it were invested. The memorial foundation of Master Heidenreich Vincke von Overberg, made in 1447, shows his wish to create prospective *memoria* of his successors, and thus to strengthen their positions in the future.

The Livonian Master was the only official of the Order to be commemorated also outside the Order, by the cities of which he was lord. The records of Reval show that during the fifteenth century the city council organized *memoria* of the deceased Livonian Masters and some Grand Masters of the Order. These communal commemorations concluded the relationships between the deceased Masters and the city that were created when the latter swore an oath of fealty.

We know little about the commemoration of other officials of the Livonian branch. Thus the case of *Landmarschall* Andreas von Steinberg and his memory is an astounding example of the variety of media used for remembering an Order's official. The inscription on his grave slab found during the archaeological excavations of the rural parish church in Ascheraden has the same content and message as a reference to his death in the chronicle of Wartberge. The Livonian commander of the Order's unfortunate death caused by a falling tree was also mentioned in the correspondence of the Order's officials. Thus after his death Andreas von Steinberg was present both in the in the Teutonic Order's communicative memory in the form of oral communication and cultural memory in the form of an inscription on the grave slab and written texts (chronicles, necrologies, annals, letters etc.).

The collective memory of the Church of Riga relied as much on the commemoration of the bishops and archbishops as on the remembrance of its cathedral canons, who in numerous episodes played decisive roles in the

---

177 LUB 10, no. 297.

struggle for the very existence of the Church of Riga as an independent entity. Dietrich Nagel's foundation shows how the remembrance of the cathedral canons was created and promoted in late medieval Livonia. This is particularly important since few testaments or foundation charters of the Livonian canons have survived. The foundation charter of 1447 drafted by Nagel shows both the intellectual and financial resources that the provosts possessed and were able to invest in *memoria*. Nagel institutionalized his own *memoria*, binding it to the provost's office. He also used the chapter's resources for it and seventeen years later was able to attract an additional endowment from the archbishop. Nagel, like any other ecclesial office holder, sought to imprint his name on the collective memory of the group alongside his predecessors and successors; his memorial foundation was one of the instruments for fulfilling this desire. The example of Dietrich Nagel's foundation shows how important *memoria* was for the continuity of an office and how the resources of a community were used for the remembrance of an individual. In Nagel's case, individual commemoration was intertwined with the commemoration of the office and institution.

CHAPTER 3

Networks of Memory – Livonia and Beyond

The fabric of Livonia was not densely woven with networks of religious institutions like similar regions in Western Europe.[1] Even the very scarce sources demonstrate that like elsewhere in late medieval Europe, Livonian religious institutions served as commemorators of the townspeople or nobility (in the case of the Cistercian abbeys and convents), but they also strove to create bonds of mutual commemoration with other religious institutions or communities. Thus, they created networks of commemoration in which, as it was practice elsewhere, names of the dead were exchanged, and mutual remembrance of the dead was practiced. Not only were the names of the dead exchanged but as a case of the so-called Dünamunde annals demonstrates, the pasts and histories of the groups were also shared. This chapter begins with the analysis of the role of these institutions in the commemoration of the townspeople and nobility and continues as an analysis of the commemorative networks in late medieval Livonia.

There were only two monasteries – Cistercian abbeys in Dünamunde (1205–1305), later Padis (1310–1560), and Valkena (Falkenau) (1234–1558).[2] The female monastic landscape in Livonia was dominated by the Cistercians. In Livonia there were five Cistercian convents: St Mary Magdalene in Riga (1257–1582), St Michael in Reval (c. 1250–1543), St Catherine of Alexandria in Dorpat (b. 1345–c. 1550), Leal (before 1238– after 1553), and St Anne in Lemsal (fifteenth century – 1539), which had a close relationship with the Riga convent.[3] There was another female monastic institution – a

---

1 Parts of this chapter have been published in the article: Strenga, 'Cistercian Networks of Memory', pp. 212–31.
2 Schmidt, 'Die Zisterzienser im Baltikum und in Finnland', pp. 1–286; Lore Poelchau, 'Das Zisterzienserkloster Dünamunde', in *Benediktiner, Zisterzienser*, ed. by Christof Römer (Berlin: Lukas-Verlag, 1999), pp. 172–83; Lore Poelchau, 'Die Geschichte des Zisterzienserklosters Dünamunde bei Riga (1205–1305)', *Studien und Mitteilungen zur Geschichte des Benediktiner Ordens und seiner Zweige*, 115 (2004), 65–199; Maja Gąssowska, 'Die Zisterzienser im mittelalterlichen Livland', in *Die Kirche im mittelalterlichen Livland*, ed. by Radosław Biskup, Johannes Götz, and Andrzej Radzimiński (Toruń: UMK, 2019), pp. 159–82.
3 Schmidt, 'Die Zisterzienser im Baltikum und in Finnland', pp. 156–238; Erki Russow, 'Die Klöster in der Stadt Reval (Tallinn)', in *Lübecker Kolloquium zur Stadtarchäologie im Hanseraum, IX: Klöster*, ed. by Manfred Gläser (Lübeck: Schmidt-Römhild, 2014), pp. 531–43, p. 534; Ieva Ose, 'Mittelalterliche Klöster in Riga im 13.–16. Jahrhundert', in *Lübecker Kolloquium zur Stadtarchäologie im Hanseraum, IX: Klöster*, pp. 509–20, pp. 511–12; Maja Gąssowska, 'Portret cysterek rewalskich "we wnętrzu"', in *Ambona. Teksty o kulturze średniowiecza ofiarowane Stanisławowi Bylinie*, ed. by Krzysztof Bracha

Birgittine convent in Mariendal (1407–1577), which had a close bonds with the townspeople of Reval and the nobility of Harrien–Wierland.[4]

In the cities and towns, mendicant friaries were represented. Dominicans had their friaries in Riga (1234–1524), Reval (1246–1525), and Dorpat (late thirteenth century – *c.* 1525).[5] In Reval, in contrast to Riga and Dorpat, the surviving sources – medieval last wills and even some sources from the friary itself – provide insight into the activities and the role of the friars in the local community.[6] Franciscans were present in Riga (1238/1253–1524) and later during the late Middle Ages had their houses in Dorpat, Lemsal, Hasenpoth, and Fellin.[7] Despite the fact that the Franciscans had more friaries in Livonia than the Dominicans, almost no Franciscan sources survive, thus their role as commemorators remains completely obscure.

Cistercian Nuns and Dominican Friars as Commemorators in the City

The dead of urban communities were commemorated not only in parish churches but also in urban religious communities: convents, friaries, and

---

and Wojciech Brojer (Warszawa: IH PAN, 2016), pp. 109–25; Maja Gąssowska, 'Klasztory żeńskie w średniowiecznym Rewalu (Tallinie)', in *Aktywność publiczna kobiet na ziemiach polskich. Wybrane zagadnienia*, ed. by Tomasz Pudłocki and Katarzyna Sierakowska (Warszawa: Neriton, 2013), pp. 11–18; Maja Gąssowska, 'Cysterki w Rewalu (Tallinie) w XIII–XV wieku', in *Przestrzeń klasztoru, przestrzeń kultury*, ed. by Joanna Pietrzak Thebault and Łukasz Cybulski (Warszawa: UKSW, 2017), pp. 35–49; Gąssowska, 'Die Zisterzienser im Mittelalterlichen Livland', pp. 171–81; Maja Gąssowska, 'Kto i kiedy zainicjował fundację klasztoru cysterek w Dorpacie?', *Studia z Dziejów Średniowiecza*, 25 (2022), 75–95; Inna Põltsam-Jürjo, 'Lihula isepäised nunnad', *Läänemaa Muuseumi toimetised*, 18 (2015), 175–194.

4 Juhan Kreem and Kersti Markus, 'Kes asutas Pirita kloostri?', *Kunstiteaduslikke Uurimusi*, 4 (2007), 60–74; Ruth Rajamaa, 'Pirita kloostri asutamine ja ülesehitamine 1407–1436 Rootsi allikate valguses', *Kunstiteaduslikke Uurimusi*, 4 (2007), 75–92; Ruth Rajamaa, *Katkenud laul: Pirita klooster 1407–1607*, ed. by Andres Adamson (Tallinn: Argo, 2018); Kersti Markus, 'The Pirita Convent in Tallinn. A Powerful Visual Symbol for the Self-Consciousness of the Birgittine Order', *Kungl. Vitterhets Historie Och Antikvitets Akademien. Konferenser*, 82 (2013), 95–110; Hägglund, *Birgittine Landscapes*, pp. 77–117.

5 Gertrud von Walther-Wittenheim, *Die Dominikaner in Livland im Mittelalter: Die Natio Livoniae* (Roma: Institutum historicum FF Praedicatorum, 1938); Marek Tamm, 'When did the Dominicans Arrive in Tallinn?' *Tuna. Ajalookultuuri ajakiri*, 4 (2009): 35–45; Tiina Kala, 'Das Dominikanerkloster von Reval/Tallinn und die lutherische Reformation' in *Die Stadt im europäischen Nordosten: Kulturbeziehungen von der Ausbreitung des Lübischen Rechts bis zur Aufklärung*, ed. by Robert Schweitzer and Waltraud Basman-Bühner (Helsinki: Aue-Stiftung, 2001), 83–93; Siiri Rebane, 'Geschichte des Dominikanerklosters in Tartu (Dorpat)', in *Estnische Kirchengeschichte im vorigen Jahrtausend*, ed. by Riho Altnurme (Kiel: Friedrich Wittig Verlag, 2001), pp. 55–60; Johnny Grandjean Gøgsig Jakobsen, 'Friars Preachers in Frontier Provinces of Medieval Europe', in *Medieval East Central Europe in a Comparative Perspective: From Frontier Zones to Lands in Focus*, ed. by Gerhard Jaritz and Katalin Szende (London: Routledge, 2016), pp. 123–36, p. 128.

6 Walther-Wittenheim, *Die Dominikaner in Livland im Mittelalter*, 92–121; Kala, 'Das Dominikanerkloster von Reval/Tallinn', pp. 83–93; Strenga, 'Bidden vor myner sele', pp. 111–32; Hahn, *Revaler Testamente*.

7 About the Franciscans in Livonia, see Leonhard Lemmens, *Die Franziskanerkustodie Livland und Preußen* (Düsseldorf: Schwann, 1912); Anti Selart, 'Die Bettelmönche im Ostseeraum zur Zeit des Erzbischofs Albert Suerbeer von Riga (Mitte des 13. Jahrhunderts)', *Zeitschrift für Ostmitteleuropa-Forschung*, 56, 4 (2007), 475–99, p. 485.

monasteries located within the town walls or in close proximity. Religious communities, unlike parishes or chapels, offered prayers by their members – nuns, monks, and friars – professional religious. This professionalism attracted townspeople, who made large endowments for the houses and smaller donations to individual nuns and friars, expecting commemoration in return. For example, in Reval the Dominican friars and Cistercian nuns dominated the offering of *memoria* in the urban space. *Memoria* served as the means for the creation of relationships between religious communities and laymen.

The Cistercian convents in the largest Livonian cities during the late Middle Ages, as the example of St Magdalene in Riga shows, were monastic institutions of considerable size counting around fifty nuns, yet were not fully integrated in the urban social fabric because most of the nuns were of the noble descent.[8] These Livonian convents were not bound together by institutional ties, but each was founded by local noble families and were home to the daughters of such families.[9] Noble families sustained strong ties with their kinswomen in the convents and supported them with individual donations and annuity rents.[10] Although the convents were situated within the town walls, the townspeople perceived them as somewhat 'foreign' because of these strong ties with the nobility. As Kadri-Rutt Hahn's analysis of wills in Reval has shown, St Michael enjoyed less support and trust from urban testators than other religious institutions in Reval, and it was somewhat more isolated than other institutions, for example, the Dominican friary.[11]

It is evident that the convents were strong and reliable partners for rich and influential Livonians who wished to secure lasting and solemn commemoration. The Cistercian convent in Riga was a place of remembrance not only for noble families but also for rich townspeople and individuals affiliated to the Teutonic Order. The city councillor Hartwich Segefridt created his memorial chantry at the convent in 1434, where two priests were appointed in 1442 after the death of his son.[12] Before 1495, the burgomaster Peter Hinrickes endowed

---

8 In 1495 only two of the fifty-three nuns of St Mary Magdalene were not of noble descent: Margreta Visch and Anna Stalbyter. Rīga, Latvijas Nacionālais arhīvs, Latvijas Valsts vēstures arhīvs (Latvian National Archive, Latvian State Historical Archives) (LVVA) 4038 f., 2 apr., 1089 l., fols. 52ª–53ª; LUB 2/1, no. 252; Andris Levāns and Gustavs Strenga, 'Medieval Manuscripts in the Riga Jesuit College Book Collection: Manuscripts of the Riga St. Mary Magdalene Cistercian Nunnery and Their Tradition', in *Catalogue of the Riga Jesuit College Book Collection (1583–1621). History and Reconstruction of the Collection*, ed. by Gustavs Strenga and Andris Levāns (Riga: Latvijas Nacionālā bibliotēka, 2021), pp. 166–87, pp. 168–69.
9 For St Mary Magdalene supporters were the archbishop's vassals, for St Michaelis noblemen of Harrien and Wierland – a locality around Reval in the northern Estonia) – and for St Catherine vassals of the bishop of Dorpat. Schmidt, 'Zisterzienser', p. 156, 169, 184, Johansen and von zur Mühlen, *Deutsch und Undeutsch*, p. 79.
10 Nobleman Claus Üxküll since 1509 paid an annuity rent of 9 marks to his nieces Anne and Gretken (Gerdrut) Üxküll, nuns of the convent in Riga. LUB 2/3, no. 552; LUB 2/1, no. 190.
11 Hahn, *Revaler Testamente*, p. 89.
12 LUB 8, no. 782, 790, 792; LUB 9, no. 844; Rīga, LUAB, R, Ms. 61, fols. 44a–45b, 66a; Bothführ, *Rathslinie*, no. 355.

1000 marks for the convent to commemorate his soul (*alle tiid begaen szyn*) and the souls of all other Christians.[13] In 1445 Johan Kerssenbrugge, physician to the Master of the Order, founded a memorial chantry in the convent, which was to be served by two priests.[14]

Many townspeople requested *memoria* from the Cistercian convents, but most big donors were noblemen who were kin to the nuns. The archbishop's vassal Christopher von Ungern, whose three kinswomen Otilia, Margreta, and Anna von Ungern were nuns in Riga in 1495, endowed St Mary Magdalene with 100 Riga marks in 1517 for a weekly sung mass on Thursdays. This endowment was made in support of the cult of Corpus Christi and for the soul of his brother Hinrich von Ungern.[15]

The convents in Reval and Dorpat also commemorated local noblemen.[16] In 1460 Hermann Soye (Zöge), a nobleman from Harrien–Wierland, founded a memorial chantry in the St Michael convent in Reval with the consent of his brothers. The initial endowment was 300 Riga marks and a further 100 marks were added ten years later.[17] In his will of 1470, Hermann Soye requested that the nuns sing the office *Deus eterne* every morning in remembrance of him and his kin (*vrunden*) in the chancel of their church.[18] Soye's permanent commemorative presence in the Cistercian church was reinforced by services at the Corpus Christi altar. In addition, Soye made a smaller endowment of 100 marks for his own remembrance in the Birgittine convent of Mariendal. He requested that the sisters and brothers celebrate two memorial masses and vigils annually. During the 1450s, he had made two agreements with the Birgittines in Mariendal about landed properties.[19]

During the fifteenth century, several noblemen from the bishopric of Dorpat and Harrien–Wierland included the Cistercian convent of Dorpat in their memorial strategies. Otto von Üxküll, vassal of the bishop of Dorpat, who also founded a memorial mass in the Cistercian monastery of Valkena, made an endowment of 150 marks in 1417 to the convent of St Catherine in Dorpat, in return for commemoration in nuns' prayers and the celebration of a vigil on the anniversary of his death in the chancel of their church.[20] In 1412 Johann von Lechtes from Harrien–Wierland chose three Livonian religious communities in which he wanted to be commemorated – the Cistercian nuns in Dorpat, the Franciscans in Riga, and the Cistercians in Padis – endowing each of them with

---

13 LUB 2/1, no. 253; Bothführ, *Rathslinie*, no. 388.
14 LUB 10, no. 150, 151, 179;
15 LUB 2/1, no. 252; LGU 2, no. 238.
16 On commemorative practices of the late medieval European nobility, see Saul, *Death, Art and Memory in Medieval England*; *Adelige und bürgerliche Erinnerungskulturen*.
17 LUB 12, no. 36; Schmidt, 'Zisterzienser', p. 222.
18 Tartu, Rahvusarhiiv (National Archives of Estonia) (EAA), f. 2069, n. 2, s. 128.
19 Tartu, EAA, f. 2069, n. 2, s. 128; LUB 11, no. 514, 772; Hägglund, *Birgittine Landscapes*, pp. 94–95, 113–15.
20 LGU 1, no. 197; Schmidt, 'Zisterzienser', p. 184.

100 marks.²¹ All three communities were obliged to commemorate Johann, his parents, his wife Margarethe, and souls of all his relatives. The services were to be celebrated each quarter, a vigil on Friday and a mass on Saturday; during both of these services, a bier had to be placed in front of an altar, as if a body lay on it.²² These noblemen also founded their remembrance in other locations, but the Cistercian nuns were among the main commemorators.

The Dominicans played a different role as commemorators in Livonian cities and towns. They were present in the cities since the thirteenth century. The friary of St John the Baptist in Riga was founded in 1234, when bishop Nicholas, immediate successor of the city's founder bishop Albert, donated his old castle to the friars.²³ In Reval the Dominicans first settled on the cathedral hill in 1229 but left four years later only to return in 1246.²⁴ In 1262 they received a large plot next to the town wall, where they had a friary built, dedicated to St Catherine of Alexandria.²⁵ In Dorpat the friary was founded during the late thirteenth century.²⁶

Dominicans in Riga and Reval were active commemorators of townspeople and local nobility. Dominicans were closer to the urban population to whom they preached and from whom they were recruited; before the late fifteenth-century observant reform, most of the friars were locals.²⁷ Reval's source material offers unique insight into the role of the Dominicans as commemorators.²⁸ According to Kadri-Rutt Hahn, the Dominican friary in Reval, together with the parish churches of St Nicholas and St Olav, received most testamentary donations. They were clearly closer to the 'testators' hearts than the cathedral or the Cistercian convent.²⁹ From the late fourteenth century until the Reformation, 70 per cent of Reval's testators made donations to the Dominican friary.³⁰ In comparison with German medieval cities, this is a high number indeed. In Cologne in the fifteenth century, around 85 per cent of lay testators donated something to the mendicant orders;³¹ in Lübeck in the second half of the fourteenth century, 26 per cent of testators were donors to

---

21 *Revaler Urkunden und Briefe von 1273 bis 1510*, ed. by Dieter Heckmann (Köln: Böhlau, 1995), no. 140; Schmidt, 'Zisterzienser', p. 184.
22 *Revaler Urkunden*, no. 140.
23 Walther-Wittenheim, *Dominikaner in Livland*, p. 7.
24 Walther-Wittenheim, *Dominikaner in Livland*, p. 8; Tamm, 'When Did the Dominicans Arrive in Tallinn?', 35–45; Jaan Tamm, *Eesti keskaegsed kloostrid. Medieval Monasteries of Estonia* (Tallinn: Eesti Entsüklopeediakirjastus, 2002) p. 168.
25 Walther-Wittenheim, *Dominikaner in Livland*, p. 10.
26 Walther-Wittenheim, *Dominikaner in Livland*, p. 12.
27 Johnny Grandjean Gøgsig Jakobsen, 'The Dominicans and the Reformation in Northern Europe', in *The Dissolution of Monasteries: The Case of Denmark in a Regional Perspective*, ed. by Per Seesko, Louise Nyholm Kallestrup, and Lars Bisgaard (Odense: University Press of Southern Denmark, 2019), pp. 75–103, p. 79.
28 For relationships between the Reval Dominicans and the townspeople, see Strenga 'Bidden vor myner sele', pp. 111–32.
29 Hahn, *Revaler Testamente*, pp. 177, 183–84.
30 Hahn, *Revaler Testamente*, p. 184.
31 Klosterberg, *Zur Ehre Gottes*, p. 121.

the Dominicans, and around the same percentage of testators made gifts to the Franciscans.[32] The Dominican friary in Reval may have received donations from testators more frequently than in other cities because it was the only mendicant community there. Most of these donations (70 per cent) were smaller than ten Riga marks, and only 3 per cent of them exceeded 100 Riga marks.[33] The majority of the donations were small because the donors were men and women of all social classes.[34]

Dominicans and other mendicants were popular with the laity because of the high reputation of the liturgical services they provided.[35] Townspeople in Reval often chose the Dominican church as their burial place over their parish churches.[36] Yet the parish – the centre of social life – was also a centre for *memoria*; most of the testators wanted to be primarily commemorated in the parish churches, but the friars were additional commemorators.

Testators sought not only commemoration at masses but also the friars' individual involvement.[37] Between 1378 and the 1470s, more than half of those testators who donated to the Dominicans also provided money gifts to individual friars (*in de hande to delende*).[38] Such donations were made alongside the endowments towards the church fabric or liturgical services; for example, Martin Busch in 1449 donated to the construction of St Catherine's church and also gave three marks to be distributed between 'young and old friars.'[39]

Testators valued the Dominicans as a group, but they wanted to oblige each friar to commemorate them privately. Regular payments of money reminded the beneficiary of prayer and created a personal bond between commemorator and beneficiary. In 1510, Reynold Korner, Reval's city clerk, donated to each friar four schillings to pray for him on the anniversaries of his death, paying two schillings for masses and two for vigils.[40] Testators in Reval and in other medieval cities engaged friars, priests, nuns, and poor people in individual commemorative praying for their souls.[41] In Reval, as in Lübeck, testators valued friars who were ordained priests more, and their liturgical services had

---

32 Noodt, *Religion und Familie*, p. 237.
33 Hahn, *Revaler Testamente*, p. 184.
34 Hahn, *Revaler Testamente*, p. 184.
35 Hahn, *Revaler Testamente*, p. 184.
36 Twelve grave slabs of the townspeople have survived in the former Dominican church of St Catherine, and seven requests of burials there were made in the last wills. See Eugen von Nottbeck and Wilhelm Neumann, *Geschichte und Kunstdenkmäler der Stadt Reval* (Reval: Kluge, 1904), pp. 174–80; Mari Loit, 'Keskaegsest surmakultuurist ja hauatähistest reformatsiooonieelse Tallinna kirikustes ja kloostrites', *Vana Tallinn*, 17 (21) (2006), 15–190.
37 Hahn, *Revaler Testamente*, p. 184.
38 Eight of fifteen donors requested to be commemorated by individual friars. *Revaler Urkunden*, no. 20; *Revaler Regesten*, no. 4, 6; LUB 3 no. 1263; LUB 8, no. 1965, 896; LUB 9, no. 911; LUB 10, no. 334, 582; LUB 11, no. 442, 385, 397; LUB 12, no. 297, 303; *Revaler Regesten*, no. 24.
39 LUB 10, no. 582.
40 LUB 2/3, no. 849.
41 Priests: *Revaler Urkunden*, no. 20; *Revaler Regesten*, no. 3, 42, 48, 50, 52, 53, 57, 93, 105, 106, 110, 118; LUB 11, no. 397. Nuns: LUB 3, no. 1263; *Revaler Regesten*, no. 4, 6, 36, 50; LUB 9, no. 911; LUB 10, no. 334, 582; LUB 12, no. 303; LUB 2/3, no. 849. Poor people: LUB 8, no. 1965; LUB 9, no. 911; LUB

more value than the prayers of simple brethren.[42] Wilm vame Schede in his will of 1447 donated one Riga mark for the prior, lector, and old friar called Johann, and one *ferding* for each ordained friar, but others received only five shillings each.[43] Other testators also donated larger sums to the priests, lectors, and preachers than to others, showing that for them the status of friars mattered.[44]

The frequency of personal donations decreased in the late fifteenth century. After the 1470s only three testators donated money to individual friars.[45] This may have been caused by the Dominican reform in Reval in 1474/1475, when the friary became part of the reformed *Congregatio Hollandiae*.[46] In the first half of the fifteenth century, the Dominican Order and its religious life were in decline; the reform aimed to restore an ideal of poverty promoted in the first constitutions and to prohibit the use of private property by the brethren.[47] Individual donations were to be received by the community as a whole.

Modification of general donation habits for individuals in religious communities may have been influenced by the Dominican reform. It is no surprise that after the reform, relationships between the townspeople and the friars may have changed because the friaries were no longer manned with 'local boys' from influential and well-connected families but were instead replaced by the friars from other cities.[48] Yet, the decrease of individual donations for friars may have also followed a general trend. Donations to individual religious decreased in the case of the Cistercian nuns and even to the poor in hospitals. The bond between testators and individual friars was important for *memoria*; it created a certain intimacy, and the abolition of individual donations and changes of the recruitment of friars affected this bond.

Testamentary donations did not assure long-term commemoration, which needed large endowments that only few could make. Gherwen Bornemann

---

10, no. 582; LUB 11, no. 442, 385; LUB 12, no. 303; *Revaler Regesten*, no. 24, 35, 36, 44, 50; LUB 2/2, no. 264.

42 Dietrich W. Poeck, 'Klöster und Bürger. Eine Fallstudie zu Lübeck (1225–1531)', in *Starptautiska Konference Hanza Vakar – Hanza Rīt, Rīga*, pp. 423–52, p. 186.

43 LUB 10, no. 334.

44 LUB 3, no. 1263; LUB 9, no. 911.

45 *Revaler Regesten*, no. 36, 50; LUB 2/3, no. 849.

46 Walther-Wittenheim, *Dominikaner in Livland*, pp. 105–21; Servatius Petrus Wolfs, 'Dominikanische Observanzbestrebungen. Die Congregatio Hollandiae (1464–1517)', in *Reformbemühungen und Observanzbestrebungen im spätmittelalterlichen Ordenswesen*, ed. by Kaspar Elm (Berlin: Duncker und Humblot, 1989), pp. 273–92, p. 286;

47 Kaspar Elm, 'Reform- und Observanzbestrebungen im spätmittelalterlichen Ordenswesen. Ein Überblick', in *Reformbemühungen und Observanzbestrebungen im spätmittelalterlichen Ordenswesen*, ed. by Kaspar Elm (Berlin: Duncker & Humblot, 1989), pp. 3–19, p. 16; Bernhard Neidiger, 'Die Reformbewegungen der Bettelorden im 15. Jahrhundert', in *Württembergisches Klosterbuch: Klöster, Stifte und Ordensgemeinschaften von den Anfängen bis in die Gegenwart*, ed. by Wolfgang Zimmermann (Ostfildern: Thorbecke, 2003), pp. 77–90, p. 80; Anne Huijbers, *Zealots for Souls: Dominican Narratives of Self-Understanding during Observant Reforms, c. 1388–1517* (Berlin: de Gruyter, 2018), pp. 177–217; in Reval also reformers demanded to abandon private property. Tallinn, TLA, f 230, n 1, s Bk 3, fol. 11ʳ.

48 Jakobsen, 'The Dominicans and the Reformation in Northern Europe', 79.

(1480) was the only known testator who made a large endowment; he requested a memorial mass read every week on the *broderschopp* altar, endowing 100 marks for the purpose.[49] Yet the city council's ledgers record large endowments made to the Dominicans for the memorial chantries by the city councillors Herman van der Hove (1415–1426),[50] Bertold Hunninghusen (1434–1524),[51] and burgher Woldemar Reval (1434–1463).[52] These chantries strengthened the bonds between the elite families and the friars.

Like the Cistercian convents, the Dominican friaries were the chosen spaces for commemoration of the Livonian noble families. The friars in Livonia were deeply rooted in urban environments, but they also managed to create close relationships with local nobilities. Until the Reformation, the nobility of Harrien–Wierland held their regular assemblies (*manntags*) in the Dominican church of St Catherine in Reval.[53]

Few foundation charters survive to demonstrate the long–term obligations undertaken by the Dominicans, but two examples explicitly show the place of the friars in the memorial strategies of the Livonian noblemen.[54] On the vigil of Epiphany (5 January) 1436 in the Dominican friary in Riga, nobleman Detlef von der Pahlen, the archbishop's vassal, endowed 100 Riga marks for liturgical services.[55] Prior Johan Schaffer and his brethren promised to celebrate a daily mass on one altar in the church during Detlef's lifetime.[56] At each mass the living and dead members of the von der Pahlen family had to be commemorated (*dencken derghenen, beide levendigen und doden*). It specified the living – Detlef himself, his wife Margrete, and his son Detlef – and the dead: his parents, Ludeke and Ylsebe, brothers Johannes and Gotschalk, and 3 more relatives.[57] Remarkably, after Detlef von der Pahlen's death the number of services was to be reduced to two weekly memorial masses for all individuals mentioned.[58]

By requesting frequent services during his lifetime, and less frequent commemoration after his death, Detlef von der Pahlen sought to benefit from *memoria* of his kin while alive. The benefits were spiritual as well as social and political, strengthening his position and that of his family, which had been in Livonia since the late thirteenth century.[59] Detlef von der Pahlen was also

---

49 Tallinn, TLA, f. 230, n.1, BN 1/I, Gherwen Borneman, fol. 1.
50 Tallinn, TLA, f. 230, n. 1, 107 Aa 7, fol. 10, 23; LUB 7, no. 451.
51 *Kämmereibuch der Stadt Reval 1432–1463*, p. 701; *Kämmereibuch der Stadt Reval 1463–1507*, p. 896; Tallinn, TLA, f. 230, n. 1, A.d. 32. fols. 16, 27, 33, 39, 46, 58, 158.
52 *Kämmereibuch der Stadt Reval 1432–1463*, p. 722; *Kämmereibuch der Stadt Reval 1463–1507*, no. 1206.
53 Ritscher, *Reval an der Schwelle*, p. 117.
54 On the Livonian noblemen as the benefactors of the Dominicans, see Walther–Wittenheim, *Dominikaner in Livland*, pp. 98–100.
55 LUB 9, no. 4; on family von der Pahlen, see Astaf von Transéhe-Roseneck, *Genealogisches Handbuch der livländischen Ritterschaft*, vol. 1 (Görlitz: Starke, 1930), pp. 532–51, 542.
56 Ibid.
57 LUB 9, no. 4; LUB 7, no. 106; Detlef's father Ludeke or Ludecinus de Pale has been mentioned in the sources between 1385–1397, see Transehe-Roseneck, *Genealogisches Handbuch*, p. 542.
58 LUB 9, no. 4.
59 Transehe-Roseneck, *Genealogisches Handbuch*, p. 532, 542.

involved with other institutions that commemorated him and his family. In 1438, Detlef von der Pahlen and his kin, both living and dead, were received into the confraternity of the Birgittine convent of Mariendal, where commemoration and prayers were offered in return for his membership, already during Detlef's lifetime.[60] In the summer of 1436, archbishop Henning Scharpenberg confirmed Detlef von der Pahlen's earlier endowment of 100 marks for the memorial chantry in the cathedral of Riga.[61] All these memorial efforts were made at a time when the influence of Detlef and his family was on the rise; in 1444 Detlef van der Pahlen received new fiefs in bishoprics of Dorpat and Ösel once held by his uncle Hans von der Rope.[62]

The friars of Reval also became commemorators to noble families. On 1 February 1411, Johan van dem Rode, the prior of the Reval Dominicans, and eight brethren promised to commemorate in their masses all living and dead members of the von Vietinghoff family, particularly Dietrich von Vietinghoff, his living wife Anne, and his sons Heinrich and Arnd, as well as Dietrich's deceased wife Adelheid.[63] Dietrich von Vietinghoff, like Detlef von der Pahlen, was an influential nobleman, a leader of the local nobility in Harrien–Wierland, and this request of remembrance can be likewise interpreted as an attempt to gain spiritual benefit as well as social prestige even during his lifetime.[64] The Dominicans were first to commemorate the founders of this endowment and then all deceased belonging to this family.[65] For five marks, the Dominicans had to commemorate the Vietinghoffs each week with a mass celebrated on Sunday, at the altar of St Anthony in the Dominican church of St Catherine, and also to speak their names from the ambo (*der selen to denkende van deme predyckstole*).[66]

Livonian noblemen requested commemoration even during their lifetimes. The Livonian Dominicans fulfilled commemorative roles undertaken by the monastic communities that commemorated their benefactors.[67] In 1495 the prior of the Riga friary, Jacob von Brugen, accepted Hermann Keyserlingk and his wife Anna and their children into the benefits of the convent's good deeds, granting them continuous prayers.[68] The Keyserlingks were also promised that after their deaths the friars would commemorate them during daily prayers.[69]

---

60 LGU 1, no. 293; Hägglund, *Birgittine Landscapes*, p. 96.
61 These services had to begin on the day Detlef von der Pahlen died. LUB 8, no. 691; LUB 9, no. 71.
62 LUB 10, no. 2; on the status of the noble families and funerary monuments, see Saul, *Death, Art and Memory in Medieval England*, pp. 241–42.
63 Walther-Wittenheim, *Dominikaner in Livland*, pp. 99–100; *Revaler Urkunden*, no. 89; Otto Magnus von Stackelberg, *Genealogisches Handbuch der estländischen Ritterschaft*, vol. 1, (Görlitz: Starke, 1931), pp. 520–34.
64 Stackelberg, *Genealogisches Handbuch*, p. 521.
65 *Revaler Urkunden*, no. 89.
66 *Revaler Urkunden*, no. 89.
67 Sauer, *Fundatio und Memoria*, pp. 22–23.
68 Walther-Wittenheim, *Dominikaner in Livland*, p. 99; LUB 2/1, no. 189.
69 Ibid.

This involvement of the Keyserlingks with the Dominicans was important for this family, recently arrived in Livonia from Westphalia, following receipt of a fief in Courland in 1493.[70] The Keyserlingks formed a bond with the Dominicans in their new country of residence.

The Reformation ended the relationships between the Dominicans and those groups for whom they once prayed. The quick rift possibly took place because of the observant reform and alienation of the friars from the urban communities.[71] In Reval, already at the beginning of 1524, members of the city council arrived in the friary and demanded an audit of its property and prohibited friars from delivering sermons.[72] The council also declared that the friars should accept for burial in the Dominican church and cemetery only those laypeople who had requested it in their wills.[73] This meant that the performance of *memoria* in the friary was halted because the friars could not freely use resources needed for memorial services. In Riga the Dominicans were expelled from the city in early 1524; in Reval the city council officially closed the Dominican friary on 12 January 1525 and confiscated its property.[74]

In contrast to the Cistercian nuns, the Dominicans were commemorators who were popular not only among one social group, but also among individuals from all classes of the townspeople and the local noblemen. The testators created closer bonds with the friars by making individual donations in order to receive personalized commemoration. Yet, in Reval the practice decreased after the Dominican reform.

Cistercian Networks of Memory

Since the early Middle Ages, communities involved outsiders – individuals and groups – in their religious and social practices. One of the forms of involvement was the confraternity, or association of prayer, usually formed by monastic communities and within which they exchanged the names of their living and dead and mutually prayed for them.[75] Confraternities of prayer were created between two communities or an individual and a community by legal acts, which enshrined spiritual and material benefits for both sides in

---

70 Oskar Stavenhagen, *Genealogisches Handbuch der kurländischen Ritterschaft*, vol. 1, (Görlitz: Starke, 1939), p. 119.
71 Jakobsen, 'The Dominicans and the Reformation in Northern Europe', pp. 77, 83–84.
72 Kala, 'Dominikanerkloster', p. 86.
73 Tiina Kala, *Euroopa kirjakultuur hiliskeskaegsetes õppetekstides: Tallinna dominiiklase David Sliperi taskuraamat* (Tallinn: Linnaarhiiv, 2001), Appendix no. 1; Kala, 'Dominikanerkloster', p. 86.
74 Arbusow, *Die Einführung*, p. 300; Kala, 'Dominikanerkloster', p. 89.
75 Schmid and Wollasch, 'Societas et Fraternitas', pp. 1–48; Schmid, 'Das liturgische Gebetsgedenken in seiner historischen Relevanz', pp. 620–44; Karl Schmid, 'Mönchtum und Verbrüderung', in *Monastische Reformen im 9. und 10. Jahrhundert*, ed. by Raymund Kottje and Helmut Maurer (Sigmaringen: Thorbecke, 1989), pp. 117–46; Herbert E. J. Cowdrey, 'Legal Problems Raised by Agreements of Confraternity', in *Memoria, der geschichtliche Zeugniswert*, pp. 233–54.

perpetuity.[76] The abbey of Reichenau is an outstanding example for the scale that such a confraternity could reach. Since the early ninth century, the abbey was bonded with other communities over vast distances within the territories of the Frankish kingdom – in northern France, Italy, Burgundy, and Bavaria, and in their confraternity book around 40,000 names of monks and lay patrons were recorded.[77]

The confraternities of prayer were part of medieval memorial culture. The partners involved in the confraternity commemorated each other's dead using their own resources and the institutional character of this kind of *memoria* made it more secure in the long term. Through the recording of the names of confraternity members in *libri memoriales*, their commemoration became part of a long–term cultural memory.[78] In many occasions confraternity books were used for centuries as sources of names of those who had to be commemorated during masses.

Prayer associations were not just social, religious, and memorial phenomena. As a constitutive phenomenon, *memoria* played an important role in shaping groups and their identities.[79] In the context of the confraternity, this aspect of *memoria* was indeed important – the prayers for individuals from other institutions created a spiritual community that never was physically in one location and formed a certain feeling of togetherness. The prayer associations appear to have been imagined communities bonding the absent living and the absent dead.

The confraternity exemplified in itself exchange of resources between the partners, both material and spiritual. The confraternity agreements laid out what was to be given and what was to be received back. As numerous prominent medievalists have shown, the Maussean concept of gift allows us to analyse relationships between early medieval monastic communities and their lay patrons as cases of gift–giving in which commemorative prayers of monks and nuns were counter–gifts for foundations and donations made by the laymen.[80] Yet, the exchange of prayers, spiritual benefits, and good deeds between the communities, as in case of the prayer associations, also has to be

---

76 Cowdrey, 'Legal Problems Raised by Agreements of Confraternity', p. 233.
77 *Das Verbrüderungsbuch der Abtei Reichenau*, ed. by Johanne Autenrieth, Dieter Geuenich, and Karl Schmid (Hannover: Hahnsche Buchhandlung, 1979); Schmid and Wollasch, 'Gemeinschaft der Lebenden und Verstorbenen', pp. 374, 377.
78 Schmid, 'Das liturgische Gebetsgedenken', pp. 620–44; Eva-Maria Butz and Alfons Zettler, 'The Making of the Carolingian Libri Memoriales: Exploring or Constructing the Past?', in *Memory and Commemoration in Medieval Culture*, ed. by Elma Brenner, Mary Franklin-Brown, and Meredith Cohen (Farnham: Ashgate, 2013), pp. 79–92; Assmann, *Das kulturelle Gedächtnis*, pp. 52–54.
79 Oexle, 'Die Gegenwart der Toten', p. 34; Oexle, 'Die Gegenwart der Lebenden und der Toten', p. 75.
80 Oexle, 'Memoria und Memoriaüberlieferung im frühen Mittelalter', p. 87; Oexle, 'Die Gegenwart der Toten', p. 52; Borgolte, 'Totale Geschichte' des Mittelalters, p. 12; Ilana F. Silber, 'Gift-Giving in the Great Traditions: The Case of Donations to Monasteries in the Medieval West', *European Journal of Sociology / Archives Européennes de Sociologie*, 36.2 (1995), 209–43.

received as a form of gift-giving where gift and counter-gift both were spiritual commodities.

As the research of Cistercian monastic communities in England, for example, demonstrates, the professed were eager to bond and create networks with partners outside their group by trading, and exchanging gifts and prayers.[81] If the mendicant orders had their territorial structures, such as provinces or later also observant congregations, the Cistercian monasteries and convents were not bound together in territorial structures; thus they were independent in their relationships with the outside world.

The role of the Cistercians in the Livonian mission has been recently reemphasized by scholars.[82] The Cistercians were active in the communication of the Baltic crusades in Western Europe, and the brethren were also involved in the mission itself.[83] During the crusading period and after it, the Cistercian monasteries were centres of economic, religious, and cultural life.[84] The Cistercian convents in the late medieval Livonian cities were an integral part of the urban sacral space, despite their 'aristocratic otherness'.[85]

Most of the surviving sources from Livonia pertain to the commemoration of laypeople as shown above, while little is known about commemoration of fellow brothers and sisters by the communities. Yet numerous sources reveal remembrance exchanged by the communities. The bonding between Livonian religious communities and their mutual *memoria* has attracted limited attention of scholars until now. Thus, this chapter will focus on the two case studies of the Cistercians – memorial networks forged by the Livonian convents in the late Middle Ages and the historical tradition of the Dünamunde abbey (later Padis), particularly the so-called Annals of Dünamunde (*Annales*

---

81 Emilia Jamroziak, 'Making and Breaking the Bonds: Yorkshire Cistercians and Their Neighbours', in *Perspectives for an Architecture of Solitude: Essays on Cistercians, Art and Architecture in Honour of Peter Fergusson*, ed. by Terryl Nancy Kinder (Turnhout: Brepols, 2004), pp. 63–70; Emilia Jamroziak, *Rievaulx Abbey and Its Social Context, 1132–1300: Memory, Locality, and Networks* (Turnhout: Brepols, 2005), pp. 203–18.

82 Poelchau, 'Das Zisterzienserkloster Dünamünde', pp. 172–83; Poelchau, 'Die Geschichte des Zisterzienserklosters Dünamünde bei Riga (1205–1305)', pp. 65–199; Marek Tamm, 'Communicating Crusade. Livonian Mission and the Cistercian Network in the Thirteenth Century', *Ajolooline Ajakiri*, 3.4 (2009), 341–72; Tamm, 'When Did the Dominicans Arrive in Tallinn?', pp. 35–45.

83 Poelchau, 'Die Geschichte des Zisterzienserklosters Dünamünde bei Riga (1205–1305)', p. 134–39; Tamm, 'Communicating Crusade', pp. 341–72; Marek Tamm, 'The Livonian Crusade in Cistercian Stories of the Early Thirteenth Century', in *Crusading on the Edge: Ideas and Practice of Crusading in Iberia and the Baltic Region, 1100–1500*, ed. by Torben Kjersgaard Nielsen and Iben Fonnesberg-Schmidt (Turnhout: Brepols, 2016), pp. 365–89.

84 Schmidt, 'Die Zisterzienser im Baltikum und in Finnland', pp. 47–53, 86–106, 141–47; Poelchau, 'Die Geschichte des Zisterzienserklosters Dünamünde bei Riga (1205–1305)', pp. 166–76; Kersti Markus, 'Misjonär või mõisnik? Tsistertslaste roll 13. sajandi Eestis', *Acta Historica Tallinnensia*, 14 (2009), 3–30.

85 Schmidt, 'Die Zisterzienser im Baltikum und in Finnland', pp. 156–237; Russow, 'Die Klöster in der Stadt Reval (Tallinn)', pp. 531–43; Ose, 'Mittelalterliche Klöster in Riga im 13.–16. Jahrhundert', pp. 509–20; Gąssowska, 'Klasztory żeńskie w średniowiecznym Rewalu (Tallinie)', pp. 11–18; Maja Gąssowska, 'Portret cysterek Rewalskich "we wnętrzu"', pp. 109–25; Gąssowska, 'Cysterki w Rewalu (Tallinie) w XIII–XV wieku', pp. 35–49; Gąssowska, 'Die Zisterzienser im Mittelalterlichen Livland', pp. 171–81.

Dunamundenses), in which the Teutonic Order played an important role. I will pursue several questions: in what kind of confraternity bonds were the Livonian Cistercian convents involved, and how long did they last? How do the *Annales Dunamundenses* reveal the relationship between the Cistercians of Dünamunde, later Padis, and the Livonian branch of the Teutonic Order in the fourteenth century? Why can these annals be perceived as a memorial text and to which historical tradition – that of the Dünamunde (Padis) Cistercians or the Teutonic Order – did they belong?

Memorial Networks of the Cistercian Nuns in Livonia

Only a handful of sources that show daily life and religious practices of the Cistercian convents survive.[86] Names of numerous Cistercian abbesses and prioresses in Livonia are known, but little is known about the number of nuns in the convents and their daily lives.[87] Even though the value and importance of confraternity agreements declined during the Middle Ages, and in most cases we cannot tell whether the prayers and good deeds were delivered, they demonstrated spiritual and social relationships between communities. In the case of Livonian Cistercians, it is particularly relevant because it contextualizes the place of the female religious communities in the local societies.

The Cistercian convents in Livonia forged confraternal ties with numerous partners, and they bonded not only with other monastic communities but also with lay institutions. Most of such agreements have survived for the St Mary Magdalene convent in Riga showing their attempts to bond with institutions outside Livonia as well. In the mid–fifteenth century, they entered into a confraternity of prayer with a religious community at the other end of Livonia. On 4 September 1428, Gerlach, the superior (*pater*) of the Birgittine convent in Mariendal, near Reval, issued a charter including the Cistercian nuns from St Mary Magdalene in the good deeds and prayers of this Birgittine convent.[88] In addition, the Birgittine community of nuns and brothers promised individual *memoria* of the deceased Cistercian nuns from Riga.[89]

---

[86] For information on the surviving prayer books of the Riga convent, see Levāns and Strenga, 'Medieval Manuscripts in the Riga Jesuit College Book Collection'; Laine Tabora, 'Psalterium Davidis of the Cistercian Nunnery of Riga (LMAVB RS F 22–96) and Its Liturgical Calendar', *Analecta Cisterciensia*, 71 (2021), 119–69; Gustavs Strenga and Andris Levāns, 'Gradual Formation and Dramatic Transformation. Mendicant and Cistercian Book Collections in Late Medieval and Post-Reformation Riga', in *The Baltic Battle of Books: Formation and Relocation of European Libraries in the Confessional Age (c. 1500-c. 1650) and Their Afterlife*, ed. by Jonas Nordin, Gustavs Strenga, and Peter Sjökvist (Leiden: Brill, 2023), pp. 37–61.

[87] Schmidt, 'Die Zisterzienser im Baltikum und in Finnland', pp. 279–83.

[88] LUB 7, no. 740; Schmidt, 'Die Zisterzienser im Baltikum und in Finnland', p. 164; Tore Nyberg, *Birgittinische Klostergründungen des Mittelalters* ([Lund]: Gleerup, 1965), p. 115.

[89] LUB 7, no. 740; Hans Cnattingius, *Studies in the order of St. Bridget of Sweden: The crisis in the 1420s*, vol. 1 (Stockholm: Almqvist & Wiksell, 1963), p. 15.

The Birgittine community in Mariendal was founded in 1407 as a *filia* of the first Birgittine foundation in Vadstena, Sweden. Initially the city of Reval opposed its foundation because of its strategic location dangerously close to the city.[90] But the Birgittines had numerous supporters. It has been thought that the founders of Mariendal were Reval merchants, but as the recent research shows, at least two of them were priests active in Vadstena and Söderköping (Sweden).[91] In the community's initial stage, local nobility and the Teutonic Order were also its patrons.[92] For example, the Birgittines of Mariendal also accepted lay noblemen in their spiritual confraternity. In 1418, Otto Lode and his wife Köne were admitted in the confraternity of the Birgittines like nobleman Detlef van der Pal and his whole kin, living and dead, were in 1438.[93] Cooperation with other religious communities in Livonia and noblemen was necessary for them to strengthen the position of the Birgittines on the Eastern shore of the Baltic Sea.[94]

The bonds of a spiritual confraternity between the communities of St Mary Magdalene in Riga and the Birgittines Mariendal may have lasted for centuries. Although most of the liturgical manuscripts of the Mariendal monastery have been lost, two leaves have survived of a calendar once used by it.[95] The names and dates of death of five nuns and clergymen have been recorded in these four pages.[96] Alongside the names of the late fifteenth–century sisters is Dorothea van Aalen (*Soror Dorothea van Aalen obijt anno mo vco xliiij. Schwester*) (†1544).[97] A noblewoman with the same name was a nun of the Cistercian convent in Riga in 1495.[98] Paul Johansen argues that the Dorothea van Aalen mentioned in the calendar of the Birgittines of Mariendal was unlikely to be the nun from Riga.[99] Yet, it is possible that she was the nun mentioned in 1495 who died in Riga as a Cistercian and was commemorated in

---

90 In 1413 the city asked the Grand Master of the Teutonic Order to move the convent, which was located close to the coast at the mouth of the river Mariendal, approximately four kilometres from Reval, inland. Nyberg, *Birgittinische Klostergründungen des Mittelalters*, pp. 95–99; Cnattingius, *Studies in the order of St. Bridget of Sweden*, p. 27; Kreem and Markus, 'Kes Asutas Pirita Kloostri?', p. 73; Rajamaa, 'Pirita kloostri asutamine ja ülesehitamine 1407–1436', pp. 75–92; Markus, 'The Pirita Convent in Tallinn', pp. 95–110.

91 Rajamaa, 'Pirita kloostri asutamine ja ülesehitamine', p. 84.

92 Kreem and Markus, 'Kes Asutas Pirita Kloostri?', pp. 60–74; Hahn, *Revaler Testamente im 15. und 16. Jahrhundert*, pp. 247–49.

93 LGU 1, no. 293; Hägglund, *Birgittine Landscapes*, p. 93, 96.

94 A spiritual confraternity of Mariendal has been described by Anna–Stina Hägglund in detail, see her *Birgittine Landscapes*, pp. 95–100.

95 Paul Johansen, *Ein Kalenderfragment aus dem Sankt Brigittenkloster zu Tallinn für den Mai und den Juni 1474–1544* (Pirita: Pirita Kaunistamise Selts, 1939).

96 May 2, 1474 Brigitte Eppenscheden; May 6, 1477 Elisabeth Stoltevoet; May 15, 1486 her Hermen Schulte, diaconus, May 1, 1492 Gerdrut Lode; June 1, 1544 Soror Dorothea van Aalen obijt anno mo vco xliiij. *Schwester*. Johansen, *Ein Kalenderfragment aus dem Sankt Brigittenkloster*, p. 16; Hägglund, *Birgittine Landscapes*, p. 92.

97 Johansen, *Ein Kalenderfragment aus dem Sankt Brigittenkloster*, p. 16, 22.

98 LUB 2/1, no. 252.

99 Johansen, *Ein Kalenderfragment aus dem Sankt Brigittenkloster*, p. 27; Mänd, 'Memoria and Sacral Art in Late Medieval Livonia', p. 248.

Mariendal because of the confraternity agreement. Even after the Reformation, the two communities – the Cistercians in Riga and the Birgittines in Mariendal – survived because of their bonds with the local nobilities. The convent of Mariendal was only destroyed in 1575/77 during a siege of Muscovite troops, and the last nuns of the Cistercian convent in Riga died in the 1580s, as claimed by the Jesuits, who described the nuns as being at least ninety years old.[100] Thus, it is possible that the institutions continued to commemorate their dead mutually throughout the period of unrest and disruption that began in 1524.

There is another case that may reveal possible memorial bonds between the convent in Riga and a religious community that likewise outlasted the Reformation. In the Uppsala University Library, there is a breviary from the Cistercian convent of Riga in which there is a record commemorating Margarete Brinken (*Margrete Brynckke*), who had died in 1548.[101] Von Bryncke or Bryncken were a family of vassals of the Teutonic Order in Courland. A certain Margarete von Bryncken has been mentioned as the abbess of the Cistercian convent in Reval in 1497, although that may have been a mistake, because between the 1490s and 1511 Elisabeth Brinke was the abbess of the convent.[102] Was this the same nun or were they two different ones, and thus did the prayer book of Riga's Cistercians mention the abbess from Reval or a nun from Riga's convent? Still, there is a possibility that a late fifteenth–century nun from Reval was commemorated in the prayer book used in the Riga Cistercian convent in the second half of the sixteenth century. However, it is also plausible that both late fifteenth–century nuns – Dorothea van Aalen from Riga and Margarete Brinken from Reval – or one of them could have had namesakes who had died in the mid–sixteenth century.

The Cistercian nuns in Reval had also forged confraternal ties with other religious communities. On 22 March 1431, abbot Alexander of the Cistercian abbey of Roma in Gotland issued a confraternity charter, which shared prayers and good works with the nuns of St Michael.[103] The Cistercians of Roma owned an estate called Kolk in Harrien, northern Estonia, and a house in Reval; thus the two communities already had a degree of geographical proximity, and they exchanged the names of the nuns and monks for whom they mutually agreed to pray.[104]

---

100 Johansen, *Ein Kalenderfragment aus dem Sankt Brigittenkloster*, p. 15; Schmidt, 'Die Zisterzienser im Baltikum und in Finnland', pp. 173–74; *Livlands Geistlichkeit*, p. 152; Levāns and Strenga, 'Medieval Manuscripts in the Riga Jesuit College Book Collection', p. 174.
101 'Item domen schref ynt yar xlyx [1548] do vor starf selyge margrete brynckke des frydages vor yubylate dat er got gnedych sy vnde barmehertych'. Uppsala, Uppsala universitetsbibliotek (Uppsala University Library) (UUB), C 436, fol. 167ʳ; Levāns and Strenga, 'Medieval Manuscripts in the Riga Jesuit College Book Collection', p. 180.
102 LUB 2/1 no. 597.
103 LUB 8, no. 417.
104 Schmidt, 'Die Zisterzienser im Baltikum und in Finnland', pp. 151–56.

Reval Cistercians were involved in another kind of a relationship that created commemorative bonds. In 1497 the Franciscan custodian Henning Schelp issued a charter in which he included the abbess of the Reval convent Margarethe Brincke in the prayers, masses, vigils, and all other spiritual deeds of the convents in Livonia and Prussia.[105] In addition to the prayers during her lifetime, the abbess was promised commemoration after death by the Franciscans. However, Henning Schelp had possibly made a mistake in writing down abbess's name because at the time, the abbess of the convent was Elisabeth Brinke, not Margarethe.[106] Although this was not a prayer association that involved two communities, it appears that the abbess mentioned during the prayers of the Franciscans represented not only herself but also the community of nuns.

The Cistercians in Riga created prayer associations not only with religious communities, but they also bonded with secular institutions. In late fifteenth-century Riga, the nuns entered into an unusual partnership. On 20 August 1495 in the church of St Mary Magdalene, an agreement to create a confraternity between the Cistercian nuns and the Beer Carters' guild was established.[107] According to the agreement, abbess Gerdrut Vitingess and 'all honourable and virtuous virgins (nuns)' were accepted into 'the guild and brotherhood' of the Beer Carters.[108] In the event of the death of a nun, the beer carters had to be 'perpetually ready' to attend the funeral with lights and a pall and to offer prayers at the vigils and requiem masses.[109] In return for the guild members' presence at the funerals and commemorations, the nuns promised to commemorate the deceased brothers and sisters of the Beer Carters' guild with vigils and masses. The charter lists the names of fifty-three nuns; the names of the beer carters were not included.

This agreement created a confraternity of prayer between the nuns and the beer carters. Such type of confraternity between a religious community and a guild was, however, unique. The co-operation benefited both parties, and it was clearly motivated by *memoria*. The confraternity enabled the nuns to have large funeral processions including lights and a pall; in turn the beer carters were promised regular liturgical remembrance of their dead in the Cistercian church.[110] By joining the Beer Carters' guild, the nuns attained something they could not have achieved without the help of a large group that had many male members. During a funeral procession, the guild members were able to carry the corpse to the grave, covered by a pall, and other members provided a large crowd of mourners. This confraternity between the nuns and the beer carters was created just as the city council of Riga was pressing the convent towards

---

105 LUB 2/1, no. 597.
106 Schmidt, 'Die Zisterzienser im Baltikum und in Finnland', p. 282; *Livlands Geistlichkeit*, p. 33.
107 LUB 2/1, no. 252; Mänd, 'Memoria and Sacral Art in Late Medieval Livonia', pp. 245–46.
108 LUB 2/1, no. 252.
109 LUB 2/1, no. 252.
110 LUB 2/1, no. 252.

reform, a pressure the nuns resisted; they also involved the Livonian Master Wolter von Plettenberg in their defence.[111]

With around two hundred members, the Beer Carters' guild was one of the largest brotherhoods in late fifteenth–century Riga (1494–1535).[112] Though the core of its members were transport workers and their spouses, it was not strictly a professional group. Amongst its members were numerous male and female artisans of indigenous descent (Latvians and Livs), servants and maids, and even individuals belonging to the social elites – the city councillors and their spouses, merchants and clergymen. The guild of the Beer Carters must have been appealing to the nuns because of its size, which granted a large number of mourners and commemorators.[113] Moreover, the social and ethnic division – different backgrounds of the noble nuns and indigenous beer carters – did not hinder the exchange of commemoration.[114] The commemorative obligations the guild accepted were not easy to fulfil, but the guild's *memoria* also benefited greatly by the addition of more than fifty nuns, who were 'professional commemorators' and providers of prayer. Moreover, the beer carters achieved this without having to invest significant financial resources. Another reason for this cooperation may have been the fact that one of the two guild's altars was located in St Jacob's parish church, right next to the convent.[115]

The agreement bound the two groups financially as well. The Beer Carters' guild had to pay the abbess two marks a year.[116] According to the account book of the Beer Carters' guild, the nuns were considered part of the guild. Between 1495 and 1511, the abbess paid an annual membership fee of three marks for all the nuns during every drinking feast, and in 1504, the nuns were described as full members of the guild.[117] The nuns' membership in the guild did not demand their presence in all secular activities of the brotherhood. It appears that the membership of the nuns in the Beer Carters brotherhood was meant to provide memorial benefits, not social participation.

The Cistercian nuns in Riga also commemorated deceased individuals, most likely from Riga, who did not belong to the community or were not members of any other religious institution. There is an entry in the calendar of the fifteenth–century psalter from the convent of St Mary Magdalene. It commemorates a certain *dominus* Conrad and his kin (*Anniuersarium domini conradi et so[ciorum]*').[118] This is the only memorial record present in the

---

111 LUB 2/1, no. 253.
112 Arbusow, 'Studien zur Geschichte der lettischen Bevölkerung Rigas', pp. 88–89;
113 Strenga, 'Turning Transport Workers into Latvians?', pp. 61–83; Strenga, 'Donations, Discipline and Commemoration', pp. 103–28.
114 Mänd, 'Memoria and Sacral Art in Late Medieval Livonia', pp. 245–46.
115 Arbusow, 'Studien zur Geschichte der lettischen Bevölkerung Rigas', p. 83.
116 Rīga, LVVA, 4038 f., 2 apr., 1089 l. fol. 52^a.
117 Presumably the Cistercian nuns continued to pay their membership fees also after 1511. Rīga, LVVA, 4038 f., 2 apr., 1089 l. fols. 14^b, 17^a, 20^b, 29^a, 29^b; Rīga, LVVA, 4038 f., 2 apr., 1159 l. fol. 16^a.
118 Tabora, 'Psalterium Davidis of the Cistercian Nunnery of Riga', pp. 119–69.

calendar of the psalter, a book that was used by a nun for individual piety because 'the Office of the Dead occupied a considerable amount of time of the nuns' prayer life'.[119] *Dominus* could have been the priest or a city councillor, but it is impossible to find out who Conrad was and in what context he was commemorated. As Laine Tabora demonstrates when analysing the only surviving calendar from the Rigan convent, the nuns followed the Order's tradition and annually commemorated the deceased, both the members of the Cistercian Order (the abbots and deceased bishops on 11 January; the Order's first martyrs on 18 September) and also parents and kin (20 November) of the nuns.[120]

These few surviving testimonies regarding the confraternity strategies of the Livonian Cistercian convents show that the bonds of confraternity were forged over the long term. The confraternity of the convent of St Mary Magdalene in Riga and the Birgittine convent in Mariendal was created in 1428, and nuns from Riga were presumably commemorated there in the sixteenth century as well, as the records in the Birgittine calendar testify. Likewise, the memorial bonds between the Cistercian nuns and the guild of Beer Carters in Riga lasted from the late fifteenth century until the Reformation. These confraternity agreements were attempts to secure commemoration of the dead members by inviting into the commemoration larger number of institutions. We can assume that the Cistercian convents in Livonia each had several bonds of confraternity with religious institutions in the province and beyond. As the exceptional case of the Riga Cistercian nuns joining the local Beer Carters guild demonstrates, the potential partners were not only religious communities but also secular groups which had commemorative potential – a large number of members who could take part in the remembrance of deceased nuns.

Annales Dunamundenses: Bonding of the Historical Traditions between the Cistercians and the Teutonic Order

Monastic groups in late medieval Europe had strong memorial traditions and hosted *memoria* of individuals not belonging to them. This practice reveals not only commemoration itself but also relationships between groups involved in the exchange of prayers and memory. As already mentioned, there were only three male monasteries outside cities in medieval Livonia, all of which were

---

[119] Laine Tabora, 'Fifteenth-Century Manuscripts: The Liturgical and Musical Testimonies from the Cistercian Nunnery in Riga', in *The Baltic Battle of Books: Formation and Relocation of European Libraries in the Confessional Age (c.1500–c.1650) and Their Afterlife*, ed. by Jonas Nordin, Peter Sjökvist, and Gustavs Strenga (Leiden: Brill, 2023), 13-36.

[120] Tabora, 'Fifteenth-Century Manuscripts'; Tabora, 'Psalterium Davidis of the Cistercian Nunnery of Riga', p. 150, 162, 165; Vilnius, Lietuvos mokslų akademijos Vrublevskių biblioteka (The Wroblewski Library of the Lithuanian Academy of Sciences) (LMAVB) RS F 22–96.

Cistercian: Dünamunde, later Padis, and Valkena.[121] Although no necrologies from these Cistercian communities have survived, there is one piece of evidence on their memorial traditions concerning the Teutonic Order. *Annales Dunamundenses* of the Livonian Cistercians present a mid-fourteenth century narrative of crusading and Christianization of Livonia that refers to those who lost their lives during these crusades. This section will deal with the *memoria* in the Dünamunde annals in the context of the relationship between the Livonian Cistercians and the Teutonic Order.

The Cistercians were actively involved in the Christianization of Livonia and in promoting crusades.[122] The Cistercians, according to Marek Tamm, 'held a crucial position in integrating Livonia with the Christian world' until the 1230s.[123] They played an important role in the communication of the Baltic crusades through their network of abbeys in Europe, thus fostering both the Christianization and implantation of European institutions in Livonia. Within Livonia itself, the Cistercians were also deeply involved in missionary work and military activities, playing key roles in the newly established Christian church even before the foundation of a Cistercian abbey.[124] Three Cistercian missionaries and bishops, Berthold Schulte (†1198),[125] Theoderic von Treiden (†1219),[126] and Bernhard zur Lippe (c. 1140–1224),[127] contributed greatly to the Livonian mission in which they combined the roles of military and religious leaders; Theoderic and Bernard were the first two abbots of Dünamunde abbey and later became bishops of Estonia and Semigallia respectively.

Once the Teutonic Order arrived in Livonia in 1237, the role of the Cistercians within the Livonian church gradually began to diminish. The Cistercians still played a part in the mission, as in the religious and economic life of Livonia through the work of their abbeys. The first Cistercian foundation in Livonia was the abbey of Dünamunde, founded in 1205 as a daughter of

---

121 Schmidt, 'Die Zisterzienser im Baltikum und in Finnland', pp. 32–151; Poelchau, 'Die Geschichte des Zisterzienserklosters Dünamünde bei Riga (1205–1305)', pp. 65–199.
122 Bernhart Jähnig, 'Zisterzienser und Ritterorden zwischen geistlicher und weltlicher Macht in Livland und Preußen zu Beginn der Missionszeit', in *Die Ritterorden zwischen geistlicher und weltlicher Macht im Mittelalter*, ed. by Zenon Hubert Nowak (Toruń: UMK, 1990), pp. 71–86.
123 Tamm, 'Communicating Crusade', p. 346.
124 Kaspar Elm, 'Christi cultores et novelle ecclesie plantatores. Der Anteil der Mönche, Kanoniker und Mendikanten an der Christianisierung der Liven und dem Aufbau der Kirche von Livland', in *Gli inizi del cristianesimo in Livonia–Lettonia: atti del Colloquio internazionale di storia ecclesiastica in occasione dell'VIII centenario della Chiesa in Livonia (1186–1986), Roma, 24–25 Giugno 1986*, ed. by Michele Maccarrone (Città del Vaticano: Libreria editrice Vaticana, 1989), pp. 132–45.
125 Jähnig, 'Bertholt Schulte', pp. 644–45.
126 Benninghoven, *Der Orden der Schwertbrüder*, pp. 20–24, 39; Bernhart Jähnig, 'Dietrich (Theoderich) von Treiden', in *Die Bischöfe des Heiligen Römischen Reiches*, pp. 144–45; Poelchau, 'Die Geschichte des Zisterzienserklosters Dünamünde bei Riga (1205–1305)', pp. 81–91.
127 Benninghoven, *Der Orden der Schwertbrüder*, pp. 29–33; Bernhart Jähnig, 'Bernhard zur Lippe', in *Die Bischöfe des Heiligen Römischen Reiches*, pp. 727–28; Wolfang Bender, 'Bernhard II. zur Lippe und die Mission in Livland', in *Lippe und Livland: mittelalterliche Herrschaftsbildung im Zeichen der Rose*, ed. by Jutta Prieur, Wolfgang Bender, and Gerhard Milting (Gütersloh: Verlag für Regionalgeschichte, 2008), pp. 147–68; Mänd and Selart, 'Livonia – a Region without Local Saints?', pp. 98–102.

Marienfeld abbey in Westphalia; it belonged to the German houses of Morimond filiation.[128] Dünamunde was located 10 kilometres north of Riga, on the right bank of the Daugava on the high sand dune near the river mouth.[129] This was a strategically important location from which all activities in the river mouth could be controlled. Exactly one hundred years later, the strategic location of the abbey influenced the relationship between the Teutonic Order and the Cistercians. The Order convinced the Cistercians to sell the abbey in 1305, during the war that broke out between the city of Riga and the Teutonic Order (1297–1330).[130] Thus, the Cistercians withdrew from the agreement with Riga (1263) not to sell their abbey without the consent of the city. This transaction was contested by Riga and confirmed only in 1318 by Pope John XXII (p. 1316–1334).[131] Despite these objections the Teutonic Order immediately began to rebuild the abbey into a castle. Meanwhile, the Cistercians moved to Padis, where they founded a new abbey in 1317, but the abbey was transformed into the castle of the Teutonic Order.[132]

Cistercian abbeys and their churches were not only centres of political, economic, and religious life, they were also important burial grounds and places of commemoration. They commemorated their founders, benefactors, and supporters.[133] Despite the prohibition of lay burials in Cistercian churches, which existed until the thirteenth century, Cistercians in neighbouring Scandinavia hosted the tombs of kings and princes, commemorating them as founders and supporters of their abbeys.[134] Similarly, in Silesia Cistercian monasteries and convents were burial sites of the ruling families.[135] Such commemoration of rulers as benefactors was an essential part of the *memoria* offered by monastic houses, and it created strong relationships between monasteries and regional political elites.

---

128 Schmidt, 'Die Zisterzienser im Baltikum und in Finnland', pp. 37–38; Poelchau, 'Das Zisterzienserkloster Dünamünde', p. 175; Poelchau, 'Die Geschichte des Zisterzienserklosters Dünamünde bei Riga (1205–1305)', pp. 73, 76–77; Tamm, 'Communicating Crusade', pp. 352, 356.
129 Poelchau, 'Das Zisterzienserkloster Dünamünde', pp. 172–73.
130 LUB 2, no. 614; Poelchau, 'Die Geschichte des Zisterzienserklosters Dünamünde bei Riga (1205–1305)', pp. 185–91.
131 LUB 1, no. 374; LUB 2, no. 670; Schmidt, 'Die Zisterzienser im Baltikum und in Finnland', p. 63; Caune, 'Rīgas pilsētas un Livonijas ordeņa karš 1297.–1330. gadā', pp. 63–74.
132 Schmidt, 'Die Zisterzienser im Baltikum und in Finnland', pp. 55–56; Poelchau, 'Die Geschichte des Zisterzienserklosters Dünamünde bei Riga (1205–1305)', pp. 185–91; *Keskaja sild Padise ja Vantaa vahel = Keskiajan silta Padisen ja Vantaan välillä*, ed. by Erki Russow (Padise: Padise Vallavalitsus, 2012); on the transformation of the abbey in to the castle, see Caune and Ose, *Latvijas viduslaiku mūra baznīcas*, pp. 136–40.
133 On the commemoration of the founder by the Cistercian community, see Jamroziak, *Rievaulx Abbey and Its Social Context*, pp. 21–40.
134 Sauer, *Fundatio und memoria*, p. 156; Thomas Hill, '"es für mich sehr nützlich ist, mir die Armen Christi zu Freunden zu machen". Voraussetzungen und Motive der Anlage von Zisterzienserklöstern in Dänemark', in *Zisterzienser: Norm, Kultur, Reform – 900 Jahre Zisterzienser*, ed. by Ulrich Knefelkamp (Berlin: Springer, 2001), pp. 65–90, p. 82.
135 Kaczmarek, 'Die schlesischen Klöster und ihr Beitrag zur Memorialkultur', pp. 29–58.

Upon arrival in Livonia the Cistercians found no kings or nobles to commemorate. Since the mid–thirteenth century, the Teutonic Order had tried to gain the upper hand first over the archbishop of Riga, and later over the city of Riga, in a struggle for leadership in Livonia. The Cistercians had to choose between the two. The war between Riga and the Teutonic Order (1297–1330) and the sale of Dünamunde abbey (1305) show that the Livonian Cistercians maintained a close relationship with the Livonian branch of the Order, like the Cistercian institutions in Prussia did.[136] Remembering the common past and the deceased was important for the relationship between the two parties in Livonia.

The Dünamunde annals record the influence of the Teutonic Order on both Cistercian historical writing and on the memorial culture in Livonia. Although described as a historical text, the annals contain numerous commemorational references, which reflect the memorial practices of the community in which they were composed.[137] The presence of memorial references does not contradict the historiographical character of annals; monastic annals in the Middle Ages were often used to commemorate benefactors, donations, and prominent members of communities.[138] In this respect the *Annales Dunamundenses* differ from other fourteenth-century Cistercian annals produced in the Baltic region, for example, the annals of the Cistercian abbey of Pelplin (Prussia), which refer exclusively to historical events and make no mention of the dead.[139]

To understand better the *memoria* embedded in the annals, the manuscript itself has to be examined closely. The annals are written on a single folio and bound within a larger codex, now held in the Tallinn City Archives.[140] The annals have several editions, and there are two later manuscripts that are described as later versions of the Dünamunde annals.[141] The whole text or sections of the Tallinn manuscript have been named as the *Kleine Dünamünder Chronik*, *Die Chronik von Dünamünde*, the *Annales Rigenses*, but

---

136 Rafał Kubicki, 'Cistercian Nuns of Zarnowitz (Żarnowiec) and the Teutonic Order in the Years 1309-1454', *Ordines Militares Colloquia Torunensia Historica. Yearbook for the Study of the Military Orders*, 25 (2020), 363–83.
137 Angermann, 'Die mittelalterliche Chronistik', p. 12.
138 Eckhard Freise, 'Kalendarische und annalistische Grundformen der Memoria', in *Memoria, der geschichtliche Zeugniswert*, pp. 441–577; Goetz, *Geschichtsschreibung und Geschichtsbewußtsein*, p. 299.
139 Jarosław Wenta, 'Über die ältesten preußischen Annalen', *Preussenland*, 32 (1994), 1–15, (1–8); Päsler, *Deutschsprachige Sachliteratur im Preußenland bis 1500*, pp. 295–98.
140 Tallinn, TLA, f. 230, n. 1, Cm 8, fol. 29ᵛ; *Mittelalterliche Handschriften in den Sammlungen des Stadtarchivs Tallinn und des Estnischen Historischen Museums: Katalog*, ed. by Tiina Kala (Tallinn: Tallinna Linnaarhiiv, 2007).
141 'Die Chronik von Dünamünde', in *Hermanni de Wartberge Chronicon Livoniae*, ed. by Ernst Gottfried Wilhelm Strehlke (Leipzig: Hirzel, 1863), pp. 131–34; Höhlbaum, 'Die Annalen von Dünamünde', pp. 612–15; Schmidt, 'Die Zisterzienser im Baltikum und in Finnland', pp. 284–86; According to Höhlbaum, later versions of the Dünamunde annals – Lviv manuscript and so-called *Annales Ronneburgenses*, see Konstantin Höhlbaum, 'Beiträge zur Quellenkunde Alt-Livlands', *Verhandlungen der Gelehrten Estnischen Gesellschaft zu Dorpat*, 7 (1873), 21–77.

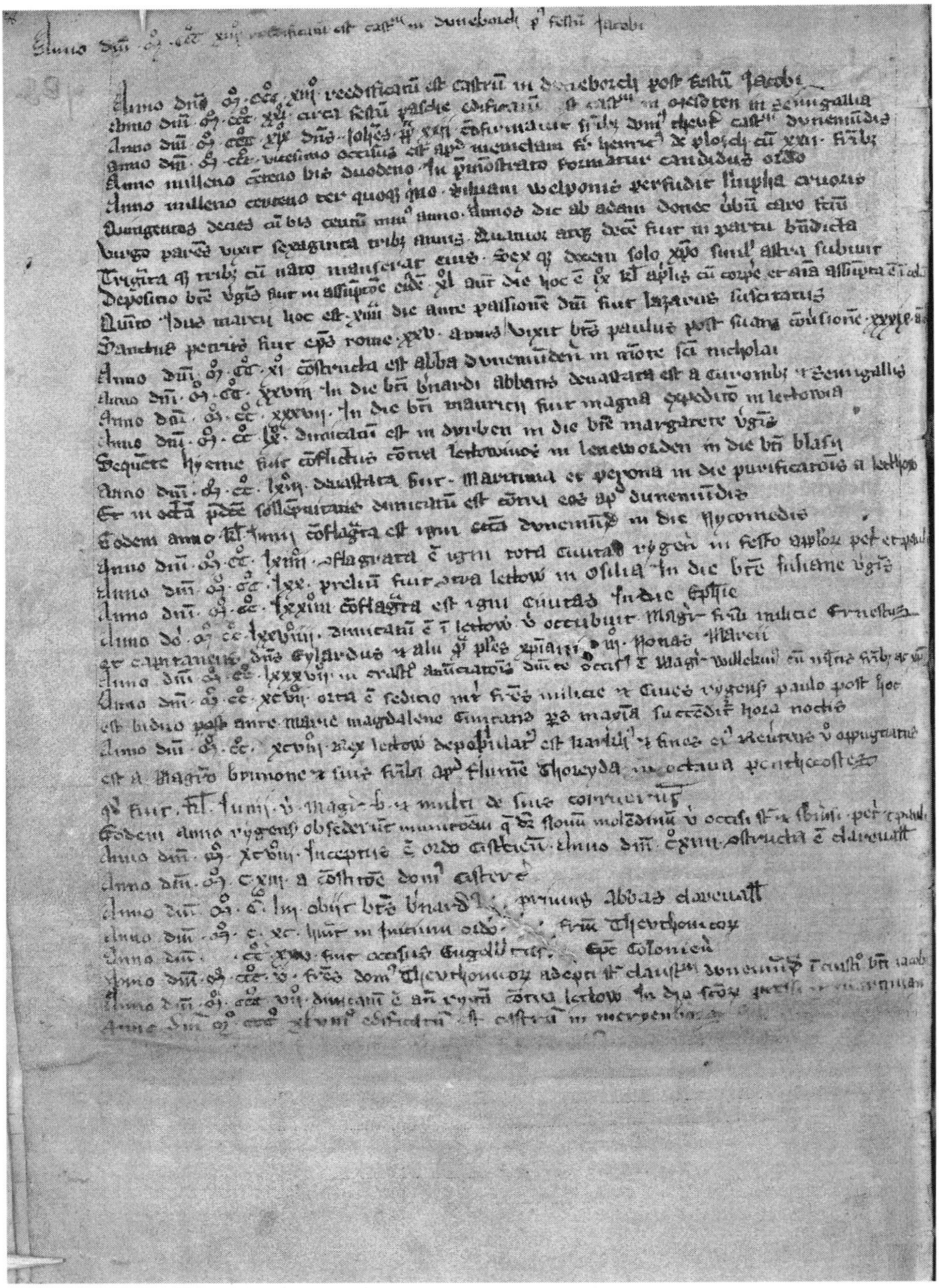

Figure 8: Dünamunde annals. Tallinn, TLA f. 230, n. 1, Cm 8, fol. 29ᵛ. Photo: Tallinn City Archives

it is most frequently referred to as the *Annales Dunamundenses* or *Annalen von Dünamünde*.[142] The examination of the annals by nineteenth-century Baltic German scholars suggested that they were initially compiled in the Cistercian abbey of Dünamunde. After the sale of the abbey in 1305, the annals were continued in Riga and at the archbishop's residence of Ronneburg until 1348, or later in the Cistercian abbey of Padis to which the Dünamunde Cistercians moved.[143] The history of the codex is equally unclear, and it can only be assumed that Tallinn City Archives acquired it after the dissolution of the abbey of Padis in 1559.[144]

Although most scholars have attributed the annals to the abbey of Dünamunde, the text was compiled long after 1305, using sources that cannot be securely linked to Dünamunde.[145] Despite the claims that parts of the text may be older than the mid-fourteenth century, an analysis of the manuscript shows that the text, with the exception of only one insertion, was written by a single hand at some point after 1348.[146] The annals may represent an attempt to reconstruct collective memory of a destroyed community. During the St George's night uprising in 1343, the abbey of Padis was badly damaged, and its monks were killed.[147] However, as it will be discussed below, it was not a very successful attempt to reconstruct the Cistercian past. Thus, the text may therefore represent remnants of historical tradition of the Dünamunde abbey; however, the text shows strong influence of other historical and memorial traditions, namely those of the Teutonic Order.[148]

The influence of the Teutonic Order's Livonian branch on the narrative of the Dünamunde annals is evident in its depiction of historical events that took place in Livonia between 1211 and 1348.[149] The earliest recorded event is the foundation of Dünamunde abbey itself (the annals incorrectly date the foundation of the abbey with the year 1211), and the last is the construction of the Teutonic Order's castle in Livonian Marienburg.[150] Although these were Cistercian annals, the events and actions of the Teutonic Order's Livonian branch are given a dominant position in the text. Thus, the annals mention the acquisition of the abbey of Dünamunde by the Teutonic Order in 1305, the papal privilege issued by Pope John XXII confirming this transaction in 1319,

---

142 Wilhelm Arndt, 'Neu Entdeckte Livländischen Chroniken', *Archiv für die Geschichte Liv-, Est- und Kurlands*, 4 (1845), 269–71, p. 269; 'Die Chronik von Dünamünde', pp. 131–32.

143 'Die Chronik von Dünamünde', pp. 131–34; Höhlbaum, 'Die Annalen von Dünamünde', p. 613; Schmidt, 'Die Zisterzienser im Baltikum und in Finnland', pp. 284–86.

144 Höhlbaum, 'Die Annalen von Dünamünde', p. 613.

145 Poelchau, 'Die Geschichte des Zisterzienserklosters Dünamünde bei Riga (1205–1305)', pp. 191–92.

146 Schmidt, 'Die Zisterzienser im Baltikum und in Finnland', p. 127; Tallinn, TLA, f. 230, n. 1, Cm 8, fol. 29ᵛ.

147 Schmidt, 'Die Zisterzienser im Baltikum und in Finnland', p. 81; Kaur Alttoa, 'Padise kloostri ehitusloo probleeme', in *Keskaja sild Padise ja Vantaa vahel*, pp. 63–80.

148 Angermann argues that the annals represent monastic history writing. See Angermann, 'Die mittelalterliche Chronistik', p. 12.

149 Schmidt, 'Die Zisterzienser im Baltikum und in Finnland', pp. 284–86.

150 Poelchau, 'Die Geschichte des Zisterzienserklosters Dünamünde bei Riga (1205–1305)', pp. 73, 192.

and the construction of the Teutonic Order's castles.¹⁵¹ Furthermore, the annals offer detailed descriptions of the Teutonic Order's military campaigns, in which context the deaths of numerous brethren are noted.

Although the annals contain the names of several dead men, no Cistercian monks – with the exception of Bernard of Clairvaux (1090–1153) – appear in it.¹⁵² Remarkably, the annals omit the illustrious thirteenth-century Livonian Cistercian, the second abbot of Dünamunde, Bishop Bernhard zur Lippe, believed to be buried in the abbey, and who was honoured as a saint with the hagiographical work of master Justinus, the *Lippiflorium*.¹⁵³

All aspects of the text demonstrate the author's – or authors' – interest in the liturgical and historical texts of the Teutonic Order. Just as in the Order's chronicles and necrologies, five prominent dead brethren from the Livonian branch were recorded in the annals: Master Ernest von Ratzeburg (†1279), Master Wilhelm von Nindorf (†1287), Master Bruno (†1298), and brother Heinrich von Plotzke (*Henricus de Plozch*) (†1320).¹⁵⁴ The defeat of the Order at Durbe (1260) was also recorded in the annals.¹⁵⁵ These names have been selected according to the same principle used in the necrologies and chronicles of the Order, all were brethren fallen during battles with the pagans. The records of their deaths in the annals are brief and thus resemble the commemorational inscriptions of the necrologies. For example, according to the annals, Master Ernest von Ratzeburg and *dominus* Eilard, Danish captain of Reval, were killed in Lithuania on 5 March 1279 along with 'numerous Christians'.¹⁵⁶ Ernest is also commemorated together with seventy brethren in the necrology of the Teutonic Order's commandery in Mergentheim (bailiwick Franken), and there the circumstances of his death are likewise omitted.¹⁵⁷ Ernest's death is described in detail in the Livonian Rhymed Chronicle and the Chronicle of Hermann Wartberge.¹⁵⁸ Equally, *dominus* Eilard commemorated in the annals also appeared in the Livonian Rhymed Chronicle, where he merited a

---

151 Schmidt, 'Die Zisterzienser im Baltikum und in Finnland', p. 284.
152 'Anno domini m c liii (1153) obiit beatus Bernardus primus abbas Clarevallis'. Schmidt, 'Die Zisterzienser im Baltikum und in Finnland', p. 286.
153 Jähnig, 'Bernhard zur Lippe', pp. 727–28; Lore Poelchau, 'Bernhards von Lippe Lebensende (1224) und seine Darstellung im „Lippiflorium". Ergänzende Interpretationen', *Zeitschrift für Ostforschung*, 51 (2002), 253–58; Erhard Wiersing, 'Ein Mensch im Wandel seiner Rollen. Zur Darstellung mittelalterlicher Personalität am Beispiel des Edelherrn Bernhard II. zur Lippe', in *Lippe und Livland*, pp. 17–32, pp. 18–20; Bender, 'Bernhard II. zur Lippe und die Mission in Livland', pp. 147–68; Tamm, 'The Livonian Crusade in Cistercian Stories', pp. 374–75; Mänd and Selart, 'Livonia – a Region without Local Saints?', pp. 99–101.
154 *Ritterbrüder*, no. 695, 624, 126, 27.
155 See Chapter 1 on the commemoration of the battle at Durbe. 'Anno domini m cc lx (1260) dimicatum est in durben in die beate margarete virginis'. Schmidt, 'Die Zisterzienser im Baltikum und in Finnland', p. 285.
156 'Anno domini m cc lxxviiii (1279) dimicatum est in lettowia, ubi occubuit magister fratrum milicie Ernestus et capitaneus, dominus Eylardus et alii quam plures christiani 3 nonas marcii'. Schmidt, 'Die Zisterzienser im Baltikum und in Finnland', p. 285.
157 Ludwigsburg, StAL B 279 II U 1, fol. 15.
158 *Livländische Reimchronik*, vers. 8511–36; *Vartberges Hermaņa Livonijas hronika*, p. 40.

long description of his struggle with Lithuanians and his tragic death on the battlefield.[159]

The other Master mentioned in the Dünamunde annals was Wilhelm von Nindorf (alias Willekin or Wilhelm von Staden), who was killed 'together with many brethren and Christians' in the battle with the Semigallians in 1287.[160] Wilhelm's *memoria*, like Ernest's, was noted in the two Livonian chronicles of the Teutonic Order and also in the necrology of Alden Biesen.[161]

The Dünamunde annals, in contrast to the Livonian Rhymed Chronicle and the Teutonic Order's necrologies in western Europe, holds records of the brethren killed in Livonia after the end of the crusading era. The annals reported the death of Master Bruno during the Order's war against Riga and its Lithuanian allies (1297–1330). Master Bruno was killed in a battle with the Lithuanians near Wenden, by the river Aa in 1298.[162] The contemporary chronicler, Albrecht von Bardewik gave a gruesome description of the battle's aftermath, when the pagan Lithuanians nailed Bruno's dead body on a cross.[163] The death of Bruno in battle is not included in the Livonian Rhymed Chronicle because the chronicle only referred to events before 1290, but Bruno's death is mentioned in the Chronicle of Wartberge.[164] The death of Bruno was part of a broader narrative describing the Teutonic Order's struggle against the enemies of the Christian faith.

The Dünamunde annals also include the names of brethren who were missing from the Order's historical texts. They mention the death of Heinrich von Plotzke, who was killed near Memel in 1320, together with twenty-two brethren.[165] Heinrich was probably a commander of the commandery at Årsta in Sweden, yet his name does not appear in other contemporary charters or historiographical texts of the Livonian branch.[166] The exception is the so-called Necrology of Runa, the late sixteenth-century Polish copy of the necrology, in which *Henrik Kontor z Pleczka* and another twenty-nine brethren

---

159 *Livländische Reimchronik*, vers. 8322–89.
160 'Anno domini 1287 in crastino annunciacionis dominice occisus est magister Willekinus cum multis fratribus ac christianis'. Schmidt, 'Die Zisterzienser im Baltikum und in Finnland', p. 285; *Ritterbrüder*, no. 624.
161 Wien, DOZA Hs. 427c, fol. 12ᵇ; Perlbach, 'Deutsch–Ordens Necrologe', no. 9, p. 363; *Livländische Reimchronik*, vers. 10675–86; *Vartberges Hermaņa Livonijas hronika. Hermanni de Wartberge Chronicon Livoniae*, p. 60.
162 '[…] Revertrens vero oppugnatus est a magistro Brunone et suis fratribus apud flumen Thoreyda in octava penthecostes, quod fuit Kal. Iunij ubi magister et multi de suis corruerunt'. Schmidt, 'Die Zisterzienser im Baltikum und in Finnland', p. 286; Caune, 'Rīgas pilsētas un Livonijas ordeņa karš 1297.–1330. gadā', pp. 67–68; *Ritterbrüder*, no. 126.
163 'Chronik des Kanzlers Albrecht von Bardewik vom Jahre 1298 bis 1301. Ein Fragment', in *Die lübeckischen Chroniken in niederdeutscher Sprache*, vol. 1. ed. by Ferdinand-Heinrich Grautoff (Hamburg: Perthes und Besser, 1829), pp. 411–28, p. 426.
164 *Vartberges Hermaņa Livonijas hronika*, p. 47.
165 'Anno domini 1320 occisus est apud memelam frater Henricus de Plozch cum 22 fratribus'. Schmidt, 'Die Zisterzienser im Baltikum und in Finnland', p. 284.
166 *Ritterbrüder*, no. 27.

fallen at Memel are mentioned.[167] Heinrich's death is commemorated in the necrology of Alden Biesen in an indirect way; on 3 February the necrology memorialized seventeen anonymous brethren killed near Memel.[168]

Although events in the Dünamunde annals are not arranged in a chronological order, the text contains the dates of death for the brethren that a liturgical commemoration would require.[169] In most cases there was a direct correlation between the dates of death in the necrologies and in the Cistercian annals. Ernest von Ratzeburg's anniversary was celebrated on 5 March both in the annals and in the Mergentheim necrology.[170] In the case of Master Wilhelm von Nindorf, there was a slight discrepancy between the anniversary in the necrologies and that in the annals; the annals reported his death on 26 March, while the necrology of Alden Biesen gave it as 25 March.[171]

These examples show that the Livonian Cistercians knew well the memorial tradition of the Teutonic Order and its Livonian branch. The source of the information may have been the Livonian Rhymed Chronicle, the Chronicle of Wartberge, or memorial texts (necrologies) of the Livonian branch. Yet it is possible that the Livonian Cistercians were commemorators of the Knight Brethren, and this information about their deaths was taken from the Cistercian liturgical manuscripts.

The memorial character of these annals is also visible when they are analysed in the context of the codex within which the annals are bound. The forty-seven leaves of 'Codex 8' contain numerous theological and liturgical texts. They include a treatise on the art of preaching by a Cistercian theologian Alain de Lille (*c.* 1120–1202), *Summa de arte predicatoria*, and several contemplative texts, such as *De contemptu mundi*, *De corpore Christi*, and *De nativitate beate virginis* etc.[172] All the texts of the codex were written in the fourteenth century, although the treatise of Alain de Lille may have been copied earlier. The annals were entered on the last page of the quire that contains de Lille's work, thus it is possible that the scribe filled in an empty folio (29v). The hand of the annals can also be found on the last folio of the codex (47r–v); it was bound during the Middle Ages, shortly after 1348 (the last record in the annals), and the scribe of the annals was involved in it too.[173]

---

167 'Die Annalen und das Necrologium von Ronneburg', in *Hermanni de Wartberge Chronicon Livoniae*, pp. 142–48, p. 145.

168 Wien, DOZA, Hs. 427c, fol. 3ᵇ; Perlbach, 'Deutsch-Ordens Necrologe', no. 9.

169 With the exception of Heinrich von Plotzke, all the other brethren had dates of their death listed. Schmidt, 'Die Zisterzienser im Baltikum und in Finnland', p. 284–86.

170 Ludwigsburg, StAL B 279 II U 1, fol. 15; Schmidt, 'Die Zisterzienser im Baltikum und in Finnland', p. 285.

171 Wien, DOZA, Hs. 427c, fol. 12ᵇ; Perlbach, 'Deutsch-Ordens Necrologe', no. 9, p. 363; Schmidt, 'Die Zisterzienser im Baltikum und in Finnland', p. 127.

172 Tallinn, TLA, f. 230, n. 1, Cm 8; Höhlbaum, 'Die Annalen von Dünamünde', p. 612; Schmidt, 'Die Zisterzienser im Baltikum und in Finnland', p. 127.

173 *Mittelalterliche Handschriften in den Sammlungen des Stadtarchivs Tallinn und des Estnischen Historischen Museums*, p. 85–86.

Because there was a close relationship between annalistic and liturgical texts, this codex may have supported liturgical activities at which important events or the deceased were commemorated.[174] In this way the annals formed part of the 'liturgical past' and a history of salvation into which the life of the Virgin, the lives of Saint Paul and Saint Peter, and the foundation of the Cistercian (1098) and Teutonic Orders (1190), all of which were mentioned in the annals, also fitted.[175]

The presence of the dead Teutonic Knights in the Cistercian annals was not coincidental but formed part of an exchange of *memoria* between the Cistercians and the Order's Livonian branch that had begun at least half a century before the production of the annals. The two groups were bound by promises of mutual *memoria*; a historic bond was created or reinforced by the sale of Dünamunde abbey in 1305.

The sale of the Dünamunde abbey to the Teutonic Order in 1305 was not solely a financial transaction, but the beginning of a long-term relationship with obligations for both sides. The charter of sale and its surviving draft recorded in detail the obligations of both parties.[176] The Cistercians agreed to hand the abbey over intact, and in return the Teutonic Order paid 4000 silver marks. In addition, the Master, his successors, and the whole Teutonic Order were compelled to continue the *memoria* of those Cistercian monks buried in the abbey's cemetery next to the chapel of St Catherine.[177] In the charter of 1305, the Cistercian abbots of Dünamunde and Valkena, Libert and Dithmar, stipulated a weekly memorial mass for the deceased Cistercians, continuing the *memoria* in perpetuity.[178] Moreover, the two abbots expressed their confidence in the *memoria*'s continuity once the Teutonic Order was in charge.[179] The presence of the dead Teutonic Knights in the Cistercian annals is part of the long-term relationship created by the sale of the abbey in 1305.

The charter of sale described the process as a *translatio* of the community.[180] The community was moved from Dünamunde to Padis, where the Cistercians already had a church, and this *translatio* also included the transfer of the historical tradition.[181] The annals served as one of the channels of this transfer, as the community entered into its new environment. The extent to which this transferred tradition survived the devastation of the Padis abbey in 1343 remains obscure. In the second half of the fourteenth century, the history and *memoria* of the Teutonic Order were added to the historical narrative of

---

174 Goetz, *Geschichtsschreibung und Geschichtsbewußtsein*, p. 299.
175 Schmidt, 'Die Zisterzienser im Baltikum und in Finnland', pp. 284–85.
176 LUB 2, no. 614; LUB 3, no. 614a; Schmidt, 'Die Zisterzienser im Baltikum und in Finnland', p. 55.
177 LUB 2, no. 614; Poelchau, 'Die Geschichte des Zisterzienserklosters Dünamünde bei Riga (1205–1305)', p. 187, 188.
178 This document was a draft of the contract; see LUB 2, no. 614; LUB 3, no. 614a; Schmidt, 'Die Zisterzienser im Baltikum und in Finnland', p. 55.
179 LUB 2, no. 614.
180 LUB 2, no. 614; LUB 3, no. 614a.
181 Schmidt, 'Die Zisterzienser im Baltikum und in Finnland', pp. 68–76.

the annals. These merged into a future mutual tradition, and the dead were part of the common history shared by the two groups.

Although no confraternity agreements between the Teutonic Order and the Dünamunde/Padis abbey have survived, the exchange of the names of the dead had taken place. The annals and the documents of the sale demonstrate a close relationship between the two communities in that both sides mutually commemorated their dead – the Teutonic Order promised *memoria* in the former abbey, and the Cistercians in the newly founded abbey of Padis maintained in their tradition the names of the deceased Knight brethren. Apparently, the sale of the abbey was one of the elements that created or strengthened an already existing bond.

As historical writing, the annals were part of historical and memorial traditions. Even if the annals were not used as a source of information for the performance of memorial services, they certainly reflected the memorial tradition of the environment in which they were written. It is not clear where the annals were compiled, but the strong influences of the historical and memorial traditions of the Cistercian and Teutonic Orders are visible in the text. In that sense the text belonged to both groups, although Cistercian origins for its creation are more plausible. The text offers insight into the memorial culture of the Livonian Cistercians because it shows the transfer of their historical tradition from Dünamunde to Padis.

Conclusion

Both the Cistercian nuns and the Dominican friars were active commemorators in Livonian cities. The nuns of Reval were less attractive commemorative partners to the townspeople than the friars were, but the local noble families were eager to use their commemorational services, as the nuns belonged to those families. The Dominicans in Reval were popular amongst testators, many of whom wanted to be commemorated by the friars. The Livonian nobility also used their services by founding chantries in the Dominican churches and holding their political meetings there, as was custom in Reval.

As the scarce written sources testify, the Livonian Cistercian communities created spiritual bonds, created confraternities of prayer by exchanging names of the dead, and in some circumstances even adapted the historical tradition of other institutions. These communities chose other religious or sometimes even secular institutions with whom to bond in mutual liturgical commemoration of their members: they created networks of commemoration. What made these relationships to be network–like structures? The communities usually were involved in numerous commemorational relationships. The goals of such relationships were to offer additional security for the groups and also allowed the groups to strengthen their relationships (legal, economic, political etc.).

The confraternity of prayer ensured participation in the good deeds of other communities. Although in the late Middle Ages the role of the confraternity of prayer had declined, one of its primary aims was still to commemorate the dead. The Cistercian nuns in the Livonian convents after their death were commemorated not only by their sisters but also by the members of other religious communities – Cistercian nuns in other cities, the Birgittines, the Livonian Franciscans, the Cistercian monks, and even lay guild members. These networks of commemoration lasted for centuries. As two examples presented in this chapter show, it is plausible that after the Reformation in the Livonian cities, the remaining female religious communities – the Cistercian convents in Riga and Reval, and the Birgittine convent in Mariendal, mutually commemorated their dead. Also the unusual entry of the Cistercian nuns in the Beer Carters' guild in Riga was designed to sustain *memoria* of the nuns and guild members; both parties had agreed to exchange mutual services – the presence of the guild members in the funerals with lights and a pall benefited the nuns, and the guild members could expect the prayers for their souls from the 'professional commemorators' in return.

Historical traditions during the Middle Ages intertwined with commemoration and memorial traditions. The *Annales Dunamundenses* are exceptional because they reveal the adopted historical tradition of the group – the Cistercians of Padis – that was almost fully destroyed. Despite the claims of the existing research, the annals were not written in the Dünamunde abbey (prior 1305), and they most likely belong to a re-constructed historical tradition after most of the monks were killed in Padis in 1343, during St George's night uprising. This rift in the Dünamunde/Padis tradition may have influenced the narrative represented in the annals. Although they have been considered to be a reflection of Cistercian historical tradition of the Dünamunde abbey, it is actually content-wise a historiographical text of the Teutonic Order. The annals reveal that at least in the Cistercian monastery of Padis in the mid-fourteenth century, there was a firm presence of the Teutonic Order's historical experiences in the narrative of the Cistercians. The events from the past of the Teutonic Order's Livonian branch were recorded alongside necrology-like records of the Knight brethren killed in the struggle against pagans. Even though it is evident that the annals were not used directly during the liturgy to commemorate the dead, they do represent the memorial tradition of a certain community – most likely the one of the Padis abbey.

In the case of the Cistercians convents and monasteries in Livonia, it is evident that the remembrance shared with other communities helped to create bonds of mutual assistance and support, benefiting all parties involved. Memorial networking was an indispensable element that internally secured commemoration of each community member, strengthening the group's identity.

CHAPTER 4

Conflict and Memory

Memoria was affected by periods of conflict. In an institutional context, *memoria* usually granted a sense of continuity, but during crises and conflicts *memoria* was used as a defensive mechanism.[1] The *memoria* of the Church of Riga was directly influenced by the conflict between the archbishops, the cathedral chapter, and the Teutonic Order. Memory often becomes crucial when identity is weak or threatened.[2] In the hands of the archbishops and the cathedral canons, *memoria* was as powerful tool as arms; it enabled them to defend something more valuable than a single life, the identity of their community. Yet, as Mihkel Mäesalu has argued, the memory of the two conflicting parties – the Teutonic Order and the Church of Riga – not only instrumentalised the past in their political struggle, but the conflicting memories also shaped identities of the two groups and further fuelled the conflict and made a lasting solution impossible.[3] This chapter focuses on the role of memory in this centuries–long conflict.

The Livonian political system had an inbuilt problem of power imbalance. When the Teutonic Order arrived in Livonia in 1237, it inherited the rights and territorial possessions of the Sword Brethren, thus taking charge of one–third of the conquered territories.[4] Soon after its arrival, the Teutonic Order struggled to free itself from the bishop (later archbishop) of Riga, under whose lordship the Sword Brethren had been.[5] The Order sought to obtain in Livonia the favourable position it had in Prussia, with large territorial possessions and control of all bishoprics. However, the Order was not intending to unify Livonia under its sole authority, but it did attempt to gain unlimited control over different political subjects.[6] Thus from the fourteenth century on, the Order

---

[1] On *memoria* and crises, see Gerd Althoff, 'Zur Verschriftlichung von Memoria in Krisenzeiten', in *Memoria in der Gesellschaft des Mittelalters*, pp. 56–73.

[2] Allan Megill, *Historical Knowledge, Historical Error: A Contemporary Guide to Practice* (Chicago: University of Chicago Press, 2007), p. 46.

[3] Mihkel Mäesalu, 'Historical Memory as the Cause of Conflict in Medieval Livonia', *Vestnik of Saint Petersburg University. History*, 64.3 (2019), 1014–30.

[4] In Courland the Order controlled two–thirds of the territory. Benninghoven, *Der Orden der Schwertbrüder*, p. 357; Jähnig, *Verfassung und Verwaltung*, pp. 12–32, 14, 31.

[5] The Order remained the archbishop's subject until 1366. See Bernhart Jähnig, 'Der Kampf des Deutschen Ordens um die Schutzherrschaft über die livländischen Bistümer', in *Ritterorden und Kirche im Mittelalter*, ed. by Zenon Hubert Nowak (Toruń: UMK, 1997), pp. 97–111.

[6] Jähnig, *Verfassung und Verwaltung*, p. 78; Hellmann, 'Deutsche Orden und die Stadt Riga', p. 32.

tried to establish control over the Livonian bishoprics and their cathedral chapters, particularly focusing on the cathedral chapter of Riga.[7]

The Teutonic Order in Livonia aspired to gain political hegemony, and this aspiration for more power resulted in a two-century long legal and sometimes also a military struggle in which the two sides – the Teutonic Order and the archbishop of Riga with his allies – attempted to weaken each other and doubted the legitimacy of each other's power, possessions, and territories.[8] These conflicts had an impact on memory culture of numerous groups involved in them.[9] After the conclusion of the struggle against the pagans in 1290, the Order confronted internal enemies, the archbishop, and the city of Riga for the next two hundred years.[10] This rivalry continued until the late fifteenth century and resulted in numerous diplomatic standoffs and wars, for example, the civil war of 1297–1330 and military conflicts with Riga in the 1480s and 1490s.[11] The dynamics of the relationship between the main actors in Livonia changed considerably in the late fifteenth century, when the Order's influence was extended by Master Wolter von Plettenberg.[12] These conflicts were reflected in the memory cultures of the groups involved.

Memory and the Struggle between the Teutonic Order and the Church of Riga

Riga cathedral as a memorial site was framed by internal Livonian politics and the struggle for the memorial site was also the struggle for power and control over the cathedral chapter and the archbishop's office. After the burial of Johannes von Vechta (†1294) in the cathedral, no other archbishop was buried there for 140 years. This was a result of the Teutonic Order's constant pressure on the archbishops, who were forced to seek refuge in the papal curia; some, between 1294 and 1424, even died there.[13] Johannes von Vechta's successor, Johannes II (e. 1294/95–1300), was incarcerated by the Order in the castle of Fellin after the beginning of the civil war between the archbishop, the city of Riga and the Teutonic Order (1297–1330). Once freed, he left for the papal

---

7 On the influence of the Teutonic Order on the Livonian bishoprics, see, Jähnig, 'Kampf des Deutschen Ordens', p. 97; Bernhart Jähnig, 'Die Verfassung der Domkapitel der Kirchenprovinz Riga. Ein Überblick', in *Kirchengeschichtliche Probleme des Preussenlandes aus Mittelalter und früher Neuzeit*, ed. by Arnold Bartetzky and Bernhart Jähnig (Marburg: Elwert, 2001), pp. 53–72, at pp. 65–72; Glauert, 'Bindung des Domkapitels', pp. 269–316.
8 Eihmane, *Rīgas arhibīskapa un Vācu ordeņa cīņas par varu*, pp. 51–117.
9 Mäesalu, 'Historical Memory', 1014–30.
10 Jähnig, *Verfassung und Verwaltung*, pp. 40–41.
11 On the conflicts between Riga and the Order, see Hellmann, 'Deutsche Orden und die Stadt Riga', pp. 1–33; Šterns, *Latvijas Vēsture. 1290–1500*, pp. 350–86; Caune, 'Rīgas pilsētas un Livonijas ordeņa karš 1297.–1330. gadā', pp. 63–74; Eihmane, *Rīgas arhibīskapa un Vācu ordeņa cīņas par varu*, pp. 16–25.
12 See, *Wolter von Plettenberg und das mittelalterliche Livland*.
13 In Avignon: Friedrich von Pernstein (1304–1341), Engelbert (1341–1347), Siegfried Blomberg (1370–1374). Fromhold von Vifhusen (1348–1369) died in Rome. 'Cronica episcoporum', pp. 175–77.

curia and died in Anagni on 19 December 1300.[14] Because of the distance between southern Europe and Livonia, no attempt was made to transfer the archbishops' remains to Livonia.

The absence of archiepiscopal burials over such a long time affected the memorial culture of the community. The reconstruction and elaboration of Meinhard's tomb during the late fourteenth century was possibly intended to compensate for the memorial absence of contemporary archbishops and to reinforce the identity of the cathedral chapter in the face of mounting pressure from the Order.[15] The new tomb was a copy of that of Pope Urban V (†1370), influenced by the archbishop's entourage from its stay with the papal curia.

Riga Cathedral was a contested memorial space for the Order, the archbishops, and the cathedral chapter.[16] This struggle over the memorial significance of the cathedral was a facet of the Order's aspirations to control elections to the see. The Livonian branch of the Order, with the assistance of well-disposed archbishops, attempted to incorporate Riga's cathedral chapter into the Order on two occasions, in 1394 and 1451, by changing the chapter's statutes and imposing its white habit on the canons.[17] By doing so the Order followed the approach used in Prussia and Livonia, where the cathedral chapters of Kulm, Samland, Pomesania and Courland had already been incorporated into the Order by the late thirteenth century.[18] Yet the Order was not fully successful in its attempts; the first incorporation was cancelled by a papal bull in 1423, and although the chapter formally followed the Order's statutes after 1451, it never came under its full control.[19] The Order experienced continuous opposition from the cathedral canons, who struggled for their institutional independence. This was a dangerous game, which sometimes ended in bloodshed: in 1428 the representatives of the Order in southern Livonia, at the lake of Liva (Liepāja), slaughtered sixteen envoys of Livonian bishops, who were on their way to Rome; among them were a number of canons from Riga.[20]

The struggle between the Order, the archbishop, and the cathedral chapter affected the *memoria* of the Church of Riga. The death of archbishop Silvester Stodewescher and its aftermath demonstrates this impact in detail. Silvester turned from the Order's close ally into an enemy.[21] Following a decade-long feud between him and the Order, Silvester was arrested in 1479 and held in the castle of Kokenhusen; although he was later released from arrest, he died

---

14 Bernhart Jähnig, 'Johannes, Graf von Schwerin', in *Die Bischöfe des Heiligen Römischen Reiches*, p. 650; Caune, 'Rīgas pilsētas', pp. 63–74.
15 See Chapter 1. Löffler, *Grabsteine*, pp. 45–47; Campe, 'Fragment', p. 307, 309–10; Bruiningk, 'Frage der Verehrung', p. 10.
16 Neitmann, 'Riga und Wenden als Residenzen', pp. 78–79.
17 Jähnig, 'Der Kampf des Deutschen Ordens', pp. 310–13;
18 Jähnig, 'Verfassung der Domkapitel', pp. 68–69; Glauert, 'Bindung des Domkapitels', p. 271.
19 Glauert, 'Bindung des Domkapitels', pp. 296, 310–13.
20 Schwarz, 'Prälaten', p. 503; Eihmane, 'Livonijas bīskapu delegācijas slepkavība 1428. gadā', pp. 29–59.
21 For Stodewescher's relationship with the Teutonic Order, see Boockmann, 'Der Einzug des Erzbischofs', p. 3; Strenga, 'Gifts and Conflicts', pp. 77–102.

there on 12 July.²² Silvester's death was initially kept a secret because Master Bernhard von der Borch (1472–1483) wished to secure the appointment of his cousin, Simon von der Borch (e. 1475–1492), bishop of Reval, as archbishop, thus establishing the Order's control over the archbishopric.²³ According to the Master's own letter to the Grand Master in the autumn of 1479, Silvester's body was brought following tradition (*gewonheit*) by 'us' (*haben wier*) to Riga and buried beside his predecessors in the cathedral.²⁴ The Livonian Master omits, however, to mention the fact that Silvester, despite the summer heat in which a body would decay rapidly, was brought to Riga and buried nearly a month after his death, on 7 August.²⁵

The delay of Silvester's funeral was part of a political game which aimed to destroy the independence of the Church of Riga. The death offered an opportunity for Bernhard von der Borch to finally reduce the archbishop from a territorial lordship to a mere ecclesiastical office devoid of political power or lands.²⁶ In 1481 Bernhard von der Borch in a letter to the Grand Master Martin Truchsess (1477–1489) acknowledged that the Order had not forgotten that the two last archbishops – Henning Scharpenberg (†1448) and Silvester Stodewescher – had caused political trouble for the Teutonic Order, even though they were its members.²⁷ Both Masters claimed that this had happened because the archbishop exercised secular power.²⁸ In order to make the intended structural changes, the Livonian Master appealed to the Imperial court, hoping that emperor Friedrich III (r. 1452–1493) would assist with the transfer of the archbishop's territories to the Order's fief.²⁹ Like his predecessor Johann von Mengede, Bernhard von der Borch sought control over the cathedral chapter to ensure that it would elect the Order's candidates as archbishops.³⁰

The Livonian Master and the Grand Master were planning to take over the Church of Riga and reduce the archbishop and the cathedral chapter to the Order's dependants. The pope, however, did not support the Master's

---

22 'Cronica episcoporum', p. 177; Gert Kroeger, *Erzbischof Silvester Stodewescher und sein Kampf mit dem Orden um die Herrschaft über Riga* (Riga: Kymmels Buchhandlung, 1930), pp. 276–77; Bruiningk, *Messe und kanonisches Stundengebet*, p. 208; Levāns, 'Lebendigen Toten', p. 32.

23 Kroeger, *Erzbischof Silvester*, p. 277; *Livlands Geistlichkeit*, p. 29; Klaus Neitmann, 'Um die Einheit Livlands. Der Griff des Ordenshochmeisters Bernd von der Borch nach dem Erzstift Riga', in *Deutsche im Nordosten Europas*, ed. by Hans Rothe (Köln: Böhlau, 1991), pp. 109–37, p. 112; Berlin, GStA PK, XX. HA, OBA 16835; LUB 13, no. 801.

24 Kroeger, *Erzbischof Silvester*, p. 277; LUB 13, no. 801

25 Kroeger, *Erzbischof Silvester*, p. 277.

26 Jähnig, *Verfassung und Verwaltung*, p. 93; Neitmann, 'Um die Einheit Livlands', pp. 112–13; LUB 13, no. 801.

27 Neitmann, 'Um die Einheit Livlands', p. 114; Jähnig, 'Henning Scharpenberg', p. 657; Kroeger, *Erzbischof Silvester*, pp. 151–280; Berlin, GStA PK, XX. HA, OBA 16989; LUB 14, no. 457.

28 Neitmann, 'Um die Einheit Livlands', p. 114.

29 Jörg Schwarz, 'Zwischen Kaiser und Papst. Der Rigaer Erzbistumsstreit 1480–1483', *Zeitschrift für Historische Forschung*, 34, 3 (2007), 373–401; Neitmann, 'Um die Einheit Livlands', p. 117, 119.

30 Neitmann, 'Um die Einheit Livlands', p. 112.

strategy and ignored Bernhard's episcopal candidate, Simon von der Borch. On 22 March 1480, Pope Sixtus IV (p. 1471–1484) appointed Stefan Grube (e. 1480–1483) a priest of the Order in the Italian bailiwick of Apulia, as the archbishop of Riga.[31] Although a member of the Order, Grube became an enemy of the Livonian branch as his two predecessors have been. Bernhard von der Borch remained loyal to his own candidate, and the battle over the office escalated into military conflict in 1481, when the city of Riga clashed with the Order's forces.[32]

This political struggle was reflected in the *memoria* performed in the cathedral. The only surviving liturgical manuscript from the cathedral, the Riga Missal (*Missale Rigense*), belonged to the altar of the Holy Cross, next to the cathedral's chancel.[33] This missal, probably produced in the late fifteenth century,[34] includes a calendar into which names and dates of death of five archbishops and cathedral canons were inserted: Johannes Ambundi (†1424),[35] Henning Scharpenberg (†1448),[36] and Silvester Stodewescher (†1479),[37] provost Georg Holland (†1481/84),[38] and canon Hinric Netelhorst (†1477).[39] These interlinear interpolations were made on separate occasions (in different inks) by a single hand, in bastarda cursive, presumably during the 1480s.[40] These records were most likely made to provide information for the celebration of memorial masses at the Holy Cross altar on the anniversaries of their deaths.

It is notable that the calendar has only five memorial records, all of individuals who had actively fought for the autonomy of the Church of Riga and

---

31 Neitmann, 'Um die Einheit Livlands', p. 116; Schwarz, 'Zwischen Kaiser und Papst', pp. 383–86.

32 Māra Caune, 'Rīgas pēdējais bruņotais konflikts ar Livonijas ordeni (1481–1491)', *Latvijas PSR Zinātņu akadēmijas vēstis*, 8 (1975), 36–45.

33 'Istud missale pertinet a(d)/ altare sancte crucis in maiori/ ecclesia ante pedem chori subter/ ambonem ubi ewangelium/ cum epistola leguntur'. *Missale Rigense*, Rīga, LUAB, R, Ms. 1; Bruiningk, *Messe und kanonisches Stundengebet*, p. 25; Guntars Prānis, *Missale Rigense Livonijas garīgajā kultūrā: gregoriskie dziedājumi viduslaiku Rīgā* (Rīga: Neputns, 2018), pp. 135–38.

34 Bruiningk, *Messe und kanonisches Stundengebet*, p. 25; Nicholaus Busch, *Die Geschichte der Rigaer Stadtbibliothek und deren Bücher*, ed. by Leonid Arbusow (Riga: Rigaer Stadtvervaltung, 1937), p. 91.

35 16 June 'obiit Johannes Ambundy Anno etc xxiiij [1424] archiepiscopus Rigensis'. Bruiningk, *Messe und kanonisches Stundengebet*, p. 207.

36 5 April 'Obiit Hennyngus archiepiscopus Rigensis anno xlviij [1448]'. Bruiningk, *Messe und kanonisches Stundengebet*, p. 205.

37 12 July 'Anno domini m cccc lxxix [1479] obiit dominus Silvester archiepiscopus Rygenis in castro Kokenhusen'. Bruiningk, *Messe und kanonisches Stundengebet*, p. 208.

38 12 October 'Anno domini m cccc lxxxiiij [1484] obiit Georgius Hollant prepositus Rigensis in Carkhus, ubi eum dominie de ordine in exilio detenebant propter libertatis ecclesie defensionem'. Bruiningk, *Messe und kanonisches Stundengebet*, p. 211.

39 23 March 'Anno m cccc lxxvij [1477] obiit dominus Hinricus Nettelhorst canonicus Rygensis'. Bruiningk, *Messe und kanonisches Stundengebet*, p. 204.

40 This contradicts Bruiningk's claim that Ambundi's name was inserted after his death. Bruiningk, *Messe und kanonisches Stundengebet*, p. 26.

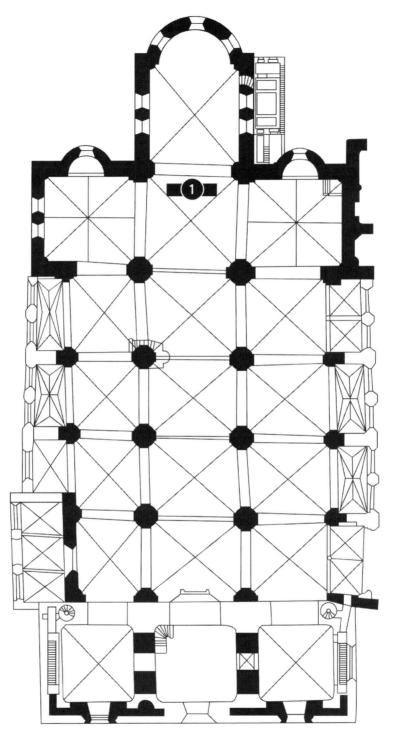

Figure 9: The plan of Riga cathedral and placement of the altar of Holy Cross (1). Designed by Una Grants, based on Prānis, *Missale Rigense Livonijas garīgajā kultūrā*, p. 135.

suffered from the hand of the Order.[41] Johannes Ambundi defended the cause of the Church of Riga at the papal curia and was successful in 1422/1423, when the chapter's first incorporation in the Order was abandoned.[42] Henning Scharpenberg and Silvester Stodewescher were celebrated enemies of the Order, who shifted from alliance with the Order to defending the Church of Riga.[43] In the case of Silvester's memorial record, the text emphasized the fact that the archbishop died in Kokenhusen (*in castro Kokenhusen*), as a prisoner of the Order.[44] The description of the circumstances of his death had mnemonic significance; remembering where Silvester had died also helped to recollect the unjustness of the Order's behaviour towards him and the cathedral chapter.

Some of these memorial records reflect the emotional reaction to the dramatic events experienced by the chapter during the late 1470s and 1480s. The provost of the cathedral chapter, Georg Holland (1469–1481/84), was captured by the Order in Dünamünde, probably in 1481, when he attempted to board a ship heading to Danzig, with 'some important documents (books)' (*etlike merklike boke*) of the Church of Riga in his baggage.[45] Holland had been involved in opposing Bernhard Borch's actions against the archbishop and the cathedral chapter after Silvester's death but failed. A letter from two cathedral canons to Stefan Grube on 18 December 1481 reported that Holland died while in the Order's captivity.[46] The calendar records that he died on 12 October 1484 in the castle of Karkhus where he was held by the Order for defending the freedom of the Church of Riga (*libertatis ecclesie defensionem*).[47] Although the memorial record contradicts the canons' letter, both sources show that the chapter was aware of the Order's wrongdoings against their provost and remembered them. 12 October 1484 may have been the date on which Holland's remains were brought to Riga from Karkhus, once relations between the Order and the church of Riga were normalized after the resignation of Bernhard von der Borch in 1483.[48]

The statement that Holland defended the independence of the Church of Riga is meaningful, and his death was like that of a martyr for a cause. This suggestion is reinforced by the fact that the martyr Bishop Berthold

---

41 The surviving sources do not enable the evaluation of the role of Hinric Netelhorst in the chapter's struggle against the Order, but he died in 1477, when the Silvester's conflict with Bernhard Borch was developing.
42 Glauert, 'Bindung des Domkapitels', p. 296; Jähnig, 'Der Kampf des Deutschen Ordens', pp. 103–04.
43 Kroeger, *Erzbischof Silvester*, pp. 218–20; Neitmann, 'Um die Einheit Livlands', p. 114; Jähnig, 'Henning Scharpenberg', p. 657.
44 Bruiningk, *Messe und kanonisches Stundengebet*, p. 208.
45 *Livlands Geistlichkeit*, p. 87; LUB 14, no. 458.
46 Holland's death in 1481 cannot be confirmed, but after 1482 his name no longer appears in the sources. See LUB 14.
47 Bruiningk, *Messe und kanonisches Stundengebet*, p. 211.
48 Jähnig, 'Der Kampf des Deutschen Ordens', p. 105.

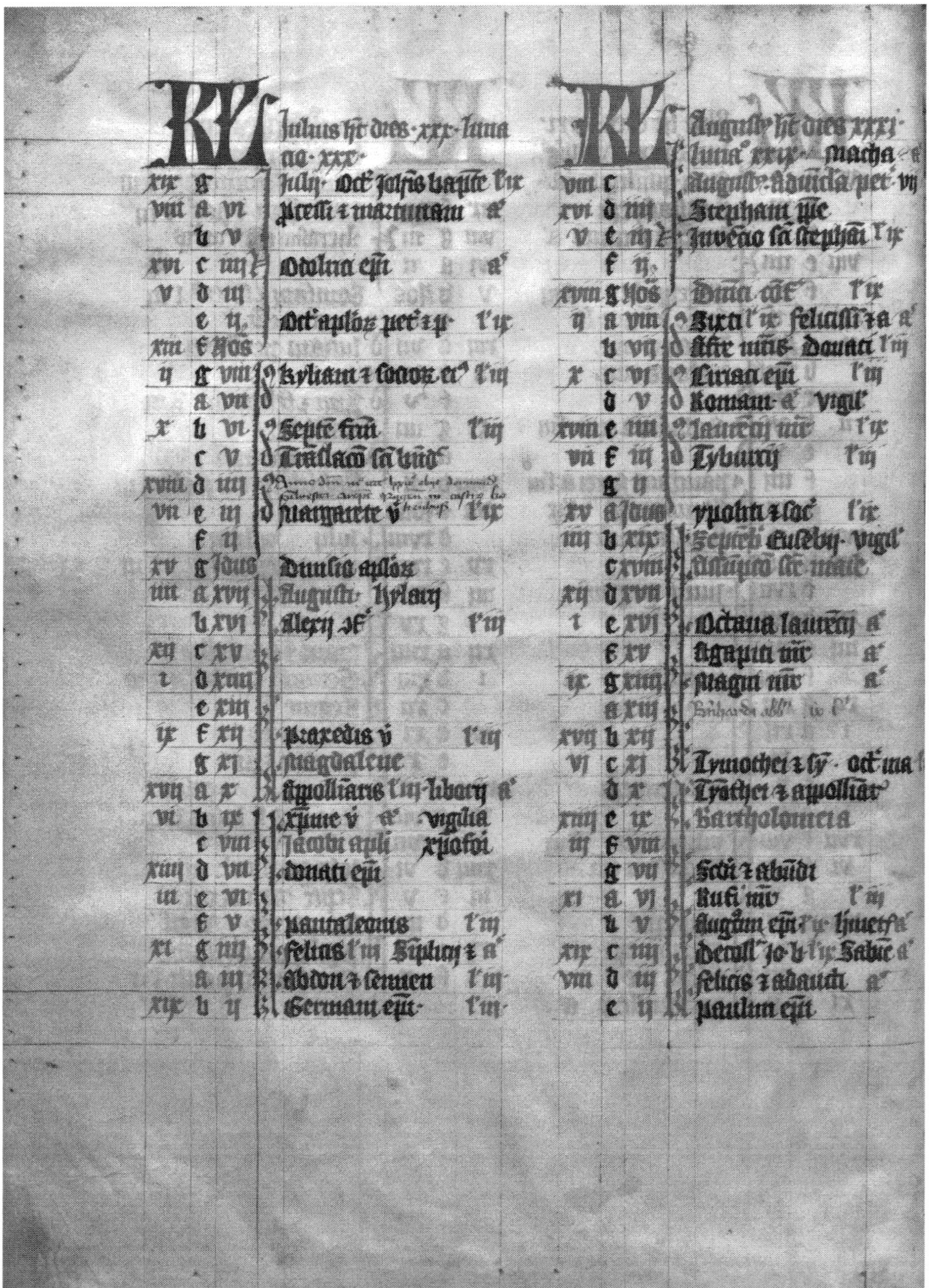

Figure 10: The record commemorating archbishop Silvester Stodewescher in the calendar of Riga Missal. *Missale Rigense*, Rīga, LUAB, R, Ms. 1. Photo: University of Latvia Academic Library

was buried near the altar of the Holy Cross.[49] The altar was just next to the chancel where all three bishops commemorated in the calendar were buried; Netelhorst and presumably also Holland were also buried in the cathedral, not far from the altar.[50] Thus, when Ambundi, Scharpenberg, Stodewescher, Netelhorst, and Holland were commemorated on the anniversaries of their deaths, their *memoria* at the Holy Cross altar took place right by their tombs.[51]

These memorial records in the calendar of the *Missale Rigense* represent a late-fifteenth-century memorial tradition aimed at strengthening the identity of a group in peril. The Livonian Master Borch hindered the *memoria* of Archbishop Stodewescher and aimed to destroy the archbishop's office and the chapter's autonomy; this struggle took place at the time when it is presumed that the memorial records in the missal were made. This *memoria* helped the cathedral chapter remember all the Order's offences against the canons and archbishops during the fifteenth century. The five liturgical memorial records were a counter-statement against the Order's attempts to destroy the traditions and identity of institutions some two centuries old. Although the missal remained in use in the sixteenth century when the daily morning mass was celebrated at the Holy Cross altar,[52] no other names were recorded after that of Georg Holland had been entered.

The Residence as a Commemorative Space

Although the residence of a medieval ruler was not a capital in the modern sense, it was a centre of power and as such was also a memorial centre of a ruler's realm. The burial place of rulers or a ruling family was one of the essential elements of a city or a castle that served as the residence of a late medieval ruler.[53] The presence of burial grounds in proximity to a residence provided an opportunity for living rulers to use the tombs of their predecessors for self-legitimation and self-representation. The tombs created a memorial space within which the deceased, present, and also future rulers were continuously commemorated by regular liturgical services. In this way the dead rulers were part of the political legitimation of their successors.[54]

---

49 'Cronica episcoporum', p. 174.
50 The grave slabs of numerous cathedral canons have survived in the cathedral of Riga, thus Netelhorst and Holland must also have been buried there. 'Cronica episcoporum', p. 117; Jähnig, 'Henning Scharpenberg', p. 657; Löffler, *Grabsteine*, pp. 22–23.
51 Zajic, 'Jahrtag und Grabdenkmal', p. 85.
52 Bruiningk, *Messe und kanonisches Stundengebet*, p. 28, 314.
53 Neitmann, 'Riga und Wenden als Residenzen', p. 79; Klaus Neitmann, 'Was ist eine Residenz? Methodische Überlegungen zur Erforschung der spätmittelalterlichen Residenzenbildung', in *Vorträge und Forschungen zur Residenzenfrage: Hans Patze zum 70. Geburtstag*, ed. by Peter Johanek and Hans Patze (Sigmaringen: Thorbecke, 1990), pp. 11–44, at p. 33.
54 Markus Thome, 'Das Bischofsgrabmal und die Visualisierung liturgischer Gemeinschaft. Die Mainzer Kathedrale als Gedächtnisraum', in *Tomb – Memory – Space: Concepts of Representation in Premodern*

Medieval rulers were not always present at their residences. As their itineraries show, the Grand Masters and the Livonian Masters of the Teutonic Order also travelled extensively throughout the Order's dominions to execute their duties; they spent only short periods of time in their residences.[55] The highest officials of the Teutonic Order, the Masters of the branches and the Grand Master himself, were still buried at their residences. They were granted a burial within the main church or chapel of the Order's branch, part of the Master's residence. There, according to the statutes, they were commemorated annually, on the anniversaries of their deaths.[56]

As the residences of the Masters were occasionally relocated due to political or military reasons, their burial grounds also changed location. In Prussia, for example, from 1341 on, most of the deceased Grand Masters were buried in the burial chapel of St Anne in the Marienburg castle, but when the Order lost its headquarters in 1457, the burial grounds of the Grand Masters were moved to the cathedral of Königsberg.[57] The burial grounds of the Livonian Masters also changed several times. However, the actual location of the burial grounds of the Livonian Masters before the mid-fifteenth century remains unknown.[58] From the time of the Order's arrival in Livonia in 1237, the Master's main residence was the castle of Riga. After the destruction of the castle in 1484, the Master's residence was relocated to Wenden, a small town seventy kilometres north of Riga.[59] Before 1484 the residence had also temporarily moved from Riga, for example, in the 1470s when the Order's castle in Fellin was briefly used as the Master's residence.

The residence in Riga was under constant threat from the city of Riga and its political ambitions. These constant political tensions frequently developed into warfare. In 1297 the townspeople of Riga destroyed the Order's castle, located within the town walls, and killed all the brethren who had defended it.[60] The castle was rebuilt after victory over the city in 1330, this time outside

---

Christian and Islamic Art, ed. by Francine Giese, Anna Pawlak, and Markus Thome (Berlin: de Gruyter, 2018), pp. 222–49.

55 On the residence and travels of the Grand Masters, see Neitmann, 'Was ist eine Residenz?', p. 20; Klaus Neitmann, 'Die Auswahl von Residenzorten. Methodische Bemerkungen zur spätmittelalterlichen geistlichen Residenzbildung', in *Spätmittelalterliche Residenzbildung in geistlichen Territorien Mittel- und Nordostdeutschlands*, ed. by Klaus Neitmann and Heinz-Dieter Heimann (Berlin: Lukas-Verlag, 2010), pp. 41–90, at pp. 43–44; Klaus Neitmann, *Der Hochmeister des Deutschen Ordens in Preussen: ein Residenzherrscher unterwegs: Untersuchungen zu den Hochmeisteritineraren im 14. und 15. Jahrhundert* (Köln: Böhlau, 1990); on residences and travels of the Livonian Masters, see Neitmann, 'Riga und Wenden als Residenzen', pp. 59–93;

56 *Statuten des Deutschen Ordens*, p. 90.

57 Szczęsny Skibiński, *Kaplica na Zamku Wysokim w Malborku* (Poznań: Wydawnictwo Naukowe UAM, 1982), pp. 151–54; *Hochmeister des Deutschen Ordens*, p. 138; Jähnig, 'Organisation', p. 52; Jóźwiak and Trupinda, *Organizacja życia*, pp. 478–81; Jóźwiak and Trupinda, 'Pogrzeby, pochówki i sposoby upamiętnienia braci', pp. 28–29.

58 Jähnig, *Verfassung und Verwaltung*, p. 168.

59 Neitmann, 'Riga und Wenden als Residenzen', p. 59.

60 Caune, 'Rīgas pilsētas', 63–74.

the town walls on the bank of Düna.[61] The relocation of the castle meant that the Order had to relocate its burial grounds as well.

The burial grounds of the Order's highest officials were usually located within the castle compounds or near the castles, as in Marienburg in the chapel of St Anne, and the cathedral of Königsberg hosted tombs of the Grand Masters residing in Prussia.[62] In Livonia before the late fifteenth century, the Order evidently lacked an prominent burial ground for the Masters comparable in status to the Prussian burial grounds, and the exact burial place of the Masters before 1469 is difficult to identify.[63]

The chapel of St Andrew, located in the immediate vicinity of the Order's castle in Riga, is the most likely burial place of the Livonian Masters before 1469.[64] There is however, no clear evidence to confirm this. The chapel, which was surrounded by a cemetery and was already described as an old building in 1450, was definitely used for the burials of the brethren.[65] In 1452 Master Johann von Mengede received a papal bull issued by Pope Nicholas V (1397–1455) that allowed the demolition of the building and the transfer of 'the earth and the remains of the dead' to another chapel nearby.[66] It has been suggested that the Order spared the chapel of St Andrew in 1452, and that it was destroyed or damaged by the Rigans in the 1480s when the castle itself was ruined.[67] Despite this destruction, St Andrew's chapel was still referred to as a burial place near the castle in the mid–sixteenth century.[68] The destruction brought by the military conflicts in the late fifteenth century also destroyed the probable resting place of the Livonian Masters.

In this way, the Order lost the memorial space where its Masters were buried and commemorated. As a result of this destruction, no grave slabs of the Masters have survived for the period prior to 1494. Another possible burial location of the Livonian Masters before 1469 was suggested by Leonid Arbusow senior, who argued that all the Livonian Masters were buried in Riga Cathedral.[69] Yet, because of the complicated relationships between the Order

---

61 Māra Caune, *Rīgas pils – senā un mainīgā* (Rīga: Jumava, 2004), pp. 7–8; Māra Caune, *Rīgas pils* (Rīga: Zinātne, 2001), pp. 11–14.
62 Jóźwiak and Trupinda, *Organizacja życia*, pp. 478–81.
63 Jähnig, *Verfassung und Verwaltung*, pp. 167–68.
64 Caune, *Rīgas pils – senā un mainīgā*, pp. 95–96.
65 Hermann Bruiningk, 'Die ehemalige Andreaskapelle bei dem Schlosse des Deutschen Ordens zu Riga', in *Sitzungsberichten der Gesellschaft für Geschichte und Alterthumskunde der Ostseeprovinzen Russlands 1900* (Riga: W. F. Häcker, 1901), pp. 178–83, pp. 180–81.
66 *Repertorium Germanicum*, vol. 6, ed. by Josef Friedrich Abert and Walter Deeters (Berlin: Georg Bath, 1985), no. 3676; *Regesten verlorener Urkunden aus dem alten livländischen Ordensarchiv*, ed. by Theodor Schiemann (Mitau: Behre, 1873), p. 18.
67 Bruiningk, 'Ehemalige Andreaskapelle', pp. 181, 182; Caune, *Rīgas pils*, pp. 12, 95–96.
68 Heinrich J. Böthführ, 'Jürgen Padel's und Caspar Padel's Tagebücher', *Mittheilungen aus dem Gebiete der geschichte Liv–, Est– und Kurlands*, 13 (1886), 291–404 (315); Caune, *Rīgas pils*, pp. 95–96.
69 Leonid Arbusow sen., 'Johannn von dem Broele gen. Plate im Deutschen Orden in Livland', *Jahrbuch für Genealogie, Heraldik und Sphragistik*, (1905/1906), 182–209, (200).

and the archbishops and the Riga cathedral chapter, this seems improbable. The only known attempt to bury and commemorate a Master there turned into conflict.[70]

New Friends and Old Enemies: The Conquest of Memorial Space by the Teutonic Order

Several developments in the mid–fifteenth century show that the Livonian branch wished to gain a more appropriate memorial space for its Masters. The transfer of the memorial space from the chapel of St Andrew to a new location in the 1450s is a good example. The decision to change the location of the burial ground of the Livonian Masters must have taken place around 1450, when the leadership of both the Livonian branch and the archbishopric of Riga had changed. On 11 August 1450, forty days after Heidenreich von Vincke's death, Johann von Mengede called Osthof, a Westphalian, was elected as the Livonian Master.[71] Two years earlier, Nicholas V had nominated Silvester Stodewescher, the Grand Master's chaplain and chancellor, as the new archbishop of Riga (1448–1479), after gifts and bribes were given by the Order's representatives to the pope and cardinals.[72] In total the Order invested an impressive sum – 6240 Rhenish Guldens – into their candidate's appointment.[73] The ascent of these two men to power marked a new phase in the relationship between the Livonian branch and the church of Riga. This also led to new developments in the Order's memorial policies.

The rise of Silvester Stodewescher, a priest brother of the Teutonic Order, and Johann von Mengede, the Livonian Master, reinitiated the relationship between the church of Riga and the Order.[74] Since the fourteenth century, the Livonian branch had aspired to establish control over the archbishopric of Riga by incorporating the cathedral chapter into the Teutonic Order.[75] Despite the Order's protracted efforts, the cathedral chapter had successfully defended its independence. The chapter was incorporated into the Order in 1394 with the assistance of Archbishop Johann von Wallenrode, but in 1426/28 Archbishop Henning Scharpenberg helped to restore the Augustinian habit and the statutes.[76] However, the arrival of two new leaders, the archbishop, who in the first years of his reign faithfully followed the Order's policies,

---

70 Neitmann, 'Riga und Wenden als Residenzen', p. 79; Kroeger, *Erzbischof Silvester*, p. 168.
71 LUB 11 no. 51; *Ritterbrüder*, no. 912, no. 584.
72 Boockmann, 'Der Einzug des Erzbischofs', pp. 1–17; Kroeger, *Erzbischof Silvester*, pp. 151–58; Strenga, 'Gifts and Conflicts', pp. 77–102.
73 Klaus Militzer, 'Die Finanzierung der Erhebung Sylvester Stodeweschers zum Erzbischof von Riga', in *Zentrale und Region: gesammelte Beiträge zur Geschichte des Deutschen Ordens in Preussen, Livland und im Deutschen Reich, aus den Jahren 1968 bis 2008*, by Klaus Militzer (Weimar: VDG, 2015), pp. 113–29.
74 On the Grand Master's chaplains, see Jähnig, 'Organisation', p. 59.
75 Jähnig, 'Kampf des Deutschen Ordens', pp. 100–06; Jähnig, *Verfassung und Verwaltung*, pp. 89–93.
76 Jähnig, *Verfassung und Verwaltung*, p. 91; Glauert, 'Bindung des Domkapitels', pp. 275–313.

and an energetic and ambitious Livonian Master, made possible the cathedral chapter's integration into the Teutonic Order.[77]

The first agreement between the Teutonic Order, the archbishop of Riga, and the cathedral chapter was made soon after the two leaders had taken office, in Wolmar on 6 July 1451.[78] According to the terms of this agreement, all future cathedral canons would wear the habit of the Teutonic Order and would be presented to the Livonian Master before election, and the Order also gained the right to make visitations of the cathedral chapter.[79] This agreement thus incorporated the Riga cathedral chapter into the Teutonic Order once again.[80] The Order not only took over the church as an institution, but it also aimed to establish control over the physical and memorial space of the cathedral.

The final article of the agreement announced that from then on all Livonian Masters would be buried in the cathedral of Riga.[81] As the agreement called it, the burial of the Masters in the cathedral was intended as a 'sign' (*czeichen*) of 'friendship and love' (*frundschafft und liebe*) between the Order and the archbishop, as well as the cathedral chapter.[82] The Master declared that he had decided with the consent of his officers: 'we and our successors, the Livonian Masters will be buried in the cathedral of Riga in the chancel'.[83] For their part, the archbishop, provost, dean, and chapter agreed to 'gratefully host' the Master's tomb in the cathedral and promised commemoration of the Master; the archbishop and the chapter had to commemorate the current Master with one annual anniversary. In addition to the posthumous remembrance of von Mengede, the archbishop and the chapter promised to perpetually commemorate his predecessors and successors with annual anniversaries, using the Order's endowment of 2000 marks and the village of Bowsel for the purpose.[84] This request to hold anniversaries of the former and future Livonian Masters symbolically transformed the cathedral of Riga into a memorial space of the Livonian branch even though no Masters were as yet buried there. This remembrance was added to the already existing annual memorial services

---

77 Klaus Eberhard Murawski, *Zwischen Tannenberg und Thorn : die Geschichte des Deutschen Ordens unter dem Hochmeister Konrad von Erlichshausen 1441–1449* (Göttingen: Musterschmidt, 1953), p. 171; Boockmann, 'Der Einzug des Erzbischofs', p. 6.

78 *Akten und Rezesse* 1, no. 537; *Visitationen im Deutschen Orden im Mittelalter: 3 : 1528–1541 sowie Nachträge, Korrekturen und Ergänzungen, Orts– und Personenverzeichnis*, ed. by Marian Biskup (Marburg: Elwert, 2008), No. 160a; Kroeger, *Erzbischof Silvester*, p. 168; Glauert, 'Bindung des Domkapitels', pp. 310–13.

79 *Akten und Rezesse* 1, no. 537; Kroeger, *Erzbischof Silvester*, p. 168.

80 Murawski, *Zwischen Tannenberg und Thorn*, pp. 171–72; Jähnig, 'Kampf des Deutschen Ordens', p. 104.

81 *Akten und Rezesse* 1, no. 537, § 14; Neitmann, 'Riga und Wenden als Residenzen', p. 78; Jähnig, *Verfassung und Verwaltung*, p. 168.

82 *Akten und Rezesse* 1, no. 537, § 14.

83 *Akten und Rezesse* 1, no. 537, § 14.

84 Later, in the report of the Order's officials in 1470, it was claimed that the Masters not only had to be buried in the cathedral, but that they also were granted a participation in the good deeds (liturgical services) which would take place in the cathedral. *Akten und Rezesse* 1, no. 537, § 14; LUB 12, no. 768, pp. 440–41.

in the cathedral commemorating the Masters and the deceased brethren of the Order, which had begun in 1428 when the chapter regained its independence.[85] In short, the plan of von Mengede was to confirm the cathedral as a memorial space for the Order, using his own physical remains for this purpose. The tomb of the Master was to serve as the political legitimation of the Order's presence in the cathedral and its control over the archbishopric.[86]

The agreement was a triumph for the Order, yet the gains were fragile.[87] In co-operation with the new archbishop, the Livonian branch established control over the cathedral chapter and gained new, prestigious, and politically significant memorial space, by taking over the cathedral chapter and thus the archbishopric itself. Eighteen years later, in 1469, when the Order's Master Johann von Mengede died, this initial triumph was reversed into a political defeat.

Archbishop Silvester went from being the Order's friend in 1451 to its opponent almost two decades later; the tradition of his office transformed him into the Order's enemy.[88] Although tensions had arisen in the 1460s between the archbishop, who was becoming more independent in his policies, and the Order, Silvester had not engaged in an open conflict with the Livonian branch before 1469.[89] The death of Johann von Mengede made the latent conflict visible.[90]

In 1469, after the burial of Johann von Mengede in the chancel of the cathedral, the archbishop refused to give consent for the placing of a slab over the Master's grave.[91] This may have been due to the fact that in the text of the agreement of 1451, the Masters were promised burial in the cathedral, but the grave slab was not even mentioned.[92] Silvester may have used this imprecise formulation as a pretext for not placing the grave slab on the Master's grave, but Johann von Mengede and his advisors in 1451, in orchestrating the conquest of the memorial space, undoubtedly perceived the grave slab as an integral part of the burial. Likewise, the archbishop himself must have been aware that the absence of a grave slab on the grave would hinder the Master's commemoration.

The absence of the grave slab meant that the Master was effectively 'defaced', and his *memoria* could not be performed. Moreover, the archbishop's action constituted the destruction of the Master's memorial image (*Memorialbild*), which was constituted by numerous elements, among them a pictorial

---

85 These memorial services were instigated in 1428 as a compensation for the Order's concession of its patronage over the chapter. LUB 7, no 733, p. 524; Glauert, 'Bindung des Domkapitels', p. 300.
86 On a tomb as a political tool, see Rader, 'Legitimationsgenerator Grab', pp. 7–20.
87 Glauert, 'Bindung des Domkapitels', p. 316.
88 Neitmann, 'Um die Einheit Livlands', p. 111.
89 On the development of the conflict between the archbishop and the Order, see Kroeger, *Erzbischof Silvester*, pp. 211–20.
90 Hellmann, 'Deutsche Orden und die Stadt Riga', p. 28.
91 LUB 12, no. 768, p. 439.
92 Neitmann, 'Riga und Wenden als Residenzen', p. 79; *Akten und Rezesse* 1, no. 537, § 14.

representation of the dead individual – a grave slab – as well as liturgical *memoria*.[93] The two elements – pictorial representation and evocation of a dead man's name in the liturgy – were interdependent.[94] As the Order's representatives later wrote, the grave slab had to be placed for 'eternal memory'. Its absence therefore endangered the memory of the Master.[95] Silvester had effectively attacked the Order where it was vulnerable.

This conflict over the Master's grave slab had many implications. First, it was a struggle over the memorial space and against political dependency. By denying the Master a grave slab, Archbishop Stodewescher presumably attempted to nullify the agreement of 1451, which determined not only the Masters' burials in the cathedral but also incorporated the cathedral chapter within the Teutonic Order.[96] Secondly, the death of Johann von Mengede was an opportunity for the archbishop to oppose the Order's aspirations to make the archbishop and his chapter submit to its control. The struggle over the burial and *memoria* of the Master was a symptom of the deeper antagonism between the Order and the archbishop. Mengede wanted to use his own body in order to complete the conquest of the cathedral as a memorial space for the Teutonic Order, but it turned out to be a misfortune for him and the Livonian branch. The Order's wish to increase its influence and gain new memorial space was doomed to failure because of the archbishop's symbolic action, the denial of the grave slab. It was an act of aggression which disrupted the Order and its memorial practices.

The archbishop's passive aggressive blocking of Mengede's *memoria* had to be countered. To solve the problem of the faceless grave, the Order had to take on the struggle against the archbishop, tackling the case with political and legal arguments.[97] In 1470 the Order's representatives composed a long text which accused the archbishop and defended the deceased Master Johann von Mengede, his deeds, and his rights to have a grave slab on his grave. Mengede was portrayed as a victim of the archbishop's duplicity, who in the presence of the Master always spoke 'beautiful, sparkling, shiny and friendly words', but changed his attitude in the Master's absence.[98] It was claimed that Mengede could have chosen the burial grounds of his predecessors, though not mentioning where it was located. The Master had, however, listened instead to the archbishop's advice that he should choose the cathedral's chancel as the burial place for himself and all the future Livonian Masters.[99] The archbishop

---

93 Oexle, 'Memoria und Memorialbild', p. 391; Horch, *Memorialgedanke*, p. 15.
94 Oexle, 'Memoria und Memorialbild', p. 387.
95 LUB 12, no. 768. p. 440.
96 *Akten und Rezesse* 1, no. 537.
97 In the Order's document of 1470, it was argued that struggle to attain the placing of the grave slab on the Master's grave should be continued by propagating information about this injustice in the documents and other written texts. p. 440.
98 'wort (…) de weren altiet schone, sote, blenckede unde frundlick (…)' LUB 12, no. 768, p. 439.
99 LUB 12, no. 768, p. 439.

had promised that by this choice the Master would become the archbishopric's protector. The authors of the text implied that if the Master had chosen the burial grounds of his predecessors, after death he would have received his grave slab and remembrance without any hindrance, apparently to emphasise the archbishop's dishonest and illegitimate actions.[100] Similarly, they argued that if the archbishop had granted the greatest honour – the Master's burial in the cathedral – why did he refuse to offer such a small one, the placement of a grave slab on the grave?[101] The Order partly reused this accusatory text eight years later in the legislative record of Weissenstein to show Silvester's evil deeds.[102]

Despite the energetic efforts of the Order's representatives, this eloquent depiction of Master Johann von Mengede as a victim had no immediate impact on his *memoria* in the cathedral. In 1474 liturgical *memoria* was still not being performed. Then the Order complained that, although Johann von Mengede had generously disposed of villages and plots of land to the cathedral chapter of Riga for his remembrance, the annual anniversaries promised in the agreement of 1451 were not being properly celebrated by the cathedral chapter.[103] The Order's representatives implied that the archbishop and the cathedral chapter should be reminded that they had to celebrate the liturgical services diligently and respectfully.

Finally, five years after the Master's burial in the cathedral, the Order achieved its aims by forcing the cathedral chapter to issue on 27 September 1474 a charter confirming the Master's *memoria* and right to place a grave slab.[104] The provost, Georg Holland, and the dean, Detmar Roper, of the cathedral chapter stated that it would commemorate Johann von Mengede, his predecessors, and successors with annual anniversaries in the cathedral in perpetuity. In order to avoid further misunderstandings, the cathedral chapter also promised not to create any future obstacles to the Masters' burials in the church chancel and promised to place grave slabs on the Masters' graves.

Despite this, the final attempt to transform the cathedral of Riga into the memorial space of the Teutonic Order failed. It is not known whether a grave slab was placed on the tomb of Johann von Mengede, but he remained the only Master to be buried in Riga cathedral.[105] The transfer of the Order's memorial space, which was initially intended as a 'sign of friendship and love',

---

100 LUB 12, no. 768, p. 440.
101 Neitmann, 'Riga und Wenden als Residenzen', p. 79; LUB 12, no. 768, p. 440.
102 Matthias Thumser, 'Geschichte schreiben als Anklage. Der Weißensteiner Rezeß (1478) und der Konflikt um das Erzstift Riga', *Jahrbuch für die Geschichte Mittel- und Ostdeutschlands*, 51 (2005), 63–75 (70).
103 Berlin, GStA PK, XX. HA, OBA no. 16502; LUB 13, no. 261; Neitmann, 'Riga und Wenden als Residenzen', p. 79.
104 Berlin, GStA PK, XX. HA, OBA no. 16510; LUB 13, no. 276; Neitmann, 'Riga und Wenden als Residenzen', p. 79.
105 Jähnig, *Verfassung und Verwaltung*, p. 168; Neitmann, 'Die Residenzen des livländischen Ordensmeisters', pp. 79–80.

resulted in a conflict that endangered not only the *memoria* of Johann von Mengede but the remembrance of all his predecessors.[106] The *memoria* of von Mengede, his predecessors, and successors had to be performed, yet they were not commemorated for five years after his death.[107] As a result of this conflict, the cathedral of Riga never became a memorial space of the Livonian branch. The next Master, who died in office, Johannn Freitag von Loringhoven (†1494), was buried in the new residence in Wenden.[108]

Conclusion

The attempt of the Teutonic Order to consolidate its power in Livonia during the mid–fifteenth century involved conquest of memorial space. The Livonian branch's Masters' remembrance was centred around their residences, where they were usually buried and where memorial services for them were celebrated. Until the mid–fifteenth century, the Livonian Masters were most likely buried in the chapel next to the Riga castle. The Order needed a more prestigious burial place for its Masters. In the 1450s, the Order, as a part of its plan to incorporate the cathedral chapter, wanted to convert the cathedral of Riga into the burial site of the Livonian Masters. The Order used the favourable situation after the appointment of its member, Silvester Stodewescher, as the archbishop of Riga to gain political benefits, including a burial site that had both prestige and symbolic meaning. When the Livonian Master Johann von Mengede was buried in the cathedral in 1469, and the archbishop denied him *memoria*, a long and fierce conflict broke out.

Although the struggle for memorial space and political influence began with success for the Teutonic Order, it developed into a humbling experience for the Order. The Order and its deceased Master became hostages of Archbishop Silvester Stodewescher, who by denying the grave slab for Johann Mengede and thus *memoria*, symbolically attacked the Order. Johann Mengede and his advisors had apparently decided to gain new memorial space for the Livonian Masters and the whole branch in the early 1450s. This plan had entirely the opposite effect. Although the Order tried, it did not succeed in the struggle for

---

106 *Akten und Rezesse* 1, no. 537, § 14.
107 LUB 13, no. 261; Neitmann, 'Riga und Wenden als Residenzen', p. 79.
108 Since 1494 when Johannn Freitag von Loringhoven found his resting place in the St Johannnes church of Wenden, two Livonian Masters after the Reformation were buried there: the illustrious Wolter von Plettenberg (†1535) and also Hermann von Brüggenei, named Hasenkamp (†1549) had their graves and grave slabs in the St Johannnes church. The direct successors of Johannn Freitag von Loringhoven – Johann Waldhaus von Heerse and Bernd von Borch – were ousted. Mänd, 'Visuelle Memoria', pp. 78– 84; Māra Siliņa, 'Ikonographie und Typologie der gotischen Memorialplastik in Lettland', in *Gotik im Baltikum: acht Beiträge zum 6. Baltischen Seminar 1994*, ed. by Uwe Albrecht (Lüneburg: Carl–Schirren– Gesellschaft, 2004), pp. 143–66, p. 153; Löffler, *Grabsteine*, pp. 25–26, 31–32; Jähnig, *Verfassung und Verwaltung*, p. 168; Neitmann, 'Riga und Wenden als Residenzen', pp. 79–80; Mänd, 'Visuelle Memoria', pp. 78–79.

proper *memoria*. As a result of this failed conquest, the Order left the cathedral of Riga forever and in the 1480s moved the residence as well as the burial grounds from Riga to Wenden. The Livonian Masters were buried there, in St Johannes parish church, until the dissolution of the Livonian branch in 1561.

Memoria helped the archbishops of Riga and the cathedral chapter to defend their identities and independence during the two centuries long conflict with the Teutonic Order, which saw attempts to incorporate the chapter into the Order. The death of Archbishop Silvester Stodewescher in 1479 offered another chance for the Order to achieve its aim, and this prompted an anonymous scribe to record the names of the Order's opponents – the dead archbishops and the cathedral canons – in the so-called Riga Missal in support of their *memoria*. The memorial records in this missal were part of the memorial counter-narrative against the Order's ambitions. Furthermore, this memorial counter-narrative supports Mihkel Mäesalu's suggestion that the memories of the conflicts between the Teutonic order and the Church of Riga fuelled further conflicts between the two groups that were not resolved until the very end of the fifteenth century.

CHAPTER 5

Memoria and Urban Elites

> I call all and everyone to this dance: pope, emperor, and all creatures poor, rich, big, or small. Step forward, mourning won't help now! Remember though at all times to bring good deeds with you and to repent your sins for you must dance to my pipe.[1]
>
> *Totentanz* of Reval

On 23 August 1468 Lübeck's city council issued a letter to its counterpart in Reval requesting the transfer of the properties of a Reval cleric, Diderik Notken, to Bernt Notke, painter and burgher of Lübeck. According to this letter, Diderik had bequeathed all his real property in Reval for the wellbeing of his soul and for his relatives (*to salicheid ziner zelen vnde behuff syner angeborenen vrund*).[2] The painter referenced in this letter was the same Bernt Notke (*c*. 1440–1508) who around 1463 painted a cycle called the Dance of Death (*Totentanz*) in the chapel of St Matthew in Lübeck, which he later replicated under the belfry of St Nicholas Church in Reval.[3] In the absence of other documentation of its commission, this letter has been used as evidence that Diderik Notken's donation for his soul was spent on the production of the Reval *Totentanz*.[4] It is undoubtedly the most famous surviving medieval artwork in the Baltics.[5]

---

1 'To dussen datse rope ik algemene/ Pawes, keiser unde alle creaturen/ Arm ryke groet unde kleine/ Tredet vort went ju en helpet nen truren/ Men dencket wol in aller tyd/ Dat gy gude werke myt ju bringen/ Unde juwer sunden werden quyd/ Went gy moten na myner pypen springen'. English translation in Elina Gertsman, 'The Dance of Death in Reval (Tallinn): The Preacher and His Audience', *Gesta*, 42.2 (2003), 143–59.
2 Gerhard Eimer, *Bernt Notke: Das Wirken eines niederdeutschen Künstlers im Ostseeraum* (Bonn: Kulturstiftung der Deutschen Vertriebenen, 1985), p. 195; LUB 12 no. 603.
3 Hartmut Freytag, 'Literatur- und kulturhistorische Anmerkungen und Untersuchungen zum Lübecker und Revaler Totentanz', in *Der Totentanz der Marienkirche in Lübeck und der Nikolaikirche in Reval (Tallinn): Edition, Kommentar, Interpretation, Rezeption*, ed. by Hartmut Freytag (Köln: Böhlau, 1993), pp. 13–58, p. 19; Eimer, *Bernt Notke*, pp. 91–102, at pp. 43–45, 195; Gertsman, 'Dance of Death in Reval', pp. 143–59.
4 Eimer, *Bernt Notke*, pp. 43–45.
5 Krista Andreson, 'Research on Tallinn's Dance of Death and Mai Lumiste – Questions and Possibilities in the 20th Century', *Kunstiteaduslikke Uurimusi*, 22.3–4 (2013), 96–109.

Figure 11: The Reval *Totentanz* by Bernt Notke (around 1468). Tallinn, EKM j 18761. Photo: Art Museum of Estonia, Niguliste Museum

Danse Macabre was a frequently occurring motif in medieval art.[6] The fragment of Reval's *Totentanz* reflects the main characteristics of the genre. It depicts Death, playing bagpipes, a preacher in a pulpit who alerts the audience, and several figures – a pope, a cardinal, an emperor, an empress, and a king – who are led into the dance by cadavers.[7] The other fragments of the Reval *Totentanz* have been lost. The Lübeck *Totentanz* painted by Bernt Notke contains more characters: twenty-four pairs of the living and the dead from all social classes, both secular and religious, including townspeople such as a burgomaster, a craftsman, and a merchant.[8] Both works have a familiar urban landscape as their background; the backdrop to the Lübeck *Totentanz* is recognisably the city, while in Reval the background is a more stereotypical Hanseatic scene. Along with the life-sized and life-like figures, the background served to reinforce a 'sense of actuality' for viewers.[9]

Both works were created during or directly after a plague that had visited both cities; it broke out in Lübeck in 1463/64 and reached Reval in 1464/65.[10] The Reval *Totentanz* was placed in the public space – in the parish church – near the place where the dead were buried.[11] In the *Totentanz* the images interplayed with the text written under the figures to convey a clear message: *memento mori*, death is inevitable.[12] Most members of the urban elite belonged to the parish of St Nicholas, where the altars of the elite guilds and brotherhoods were located.[13] The *Totentanz* reminded them to care for the afterlife and about their commemoration. In the *Totentanz*, Death directly addresses

---

6 Elina Gertsman, *The Dance of Death in the Middle Ages: Image, Text, Performance* (Turnhout: Brepols, 2010); Susanne Warda, *Memento mori: Bild und Text in Totentänzen des Spätmittelalters und der frühen Neuzeit* (Köln: Böhlau, 2011); Paul Binski, *Medieval Death: Ritual and Representation* (Ithaca, N.Y: Cornell University Press, 1996), pp. 152–59.
7 Hartmut Freytag, 'Der Lübeck–Revaler Totentanz. Text und Kommentar', in *Totentanz*, pp. 127–342, pp. 131–200; Gertsman, 'Dance of Death in Reval', p. 145.
8 Eimer, *Bernt Notke*, pp. 42; Warda, *Memento mori*, pp. 69–98; Gertsman, 'Dance of Death in Reval', pp. 145–46.
9 Also in the Reval's *Totentanz* Lübeck's landmarks are present. Gertsman, 'Dance of Death in Reval', pp. 148–49; Gertsman, *Dance of Death in the Middle Ages*, pp. 105–06.
10 Freytag, 'Anmerkungen', p. 15; Heinrich Reincke, 'Bevölkerungsprobleme der Hansestädte', in *Hansische Geschichtsblätter* 70 (1951), 1–33, p. 11; Mänd, 'Church Art', pp. 3–30.
11 The chapel of St Matthew also hosted tombs. Warda, *Memento mori*, p. 57; Gertsman, 'Dance of Death in Reval', p. 144; Elina Gertsman and Elina Räsänen, 'Locating the Body in Medieval Reval', in *Locating the Middle Ages: The Spaces and Places of Medieval Culture*, ed. by Julian Weiss and Sarah Salih (London: King's College London, 2012), pp. 137–58, p. 145.
12 Freytag, 'Der Lübeck–Revaler Totentanz', pp. 127–342; Eimer, *Bernt Notke*, p. 42; Warda, *Memento mori*, p. 57; Gertsman, 'Dance of Death in Reval', p. 147; Binski, *Medieval Death*, p. 152.
13 St Nicholas had altars of the city council, the Great Guild, and also of the Black Heads. Gertsman, *Dance of Death in the Middle Ages*, pp. 115–18; Gertsman and Räsänen, 'Locating the Body in Medieval Reval', pp. 145–47; Dietrich W. Poeck, *Rituale der Ratswahl: Zeichen und Zeremoniell der Ratssetzung in Europa (12.–18. Jahrhundert)* (Köln: Böhlau, 2003), p. 263; Anu Mänd, 'Über den Marienaltar der Revaler Schwarzenhäupter und seine Ikonographie', in *Die Kunstbeziehungen Estlands mit den Niederlanden in den 15.–17. Jahrhunderten. Der Marienaltar des Meisters der Lucialegende, 500 Jahre in Tallinn*, ed. by Tiina Abel (Tallinn: Eesti Kunstimuuseum, 2000), pp. 228–36, p. 233; Johansen and von zur Mühlen, *Deutsch und Undeutsch*, p. 66.

both the painted figures and the parishioners of St Nicholas: '[…] you must follow me and become what I am.'[14] The message of Reval's *Totentanz* was directed towards the elite, to remind it of the temporary nature of its own power and wealth. And so members of the late medieval urban elite were well aware of that, and they used their power and wealth to ensure the well-being of their souls through institutions by making extensive provisions for *memoria*, both individually and collectively.

This chapter focuses on the memorial practices of the urban elites of Reval and Riga. Merchant elites, including their family members, accounted for between a tenth and a fifth of the urban population in the late medieval Hanseatic cities.[15] In late medieval Riga and Reval, with approximately 6000–8000 and 5000–6000 inhabitants respectively, the merchant elites numbered several hundred individuals.[16] The elite in Riga was comprised of around 100–20 long-distance merchants who belonged to the Great Guild as well as their family members. They lived alongside a group of approximately 100 apprentices and foreign merchants.[17] According to Benninghoven, 10 per cent of all townspeople in Riga belonged to the elite.[18] In late-fifteenth century Reval, around 540 townspeople belonged to the elite long-distance merchant families, which were represented in the merchant guild and the other elite brotherhoods.[19]

Since the late-thirteenth century, merchants controlled the urban government of all Hanseatic cities and excluded artisans from political power.[20] In Riga and Reval, the city councils were controlled by the exclusive merchant Great Guilds, and only their members were allowed to join the council.[21] Membership in the Great Guild was usually combined with activities in the charitable Table Guild; before proceeding to the Great Guild, young merchants in Riga and Reval usually belonged to the brotherhood of Black Heads.[22] The merchants who were bound together socially by membership in

---

14 '[…] du most my Volghen vnd werden als ik sy'. Gertsman, 'Dance of Death in Reval', p. 148, 154.
15 Brandt, 'Gesellschaftliche Struktur', p. 212.
16 Küllike Kaplinski, 'Über die Einwohnerzahl und die Sozialstruktur Tallinns von 1369–1399', *Jahrbuch für Geschichte des Feudalismus*, 3 (1979), 111–39, p. 122, 124, 138; Johansen and von zur Mühlen, *Deutsch und Undeutsch*, pp. 92–93; Benninghoven, *Rigas Entstehung*, p. 100.
17 Thomas Brück, 'Riga in der ersten Hälfte des 15. Jahrhunderts. Das Verhältnis der Stadt zum Orden, zum Erzbischof und zur Hanse', in *Städtisches Leben im Baltikum zur Zeit der Hanse: zwölf Beiträge zum 12. Baltischen Seminar*, ed. by Norbert Angermann (München: Carl Schirren Gesellschaft, 2003), pp. 43–92, p. 58.
18 Benninghoven, *Rigas Entstehung*, p. 100.
19 Kaplinski, 'Einwohnerzahl', pp. 138–39.
20 von Brandt, 'Die Gesellschaftliche Struktur des spätmittelalterlichen Lübeck', p. 211.
21 Anu Mänd, 'Geselligkeit und soziale Karriere in den Revaler Gilden und der Schwarzhäupterbruderschaft', in *Vereinskultur und Zivilgesellschaft in Nordosteuropa: regionale Spezifik und europäische Zusammenhänge = Associational culture and civil society in North Eastern Europe*, ed. by Jörg Hackmann (Wien: Böhlau, 2008), pp. 39–76, p. 41.
22 On Livonian Table Guilds, see Anu Mänd, 'Table Guilds and Urban Space: Charitable, Devotional, and Ritual Practices in Late Medieval Tallinn', in *Space, Place, and Motion: Locating Confraternities in the Late Medieval and Early Modern City*, ed. by Diana Bullen Presciutti (Leiden: Brill, 2017),

these associations 'formed the summit of the urban elite'.[23] They controlled the economic, political, social, and religious life of these cities. Memorial activities of these elite groups will be the focus of this chapter.

Until recently, research into late medieval urban *memoria* has been primarily concentrated on individual remembrance and memorial foundations of townspeople.[24] Previous studies of group *memoria* have also focused on large groups, such as the patriciate, but less attention has been given to the commemorative practices of brotherhoods, guilds, and city councils.[25] Anu Mänd has explored the collective *memoria* of the elite associations of Reval and Riga.[26] Her work, however, has largely focused on *memoria* as a religious phenomenon and has not considered the social, political, and representational functions of *memoria*. I shall aim, therefore, to show how *memoria* was used for social purposes, both to create and strengthen the identities of different elite groups and to explore the role *memoria* played within urban politics in late medieval Riga and Reval.

Memoria in the Merchant Guilds of Riga and Reval

A scribe of the Rigan *kumpanie van den kopluden* – company of merchants – later known as the Great Guild, described the reason for recording the guild's statutes in 1354: as 'human memory is weak, so it has to be secured with documents and written text.'[27] This fragility of the human memory endangered not only memory of the past but also that of deceased predecessors. Groups had to 'record' the dead, noting their names in the account books; they had to imprint them in collective memory, through liturgical and social practices of *memoria*. Late medieval urban elite associations considered the memory

---

pp. 21–46; Anu Mänd, 'Hospitals and Tables for the Poor in Medieval Livonia', *Mitteilungen des Instituts für Österreichische Geschichtsforschung*, 115.3–4 (2007), 234–70; on the Black Heads, see Herbert Spliet, *Geschichte des rigischen Neuen Hauses, des später sogen. König Artus Hofes, des heutigen Schwarzhäupterhauses zu Riga* (Riga: Plates, 1934); Mänd, 'Geselligkeit und soziale Karriere', pp. 39–76; on Great Guilds see Benninghoven, *Rigas Entstehung*, pp. 93–97; Eugen von Nottbeck, *Die Alten Schragen der Grossen Gilde zu Reval* (Reval: Emil Prahm, 1885); Anu Mänd, *Urban Carnival: Festive Culture in the Hanseatic Cities of the Eastern Baltic, 1350–1550* (Turnhout: Brepols, 2005), p. 31.

23 Mänd, *Urban Carnival*, p. 31; Nottbeck, *Schragen*, p. 13.
24 Noodt, *Religion und Familie*; Lusiardi, *Stiftung*.
25 For *memoria* of the Hanseatic town councils, see Poeck, 'Rat und Memoria', pp. 286–335; Poeck, 'Totengedenken in Hansestädten', pp. 175–232; for *memoria* and representation of city councillors see Rüther, *Prestige und Herrschaft*; Olivier Richard has researched *memoria* of Regensburg's patriciate as a group, see him, *Mémoires bourgeoises*; Olivier Richard, 'Von der Distinktion zur Integration. Die Repräsentation des Regensburger Patriziats im Spätmittelalter', in *Repräsentationen der mittelalterlichen Stadt*, ed. by Jörg Oberste (Regensburg: Schnell Steiner, 2008), pp. 213–28; Renée Rößner has researched collective *memoria* of the Hanseatic merchants in Flanders, see *Hansische Memoria*.
26 Mänd, 'Church Art', pp. 3–30; Mänd and Randla, 'Sacred space', pp. 43–80.
27 '(…) krancken ghedechtnisse der lude, so plecht men se mit breven unde mit schrift tho bewaren (…)'. *Schragen der Gilden und Aemter der Stadt Riga bis 1621*, ed. by Wilhelm Stieda and Constantin Mettig (Riga: Stieda, 1896), no. 35, pp. 313, 555.

of their own historical past and their deceased colleagues to be of great importance as closely related practices.[28]

The elites in Riga and Reval met in exclusive associations, the merchant Great Guilds. As merchants they were involved in wholesale and long-distance trade, and from these guilds all political leaders – the city councillors – arose.[29] In this respect Riga and Reval were not unique. In the Hanseatic metropolis Lübeck, most of the city councillors were also members of the elite *Zirkelgesellschaft* (Circle Company), the oldest and most prestigious of its three merchant guilds.[30] These elite associations in Riga and Reval developed during the fourteenth century, and both were turned by the following century into the Great Guilds.[31] In Riga the merchant *kumpanie van den kopluden* was first mentioned in 1354, and in Reval it was the *kindergilde* in 1363.[32] The emergence of these merchant associations was part of a larger structural change in Livonian cities, through which guilds combining broad professional groups were abolished and new professionally distinct associations were established.[33] The 1354 statues of the Rigan *kumpanie* demonstrate these developments by excluding several professional and ethnic groups from the membership in the guild: artisans, priests, and indigenous non-Germans.[34] This process of transformation was completed during the early fifteenth century when the associations for foreign and young unmarried merchants – the brotherhoods of the Black Heads – were separated from the *kumpanie* and *kindergilde*.[35] After this separation the Great Guilds became even more exclusive, and both political and economic power laid in their hands.

In contrast to other urban guilds and brotherhoods that received their statutes from the city council, the Great Guild was autonomous and self-

---

28 On *memoria* in the Hanseatic elite groups, see Dünnebeil, *Lübecker Zirkel-Gesellschaft*, pp. 51–75.
29 Mänd, *Urban Carnival*, p. 31; Nottbeck, *Schragen*, p. 13.
30 Dünnebeil, *Lübecker Zirkel-Gesellschaft*; Sonja Dünnebeil, 'Die drei großen Kompanien als genossenschaftliche Verbindungen der Lübecker Oberschicht', in *Genossenschaftliche Strukturen in der Hanse*, ed. by Nils Jörn (Köln: Böhlau, 1999), pp. 205–22; Roman Czaja, 'Patrician Guilds in Medieval Towns on the Baltic Coast', *Acta Poloniae Historica*, 92 (2005), 31–52 (35–37).
31 Nottbeck, *Schragen*, pp. 10–11; Benninghoven, *Rigas Entstehung*, pp. 93–97.
32 Johansen and Mühlen, *Deutsch und Undeutsch*, p. 65.
33 These social changes took place simultaneously with other events: the Estonian uprising (1343), the acquisition of Estonia by the Teutonic Order (1346), the plague (1349/1350), and the capitulation of Riga after the war with the Order (1330). Knut Schulz, 'Gewerbliche Strukturen des Hanseraumes unter besonderer Berücksichtigung der baltischen Städte (Riga, Reval) im Spätmittelalter', in *Von der Geschichte zur Gegenwart und Zukunft: Mittelständische Wirtschaft, Handwerk und Kultur im baltischen Raum*, ed. by Burghart Schmidt (Hamburg: DOBU, 2006), pp. 84–108, at pp. 96–98; *Schragen der Gilden und Aemter*, pp. 85–100; Heinz von zur Mühlen, 'Zur Frühgeschichte der Revaler Gilden', in *Reval: Handel und Wandel vom 13. bis zum 20. Jahrhundert*, ed. by Norbert Angermann and Wilhelm Lenz (Lüneburg: Verlag Nordostdt. Kulturwerk, 1997), pp. 15–42, pp. 15, 18–20; Thomas Brück, 'Zwischen ständischer Repräsentanz und Interessenkonflikten–Bemerkungen zur Entwicklung der Großen Gilde in Riga im ersten Drittel des 15. Jahrhunderts', in *Genossenschaftliche Strukturen in der Hanse*, ed. by Nils Jörn, Detlef Kattinger, and Horst Wernicke (Köln: Böhlau, 1999), pp. 239–71, pp. 240–41; Benninghoven, *Rigas Entstehung*, p. 95; Mänd, 'Geselligkeit', pp. 40–41.
34 *Schragen*, p. 314, § 5–6.
35 Mänd, *Urban Carnival*, pp. 32–38; Mühlen, 'Zur Frühgeschichte', p. 39.

governing.³⁶ *Memoria* within it played an even greater role than in other urban groups. Urban elite groups created, maintained, legitimated, and represented their power and status by remembering their past and predecessors.³⁷ This *memoria* was not only aimed at its members, but it also reached out to external audiences, thus presenting its power and status to other townspeople. To attain these aims, the elite urban associations invested considerable resources in elaborate memorial services, and in the founding of chapels, the provision of liturgical vessels and utensils, the commissioning of altarpieces, and the arrangement of commemoration during the communal meals.

The importance of *memoria* for elite associations can be observed, for example, within the Lübeck's Circle Company, which assembled representatives of the city's most influential families. Directly after its foundation in 1379, the Circle Company requested *memoria* for its members from the Franciscans in St Catherine's church, and invested significant resources in the acquisition of the chapel there, where the brethren were later buried.³⁸ Even before the establishment of this association, its founders provided wine for future commemoration performed by its members. The brethren later made further numerous substantial memorial endowments for the Circle Company, thus supporting its collective *memoria*.³⁹ During the fifteenth century, *memoria* gradually lost its importance within the Circle Company, as it turned from spiritual brotherhood into professional association, but in its initial stages, *memoria* had constituted and consolidated this elite group.⁴⁰

In Riga and Reval, collective *memoria* was 'a constitutive element' that formed the merchant guilds as social groups.⁴¹ In contrast to the Circle Company, however, the *memoria* of the elite groups in Riga and Reval was not performed in the Great Guilds alone. The statutes of both Great Guilds describe only very briefly the commemorative activities of these groups, and it is evident that some of these were delegated to charitable sub-organizations, known as Table Guilds (*tafelgilde*).⁴² In their statutes the Great Guilds still promised their members basic commemorative services, though with greater pomp than those organized by other urban associations.

The first statutes of the Rigan *kumpanie*, issued in 1354, decreed that on the day after the *drunke* (drinking feast), the guild's brethren in remembrance of all the guild's dead had to spread a pall (coffin cover) in the church, light four candles, and then sing a vigil; five memorial masses followed on the next

---

36 Benninghoven, *Rigas Entstehung*, p. 93.
37 Vincent Robijn, 'Brothers in Life and Death. The "Schepenmemorie" of Kampen (1311–c. 1580)', in *Trade, Diplomacy and Cultural Exchange : Continuity and Change in the North Sea Area and the Baltic, c. 1350–1750*, ed. by Hanno Brand (Hilversum: Uitgeverij Verloren, 2005), pp. 171–85, p. 172.
38 Dünnebeil, *Lübecker Zirkel-Gesellschaft*, pp. 49–75; Dünnebeil, 'Drei großen Kompanien', p. 206.
39 Dünnebeil, *Lübecker Zirkel-Gesellschaft*, pp. 65, 73–75.
40 Dünnebeil, 'Drei großen Kompanien', p. 207; Oexle, 'Soziale Gruppen', p. 31.
41 Oexle, 'Gegenwart der Lebenden', p. 75.
42 *Schragen der Gilden und Aemter*, p. 318–19, § 52–53; Nottbeck, *Schragen*, p. 43, §26–31; Mänd, *Urban Carnival*, pp. 39–40; Mänd, 'Church Art', pp. 7–9.

morning.[43] In Reval the statutes ordained that memorial services – a vigil and three memorial masses sung the next morning – were to be performed at the death of every brother in the presence of a pall and lights.[44] In Riga each deceased member of the Great Guild was commemorated with one memorial mass in the parish churches of St Peter or St Jacob, like 'every poor man'.[45] In addition, the guild was committed to the organization of ten memorial masses a year to be celebrated after All Souls, for the consolation and salvation of all souls.[46] These two obligations of the guild, which were later – probably after the Reformation – annotated on the margin of the statutes as being no longer valid (*dit is dot*), demonstrate the guild's investment in both individual and collective memorial services.

The statutes of the Rigan *kumpanie* motivated all brethren to take part in the memorial services, not only by imposing fines for absence but also by encouraging brethren to treat 'our predecessors' as they would like to be treated after their death.[47] This obligation reveals the prospective character of the guild's *memoria*; it implied that those who commemorated would be commemorated in turn.[48] This reciprocity was essential as it transmitted *memoria* from generation to generation. The Great Guilds also took responsibility for *memoria* of their impoverished members by granting them funerals with a pall and lights. This followed a lifetime provision whereby poor members were offered free participation in all the feasts, as was the case in the Reval Great Guild.[49]

As a result of the ample resources at their disposal, the Great Guilds were able to organise memorial services not only during their annual assemblies but throughout the year. The statutes of the Reval Great Guild stated that the guild had to pay one *ferding* to the priests of St Nicholas church on Shrovetide for monthly remembrance.[50] In St Nicholas church, the guild had two altars, dedicated to St Blaise and St Christopher at which, priests celebrated the memorial services.[51] In addition to the priests of St Nicholas, the Great Guild also involved other institutions in remembrance of their deceased members, including the parish church of St Olaf, the church of Holy Spirit, and the Dominican church of St Catherine, by regularly paying them fees for memorial

---

43 *Schragen der Gilden und Aemter*, p. 318, § 52.
44 Nottbeck, *Schragen*, p. 43, § 26.
45 *Schragen der Gilden und Aemter*, p. 318, § 53.
46 *Schragen der Gilden und Aemter*, p. 318, § 53; Mänd, 'Church Art', p. 7.
47 *Schragen der Gilden und Aemter*, p. 318, § 52.
48 Assmann, *Das kulturelle Gedächtnis*, p. 61.
49 Nottbeck, *Schragen*, p. 43, § 28.
50 Nottbeck, *Schragen*, p. 43, § 31.
51 Schulz, 'Gewerbliche Strukturen', p. 97; Mänd, 'Saints' Cults in Medieval Livonia', p. 204; Johansen and Mühlen, *Deutsch und Undeutsch*, p. 66.

services.[52] The greater the number of commemorating institutions involved, the more prestige and influence was attained by the guild.[53]

As a merchant guild, the Great Guild in Reval also provided *memoria* for those brethren who had died abroad by organising a vigil and memorial mass.[54] The statutes also ordained that if a brother died abroad in poverty, the brethren who were closest to his place of death would cover the costs of a funeral and be reimbursed by the Great Guild.[55] In addition, the brethren of the Riga and Reval merchant guilds, who were also members of the charitable Table Guilds and died outside Livonia, were commemorated with special services by these sub-organizations of the Great Guilds.[56] The Great Guilds adjusted to the dynamic lifestyle of the merchants, and acted as custodians of the group memory of deceased brethren who died on business trips away from home.

No records of the performance of commemorative activities have survived. Nor is there much information about donations and endowments made by the merchants to the Great Guild. A copy of one endowment document that shows a relationship motivated by *memoria* between the Reval Great Guild, its officials, and a priest has survived. In 1456, a priest of Reval's Holy Spirit church, Ludeke Karwel, made an endowment of 500 Riga marks to the Great Guild for the salvation of his own and souls of his relatives.[57] Karwel was a member of the Table Guild between 1457 and 1470 and also its priest.[58] His relationship with the Great Guild was determined by the fact that the Holy Spirit church, located next to the Great Guild's guildhall, was the memorial and charitable centre of the Great Guild and its Table Guild. Ludeke Karwel died fourteen years after the endowment, and on Easter of 1470, he was commemorated by the members of the Table Guild.[59]

The main objective of Karwel's endowment was to support the institutions of the Great Guild: the guild's altar of St Blaise in St Nicholas Church and the Table Guild.[60] The annuity rent from part of Karwel's endowment (300 marks) had to support a priest who would serve at the altar of St Blaise; Karwel even chose two young men, who when ordained, could become the chantry

---

[52] Mänd, 'Church Art', p. 6; Ivar Leimus, Rein Loodus, Marta Männisalu, and Mariann Raisma, *Tallinna Suurgild ja gildimaja* (Tallinn: Eesti Ajaloomuuseum, 2011), pp. 457–58.
[53] Sonja Dünnebeil, 'Soziale Dynamik in spätmittelalterlichen Gruppen', in *Menschenbilder – Menschenbildner: Individuum und Gruppe im Blick des Historikers*, ed. by Ulf-Christian Ewert and Stephan Selzer (Berlin: de Gruyter, 2002), pp. 153–75.
[54] Nottbeck, *Schragen*, p. 43, § 27.
[55] Nottbeck, *Schragen*, § 28.
[56] *Schragen der Gilden und Aemter*, p. 663, § 14; Nottbeck, *Schragen*, p. 102, § 13; Mänd, *Urban Carnival*, p. 39.
[57] LUB 11, no. 524; Mänd 'Church Art', p. 7.
[58] Nottbeck, *Schragen*, p. 100, § 3; Torsten Derrik, *Das Bruderbuch der Revaler Tafelgilde (1364–1549)* (Marburg: Tectum Verlag, 2000), pp. 372, 380; Mänd 'Church Art', p. 7; Mänd, 'Hospitals', p. 257.
[59] Tallinn, TLA, f. 191, n. 2, s. 2, fol. 35ᵃ.
[60] Johansen and Mühlen, *Deutsch und Undeutsch*, p. 66; LUB 11, no. 524, p. 417.

priests.⁶¹ The money provided for the Table Guild was to be spent on alms (*gifte*) distributed on the feast of the Holy Cross. The guild's warden was to give six *ferdings* four times a year to individual recipients at the Hospital of the Holy Spirit. The charter stated that all payments for these activities had to be made after Ludeke's death.

In his charter Ludeke Karwel expressed his desire to be commemorated by the Great Guild with a perpetual soul mass that was to be celebrated in the Holy Spirit church.⁶² An annuity rent of 12 marks was also to be paid to Karwel's mother during her lifetime, a sum that after her death was to be used to maintain this *memoria*.⁶³ Although the aim of the endowment was the commemoration of himself and his relatives, Karwel integrated his remembrance within the collective *memoria* of the Great Guild. During the memorial masses celebrated on days chosen by a chantry priest and particularly on Easter, Pentecost, and Christmas, the souls of all deceased brothers and sisters of the Great Guild were also to be remembered.⁶⁴

Memoria was essential to the life of the Reval and Rigan Great Guilds. The statutes of the Riga Great Guild stated that the commemoration of their predecessors was as important as remembrance of the current members after their death. *Memoria* not only ensured salvation but also helped merchant groups to develop their distinctiveness, to legitimize their economic and political leadership, and to maintain their status. Equally, the Great Guilds had rich resources at their disposal to invest in their collective *memoria* with splendour that demonstrated their status. Yet, sources about their commemorative activities are scarce, perhaps because the Great Guilds delegated part of their *memoria* to the Table Guilds, their sub-organizations.

Merchant Table Guilds in Riga and Reval: Between Poor Relief, *Memoria*, and Social Capital

In Lent of 1425, all members of the Great Guild of Riga gathered with the consent of the city council – and for sake of the Lord, the Virgin Mary, all the saints, and the poor (*nottroftigen armen*) – to found a 'table guild'.⁶⁵ The foundation was justified by reference to the Gospel: 'to the one who will give a sip of water (*de enen drunk waters ghevet*) to the needy poor (*den nottroftigen armen*) in my name, I will give in return twice as much in the eternal life.'⁶⁶ The

---

61 One of them was the son of Gise Vos, a long-term alderman of the *kindergilde* and also member of the Table Guild; the other was the son of Karwel's brother. Derrik, *Bruderbuch*, p. 40, 323; LUB 11, no. 524, p. 417.
62 Tallinn, TLA, f. 230, n. 1, Aa 7, fol. 11ᵃ.
63 LUB 11, no. 524, p. 418; Mänd 'Church Art', p. 8.
64 LUB 11, no. 524, p. 418.
65 *Schragen der Gilden und Aemter*, p. 660. no. 123
66 *Schragen der Gilden und Aemter*, pp. 660–61; Matthew 10:42

preamble to the statutes stated that the guild would distribute nineteen alms on every Sunday in the belfry of St Peter's church (*under deme clokthorne*), for the benefit of the souls of the Table Guild's founders (*begynnere*) and its future benefactors (*hulpere*).[67] The statutes made the aims of *tafelgilde* clear: devotion to the Lord and His saints, care of the poor, and commemoration of those who provided the alms. These objectives of the *tafelgilde* were inseparable and interlinked as poor–relief was both a pious act and a commemorative one.[68]

Poor–tables, charitable associations created for the distribution of alms, clothing and food were established in numerous European regions; they were found in the cities of the Low Countries, the Empire, France and the Iberian peninsula.[69] As elsewhere in late medieval northern Europe, in Riga and Reval, the guild was named after the table – *tafel* – set up in the churches and at which food and clothing were handed out on Sundays and certain feasts.[70] The Table Guilds also had other functions besides poor relief. Their charity, piety, and *memoria* were instruments of social and political communication, legitimation, and community building. Moreover, the Table Guilds were institutions for which *memoria* was not only a social practice but one of the purposes for their existence.[71] Such practices of *memoria* and almsgiving in the Table Guilds contributed to the definition and legitimation of the elite and its privileges.

The Table Guilds of the Great Guilds in Reval and Riga were not occupational groupings, and most members joined them voluntarily. They were founded in 1363 and 1425 respectively and were both exclusive associations formed by the local prosperous and influential townspeople. Most of the Table Guild's members belonged to the Great Guild, yet they had separate leadership and meetings.[72] Among the members were the city councillors, and so the Table Guilds were also informal political meeting places.[73] Many burgomasters and city councillors were leaders of the *tafelgilde*; of the three thousand names of the brethren of the Reval's Table Guild recorded between 1364 and 1549,

---

67 *Schragen der Gilden und Aemter*, p. 661.
68 Torsten Derrik implies that possibly the *tafelgilde* of Reval in its initial stages focused more on poor relief, than on *memoria*, because *memoria* does not appear in the first statutes (1363), see his, *Bruderbuch*, p. 16.
69 On the poor tables in the Low Countries see David Nicholas, *The Later Medieval City 1300–1500* (London: Longman, 1997), p. 254; Michael Galvin, 'Credit and Parochial Charity in Fifteenth–Century Bruges', *Journal of Medieval History*, 28.2 (2002), 131–54; on the poor tables in Catalonia, see James Brodman, *Charity and Welfare: Hospitals and the Poor in Medieval Catalonia* (Philadelphia: University of Pennsylvania Press, 1998), pp. 18–21.
70 In Riga and Reval there were also other associations named Table Guilds, organized by the artisan guilds and parishes, about which little is known. Here I exclusively refer to *tafelgilde* of the Great Guilds. Mänd, 'Hospitals', p. 257; Mänd, *Urban Carnival*, pp. 39–40.
71 Derrik, *Bruderbuch*, p. 23.
72 Derrik, *Bruderbuch*, p. 39; Leimus, Loodus, Männisalu, and Raisma, *Tallinna Suurgild*; Derrik, *Bruderbuch*, p. 17.
73 Derrik, *Bruderbuch*, p. 17; Thomas Brück, 'Die Tafelgilde der großen Gilde in Riga im 15. und 16. Jahrhundert', in *Buch und Bildung im Baltikum: Festschrift für Paul Kaegbein zum 80. Geburtstag*, ed. by Heinrich Bosse and Paul Kaegbein (Münster: LIT, 2005), pp. 59–88, at p. 64, 85.

at least two hundred were city councillors.⁷⁴ The Table Guilds drew members from consecutive generations of the councillors' families.⁷⁵ Alongside the local elites, the Table Guilds hosted also rich merchants and city councillors from other Livonian and Hanseatic cities.⁷⁶ High status clergymen were admitted to the *tafelgilde* too. The first list of the Reval *tafelgilde* members of 1364 opened with the name of the bishop of Reval, Ludwig von Münster (1352–1389).⁷⁷ As Torsten Derrik's study of the Reval *tafelgilde* shows, the size of the guild fluctuated between 250 and 700, with more numerous membership during the fifteenth century.⁷⁸

Poor relief and *memoria* organized by the Table Guilds helped local elites to gain a 'reward from God' (*lon vor Gode*) while securing their social standing. This was done by the accumulation of social capital out of bonds created between the powerful rich and powerless poor.⁷⁹ Social capital is created by interpersonal networks; therefore elites had to join others in conduct of material and symbolic exchanges.⁸⁰ Poor relief and *memoria* offered such forms of reciprocal material and symbolic exchanges.⁸¹ Elite members initiated these exchanges by providing resources for almsgiving and distributing them to the poor; as a counter-gift, the poor offered *memoria*.⁸² The elites converted the social capital accumulated during this exchange with the 'poor' into their exclusive status.

The elites of Riga and Reval, like the ruling groups of other Hanseatic cities, were aware that poor-relief had political significance. During the 1420s the political elite of Riga gained in self-assurance and aimed to abolish the Teutonic Order's overlordship, and to gain the status of a free city.⁸³ Thomas Brück argues that the establishing of the *tafelgilde* manifested the city elite's care for the poor without the involvement of the archbishop or the Teutonic

---

74 For biographies of the city councillors members of the Reval *tafelgilde*, see Derrik, *Bruderbuch*, p. 44, pp. 48–327.

75 At least twenty-two Reval families had numerous representatives in *tafelgilde*. ` see Derrik, *Bruderbuch*, pp. 32–36; Roman Czaja, 'Das Patriziat in den livländischen und preußischen Städten. Eine vergleichende Analyse', in *Riga und der Ostseeraum*, pp. 211–22, pp. 215–16.

76 In Reval's *tafelgilde* there were members from Lübeck's *Zirkel-Gesellschaft* and also city councillors from Dorpat, Narva, Fellin, Pernau, Riga, Visby and Danzig. Individuals from other cities composed around 5 per cnet of all guild members. Derrik, *Bruderbuch*, pp. 24–25, 28–30.

77 Tallinn, TLA, f. 191, l. 2, s. no. 1, fol. 1ʳ; Klaus Neitmann, 'Ludwig von Münster', in *Bischöfe des Reiches*, p. 640.

78 The Reval Table Guild in the early and late-fifteenth century had between 200 and 300 members, but between 1424 and 1460, the guild enjoyed the largest number of members – around 400, reaching a maximum in 1442 – 787 members. In the late-fifteenth and early sixteenth century, the guild experienced a decrease of members. See Derrik, *Bruderbuch*, p. 24.

79 Pierre Bourdieu, 'The Forms of Capital', in *Handbook of Theory and Research for the Sociology of Education*, ed. by John G. Richardson (Westport: Greenwood Press, 1986), pp. 241–58.

80 Bourdieu, 'The Forms of Capital', p. 51.

81 On poor relief and *memoria*, see Wollasch, 'Gemeinschaftsbewußtsein', pp. 268–86.

82 Oexle, 'Adel, Memoria und kulturelles Gedächtnis', p. 344; Poeck, 'Totengedenken in Hansestädten', p. 200.

83 Brück, 'Tafelgilde', p. 64.

Order. Their ability to provide poor relief on their own was a sign of autonomy and freedom.[84] It helped to demonstrate their good rule and legitimate it.[85]

The high social status of the Table Guild was also manifested during the mid–fifteenth century *Corpus Christi* procession in Reval, where its members marched directly before a priest carrying the Eucharist.[86] The exclusivity of these guilds was reflected in their statutes. In Riga they instructed that 'one who wants to enter this brotherhood' had to be a 'brother of the Great Guild before'.[87] Similarly, the Reval *tafelgilde* only accepted members of the Great Guild.[88] In Riga prospective members paid 6 ores as admission fee, and were encouraged to give more in charity (*meer gudes to don*), which would be rewarded richly in the afterlife.[89] In Riga 'honourable women' – wives or widows of the Great Guild members – could also join the *tafelgilde*.[90] In contrast to Riga, the statutes of Reval *tafelgilde* mention only brothers, and the members' lists include only few women.[91]

Memoria of deceased members was equally important to the Reval and Rigan Table Guilds.[92] Poor relief and *memoria* were interconnected, yet commemorative activities of the annual assemblies did not involve the 'poor' as commemorators.[93] The *memoria* of the *tafelgilde* performed at their annual assemblies was self–centred and its performance was intended to strengthen group identity and communal bonds. This emphasis on remembering its past and dead members is very clearly expressed in the guilds' statutes; the Table Guilds were founded particularly to foster *memoria* of elite members by elite members.[94] Although they were not independent guilds, the Table Guilds in Riga and Reval granted burial and commemoration to all their members, most of whom were also brethren of the Great Guilds.[95] The statutes of both guilds precisely laid out when and how the members were to be commemorated, combining both liturgical (memorial masses and prayers) and social (communal meals) practices of *memoria*.

Like most late medieval associations, the Table Guilds required two types of commemorative events: funerals and anniversaries of individual deceased members and vigils and masses of remembrance for 'all who had died in this

---

84 Rüther, 'Strategien der Erinnerung', pp. 112–13; Queckenstedt, *Armen und die Toten*, p. 144.
85 Queckenstedt, *Armen und die Toten*, p. 143.
86 Mänd, *Urban Carnival*, p. 166; on hierarchies in *Corpus Christi* processions, see Miri Rubin, *Corpus Christi: The Eucharist in Late Medieval Culture* (Cambridge: Cambridge University Press, 1991), p. 248.
87 *Schragen der Gilden und Aemter*, p. 661, § 3.
88 Mänd, 'Hospitals', p. 257; Tallinn, TLA, f. 191, n. 2, s. no. 2, fol. 2; Nottbeck, *Schragen*, p. 96, § 1.
89 In Reval the fee was 3 ores. *Schragen der Gilden und Aemter*, p. 661, §2; Nottbeck, *Schragen*, p. 96, §2.
90 *Schragen der Gilden und Aemter*, p. 661, § 2; Mänd, 'Church Art', p. 6.
91 Nottbeck, *Schragen*, pp. 96–100, 104–07; Mänd, 'Hospitals', p. 258.
92 Brück, 'Tafelgilde', p. 60.
93 Poeck, 'Totengedenken in Hansastädten', p. 200.
94 *Schragen der Gilden und Aemter*, p. 660–63; Nottbeck, *Schragen*, pp. 96–107; Derrik, *Bruderbuch*, p. 23; on *memoria* of the Table Guilds in Reval and Riga see Mänd, 'Church Art', pp. 7–9; Mänd, 'Hospitals', p. 259–60.
95 *Schragen der Gilden und Aemter*, p. 661, § 6; Nottbeck, *Schragen*, p. 98, § 14;

brotherhood' (*alle dejenne, de ute desser broderschop vorstorven sin*).⁹⁶ The latter took place during the general assemblies, and the statutes laid down the exact time, place, and form for such events.⁹⁷ In Riga and Reval the Table Guilds organized their *memoria* in the churches where they managed their charitable activities. In Riga the dead were commemorated in St Peter's church, where the guild distributed its alms on Sundays in the belfry. In Reval the memorial space of the *tafelgilde* – the Holy Spirit Church – served the same purpose.⁹⁸ In Riga the *tafelgilde* organized a vigil on the second Sunday after Michaelmas and a memorial mass in the morning.⁹⁹ In Reval, the *tafelgilde* gathered for the commemoration of all dead brethren twice a year; vigils and memorial masses were celebrated on the second Saturday and Sunday after Easter and Christmas, when following the election of a new warden, his predecessor in the office organized commemorative services.¹⁰⁰ The costs of these services were covered by income from membership fees; in the Riga *tafelgilde*, each brother and sister had to donate two *artigs* for the annual vigil and memorial mass.¹⁰¹

The annual commemorations of *tafelgilde* were preceded by bell ringing. In Riga, guild wardens provided ringing of the 'large' church bells on the vigil.¹⁰² In both Riga and Reval, the guild's pall (*gildestoven boldeke*), a bier (*bare*), and candles (*lichten*) were set up in the church.¹⁰³ The following morning, memorial masses were celebrated.¹⁰⁴ In Reval, for the annual memorial mass, priests of the Holy Spirit church were employed for half a mark, with an additional five schillings for expenses.¹⁰⁵

During the commemoration of the dead, hierarchy and political power were manifested too. The statutes of the Riga *tafelgilde* regulated the ceremony of offertory (*offer*) – donation of liturgical gifts and money at the altar – during the annual memorial mass on Monday two weeks after Michaelmas.¹⁰⁶ During the offertory, the wives of the guild wardens first carried a memorial candle each, and then the other sisters followed and made an offering.¹⁰⁷ The

---

96 *Schragen der Gilden und Aemter*, p. 661, § 6.
97 Mänd, *Urban Carnival*, p. 51.
98 *Schragen der Gilden und Aemter*, p. 660; Mänd, 'Church Art', p. 7; Mänd, 'Hospitals', p. 257; Nottbeck, *Schragen*, p. 100, § 3.
99 *Schragen der Gilden und Aemter*, p. 662, § 10.
100 Nottbeck, *Schragen*, p. 100, § 3; p. 99, § 18; Mänd, 'Hospitals', p. 259.
101 *Schragen der Gilden und Aemter*, p. 662, § 6.
102 *Schragen der Gilden und Aemter*, p. 662, § 7.
103 *Schragen der Gilden und Aemter*, p. 662, § 6, 7.
104 *Schragen der Gilden und Aemter*, pp. 661–62, § 6, 10; Nottbeck, *Schragen*, p. 100, § 3, p. 103, § 5.
105 Nottbeck, *Schragen*, p. 100, §3, p. 103, § 5, 6.
106 On offertories, see Arnold Angenendt, 'Das Offertorium. In liturgischer Praxis und symbolischer Kommunikation', in *Zeichen – Rituale – Werte. Internationales Kolloquium des Sonderforschungsbereichs 496 an der Westfälischen Wilhelms-Universität Münster*, ed. by Gerd Althoff (Münster: Rhema, 2004), pp. 71–150; David Ganz, 'Giving to God in the Mass: The Experience of the Offertory', in *The Languages of Gift in the Early Middle Ages*, ed. by Wendy Davies and Paul Fouracre (Cambridge: Cambridge University Press, 2010), pp. 18–32.
107 *Schragen der Gilden und Aemter*, p. 662, § 7; similar ritual was practiced in Reval, see Nottbeck, *Schragen*, p. 100, § 3; p. 103, § 7.

burgomasters and the city council, the alderman of the Great Guild, and the wardens of *tafelgilde* followed, and finally the common brethren made their gifts.[108] This ceremony created a public image of the guild and its contribution to the city's wellbeing.[109]

Following the liturgical *memoria* the deceased were also remembered during the communal meal. The statutes of the Rigan *tafelgilde* instructed that the communal meal should consist of three courses and 'good beer'.[110] Following the meal, a bell was rung to mark the reading of the names of the guild members of brothers and sisters who had died during the last year.[111] Similarly, in Reval the *tafelgilde* remembered the dead during the communal meal celebrated at an annual assembly two weeks after Easter. The instruction of the guild's annual assembly (1514) stated that during a meal, after eating and drinking the chant 'Christ is risen' (*krystes vpgestanden*) had to be sung; as in Riga a servant had to ring a bell, and then the guild's warden named the dead brothers.

This naming of the brothers and sisters who had died within the past year was a commemorative act, and the meal was a continuation of the Eucharist with a commemoration.[112] The subsequent almsgiving or distribution of the leftover food by Reval's *tafelgilde* further extended this commemorative work.[113] Liturgical and social forms of *memoria* merged during the meal.

At the communal meals, the Table Guilds recorded the names of their deceased members for liturgical and non–liturgical commemoration.[114] Between 1448 and 1549, the Reval *tafelgilde* recorded the names of the dead brethren alongside those of newly admitted ones[115] three times annually, at Shrovetide, Easter, and Christmas.[116] The records of the Reval *tafelgilde* show that during periods of great mortality, the guild's ability to provide such *memoria* was tested. In 1464/1465, a year of devastating plague, fifty guild members died over four months and several consecutive leaders of the Great Guild and *tafelgilde* died too.[117] According to the members' lists, such periods of great mortality were also experienced in Reval in 1474, 1481/82, 1495, 1503/04, and 1520/21.[118] During the Reformation the recording of names was interrupted,

---

108 Nottbeck, *Schragen*, § 8.
109 Brück, 'Tafelgilde', p. 64.
110 *Schragen der Gilden und Aemter*, p. 662, § 10; Mänd, 'Hospitals', p. 259.
111 *Schragen der Gilden und Aemter*, pp. 662–63, § 13.
112 Oexle, 'Gegenwart der Lebenden', p. 81; on evocation of the names and *memoria* see Oexle, 'Gegenwart der Toten', p. 31; Gervase Rosser, 'Going to the Fraternity Feast. Commensality and Social Relations in Late Medieval England', *Journal of British Studies*, 33.4 (1994), 430–46, at p. 434;
113 Nottbeck, *Schragen*, p. 102, § 17; Oexle, 'Mittelalterlichen Gilden', p. 213.
114 Mänd, 'Church Art', p. 9.
115 After 1500 the recording of the deceased names was not regular. Tallinn, TLA, f. 191, 1. 2, no. 1, fol. 20ᵛ–72ʳ; Derrik, *Bruderbuch*, pp. 331–32.
116 Mänd, 'Church Art', p. 9; Derrik, *Bruderbuch*, p. 331; *Schragen der Gilden und Aemter*, p. 663, § 14; Nottbeck, *Schragen*, p. 102, § 13.
117 Tallinn, TLA, f. 191, l. 2, no. 1, fols. 30ᵛ–31ʳ; Derrik, *Bruderbuch*, p. 21.
118 Derrik, *Bruderbuch*, p. 332; Mänd, 'Church Art', p. 9.

with the last deceased member recorded in 1521, and then a few more were added during the 1530s.[119] Liturgical *memoria* was abolished in 1523/24. The interruption of the recording shows the close relationship between it and the liturgical practices. Remarkably, in 1547 guild wardens sought to reconstruct the lists of the dead for the missing years, but this was no longer possible.[120] The lists of deceased brethren reveal the inner hierarchy in the Reval *tafelgilde* with the names of the city councillors recorded at the top of the lists.[121]

The group's history was also remembered during the communal meal of the *tafelgilde*. The fifteenth–century ordinance for the annual assembly in Reval stipulated that during the communal meal, the guild's five youngest members read an account describing: the foundation of the 'poor–table', where the alms should be distributed, and why the assembly took place on this day.[122] In this way the communal meal reaffirmed the group's identity, making the guild's members aware of its origins, history, their predecessors, and the purpose of the guild's existence.[123]

Alongside the collective *memoria* of deceased members, the Table Guilds also organized the funerals and individual commemorative services of their brothers and sisters. The statutes of the Reval *tafelgilde* stipulated that every dead brother had to be carried to the grave by his fellow brethren.[124] The guild expected that all brothers present in the city at the time would take part in the funeral procession of each deceased guild member.[125] A fine was imposed on those who failed to do so.

In addition to the presence at funerals of fellow brothers and sisters, members also covered the costs of individual memorial services celebrated after burial. When a brother or sister of the Riga *tafelgilde* died, guild wardens collected one *artig* from each member for memorial masses.[126] In Reval every brother of the *tafelgilde* had to arrange a memorial mass for each deceased member and to make donations for the poor table as part of these commemorative actions.[127] *Tafelgilde* offered *memoria* even for impoverished members who could not afford a proper burial. In Riga the Table Guild granted to its members burials with the value of two Rhenish gulden.[128] In addition, both guilds took care to remember those brothers and sisters who died abroad and were buried outside Riga and Reval.[129]

---

119 Tallinn, TLA, f. 191, 1. 2, no. 1, fols. 60^r–60^v.
120 Tallinn, TLA, f. 191, 1. 2, no. 1, fol. 60^r.
121 Tallinn, TLA, f. 191, 1. 2, no. 1, fols. 20^v–72^r.
122 Nottbeck, *Schragen*, p. 101, § 8.
123 Oexle, 'Liturgische Memoria', p. 333.
124 Nottbeck, *Schragen*, p. 101, § 8.
125 Nottbeck, *Schragen*, p. 98, § 14.
126 Nottbeck, *Schragen*, p. 663, § 13; Mänd. 'Church Art', p. 6.
127 Nottbeck, *Schragen*, p. 98, § 14.
128 *Schragen der Gilden und Aemter*, p. 663, § 19.
129 *Schragen der Gilden und Aemter*, p. 663, § 14; Nottbeck, *Schragen*, p. 104, § 13.

Memoria of benefactors within late-medieval urban associations played a role similar to that in medieval monastic communities.[130] Urban associations prayed for their benefactors just as monastic ones did, and this fostered memory not only of benefactors but also of the group's past.[131] For elite associations, such *memoria* was also an important political exercise; commemoration of the benefactors was widespread in elite institutions of the Hanseatic cities.[132] Internal charitable gift giving formed part of the *Ratsmemoria* and served to present the group to the world as much as to itself.[133] In contrast to monastic communities, most benefactors of urban elite associations were themselves members of these groups. Since the merchant groups were also internally diversified, these associations maintained inner hierarchy too.[134]

As for the poor tables in Flemish cities, the administration of the benefactors' *memoria* in Riga and Reval was as important as almsgiving.[135] The statutes of the Riga *tafelgilde* state that it was expected that the brethren would 'do good deeds', and donate money for the poor.[136] 'All those who have died in this guild' were promised an annual vigil and requiem mass, but the statutes stated that those who had 'done something good', or at least had such an intention to do so, were to be particularly commemorated.[137] Praise of benefactors in the Rigan *tafelgilde* was practiced every Sunday, when in a church – most likely St Peter's church – a priest prayed for brothers and sisters of the guild, for those were benefactors, and also for those who would do good in the future.[138] From the pulpit the priest called out the names of all living members and benefactors as well as the dead. These prayers involved not only members but also the parish community gathered there for Sunday mass.[139] Commemoration of living and dead guild members and benefactors in the parish church of St Peter's became an act of a self-representation of the elites to the urban community.

Who were the benefactors of *tafelgilde*? Individual wills and account books show that in Riga and Reval, gifts of money were bequeathed to the guilds

---

130 On *memoria* and benefactors of monastic communities, see Geary, *Phantoms of Remembrance*, p. 76; Oexle, 'Memoria und Memorialbild', p. 385; Oexle, 'Gegenwart der Toten', p. 22, 25.
131 Oexle, 'Liturgische Memoria', p. 332.
132 Poeck, 'Rat und Memoria', p. 319.
133 Poeck, 'Rat und Memoria', pp. 286–335.
134 Czaja, 'Patrician Guilds', p. 50.
135 Galvin, 'Credit and charity', p. 133.
136 *Schragen der Gilden und Aemter*, p. 661, § 2.
137 *Schragen der Gilden und Aemter*, p. 661, § 6.
138 *Schragen der Gilden und Aemter*, p. 663, § 15.
139 For a public commemoration of elite benefactors, see Speer, *Frömmigkeit und Politik*, pp. 287–88; Poeck, 'Rat und Memoria', p. 319.

by city councillors, wardens of the Great Guild and *tafelgilde*, and wealthy merchants.[140] Most of the benefactors came from a small group of members.[141]

The few surviving sources on endowments made to the Table Guilds indicate the existence of memorial expectations. The *Bock der Breve* of the Rigan *tafelgilde* contains copies of three charters that reveal the memorial wishes of the benefactors, most of whom were city councillors or their family members.[142] In 1494 the Riga city councillor Hinrik Krivitz and his wife Margrete made a generous endowment to the *tafelgilde*, bequeathing 710 Riga marks, for the welfare of their souls and the glory of God.[143] The endowment was secured by six properties yielding a rent of 43 marks annually, and it secured almsgiving by the Table Guild under the belfry of St Peter's church; two portions of food (*schottele*), three pieces of Rostockian cloth for the poor, and an unspecified number of shoes were to be distributed on regular occasions.[144] The distribution of the alms was to begin after the death of one spouse and to operate in full after the death of the other.[145]

Two endowments were made by the widows of Riga city councillors, who may have been guild members.[146] Margaret, widow of the city councillor Johan Scheding, bequeathed 300 Riga marks for the Table Guild in 1502.[147] Like Hinrik and Margrete Krivitz, Margaret Scheding identified the welfare of her soul and that of her husband's and their descendants as the purpose for the endowment. Yet, the charter provides little detail on the activities foreseen. In 1496 Anna, widow of the councillor Cord Visch junior, made an endowment of 200 marks for the Table Guild for distribution of alms in the belfry of St Peter's church in remembrance of her husband and his family.[148]

---

140 In Reval between 1414 and 1524, ten testators made bequests for *tafelgilde*: brother Hans Lyndenbeke (1414), brother Gert van Lynden (1442), warden Evert van der Lynden (1455), warden Dethart Helpyn (1465), warden Gerwin Borneman (1480), city councillor Hinrik Schelewent (1490), brother Gerd Strobuck (1497), brother Hans van Epen (1511), (not in the members list) Hans Bouwer (1519), and city councillor Johann Viant (1524); LUB 5, no. 1965; LUB 9, no. 911; LUB 11, no. 385; LUB 12, no. 303; LUB 2/1, no. 545; *Revaler Regesten*, nos. 104, 118, 127; Derrik, *Bruderbuch*, pp. 40, 342, 345, 290, 256, 267, 181, 385, 396, 222; Friedrich Georg von Bunge, *Die Revaler Rathslinie* (Reval: Kluge, 1874), pp. 128, 94; Mänd, 'Hospitals', p. 261; in Riga the city councillor Cord Visch (1425); LUB 7, no. 372; Heinrich J. Böthführ, *Die Rigische Rathslinie von 1226 bis 1876* (Riga: J. Deubner, 1877), no. 236.

141 In the Reval *tafelgilde* between 1363 and 1549, the local and foreign city councillors constituted around ten per cent of all brethren, but among the known benefactors their ratio was greater. Derrik, *Bruderbuch*, pp. 44–45.

142 Rīga, LVVA 223 f., 1 apr., 369 l., fols. 44ʳ–45ʳ, 52ʳ.

143 Hinrik Krivitz was councilor between 1469 and 1506. Böthführ, *Rathslinie*, no. 365; Rīga, LVVA 223 f., 1 apr., 369 l., fol. 45ʳ; Brück, 'Tafelgilde', p. 84.

144 Rīga, LVVA 223 f., 1 apr., 369 l., fol. 45ʳ; Brück, 'Tafelgilde', p. 84.

145 Brück, 'Tafelgilde', p. 84.

146 *Schragen der Gilden und Aemter*, p. 661, § 2; Böthführ, *Rathslinie*, no. 349.

147 Rīga, LVVA 223 f., 1 apr., 369 l., fol. 52ʳ.

148 Rīga, LVVA 223 f., 1 apr., 369 l., fol. 44ʳ; Cordt Visch was the warden of *tafelgilde* (1477), the councillor (1448–1473), and a burgomaster (in the 1470s). His father, Cord Visch senior also had donated to the *tafelgilde* (1425). Böthführ, *Rathslinie*, no. 236, 334; Brück, 'Tafelgilde', p. 85; LUB 7, no. 372.

Widows of city councillors or guild officials of Reval also made charitable endowments as part of elite *memoria*. In 1488 the widow of the Reval city councillor Ewert Smed endowed 200 marks for one portion of alms.[149] In 1475 the widow of Gise Voss, once alderman of the Great Guild and warden of *tafelgilde*, endowed 50 marks for the distribution of food on the feast of St Blaise.[150] Likewise, in the Reval *tafelgilde* city councillors supported the guild with endowments; city councillor Johan Super in the late-fifteenth century increased the number of prebends distributed by *tafelgilde* by endowing it with 150 Riga marks.[151]

These examples of city councillors and their widows providing considerable resources for almsgiving and *memoria* in the Riga and Reval *tafelgilde* demonstrate the essential role of political leaders as civic benefactors. The endowments intended for feeding and clothing the poor were part of the urban government's political *memoria*.[152]

As already stated, the poor played an important role in the commemoration of benefactors. The existing source material — account books and testaments — is deceptive in showing the poor as objects of the elite's charity. For, as Dietrich Poeck observes, the poor were also active participants who had to deliver a counter-gift in the form of prayers.[153] Feeding the poor was a memorial practice, in which the poor were perceived as representatives of the dead.[154] Moreover, the relationship between the benefactors and the recipients of the gifts was not anonymous; benefactors frequently stated that alms were to be given to each recipient individually, with the knowledge of who the giver was.[155] This was a process of a communication between dead benefactors and living poor.

The recipients of alms in the Livonian *tafelgilde* were not an anonymous group. As was the case with the poor tables in Bruges, the Table Guilds of Riga and Reval selected the recipients of alms as 'a select group of a select group'.[156] Like most late medieval charitable associations, the Reval *tafelgilde* supported the house poor (*armen husarme*),[157] and the 'shamefaced poor', who had a residence and were not beggars.[158] Additionally the statutes of the Riga *tafelgilde* stated that the wardens had to distribute alms to the 'poorest'

---

149 Derrik, *Bruderbuch*, p. 41.
150 Derrik, *Bruderbuch*, pp. 40, 323.
151 Derrik, *Bruderbuch*, p. 41; Bunge, *Rathslinie*, p. 134.
152 *Ratsmemoria* — remembrance of city councils — is discussed in the subchapter below.
153 Poeck, 'Totengedenken in Hansestädten', p. 200.
154 Wollasch, 'Gemeinschaftsbewußtsein', p. 279; Oexle, 'Mahl und Spende', pp. 401–20; Oexle, 'Gegenwart der Toten', pp. 48–58.
155 Poeck, 'Totengedenken in Hansestädten', p. 200.
156 Galvin, 'Credit', p. 132.
157 Nottbeck, *Schragen*, p. 96, § 5.
158 Mänd, 'Hospitals', p. 262; on shamefaced poor, see Bronisław Geremek, *Poverty: A History*, trans. by Agnieszka Kolakowska (Oxford: Blackwell, 1994), p. 24, 43; Ernst Schubert, '"Hausarme Leute", "starke Bettler". Einschränkungen und Umformungen des Almosengedankens um 1400 und um 1500', in *Armut im Mittelalter*, ed. by Otto Gerhard Oexle (Ostfildern: Thorbecke, 2004), pp. 283–348, pp. 295.

individuals they knew.[159] As elsewhere in medieval Europe, the Riga *tafelgilde* distributed lead tokens (*teken van blye*) to the poor for the reception of alms.[160] An example of one of these tokens on which the initials of a benefactor were inscribed has survived from post-Reformation Reval.[161] The tokens enabled the Table Guild to control who received alms, as well as to inform recipients who their benefactors were.

Brethren of the guild who had fallen on hard times also received alms from *tafelgilde*. Impoverished *tafelgilde* members in Riga and Reval were granted alms, sometimes even a double portion.[162] Many townspeople lived under the constant threat of poverty, due to fluctuating food prices and periods of economic downturn.[163] Although the Table Guilds were elite associations, they were socially diverse: alongside wealthy merchants there were skippers and even some servants.[164] The dynamic Hanseatic economy posed risks even to wealthy Riga and Reval merchants, who could lose all and 'cease living according to the standards of (their) status'; to such members some support was directed by the *tafelgilde*.[165] The existence of the 'poor' within *tafelgilde* meant that the commemorators could be readily found within the group.

The distribution of alms was a demanding process. In Reval there were almost one hundred occasions in every year when the *tafelgilde* distributed portions of food, usually bread, but also fresh meat, fish, and peas.[166] It has been estimated that the Reval *tafelgilde* regularly fed approximately 160 people.[167] In Reval the distributions of alms took place in the morning 'before the High Mass [was] sung' in the belfry of the Holy Spirit church, where *tafelgilde* commemorated their dead members and benefactors.[168] This church was both a charitable and a memorial space. A prayer in the church for the benefactor was a fitting return from the 'poor' for food and clothing distributed in the belfry.

The *tafelgilde* was a sub-organization of the Great Guild, which functioned as a charitable association, but it had a complex set of aims. In the *tafelgilde* charity and *memoria* were intertwined. As the statutes of the Table Guilds show, commemorative practices took place with regularity and were strictly regulated, involving all the guild members and investing considerable

---

159 *Schragen der Gilden und Aemter*, p. 661, § 3.
160 Mänd, 'Hospitals', p. 263; *Schragen der Gilden und Aemter*, p. 661, § 4;
161 Mänd, 'Hospitals', p. 263.
162 *Schragen der Gilden und Aemter*, p. 661, § 4; Nottbeck, *Schragen*, p. 97, § 7.
163 Valentin Groebner, 'Mobile Werte, informelle Ökonomie. Zur "Kultur" der Armut in der spätmittelalterlichen Stadt', in *Armut im Mittelalter*, ed. by Otto Gerhard Oexle (Ostfildern: Thorbecke, 2004), pp. 165–88, at p. 170; Otto Gerhard Oexle, 'Armut und Armenfürsorge um 1200. Ein Beitrag zum Verständnis der Freiwilligen Armut bei Elisabeth von Thüringen', in *Sankt Elisabeth, Fürstin, Dienerin, Heilige: Aufsätze, Dokumentation* (Sigmaringen: Thorbecke, 1981), pp. 78–100, p. 80.
164 Derrik, *Bruderbuch*, pp. 36–38.
165 Mänd, 'Hospitals', p. 262.
166 Mänd, 'Hospitals', p. 261; Derrik, *Bruderbuch*, pp. 42–43.
167 Mänd, 'Hospitals', p. 261.
168 Nottbeck, *Schragen*, p. 96, § 5.

resources. The liturgical commemoration performed during the Table Guilds' annual assemblies was complemented by individual memorial services organized by the guilds and social *memoria* of the dead members at the communal meals. Although these were sub-organizations of the Great Guilds, their memorial policies were independent from those of their 'mother' associations.

The charitable activities of the Table Guilds demanded significant resources, accumulated from the gifts of rich merchants and their families. These guilds granted additional commemoration to their benefactors, offering praise and thanks not only within the guild but also in parish churches. Most of the benefactors were local political leaders and their family members, thus charity was part of political *Ratsmemoria* too. The benefactors were commemorated not only by their fellow guild members but also by the poor, who received food and clothing each week in the belfries of the churches where the Table Guilds commemorated their dead.

The Remembrance of Rich Men: The Botherhoods of the Black Heads in Riga and Reval

Beginning with their foundation in the thirteenth century, Livonian cities welcomed travelling tradesmen alongside their population of settled merchants. As merchants from other Hanseatic cities passed through Riga, Dorpat, and Reval, it became clear that they and also young local merchants had to be distinguished from the rest of the merchant population in terms of political rights and commercial privileges. From the late-fourteenth century onwards, young, unmarried, and foreign merchants interacted in the brotherhoods of the Black Heads in the three largest Livonian cities.[169]

The brotherhoods of the Black Heads emerged in Riga and Reval at the same time. The Black Heads are first mentioned in Reval in 1400; in Riga the account book of the brotherhood's Shrovetide warden (*Fastnachtschafferbuch*) was created in 1413, although the first statutes were issued in 1416.[170] Yet the brotherhoods must have existed prior to these first references. These were a Livonian phenomenon similar to the exclusive Prussian urban associations, the Arthur's Courts (*Arthushöfe*).[171] In contrast to the Arthur's Courts and other

---

[169] In the early scholarship, the origins of the Black Heads were related to the fourteenth-century group known as Stable Brethren (*Stallbrüder*), the servants and guards of the Teutonic Order in Livonia. However, the urban Black Heads and the associations of *Stallbrüder* were different groups. Spliet, *Geschichte*, pp. 2–6; Herbert Spliet, 'Die Schwarzhäupter in ihrem Verhältnis zur deutschen kolonialen Ständegeschichte in Livland', *Zeitschrift für Ostforschung*, 3 (1954), 233–47; Mänd, *Urban Carnival*, pp. 32–33.

[170] LUB 4, no. 1503; *Schragen der Gilden und Aemter*, pp. 549–44; Marburg, Dokumentesammlung des Herder–Instituts in Marburg Lahn, 120 Schwarzhäupter Riga (DSHI), no. 64. fol. 2.

[171] In Riga the Black Heads also called their guild hall – *konyngk Artushoff*. Stephan Selzer, *Artushöfe im Ostseeraum: ritterlich–höfische Kultur in den Städten des Preussenlandes im 14. und 15. Jahrhundert* (Frankfurt am Main: Lang, 1996); *Schragen der Gilden und Aemter*, p. 556.

Hanseatic urban elite associations that welcomed 'sisters' — wives or widows of the brethren — the Black Heads were exclusively male groups.[172]

Although the Black Heads were excluded from urban government, they still formed part of the urban elite.[173] Young merchants, future urban economic and political leaders, were trained, gained business contacts, and engaged in religious and social activities within these brotherhoods.[174] Entitled *swarten hovede*,[175] these groups had as their patrons St Maurice (visualised as a head of a black man) and the Virgin Mary.[176] The prestige of these brotherhoods was manifested by the locations of their guildhalls. In Riga, the house of the Black Heads, also known as 'the New House', was located on the marketplace, opposite the city hall. This house had been erected before the establishment of the brotherhood and for a time after 1413/1416, was shared with the Great Guild (see Figure 2).[177] The brotherhood also rented a house in a central location in Reval — on Long Street — where the guildhalls of all major associations were located (see Figure 3); during the sixteenth century they acquired their own house there.[178] Additionally, both in Riga and in Reval, the Black Heads established altars and also chapels in the churches of St Catherine (of Alexandria); in Riga this was the Franciscan church but in Reval it was the Dominican church.[179] Both institutions became religious centres for the brotherhoods, and they received generous support from the Black Heads.

Although they commanded resources and established great pomp, these brotherhoods were smaller in size than the senior Great Guilds. From small groups with only a few dozen members in the early fifteenth century, the Black Heads nonetheless grew into associations which numbered around one hundred brethren by mid–century. During one of the first known *drunke* of the Riga brotherhood in 1413, forty-one Black Heads paid a membership fee of 10 ore. The number of the Black Heads in Riga clearly fluctuated: 63 brethren in 1416; 105 in 1417; 91 in 1419, and 90 in 1424.[180] According to the lists of

---

172 Selzer, *Artushöfe*, p. 115.
173 Tiina Kala, Juhan Kreem, and Anu Mänd, 'Die Bruderschaft der Schwarzenhäupter im Mittelalter', in *Tallinna Mustpead : Mustpeade vennaskonna ajaloost ja varadest = Die Revaler Schwarzhäupter. Geschichte und Schätze der Bruderschaft der Schwarzhäupter*, ed. by Urmas Oolup and Juhan Kreem (Tallinn: Tallinna Linnarhiiv, 1999), pp. 61–66, at p. 64.
174 Brück, 'Bemerkungen', p. 116.
175 *Schragen der Gilden und Aemter*, p. 549; LUB 9, no. 695;
176 The brotherhoods in Riga and Reval had also other patron saints, see Spliet, *Geschichte*, pp. 6–7, 119–23; Kala, Kreem, and Mänd, 'Bruderschaft', p. 62.
177 Benninghoven, *Rigas Entstehung*, p. 96.
178 Mänd, *Urban Carnival*, p. 257.
179 Spliet, *Geschichte*, pp. 116–17; Kala, Kreem, and Mänd, 'Bruderschaft', p. 63; Anu Mänd and Anneli Randla, 'Sacred Space and Corporate Identity. The Black Heads' Chapels in the Mendicant Churches of Tallinn and Riga', *Baltic Journal of Art History*, 4 (2012), 43–80.
180 Marburg, DSHI 120, no. 64, fols. 4, 17, 32–33, 53–55; Thomas Brück, 'Bemerkungen zur Kaufmannschaft Rigas in der ersten Hälfte des 15.Jahrhunderts unter besonderer Berücksichtigung der Schwarzhäupter zwischen 1413 und 1424', in *'Kopet uns werk by tyden': Beiträge zur hansischen und preußischen Geschichte. Festschrift für Walter Stark zum 75. Geburtstag*, ed. by Nils Jörn and Walter Stark (Schwerin: Helms, 1999), pp. 113–30, p. 113.

guests at their feasts between 1450 and 1557, the Black Heads in Reval had on average around one hundred members. Membership fluctuated, affected by outbreaks of plague and by the changing economic climate.[181]

Most of the brotherhood members were the sons of merchants of the Great Guild, and they entered the Black Heads after turning eighteen; when a Black Head married, he took the burgher's oath and was then admitted to the Great Guild, thus leaving the Black Heads brotherhood.[182] The Black Heads also had members from the other Hanseatic cities (in Riga these accounted for at least half of all Black Heads), who after some time either left the city or acquired burgher rights.[183] Thus these brotherhoods can be considered as transitional groups, in which membership usually lasted no longer than a few years. An analysis of the members' lists of the Reval Black Heads shows that merchants spent an average of five years in the association before entering the Great Guild.[184] There are few known merchants who stayed in the brotherhood longer and even fewer are known to have died as members of the group.[185] Most of the Black Heads at some point left the brotherhood and ended their lives as members of the Great Guild or in associations of other Hanseatic cities.

The remembrance of the Black Heads can be seen as part of the *memoria* of the urban elites, but it differed from the collective *memoria* of the other elite associations. Firstly, the connection between the individuals and the brotherhood was not lifelong. *Memoria* in the urban associations was usually the extension of bonds created during a lifetime. Because no lists of the members commemorated have survived, it is unknown whether the brotherhoods remembered those members who died as brethren of the Great Guild or as burghers of other cities. The Black Heads certainly had their own dead, commemorated intensively even though membership of these brotherhoods was so short. Secondly, for the Black Heads, like the Prussian Arthur's Courts, *memoria* was a constitutive element, a vehicle for social prestige.[186] *Memoria* was also an occasion for self–representation by the brotherhoods, which was manifested during the annual feasts, directed towards members themselves and also other groups.[187]

In the Riga and Reval Black Heads brotherhoods, the genesis and development of commemoration allows us to witness how these merchant groups emerged, developed, and changed. In general, *memoria* can be considered as

---

181 Mänd, *Urban Carnival*, pp. 91–92.
182 Some brethren also remained in the brotherhood after the marriage, and in Riga not all brethren became members of the Great Guild, see Mänd, *Urban Carnival*, p. 36; Mänd, 'Geselligkeit', pp. 48–51; Spliet, *Geschichte*, p. 57; Brück, 'Bemerkungen', p. 117.
183 In Riga most of the foreign Black Heads were from Lübeck, Danzig, and Reval, as well as Cologne and Dortmund. Brück, 'Bemerkungen', p. 114, 116.
184 Mänd, 'Geselligkeit', p. 49.
185 A long term member Bernd Pal died in 1503 as a Black Head, see Carsten Jahnke, 'Bernd Pal, ein Kaufmann des 15. Jahrhunderts. Eine biographische Skizze', *Vana Tallinn*, 15 (2004), 158–76.
186 Selzer, *Artushöfe*, p. 121.
187 Mänd, *Urban Carnival*, pp. 55–159, 256–80.

one of the signs of a group's existence; it created and constituted a group and provided an identity that secured its existence.[188]

Because *memoria* was a tool that perpetuated a group's continuity,[189] it was practiced even at the initial stages of the group's formation when there were as yet no deceased members to commemorate. This practice projected the sustaining of a long-term identity. At this early stage it was essential to ensure members that a prospective *memoria* would be granted to them after their death.[190] Although we do not know exactly when the brotherhoods of the Black Heads in Riga and Reval were established, the presence of liturgical *memoria* in the groups' early activities shows that they were already active in imagining the past and future. As communities in which foreigners dominated, they needed secure spaces in which to fulfil their religious obligations because most of them had no families or relatives in the cities.[191] By the time they first appear in the records, the Black Heads had already chosen their memorial spaces, which remained unchanged until the Reformation.

The Reval Black Heads were mentioned for the first time in 1400, in a charter issued by the local Dominicans, confirming the brotherhood's right to an altar of the Virgin Mary in St Catherine's church.[192] The leaders of the Black Heads agreed with the Dominicans that the vestments, books, altarpieces, chalices, and all other objects they would give to this church should remain in the brotherhood's possession.[193] Evidently, the Black Heads had begun – or intended to begin – liturgical services at the altar where the Dominicans promised to celebrate masses.[194] The charter does not specifically identify the masses as memorial ones (*selemisse*), but presumably the dead were commemorated during every mass.

The link between the Black Heads and the mendicant orders occurs in Riga as well.[195] There the brotherhood likewise founded its first chantry in 1421 in the mendicant church, at the Franciscan church of St Catherine.[196] These choices were determined by numerous factors. The Black Heads as journeymen merchants were not burghers and did not belong to the congregations of the parish churches, thus they could not found chapels there.[197] As Anneli Randla and Annu Mänd point it out, at least for the Black Heads

---

188 Oexle, 'Gegenwart der Lebenden', p. 75.
189 Oexle, 'Soziale Gruppen', p. 31.
190 Assmann, *Das kulturelle Gedächtnis*, p. 61.
191 Mänd and Randla, 'Sacred space', p. 47.
192 This altar devoted to the Virgin Mary, St Gertrude, and St Dorothy was consecrated in 1403. LUB 4, no. 1503; LUB 6, no. 2958; Mänd and Randla, 'Sacred space', p. 50.
193 Later, in 1403 the brotherhood's altar received an altarpiece of the Virgin Mary. LUB 4, no. 1503; LUB 6, no. 2958; Mänd and Randla, 'Sacred space', p. 50.
194 LUB 4, no. 1503.
195 On the mendicants and the Black Heads in Riga and Reval, see Mänd and Randla, 'Sacred space', pp. 43–80.
196 LUB 9, no. 704.
197 Mänd and Randla, 'Sacred space', p. 47; Antje Grewolls, *Die Kapellen der norddeutschen Kirchen im Mittelalter: Architektur und Funktion* (Kiel: Ludwig, 1999), p. 104.

in Reval, St Catherine's church 'was a natural choice'; in Riga the proximity of the Franciscan friary to the house of the Great Guild may have played a role in the choice.[198] The Black Heads in both Riga and Reval may have imitated Lübeck, the city of origin of numerous Black Heads.[199] In Lübeck St Catherine's Franciscan church hosted *memoria* and religious activities of prestigious merchant groups, like Circle Company.[200] Yet, St Catherine does not appear among the main patrons of either brotherhood.[201]

The Reval Black Heads remained linked to the Dominicans for 125 years.[202] In 1418 they founded another altar in St Catherine's church, dedicated to the Holy Trinity.[203] Since the early fifteenth century, the Black Heads had a chapel of the Virgin Mary in St Catherine's church.[204] According to the brotherhood's chantry account book for the period 1418–1517, the Black Heads endowed their altars lavishly: they commissioned altarpieces, liturgical vessels, utensils, and garments, donated missals and candlesticks, in addition to annually supporting the Dominicans with payments and donations of food.[205] According to an inventory prepared by the Dominicans in 1495, the Black Heads chantry possessed impressive quantities of liturgical vessels and vestments donated by the brethren.[206] In the late–fifteenth century, the Black Heads also had church pews in the parish church of St Nicholas, though the Dominican church remained their religious centre.[207]

The relationship between the Black Heads and the Dominicans was a close one. The Black Heads were involved in the internal processes of the friary, such as its reform in 1474/1475.[208] From this relationship – of which *memoria* formed a part – the brotherhood benefited not only spiritually but also in terms of social prestige. The Reval Black Heads received at least two charters from the highest officials of the Dominican Order securing prayers and *memoria*. In 1460 Ludolph, the Provincial of the Danish Dominican province to which the Reval friary belonged, issued a charter ensuring the participation of the Black Heads in the good deeds accumulated by the Dominicans of that province.[209] In addition, the Provincial promised that all friaries of the province would pray

---

198 Mänd and Randla, 'Sacred space', pp. 47–49.
199 Brück, 'Bemerkungen', p. 114, 116.
200 Dünnebeil, *Lübecker Zirkel-Gesellschaft*, pp. 49–75; Dünnebeil, 'Drei großen Kompanien', p. 206; Brück, 'Bemerkungen', p. 116.
201 Spliet, *Geschichte*, pp. 119–22; Kala, Kreem, and Mänd, 'Bruderschaft', p. 62; LUB 2/1, no. 106, p. 84.
202 Kala, Kreem, and Mänd, 'Bruderschaft', p. 63.
203 Hamburg, Staatsarchiv der Freien und Hansestadt Hamburg (StAH), coll. 612-2/6, no. E 1, fol. 3.
204 Mänd and Randla, 'Sacred space', pp. 68–72.
205 Hamburg, StAH, coll. 612-2/6, no. E 1, fols, 2–190; after the reform the friars no longer consumed meat, so the Black Heads donated to them fish and peas. See Kala, Kreem, and Mänd, 'Bruderschaft', p. 63; Tallinn, TLA, f 230, n 1, s Bk 3, fols. 11^r, 22^r, 77^r.
206 LUB 2/1, no. 106.
207 Mänd, 'Über den Marienaltar der Revaler Schwarzenhäupter', p. 233.
208 Tallinn, TLA, f 230, n 1, s Bk 3, fol. 11^r.
209 LUB 12, no. 34.

for the souls of deceased Black Heads.[210] Another charter was issued by Master General Leonardo Mansueti (1474–1480), in Rome in 1478, which praised the Black Heads' piety and their support for the local friary, while promising prayers by all of the Order's houses.[211] These charters, which were kept in the brotherhood's collection of its most important documents, established the spiritual confraternity between the two groups and helped to enhance the brotherhood's status.[212] Such charters were most likely bought, and all deceased Black Heads would likely not have been commemorated in all the friaries of the Danish province. Yet the promise of *memoria* was a gesture of partnership between the friars and the brotherhood. Thus the choice of location for their religious activities and commemoration affected the brotherhood's status; the friars were not simply commemorators but also long-term allies.

The records of the Riga Black Heads reveal how *memoria* was performed in practice, how the brotherhood's memorial activities changed, and how their memorial chantries functioned. The Riga Black Heads had two memorial spaces from the very beginning: the Franciscan friary of St Catherine and the parish church of St Peter.[213] As in Reval, the Riga Black Heads used these memorial spaces until the Reformation, although their relative importance changed over time.

The Black Heads commemorated their dead in Riga, even before they were able to accumulate the substantial resources necessary to establish a chantry, an altar, and regular liturgical services. Until the establishment of the chantry in St Catherine's church in 1421, the Black Heads sustained *memoria* by requesting prayers from parish priests. Its earliest statutes of 1416 stipulated payment to the priests of St Peter's church of four ores, for commemoration of the Black Heads every Sunday from the pulpit.[214] In this respect the Black Heads followed the example of the Table Guild, where brothers and sisters were likewise remembered every Sunday in St Peter's church.[215] As in the case of the Table Guild, this commemoration of the deceased Black Heads was directed not only to group members but also to the parish community present at Sunday services. Before the foundation of the chantry, these prayers were financed by the guild at a relatively low cost: the vigils cost four ores, and priests received three ores for singing the vigils while the musicians – pipers (*pyperen*) and drummers (*bungeren*) – were paid 6 ores for their part in the

---

210 LUB 12, no. 34.
211 The charter was given in gratitude from the Master for the Black Heads's involvement in reforming the Dominican friary in 1474. Tallinn, TLA, f. 87, n. 1, no. 91; Tallinn, TLA, f. 230, n. 1, s. Bk 3, fol. 11ʳ; Kala, Kreem, and Mänd, 'Bruderschaft', p. 64; Mänd and Randla, 'Sacred space', p. 48.
212 Kala, Kreem, and Mänd, 'Bruderschaft', p. 64; Spliet, *Geschichte*, p. 117.
213 Spliet, *Geschichte*, pp. 116–17, 125.
214 *Schragen der Gilden und Aemter*, p. 553, § 27; Marburg, DSHI 120, no. 64, fol. 23, 36.
215 *Schragen der Gilden und Aemter*,

liturgical services.²¹⁶ These, however, were activities whose regularity cannot be traced, and they probably did not continue in the long term.

The foundation of an altar as a memorial space of the brotherhood added prestige to the Black Heads' religious activities and helped sustain *memoria* in the long run. In 1421 the 'whole brotherhood' of the Black Heads, with the consent of the Great Guild's brethren, founded a chantry and an altar in St Catherine's church.²¹⁷ The foundation was secured by an endowment of 47 marks provided by the brotherhood itself, and the charter of foundation was kept in the brotherhood's chest.²¹⁸ In return for liturgical *memoria*, the Franciscans received an annuity rent of 4 marks and, as in Reval, donations of food.²¹⁹

After the erection of the chapel and the altar, the chantry began receiving donations of useful objects from the brethren as well as from members of the Great Guild.²²⁰ According to the inventory, the chapel gained its grandeur gradually; by 1441 it had received mensa stones for the altar, altarpieces, liturgical books, chalices, liturgical vessels and utensils, candlesticks, and other items.²²¹ Among these objects were those used in commemorative activities or created for commemoration of an individual. In 1422 the chapel acquired a silver chalice inscribed with the brotherhood's coat of arms, which was a memorial donation of the Black Head Cord van der Heyde.²²² A pall (*boldyk*), for use at funerals and commemorative services, was obtained in 1423.²²³ In the 1420s the brotherhood also acquired a grave slab, which was placed directly in front of the Black Heads altar in their chapel and was possibly used as a collective grave slab for the brotherhood.²²⁴ A decade after the chantry's establishment, the brotherhood obtained other objects that may have been used for commemorative purposes, namely stained-glass windows and an altarpiece.²²⁵ Two stained-glass windows were commissioned for the brotherhood's chapel

---

216 Marburg, DSHI 120, no. 64, fol. 36.
217 Marburg, DSHI 120, no. 64, fol. 42; Spliet, *Geschichte*, p. 117; Mänd and Randla, 'Sacred space', pp. 53–55.
218 Marburg, DSHI 120, no. 5, fols. 5–6; DSHI 120, no. 64, fol. 64; Spliet, *Geschichte*, p. 117.
219 Marburg, DSHI 120, no. 64, fols. 19 (1416), 36 (1419), 48 (1422); Marburg, DSHI 120, no. 5, fols. 24 (1442), 27 (1443), 42 (1446), 43 (1447), 124, 125 (1469); Spliet, *Geschichte*, p. 119.
220 Neither the chapel nor St Catherine's church have survived. LUB 9, no. 704, p. 491; Spliet, *Geschichte*, p. 117; Arbusow, *Einführung*, p. 300.
221 LUB 9, no. 704; Marburg, DSHI 120, no. 64, fols. 57–75.
222 LUB 9, no. 704; Rīga, LVVA, f. 4038, apr. 2, l. 1159.
223 LUB 9, no. 704. p. 491;
224 The tombstone was received from Hans Witte, corrodian (*provener*) of St Catherine's church. LUB 9, no. 704. p. 492. Similarly in Reval the merchants from Cologne had a collective tombstone in the Dominican church. See Nottbeck and Neumann, *Geschichte und Kunstdenkmäler*, p. 178.
225 On altarpieces as commemorative objects, see Elisabeth Vavra, 'Kunstwerke als religiöse Stiftung. Überlegungen zum Stifterbild in der deutschen Tafelmalerei des Spätmittelalters', in *Artistes, artisans et production artistique au Moyen Âge. 2: Commande et travail*, ed. by Xavier Barral i Altet (Paris: Picard, 1987), pp. 257–72, p. 261; Oexle, 'Gegenwart der Toten', p. 47.

in 1430 at a cost of 107 marks, and a year later, an altarpiece was received from Lübeck, valued at an impressive 74 Riga marks.[226]

All objects were given by patrons who wished to be commemorated by the brotherhood. An early fifteenth-century Riga testament reveals how brotherhood members supported the group's *memoria* and shaped its commemorational spaces by their donations and endowments. In 1420, Cord van der Heyde, a Black Head (*eyn koepgeselle*), named the brotherhood and the churches where it had its religious activities as beneficiaries in his will.[227] Van der Heyde may have belonged to a family of the city councillors, and he himself was alderman when the brotherhood's first statues were issued in 1416.[228] He donated three marks to the construction of St Peter's church, where the brotherhood prayed for their dead, and asked to be commemorated in return.[229] Likewise, he donated five marks to the Franciscans of St Catherine's church, where a year later the Black Heads chantry was established.[230] Cord van der Heyde chose to be buried there and requested prayers for his soul.[231]

Van der Heyde also donated to the brotherhood a silver chalice for the celebration of mass. He gave the silver for its production on the condition that the chalice remained in the chantry in perpetuity.[232] The chalice was to serve the eternal commemoration of the donor and to ensure prayers in return.[233] In 1441 it was recorded in the chantry inventory, when its donor's name was given as well.[234] Embossed with the brotherhood's coat of arms, it was the sole chalice of the brotherhood's altar; usually the coat of arms ensured that the chalice would continue to be used for the brotherhood's services.[235] Van der Heyde's donation was used in all masses celebrated at the brotherhood's altar, and in this way the donor was commemorated at every mass.[236] Van der Heyde had created *memoria* in which space his grave slab in the Franciscan church, an object, the chalice of the Black Heads, and prayers by the Franciscans combined effectively with the collective *memoria* of the brotherhood.[237]

Memoria was maintained through objects. The Riga brotherhood had numerous altarpieces in St Catherine's and St Peter's churches, none of which

---

226 LUB 9, no. 704. p. 492; Mänd and Randla, 'Sacred space', p. 54.
227 Rīga, LVVA, f. 4038, apr. 2, l. 1159.
228 On de Heyde family, see Böthführ, *Rathslinie*, nos. 196, 273; Cord van der Heyde was dead by 1441. *Schragen der Gilden und Aemter*, p. 550; Marburg, DSHI 120, no. 64, fol. 17; Rīga, LVVA, f. 4038, apr. 2, l. 1159; LUB 9, no. 704.
229 Rīga, LVVA, f. 4038, apr. 2, l. 1159; *Schragen der Gilden und Aemter*, p. 553, § 26.
230 *Schragen der Gilden und Aemter*, p. 553, § 25.
231 Rīga, LVVA, f. 4038, apr. 2, l. 1159; LUB 9, no. 704.
232 Rīga, LVVA, f. 4038, apr. 2, l. 1159.
233 Chalices for memorial purposes were also donated in other Hanseatic towns, see Lusiardi, *Stiftung*, p. 53.
234 LUB 9, no. 704.
235 Lusiardi, *Stiftung*, p. 53.
236 Oexle, 'Gegenwart der Toten', p. 47.
237 On the roles of a tombstone, donated objects, and liturgy in *memoria*, see Zajic, 'Jahrtag und Grabdenkmal', p. 85.

survives.[238] In Reval, however, the Black Heads' altarpiece of the Virgin Mary in St Catherine's church survived the Reformation.[239] It is a triptych with two pairs of wings, produced by 1493, and depicts the Virgin Mary with the infant Jesus on the central panel, saints on its wings, as well as its patrons, the Black Heads.[240] The altarpiece was produced in Bruges by the workshop of the master of the St Lucy Legend.[241] Although scholars are not sure of the date of the commission and its arrival in Reval, citing 1481 or 1495 as possible dates of arrival, a record in the account book of the Great Guild notes that in 1493 a guild member Gosschalk Remmelinkrade acquired an altarpiece for an altar in the Dominican church.[242] The members of the Great Guild took part in the acquisition, but the patrons of the altarpiece were the Black Heads, and it was placed at their altar in St Catherine's church, where it remained until the Reformation.[243]

The altarpiece of the Virgin Mary was a memorial foundation commissioned to sustain the *memoria* of its patrons. The patrons aimed to remain perpetually present through the mediation of an image or an important object.[244] The memorial image of a patron in an altarpiece supplemented liturgical commemoration performed at the altar, thus enhancing the presence of the patron and strengthening *memoria*.[245] The patrons of the altarpiece, the Black Heads, were represented on two wings as a group of thirty young men, kneeling, hands together in prayer, fifteen at the feet of the Virgin Mary on one wing, and the rest in front of St John the Baptist on the other.[246] The altarpiece with its wings could be used in three different positions according to the season and as appropriate for specific feast days. One might suggest that the wings, which depicted the Black Heads, were displayed during the memorial masses.[247]

As usual for such group portraits, most individuals posses few distinguishing features, yet Anu Mänd has suggested that the two men in the foreground of each panel are 'depicted much more realistically and reveal deep individualism'; it has been suggested that at least one of them was the altar warden or

---

[238] LUB 9, no. 704. p. 491; Spliet, *Geschichte*, p. 145.

[239] The altarpiece of the Virgin Mary now is part of the collection of the Art Museum of Estonia EKM j 18760.

[240] The altar next to the enthroned Virgin depicts another image of the Virgin (*Maria lactans*), God the Father, the Holy Spirit (in a form of white dove), Christ, St George, St Maurice or Victor, St Francis of Assisi, and abbess St Gertrude of Nivelles. Anu Mänd, 'The Altarpiece of the Virgin Mary of the Black Heads in Tallinn: Dating, Donors, and the Double Intercession', Acta Historiae Artium Balticae, 2 (2007), 35–53.

[241] Ravo Reidna, *The Altar of Holy Mary of the Tallinn Brotherhood of the Blackheads* (Tallinn: Eesti Kunstimuuseum, 1995), pp. 9–10.

[242] Amelung and Wrangell *Geschichte*, p. 36; Mänd, 'The Altarpiece of the Virgin Mary', p. 39.

[243] Mänd, 'The Altarpiece of the Virgin Mary', p. 41; Mänd, 'Über den Marienaltar der Revaler Schwarzenhäupter', p. 228; Kala, Kreem, and Mänd, 'Bruderschaft', p. 64.

[244] Vavra, 'Kunstwerke', p. 261.

[245] Oexle, 'Gegenwart der Toten', p. 47; Oexle, 'Memoria und Memorialbild', pp. 387–88.

[246] Mänd, 'The Altarpiece of the Virgin Mary', p. 41.

[247] Mänd, 'Church Art', p. 10.

Figure 12: Altarpiece of the Virgin Mary of the brotherhood of the Black Heads in Reval in a half-opened position. Tallinn, EKM j 18760. Photo: Art Museum of Estonia, Niguliste Museum

alderman of the Black Heads.[248] The Black Heads had two altar wardens, and likely they were the two men in the foreground.[249] In fact, the status of their altar wardens was different from that of other brotherhood's officials. The altar wardens of both the Reval and Riga Black Heads were already members of the Great Guild when elected, and remained in office for ten years on average, sometimes even becoming city councillors during their term of office.[250] As a transitional group of young and foreign merchants, with membership lasting only a few years and being mobile and somewhat inexperienced, the brotherhood required officials who could ensure institutional continuity.[251] Although the altar wardens were not members of the brotherhood, they were perceived as part of it. The two officials at the time of the altarpiece's commission, who may have been portrayed, were: altar warden Hans Kullert, elected to office in

---

248 Because the Reval Black Heads did not have one alderman but a group of leaders, the suggestion that one of the two men was an alderman can be doubted. Amelung and Wrangell, *Geschichte*, pp. 20–21; Mänd, 'Geselligkeit', p. 52; Mänd, 'The Altarpiece of the Virgin Mary', p. 42.
249 Amelung and Wrangell, *Geschichte*, pp. 35–36; Mänd, 'The Altarpiece of the Virgin Mary', pp. 42–44.
250 Evert van der Schuren, the altar warden of the Black Heads (1476–1486), was elected into the office after becoming a burgher in 1466, thus entering the Great Guild. *Tallinna Kodanikkuderaamat 1409–1624 = Das Revaler Bürgerbuch 1409–1624*, ed. by Otto Greiffenhagen (Tallinn: Tallinna Eesti Kirjastus Ühisus, 1932), p. 25; Mänd, 'The Altarpiece of the Virgin Mary', pp. 43–44; Spliet, *Geschichte*, pp. 124–25, 138.
251 Mänd, 'Geselligkeit', p. 49; Mänd, 'The Altarpiece of the Virgin Mary', p. 44.

1486, who served until 1496 and was also burgomaster, and Israhel van Mer, elected in 1484.²⁵² If the altarpiece was commissioned before 1484, then one of the candidates may have been Evert van der Schuren, altar warden between 1476 and 1486.²⁵³

If the men depicted in the foreground of the wings were the altar wardens, this indicates their special role in the brotherhood's work of *memoria*. In the Riga brotherhood the altar wardens were also founders of individual and collective memorial services in the brotherhood's chantry.²⁵⁴ The altar wardens commissioned altarpieces for the Livonian Black Heads brotherhoods as did those of the fifteenth–century Italian confraternities.²⁵⁵ They were acting as co–patrons of sorts and their preferences, including memorial ones, may have been considered in the commissioning of an altarpiece. However, the account books do not record the specific commemoration of the altar wardens but only that of the brotherhood's leaders.²⁵⁶

The wings of the Virgin Mary altar represent the collective *memoria* of the Black Heads. Although, as Anu Mänd has argued, it cannot be ruled out that some Black Heads who commissioned the altarpiece and went to Bruges actually sat for the artist, the altarpiece most likely depicts a stereotypical group of young, rich, and handsome

Figure 13: Altarpiece of the Virgin Mary, a fragment. Photo: Art Museum of Estonia, Niguliste Museum

---

252 Mänd, 'The Altarpiece of the Virgin Mary', p. 44; Bunge, *Rathslinie*, p. 89, 115.
253 Mänd, 'The Altarpiece of the Virgin Mary', p. 44; *Revaler Bürgerbuch*, p. 25.
254 Spliet, *Geschichte*, p. 126.
255 In Riga the altar warden of the Black Heads Hans (Johannes) Schroder commissioned an altarpiece from Lübeck in 1493. Ellen Schiferl, 'Italian Confraternity Art Contracts. Group Consciousness and Corporate Patronage, 1400–1525', in *Crossing the Boundaries : Christian Piety and the Arts in Italian Medieval and Renaissance Confraternities*, ed. by Konrad Eisenbichler (Kalamazoo: Western Michigan University, 1991), pp. 121–40; Marburg, DSHI 120, no. 7, fol. 36.
256 In 1450 the Reval Black Heads paid eight marks to commemorate the deceased brotherhood's leaders Reincke Grote and Hinrick Kothusen with sung memorial masses. Hamburg, StAH, coll. 612–2/6 no. D1, fol. 10ᵛ.

upper-class men.[257] Within the context and location of the altarpiece, it is a specifically designated group. Even if stereotypical, it portrays the Reval Black Heads as a youthful, pious, and wealthy merchant group destined for the elite, at prayer, and invites spectators to join in commemoration.[258] As part of collective *memoria*, it reminded the living brethren attending memorial masses that they also belonged to this group, and they should commemorate their dead predecessors.

All the objects created to assist *memoria* and to create memorial images of their patrons were passively or actively used in commemorational practices. In the case of the Riga Black Heads, these memorial practices can be at least partially reconstructed. Although by the end of the fifteenth century, *memoria* of the brotherhood was performed on a regular basis, there were periods when such activities were intensive. The commemorative activities of the Riga Black Heads were described in the brotherhood's statutes of 1416, and later ordinances add information, particularly about carnival, when the brotherhood annually celebrated its *drunke*.[259] During the fifteenth century, the carnival *drunke* began on Wednesday preceding Lent and ended on the Sunday after Shrovetide.[260] According to the carnival regulations of 1510, the *drunke* ended on the first Tuesday in Lent, after eight days.[261] Running to 216 paragraphs, the carnival regulations scrupulously describe each stage of the *drunke*; they reflect the brotherhood's wish to sustain the identity and unity of the group in the long term, just as *memoria* did.[262]

Carnival was a busy time for the brotherhood's members. Memorial rituals took place at the start and end of the *drunke*, and between them the Black Heads and their guests drank, ate, and danced.[263] Two days into the *drunke*, on Friday, the Riga brotherhood commemorated 'the Black Heads, who are dead' in St Catherine's church with a vigil, and memorial masses followed on Saturday morning.[264] The wardens of carnival prepared three candles and hired women to carry them during the memorial masses.

The statutes stipulated that the commemoration at *drunke* continued into Lent. On Ash Wednesday the Riga Black Heads held a vigil, and on Thursday morning, memorial masses were celebrated in St Peter's church.[265] The

---

257 Gerhard Jaritz, '"Young, rich, and beautiful". The Visualization of Male Beauty in the Late Middle Ages', in *The man of many devices, who wandered full many ways: Festschrift in honor of János M. Bak*, ed. by Balázs Nagy (Budapest: Central European University Press, 1999), pp. 61–77; Mänd, 'The Altarpiece of the Virgin Mary', p. 45.
258 Reidna, *The Altar of Holy Mary*, p. 10; Mänd, 'The Altarpiece of the Virgin Mary', p. 45; Mänd, 'Church Art', pp. 10–11.
259 Mänd, *Urban Carnival*, pp. 67–89.
260 *Schragen der Gilden und Aemter*, p. 551, § 9.
261 *Schragen der Gilden und Aemter*, p. 584, § 24.
262 *Schragen der Gilden und Aemter*, pp. 559–623; Mänd, *Urban Carnival*, pp. 87–88.
263 Mänd, *Urban Carnival*, pp. 75–76.
264 *Schragen der Gilden und Aemter*, p. 553, § 25.
265 *Schragen der Gilden und Aemter*, p. 553, § 26.

carnival regulations of 1510 laid down that on Thursday morning at 8 o'clock, all Black Heads took part in a memorial mass if they wished to be commemorated after their own death.[266] Members gathered at the brotherhood's house in the marketplace and processed in pairs, led by an alderman to St Peter's church for the celebration of a memorial mass at the brotherhood's altar.[267] After the morning commemoration, the *drunke* continued with a meal, followed by another in the evening in the Black Heads house, to which the members of the Great Guild and their wives were invited.[268] *Drunke* were lively events, so the wardens reminded the Black Heads that they must appear for the memorial mass on the next morning, as did the Reval brotherhood during the Christmas drinking feast.[269]

These collective commemorations were important for the group, not least because during carnival new members were admitted and inducted.[270] Thus new members were introduced to the group's traditions, to its past and its dead. This was an intensive introduction; while other urban associations commemorated their dead with vigils and masses only once during *drunke*, the Black Heads did so twice.[271] During these intensive festivities of carnival and remembrance of the dead, the Black Heads strengthened their group identity.[272]

Although funerals of members were a central obligation of all medieval confraternities, only limited information survives about the funerals of the Black Heads. Most of the Black Heads left the brotherhoods before their death, yet the brotherhood took care of the bodies and souls of those who died as members. The Black Heads in Riga and Reval possessed all that was required: biers, numerous palls, and in Riga, as we have seen, the brotherhood had a confraternity grave slab in its chapel.[273] The palls, presumably decorated with associations' emblems, reflected the brotherhoods' desire for prestige and ceremony and generated income for the group.[274] In Reval, the Black Heads had a red pall donated by an Augustinian preacher, Tibursius, in addition to the brotherhood's own pall decorated with gold.[275] One pall of the Riga Black Heads was of blue and yellow woollen cloth, lined with fine blue linen; the other was completely blue. Both palls and the bier were also rented to other

---

266 *Schragen der Gilden und Aemter*, p. 615.
267 *Schragen der Gilden und Aemter*, p. 615, § 174.
268 *Schragen der Gilden und Aemter*, pp. 615–16, § 176–80.
269 Mänd, *Urban Carnival*, p. 294, § 61.
270 Mänd, *Urban Carnival*, p. 89.
271 The Great Guild had only one vigil and memorial mass during their *drunke*. *Schragen der Gilden und Aemter*, p. 318, § 52.
272 Oexle, 'Gegenwart der Toten', p. 33; Oexle, 'Liturgische Memoria', p. 333.
273 LUB 9, no. 704. p. 491, 492; Hamburg, StAH, coll. 612–2/6, no. E 1, fol. 24; Hamburg, StAH, coll. 612–2/6, no. D1, fols. 4ᵛ, 6ʳ, 7ʳ; Marburg, DSHI 120, no. 5, fol. 5; LUB 2/1, no. 106.
274 Mänd, 'Church Art', p. 6.
275 StAH, coll. 612–2/6, no. E 1, fol. 24; Hamburg, StAH, coll. 612–2/6, no. D1, fol. 27ʳ; LUB 2/1, no. 106, p. 85.

individuals and associations.²⁷⁶ In addition, the Rigan Black Heads rented out torches (*bome*) for funeral ceremonies, raising additional revenue in this manner.²⁷⁷

The statutes of neither group provide details about the forms of funerals, but in Reval the brotherhood encouraged its brethren to help bury deceased brothers.²⁷⁸ The commemorative practices of the Black Heads were known to other townspeople too. In Riga in 1451, a female donor made donations to the Black Heads on the condition that they bury her according to their customs and commemorate her like the brethren, that is with vigils and memorial masses.²⁷⁹ The Rigan brotherhood also hired a gravedigger (*doden greuer*) in 1469, paying him 3 schillings for his work.²⁸⁰ Possession of palls, biers, and grave slabs and the rental of some of these objects shows that the Black Heads were well prepared for funerals of their brethren.

During the late–fifteenth century in Riga, the focus of memorial activities shifted from the altar and chantry in St Catherine's church to the main parish church, St Peter's. This coincided with a period of intensified *memoria*. Although the Black Heads had used St Peter's church as their commemorational space since 1416, paid parish priests for commemorative prayers, and donated a stained–glass window in 1470, the chantry with its altar was established there only in 1481.²⁸¹ The city council allocated a prestigious place in St Peter's church for the erection of the Black Heads altar, next to the altar of the Porters' guild (*losdreger altar*) (see Chapter 6), in the chapel on the south side of the church.²⁸² The brotherhood clearly sought to be represented in the largest and most prestigious parish church, and probably as non–burghers the Black Heads required permission from the city government to do so.²⁸³ In order to secure the chantry and to enhance its status, the Black Heads acquired a confirmation charter from archbishop Michael Hildebrand in 1487.²⁸⁴ After the establishment of the new altar, an influx of considerable resources for commemoration can be observed, and it appears that the support exceeded that given to the chantry in St Catherine's.²⁸⁵

With access to the altar in St Peter's church, the Black Heads intensified their collective liturgical *memoria*. In 1483, two years after the foundation of the altar, the brotherhood founded daily commemorative services there. The aldermen of the brotherhood recruited two priests to celebrate a daily mass or

---

276 Marburg, DSHI 120, no. 5, fol. 5; Spliet, *Geschichte*, p. 119.
277 Marburg, DSHI 120, no. 5, fols. 218, 236, 240, 246, 266, 271.
278 LUB 9, no. 696, § 13.
279 Marburg, DSHI 120, no. 5, fol. 1.
280 Marburg, DSHI 120, no. 5, fol. 126.
281 *Schragen der Gilden und Aemter*, p. 553, § 25, 26; Spliet, *Geschichte*, p. 125; Marburg, DSHI 120, no. 5, fol 129; Mänd and Randla, 'Sacred space', p. 55.
282 Marburg, DSHI 120, no. 7, fols. 31–33.
283 Mänd and Randla, 'Sacred space', p. 55.
284 Marburg, DSHI 120, no. 7, fols. 32–33.
285 Spliet, *Geschichte*, pp. 125–42.

three weekly masses – requesting that it be a morning mass – with an annual wage of 40 marks.[286] The probable reason for this two–year delay was Riga's war with the Teutonic Order (1481–1491), which affected the activities of the urban associations, and the foundation took place during a short armistice.[287]

This commemorative service was supported by the foundation made by a brotherhood official in 1487. Hans Siveke, the warden of the Black Heads altar in St Peter's church between 1484 and 1511, founded a *requyem* – a daily vigil and memorial mass for the support of all Christian souls – which had to be perpetually celebrated at the altar of the brotherhood in St Peter's church.[288] More specifically, Hans Siveke requested that the souls of his mother, himself, and all Christians be commemorated at these services. Although Siveke's aim was perpetual commemoration, there was a plan for five years, during which five priests had to celebrate the daily services and receive 20 marks annually each.[289] The priests could be hired anew each year, and they were not to be substituted by choirboys (*korscholer*).[290] The brotherhood was in charge of supporting these memorial services.[291] The foundation was meant to augment the morning masses created in 1483 by adding daily vigils to them. It seems that the services were begun in 1487 and were performed at Hans Siveke's death in 1511, as recorded in the chantry's account book, and the brotherhood received on that occasion 300 Riga marks for the chantry.[292]

Siveke's requiem reveals the schedule of daily memorial services for the brotherhood. The five priests of the chantry were expected to sing a memorial mass every morning 'at six or seven', and to offer a vigil in the afternoon at around one o'clock.[293] For a time, the memorial mass of the brotherhood had to be celebrated at six because the requiem founded by burgomaster Peter Hinriks was celebrated in St Peter's church at seven.[294] After Hinriks' death the memorial mass of the Black Heads was again celebrated at seven o'clock.[295] These memorial masses of the Black Heads were additionally supported by an annual payment of 6 marks.[296] After Siveke's death an additional 10 marks were given to the chantry's priests.[297] Siveke's requiem shows how the memorial efforts of the brotherhood's officials were blended into existing commemorative practices. The collective *memoria* of the Black Heads was also sustained by 'the

---

286 Spliet, *Geschichte*, p. 126; Marburg, DSHI 120, no. 7, fol. 31.
287 Spliet, *Geschichte*, p. 126; Caune, 'Rīgas pēdējais bruņotais konflikts', p. 37, 39.
288 Spliet, *Geschichte*, p. 129; Marburg, DSHI 120, no. 8, fol. 43.
289 Marburg, DSHI 120, no. 7, fol. 32.
290 Marburg, DSHI 120, no. 7, fol. 33.
291 Spliet, *Geschichte*, p. 126; Marburg, DSHI 120, no. 7, fol. 32.
292 Marburg, DSHI 120, no. 7, fol. 38
293 Marburg, DSHI 120, no. 7, fol. 32.
294 Bruiningk, *Messe*, p. 63; Böthführ, *Rathslinie*, no. 388.
295 Spliet, *Geschichte*, p. 127.
296 Marburg, DSHI 120, no. 8, fol. 45.
297 Marburg, DSHI 120, no. 7, fol. 33.

book of dead', which presumably lay on the brotherhood's altar and was used during the liturgy.[298]

Intensive *memoria* demanded considerable resources and the chantry of the Black Heads in St Peter's church possessed such support. From its foundation until the Reformation, there was a constant flow of funds for the chantry.[299] In 1514 the chantry's income from the annuity rents alone was an impressive 136 Riga marks; by the Reformation in 1525 this sum had risen to 208 marks.[300] Several houses owned by the chantry provided a regular income.[301] The chantry also received non–monetary donations from individual Black Heads. By 1521, forty years after the chantry's establishment, it had a rich collection of objects: liturgical books, altar cloths, small altarpieces, water and wine cruets, chalices, and also some very valuable objects, such as a silver statue of St George worth 600 marks.[302] In addition to rents, the memorial donations of members provided financial resources for the chantry too. In 1491 the chantry received 50 marks from Hinrick Sarrenhagen for commemoration of a certain Hans Wulff. The rents had to be spent on vigils and memorial masses in the Black Heads chantry, which continued for six years.[303]

For the Black Heads brotherhoods in Riga and Reval, as transitional groups, the commemoration of their dead was not only a practice of caring for the souls of former members, but it was also essential to expose new members to the group's past. Like their secular activities, the commemorative practices of the Black Heads were intensive and aimed at effectively forming a collective identity of a vibrant and constantly changing group. The importance of *memoria* for these groups is demonstrated by the amount of resources invested in the construction of altars, the commissioning of altarpieces, and the investment in funerals and memorial services.

Ratsmemoria: The Commemoration of the Political Elites

On 5 September 1425, Lübeck's city councillors sent a letter to their counterparts in Reval. They requested the restoration of the grave slab of their deceased fellow councillor Johann Lüneburg (*Johannis Luneborch*), who had died in Reval in 1373 while on a diplomatic mission, and who had been buried in the chancel of St Olaf's parish church.[304] The Lübeckians expressed the concern about the grave slab's removal during reconstruction of the chancel

---

298 Marburg, DSHI 120, no. 7, fols. 306.
299 For the Black Heads chantry's annuity rents and properties, see Spliet, *Geschichte*, pp. 121–38.
300 Spliet, *Geschichte*, p. 134.
301 Spliet, *Geschichte*, pp. 129–34.
302 Marburg, DSHI 120, no. 7, fols. 306–306a; Spliet, *Geschichte*, pp. 139–41.
303 Marburg, DSHI 120, no. 8, fol. 124.
304 LUB 7, no. 344; in the Lübeck's *Rathslinie* certain *Johann Luneborch* appears in 1367. Friedrich Bruns, 'Die ältesten lübischen Ratslinien', *Zeitschrift des Vereins für Lübeckische Geschichte und Altertumskunde*, 27 (1933), 31–99 (53).

and they 'kindly asked' the Reval council to return it to Lüneburg's grave.³⁰⁵ In reality, Lübeck's political leaders were concerned not about the grave slab alone but about the fact that the absence of the grave slab meant the end of Lüneburg's *memoria*.³⁰⁶

Johann Lüneburg died in a foreign city while trading for the 'common good' (*gemeynen besten*) of his community. He was still remembered by Lübeck's city council fifty years after his death. This memory was part of the carefully preserved institutionalized *memoria* of the Lübeck city council. The surviving lists of names of deceased councillors contain hundreds of entries with dates of death recorded between the mid-fourteenth and mid-sixteenth centuries.³⁰⁷ From the 1350s the city clerk recorded these names; he also served as a priest of the council's altar in the church of St Mary and was thus actively involved in the commemoration of the deceased councillors whose names he listed.³⁰⁸

Why was it important to preserve grave slabs and to record names and death dates of deceased city councillors? As Vincent Robijn has pointed out, 'the care for the salvation of late medieval city governors' served 'both religious and social-political ends.'³⁰⁹ Jan Assmann has argued that every 'power requires origin', thus for the political institutions, it is important to remember the past.³¹⁰ The liturgical remembrance of city councillors – *Ratsmemoria* – helped to legitimize their political power in the urban space, just as *memoria* legitimated the power of the medieval aristocracy.³¹¹ For aristocrats, kinship helped to build political *memoria*, but within a city council's *memoria*, two elements were important: kinship and membership in an institution. Thus *Ratsmemoria* consisted of three equally essential components: *memoria* of deceased city councillors kept by an institution, *memoria* of a city councillor founded individually but often also fostered institutionally, and *memoria* sustained by a councillor's family. These elements composed *Ratsmemoria*, and they often overlapped.³¹² *Memoria* of city councillors' families could also serve as representation of power and status through pious deeds.³¹³ This section focuses on two elements of Livonian *Ratsmemoria*: the institutional forms it took and memorial efforts of families represented on the council in successive generations. Despite scarce sources, the *Ratsmemoria* of specific individuals in Riga and Reval illustrates long-term continuity from the late-fourteenth or early fifteenth century, which can be traced up until the Reformation.

---

305 LUB 7, no. 344.
306 On *memoria* and a tombstone see Fehrmann, 'Grabmal', pp. 281–98.
307 Poeck, 'Rat und Memoria', pp. 300–28; Poeck, 'Totengedenken', p. 226.
308 Poeck, 'Rat und Memoria', p. 316.
309 Robijn, 'Brothers in Life and Death', p. 172.
310 Assmann, *Cultural Memory and Early Civilization*, p. 54.
311 Oexle, 'Adel, Memoria und kulturelles Gedächtnis', p. 340.
312 Poeck, 'Rat und Memoria', pp. 287–88.
313 Plate, 'Biddet vor dat geslecht', p. 179.

The city councils in Riga and Reval emerged during the thirteenth century: in Riga in 1226 and in Reval soon after 1243.[314] All city councillors were wealthy merchants and members of the Great Guilds, and refusal to serve on the council was a punishable offence.[315] As in other towns of northern Europe, council membership in Livonian cities comprised different combinations of the symbolic number twelve.[316] In Reval the city council had twenty–four to twenty–six councillors, including four to five burgomasters, until 1457, after which the city council was reduced to fourteen councillors and four burgomasters.[317] In Riga the city council originally numbered twelve, which later rose to sixteen.[318] During the fifteenth century the city councils were elected annually on Sunday at Michaelmas in Riga, and on St Thomas Day in Reval.[319] In Reval half the councillors were selected each year, leaving the other half of the 'old' council in office for one more year, thus enabling a smooth change of power.[320] In Riga twelve councillors were chosen before Michaelmas, and the other four were selected some weeks later from candidates who had not been on the council for the two previous years; together with the 'old' members, they elected the burgomaster.[321] This system meant that new representatives regularly entered government; yet numerous councillors had political careers lasting decades.

Although access to political power was restricted to a small merchant group, the ruling elites of the Hanseatic cities were in a constant state of flux, as families both entered and left the ranks of the political elite.[322] Both in Riga and Reval, there was also significant social mobility among the families that served on the city council. Although there were periods during the thirteenth and fourteenth centuries when both city councils became more exclusive and admitted a smaller number of new families, those represented by consecutive generations or numerous members were never the majority.[323] Between 1360 and the late sixteenth century, two–thirds of the city councillors were members of new families; during the same time period, around half of the families held seats on the council only once.[324] This was a socially dynamic environment in which councillors' families aimed to create continuity and to secure represen-

---

[314] Poeck, *Rituale*, p. 253, 256; Benninghoven, *Rigas Entstehnung*, p. 84.
[315] Johansen and Mühlen, *Deutsch und Undeutsch*, p. 61.
[316] Dietrich W. Poeck, 'Zahl, Tag und Stuhl. Zur Semiotik der Ratswahl', *Frühmittelalterliche Studien*, 33 (1999), 396–427 (407–13).
[317] Johansen and Mühlen, *Deutsch und Undeutsch*, p. 61.
[318] Poeck, *Rituale*, p. 253.
[319] Johansen and Mühlen, *Deutsch und Undeutsch*, p. 61; Poeck, *Rituale*, pp. 253–54, 258.
[320] Johansen and Mühlen, *Deutsch und Undeutsch*, p. 61.
[321] Poeck, *Rituale*, pp. 253–54.
[322] Rüther, *Prestige und Herrschaft*, p. 2.
[323] Czaja, 'Das Patriziat in den livländischen und preußischen Städten', pp. 215–16; Thomas Brück, 'Zwischen Autonomie und Konfrontation. Bemerkungen zur Politik des Rates von Riga in der ersten Hälfte des 15. Jahrhunderts', in *Riga und der Ostseeraum*, pp. 144–68, at p. 144.
[324] Czaja, 'Das Patriziat in den livländischen und preußischen Städten', pp. 216, 221–22.

tation over consecutive generations. Some, like the Hunninghusens, succeeded in serving on Reval's council from the early 1400s until the 1550s.[325]

City councils maintained chapels and pews in local churches. The *Ratskapelle* was a place not only for religious activities but for political and memorial ones too.[326] *Ratskapellen* and the liturgical services celebrated there were part of urban politics and provided a 'sacral legitimation' of government.[327] In their pews and chapels, city councillors were physically separated from the other worshippers during services and thus fostered their distinct identity.[328] There they gathered for the masses celebrated before or after their meetings in the city hall, and there they commemorated their deceased predecessors.[329] *Ratskapellen* and pews were places where the past of a city and its government were remembered.[330]

In Riga and Reval, the city councils did not have a central chapel but were present in numerous churches. In Reval the city council had pews (*radestale*) and altars in the Dominican church of St Catherine and in the churches of the Holy Spirit and St Nicholas.[331] They invested significant resources in the establishment of their pews and altars, which received regular financial support.[332] In Reval the city council had a special relationship with the church of the Holy Spirit.[333] They gathered there before elections and after a mass in the council's chapel, went in a procession to the nearby city hall.[334] In 1483, the city council's altar received a valuable carved altarpiece produced by Bernt Notke.[335] Moreover, the Holy Spirit church also provided a burial ground for the councillors; in 1510 burgomaster Borchard Heerde was buried there.[336]

Riga was exceptional among Hanseatic cities in this respect. The city council's pews were located in all the major churches: in the parish churches of St Peter and St Jacob, in the cathedral of St Mary, the Dominican church

---

325 Bunge, *Rathslinie*, pp. 106–07.
326 On *Ratskapelle* in the Hanseatic towns, see Grewolls, *Kapellen*, pp. 96–98; Poeck, 'Rat und Memoria', pp. 320–24.
327 Rößner, *Hansische Memoria*, p. 221.
328 Czaja, 'Das Patriziat in den livländischen und preußischen Städten', p. 218.
329 Uwe Heckert, 'Die Ratskapelle als religiöses und politisches Zentrum der Ratsherrschaft in deutschen Städten des späten Mittelalters' (unpublished PhD Thesis, University of Bielefeld, 1997), pp. 123–27.
330 Rößner, *Hansische Memoria*, p. 221.
331 *Raetstole* in St Catherine's church was first mentioned in 1386, in Holy Spirit in 1420, in St Nicholas in 1459. LUB 5, no. 2502; Poeck, *Rituale*, pp. 258, 263; *Revaler Urkunden*, no. 44; *Kämmereibuch der Stadt Reval: 1432–1463*, no. 1098.
332 *Kämmereibuch der Stadt Reval 1432–1463*, no. 1098; *Kämmereibuch der Stadt Reval: 1463–1507*, nos. 2036, 2744, 2750, 2166; Tallinn, TLA, f. 230, n. 1, A.d. 32, fol. 21.
333 Poeck, *Rituale*, p. 263.
334 Poeck, *Rituale*, p. 258.
335 Eimer, *Bernt Notke*, pp. 91–102; Neumann and Nottbeck, *Geschichte und Kunstdenkmäler*, pp. 109–10.
336 Heerde was in the office between 1493 and 1510. Tallinn, TLA, f. 230, n. 1, 107 Aa 7, fol. 198; Bunge, *Rathslinie*, pp. 69, 101.

of St John, and the Franciscan church of St Catherine.[337] In St Peter's church, the council's pews stood directly in front of their altar, dedicated to St Peter, the city's patron.[338] The city council had employed its own chantry priest there since the 1350s, and the chantry was named *vicaria civitatis*.[339] In the fifteenth century, the chantry employed priests coming from councillors' families, like Johann Woynckhusen between 1405 and 1422.[340] The city council in the 1460s paid for sung masses in the Franciscan church 'for [the] benefit of the city' and also for such services in 'all churches' of Riga.[341] Through their pews in every church and the communal masses celebrated there, the city council was able to involve the whole community in praying for them and their deceased predecessors.

In many Hanseatic cities, *Ratsmemoria* was institutionalized, as councils made their own memorial foundations and liturgically commemorated city councillors in their chapels.[342] In Reval the city council had its own liturgical service with memorial overtones. On 14 January 1386, the prior of Reval's Dominican friary Johannes Vrolinck promised the city council that the friars would celebrate a daily mass at St Dominic's altar in front of the city council's pews in St Catherine's church.[343] Although *memoria* is not explicitly mentioned in the charter, the annual 6 marks needed for the daily masses came from the endowment of the deceased city councillor Herman van der Houe. He was an important local politician, who had been active in the city's government since 1358, and served as the burgomaster in the 1360s and 1370s.[344] It would appear that the endowment was intended to ensure the remembrance of Herman van der Houe and other deceased city councillors. Van der Houe was remembered by his successors in the long term. Between 1415 and 1426, the city council paid annually two Riga marks from Herman van der Houe's endowment for the chantry in front of its pews in the Dominican church, where the friars celebrated masses.[345] The presence of van der Houe's name in the payment records shows that the city council and the Dominicans were aware of the source of this bounty even forty years after it was given.

The city council supervised memorial endowments based on long-term annuity rents secured by property, and was also responsible for distributing the income to the chantries for memorial services. By controlling these finances

---

337 Czaja, 'Das Patriziat in den livländischen und preußischen Städten', p. 219; Poeck, *Rituale*, p. 254; *Kämmerei-Register der Stadt Riga 1348–1361 und 1405–1474*, p. 107, 154, 172, 174, 274, 276, 300, 305, 309, 313, 315, 317, 332.
338 Bruiningk, *Messe*, pp. 521–24.
339 *Kämmerei-Register*, pp. 28, 59, 60, 64; Czaja, 'Das Patriziat in den livländischen und preußischen Städten', p. 219.
340 *Livlands Geistlichkeit*, p. 232.
341 *Kämmerei-Register*, pp. 304, 312, 316, 325.
342 Poeck, 'Rat und Memoria', pp. 320–24.
343 *Revaler Urkunden*, no. 44.
344 Bunge, *Rathslinie*, p. 105.
345 Tallinn, TLA, f. 230, n. 1, 107 Aa 7, fols, 10, 23; LUB 7, no. 451.

the city council effectively controlled *memoria*.[346] This financial control also affected the initial objectives of an endowment and to transform it. With the support of the city council, the endowments of the city councillors survived longer than the endowments of other urban dwellers. This is evident in the cases of the city councillors Johann Bremen, Johann Gotland, and Bertold Hunninghusen.[347]

Rent income for an endowment made by the councillor Johann Bremen appears in the ledger of the Reval city council in the 1430s; Bremen, however, had died in 1346.[348] Between 1436 and 1455, annual rent payments of six to seven marks for 'Johann Bremen's poor relatives in Dorpat were made.[349] For ten years Bremen's rent disappears from the city council's ledger, only to reappear in the ledger on 26 April 1466, this time with a formulation that it is for Johann Bremen's commemoration (*memorien*).[350] The city council may have transformed this endowment from a charitable to a memorial one when a century later, none of Bremen's relatives remained in Dorpat. Not only did the use of the rent change, but the amount did too; six marks were paid twice a year, thus doubling the original sum. This means that the city council itself must have reorganised the endowment.

Bremen's *memorien* were performed in the church of the Holy Spirit, where the city council had its altar.[351] Rents were paid to an individual priest and on some occasions to all the priests of the Holy Spirit church.[352] The memorial payments were made until the early sixteenth century, with a short pause between 1482 and 1492.[353] Judging by the 12 marks allocated to this purpose, these *memorien* must have been regular memorial services. Similar long–term memorial payments are recorded for another fourteenth–century Reval city councillor – Johann Gotland – who was also commemorated in the Holy Spirit church during the fifteenth and early sixteenth centuries.[354]

The endowments of Bremen and Gotland were long–term foundations that survived into the fifteenth century and were transformed over time, perhaps contradicting the founders' original aims.[355] They were created in the mid–fourteenth century, a period when social mobility in the Reval city council di-

---

346 Richard, 'Von der Distinktion', p. 226.
347 *Kämmereibuch der Stadt Reval 1432–1463*, pp. 701–03; *Kämmereibuch der Stadt Reval 1432–1463*, pp. 884–85, 891, 896.
348 Bremen was councillor between 1325 and 1346. Bunge, *Rathslinie*, p. 83.
349 *Kämmereibuch der Stadt Reval 1432–1463*, p. 702.
350 *Kämmereibuch der Stadt Reval 1463–1507*, no. 1288.
351 Poeck, *Rituale*, p. 263.
352 *Kämmereibuch der Stadt Reval 1432–1463*, no. 1307, 1373.
353 The payments were still made in 1507, 1508, 1509, and 1510. *Kämmereibuch der Stadt Reval 1463–1507*, no. 1827, 2164; Tallinn, TLA, f. 230, n. 1, A.d. 32, fols. 4, 13, 21, 29.
354 *Kämmereibuch der Stadt Reval 1432–1463*, p. 703; *Kämmereibuch der Stadt Reval 1463–1507*, p. 891.
355 On foundations and their transformation, see Michael Borgolte, 'Stiftung, Staat und sozialer Wandel. Von der Gegenwart zum Mittelalter', in *Strukturwandel der Armenfürsorge und der Stiftungswirklichkeiten in Münster im Laufe der Jahrhunderte*, ed. by Franz–Josef Jakobi (Münster: Aschendorff, 2002), pp. 9–24.

minished and became more exclusive.[356] Large, long-term endowments show that the city councillors sought to strengthen the positions of their successors in this exclusive environment. In the fifteenth century, the city council transformed these endowments to support collective *memoria* of the city council. Because Holy Spirit Church was the city council's religious centre, it is plausible that the endowments of Bremen and Gotland supported memorial services at the council's altar there.[357]

The city council took charge of the individual *memoria* of city councillors, even those from other Livonian towns. Rothger van Lare, a councillor from Fellin, founded a chantry in front of the chancel of St Olaf's church in Reval.[358] His testament executors were two Reval councillors, and the council took over the chantry in perpetuity on 16 November 1475. This meant that the council would cover the costs of the chantry, and van Lare's *memoria* was secured in the long-term.

The *memoria* of Riga and Reval city councillors was institutionalized in the late Middle Ages. The councils organized and covered the costs of the burial and commemoration of their members and individuals with close associations. On four occasions between 1514 and 1516, Riga city council paid 4 marks for 'commemoration' (*begencknysse*) and candles, presumably for the liturgical *memoria* of its members.[359] The costs of individual funerals were also covered by the city council. In 1515 the Riga council paid for the funeral of master Bernt Brand (*meyster Bernt*), the council's clerk.[360] It paid for wax, the bier, candles, and the commemorative ringing of the bells of the cathedral, the churches of Sts Peter and Jacob, and also other funeral costs worth 20½ marks.[361] In addition, it repaid 20 marks that Brand owed to a city councillor and the 21 marks spent on the preparation of Brand's body and the funeral to another two. This support for the clerk's funeral can be explained by the fact that the city clerks (*scryuer*) were usually salaried officials, men with university degrees (*magister, meister*), who although not council members, were deeply involved in the council's activities. They also played an important role in the creation of a communal memory. Hermann Helewegh (*c*.1420/30–1489), a clerk who later became a city councillor, wrote a chronicle in the 1480s at the behest of the council describing Riga's struggle against the Teutonic Order.[362]

---

356 Czaja, 'Das Patriziat in den livländischen und preußischen Städten', p. 216.

357 Poeck, *Rituale*, p. 263.

358 Tallinn, TLA, f. 230, n. 1, 107 Aa 7. fol. 198.

359 *Zwei Kämmerei-Register der Stadt Riga: ein Beitrag zur Deutschen Wirtschaftsgeschichte*, ed. by August von Bulmerincq (Leipzig: Duncker & Humblot, 1902), p. 57.

360 *Zwei Kämmerei-Register der Stadt Riga*, pp. 57, 59, 215.

361 *Zwei Kämmerei-Register der Stadt Riga*, p. 59.

362 The chronicle has survived only in a seventeenth century copy, see Thomas Brück, 'Hermann Helewegh – Ratssekretär und Ratsherr in Riga im Spannungsfeld zwischen Stadt und Stadtherren im 15. Jahrhundert', in *Akteure und Gegner der Hanse: zur Prosopographie der Hansezeit*, ed. by Detlef Kattinger and Konrad Fritze (Weimar: Böhlau, 1998), pp. 145–63; Thomas Brück, 'Helewegh, Hermann', in *Encyclopedia of the Medieval Chronicle. 1. A–I*, ed. by Graeme Dunphy and Cristian Bratu (Leiden:

Ratsmemoria was not only institutionalized, organized, and maintained by city councils but likewise created and sustained by individual councillors and their families.³⁶³ Wills made by councillors reveal memorial strategies chosen with the aim of fostering individual and *Ratsmemoria*. Cord Visch's last will drafted in 1425 is a good example with which to illustrate the intertwining of individual, family, and council *memoria*. Visch, who was dead by 1430, was a city councillor and burgomaster of Riga between 1391 and 1425, active in trade with Flanders, who served on various diplomatic missions.³⁶⁴ When he was drafting his will, he was the first representative of his family on the council, and his two sons, Gottschalk and Cord, were approaching the age when they could also be members.³⁶⁵

Cord Visch's will focuses on the creation of *memoria* and pious donations, with only few bequests to family members and fellow merchants. His aim was to promote the salvation of his and his wife's souls, by use of property 'given and lent' (*gegenven unde vorlenet*) to him by God.³⁶⁶ Visch involved in his *memoria* all the urban religious institutions and their members and established numerous foundations in the main churches of the city. He donated to the fabric of all Riga's churches, friaries, and convents, even including the Russian Orthodox church. The largest amounts went to the parish church of St Peter, 25 marks, and to the cathedral, 10 marks, while two marks were allocated each to the parish church of St Jacob, hospitals of St George and St John, and the hospital in *Ellerrbroke*, the Dominican and Franciscan friaries, the beguines of St Peter, and the Cistercian nuns. These donations to the fabric of these institutions were memorial in nature. Visch specified that the donation for the cathedral had to serve for perpetual commemoration. In the case of all hospitals, friaries, and convents, each sick person, friar, and nun received 3 ores and had to pray to God for the testator. This combining of donations for the construction of monastery or hospital churches with donations to individual members was practiced by city councillors and other testators elsewhere in the fifteenth-century Hanseatic region.³⁶⁷

Visch also cared for the poor in his will; he left 25 marks for the distribution of alms by the Table Guild, 50 marks for clothing, and endowed 7½ marks for the 'house poor' (*husarmen*), who were to receive an annual rent of half a mark.³⁶⁸ Among the recipients of these donations was the Birgittine convent in

---

Brill, 2010), p. 763; Thomas Brück, 'Konflikt und Rechtfertigung in der Geschichtsschreibung im Alt–Livlands Christoph Forstenau – Silvester Stodewescher – Hermann Helewegh', in *Geschichtsschreibung im mittelalterlichen Livland*, pp. 87–132; Böthführ, *Rathslinie*, no. 379.

363 Poeck, 'Ratsmemoria', pp. 287–88.
364 LUB 8, no. 383; Böthführ, *Rathslinie*, no. 236; Rößner, *Hansische Memoria in Flandern*, p. 429, no. 257; LUB 5, no. 1970, 2006, 2067, 2108, 2286, 2521.
365 Böthführ, *Rathslinie*, no. 315, 334.
366 LUB 7, no. 372, p. 264.
367 Rüther, 'Strategien der Erinnerung', p. 103.
368 LUB 7, no. 372, p. 264.

Mariendal.³⁶⁹ By incorporating in his *memoria* all churches and also all friars, nuns, hospital patients, and the 'house-poor' of Riga, Cord Visch created a communal *memoria* network involving the whole urban community in his remembrance.³⁷⁰ This was a common memorial practice among political leaders of Hanseatic cities.³⁷¹

The involvement of the whole community in prayer was not all Cord Visch did in search of *memoria*. Visch supported memorial chantries and involved individuals in remembrance; he left his clothing to poor priests in return for prayers. Visch and his wife sought to send a good man, preferably a priest, on pilgrimage to the Church of the Holy Sepulchre in Jerusalem (*thee tho deme hilgen grave*).³⁷² Visch also bequeathed 100 marks to his wife for his soul's remembrance.³⁷³ His executors were charged with finding a priest who would be paid 5 marks for celebrating 52 masses in remembrance of Visch's soul. All these acts not only expressed Visch's individual piety but were also evidence of his suitability for political office.³⁷⁴

For one of his memorial chantries, Visch chose an existing chantry that sustained the altar of St Anne.³⁷⁵ The objective of this chantry was not to commemorate Visch or his family but to remember the souls of burgomaster Arnd Plagal, his wife Margrete, and their children (*vor heren Plagales zele, Margreten, syner husvruwen, unde erer kinder zele*).³⁷⁶ Plagal, who had presumably founded the chantry, was a contemporary of Visch on the city council during the early 1390s.³⁷⁷ This support for *memoria* of a fellow city councillor has to be seen as part of a wider *Ratsmemoria*. In order to pursue these aims, Visch endowed 200 marks, in addition to allocating 10 Rhenish guldens in gold to a priest of this chantry.³⁷⁸ From his wage the priest also had to provide two candles; if he did not do that, the relatives had to provide these, taking two guldens of a priest's wage. The friendship of Visch and Plagal could have been a reason for this support, but links of service, business, and experience may also explain this remarkable act.

With the consent of the city council Cord Visch founded his own memorial chantry too. He had an altar built for it in the chancel of the church, within a chapel on the south aisle of St Peter's church. The charter does not reveal the

---

369 LUB 7, no. 372, p. 265.
370 On communal *memoria*, see Richard, 'Von der Distinktion', pp. 225–28.
371 For Lübeck, see Rüther, 'Strategien der Erinnerung', pp. 101–22; Rüther, *Prestige und Herrschaft*, pp. 58–71.
372 LUB 7, no. 372, p. 265; on pilgrimages as part of *memoria* see Norbert Ohler, 'Zur Seligkeit und zum Troste Meiner Seele. Lübecker Unterwegs zu Mittelalterlichen Wallfahrtsstätten', *Zeitschrift des Vereins für Lübeckische Geschichte und Altertumskunde*, 63 (1983), 83–103.
373 LUB 7, no. 372, p. 265.
374 Rüther, *Prestige und Herrschaft*, pp. 72–73.
375 Bruiningk, *Messe*, p. 359.
376 LUB 7, no. 372, p. 265.
377 Plagal was in the council between 1383 and 1393. Böthführ, *Rathslinie*, no. 216; *Kämmerei-Register*, p. 290.
378 LUB 7, no. 372, p. 265.

patron saint of this altar, but later donations made by Visch's successors show that it was dedicated to St Andrew.[379] There the souls of Cord, his wife, their children, and all of their friends and relatives were to be commemorated.[380] Visch endowed his chantry with 200 Riga marks – the same sum as Plagal's chantry – in addition to providing all necessary liturgical vestments, books, vessels, palls, and candlesticks. The chantry priest received an annual wage of 10 Rhenish guldens and was expected to provide the required candles from it. Both chantries were secured by Visch's real property until the time when his relatives would provide the two promised endowments of 200 marks each. Visch had founded for his remembrance an altar of St Andrew that was supported both by his relatives and by his successors in the council.

The two foundations were part of the long-term memorial strategy of the Visch family, and they were sustained and supported by Cord Visch's successors. According to the financial records of the city council between 1447 and 1474, a chantry of Arnd Plagal and Cord Visch in St Peter's church, with altars dedicated to St Anne and St Andrew, received 15 marks annually.[381] For the first four years, the rent was paid to Andreas Soppelbecke, and between 1451 and 1453 city councillor Gottschalk Visch, presumably Cord's son, received money for the chantry.[382] For two decades after 1454, Cord Visch junior (†1486), also a city councillor, was the only contributor to the chantry.[383] Both Conrad's sons also invested in the chantry supported by their father. In 1475, Cord junior and Gottschalk Visch each paid 18 marks for the altar of St Andrew 'in the chapel, in the chancel'.[384] These payments continued after 1475 when the financial records of the city council end; the chantry of Plagel–Visch was dissolved in 1518 by the council probably because the Visch family were no longer represented in it.[385]

Family *memoria* was also fostered after the death of Cord junior and Gottschalk. In 1495 Drude Visch, Gottschalk's widow, donated 18 marks to the altar of St Anne.[386] A year later, in 1496, Anna, widow of Cord junior made an endowment of 200 marks for the Table Guild, for distribution of alms in the belfry of St Peter's church in remembrance of her husband and his family.[387] She requested that one portion of alms should be distributed to the poor every Sunday in the belfry of St Peter's church for her and her husband's souls, as well as the souls of both their families and friends. These two donations by

---

379 Bruiningk, *Messe*, p. 358.
380 LUB 7, no. 372, p. 265.
381 *Kämmerei–Register*, pp. 236, 239, 242, 245, 249, 253, 256, 262, 262, 269, 272, 278, 280, 284, 286, 290, 293, 297, 299, 304, 307, 311, 315, 319, 323, 327, 331, Bruiningk, *Messe*, pp. 357–58.
382 Böthführ, *Rathslinie*, no. 315; *Kämmerei–Register*, pp. 249, 256.
383 Böthführ, *Rathslinie*, no. 334.
384 Bruiningk, *Messe*, p. 358.
385 *Kämmerei–Register*, Erläuterungen, p. 85.
386 Bruiningk, *Messe*, p. 359.
387 Rīga, LVVA 223 f., 1 apr., 369 l., fol. 44ʳ.

widows clearly indicate that *memoria* in St Peter's church was a long-term strategy of the *Ratsfamilie* Visch.

Long term memorial foundations such as these supported the political and social prestige of a *Ratsfamilie*. In Reval, the Hunninghusen family similarly supported *memoria* in the long term. The testament of Reval city councillor Bertold Hunninghusen has not survived, but his chantry founded in the Dominican St Catherine's church has left numerous records within the city's ledger from the 1430s until the early sixteenth century.[388] The Hunninghusens, like the Vischs, served on the city council for several consecutive generations between the early fifteenth century and the 1540s.[389] Like Cord Visch, Bertold Hunninghusen was the first representative of his family on the city council. The Hunninghusens were one of the most significant merchant families in Reval; from the late fourteenth century until the 1530s at least ten Hunninghusens belonged to the elite Table Guild.[390]

Bertold Hunninghusen died in 1433 or 1434. On 13 April 1433, 200 Riga marks were endowed 'for Bertold Hunninghusen' according to his wish for the perpetual memorial mass celebrated at the altar of Virgin Mary 'under the chancel' (*vnser leuen vrowen altare vnder deme kore*) in St Catherine's church.[391] Every Easter, 12 marks were to be paid for the chantry annually: 8 marks to the friars for the services and 4 marks for the illumination of the altar.[392] From 1434 until 1523 payments were made to the Dominicans annually.[393]

For almost the whole life of the chantry, from 1434 to the Reformation, Hunninghusens served on the city council, which was in charge of these payments; Bertold's son Heinrich I (1456–1480), Gert (1473), and Heinrich II (1495–1514) were part of the city government.[394] From 1495 on, the payments for Hunninghusen's chantry were made twice a year; 13 marks were paid after Easter and 13 marks after Michaelmas.[395] This means that either Heinrich II Hunninghusen, in service from 1495, or the council itself had increased the endowment. The increase could be considered to be a re-foundation of the chantry, adding the *memoria* of other Hunninghusens. The presence of the family on the council was essential to this re-foundation.

Attempts to strengthen the family memory of the city councillors in the long term have also left visual traces. As Anu Mänd claims, in Reval around

---

[388] Bertold Hunninghusen became burgher in 1409, a councillor in 1413, and a burgomaster in 1427; he died between 1427 and 1437. Bunge, *Rathslinie*, p. 106.

[389] Bunge, *Rathslinie*, p. 106; Derrik, *Bruderbuch*, pp. 107–09.

[390] For the time period 1399–1529 there were 10 Hunninghusens in the *tafelgilde*. Derrik, *Bruderbuch*, p. 33.

[391] *Das Revaler Pergament-Rentenbuch 1382–1518*, ed. by Artur Plästerer (Reval: Revaler Estnische Verlagsgenossenschaft Tallinn Eesti Kirjastus Ühisus, 1930), no. 868; this was the Black Heads' altar. LUB 4, no. 1503; LUB 6, no. 2958.

[392] *Revaler Pergament Rentenbuch*, no. 868.

[393] *Kämmereibuch der Stadt Reval 1432–1463*, p. 701; *Kämmereibuch der Stadt Reval 1463–1507*, p. 896; Tallinn, TLA, f. 230, n. 1, A.d. 32. fols. 16, 27, 33, 39, 46, 58, 158.

[394] Bunge, *Rathslinie*, p. 106.

[395] *Kämmereibuch der Stadt Reval 1463–1507*, no. 2289, p. 896.

1520 Gertrud van Grest (also Surenpe, Lippe), a daughter of the influential councillor and burgomaster Johann van Grest, and her husband Victor van der Lippe, a son of the councillor Evert van der Lippe, probably promoted *memoria* of their fathers by adding their coats of arms to the outer wings of the Passion altarpiece in the Dominican church of St Catherine.[396] Here, not only were two city councillor families united by family ties, but the commemorative efforts of two councillor families were combined, thus potentially strengthening political possitions of their descendants.

Like many late medieval merchant families, the ones mentioned here attempted to create a dynasty with the help of their long-term *memoria* and thus legitimize and sustain their status and power.[397] Ancestry and continuity strengthened such families as they did the well-known Fuggers of Augsburg, who also used *memoria* to demonstrate their long familial history.[398] In the cases presented here, each generation fostered *memoria* of the previous one, thus maintaining political continuity. Most families with members on the city councils in Riga and Reval failed to sustain their place into the second, third, or fourth generations.[399] The *memoria* founded by Cord Visch and Bertold Hunninghusen influenced the political status of their successors long after their deaths. *Ratsmemoria* was a form of *memoria* in which institutional efforts to preserve the memory of their deceased members became intertwined with the efforts of families to remember previous generations. In Riga and Reval, the city councils prayed for their deceased members during the services celebrated at their altars and chapels, which were located in the major urban churches. As in other Hanseatic cities, *Ratsmemoria* helped to represent and legitimate the power held by a small group of individuals belonging to the merchant Great Guilds. In Riga and Reval, *memoria* that survived over generations was a unique characteristic of the families belonging to the urban political elites. By the help of *memoria*, these families, continuously present in the city council, legitimated their political status, and in turn, political status helped to foster *memoria*.

Conclusion

Memoria of urban elites was the remembrance of a minority that controlled power and resources. All male members of urban elites in Livonian cities were current or former brethren of the Black Heads brotherhoods, the Great Guilds, and the Table Guilds; some of them were also city councillors. These groups offered *memoria* for their members and used it as a tool for representation and legitimation of their exclusive status.

---

396 Mänd, 'Women Shaping Sacred Space', pp. 87-88.
397 Richard, 'Von der Distinktion', pp. 223–24.
398 Oexle, 'Adel, Memoria und kulturelles Gedächtnis', p. 340.
399 Czaja, 'Das Patriziat in den livländischen und preußischen Städten', pp. 221–22.

The Great Guilds in Riga and Reval were the largest elite groups, uniting the long–distance merchants, who controlled most of city's economic resources and held political power. Founded during the mid–fourteenth century, the Great Guilds in both cities established intensive memorial practices from their first statutes, which were performed during their drinking feasts at their altars in the main churches of these cities. Yet, most of the commemorative work for these groups was done by the Table Guilds, which were sub–organizations of the Great Guilds. The Table Guild combined charitable activities with *memoria* of its members. The *tafelgilde* commemorated dead members during the communal meals and kept lists of the deceased names. The poor were also involved in the commemorative activities of the wealthy benefactors through the distribution of food and clothing in the belfries of the churches. This charity and *memoria* strengthened both the identities of these elite groups and their awareness of their exclusivity.

The brotherhoods of the Black Heads in Riga and Reval, which developed during the early fifteenth century, were transitional groups in which members usually stayed only for a few years, leaving the brotherhoods when they married. Therefore for the Black Heads *memoria* was an essential tool in the maintaining and fostering of their identities. The Black Heads invested in their commemoration from the very early stages of their existence, creating centres of their spiritual life; one such centre in Reval was the Dominican church, while in Riga it was the Franciscan church and later also the parish church of St Peter.

The *Ratsmemoria* consisted of institutional remembrance carried out by city councils and also individual efforts by the city councillors' families. The city councils in Reval and Riga never created memorial foundations, but they organized – and, when needed, financially supported – the *memoria* of its councillors. Church pews, altars, and chapels of the councils served as places where predecessors in office were commemorated. Yet, for *Ratsmemoria* the individual efforts of councillors and their families were important. The councillors' families, like Visch in Riga or Hunninghusen in Reval, strengthened their political positions by commemorating their predecessors.

CHAPTER 6

Memoria and the Non–elites

Memoria has been described as a 'total social phenomenon' that influenced every sphere of life, but it was also literally socially total.¹ *Memoria* transcended all kinds of social differences and had no social boundaries. *Memoria* was practised by everyone, and everyone longed to be commemorated after their death; only the forms of commemoration differed according to social status and material wellbeing. Rich and poor, powerful and powerless, privileged and marginalized, all memorialised their dead and also cared about their own commemoration.

Although scholars who deal with medieval remembrance have been fully aware of *memoria's* social 'totality', there is little empirical research to confirm the existence of medieval remembrance as a practice across all social groups. *Memoria* scholarship deals mainly with the *memoria* of elites. Research on commemoration within the urban non–elites has barely been conducted, and there are only a small number of studies on *memoria* performed by the poor and the socially marginalized, which I shall call the urban 'non–elites'.² The existing studies of remembrance among the poor have created a firm theoretical and methodological framework, but they offer only narrow perspectives in terms of period and location. They focus more on the involvement of the poor in remembrance of elites, rather than on their own commemorative practices.

This chapter is intended as a case study of the social role of *memoria* for 'non–elite' folk in late medieval Riga. The Livonian cities of Riga, Reval, and Dorpat were ethnically diverse and socially differentiated between the immigrant Hanseatic (German) elites and indigenous non–German (Livonian, Estonian, and Latvian) non–elites. This adds an additional angle to the study of *memoria*, a primarily ethnic one.

Research on the indigenous population of Livonia, 'non–Germans' (*Undeutsche*) – Baltic Latvians (until the fifteenth century– Curonians, Latgalians, Selonians, and Semigallians), Finno–Ugric Livs, and Estonians – has a rich tradition, and it shall not be ignored when studying urban commemoration.³ The

---

1 See Oexle, 'Memoria als Kultur', p. 39.
2 Rexroth, 'Armut und Memoria', pp. 336–60; Frank Rexroth, *Deviance and Power in Late Medieval London*, trans. by Pamela E. Selwyn (Cambridge: Cambridge University Press, 2007), pp. 246–65; Queckenstedt, *Die Armen und die Toten*; Wollasch, 'Toten– und Armensorge', pp. 9–38; Wollasch, 'Gemeinschaftsbewußtsein', pp. 268–86.
3 Arbusow, 'Studien zur Geschichte der lettischen Bevölkerung Rigas', 76–100; Leonid Arbusow, 'Zwei lettische Handschriften aus dem XVI und XVII Jahrhundert', *Latvijas Augstskolas Raksti*.

term *Undeutsche* has been borrowed from the late medieval sources in which locals from the indigenous population – notwithstanding ethnic differences – were called *undutsch* in Middle Low German; this term, however, was not used for Russians, Swedes, Finns, and Lithuanians present in Livonia.[4] The historiography of the non–Germans began as research with an ethnic focus, aimed at validating the importance of one or another ethnic group in Livonian society. Most contemporary researchers consider the medieval *undutsch* in Livonia more as a social category and less as an ethnic one.[5] Writing about non–German literacy, Anti Selart has argued that non–German in Livonia belonged to the realm of the non–elites and oral communication, and thus German could be perceived as something that belonged to the realm of elites and literacy.[6] In order to emphasise *Undeutsch* as a social category, I shall most frequently use the term 'non–elite'. The term non–elite is a broad one but is here used primarily to describe individuals who were socially and economically marginalized for ethnic and/or economic reasons.

Non–elites, which were dominated by the indigenous population, existed in all of the three largest Livonian cities. There is only surviving source material, however, for the transport workers' guilds in Riga, since the archival sources of such groups in Reval and Dorpat have vanished.[7] This chapter discusses

---

Acta Universitatis Latviensis, 2 (1922), 19–57; Leonid Arbusow, 'Kirchliches Leben der Rigaschen Lostrāger im 15. Jahrhundert', *Latvijas Universitātes Raksti. Acta Universitatis Latviensis*, 6 (1923), 185–224; Johansen and von zur Mühlen, *Deutsch und Undeutsch*; Niitemaa, *Undeutsche Frage*; Manfred Hellmann, 'Gilden, Zünfte und Ämter in den livländischen Städten unter besonderer Berücksichtung der "Undeutschen"', in *Festschrift für Berent Schwineköper. Zu seinem siebzigsten Geburtstag*, ed. by Helmut Maurer and Hans Patze (Sigmaringen: Thorbecke, 1982), pp. 327–35; Šterns, *Latvijas Vēsture. 1290–1500*, pp. 268–82; Norbert Kersken, 'Städtische Freiheit und die nichtdeutsche Bevölkerung. Livland und Oberlausitz im Vergleich', *Zeitschrift für Ostmitteleuropa-Forschung*, 57, 1 (2008), 4–22; Kala, 'Gab es eine "Nationale Frage" in mittelalterlichen Reval?', pp. 11–34; Selart, 'Non–German Literacy in Medieval Livonia', pp. 37–63; *Estnisches Mittelalter: Sprache – Gesellschaft – Kirche*, ed. by Kadri-Rutt Hahn, Matthias Thumser, and Eberhard Winkler (Berlin: LIT, 2015) and especially the article of Heiki Valk, 'Die ethnischen Identitäten der undeutschen Landbevölkerung Estands vom 13. bis zum 16. Jahrhundert. Ergebnisse der Archäologie', pp. 55–92; Põltsam-Jürjo, 'Die autochthone Bevölkerung', pp. 341–75; Strenga, 'Turning Transport Workers into Latvians?', pp. 61–83; Misāns, 'The Western Model and the Autochthons', pp. 83–104; Arvi Haak, 'Problems in Defining Ethnic Identity in Medieval Towns of Estonia on the Basis of Archaeological Sources', in *Today I Am Not the One I Was Yesterday: Archaeology, Identity, and Change*, ed. by Arvi Haak (Tartu: University of Tartu, 2015), pp. 13–27; Magdalena Naum, 'Multi-Ethnicity and Material Exchanges in Late Medieval Tallinn', *European Journal of Archaeology*, 17.4 (2014), 656–77.

4 On the usage and different meanings of *Undeutsch*, see Kala, 'Gab es eine "Nationale Frage" in mittelalterlichen Reval?', pp. 15–20; Wilhelm Lenz, 'Undeutsch. Bemerkungen zu einem besonderen Begriff der baltischen Geschichte', in *Aus der Geschichte Alt-Livlands: Festschrift für Heinz von zur Mühlen zum 90. Geburtstag*, ed. by Bernhart Jähnig and Heinz von zur Mühlen (Münster: LIT, 2004), pp. 169–84; Hellmann, 'Gilden', p. 328; Selart, 'Non–German Literacy in Medieval Livonia', pp. 39, 50–51.

5 Kala, 'Gab es eine "Nationale Frage" in mittelalterlichen Reval?', p. 26.

6 Selart, 'Non–German Literacy in Medieval Livonia', p. 63.

7 Main sources used in this chapter are: the account book of Riga's Porters guild (1450–15??) Rīga, LVVA, 4038 f., 2 apr., 1087 l., which is inaccurately described in the catalogue as a Beer Carters' account book; Account book of Riga's Beer Carters guild (1521–1524) Rīga, LVVA, 4038 f., 2 apr., 1159 l; in this book I use the archival reference 1159 l. for this account book, yet elsewhere it has been referred to as 1089 l. Account book of Riga's Beer Carters (1461–1686) Rīga, LVVA, 4038 f., 2 apr.,

the importance of remembrance for the two transport workers' guilds – the guilds of the Porters and of the Beer Carters– which included most of the non–German townspeople in medieval Riga.[8]

The main questions which form this chapter are the following: how did non–elite guild members participate in the creation and performance of *memoria*? What role did the urban elites play in the remembrance of non–elite guilds in late medieval Riga, and how did it influence relations between elites and non–elites? How did the involvement of elites within the two guilds change the practices of commemoration? What effect did the abolition of *memoria* during the Reformation have on the Beer Carters and Porters guilds? Since the memorial practices of these groups were grounded in their social position, I shall begin with the social context and then address their *memoria*.

Non–elites in Late Medieval Riga and the Transport Workers' Guilds

Riga was a seaport and long–distance trade was at the core of the urban economy.[9] Economic prospects and social structures were shaped by long–distance trade. Trade was dominated by the German merchants, but it involved the employment of large numbers of people for packing, transporting, guarding, and storing goods. Merchant activities would have been impossible without porters, who transported goods between the ships in the harbour and the warehouses. From the late fourteenth century, there was no ethnic diversity within the groups involved in trade; the merchant business was German, and those who transported goods were overwhelmingly non–Germans, i.e. Livs and Latvians.[10]

Because no trading activity could take place without it, the profession of transport worker was one of the oldest in medieval Riga.[11] The porters, however, are mentioned relatively late in the sources, only in the mid–fourteenth century.[12] Nor is there mention of transport workers' brotherhoods until the

---

1089. l.; in this book I use the archival reference 1089 l. for this account book, yet elsewhere it has been referred to as 1088 l.; the chantry book of the Porters guild is published in Arbusow, 'Kirchliches Leben', pp. 202–21, original Rīga, LVVA, 7363 f., 1 apr., 367 l. most of which has perished.

8 The two articles of Leonid Arbusow on non–German population and the Beer Carters and Porters guilds in the late medieval Riga contain also publication of fragments from the Porters guild's account books. Following Arbusow and the sources in this chapter both brotherhoods will be called 'guilds'. Arbusow, 'Studien zur Geschichte der lettischen Bevölkerung Rigas', pp. 76–100; Arbusow, 'Kirchliches Leben', pp. 185–224.

9 O'Connor, *The House of Hemp and Butter*, pp. 69–95.

10 Arbusow, 'Studien zur Geschichte der lettischen Bevölkerung Rigas', pp. 82, 83.

11 Arbusow, 'Kirchliches Leben', p. 186; Constantin Mettig, 'Die Gilde der Losträger und die mit ihr verwandten Aemter in Riga', in *Sitzungsberichten der Gesellschaft für Geschichte und Alterthumskunde der Ostseeprovinzen Russlands für das Jahr 1902* (Riga: W. F. Häcker, 1903), pp. 56–69, p. 57.

12 Mettig, *Gewerbe*, p. 75; *Die Libri redituum der Stadt Riga*, ed. by Jakob Gottlieb Leonhard Napiersky (Leipzig: Duncker & Humblot, 1881), pp. 95, 277.

late fourteenth century. These brotherhoods emerged when, between 1360 and 1450, new urban social structures – merchant and craft guilds – were created.[13]

The emergence of the new transport workers' groups coincided with the marginalisation of the 'non-Germans', who comprised the majority of these groups' members. From its beginnings until the mid-fourteenth century, a degree of equality existed between locals and immigrants in Riga. The status of non-Germans began to change gradually in the late fourteenth century, and from then on Germans, monopolized all lucrative business – both in trade and in crafts – thus marginalising the indigenous Livonians and Latvians.[14] Presumably such marginalization was a result of demographic changes brought about by the plague in the late-fourteenth century and the urban mortality it caused.[15] In general, medieval cities relied on immigration from the countryside or from other towns because even in times when the plague was absent, urban mortality exceeded the birth-rate.[16] As a colonial city, Riga relied completely on immigration from northern German Hanseatic cities, and a decrease in such migration endangered the position of the German population in every sphere of social life.[17]

Exclusion of non-Germans from a number of social positions seems to have been an attempt to secure dominance for the 'colonists' who, although they constituted the majority of Riga's townspeople, could be overrun by indigenous migrants from the Livonian countryside.[18] Recent research has shown that the 'non-Germans' were not all townspeople of the indigenous origin but the first generation migrants – the former peasants.[19] The policy of exclusion in Livonian cities was not legally compelled by the official city governments but rather resulted from the initiatives of craft and merchant associations.[20] By the mid-fifteenth century, non-Germans could no longer participate in trade and were banned from the merchant Great Guild and the most prestigious artisan brotherhoods.[21] It was similar to the so-called 'Wendish Paragraphs' (*Wendenparagraphen*) in the statutes of the guilds in

---

13 Niitemaa, *Undeutsche Frage*, p. 62.
14 Arbusow, 'Studien zur Geschichte der lettischen Bevölkerung Rigas', 79–81.
15 Heinrich Reincke, 'Bevölkerungsverluste der Hansestädte durch den Schwarzen Tod 1349/50', *Hansische Geschichtsblätter*, 72 (1954), 88–90; Reincke, 'Bevölkerungsprobleme der Hansestädte', pp. 1–33.
16 Brandt, 'Die gesellschaftliche Struktur', p. 211.
17 Benninghoven, *Rigas Entstehung*, p. 105.
18 Benninghoven, *Rigas Entstehung*, p. 101.
19 Kala, 'Gab es eine "Nationale Frage" in mittelalterlichen Reval?', p. 26; Selart, 'Non-German Literacy in Medieval Livonia', pp. 50–51; Strenga, 'Turning Transport Workers into Latvians?', p. 66
20 Niitemaa, *Undeutsche Frage*, p. 65.
21 Non-Germans were banned from the merchant Great Guild in 1354 and from the artisan guilds: coopers (1375), cloth cutters (1383), masons (1390), tailors (end of 14th century) and shoemakers (end of 14th century). Arbusow, 'Studien zur Geschichte der lettischen Bevölkerung Rigas', p. 80; Niitemaa, *Undeutsche Frage*, p. 63.

north–east German cities.²² In historiography it has been claimed that in Riga the non–Germans were also prohibited from owning real property, but the newest research contradicts this assumption.²³ This exclusion meant that non–Germans were relegated to lower class jobs, though it cannot be claimed that individual social mobility was not possible.

The first brotherhood for those employed in transport was formed in 1386, when the city council confirmed the statutes of the Beer Carters (Draymen) guild (MLG *beerdreger gilde*, Ger. *Bierträger*).²⁴ It is hard to say who the members were in 1386, all of Riga's transport workers or only porters of beer, wine and other liquids, as is mentioned in the later edition of the statutes dating from the mid–fifteenth century. Leonid Arbusow argues that there was a larger group of transport workers in late–fourteenth century Riga from which the guild of Beer Carters had split.²⁵ It is more likely that in the mid–fifteenth century other groups of transport workers – the Porters guild (MLG *ghylde der losdreger*, Ger. *Losträger*) (first surviving statutes from 1450) and the Dockers guild (*Ligger*) (first statutes from 1463) – split off from the Beer Carters guild.²⁶ The porters and dockers had similar professional obligations, thus after the Reformation the brotherhoods of the Porters and Dockers were united in a single guild.²⁷

The Beer Carters guild was the biggest non–elite brotherhood in late medieval Riga. Between 1485 and 1519, it had on average 200 members, more than either the Porters or the Dockers guilds; before the Reformation all three guilds together numbered 500 to 600 members.²⁸ The number of members in the Beer Carters and Porters guilds fluctuated constantly by season, economic fortune, or political stability, war and disease; the Beer Carters guild between 1485 and 1519 had on average around 200 annual members.²⁹ Just before the Reformation, both transport workers' guilds experienced growth and the Beer Carters guild had around 300 members in 1517.³⁰ These guilds brought together not only Riga's non–German population but also numerous German elite members (their membership will be discussed in detail below). The

---

22 Winfried Schich, 'Zur Diskriminierung der wendischen Minderheit im späten Mittelalter: die Ausbildung des "Wendenparagraphen" in den Zunftstatuten nordostdeutscher Städte', *Europa Regional*, 10.2 (2002), 57–61; Selart, 'Non–German Literacy in Medieval Livonia', pp. 43–45.
23 Arbusow, 'Studien zur Geschichte der lettischen Bevölkerung Rigas', pp. 80–81; Indriķis Šterns, 'Latvieši un krievi viduslaiku Rīgā', *Latvijas Vēstures Institūta Žurnāls*, 2 (1996), 22–54 (25).
24 *Schragen der Gilden und Aemter*, no. 12, pp. 252–58.
25 Arbusow, 'Studien zur Geschichte der lettischen Bevölkerung Rigas', p. 83.
26 *Schragen der Gilden und Aemter*, no. 77, no. 74; Arbusow, 'Studien zur Geschichte der lettischen Bevölkerung Rigas', p. 83.
27 *Schragen der Gilden und Aemter*, no. 78, p. 418.
28 Arbusow, 'Studien zur Geschichte der lettischen Bevölkerung Rigas', p. 88; Strenga, 'Turning Transport Workers into Latvians?', pp. 71–72.
29 Arbusow, 'Studien zur Geschichte der lettischen Bevölkerung Rigas', p. 90; Strenga, 'Turning Transport Workers into Latvians?', pp. 71–73.
30 Arbusow, 'Studien zur Geschichte der lettischen Bevölkerung Rigas', p. 91; Strenga, 'Turning Transport Workers into Latvians?', p. 71.

Reformation appears to have dealt a final blow to the strength of the Beer Carters and Porters guilds. During the Reformation both guilds lost all elite members and a considerable number of non-elite members too. Between 1524 and 1540, the Beer Carters guild accepted no new members.[31] The Porters guild experienced a grave crisis between 1523 and 1532, and when it resumed its activities, the guild had only fifty-six male members.[32]

Although both guilds were officially professional associations of Beer Carters and Porters, in reality, a considerable number of the guild members were individuals from other professional groups: Latvian and Livonian artisans, wage-workers, and their spouses.[33] Arbusow suggests that the influx of artisans into transport workers' guilds was influenced by the gradual exclusion of non-Germans from a number of craft guilds, so that both guilds hosted those Latvian and Livonian artisans who had no chance of being integrated in the craft guilds.[34] The Porters and Beer Carters guilds were also suitable for those artisans whose crafts were not organized into guilds, and who were labelled as an unskilled labour force by the city government.[35] In the lists of members of both guilds, one finds mention of non-German artisans: carpenters, masons, belt makers, coopers, bakers, sail and candle makers, and others.[36] Although they were non-Germans, their names and professions in the records were usually Germanized.[37]

Members of the Beer Carters and Porters guilds also came from outside the urban space. In both guilds there were people who either lived in or were descended from the villages in the *Stadtmark*, the territory located outside the town walls but still under the city's government.[38] Among the members of the two guilds were first generation immigrants from the countryside.[39] This meant that the guilds attracted individuals who had only recently entered the urban environment and who had yet to develop social networks.

Like most of their members, the Beer Carters and Porters guilds were themselves socially marginal, even spatially within the city as their guildhalls were placed on the periphery. For a long time they had no guildhalls, and when

---

31 Arbusow, 'Studien zur Geschichte der lettischen Bevölkerung Rigas', p. 92.
32 Rīga, LVVA, 4038 f., 2 apr., 1087 l., fols. 63^b–64^a; Strenga, 'Turning Transport Workers into Latvians?', p. 75.
33 Arbusow, 'Studien zur Geschichte der lettischen Bevölkerung Rigas', p. 84.
34 Arbusow, 'Studien zur Geschichte der lettischen Bevölkerung Rigas', p. 84.
35 Arbusow, 'Studien zur Geschichte der lettischen Bevölkerung Rigas', p. 85.
36 There were more craftmen listed in two members' books of the guild. Rīga, LVVA, 4038 f., 2 apr., 1159 l., fols. 20^a, 37^a, 29^b, 19^b; Rīga, LVVA, 4038 f., 2 apr., 1087 l., fols. 36^a, 48^a; Arbusow, 'Studien zur Geschichte der lettischen Bevölkerung Rigas', p. 85.
37 Arbusow, 'Studien zur Geschichte der lettischen Bevölkerung Rigas', p. 81; for the transcribed names from the members' lists of the both groups, see Ernests Blese, *Latviešu personu vārdu un uzvārdu studijas*, I (Rīga: Ansis Gulbis, 1929).
38 Rīga, LVVA, 4038 f., 2 apr., 1089 l. fol. 47^a; Arbusow, *Einführung*, p. 727.
39 Arbusow, 'Studien zur Geschichte der lettischen Bevölkerung Rigas', p. 89; Strenga, 'Turning Transport Workers into Latvians?', p. 66.

these were created, they were located in *Swinenstrate* (Swine street) where mostly warehouses were located.[40]

As a result of the processes of social and ethnic urban segregation in late-fourteenth and early fifteenth century Riga, these guilds acted as organizations in which members could easily enter and receive social recognition and protection. The entrance fees were low: only 6 old ores for the Porters and 6 schillings for the Beer Carters guild.[41] Yet the members were not allowed to concurrently hold membership of any other guild, and they had to possess burgher rights before admission.[42] In other medieval cities, wage-workers, merchants' helpers (also transport workers), servants, and self-employed women belonged to the group of *nichtzünftige*, who could not be part of artisan associations.[43] In Riga the Beer Carters and Porters guilds offered exclusive opportunities for these people.

In both brotherhoods a considerable number of members were male and female non-German artisans and servants.[44] Not all members recorded in the lists have their occupations noted, but the largest named occupations in the guilds' lists are female maidservants, weavers, and hemp spinners, leaving male artisans in a minority.[45]

Women played an important role in both brotherhoods. Between 1462 and 1479, 466 women were registered as members of the Beer Carters guild.[46] A high percentage of women in the guild is evident in the records of all of the guild's members for the early sixteenth century. In 1507 more than a half of the altogether 222 individuals, who had paid their members' fees, were female.[47] The number of the Beer Carters guild's female members was even higher than recorded in the member lists because in 1495 the Cistercian nuns of the local convent joined the guild, and their prioress paid annual membership fees on

---

40 The Porters bought their house in 1466, but the Beer Carters guild rented a hall between 1441 and 1474 for annual drinking feasts from the Black Heads. Arbusow, 'Kirchliches leben', p. 210; *Die Erbebücher der Stadt Riga, 1384–1579*, ed. by Jakob Gottlieb Leonhard Napiersky (Riga: Kymmel, 1888), no. 45; Marburg, DSHI 120, no. 5, fols. 22, 25, 41, 44, 62, 66, 70, 72, 81, 85, 91, 104, 113, 123, 126, 131, 136, 140, 141.

41 *Schragen der Gilden und Aemter*, no. 77, § 1, no. 12, § 3.

42 *Schragen der Gilden und Aemter*, no. 12, § 12, no. 77, § 27, 28.

43 Erich Maschke, 'Die Unterschichten der mittelalterlichen Städte Deutschlands', in *Gesellschaftliche Unterschichten in den südwestdeutschen Städten*, ed. by Erich Maschke and Jürgen Sydow (Stuttgart: Kohlhammer, 1967), pp. 1–74, p. 1.

44 Arbusow, 'Studien zur Geschichte der lettischen Bevölkerung Rigas', p. 85; Gustavs Strenga, 'Donations, Discipline and Commemoration', pp. 108–09.

45 Between 1462 and 1523, seventy-seven maids can be identified in the Beer Carters guild and thirty-nine in the Porters guild for the time period 1453–1519. Rīga, LVVA, 4038 f., 2 apr., 1089 l., fols. 46^a–48^b; Rīga, LVVA, 4038 f., 2 apr., 1159 l., fols. 1^a–37^a; Rīga, LVVA, 4038 f., 2 apr., 1087 l. fols. 24^b–87^b; Rīga, LVVA, 4038 f., 2 apr., 1089 l. fols. 46^a, 46^b, 47^b, 48^a, 48^b, 55^b; Rīga, LVVA, 4038 f., 2 apr., 1159 l., fols. 11^b, 16^a, 18^a, 20^b, 31^b, 35^b; Rīga, LVVA, 4038 f., 2 apr., 1087 l., fol. 49^b.

46 Rīga, LVVA, 4038 f., 2 apr., 1089 l., fols. 46^a–48^a.

47 Rīga, LVVA, 4038 f., 2 apr., 1159 l., fols. 9^a–11^b.

their behalf.⁴⁸ It seems that in the Porters guild, the tendency to have many female members was shared, though no full member lists have survived.⁴⁹ The large number of female members definitely did not contribute to the guilds' status and economic power; in fact, it even weakened it.

The majority of non–elite members in the guilds of Beer Carters and Porters as wage–workers were 'working poor'.⁵⁰ According to Bronisław Geremek, 'material instability was a permanent and inevitable feature of the lives' of medieval wage–workers.⁵¹ Seasonal change, weather conditions, and economic and political factors in the city and region directly affected the wellbeing of beer carters, porters, servants, and maids in Riga; their numbers fluctuated depending on the navigation season, navigation conditions, and with the number of merchant fleets arriving in the harbour.⁵² Medieval wage–earners spent most of their income on food, and were always at risk of falling into mendicancy to avoid starvation.⁵³ In Riga, transport workers' wages depended on services offered and were not high.⁵⁴

Medieval poverty cannot be described solely as a material experience. In fact, 'in medieval society, anyone – independent of gender, actual social status or original wealth – could, in specific situations, have been defined or have wanted to be characterised and recognised as being poor.'⁵⁵ Poverty has to be seen as a complex phenomenon, which depending on context involved lack of food, property, political power, social status, physical strength, and also lack of protective social networks, knowledge, and judicial rights.⁵⁶ This definition of poverty helps to distinguish between individuals who experienced temporary material need but had social status and protection and those who were exposed to the permanent threat of poverty. The non–Germans in both brotherhoods belonged to latter category.

Although most of the non–elite guild members were 'working poor' not all members were such. Katharina Simon–Muscheid's analysis of late medieval artisan guilds in Basel shows that there were guilds that had higher numbers

---

48 Constantin Mettig, 'Bücher der Rigaschen Bierträgergilde', in *Sitzungsberichten der Gesellschaft für Geschichte und Alterthumskunde der Ostseeprovinzen Russlands für das Jahr 1890* (Riga: W. F. Häcker, 1891), pp. 120–25, at p. 123; Rīga, LVVA, 4038 f., 2 apr., 1089 l., fols. 14^b–17^a; 20^b; 29^a–29^b, 52^a–53^a.

49 In 1512, of twenty–seven new members accepted in the Porters guild, twelve were women. Rīga, LVVA, 4038 f., 2 apr., 1087 l., fols. 53^a–53^b; Arbusow, 'Studien zur Geschichte der lettischen Bevölkerung Rigas', p. 88.

50 On poor servants, maids, and workers as 'working poor', see Groebner, 'Mobile Werte', p. 171.

51 Geremek, *Poverty*, p. 67.

52 Arbusow, 'Studien zur Geschichte der lettischen Bevölkerung Rigas', pp. 88–89.

53 Schubert, 'Hausarme Leute', p. 287; Geremek, *Poverty*, p. 60.

54 *Schragen der Gilden und Aemter*, No. 77, § 30; *Kämmerei-Register 1405–1474*, pp. 272, 316, 137.

55 Gerhard Jaritz, 'Poverty Constructions and Material Culture', in *The Sign Languages of Poverty: International Round Table–Discussion, Krems an Der Donau, October 10 and 11, 2005*, ed. by Gerhard Jaritz (Wien: Verlag der Österreichischen Akademie der Wissenschaften, 2007), pp. 7–18, p. 9.

56 Katharina Simon–Muscheid, 'Sozialer Abstieg im Mittelalter', in *The Sign Languages of Poverty*, pp. 95–117, at p. 96; Oexle, 'Armut und Armenfürsorge', p. 82; Miri Rubin, *Charity and Community in Medieval Cambridge* (Cambridge: Cambridge University Press, 1987), pp. 7–8.

of 'poor', and that even the poorest guilds had a small minority of members who were better off.[57] Also in Riga both brotherhoods had such a minority, who were better off than others and even owned houses and gardens in the city despite the restrictions on non–Germans owning real properties within the town walls.[58] Peter Lybete was an official of the Porters guild and owned a house in the city in 1473.[59] Lybete's colleague, Michael van der Nygemolen, owned a house in the city around 1464;[60] when in 1458 the guild's chantry was created, he donated a silver chalice and paten for its altar.[61] He also supported the guild when it experienced a monetary shortage by lending it 10 marks.[62] Claus Lachermunt, a non–German beer carter, together with his German wife Ilsebe, owned a garden; however, they had to endow it because as the record claimed, the non–Germans had no right to own real properties.[63]

The guilds of Beer Carters and Porters were not the most prestigious urban associations, but during the mid–fifteenth century their status evolved. These groups at the time experienced a 'new beginning' by gaining a greater social prestige and more prominent spaces for their religious activities.[64] After the mid–fifteenth century, these groups were reminiscent of confraternities that emphasised 'typically confraternal elements': memorial activities, the cult of a patron saint, and the welcoming of members of different occupations.[65] According to their statutes, members the Beer Carters guild were exposed to stigmatising obligations, but they freed themselves from these during the fifteenth century. The concluding paragraph of the guild's statutes of 1466 stated that none of its present or future members would ever act as city executioner.[66] This can be interpreted as a rejection of duties the Beer Carters fulfilled for some time before 1466, which were forced on them by the city government. There is no doubt that acting as executioners stigmatized the group, lowering its status. In medieval society sanguinary professions, especially the ones of the butcher, executioner, and soldier, were considered in some places to be illicit.[67]

---

57 Katharina Simon-Muscheid, *Basler Handwerkzünfte im Spätmittelalter: zunftinterne Strukturen und innerstädtische Konflikte* (Bern: Lang, 1988), pp. 141–42, 161, 230, 232.
58 Šterns, *Latvijas Vēsture. 1290–1500*, p. 270; Arbusow, 'Studien zur Geschichte der lettischen Bevölkerung Rīgas', pp. 80–81.
59 Arbusow, 'Kirchliches Leben', p. 204; *Erbebücher* I, no. 1040.
60 Arbusow, 'Kirchliches Leben', p. 209.
61 Arbusow, 'Kirchliches Leben', p. 205.
62 Arbusow, 'Kirchliches Leben', p. 219.
63 Rīga, LVVA, 4038 f., 2 apr., 864 l. fol. 24ᵇ–25ᵃ; *Erbebücher* I, § 998; Arbusow, 'Studien zur Geschichte der lettischen Bevölkerung Rīgas', p. 81; Rīga, LVVA, 4038 f., 2 apr., 1089 l. fol. 46ᵃ; Strenga, 'Turning Transport Workers into Latvians?', p. 67.
64 Strenga, 'Turning Transport Workers into Latvians?', pp. 68–69.
65 Paul Trio, 'Confraternities as Such, and as a Template for Guilds in the Low Countries during the Medieval and the Early Modern Period', in *A Companion to Medieval and Early Modern Confraternities*, ed. by Konrad Eisenbichler (Leiden: Brill, 2019), pp. 23–44.
66 *Schragen der Gilden und Aemter*, no. 12, § 17.
67 Jacques Le Goff, 'Licit and Illicit Trades in the Medieval West', in *Time, Work, and Culture in the Middle Ages*, ed. by Jacques Le Goff, trans. by Arthur Godlhammer (Chicago: University of Chicago Press, 1980), pp. 58–70, p. 59.

Riga's Beer Carters were aware of the ignobleness of the executioner's office, describing it as a 'shaming and dirtying job', and wished to be freed of it.[68]

The change in its status is also manifested in the brotherhood's desire to prevent immoral individuals, for example, 'openly loose women', from joining the group or to invite weavers, blood-letters, and public bath custodians as guests of the guild.[69] The simultaneous attempts made during the mid-fifteenth century to restrict people considered to be morally corrupt from entering the group may show that both brotherhoods were dissatisfied with their status and wanted to improve it. This took place exactly at the time when both brotherhoods were intensifying their religious life and were investing in memoria.

The 'poor' were important agents of *memoria* since their prayers had remarkable value. Through distribution of alms, they became involved in commemoration of institutions and individuals.[70] The brotherhoods of the Beer Carters and Porters were associations in which most of the members can be considered to have been 'poor', both because of their economic vulnerability, and of their social marginalisation too. These groups were professional brotherhoods, but they were open to all townspeople, with the exception of a few illicit occupations. This allowed them to become groups that united not only professional porters and beer carters but also most of Riga's non-German artisans, maids, and servants. These were groups that enabled the city government to control the non-elites by gathering them in these brotherhoods. These groups were used by the urban government for the fulfilment of shameful tasks before the mid-fifteenth century, but after 1450, when both groups intensified their religious activities, their status changed.

Commemoration within the Non-elites in Late Medieval Riga

Memoria was equally important to the elite and non-elite guilds because it formed and sustained their identities.[71] Yet in the case of Riga's non-elite guilds *memoria* was even more crucial for their existence because it was one of the main ways of bringing together individuals of various backgrounds: transport workers, male and female artisans, servants, and even elite members.

---

68 *Schragen der Gilden und Aemter*, no. 12, § 17.
69 *Schragen der Gilden und Aemter*, no. 12, § 11, no. 77, § 23; on the status of weavers, blood letters, and public bath custodians, see Bronisław Geremek, 'The Marginal Man', in *Medieval Callings*, ed. by Jacques Le Goff, trans. by Lydia G. Cochrane (Chicago: University of Chicago Press, 1990), pp. 346–73; linen weavers also had a low social status in the northern German cities and in the Livonian cities as well, see Glenn M. Bülow, 'Leineweber(innen). Handwerker zwischen Zunftausschluß, Verketzerung und Armutsspott', in *Randgruppen der spätmittelalterlichen Gesellschaft: ein Hand- und Studienbuch*, ed. by Bernd-Ulrich Hergemöller (Warendorf: Fahlbusch, 2001), pp. 198–218; Selart, 'Non-German Literacy in Medieval Livonia', p. 44.
70 Geremek, *Poverty*, p. 37; Wollasch, 'Toten- und Armensorge', pp. 9–38.
71 Oexle, 'Liturgische Memoria', p. 332; Oexle, 'Mittelalterlichen Gilden', p. 214.

Memoria was both a reason for joining these guilds and also a guarantee for their existence and successful development. *Memoria* also helped to sustain groups' identities in circumstances when the number of members constantly fluctuated.

The statutes of Riga's non-elite guilds treat commemoration as an important activity. The Porters statutes (1450) emphasized the commemoration of all deceased guild members during the annual drinking feast on All Saints.[72] The statutes of the Dockers guild (1463) declared that all deceased brothers and sisters of the guild should be commemorated annually with masses, vigils, and almsgiving during the drinking feast on Pentecost, and that the priests of St Peter's church should be paid 6 ores and sent one jug of beer on that occasion.[73] The statutes of the Dockers, Porters, and Beer Carters guilds focused more on regulating the funerals of deceased members than on events that followed funerals, such as regular memorial masses and vigils.

The funeral, memorial mass, vigils, and almsgiving marked the beginning of *memoria*, and the guilds guaranteed that every member would be buried with respect. The alderman of the Porters guild was instructed to pay for the burial of those too poor to afford a proper funeral and to provide it with bell ringing.[74] This guild also assured all members that it would take care of a member's body if he or she was murdered or drowned within a mile radius of Riga.[75] Medieval guilds also guaranteed a large body of mourners at funerals, which was considered to benefit the souls of the dead.[76] They aimed to have all members present at every commemorational event, although frequently guilds and confraternities failed to gather large crowds.[77] Medieval guilds in general, and Riga's transporters' brotherhoods in particular, ensured attendance of the funerals by imposing fines for absence during any part of the funeral.[78] As the fine book of the Porters guild shows, although guilds were committed to gathering a large number of members at burials, in numerous cases they failed to do so.[79]

---

72 *Schragen der Gilden und Aemter*, no. 77, § 2, p. 414.
73 *Schragen der Gilden und Aemter*, no. 74, § 2, 32, p. 407, 411.
74 *Schragen der Gilden und Aemter*, § 18, p. 416.
75 *Schragen der Gilden und Aemter*, § 17.
76 Paul Trio, 'The Social Positioning of Late Medieval Confraternities in Urbanized Flanders: From Integration to Segregation', in *Mittelalterliche Bruderschaften in Europäischen Städten : Funktionen, Formen, Akteure = Medieval Confraternities in European Towns: Functions, Forms, Protagonists*, ed. by Monika Escher-Apsner (Frankfurt am Main: Peter Lang, 2009), pp. 99–110, p. 101.
77 Katharina Simon-Muscheid, 'Zunft-Trinkstuben und Bruderschaften. "Soziale Orte" und Beziegungsnetz im spätmittelalterlichen Basel', in *Geschlechtergesellschaften, Zunft-Trinkstuben und Bruderschaften in spätmittelalterlichen und frühneuzeitlichen Städten*, ed. by Gerhard Fouquet, Matthias Steinbrink, and Gabriel Zeilinger (Stuttgart: Thorbecke, 2003), pp. 147–62, p. 158; John Henderson, 'Religious Confraternities and Death in Early Renaissance Florence', in *Florence and Italy: Renaissance Studies in Honour of Nicolai Rubinstein*, ed. by Peter Denley and Caroline Elam (London: Westfield College, University of London, Committee for Medieval Studies, 1988), pp. 383–94, p. 384.
78 *Schragen der Gilden und Aemter*, no. 12, § 14, no. 74, § 24, no. 77, § 17.
79 Arbusow, 'Kirchliches Leben', pp. 221–24.

The statutes of Riga's non–elite guilds also described the funeral procession as the body of the deceased was carried from church to grave.[80] The Dockers guild specified elements of the funeral granted to every member: two priests, one schoolboy, and a sacristan led the procession with funeral songs and ringing bells.[81] The ringing of small bells during the funeral was part of the Porters guild's funeral procession too.[82] In addition to bell ringing, the Porters guild provided a pall and lights for the procession.[83] In the case of the Porters, deceased members were most likely buried in the cemetery of St Peter's church, where the guild's altar was located, and the results of recent archeological excavations in the location of that cemetery support such an assumption. Among the late medieval human skeletal remains excavated there, many have bone defects caused by lifting heavy objects.[84]

Funerals required the purchase of torches for the procession, the engagement of the services of priests, gravediggers, and more. Non–elite guilds used donations and fines in wax to cover these expenses. Every member of the Dockers and Porters guilds who failed to attend a funeral, memorial mass, or vigil, had to pay a fine ranging from one to five pounds of wax.[85] Other wrongdoings, such as spilling a beer or sleeping during the drinking feast, were punished by a fine in wax, and the fine book of the Porters guild for the years 1450–1459 shows that such infractions were common.[86] The wax acquired in this way was most likely used to supply lights for the church altar and torches for the procession.

Memoria began with the funeral, and was followed by other memorial rituals, both liturgical and non–liturgical. Guilds were expected to deliver 'perpetual remembrance' (*ewige dechtnisse*) for all of their members.[87] This was particularly important in the non–elite guilds, as the majority of their members could not afford large private investments in remembrance. To achieve long-term liturgical commemoration, guilds created their own altars: the Porters established their altar in 1458 in St Peter's, and the Beer Carters had one altar in St Jacob's and from 1473 another in St Peter's.[88]

The altar of the chantry was the centre of a group's religious life and commemorative activities. There is some information on the liturgical

---

80 *Schragen der Gilden und Aemter*, no. 77, § 17; no. 74, § 31.
81 *Schragen der Gilden und Aemter*, no. 74, § 31, p. 410.
82 *Schragen der Gilden und Aemter*, no. 77, § 18, p. 418.
83 *Schragen der Gilden und Aemter*, § 17.
84 Guntis Gerhards, 'Traumas un ievainojumi Rīgas 13.–18. gadsimta iedzīvotājiem', in *Senā Rīga: pētījumi pilsētas arheoloģijā un vēsturē*, vol. 7, ed. by Ieva Ose (Rīga: Latvijas vēstures institūta apgāds, 2012), 128–48; Strenga, 'Turning Transport Workers into Latvians?', p. 70.
85 *Schragen der Gilden und Aemter*, no. 77, § 18, no. 74, § 24.
86 Rīga, LVVA, 4038 f., 2 apr., 1087 l. fols. 1ᵃ–23ᵇ.
87 In the late Middle Ages, a funeral of an individual was usually followed by anniversaries on the third, seventh, and thirtieth day after death and also a one after a year. Babendererde, *Sterben*, p. 148; Arbusow, 'Kirchliches Leben', p. 207.
88 Arbusow, 'Kirchliches Leben', p. 204, Arbusow, 'Studien zur Geschichte der lettischen Bevölkerung Rigas', p. 83; Rīga, LVVA, 4038 f., 2 apr., 1089 l., fol. 75ᵃ.

commemoration of the Porters guild in its altar account book.[89] We know little about the commemoration performed after funerals for the time period before the foundation of a chantry in 1458.[90] It remains unknown whether the Porters guild between 1450 and 1459 had memorial practices other than the funerals of their members. In the fine book (1450–1459), only absences from funeral ceremonies are recorded, but other commemorational events are not mentioned.[91] The guild had its own dead that would have needed long-term remembrance; between 1450 and 1459, the guild organized funerals for at least eleven guild members.[92] During that time the Porters guild apparently had neither the infrastructure – an altar – nor the resources – a chantry – for long-term *memoria*. The fine book shows that, despite the lack of resources for institutionalized long-term commemorational practices, the guild still managed to organise the remembrance of its members.

While the Porters' chantry was founded around 1458, the first regular commemorative masses for the guild were celebrated in 1460, when a chaplain of the guild's altar in St Peter's church received his annual wage, 12 Riga marks.[93] Until the Reformation the guild continued to employ a single chantry priest charged with celebrating four memorial masses a week.[94] This was not a busy schedule by the standards of the chantries of the more prestigious guilds in late medieval Riga. The brotherhood of the Black Heads, which also had a chantry in St Peter's, employed five priests for the same duties during the 1480s.[95] The Black Heads brotherhood paid every priest 20 marks a year, compared to the 12 marks received by Porters guild's chaplain.

Even with its sole priest, the Porters chantry did not lack impressiveness. In 1460 the chantry paid 4 Riga marks to a schoolmaster (*scholemester*) to be present at the masses all year round together with singing schoolboys (*scholeren*).[96] 10 ferdings were paid to an organist and one mark for the person who operated the bellows.[97] In addition, two sacristans were appointed for the altar.[98] A continuous flow of donations, liturgical books, chalices, and other objects, supported the services during the 1460s and 1470s.[99]

Regular memorial masses celebrated at the guild's altar and financed by the chantry were important because they constituted the guild as a community. Yet it was not the only the way to commemorate the deceased. The records of

---

89 The text of this account book has been edited and published by Leonid Arbusow, see his 'Kirchliches Leben', pp. 204–21.
90 Arbusow, 'Kirchliches Leben', p. 204.
91 Riga, LVVA, 4038 f., 2 apr., 1087 l. fols. 1^a–23^b.
92 Riga, LVVA, 4038 f., 2 apr., 1087 l. fols. 1^b–21^b.
93 Arbusow, 'Kirchliches Leben', p. 202.
94 LUB 12, no. 288.
95 Marburg, DSHI 120 no. 8, fol. 43.
96 Arbusow, 'Kirchliches Leben', p. 202, 205.
97 Arbusow, 'Kirchliches Leben', p. 202.
98 Arbusow, 'Kirchliches Leben', p. 202.
99 Strenga, 'Donations, Discipline and Commemoration', pp. 114–21.

the Porters guild show payments for individual priests and Franciscan friars. In 1452, six years before the creation of the chantry, the porters donated to the Franciscan friars 8 shillings and one jug of beer for *memoria* of their deceased brothers and sisters; the Franciscan friars had to commemorate (*bedenken*) the guild's deceased from the pulpit of St Catherine's church.[100] Even in 1460, when the chantry was up and running, similar records appear in the account book, requesting the Franciscan friars to commemorate the guild members. The naming of the dead during prayers did not have such a representative meaning as the memorial mass had, but it required fewer resources. Yet the Porters guild – for unknown reasons – decided to cease this memorial cooperation with the Franciscans; the record of 1460 was crossed out, and henceforward they were never mentioned again.[101] Possibly the disruption of this practice was influenced by the creation of the guild's own chantry.

The Porters guild also involved individual priests in its *memoria*. The parish priest of St Peter's church received an annual salary during the annual drinking feast, as well as donations; before 1460 this amounted to 8 or 9 ferdings, and a jug of beer for commemorating 'the deceased brothers and sisters all year around'.[102] The guild did not specify how the priest was to commemorate its members. Since his salary was nine times that of the Franciscans,[103] his duties were probably more extensive than just individual prayers. The relationship could become quite close between parish priest and the guild; the St Peter's parish priest and cathedral canon Hinrik Netelhorst (†1479) donated a corporal to the guild's chantry, sometime between 1459 and 1475, and his mother Bele donated a white surplice.[104]

A record in the Porters' chantry account book reveals the rhythm of remembrance during the annual drinking feasts. The Porters guild stated in 1461 that every year during the main drinking feast of All Saints and the one of *Corpus Christi* (Thursday after Trinity Sunday), all guild members would gather to remember deceased guild members (*beghan unse vorstorven brodere und sustere*).[105] In fact the brotherhood was named after *Corpus Christi*, and the cult, popular in medieval Europe, played an important role in its religious activities, yet little is known about what the group did during the feast, in constrast to *Corpus Christi* confraternities, for example in Lübeck.[106] On the

---

100 Rīga, LVVA, 4038 f., 2 apr., 1087 l., fol. 0.
101 Arbusow, 'Kirchliches Leben', p. 202.
102 Arbusow, 'Kirchliches Leben', p. 202.
103 The Franciscans received 8 schillings, a sum 9 times smaller than the 8 ferdings or 72 schillings received by the parish priest.
104 Arbusow, 'Kirchliches Leben', p. 206; Bruninigk, *Messe*, p. 204; *Livlands Geistlichkeit*, p. 148.
105 Arbusow, 'Kirchliches Leben', p. 207.
106 Strenga, 'Turning Transport Workers into Latvians?', pp. 69–70; on *Corpus Christi* cult see, Rubin, *Corpus Christi*; on *Corpus Christi* guilds in Lübeck, see Carsten Jahnke, 'The Corpus Christi Guild in Lübeck', in *Guilds, Towns, and Cultural Transmission in the North, 1300–1500*, ed. by Lars Bisgaard, Lars Boje Mortensen, and Tom Pettitt (Odense: University Press of Southern Denmark, 2013), pp. 203–28; Carsten Jahnke, 'Lübeck's Confraternities', in *A Companion to Medieval Lübeck*, ed. by Carsten Jahnke

Corpus Christi feast, a vigil had to be celebrated on Wednesday evening and the mass for 'the eternal remembrance of our guild' (*tor ewiger dechnisse unser ghilde*) on Thursday morning.[107] The Beer Carters guild also had two *drunke*, one at Pentecost and the other one during the feast of Our Lady – probably the Assumption of the Virgin – at which communal meals were celebrated.[108]

In the case of Riga's Beer Carters and Porters guilds, it is easier to discover and analyse the donations made by members of the elite. The contribution of non–elite members to *memoria* is not so obvious. Individuals from the non–elites also wished to be commemorated individually, and they managed to create individual remembrance despite their relative lack of resources and status. In Riga, despite the exclusion of non–Germans from lucrative crafts and possession of real property, we have seen that some members had substantial property.[109] They were usually the leaders of their guilds, like Peter Lybete and Michael van der Nygemolen of the Porters guild.[110] They made larger donations than other members. In the 1450s and 1460s, leaders of the Porters guild were the most active donors, making larger donations than other members did, and most likely, trying to lead by example and mobilise others to follow their lead.[111]

In 1464, Michael van der Nygemolen, a deputy of the Porters guild's alderman, and his wife Ilsebe bestowed income from a house upon St Peter's church and the Porters *Corpus Christi* altar, the guild's chantry.[112] The rent from the house was to be divided after their death between the parish and the chantry. Since non–Germans possibly were denied the right to own real property, some non–Germans turned properties into endowments for local churches in order to maintain control of them in their lifetime.[113] By this arrangement the van der Nygemolens may have been avoiding the prohibition, as other non–Germans did. However, this does not mean that there were no spiritual reasons behind such bequests. By bestowing his house on the parish and the guild's altar, he became a benefactor of both institutions with the expectation of remembrance in masses at the guild's altar and in St Peter's church.[114]

The van der Nygemolens made another large donation of a clear memorial character. They gave money for the production of a pall used to cover the body

---

(Leiden: Brill, 2019), pp. 372–97, p. 374; Carsten Jahnke, *Gott gebe, dass wir alle selig werden mögen: die Mitgliederverzeichnisse der Heilig–Leichnams–, St. Antonius– und St. Leonhards–Bruderschaft zur Burg in Lübeck sowie das Bruderschaftsbuch der Heilig Leichnams– und St. Mauritiusbruderschaft der Weydelude zu St. Katharinen* (Göttingen: V&R unipress, 2022), p. 387.

107 Arbusow, 'Kirchliches Leben', p. 207.
108 Rīga, LVVA, 4038 f., 2 apr., 1089 l., fol. 75^b.
109 *Erbebücher* I, no. 1040; Rīga, LVVA, 4038 f., 2 apr., 864 l. fol. 24^b.
110 Arbusow, 'Kirchliches Leben', p. 204.
111 Strenga, 'Donations, Discipline and Commemoration', pp. 116–17.
112 Arbusow, 'Kirchliches Leben', p. 209; Strenga, 'Donations, Discipline and Commemoration', p. 117.
113 Arbusow, 'Studien zur Geschichte der lettischen Bevölkerung Rigas', p. 81.
114 Arbusow, 'Kirchliches Leben', p. 202; Strenga, 'Turning Transport Workers into Latvians?', pp. 64–65.

of the deceased during funeral processions.[115] This was a substantial donation, worth 22 marks in value and an important object; according to the statutes, it was used at every burial.[116] By commissioning a pall, both donors guaranteed their presence in all memorial activities of the guild.

Identifying the intentions behind such commemorative donations is always challenging.[117] The account books of the Beer Carters and Porters have lists of donations made by members for the guilds, their chantries, and altars, yet in most cases the intentions and requests of the donors are not mentioned.[118] This does not mean that these non-specific donations were not memorial ones. For example, in the Porters guild in the 1470s and 1480s, numerous members made donations for *Corpus Christi*, yet this does not mean that *memoria* was completely ignored.[119] Moreover, the memorial donations cannot simply be defined by the use of the donated object; the donations could have had a memorial purpose even if it was not explicitly manifested.

The account book of the Beer Carters guild contains the names of brothers and sisters who donated objects 'for the commemoration' (*to ener dechtnisse*).[120] Between 1460 and 1515, a total of 154 guild members donated tableware: tablecloths, towels, jugs, plates, and tin glasses.[121] Donations also included portions of wax for illumination as well as small sums of money for the guild's chantry. Donations of money were rare and were mostly made by male members of the guild. Over fifty years, only thirteen of more than 150 donors donated a sum amounting to 39 Riga marks.[122] Many gifts were produced by the donors themselves.[123] For example, towels were frequent donations made by female weavers and hemp spinners. Other objects were made by the artisan guild members, e.g. the metal-caster Laurens donated a tin glass and the glazier Claus, a jug.[124]

The most active period of memorial donation in the Beer Carters guild was 1460–1465,[125] with fewer donations between 1470 and 1480, even fewer in the 1490s, and only five in the early sixteenth century.[126] Donations for the Porters chantry were collected by the guild's officials, who went 'from house to house' (*van husen to husen*) to collect them.[127] During such campaigns, glasses, jugs,

---

115 Arbusow, 'Kirchliches Leben', p. 209.
116 *Schragen der Gilden und Aemter*, No. 77, § 17.
117 Truus van Bueren, 'Care for the Here and the Hereafter. A Multitude of Possibilities', in *Care for the Here and the Hereafter*, pp. 13–34, p. 16.
118 Rīga, LVVA, 4038 f., 2 apr., 1089 l., fols. 55ᵃ–58ᵇ; Arbusow, 'Kirchliches Leben', pp. 202–21.
119 Arbusow, 'Kirchliches Leben', pp. 212–13.
120 LUB 7 no. 362, p. 266.
121 Strenga, 'Donations, Discipline and Commemoration', pp. 122–26.
122 Rīga, LVVA, 4038 f., 2 apr., 1089 l., fols. 55ᵃ–58ᵇ.
123 Arbusow, 'Studien zur Geschichte der lettischen Bevölkerung Rigas', p. 85.
124 Rīga, LVVA, 4038 f., 2 apr., 1089 l., fols. 58ᵃ, 55ᵃ.
125 Rīga, LVVA, 4038 f., 2 apr., 1089 l., fols. 55ᵃ–57ᵃ; Strenga, 'Donations, Discipline and Commemoration', p. 122.
126 Rīga, LVVA, 4038 f., 2 apr., 1089 l., fol. 58ᵇ.
127 Arbusow, 'Kirchliches Leben', p. 204.

pots, and tablecloths as well as wax and rings were collected.[128] Such gathering of donations had a sporadic character, and it took place when initiated by the guild officials.

Donations for the Porters' chantry dropped considerably during the late fifteenth and early sixteenth centuries.[129] We may ask whether this decrease in donations to both guilds had something to do with the way they were collected. Indriķis Šterns suggests that the personality of an alderman affected the guild's fortunes; more was collected under an energetic alderman.[130] But with a decrease in donations in both guilds, we should seek a more general explanation. More donations were always offered straight after the foundation of the chantry, when the collective *memoria* was just established, because it needed to be fostered in order to secure it. Later, annual rent income sustained the chantries, so they no longer needed continuous donations. This development does not mean that *memoria* lost its role in the life of the guilds, simply that the sources for its sustaining changed.

Individual donations recorded in the Beer Carters account book show the involvement of guild members in commemoration. Even small donations were the result of individual choices. The Beer Carters list states that these donations were made 'for remembrance', but the individual records rarely record the intention of the remembrance. Merten Bodeker and his wife Margrete (1500) were the only donors who specified that their gift of a pot was towards their own commemoration (*to enyger dechtnysse*). The modest formula, *to ener dechtnisse*, used by the Beer Carters scribe at the beginning of the list, does not specify the form of commemoration.[131]

The Porters also donated objects and small sums of money for individual commemoration or remembrance of others individuals; some even specified how such *memoria* was to be carried out. Only five donations between 1464 and 1523 explicitly recorded donors' expectations. In 1499 Hans Bysschop donated a black cloak once owned by a certain Albrecht for the commemoration of the latter's soul (*siner armen sele, Gade to love unde to eren*).[132] Hans Tydevogel donated in 1461–1464 15 Riga marks for commemoration and an additional two for the memorial masses and vigils.[133] Peter Ghowre and his wife donated 15 marks for the chantry.[134] Hans Swen gave 5 marks for the remembrance of Hans Lybet, and Jacob Maten's wife donated 6 ½ pounds of wax for use in commemoration.[135]

---

128 Arbusow, 'Kirchliches Leben', p. 216.
129 Arbusow, 'Kirchliches Leben', pp. 214–15.
130 Šterns, *Latvijas Vēsture. 1290–1500*, p. 282.
131 Rīga, LVVA, 4038 f., 2 apr., 1089 l., fols. 58^b, 55^a.
132 Arbusow, 'Kirchliches Leben', p. 215.
133 Arbusow, 'Kirchliches Leben', pp. 208–09.
134 Arbusow, 'Kirchliches Leben', p. 208.
135 Arbusow, 'Kirchliches Leben', p. 208, 209.

Although the majority of the objects donated were for habitual use, objects could be donated with a memorial intention even if they were later used for profane purposes.[136] Precious objects donated to the guilds could, of course, be sold. The altar keeper of Reval's Black Heads brotherhood in 1485 sold for four Riga marks a *paternoster* bead and invested the proceeds into the altar of the brotherhood.[137] In the case of the two non–elite guilds in Riga, tablecloths, towels, glasses, and other dishes of the guild given 'for remembrance' were in fact used at the communal meals.[138] The Porters guild's inventory shows that the guild owned tablecloths, towels, tin glasses, wooden and tin jugs, candlesticks, and other dishes. In 1465 the Porters had twenty–seven pieces of tablecloths and towels, fifty–three glasses, three tin jugs, four brass pots, two candle sticks, three wooden jugs, one tub, and numerous other dishes.[139] Although the donations of dishes and tablecloths continued, such objects were often lost, broken, or worn. Thus, in 1514 the guild owned as many objects as in 1465: fifty–four big and small glasses, seven tablecloths, fourteen towels, seven pillows, a frying pan, and several pots of different sizes.[140] Inventories were kept by the Carter guild until the Reformation.[141]

Objects donated by the guild members did not serve as a resource for the liturgical remembrance but were used for the non–liturgical commemoration. Similarly as liturgical objects – chalices, altarpieces, and monstrances – represented donors, profane objects also commemorated benefactors by their existence and usage, manifesting the donors' presence in the group after the death. As during a mass, the dead were made present by the invocation of their names, during communal meals the deceased members of the group were also present through the objects donated.[142]

The non–elite guilds in Riga are unique in offering detailed information on the *memoria* of groups whose social lives are usually little known. The commemoration offered by the Beer Carters and Porters guilds did not differ from that of other guilds, but they had less internal resources than other associations. The guilds of the Beer Carters and Porters provided burial and commemoration to their members; the Porters guild, even with its limited resources, had succeeded in establishing an association with the Franciscans

---

136 Gerhard Jaritz, 'Seelgerätstiftungen als Indikator der Entwicklung materieller Kultur im Mittelalter', in *Materielle Kultur und religiöse Stiftung im Spätmittelalter: Internationales Round–Table–Gespräch, Krems an der Donau, 26. September 1988*, ed. by Gerhard Jaritz (Wien: Verlag der Österreichischen Akademie der Wissenschaften, 1997), pp. 13–36, p. 16; Gerhard Jaritz, 'Seelenheil und Sachkultur. Gedanken zur Beziehung Mensch–Objekt im späten Mittelalter', in *Europäische Sachkultur des Mittelalters*, ed. by Manfred Mayrhofer (Wien: Verlag der Österreichische Akademie der Wissenschaften, 1980), pp. 57–82, p. 71; Richard, 'Fromme Klauseln', p. 78.
137 StAH Coll. 612–2/6, no. E 1, fol. 118.
138 Strenga, 'Donations, Discipline and Commemoration', p. 115.
139 Arbusow, 'Kirchliches Leben', p. 219.
140 Arbusow, 'Kirchliches Leben', p. 216.
141 Arbusow, 'Kirchliches Leben', pp. 219–21, 218.
142 Oexle, 'Gegenwart der Toten', p. 31.

and the parish priest of St Peter's church in its practices of the commemoration before they established their chantry in 1458.

Although in both guilds, the majority of members lacked the resources for large commemorative donations, they still created remembrance. For the guild members of the Beer Carters and Porters guilds, objects were the media through which they expressed their commemorative choices. Donated objects, primarily dishes or cloths, were not used for the liturgical remembrance, but for the non-liturgical commemoration during guilds' communal meals. These donations show that even those who possessed little resources were ready to invest in their individual and collective commemoration.

Practices of Commemoration: The Fine Book of the Porters Guild (1450–1459)

Such normative documents as guild statutes reflect expectations as to how the group's piety or remembrance should be practiced but fail to reflect the complex reality.[143] The book of fines and members of the Porters guild is a useful source when attempting to assess the relationship between the rule and the practice in the life of such groups.[144] It contains the names of newly accepted brothers and sisters and lists transgressions against guild statutes for the period 1450–1459. Many offences took place during the annual drinking feasts: members were most commonly fined for disobedience and ignorance of officials' orders, spilling beer, failing to pay fees, sleeping in the guildhall, wife-beating, vomiting and urinating on the floor of the guildhall.[145] Moreover, the fine book contains records of cases in which guild members failed to attend funerals, vigils, and other memorial ceremonies and were subsequently fined.[146]

The memorial masses and vigils were important elements of the guild life that demanded members' presence and their donations.[147] From the late-fourteenth century, guilds in northern Europe usually codified three memorial rituals – funerals, memorial masses, and vigils – in their statutes as events all guild members were obliged to attend.[148] In Riga the Porters' statutes of 1450 ordained that guild members must attend funerals or pay five pounds of wax and pay one pound of wax for missing a vigil or mass.[149] The guild's fine book

---

143 Strenga, 'Donations, Discipline and Commemoration', pp. 110–14.
144 Rīga, LVVA, 4038 f., 2 apr., 1087 l.
145 Constantin Mettig, 'Die ältesten Bücher der Losträgergilde in Riga', in *Sitzungsberichten der Gesellschaft für Geschichte und Alterthumskunde der Ostseeprovinzen Russlands für das Jahr 1900* (Riga: W. F. Häcker, 1901), pp. 120–35; Strenga, 'Donations, Discipline and Commemoration', p. 111.
146 Arbusow, 'Kirchliches Leben', p. 221; Strenga, 'Donations, Discipline and Commemoration', pp. 111–12.
147 Jahnke, 'Lübeck's Confraternities', p. 383.
148 Dieter Schewe, *Geschichte der sozialen und privaten Versicherung im Mittelalter in den Gilden Europas* (Berlin: Duncker und Humblot, 2000), p. 140.
149 *Schragen der Gilden und Aemter*, no. 77, § 17, 18.

shows how frequently such trespasses happened but not the amount of wax paid.[150]

The fine registers show that guild officials concentrated their attention on controlling the attendance at funerals. Between 1450–1459, guild members were absent or misbehaved during memorial events on 134 occasions.[151] Absence from funerals was the main offence with 126 incidents, absence in funeral masses followed with fifty–seven cases, and vigils had twelve cases. In forty–eight cases guild members were cited for absence from two of the rituals. They seem to have attended vigils and masses more frequently than they did funerals. This raises doubts about the importance of the funeral as a commemorational practice if so many guild members refrained from attending it. For example, in 1450 sixteen guild members were recorded as having failed to attend the funeral of Holken's wife, but only three guild members were fined for missing her funeral mass.[152]

Although the fine book cannot be used as a complete source, it shows different social patterns within the group. Between 1450 and 1459, there were eleven funerals in which some cases of misbehaviour were registered.[153] Four of these funerals were for male guild members,[154] and seven were for female ones.[155] The funerals of male members appear to have been well–attended, and the number of absentees at them never exceeded seven. When a certain Stenbreker was buried, only five guild members stayed away.[156] In the case of Versyskuls, six did not turn up to the vigil and funeral, and only one failed to attend the funeral, while seven missed the memorial mass.[157] Two other burials mentioned in the fine book were apparently well attended; Peter Bruke's funeral had no absentees,[158] and at Hans Balye's funeral, only two guild members were fined for absence.[159]

The funerals of women, on the other hand, display a different pattern. In 1456, when a certain Glasewertsche was buried, twenty guild members were absent,[160] and when Nycklawe's mother had her funeral, twenty–four guild members were not present.[161] Even greater numbers of guild members were absent from the funeral of Lelkaysschen; thrity–two guild members stayed away from her funeral and the memorial mass.[162] Overall, funerals of women

---

150 Arbusow, 'Kirchliches Leben', p. 222.
151 Rīga, LVVA, 4038 f., 2 apr., 1087 l. fols. 1ᵃ–21ᵇ.
152 Rīga, LVVA, 4038 f., 2 apr., 1087 l. fol. 3ᵃ.
153 Rīga, LVVA, 4038 f., 2 apr., 1087 l. fols. 1ᵃ–21ᵇ.
154 Rīga, LVVA, 4038 f., 2 apr., 1087 l. fols. 1ᵃ; 5ᵇ; 13ᵃ–13ᵇ.
155 Rīga, LVVA, 4038 f., 2 apr., 1087 l. fols. 3ᵃ; 5ᵇ; 8ᵇ; 16ᵇ–17ᵃ; 17ᵇ; 21ᵇ.
156 Rīga, LVVA, 4038 f., 2 apr., 1087 l. fol. 1ᵃ.
157 Rīga, LVVA, 4038 f., 2 apr., 1087 l.fol. 13ᵃ.
158 Rīga, LVVA, 4038 f., 2 apr., 1087 l. fol. 2ᵃ.
159 Rīga, LVVA, 4038 f., 2 apr., 1087 l. fol. 5ᵇ.
160 Rīga, LVVA, 4038 f., 2 apr., 1087 l. fol. 17ᵇ.
161 Rīga, LVVA, 4038 f., 2 apr., 1087 l. fol. 16ᵇ.
162 Rīga, LVVA, 4038 f., 2 apr., 1087 l. fol. 21ᵇ.

had a larger number of absentees than those of the men. As at Swekken's wife's funeral, there were nine missing guild members and at Holken's wife's funeral sixteen.[163] At only two funerals, the list of absentees was short: that of a beguine and that of the wife of a certain Hynryk Breden.[164] Even with such limited data, we note a difference between attendance at male and female funerals.

Missing funerals was against the guild's rules for collective remembrance, and it was costly too, with a fine at five pounds of wax.[165] Nonetheless, some guild members were repeatedly absent. Jacop Mate was absent from memorial services five times during the 1450s; Clawyn Stawedurs, Lawrens Samedurs, Peter Serbe, and Matyas Kursehawe were absent three times, and Peter Lybete, who would be a guild official in the 1460s, Clawyn Schapyn, and Andreas Kakkerok had two absences each.[166] Other individuals were fined only once. Those members who were regularly absent from memorial ceremonies usually had an impressive record of other forms of misbehaviour too.[167]

Funerals and other memorial ceremonies had to be well attended and also properly organized and performed in a respectful manner. The fine book shows that proper celebration of memorial activities was guided and controlled. Almost all of the wrongdoings during the commemoration were related to the funeral procession. The funeral procession was one of the most important parts of the Christian burial ritual, which retained its central role even after the Reformation. The Porters' statutes instructed that the deceased be carried to the grave in a procession, with a pall over the dead body and accompanied by lights.[168] According to Eamon Duffy, the carrying of lights in England was intended to 'banish demons'.[169] The number of torches mattered too – the higher the number of lights, the higher the status – thus the poor and women were often paid to carry torches.[170] Riga's Beer Carters guild had also developed an elaborate funeral procession. They had lights and a pall during funeral processions by end of fifteenth century; by 1495 the guild officially offered the service of carrying lights and the pall for every deceased Cistercian nun.[171]

Some members of the Porters guild were negligent of their responsibilities during funeral processions. In 1450, a man named Myssener disobeyed the

---

163 Rīga, LVVA, 4038 f., 2 apr., 1087 l. fols. 8^b, 3^a.
164 Rīga, LVVA, 4038 f., 2 apr., 1087 l. fols. 5^b, 19^b.
165 *Schragen der Gilden und Aemter*, no. 77, § 17.
166 Rīga, LVVA, 4038 f., 2 apr., 1087 l., fols. 3^a, 8^b, 13^a, 16^a, 16^b, 17^b, 21^b.
167 Peter Serbe was fined seven times over two years for misdeeds during the communal meals. Mettig, 'Ältesten Bücher', p. 123, Strenga, 'Donations, Discipline and Commemoration', p. 112.
168 *Schragen der Gilden und Aemter*, no. 77, § 17, p. 416.
169 Eamon Duffy, *The Stripping of the Altars: Traditional Religion in England, c.1400–c.1580* (New Haven: Yale University Press, 1992), p. 361.
170 Katherine L. French, *The Good Women of the Parish: Gender and Religion after the Black Death* (Philadelphia: University of Pennsylvania Press, 2008), p. 72; Duffy, *Stripping Altars*, p. 361.
171 LUB 2/1, no. 252.

treasurer's order to carry lights during the funeral procession for Peter Bruke and did not follow the procession but stayed in the marketplace through which the funeral procession proceeded.[172] Hermen Speke similarly rejected the treasurer's orders to carry lights during Hynrik Breden's wife's funeral, as did Hermen Kuylle at Stenbreker's funeral.[173]

Guild members showed their reluctance to take part in guild ceremonies not only in the case of light bearing but also when they had to deal with corpses. In 1451, during the funeral of Swekken's wife, when the guild's treasurer instructed two guild members – Stauwedur and Lapse – to place the corpse on a bier, they refused the treasurer's orders and laughed.[174] The bearing of a corpse during the funeral ceremony may have been perceived by guild members as an unattractive obligation because of the direct proximity to the dead body in its early stages of putrefaction. In the Westphalian artisan brotherhoods members also avoided bearing a coffin or a corpse on a bier, and in order to combat such reluctance, guilds imposed fines of wax and beer.[175]

An obligation to take part in the funeral ceremony as a light- or bier-bearer was not set out in the Porters guild's statutes, but attempts to avoid fulfilling instructions by the treasurer counted as disobedience.[176] A fine of 1454 issued to Clawyn Sennites expressed the scribe's opinion that he was unwilling to do anything during funerals, and that he is always the last to do 'Lord's works' (*heren arbeit*) and does not obey orders.[177] Two years later, in 1456, Hans Broken, Hynryk Pyrssejalghe, Jacob Schuppel, and Pupewal were registered in the fine book for disobeying the treasurer during the burial of Glasewertersche.[178] Hans Broken had been complaining about directions given by the treasurer and refused to obey him; Hynryk Pyrssejalghe and Jacop Schuppel had simply disobeyed, but Pupewal did not want to listen to the treasurer since he considered himself to be 'a headman'.

It was the treasurer's responsibility to deal with all of these matters.[179] The treasurer had to control all of the people taking part in memorial ceremonies because as seen in the case of Myssener, the person taking part in the procession could simply change his or her mind and leave it.[180] In the Porters guild, the treasurer was in charge of maintaining order not only during funerals but also during the communal meals in the guildhall. The treasurer gave orders to the members during different guild activities and often received insulting

---

172 Rīga, LVVA, 4038 f., 2 apr., 1087 l. fol. 2ᵃ; Mettig, 'Ältesten Bücher', p. 124.
173 Rīga, LVVA, 4038 f., 2 apr., 1087 l. fols. 1ᵇ, 19ᵇ.
174 Rīga, LVVA, 4038 f., 2 apr., 1087 l. fol. 8ᵇ.
175 Peter Löffler, *Studien zum Totenbrauchtum in den Gilden, Bruderschaften und Nachbarschaften Westfalens vom Ende des 15. bis zum Ende des 19. Jahrhunderts* (Münster: Regensberg, 1975), p. 143.
176 Rīga, LVVA, 4038 f., 2 apr., 1087 l. fol. 2ᵃ.
177 Rīga, LVVA, 4038 f., 2 apr., 1087 l. fol. 16ᵃ.
178 Rīga, LVVA, 4038 f., 2 apr., 1087 l. fol. 17ᵇ.
179 Strenga, 'Donations, Discipline and Commemoration', p. 112.
180 Rīga, LVVA, 4038 f., 2 apr., 1087 l. fol. 2ᵃ.

responses in return.¹⁸¹ The treasurer in the brotherhood had a role similar to that of a testament warden, who supervised performance of the testator's *memoria*. It is not known whether the treasurer organized the funeral, but he definitely had to act in order to prevent the failure of those ceremonies, which were so important for the individual and collective remembrance of guild members.

It is hard to judge the significance of unruly individual behaviour in the context of the wider spirit of the guild. Members' misdeeds do not prove that they did not favour commemoration and Christian religiosity, as Šterns has suggested.¹⁸² The fine book reflects the guild's efforts to ensure discipline during all guild events, especially at funerals. It was an attempt by the guild's leadership to use discipline for the formation of the group as a community.¹⁸³ The funeral processions of guild members were public events that represented the group and its *memoria*. It was, therefore, important to maintain discipline and involve all members in it. For a group that lacked social status, like the Porters guild, successful presentation of its commemoration was crucial. The fine book of the Porters guild demonstrates that organization of *memoria* did not solely depend on financial resources but also on the guild's ability to ensure discipline and order. These were the challenges the guild faced in the performance of its own *memoria*.

Entfengen in unse broderschop: Elite Members in the Brotherhoods of the Beer Carters and Porters

In the late-fifteenth and early sixteenth centuries, rich merchants, city councillors, clergymen, and their families joined the two non-elite guilds of transport workers, the Porters and Beer Carters.¹⁸⁴ An influx of high-status individuals to these brotherhoods is a phenomenon found not only in medieval Riga but also in other Hanseatic cities. Transport workers of all kinds were part of the Hanseatic mercantile economy, in charge of transporting goods to and from the harbour. In Stralsund and Stettin, city councillors, clergymen, noblemen, and even local princes founded, joined, and supported transport workers' brotherhoods.¹⁸⁵ The brotherhood of Porters in Stettin was founded by Pomeranian duke Otto I (1295–1344) in 1283; he also endowed the guild's St Lawrence chantry in St Jacob's church in Stettin.¹⁸⁶ In Stralsund the

---

181 Mettig, 'Ältesten Bücher', p. 123; Strenga, 'Donations, Discipline and Commemoration', p. 112.
182 Šterns, *Latvijas Vēsture. 1290–1500*, p. 282.
183 Strenga, 'Donations, Discipline and Commemoration', p. 111.
184 Strenga, 'Turning Transport Workers into Latvians?', p. 69.
185 Otto Blümcke, 'Die S. Laurentius-Bruderschaft der Träger in Stettin', *Baltische Studien*, 35 (1885), 267–359 (275); Konrad Fritze, 'Kompanien und Bruderschaften im Spätmittelalterlichen Stralsund', in *Einungen und Bruderschaften in der spätmittelalterlichen Stadt*, ed. by Peter Johanek (Köln: Böhlau, 1993), pp. 31–43, pp. 41–42.
186 Blümcke, 'S. Laurentius-Bruderschaft', p. 275.

brotherhood of Porters was founded by 1325, and Vitslav III, prince of Rügen (1303–1325), was one of its founding members. In 1329 the brotherhood had already received a papal privilege, which was copied into the brotherhood's account book, listing hundreds of names of living and dead members of the group.[187] Among those included were numerous members of the princely family, four dukes of Pomerania, the bishop of Roeskilde, many members of the local nobility, city councillors and burgomasters of Stralsund, clergymen, and, finally, porters themselves.

So far scholars have rarely explored this form of cooperation between elite and non–elite townspeople in brotherhoods. Konrad Fritze, who has studied these brotherhoods in Stralsund, sees this cooperation of political, economic, and social elites and transport workers as 'scarcely comprehensible'.[188] Šterns sees the reason for the 'honorary membership' of the elites in non–elite guilds in Riga as stemming from 'a common interest' of the merchants and the transport workers in the transporting business.[189] Nor was the Arbusow, who has extensively researched the non–elite guilds in Riga, able to explain this phenomenon; he vaguely suggested that the city's elites joined the guilds of Beer Carters and Porters for 'religious reasons'.[190] Carsten Jahnke has described the religious guilds in Lübeck, including the *Corpus Christi* guild, as groups where elite and non–elite members practised religion together, took part in social activities, and communicated; thus the membership in a religious confraternity would not exclude broader contacts.[191] Elites and non–elites represented two opposite social poles, but in religious brotherhoods and groups like the Beer Carters and Porters, they existed side by side. Seeking the reasons and effects for this uncommon communion of 'rich' and 'poor' or patronage of 'rich' over 'poor' is the aim of my discussion.

The interaction of elite membership in non–elite guilds is a complicated phenomenon in which social, ethnic, and economic contexts intersect. As Antjekathrin Grassmann has pointed out, in the Hanseatic cities the merchants had a special relationship with the transport workers in a harbour, and they took care of them.[192] I would suggest that in addition to possible social and professional reasons, individuals from the elites of Riga joined the non–elite guilds for the sake of *memoria* and fulfilled the role of patrons in commemoration. Here I will examine the involvement of elites in these brotherhoods, their

---

187 Fritze, 'Kompanien und Bruderschaften im Spätmittelalterlichen Stralsund', p. 41, 42.
188 Fritze, 'Kompanien und Bruderschaften im Spätmittelalterlichen Stralsund', p. 40.
189 Šterns, *Latvijas Vēsture. 1290–1500*, p. 277.
190 Arbusow, 'Kirchliches Leben', pp. 185–224; Arbusow, 'Studien zur Geschichte der lettischen Bevölkerung Rigas', pp. 76–100, 84.
191 Jahnke, 'Lübeck's Confraternities', p. 380; Jahnke, *Gott gebe, dass wir alle selig werden mögen*, p. 286.
192 Antjekathrin Grassmann, 'Zwischen Nächstenliebe und Geschäft. Zum sozialen Wirken des Lübecker Kaufmanns', in *Der Lübecker Kaufmann: Aspekte seiner Lebens– und Arbeitswelt vom Mittelalter bis zum 19. Jahrhundert*, ed. by Gerhard Gerkens and Antjekathrin Grassmann (Lübeck: Museum für Kunst und Kulturgeschichte, 1993), pp. 97–102, p. 97.

MEMORIA AND THE NON-ELITES 223

contribution to the *memoria* of non–elites, and the effect of the Reformation on the relationship of elites and non–elites.

Member lists have survived in the account books of the Beer Carters and Porters guilds from the mid–fifteenth century. Individuals belonging to the urban elite can be identified, and it is also relatively easy to identify clergymen and city councillors as members of both guilds, referred to as *her* – lord,[193] and in some cases *prester* was added to a priest's name.[194] Not all individuals designated as *her* can be fully identified because of gaps in urban documentation, and this is true for priests too.[195]

According to the lists of members, the Porters guild had more clergymen and city councillors as members than the Beer Carters guild, with forty–four individuals described as *her* between 1452 and 1520, sixteen of whom were city councillors;[196] and two other may have been too;[197] four individuals in the member list of the Porters guild were priests.[198] The names of twenty–two guild members recorded as *her* cannot be found in the surviving sources.[199]

Although the Beer Carters guild was the larger of the two, there was considerably smaller representation of the city councillors in it. The Beer Carters member lists for the period between 1460 and 1520 have records of nineteen city councillors or clergymen.[200] Only for two individuals is there evidence that they were city councillors;[201] the other eight who have been referred to as *her* are not identifiable in any other sources.[202] At least two others, not named as *her* upon entering the guild, later became councillors.[203] In the member lists of the Beer Carters guild, it is easier to distinguish the clergymen from the city

---

193 The Latin term *dominus* in the member lists of both brotherhoods has been used only in rare occasions.
194 Rīga, LVVA, 4038 f., 2 apr., 1087. l. fol. 88ᵃ; Rīga, LVVA, 4038 f., 2 apr., 1089. l. fol. 17ᵇ.
195 Absence of a person's name from the registers prepeared from charters and townbooks by Bothführ (*Rathslinie*) and Arbusow (*Livlands Geistlichkeit*) does not mean that a person was not a city councillor or priest, only that there are no surviving sources validating the status, or the registers are incomplete.
196 Johan Treros (member 1453); Heinrich Beckerwerter (1453); Wennemar Harmen (1456); Johan Geresem , (1459); Hinrik Kryvitz (1472); Johan Schoning (1486); Hinrik Molner (1488); Nikolaus Golste (1491); Ewert Steven (1500); Gosswyn Mennyng (1503); Johan Meteler (1503); Peter Grawert (1510); Merten Brekerfeldt (1512); Hans Spendinckhusen (1513); Diderick Meteler (1514); Tönnies Muther (1515); Rīga, LVVA, 4038 f., 2 apr., 1087 l. fols. 84ᵇ, 85ᵇ, 87ᵃ, 87ᵇ, 25ᵇ, 34ᵃ, 35ᵇ, 37ᵇ, 46ᵇ, 47ᵃ, 52ᵃ, 53ᵃ, 54ᵇ, 55ᵃ, 56ᵇ; Böthführ, *Rathslinie*, nos. 333, 297, 325, 318, 365, 372, 371, 397, 384, 391, 418, 425, 414, 431, 375, 415.
197 Bartolomeus Meyer (1493/94); Hermen Lemensiike (1453); Rīga, LVVA, 4038 f., 2 apr., 1087 l. fols. 37ᵇ, 85ᵇ; *Erbebücher* II, No. 23, no. 97; *Erbebücher* I, no. 790, 912.
198 Johan Geresem, Geritsem junior (1459); Peter Grybowe, Bertoldus Bewnick prester (1507), her Hynryck Smyt ere vycarius unde schriwer (1512), her Jochim Moller presbyter (1518), Andreas Knopken (1517), Jakob Knopken (1517), Rīga, LVVA, 4038 f., 2 apr., 1087 l., fols. 88ᵃ, 50ᵃ, 53ᵃ, 59ᵃ, 58ᵇ; *Kämmerei–Register* II, pp. 272, 7; 221, 9; 225, 20; *Livlands Geistlichkeit*, pp. 70, 103.
199 Rīga, LVVA, 4038 f., 2 apr., 1087 l. fols. 84ᵃ, 87ᵇ, 88ᵇ, 34ᵇ, 35ᵃ, 35ᵇ, 36ᵃ, 37ᵃ, 38ᵇ, 40ᵃ, 43ᵇ, 48ᵃ, 48ᵇ, 50ᵇ, 52ᵃ, 54ᵃ, 60ᵃ, 60ᵇ, 25ᵃ.
200 Rīga, LVVA, 4038 f., 2 apr., 1159 l; Rīga, LVVA, 4038 f., 2 apr., 1089. l.
201 Johan Wenkhusen (1507); Johann Duvel (1521); Rīga, LVVA, 4038 f., 2 apr., 1159 l. fols. 10ᵇ, 1ᵃ; Böthführ, *Rathslinie*, no. 407, 440.
202 Rīga, LVVA, 4038 f., 2 apr., 1159 l. fols. 8ᵃ, 10ᵇ, 1ᵃ, 2ᵇ; no. 381.
203 Rīga, LVVA, 4038 f., 2 apr., 1159 l. fol. 18ᵃ, 34ᵇ; Böthführ, *Rathslinie*, no. 435, 432.

councillors than in the ones of the Porters. All seven clergymen in the member lists were canons of the Riga cathedral chapter and were referred as *domher*.[204]

Some of the city councillors who joined the Porters or Beer Carters guilds had remarkable careers. For example, Johan Schöning, who became a member of the Porters guild in 1486, had come to Livonia in 1456, became a city councillor of Riga in 1476 and a burgomaster in 1479.[205] His son Thomas Schöning became archbishop of Riga in the 1520s.[206] Other influential councillors also became members of the two brotherhoods. In 1459, city councillor Johan Geresem (Geresem, Geritsem) joined the Porters guild in the latter part of a thirty-year-long political career, during which he had been treasurer of the city for at least eleven years.[207] He had been amongst the first members of the Black Heads brotherhood (1416), co-founder of their chantry in St Catherine's friary (1421), and active in the city government since the 1430s.[208] A year after joining, Geresem endowed a chantry for the guild in order to foster his *memoria*.[209] Other members of the Porters guild had long and successful careers in city government; Johan Meteler, who joined in 1503, became city councillor around 1503, was treasurer in 1511, and burgomaster in 1516.[210] Ewert Steven, a member in 1500, had a rapid career; he was first mentioned as councillor in 1481, and in the same year he was burgomaster too.[211] Johan Treros (1453) was burgomaster in 1461 and in that year also represented Riga in the meeting of the Hanse in Lübeck.[212] All these councillors played important roles in the urban politics of their day.

The Beer Carters guild attracted fewer city councillors than the Porters, and those who joined seem to have been somewhat less illustrious. There was only one burgomaster, Johann Moller, who joined in 1522, the year of his service as burgomaster, although his career had begun more than forty years earlier, in 1480, as an ambassador to Rome.[213] The Beer Carters guild had as members such distinguished city councillors as Ewert Steven (1509), who a decade earlier had been a member of the Porters guild, and Peter Grawert (1516–1520), who had also been a member of the Porters guild in 1510.[214]

The Beer Carters guild lacked an extensive representation of politically and economically influential urban politicians, but it attracted the Riga cathedral canons. Some canons were provosts and priests in the parishes of St Peter's

---

204 Mettig, 'Bücher der Bierträgergilde', p. 122; LVVA, 4038 f., 2 apr., 1089 l. fols. 75ᵇ, 16ᵃ; LUB 2/1 no. 571; *Erbebücher* II no. 375, 485.
205 Rīga, LVVA, 4038 f., 2 apr., 1087 l. fol. 34ᵃ; Böthführ, *Rathslinie*, no. 372.
206 Böthführ, *Rathslinie*, no. 372.
207 Rīga, LVVA, 4038 f., 2 apr., 1087 l. fol. 87ᵇ; Böthführ, *Rathslinie*, no. 318.
208 Spliet, *Geschichte*, p. 88.
209 LUB 12, no. 6.
210 Rīga, LVVA, 4038 f., 2 apr., 1087 l. fol. 47ᵃ; Böthführ, *Rathslinie*, no. 418.
211 Rīga, LVVA, 4038 f., 2 apr., 1087 l. fol. 46ᵇ; Böthführ, *Rathslinie*, no. 384; *Erbebücher* I, no. 1147.
212 Rīga, LVVA, 4038 f., 2 apr., 1087 l. fol. 84ᵇ; LUB 12 no. 89; 91.
213 Rīga, LVVA, 4038 f., 2 apr., 1159 l. fol. 2ᵇ; Böthführ, *Rathslinie*, no. 381.
214 Mettig, 'Ältesten Bücher', pp. 121–22; Rīga, LVVA, 4038 f., 2 apr., 1087 l. fol. 52ᵃ.

and St Jacob's, where the altars of the Beer Carters were also located, which may have been the link. Riga's canons can be found in the Beer Carters guild for the first time in the 1460s, when the canons Johan Sleff and Gert van Borken, together with his father, became members of the guild.[215] The canon Martin Epinckhusen was mentioned in 1473 as a member of the guild.[216] In 1497 the guild was joined by three canons: provost Jasper Noteken,[217] dean Jasper Linde, and canon Jacob Huttini, priest of St Jacob's.[218] These were the highest-ranking officials of the diocese, and their presence in such a guild is striking. Indeed, Jasper Linde became the archbishop of Riga in 1509.[219]

By joining the guilds of the Beer Carters and Porters, elite members fostered their family's connections and other social networks. Elite women often joined with their councillor husbands, as with Hermen Lemsiike (1453),[220] Johan Schöning (1486),[221] Hinrick Molner (1488),[222] Nicolaus Golste (1491),[223] Ewert Steven (1500),[224] Gosswyn Mennyngk (1503),[225] Johan Meteler (1503),[226] and Peter Grawert (1510).[227] Some wives of city councillors joined on their own, like Lukke, wife of city councillor Johann van dem Orde, who joined the guild of Porters in 1453, though her husband apparently was not a member.[228] Two other women from elite families joined the Porters and Beer Carters guilds: in 1506 the wife of the city councillor Peter Grawert[229] joined the Beer Carters;[230] the mother of Blasius van Lessen, chantry priest and guild member, joined in 1509.[231]

Where the description *her* is absent, locating and identifying individuals from elites in the members' lists is more challenging. Some representatives of the Livonian nobility were present in both guilds. There are few members from noble families; only two noble women joined the Beer Carters guild: Katerine Üxkull in 1464 and Katarina Patkull in 1497.[232] In 1495, quite unusually, all fifty-three nuns of the Cistercian nunnery in Riga joined the Beer Carters guild

---

215 *Livlands Geistlichkeit*, p. 196, 29; Gert van Borken and his father left the guild before 1466. Mettig, 'Ältesten Bücher', p. 122.
216 Rīga, LVVA, 4038 f., 2 apr., 1089 l. fol. 75^b.
217 *Livlands Geistlichkeit*, p. 152.
218 Rīga, LVVA, 4038 f., 2 apr., 1089 l. fol. 15^a.
219 *Livlands Geistlichkeit*, p. 124.
220 Rīga, LVVA, 4038 f., 2 apr., 1087 l. fols. 85^b, 86^a.
221 Rīga, LVVA, 4038 f., 2 apr., 1087 l. fol. 34^a.
222 Rīga, LVVA, 4038 f., 2 apr., 1087 l. fol. 35^b.
223 Rīga, LVVA, 4038 f., 2 apr., 1087 l. fol. 37^b.
224 Rīga, LVVA, 4038 f., 2 apr., 1087 l. fol. 46^b.
225 Rīga, LVVA, 4038 f., 2 apr., 1087 l. fol. 47^a.
226 Rīga, LVVA, 4038 f., 2 apr., 1087 l. fol. 47^a.
227 Rīga, LVVA, 4038 f., 2 apr., 1087 l. fol. 52^a.
228 Böthführ, *Rathslinie*, no. 304; Rīga, LVVA, 4038 f., 2 apr., 1087 l. fol. 86^a.
229 Böthführ, *Rathslinie*, no. 425.
230 Rīga, LVVA, 4038 f., 2 apr., 1159 l. fol. 8^a.
231 Rīga, LVVA, 4038 f., 2 apr., 1159 l. fol. 15^b.
232 Mettig, 'Ältesten Bücher', p. 123; Rīga, LVVA, 4038 f., 2 apr., 1089 l. fol. 14^b.

as a community and as stated earlier, most of them were from the Livonian noble families.[233]

The Beer Carters and Porters guilds attracted rich and influential members, but these were always a minority. In the Beer Carters guild between 1485 and 1519, there were on average around 200 members per annum; the highest number, 300, was in 1517.[234] Among the approximately two hundred members of the Beer Carters guild in the years 1509–1514, only three *her* can be identified paying fees: vicar Blasius van Lessen,[235] priest Johan Wenkhusen,[236] and priest Thomas Dethleui.[237] Only three belonged to the urban elites, one to two per cent in all. In the Porters guild, the representation of elites may have been a bit higher.[238] Altogether, individuals from social, economic, and political elites were a numerical minority in the two guilds, but they were an influential and useful minority.

Even though the presence of elite members is evident, less is known about what status these prominent members enjoyed. Did they take full part in guild activities as full members? Johan Wenckhusen, a priest, was accepted in the Beer Carters guild in 1503 as 'a full brother' (*eynen vullen broder*),[239] but others may not have been fully integrated. Konrad Fritze argues that in late medieval Stralsund, where elites also took part in the transport workers' guilds, city councillors, priests, and noblemen were not full members.[240] Also in the Porters and Beer Carters guilds some distinction between elite members and others existed. While both guilds demanded from their non–elite members that they belong only to one guild, the elite members combined their membership with the one of the Great Guild, and some even joined both transport workers' brotherhoods.[241] As the events of the Reformation show, elite members were first to leave the guilds when the efficacy of their commemorative activities was called into question.

As Paul Trio has reminded us, many members in different brotherhoods and confraternities were members on paper alone, and their membership was restricted to participation in the association's charitable activities and other financial contributions. In his view they did not participate in other activities, and many of them enrolled in several confraternities concurrently. Trio claims that 'one should be wary to imagine all kinds of networks between the members' because 'they might have hardly ever met – at least, within the context of the corporation's activities.'[242]

---

233 Rīga, LVVA, 4038 f., 2 apr., 1089 l. fols. 52ª–53ª; LUB 2/1, no. 252.
234 Arbusow, 'Studien zur Geschichte der lettischen Bevölkerung Rigas', pp. 88; 90–91.
235 *Livlands Geistlichkeit*, p. 122; LVVA, 4038 f., 2 apr., 1159 l. fols. 16ª, 18ᵇ, 24ᵇ, 25ª, 28ª, 32ª.
236 Rīga, LVVA, 4038 f., 2 apr., 1159 l. fols. 17ᵇ, 22ª, 24ᵇ, 28ª, 32ª.
237 *Livlands Geistlichkeit*, p. 42; Rīga, LVVA, 4038 f., 2 apr., 1159 l. fols. 16ᵇ, 19ᵇ, 21ᵇ, 25ª, 28ª, 32ª.
238 Arbusow, 'Studien zur Geschichte der lettischen Bevölkerung Rigas', p. 88.
239 Rīga, LVVA, 4038 f., 2 apr., 1089 l. fol. 19ª.
240 Fritze, 'Kompanien und Bruderschaften im Spätmittelalterlichen Stralsund', pp. 40–42.
241 *Schragen der Gilden und Aemter*, no. 12, § 12, no. 77, § 27.
242 Trio, 'Social Positioning', p. 100.

Trio's comments are a useful reminder, but they do not necessarily apply to the relationships between guilds and their members when these were motivated by *memoria*. Firstly, even if it did not mean full integration in the brotherhood, membership was a meaningful gesture towards the group. Secondly, the presence of all members at all guild or brotherhood events, at least in the case of Riga's Beer Carters and Porters guilds, cannot be proven. As the fine book of the Porters guild (1450–1459) shows, the guild fined members who were absent from the guild's drinking feasts, elite and non–elite alike. In 1452 the future city councillor and burgomaster Johan Geismer (Hans Geysmer, Giesmer, Gheismer), who in 1459 had made a large endowment for the Porters guild, was fined together with other guild members for not attending the guild's drinking feast.[243] The drinking feasts were the events at which the membership fees were collected, and absence meant failure to pay them. Possibly rich members paid their fees in other ways, without being present during the communal meal.

Trio's view that one should be 'wary to imagine all kinds of networks' because the members may never have met is well taken. Even if the membership of high–status individuals in these guilds was nominal, this does not preclude the existence of meaningful networks of remembrance. Joining such networks of remembrance was a process that did not require physical presence. There were long traditions of aristocratic benefactions to monastic communities that implied 'distant' brotherhood. Late medieval urban guilds may have emulated the links between such religious communities and their aristocratic patrons and provided a similar relationship of *memoria* for benefactors and high–status members.[244] These elite members, although probably not full members, were potential contributors to the social and memorial activities of the guilds.

Both transport workers' guilds in Riga had numerous members drawn from the ranks of the elite: city councillors and their wives, rich merchants, highly placed clergymen, and ordinary priests. They formed a minority of the guild members, but their membership was a very important resource for these guilds, which promised additional resources for religious and memorial activities of the Beer Carters and Porters guilds.

City Councillors and Clergymen as Patrons of *Memoria* in the Non–elite Guilds

Collective *memoria*, in the form of memorial liturgical services, soul masses, and vigils, required investment in the form of an endowment. The foundation of liturgical *memoria* by the creation of a chantry established privileged

---

243 Böthfuhr, *Rathslinie*, no. 350; Rīga, LVVA, 4038 f., 2 apr., 1087 l. fol. 6^b.
244 Gervase Rosser, 'Finding Oneself in a Medieval Fraternity. Individual and Collective Identities in the English Guilds', in *Mittelalterliche Bruderschaften*, pp. 29–46, pp. 35–36.

memorial practices into the future.²⁴⁵ Foundations and their commemorative activities no doubt experienced change and transformations of meanings, but they were a safe form of remembrance.²⁴⁶ Larger financial investments provided constant incomes and were a preferred form of support over smaller donations of members. The endowment of a foundation supported a chaplain, choirboys, the organist, the altar, and vessels necessary for liturgical remembrance; Riga's Porters guild spent some 23 Riga marks a year on the early stages of their chantry during the 1460s.²⁴⁷ Smaller donations of money and objects fluctuated in numbers and were more influenced by external factors such as wars, disease, and economic crisis.²⁴⁸

Neither the Beer Carters guild nor the Porters guild were able to organize long-term commemorative services without substantial support from rich donors. Guild officials were often well off, e.g. owners of properties in the city, but most likely none had resources large enough for the endowment of a chantry.²⁴⁹ Yet the lack of such financial resources among non-elite guild members does not mean that they were unable to sustain or create *memoria* altogether. In 1458, appearantly without the presence of any elite guild members, the Porters created their chantry in St Peter's church.²⁵⁰ Alderman Merten Ghargesul and his deputies Clawin Schapin, Hinrick Slachter, Mychel van der Nygenmolen, and Peter Lybet acted as founders.²⁵¹ All that the chantry acquired without an endowment was the donation of one Riga mark by each of the guild officials. After receiving the consent of St Peter's churchwarden for building an altar in the southern side of the church, the guild officials went from house to house of guild members, collecting donations for the chantry.²⁵² During this fundraising campaign, thrity-three members and other benefactors made donations, money and objects, necessary for the construction and elaboration of the chantry's altar, including the chalice and paten, missal, liturgical towels, and tablecloths. A donation of 15 Riga marks was granted for the commemoration of St Peter's church former vicar Nicolaus Sasse.²⁵³ None of these contributions was large enough for perpetual endowment.

Although the chantry of the Porters guild was created without direct engagement of elite members, it was guaranteed by the efforts of two city councillors who joined the guild after the chantry's creation. The first important

---

245 Lusiardi, *Stiftung*, p. 51; Michael Borgolte, 'Die Stiftungsurkunden Heinrichs II. Eine Studie zum Handlungsspielraum des letzten Liudolfingers', in *Festschrift für Eduard Hlawitschka zum 65. Geburtstag*, ed. by Karl Schnith (Kallmünz: Lassleben, 1993), pp. 231–50, p. 232.
246 Borgolte, 'Stiftung, Staat und sozialer Wandel', p. 19.
247 Arbusow, 'Kirchliches Leben', p. 202.
248 Arbusow, 'Kirchliches Leben', p. 199.
249 Benninghoven, *Rigas Entstehung*, p. 103; *Erbebücher* II, no. 81; *Kämmerei-Register 1405–1474*, p. 284; Riga, LVVA, 4038 f., 2 apr., 1089 l. fol. 58ª; Arbusow, 'Kirchliches Leben', pp. 219, 220.
250 Arbusow, 'Kirchliches Leben', p. 204.
251 Strenga, 'Donations, discipline and commemoration', p. 116.
252 Arbusow, 'Kirchliches Leben', pp. 204–05.
253 Arbusow, 'Kirchliches Leben', p. 205.

endowment was recorded in the chantry book in 1459, when a city councillor, later burgomaster, Johan Geismer granted 50 Riga marks, the equivalent of the chantry's annuity rent of 3 marks.[254] Geismer was an aspiring urban politician, who entered the city council in the mid 1450s and had become a member of the Porters' guild in 1452.[255] The terms of this endowment are not known because its charter has not survived, but it may have requested – as was the custom – to commemorate the benefactor, his family, and also the deceased of the guild.

Geismer's example was followed a year later by city councillor Johan Geresem, who in 1460 endowed the chantry of the Porters guild; he had joined the guild a year earlier.[256] A founding charter was issued by the guild and recorded in the guild's account book.[257] Geresem gave 100 old Riga marks in return for six marks annually, which was to support the chantry after his death, but was paid to the endower during his lifetime. Two marks annually had to be paid for a memorial mass celebrated by all priests of St Peter's church on the day of Geresem's obit, and on the same day, one mark had to spent on alms for the poor for the sake of all Christian souls.[258] The endowment charter set out that other services for Geresem's remembrance could be added. From 6 marks of annual rent, three went for memorial services intended to commemorate Geresem himself, but the other three, it seems, were at the free disposal of the chantry to finance the altar and liturgical services. Not only Geresem himself bonded with the group; right after the guild's chantry's foundation, Geismer's wife Drude had donated 'a beautiful ornamented towel' for the altar.[259]

The endowments made by Geresem and Geismer created the commemoration of the donors but also benefited the collective commemoration of the guild. Incomes from endowments made to the Porters' chantry by Geresem and Geismer were used for the commemoration of all deceased guild members, not only the souls of the founders.[260] The main aim for benefactors was to be kept in the 'memory' of the guild by being named regularly in services and prayers. Geresem's and Geismer's endowments characterize the aim of the collective remembrance in the group – endowments were made for the sake of the endower's commemoration, but at the same time they helped to perform *memoria* for the whole group. By making endowments that were so crucial for the remembrance of the group, city councillors became patrons, retaining their

---

254 Rūta Brusbārde, PhD student of Kiel University has shared with me biographic entries of Geismer from her forthcoming dissertation on the Riga's city councillors in the fifteenth century. Böthfuhr, *Rathslinie*, no. 350; Arbusow, 'Kirchliches Leben', p. 206, Strenga, 'Donations, Discipline and Commemoration', p. 121.
255 Rīga, LVVA, 4038 f., 2 apr., 1087 l. fol. 24ᵃ.
256 Rīga, LVVA, 4038 f., 2 apr., 1087 l. fol. 87ᵇ.
257 Arbusow, 'Kirchliches Leben', p. 205; LUB 12, no. 6; Strenga, 'Donations, Discipline and Commemoration', p. 121.
258 LUB 12 No. 6.
259 Arbusow, 'Kirchliches Leben der Rigaschen Losträger', p. 205.
260 Arbusow, 'Kirchliches Leben'. p. 202.

roles after death, when the resources endowed started to sustain the guild's collective remembrance. Moreover, this *memoria* of the two city councillors can be seen as part of the elite *Ratsmemoria* meant to represent and legitimize their power.[261]

An example from the Beer Carters guild demonstrates the ways in which remembrance of an elite member was performed. Claus Glembeke created the chantry of the Beer Carters guild in 1473 in the parish church of St Peter's. Glembeke was not a city councillor but a rich merchant and the owner of many urban properties.[262] Glembeke's foundation reflects the founder's prosperity and a wish for self-representation.

Claus Glembeke established a new chantry and altar in St Peter's church and handed it over to the Beer Carters guild's alderman and the brethren.[263] In the foundation document, Glembeke made at least twenty-one requests for endowments and donations to be made, mostly for the newly founded chantry and the guild of the Beer Carters.[264] He requested the setting up of an altar and the placement of his grave slab near it with a statue and altarpiece; he provided a chalice, missal, lights, and a number of other objects.[265] Glembeke endowed an additional 200 marks for the chantry based on the income from two houses. The resources allocated were worth approximately 768 Riga marks, and it is the largest endowment known in late medieval Riga. This foundation was confirmed by archbishop Silvester Stodewescher, the city council, and later reconfirmed by Archbishop Michael Hildebrant in 1506.[266]

The foundation of the chantry, which became the Beer Carters own, differed from the foundation for the Porters in the same church fifteen years earlier. The Porters created the chantry for themselves and later gifts by city councillors were made to it. There is another difference. As Leonid Arbusow has argued, the Beer Carters guild already had an existing altar and chantry in St Jacob's church founded in 1386.[267] Although there are no sources that would testify to the chantry's existence in the 1470s, we may assume that the new chantry founded by Glembeke at the eastern side (*ost siden*) of St Peter's, probably in the chancel of the church, was in addition to the Beer Carters.[268] This foundation was a chance for the Beer Carters guild to establish their presence in a parish church more prestigious than St Jacob's.

A year later, in 1474, Glembeke specified that a vigil and a memorial mass be celebrated once a year for his and his family's remembrance, with two choir-

---

261 Poeck, 'Rat und Memoria', pp. 286–335.
262 *Erbebücher* I, no. 863, 1019–1021;
263 Rīga, LVVA, 4038 f., 2 apr., 1089 l. fol 75ᵃ.
264 Rīga, LVVA, 4038 f., 2 apr., 1089 l. fols. 75ᵃ–75ᵇ.
265 Rīga, LVVA, 4038 f., 2 apr., 1087 l. fol. 75ᵃ.
266 Rīga, LVVA, 4038 f., 2 apr., 1084 l. fols. 41ᵃ–47ᵇ; LUB 2/3, no. 128.
267 Arbusow, 'Studien zur Geschichte der lettischen Bevölkerung Rigas', p. 83.
268 Rīga, LVVA, 4038 f., 2 apr., 1089 l. fol. 75ᵃ.

boys participating.²⁶⁹ The chantry's priest was to celebrate a vigil and a mass on every Ember Day and a weekly mass in remembrance of all Christian souls and the souls of the chantry's founders and supporters. Glembeke instructed the guild that if a member of his family were to become a priest, he should be employed by the chantry. This was *memoria* of Glembeke and his family within the guild of the 'poor' in which future family members could become involved. Although we do not know whether Glembeke had made any other large endowments, this one shows that he entrusted the *memoria* of his whole family not to a religious community or ecclesiastical institution but to his city's non-elite guild.

Glembeke's endowment created liturgical *memoria* but also supported a non-liturgical remembrance in the Beer Carters guild. Glembeke requested that his and 'all Christian souls' be commemorated twice a year at the guild's *drunke* of Pentecost and Annunciation; one Riga mark was to be spent on beer and bread for each *drunke*. As shown in the chapter on elites, the communal meals were occasions not only of commensality but also of commemoration.²⁷⁰ In Glembeke's case, the wish to be commemorated during the communal meal shows that he sought to be effectively integrated into the *memoria* of the Beer Carters guild. Glembeke's remembrance became an integral part of the guild's *memoria*, although he did not belong to the group socially, but rather spiritually. Glembeke's relations with the Beer Carters brotherhood demonstrate a close, spiritual link between the group and the individual.

We may explore further the relation of elite members to the Beer Carters guild through the case of the priest Johan Wenckhusen, who in 1503 became member of the Beer Carters guild, and donated a coffin cover (*palle*) and a corporal (*corporall*) to the guild's chantry.²⁷¹ Master (*mester*) Wenckhusen was first mentioned in Riga around 1492 and was a longstanding member of the Beer Carters guild, paying his member's fees regularly between 1506 and 1514.²⁷² Wenckhusen was not the chantry priest of the Beer Carters guild, though he was employed by other memorial chantries.²⁷³ Although his name is absent from the guild's records after 1514, Wenckhusen was still present in Riga in 1518.

Johan Wenckhusen was received into the Beer Carters guild together with his deceased parents, who also became members of the guild, so as to 'take their part in the good deeds that happen in this guild'.²⁷⁴ The good deeds (*guden werke*) that would benefit the souls of Wenckhusen's parents were the

---

269 Rīga, LVVA, 4038 f., 2 apr., 1089 l. fol. 75ᵇ.
270 *Schragen der Gilden und Aemter*, pp. 662–63, § 13; Oexle, 'Gegenwart der Lebenden', p. 81; Rosser, 'Going to the Fraternity Feast', p. 434.
271 Rīga, LVVA, 4038 f., 2 apr., 1089 l. fol. 19ᵃ.
272 *Die Libri Redituum der Stadt Riga*, no. 174; *Livlands Geistlichkeit*, p. 232; Rīga, LVVA, 4038 f., 2 apr., 1159 l. fol. 8ᵇ, 32ᵃ.
273 *Libri Redituum*, no. 33, 34.
274 Rīga, LVVA, 4038 f., 2 apr., 1089 l. fol. 19ᵃ.

guild's religious activities: masses, vigils, and prayers as part of a memorial cycle. *Memoria* was his main reason for joining, bringing along his deceased parents to receive these benefits as well.

The Beer Carters guild acted as a spiritual confraternity of remembrance for Wenckhusen and his parents.[275] Spiritual confraternity integrated both living and dead.[276] Ralf Lusiardi has showed that in the case of the Porters guild of late medieval Stralsund, the commemorative role of this group was on par with that of local religious communities. The porters, like local monasteries, incorporated noblemen, clergymen, and city councillors, within their own remembrance.[277] Riga's Beer Carters guild was also a confraternity of remembrance that offered *memoria* within the group for individuals from other social groups and their families. In such a way the transport workers' brotherhoods in Riga and Stralsund fulfilled memorial functions formerly and elsewhere reserved for religious communities.[278]

Wenckhusen's case shows what cannot be seen in other examples where elite individuals joined both guilds. The entrance of elite members into the Beer Carters and Porters guild not only had a financial impact on the *memoria* or on the status of these organizations, but there were also spiritual ties between the guilds and their elite members. This was a long–term relationship, which involved not only the elite members themselves but also their dead and future family members. There must have been some kind of distance between both transport workers guilds and elite members of those guilds, which became evident during the Reformation.

As the member lists show, a significant group of city councillors, merchants, clergymen. and their family members joined the Beer Carters and Porters guilds, but only a few of them can be identified as donors. Not all elite members chose the two guilds as their commemorators or made donations to them. Among the elite members, there were also individuals who belonged to the city elite – high clergymen or rich merchants –who were not city councillors.

One such was Hans Grote, a burgher of Riga and most likely a merchant. In 1466 he endowed 200 marks for the chantry of the Porters guild.[279] The annual rent of 12 marks had to be divided in two: 6 marks of rent to be invested in the chantry and the other 6 to be spent on alms. Grote's endowment was indeed significant, and it can be compared to those made by the councillors Geresem and Geismer several years earlier.

Kersten van Dike (Dyke) similarly made a donation to the Beer Carters guild in 1487. A burgher and most likely a son of city councillor Johannes van Dyke, he donated 4 Riga marks for the making of pall, requesting remembrance

---

275 Confraternity in this context means a spiritual brotherhood rather than an institution. Cowdrey, 'Legal Problems Raised by Agreements of Confraternity', pp. 233–34.
276 Schmid, 'Mönchtum und Verbrüderung', p. 161.
277 Lusiardi, *Stiftung*, p. 75.
278 Oexle, 'Liturgische Memoria', p. 338.
279 *Erbebücher* I, nos. 684, 685, 950, 951, 1011; Arbusow, 'Kirchliches Leben', pp. 210–11.

for himself and all Beer Carters (*tho eyn dechnisse den berdregher*).[280] Like Grote, van Dike also cannot be found in the member list of the guild from which they requested a commemoration.

Other members of the upper classes of Riga made memorial donations for the two transport workers' guilds. Hans Tydefogel, who owned a property in the city, donated 15 marks in 1461/1464 for his *memoria* to the chantry of the Porters guild, requesting vigils and a requiem mass.[281] The account book of the Beer Carters guild in 1491 also recorded that the deceased priest of St George's chapel, Berent Vischer, had donated a number of liturgical objects for the Beer Carters guild.[282]

Those individuals from the social elite who created *memoria* for themselves and their families were probably attracted by the long–term prospect of commemoration offered by the guilds. In the two non–elite guilds, commemoration mixed their core members, transport workers and non–German townspeople of Riga, with individuals from the social elite. The *memoria* of the city councillors and rich merchants, who made large endowments to the Porters guild, was integrated into the collective *memoria* of this non–German brotherhood. Without these large endowments and also the smaller donations of elite members, long–term *memoria* of the non–elite guilds would not have been possible. Their resources sustained the *memoria* of non–German Beer Carters and porters.

Both guilds allowed elite members to integrate personal *memoria* and that of their deceased family members, as we have seen it in in the case of Johan Wenckhusen and his parents. Such a relationship could have become an intimate, long–term bond between the guilds and their benefactors, resembling the bonds created between benefactors and monastic communities. Like transport workers' brotherhoods, the Beer Carters and Porters guilds were groups, which, like monastic communities, commemorated the rich and powerful.

Elites and the Commemorational Spaces of the Non–elites

As mentioned above, the 'new beginning' of these groups in the mid–fifteenth century was marked by gaining prestigious spaces for their religiosity.[283] The charter that created the altar of the Porters guild atar in St Peter's church was issued by the city council two years after the creation of the chantry on 9 of October 1460.[284] It secured for the guild the use of an altar at the south side (*zuderziide*) of the church, behind the pillar next to the *rathstole*, the pews

---

280 Böthführ, *Rathslinie*, no. 339; *Erbebücher* I, no. 1109, 1142; Rīga, LVVA, 4038 f., 2 apr., 1089 l. fol. 4^b.
281 *Erbebücher* I, no. 757; Arbusow, 'Kirchliches Leben', pp. 208–09.
282 Rīga, LVVA, 4038 f., 2 apr., 1089 l. fol. 9^b.
283 Strenga, 'Turning Transport Workers into Latvians?', pp. 68–69.
284 LUB 12, no. 60.

of the council.²⁸⁵ In the charter the city council ordered the Porters guild to build a vault at its own expense that would stretch over the new altar and a window.²⁸⁶

The altar at the south aisle was a prominent location for the guild of poor porters and wage-workers.²⁸⁷ During the reconstruction of the church between 1456 and 1466 the old nave, dating back to the early thirteenth century, was considerably rebuilt, and the adjacent aisles were attached to the nave.²⁸⁸ The vault built by Porters guild, was part of this major enlargement project, supervised by the churchwardens, who were city councillors. An impressive sum of 100 Riga marks was spent on the vault, the price of a small house. Officials of the guild paid 100 Riga marks to the churchwardens in 1468, ten years after the creation of the chantry, but its sources remain unknown.²⁸⁹ In the chantry book there are no more details about the building process which was probably funded by members' donations. Here again the elite members may have facilitated the building project. As to the labour, some scholars have suggested that the Porters guild may have used unpaid voluntary labour of the guild members.²⁹⁰ Indeed, the guild's members supported the new chantry with their own labour; the city's carpenter (*stat tymmerman*), a certain Hinrik, member of the guild, voluntarily erected the Porters guild's altar.²⁹¹ Yet, even with unpaid labour, the costs of the vault were high.

The construction of the outstanding vault in St Peter's church was part of a larger campaign to gain prestige for the guild and its chantry. In 1464 Archbishop Silvester Stodewescher, granted the Porters guild the right to a chantry, altar, and perpetual mass in St Peter's.²⁹² His charter, in addition to the charter issued by the city council, ensured that the chantry was fully recognized by the council and by the archbishop. The archbishop's charter was a privilege; it acknowledged the chantry and the guild's right to choose its chantry priest.²⁹³ This charter secured autonomy for the chantry, and the guild spent a great deal in its efforts to secure it. The chantry's account book shows that the alderman and his deputies used the city council's letter to lobby for the charter from the archbishop, spending 22 Riga marks on gifts and other expenses, and 8 marks on the production of the document itself.

The support of elite members helped the Porters guild gain an excellent location in the church, at the very centre of St Peter's, next to the council's pews. Claus Glembeke also erected an altar for the Beer Carters guild in St

---

285 LUB 12, no. 60.
286 LUB 12, no. 60.
287 The altar of the prestigious Black Heads brotherhood was established later in the 1480s, next to their altar. Marburg, DSHI 120, no. 7, fol. 31.
288 Gunārs Zirnis, *Pētera baznīca* (Rīga: Zinātne, 1984), p. 51.
289 Arbusow, 'Kirchliches Leben', p. 211.
290 Zirnis, *Pētera baznīca*, p. 56; Rīga, LVVA, 4038 f., 2 apr., 1087 l. fols. 36ª, 48ª.
291 Arbusow, 'Kirchliches Leben', pp. 203, 205.
292 LUB 12, no. 288.
293 Arbusow, 'Kirchliches Leben', p. 210.

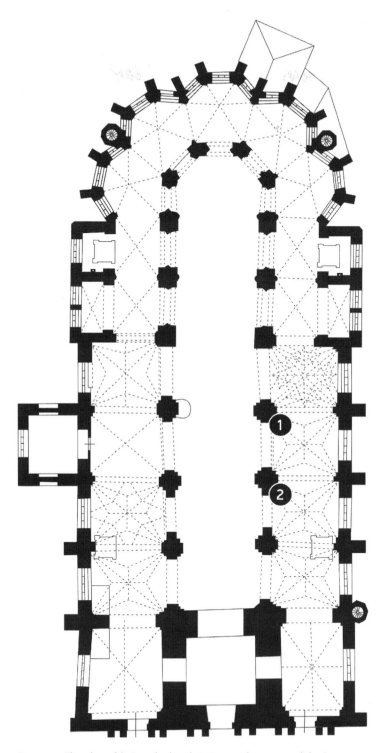

Figure 14: The plan of St Peter's church in Riga and position of the Porters guild's altar. Designed by Una Grants

Peter's, establishing a more prestigious commemorational space next to their altar in the smaller parish church of St Jacob. These shifts would not have been possible without the direct engagement of the elite and support by city councillors in charge of the parish churches.

Conclusion

The guilds of Beer Carters and Porters were the largest non–elite guilds in Riga, with several hundred members throughout the late Middle Ages, a large section of Riga's non–German (Latvian and Liv) population. The guilds were open to almost anyone who wished to join, but they maintained their profile as professional guilds of the Porters and Beer Carters. Both guilds experienced an upswing of activities, a 'new beginning', from the mid–fifteenth century when their memorial practices were established and also recognized by other social groups in Riga.

Memoria in all its forms demanded resources, and these guilds of the working poor lacked resources for lavish remembrance. In their initial stages, they maintained remembrance by gathering small donations and using the funeral ceremonies as the main commemorative events. While long–term liturgical remembrance was ensured through endowments by richer members, non–elite guild members continued to donate objects such as vessels and cloths for use at the communal meals. In this way individual donations contributed to the collective memorial practices.

Commemorative events were important for these transport workers' guilds. Yet, as the Fine Book of the Porters guild shows, they also were confronted with problems. Guild members were obliged by the statutes to commemorate their deceased brothers and sisters, but many members of the Porters guild misbehaved during funerals and occasionally were absent. The guild had to control and punish its members in order to maintain collective *memoria* properly, because without control, the commemoration could simply fail.

In my view, elite guild members – city councillors, rich merchants, and their family members – perceived the majority of the members in the Beer Carters and Porters guilds as 'poor', and that is why they joined them in *memoria*. This claim, however, cannot be directly confirmed by the sources, but it arises from the analysis offered here. Medieval elites strove to offer charity to the 'poor' and involve them in their commemoration.[294] In Riga, the guilds of the Beer Carters and Porters, with their predominance of non–German members, were in fact, the poor.

Networks of remembrance involving elites and non–elites or transport workers may have also existed in other Hanseatic cities, as in Stralsund and Stettin. This case study of the *memoria* of the guilds of Beer Carters and

---

294 Wollasch, 'Gemeinschaftsbewußtsein', pp. 271–83; Wollasch, 'Toten– und Armensorge', pp. 9–38;

Porters demonstrates that these groups were important centres of commemoration in late medieval Riga. Both guilds hosted *memoria* for elite families. Two city councillors – Geismer and Geresem – were the first endowers of the chantry of the Porters. A rich merchant, Claus Glembeke, created the chantry of the Beer Carters guild in St Peter's church, and a number of elite individuals requested remembrance from both guilds. The Beer Carters guild accepted not only living individuals from elites but also their dead kin as the members of the guild. In their commemoration of elite members and benefactors, the guilds emulated commemorative practices of religious communities.

Cooperation with leading townspeople had advantages for the guilds of working poor. Although the beer carters and porters were socially and politically marginal, their guilds received altars located at central spaces of St Peter's parish church. This would not have been possible without active support from the elites. Because of the elite endowments, they could establish long-term memorial services, which were resource consuming. Once elite members began to join the Beer Carters guild in mid-fifteenth century, the Beer Carters were also relieved from the humiliating function of executioners. The social marginality or 'poverty' of most guild members was the reason for elite interest in both guilds. This was a kind of reciprocal exchange, the non-elites counteracting their poverty by exchanging their commemorative practices for the money and benefits of the city councillors and rich merchants.

CHAPTER 7

Reformation and *Memoria*

The Reformation was not the end of *memoria*; *memoria* lost its importance centuries later with the onset of modernity.[1] The remembrance of the dead was transformed by Protestantism, yet it continued to be an important element of Catholic piety.[2] In the Protestant form, *memoria* lost its religious motivation. All reformers agreed that prayers for the suffering souls in purgatory were no longer necessary, and they enthusiastically criticised such a form of piety.[3] However, *memoria* did live on in Protestantism; Martin Luther (1483–1546) himself and other reformers were portrayed in numerous images that can be considered as memorial ones.[4] The relationship between the dead and the living gradually changed. In German towns from the early sixteenth century, the living were separated from the dead both theologically in the new Protestant views on the afterlife and also spatially by the relocation of cemeteries outside the city walls.[5]

The centres of the Reformation in Livonia were the cities – Riga and Reval – where it prevailed quickly. Riga came under the influence of the Lutheran Reformation around 1522. A vital role in it was played by Andreas Knopken (also Knopke, c. 1468–1539), a Brandenburg born clergymen who had returned from Pomerania a year earlier.[6] There he had been working at the Treptow town school together with Johann Bugenhagen (1485–1558), rector of the school, subsequent reformer and close friend of Luther.[7] Andreas had been working in Riga before his departure to Treptow, and he was well networked in the city because his older brother Jakob Knopken (Knopke)

---

1 Otto Gerhard Oexle, 'Das Ende der Memoria', in *Reformations and Their Impact on the Culture of Memoria*, pp. 315–30, p. 329.
2 Oexle, 'Die Memoria der Reformation', pp. 187–242; in a more local context, see Doreen Zerbe, *Reformation der Memoria: Denkmale in der Stadtkirche Wittenberg als Zeugnisse lutherischer Memorialkultur im 16. Jahrhundert* (Leipzig: Evangelische Verlagsanstalt, 2013); Susanne Ruf, 'Memoria im Luthertum? Sachzeugnisse des individuellen Totengedenkens in thüringischen Kirchen vom 16. bis zum 20. Jahrhundert', in *Reformations and Their Impact on the Culture of Memoria*, pp. 141–70.
3 Koslofsky, 'From Presence to Remembrance', p. 29.
4 Oexle, 'Die Memoria der Reformation', pp. 204–05, 208–15.
5 Koslofsky, *Reformation of the Dead*; Oexle, 'Das Ende der Memoria', 318.
6 Arbusow, *Die Einführung der Reformation*, pp. 171–85; *Contemporaries of Erasmus: A Biographical Register of the Renaissance and Reformation*, vol. 2, ed. by Peter G. Bietenholz and Thomas Brian Deutscher (Toronto: University of Toronto Press, 1986), p. 267; Martin Pabst, *Die Typologisierbarkeit von Städtereformation und die Stadt Riga als Beispiel* (Frankfurt am Main: Peter Lang, 2015), pp. 210–14.
7 *Contemporaries of Erasmus: A Biographical Register of the Renaissance and Reformation*, vol. 1, ed. by Peter G. Bietenholz and Thomas Brian Deutscher (Toronto: University of Toronto Press, 1985), pp. 217–19.

was the cathedral cannon and in 1517, with his brother's support, Andreas became a priest at St Peter's.[8] The Knopken brothers were involved in the aforementioned Porters guild, as members from 1517.[9] On 12 June 1522, there was a public disputation in St Peter's church between Andreas Knopken and the mendicants, during which Knopken presented twenty-four theses criticising the idolatry of the Catholic Church and its turning away from the Gospel that were later published in Nuremberg, Wittenberg, and Strasbourg.[10] That was a turning point after which numerous city councillors and the members of the merchant guilds openly supported the Reformation. When Andreas Knopken and another reformer Silvester Tegetmeyer were appointed as preachers at the city's two parish churches – St Peter's and St Jacob's – in late 1522, the Reformation was in full swing.[11] The events developed more dramatically when in the spring of 1524, Dominican and Franciscan friars were expelled, and violent crowds raided the city's churches that year in March and August smashing statues, altarpieces, and altars.[12] In 1525 the Reformation had succeeded: all the catholic institutions in the city, except the cathedral and the Cistercian convent, were taken over by the city council, and also all chantries and foundations were collected in so-called *gemeine Kasten*.[13] That meant an end of the liturgical remembrance.

The Reformation set its foot in Reval later than in Riga. Luther addressed Revalians together with Rigans in his printed letter of November 1523 to the Livonian cities, though it can be only assumed that at the time reformers were active in Reval.[14] Since the spring of 1524, the activities of the reformers became more evident. However, in Reval there was also iconoclastic violence. The procession of the feast of the Exaltation of the Holy Cross[15] on 14 September 1524 turned violent, when the mob ransacked the churches of the Holy Ghost and St Olaf. The churchwarden of St Nicholas had purposely damaged the locks to prevent the pillaging.[16] Once the Reformation took root

---

8 Arbusow, *Livlands Geistlichkeit*, p. 103.
9 Rīga, LVVA, 4038 f., 2 apr., 1087 l., fol. 58^b.
10 Arbusow, *Die Einführung der Reformation*, pp. 210–15; Pabst, *Die Typologisierbarkeit von Städtereformation und die Stadt Riga als Beispiel*, pp. 214–18; Andreas Knopken, *In epistolam ad Romanos Andreae Knopken Costerinensis interpretatio, Rigae apud Liuonios praelecta* [...] ([Nürnberg: Johann Petreius, 1524]), Andreas Knopken, *Vēstules romiešiem skaidrojums, ko kistrinietis Andreass Knopkens ir priekšlasījis livoniešiem Rīgā, kur viņš ir draudzes gans. 24 tēzes disputam 1522. gadā Sv. Pētera baznīcā*, transl. Kaspars Bankovskis (Rīga: Profesora Roberta Feldmaņa fonds, 2017).
11 Arbusow, *Die Einführung der Reformation*, p. 242; Pabst, *Die Typologisierbarkeit von Städtereformation und die Stadt Riga als Beispiel*, pp. 210–14;
12 Arbusow, *Die Einführung der Reformation*, pp. 290–312; Michalski, 'Bildersturm im Ostseeraum', p. 226; Michalski, '"Hölzer wurden zu Menschen"', pp. 147–48.
13 Arbusow, *Die Einführung der Reformation*, pp. 302–04; Schubert, 'Hausarme Leute', p. 333.
14 Arbusow, *Die Einführung der Reformation*, pp. 274–76; Alfred Ritscher, *Reval an der Schwelle zur Neuzeit. Teil I. Vom Vorabend der Reformation bis zum Tode Wolters von Plettenberg (1510–1535)* (Bonn: Kulturstiftung d. dt. Vertriebenen, 1998), p. 112; Martin Luther, *Den Auszerwelten lieben Freunden gottis, allen Christen zu Righe, Reuell vnd Tarbthe ynn Lieffland* [...] ([Wittemberg: Hans Lufft, 1523])
15 The meaning of the feast for the Livonian collective memory is described below.
16 Arbusow, *Die Einführung der Reformation*, pp. 357–58; Ritscher, *Reval an der Schwelle zur Neuzeit*, p. 114.

in the city, it had an upper hand over the old faith just as it did in Riga. By 1525 the Reformation had succeeded in all the largest Livonian cities, but the protestant beliefs were accepted in the Teutonic Order and Livonian nobility only gradually.[17]

The Teutonic Order experienced far-reaching changes during the Lutheran Reformation of the 1520s. Although the Grand Master, Albrecht von Hohenzollern (1490–1568), secularized the Prussian branch in 1525 and became a duke, the Livonian Master did not follow in his steps. The old and conservative Master Wolter von Plettenberg remained Catholic until his death in 1535, but the Livonian branch itself was affected by Protestantism even before that date. By the time the branch was dissolved in 1561, most of its members were Lutherans. Because little is known about how the Reformation transformed *memoria* practised by the Teutonic Order and Livonian nobility, this chapter focuses only on the changes that took place in Riga and Reval.

***

Just shortly before the Reformation, a new development in the local memory culture took place. It was short lived because of the Reformation but is important to mention. In the preceding chapters, the conflict between the Church of Riga and the Teutonic Order that had a great influence on the memory and commemoration in Livonia was described. These two parties had contrasting memory cultures that not only reflected but also fuelled the political conflicts between them.[18] Yet, a threat from the outside and a common enemy created the preconditions to have shared memories on one historical event.

During the late fifteenth century, Livonia anticipated a new military conflict with Muscovy that had gained regional influence under the rule of Ivan III (1462–1505). The Muscovites' conquest of Novgorod in 1484 had a direct implication on the Hanseatic trading, and Muscovy became a direct neighbour of Livonia.[19] In 1501 the Russian–Livonian war (1501–1503) began. It culminated in a battle at Lake Smolino on 13 September 1502 during which the Livonian forces – a combination of Teutonic Knights, mercenaries, and peasants under the command of the Teutonic Order's Livonian Master Wolter von Plettenberg fighting together with the archbishop of Riga Michael Hildebrand

---

17 Juhan Kreem, 'Der Deutsche Orden und die Reformation in Livland', in *The Military Orders and the Reformation: Choices, State Building, and the Weight of Tradition*, ed. by Johannes A. Mol, Klaus Militzer, and Helen J. Nicholson (Hilversum: Verloren, 2006), pp. 43–58.
18 Mäesalu, 'Historical Memory as the Cause of Conflict in Medieval Livonia', 1014–30.
19 Anti Selart, 'Switching the Tracks. Baltic Crusades against Russia in the Fifteenth Century', in *The Crusade in the Fifteenth Century. Converging and Competing Cultures*, ed. by Norman Housley (London: Routledge, 2016), pp. 90–106, 98.

– defeated the Muscovite army.[20] Scholars have doubted the battle's military relevance and have also emphasised that this was an unusual victory because the Livonian forces retreated back to Livonia after it.[21] Yet in Livonia at the time, this battle was considered to be a miracle and major victory, which was used in as anti–Russian propaganda during the indulgence campaign in the Empire to attract resources for the possible continuation of the war.[22]

The battle at Smolino was the first attempt to create a Livonian *lieu de mémoire*. In 1504 during the Livonian Landtag, it was decided that the battle and victory had to be commemorated on 14 September, the feast of the Exaltation of the Holy Cross.[23] According to '*Eynne schonne hysthorye von vunderlyken geschefften der herren tho Lyfflanth myth den Rüssen unde Tartaren*' a propaganda text of the Teutonic Order written around 1508, the archbishop of Riga ordered that the battle should be commemorated with a special service and a procession of the Blessed Sacrament, similar to that of Easter, had to take place.[24] The same text described the commemoration of the battle: the Master of the Livonian branch and the high–standing officials (*Gebieteiger*) founded numerous chantries and built chapels devoted to the Virgin Mary, which they funded lavishly. The Breviary of Riga printed in Paris in 1513 had a long introduction in which the battle at Smolino was mentioned, and the feast of the Exaltation of the Holy Cross as an event commemorating the battle was newly introduced.[25] The breviary emphasised the role of the archbishop in victory against the Muscovites, instructed the liturgy to have the festive spirit of Easter, and introduced a new chant to thank God for liberating them from the Russian power.[26] In European aristocratic and urban memory cultures, the remembrance of battles played an important role. This was the first and only time when the main Livonian powers univocally promoted the same memories. There is no information about how the remembrance of this

---

20 Alexander Baranov, 'Contra Multitudinem Ruthenorum Armatorum: The Russian–Livonian Battle of Lake Smolino (1502) Reconsidered', in *The Art of Siege Warfare and Military Architecture from the Classical World to the Middle Ages*, ed. by Michael Eisenberg, Rabei G. Khamisy, and Denys Pringle (Oxford: Oxbow Books, 2021), pp. 227–32.

21 Juhan Kreem, 'Crusading Traditions and Chivalric Ideals: The Mentality of the Teutonic Order in Livonia at the Beginning of the Sixteenth Century', *Crusades*, 12 (2013), 233–50 (238); Baranov, 'Contra Multitudinem Ruthenorum Armatorum', 227.

22 Leonid Arbusow jun., *Die Beziehungen des Deutschen Ordens zum Ablasshandel seit dem 15. Jahrhundert* (Riga: Häcker, 1909), pp. 391–409; Anti Selart, 'Switching the Tracks', 99–100.

23 *Akten und Rezesse der livländischen Ständetage (1494–1535)*, vol. 3, ed. by Leonid Arbusow (Riga: Deubner, 1909), no. 29, p. 116.

24 Uppsala, UUB, H 131, fol. 49ᵛ; Matthias Thumser, 'Antirussische Propaganda in der ‚Schönen Historie von wunderbaren Geschäften der Herren zu Livland mit den Russen und Tataren', in *Geschichtsschreibung im mittelalterlichen Livland*, ed. by Matthias Thumser (Berlin: LIT, 2011), pp. 133–53, p. 150.

25 *Breviarium Rigense* ([Paris]: [for Willem Corver (Amsterdam)], 1513); the only surviving copy of the breviary is in the collection of the University of Latvia Academic Library H 2/6, R 2522; Bruiningk, *Messe und kanonisches Stundengebet*, pp. 226–27.

26 "Grates nunc omnes / Reddamus Domino Deo / Qui sua benignitate / Nos liberavit / De Ruthenica potestate" von Bruiningk, *Messe und kanonisches Stundengebet*, 228.

battle was practised in Livonia, except the unfortunate procession in Reval in 1524 that marked the beginning of the Reformation in the city.[27] The common memories and remembrance of the victory were dismantled during the Reformation and the Livonian war (1558–1583) that followed, dissolving the Livonian branch and Livonia as a political entity.

Reformation and *Ratsmemoria*

The institutionalized *Ratsmemoria* survived until the spring of 1524, when in both Riga and Reval, the memorial services were permanently halted, and the chantries were dissolved.[28] The city councils played a crucial role in this process: they decided whether to appoint a Protestant preacher in the parish church or friary and whether to restrict or remove priests and friars from the city.[29] Likewise, city councils directly intervened in memorial affairs: in 1524 they disbanded the private and corporate chantries and consolidated all resources into *gemeine Kasten*, which were used for charitable purposes and the payment of Protestant preachers.[30] The failure of the city councils to prevent iconoclastic violence in churches where lavish altars had been erected by generations of townspeople benefited the cause of the new faith.[31] Moreover, the city councils themselves abolished liturgical *memoria* by dissolving memorial chantries and dismissing their commemorators, thus separating themselves from centuries–old traditions and also their deceased predecessors.[32]

Even on the eve of the Reformation, some city councillors demonstrated their memorial choices in their wills. In Riga, the city council openly promoted the new faith, but in Reval, although the council allowed reformers to preach in 1524, numerous councillors remained Catholic.[33] On 7 May 1524, Reval's burgomaster Joan Viandt drafted a will in which he indicated his intention to make lavish donations to churches, friaries, monasteries, and the poor.[34] He

---

27 Ritscher, *Reval an Der Schwelle Zur Neuzeit*, p. 114.
28 Arbusow, *Die Einführung der Reformation*, pp. 291–312.
29 Arbusow, *Die Einführung der Reformation*, pp. 300–01, 311–12; Ritscher, *Reval an der Schwelle*, pp. 113–17; Kala, 'Das Dominikanerkloster von Reval/Tallinn', pp. 86–87.
30 The *gemeine Kasten* was organized by the Riga council just after the iconoclasm in 1524. The principle of *gemeine Kasten* was developed in the German Lutheran towns to finance the poor. The guilds kept the resources of the chantries, but they had to make an annual payment for the sake of *gemeine Kasten*. Arbusow, *Die Einführung der Reformation*, pp. 302–04; Schubert, 'Hausarme Leute', p. 333.
31 Arbusow, *Die Einführung der Reformation*, pp. 290–96; Ritscher, *Reval an der Schwelle*, pp. 114–17; Sergiusz Michalski, 'Die protestantischen Bilderstürme. Versuch einer Übersicht', in *Bilder und Bildersturm im Spätmittelalter und in der frühen Neuzeit*, ed. by Robert W. Scribner (Wiesbaden: Harrassowitz, 1990), pp. 69–124, p. 93; Reinhard Wittram, 'Die Reformation in Livland', in *Baltische Kirchengeschichte*, ed. by Reinhard Wittram (Göttingen: Vandenhoeck & Ruprecht, 1956), pp. 35–55, at p. 40.
32 On distancing from the dead, see Koslofsky, *The Reformation of the Dead*; Koslofsky, 'From Presence to Remembrance', pp. 25–38.
33 Arbusow, *Die Einführung der Reformation*, pp. 286, 311–12.
34 Tallinn, TLA, f. 230, n. 1, s. BN 1–III Joann Viandt; *Revaler Regesten*, no. 127; Bunge, *Rathslinie*, p. 94.

aimed to leave 200 marks for the Dominicans, 300 marks for the Birgittines in Mariendal, and 100 marks to the parish church of St Olaf.[35] These were followed by minor prospective donations of 20 marks for the churches of St Nicholas, St Gertrud, and the cathedral. He wished to endow 500 marks for the *tafelgilde* and for the 'new hospital' (*nygen sekenhus*) and for the hospital of Holy Spirit 400 marks. Institutions outside Reval were also among the recipients of his pious bounty: a hospital and church in Westphalian Schwerte and nuns and the Table Guild in Dorpat.

It is remarkable that Joan Viandt, deeply involved in Reval politics and apparently tolerant of the new developments, expressed his wish to make large pious endowments for institutions which weeks later were reformed or disbanded by the city council's representatives.[36] It is possible that Viandt adhered to the traditional approach to testamentary bequests because he drafted his will while ill (*kranck an mynem licham*), and thus in case of potential death, it was more secure to rely on well-known Catholic practices.[37] Although this programme of pious and charitable endowments was impressive, it was never realised because Viandt died in 1529, when most of these institutions were already disbanded or reformed.[38]

The testament of burgomaster Viandt shows how deeply rooted pious and memorial donations were in the religious and political culture of the region. Even during the early stages of the Reformation, memorial endowments and donations played an important role for political leaders, who apparently relied on old practices. This practice, however, did not prevent their active involvement in the Reformation that dissolved *memoria* and transformed all private endowments into community property.

Reformation and *Memoria* of the Elite Guilds in Riga and Reval

The Black Heads *memoria* both in Riga and Reval was impressive. Yet the lavishly decorated altars furnished with liturgical objects and embedded within a programme of memorial services, were abandoned at the Reformation. Moreover, during the Reformation the Black Heads eagerly supported religious change; indeed, the Riga Black Heads took part in the destruction of memorial sites created by their predecessors. The Black Heads were the first in Riga to destroy the brotherhood's altars, altarpieces, statues, and other liturgical utensils.[39] As elsewhere in northern Europe and so in Riga, 'the commissioners of

---

35 Revaler Regesten, no. 127.
36 Kala, 'Das Dominikanerkloster von Reval/Tallinn', pp. 86–87.
37 Tallinn, TLA, f. 230, n. 1, s. BN 1–III Joann Viandt
38 Bunge, *Rathslinie*, p. 94; Kala, 'Das Dominikanerkloster von Reval/Tallinn', pp. 83–94.
39 Arbusow, *Die Einführung der Reformation*, p. 293.

images were the image destroyers' (*die Bilderstürmer waren die Bilderstifter*).[40] Likewise, the founders of the liturgical *memoria*, or rather their successors, abolished it as ineffectual.

According to Arbusow, the Black Heads supported the Reformation because as young men and foreigners, they were more exposed to the new reforming preaching.[41] Yet the Black Heads in Riga as a group did not destroy their own memorial spaces. In early 1524 the brotherhood's altar and chapel in St Peter's church was still repaired,[42] though on 10 March the Black Heads assembled in their house and agreed to cease payment for the altar and memorial services.[43] They decided to take the altarpiece and the chantry's objects to the Black Heads' house in the marketplace. The decision, however, was not carried out.

What happened next can be reconstructed only in part. Most likely after the assembly, some brethren, later described as 'young brothers with dull and witless heads' (*junghe broders myt ene dulle unsynnygen koppe*), went to St Peter's, where they destroyed the Black Heads altar.[44] As a result, the large altarpiece, the small ones, a missal, a corporal, chalices, candlesticks, and all the other objects belonging to the chantry were destroyed.[45] Although the destruction of the altarpiece was reported on 10 March, the brotherhood sold it and two smaller images for 236 marks after Michaelmas 1524, more than half of the amount paid for the large altarpiece produced in Lübeck in 1493.[46]

Though the brotherhoods supported the Reformation, alderman Hinrick van dem Sande and his deputies, treasurers, and the altar wardens were opposed to the violence.[47] They criticised the iconoclasts and noted down in the account book that the chantry had existed for forty-four years, 'which is a very short time'.[48] Despite the violence in St Peter's church, the hundred-year-old Black Heads chantry and altar in the Franciscan church was not ransacked, and all its belongings were handed over to the brotherhood in 1525.[49]

In contrast to the violent dissolution of the chantry in St Peter, the priests were treated better. This was a chantry of six priests, four of whom were paid their last wages by the brotherhood in November 1524, 26 Riga marks

---

40 Hermann Heimpel, 'Das Wesen des deutschen Spätmittelalters', *Archiv für Kulturgeschichte*, 35 (1954), 29–51 (50).
41 In the spring 1524, the Black Heads in Riga hired two reformers, Silvester Tegetmeyer and Andreas Knopken, as their preachers. Marburg, DSHI 120, no. 8, fol. 203; Spliet, *Geschichte*, p. 147; Arbusow, *Die Einführung der Reformation*, p. 293.
42 Marburg, DSHI 120, no. 8, fol. 46.
43 Spliet, *Geschichte*, p. 145.
44 Marburg, DSHI 120, no. 7, fol. 39; the Black Heads in Riga took part in the destruction of other altars in St Peter's and also in St Jacob's churches. See Arbusow, *Die Einführung der Reformation*, p. 295; Pabst, *Die Typologisierbarkeit von Städtereformation und die Stadt Riga als Beispiel*, p. 224.
45 Marburg, DSHI 120, no. 7, fol. 39.
46 Marburg, DSHI 120, no. 8, fol. 167; Arbusow, *Die Einführung der Reformation*, p. 294.
47 Arbusow, *Die Einführung der Reformation*, p. 293; Spliet, *Geschichte*, p. 146.
48 Marburg, DSHI 120, no. 7, fol. 39.
49 Spliet, *Geschichte*, p. 146; Arbusow, *Die Einführung der Reformation*, p. 294.

each.[50] The same amount was now directed to the salaries of two Lutheran preachers and for 'the box of the poor,' which accumulated resources from all abolished memorial chantries.[51] The process of ending traditional rituals, *memoria* among them, was concluded in June 1524, when the brotherhood finally demolished its altar, taking the altar-stones away and erecting the brotherhood's pews in their place.[52]

Although the churches of Reval, including St Catherine's, also suffered at the hand of iconoclasts, the Black Heads abolished their chantries and altars in a more organised manner. The Black Heads ceased supporting the memorial services in the Dominican church in 1524: on 1 August the brotherhood withdrew all endowments made to the two chantries in St Catherine's church, thus ending 124 years of cooperation between the two groups.[53] The brotherhood also removed the precious altarpiece of the Virgin Mary to its house, where it remained until the mid-twentieth century.[54]

Memoria had immense importance for such a transitional group like the Black Heads, yet as the attitudes towards the prayers for the dead changed, the Black Heads themselves abolished the liturgical *memoria* and objects supporting it. This, however, does not mean that the remembrance of the dead became irrelevant. Three decades after the abolition of liturgical *memoria*, the remembrance of the dead reappeared. In 1561, the Reval Black Heads commissioned an epitaph depicting ten brethren killed during the Livonian war on their knees, hands in prayer, in front of the cross, similar to the way their fellow brethren were portrayed on the Virgin Mary altarpiece sixty-five years earlier.[55] Collective *memoria* was not gone; it had been transformed, losing its liturgical character and developing instead its social forms.[56]

The Black Heads in Riga and Reval nurtured their remembrance from the earliest days of their existence. *Memoria* in these groups of young and foreign merchants is particularly interesting, since membership for most of the members was limited in time. *Memoria* constituted the groups and helped maintain their traditions and identities in conditions when membership constantly changed. The Black Heads in Riga and Reval enhanced *memoria* within local churches by commissioning memorial objects, including valuable altarpieces.

---

50 Marburg, DSHI 120, no. 8, fol. 202; Spliet, *Geschichte*, p. 147.
51 Marburg, DSHI 120, no. 8, fol. 203; Marburg, DSHI 120, no. 7, fol. 40; Arbusow, *Die Einführung der Reformation*, pp. 300–05.
52 Spliet, *Geschichte*, p. 148.
53 Kala, Kreem, and Mänd, 'Bruderschaft', p. 64; Amelung and Wrangell, *Geschichte*, p. 53; Kala, 'Das Dominikanerkloster von Reval/Tallinn', pp. 83–93.
54 Reidna, *The Altar of Holy Mary*, p. 7; Mänd, 'Über den Marienaltar der Revaler Schwarzenhäupter', p. 228.
55 Jüri Kivimäe, 'Das Scharmützel hinter dem Jerusalemer Berg Anno 1560', in *Die Revaler Schwarzenhäupter*, pp. 67–83, pp. 79–81; Mänd, 'The Altarpiece of the Virgin Mary', pp. 41–42.
56 Oexle, 'Memoria der Reformation', pp. 187–242; Koslofsky, *Reformation of the Dead*; Koslofsky, 'From Presence to Remembrance', pp. 25–38; Schmidt, *Wandelbare Traditionen*, pp. 72–84.

In Reval, the Virgin Mary altarpiece, which depicted the brethren, was a part of the Black Heads' collective *memoria*.

Although the Black Heads valued their *memoria* highly, during the Reformation in 1524, they were the first of the urban associations in Riga and Reval to abolish the liturgical *memoria* and dissolve their altars. Moreover, some Black Heads took part in the destruction of the memorial sites. Yet, although the Black Heads in both Riga and Reval wished to dissolve their altars, they also sought to hold onto their memorial objects, and transformed *memoria* to other social forms after the Reformation.

Reformation and *Memoria* of Non-elite Guilds in Riga

The Reformation swept away *memoria* in its medieval forms. The reformers in northern Europe attacked *memoria* not only theologically, but also physically. Widespread iconoclasm and the halting of commemorative services changed both the urban landscape and its social relations. The destruction of *memoria* in the guilds of the Beer Carters and Porters brought about a period of drastic change that impacted the relationships between elites and non-elites.

St Peter's church was the centre of commemoration for the guilds of Beer Carters and Porters, but St Peter's was also the centre of the Reformation in Riga during the early 1520s.[57] Located in the centre of the city, St Peter's was the largest parish church with the altars and chapels of rich elite families and influential brotherhoods and guilds. In 1524 the Reformation took a rapid course and violence broke out when the churches were run over during iconoclastic attacks. The altars of the Beer Carters and Porters in St Peter's church were also destroyed. By the end of 1524, the Reformation had triumphed in Riga.

Andreas Knopken was a central figure in the Lutheran Reformation in Riga. Leonid Arbusow claims that Andreas was appointed as the priest of the Porters guild and that he was hired to offer commemoration.[58] However, in the members' list, Andreas Knopken's status is not specified.[59] Arbusow argues convincingly that Andreas Knopken was a member of the Porters guild even after Knopken's appointment as a Lutheran preacher in 1522, but he acknowledges that nothing can be concluded about Knopken's possible influence on the guild members and the spreading of Lutheranism among them.[60]

The involvement of the reformer Andreas Knopken in the Porters guild and his possible but disputed appointment as a chantry priest of the guild poses the question of how both non-elite guilds and the non-German population

---

57 Arbusow, 'Kirchliches Leben', p. 191, 204; Rīga, LVVA, 4038 f., 2 apr., 1087 l., fol. 75ᵃ; Arbusow, *Die Einführung der Reformation*, pp. 236–43.
58 Arbusow, *Die Einführung der Reformation*, pp. 175–76; Arbusow, 'Studien zur Geschichte der lettischen Bevölkerung Rigas', p. 91.
59 Rīga, LVVA, 4038 f., 2 apr., 1087 l., fol. 58ᵇ.
60 Arbusow, 'Studien zur Geschichte der lettischen Bevölkerung Rigas', p. 91.

in general reacted towards the Reformation. The records of the Beer Carters account book show that guild officials were not enthusiastic supporters of the reforming iconoclasm in Riga. In the chantry's account book, the scribe of the Beer Carters guild described the iconoclasm carried out by the supporters of the new faith in St Peter's and St Jacob's churches in 1524. Referring to the violence, the scribe wrote that on 16 March, the 'Lutherans (*luterianer*) carried out something amazing (*wunderlick*) in Riga'.[61] The description of the *Bildersturm* appears to be opposed to the actions of the *luterianer*.[62] In depicting the destruction by the iconoclasts, the scribe takes on an apocalyptic tone, paraphrasing Isaiah:[63] 'Blind will see, mute will speak, the lame will walk and trees will become men.'[64] Next he discusses the violence in St Peter's and St Jacob's and the destruction by the crowd of the altarpieces of the Virgin Mary and reliquaries.[65] As they completed the day's destruction, the rioters sang Psalm 117 with the antiphon '*Haec dies pascale*', and a Lutheran preacher spoke in support of the violence, praising the iconoclasts for their righteous action against idolatry (*afgaderye*).[66] The destruction was not total, however, and the remaining altars were removed during the second wave of destruction in August 1524.[67]

The scribe of the Beer Carters guild, probably the chaplain of its chantry Johann Steffen, did not support the new faith and the actions of the iconoclasts despite the claims of Sergiusz Michalski, who describes this as a Lutheran text.[68] The apocalyptic tone of this story shows how distressed the author was by the events of the destruction of the Beer Carters altar in St Peter's. Steffen was dismissed from the chantry and lost his incomes; in 1524 he was not paid his annual wage, although in a number of other chantries, priests did receive their last wages.[69]

Even within guilds, attitudes to the challenges of the Reformation and to the violence related to it could differ. Steffen as a priest, who was paid for his services, did not represent the guild itself, so it could be questioned whether

---

61 '(..) don anrichtedenn de luterianer eyn wunderlick an bynnen Righe'. Arbusow, *Die Einführung der Reformation*, p. 295, 296; Rīga, LVVA, 4038 f., 2 apr., 1089 l., fol. 36ᵃ; Heinrich J. Böthführ, 'Einige Bemerkungen zu Sylvester Tegetmeier's Tagebuch', *Mittheilungen aus der livländischen Geschichte*, 13 (1881), 61–84 (66–67); Pabst, *Die Typologisierbarkeit von Städtereformation und die Stadt Riga als Beispiel*, pp. 224–25.
62 Arbusow, 'Studien zur Geschichte der lettischen Bevölkerung Rigas', p. 92.
63 Is 35: 4–6.
64 'De blinden worden sen, de stummen sprekenden, de lamen gande, de holter worden mynschen [..])' Rīga, LVVA, 4038 f., 2 apr., 1089 l. fol. 36ᵃ; Böthführ, 'Einige Bemerkungen', p. 66; Arbusow, *Die Einführung der Reformation*, p. 295; Michalski, '"Hölzer wurden zu Menschen"', pp. 152–53.
65 Böthführ, 'Einige Bemerkungen', pp. 66–67.
66 Böthführ, 'Einige Bemerkungen', p. 67; Arbusow, *Die Einführung der Reformation*, p. 296.
67 Rīga, LVVA, 4038 f., 2 apr., 1089 l. fol. 36ᵃ.
68 Arbusow, 'Studien zur Geschichte der lettischen Bevölkerung Rigas', p. 92; Arbusow, *Livlands Geistlichkeit*, p. 202; Michalski, '"Hölzer wurden zu Menschen"', pp. 152–53.
69 Arbusow, 'Studien zur Geschichte der lettischen Bevölkerung Rigas', p. 91; Arbusow, *Die Einführung der Reformation*, p. 305.

his attitudes towards the Reformation had anything in common with those of the Beer Carters. An example that shows the discrepancy of attitudes between the officials and simple guild members is the reaction of the senior officials of Riga's prestigious Black Heads brotherhood, who criticized younger members for destroying their chapel in St Peter's church on 16 March 1524.[70] Arbusow suggests that in Riga too the non-Germans, of whom many were members of the Beer Carters and Porters guilds, took part in iconoclastic acts as they did in Reval, Pernau, and Dorpat, but I can find little evidence to support this.[71] Some Beer Carters and Porters guild members took an active part in the Reformation, but these were elite members, city councillors, and priests, like the Knopken brothers who were active supporters of the Reformation.

It is hard to imagine that the disestablishment of *memoria* could have been an easy process for the guilds because it played an important role in the maintenance of their identities.[72] The deconstruction of *memoria* posed a real challenge to the guilds, even though many of their representatives took part in the Reformation theologically (clergymen), politically (city councillors), and also iconoclastically (townspeople). The deconstruction of *memoria* provoked some reluctance when the guilds' chantries were disbanded.

The guilds' officials were ambivalent about the changes the Reformation brought. When in 1525 the Beer Carters guild had to pay its share to the *gemeine Kasten*, the guild's officials entered in the account book: 'city councillors took from us' (*do nemet uns de radtlüde*) church wax.[73] Here the words 'took from us' should be emphasized. Clearly, the Beer Carters guild's officials did not show much enthusiasm for voluntarily contribution of resources, which normally would be spent on sustaining *memoria* and religious activities of the guild.

Unwillingness to pay the guild's share to the *gemeine Kasten* was a sign of reluctance to abandon *memoria* after the triumph of the Reformation in Riga. The guild's account book shows that between 1526 and 1530–1533, incomes from the chantry were spent on various secular purposes. The chantry's rents, which before the Reformation had sustained the guild's *memoria* and liturgical services, were now spent on communal meals during the annual drinking feasts and the funerals of poor guild members, distributed among the guild's members, and invested in the fabric of the guildhall.[74] Some of these acts still had commemorative meanings, particularly the communal meals, funerals, and almsgiving.[75]

---

70 Marburg, DSHI 120, no. 7, fol. 39.
71 Arbusow, 'Studien zur Geschichte der lettischen Bevölkerung Rigas', p. 91.
72 Oexle, 'Liturgische Memoria', p. 323, 333, 335.
73 Rīga, LVVA, 4038 f., 2 apr., 1089 l., fol. 36^b; Arbusow, 'Studien zur Geschichte der lettischen Bevölkerung Rigas', p. 92.
74 Rīga, LVVA, 4038 f., 2 apr., 1089 l., fols. 36^b, 37^a; Arbusow, 'Studien zur Geschichte der lettischen Bevölkerung Rigas', p. 92.
75 Wollasch, 'Gemeinschaftsbewußtsein', p. 340.

When liturgical remembrance ceased to exist, remembrance of the dead within the Beer Carters guild still carried on; communal meals, burials, and almsgiving continued non–liturgical *memoria* within the guild. For the reformers it was difficult, if not impossible, to eradicate that kind of activity. It is hard to assess how long the non–liturgical remembrance lasted in the Beer Carters guild, but it was continued at least until the mid–1530s, when Riga's transport workers guilds were reformed.[76]

The endowments made by elite guild members continued to serve for non–liturgical remembrance, even though they had left the brotherhoods when liturgical *memoria* ceased to exist. The member lists of both guilds show that the elite members had left the guilds even before the attacks of 1524. The last registered elite members of the Beer Carters guild were burgomaster Johann Moller and city councillor Tönnis Muther in 1522;[77] in the Porters guild it was priest Hynricus Ludert in 1522.[78] It is not a coincidence that the elite members cannot be found in the lists of members of the brotherhoods after 1522 because the Reformation had won the support of the elites after the disputation between Andreas Knopken and the friars in St Peter's church.[79] Theirs was a political as well as a religious decision, promoted by burgomaster Conrad Durkop.[80] The city councillors ceased their activities in the Beer Carters and Porters guilds, but the endowments made by them and other rich merchants, however, remained in the hands of both guild chantries.

The absence of elite members from the Beer Carters and Porters guilds in 1523 was just the beginning of their decline. During the Reformation the Beer Carters and Porters guilds lost all those members who were not involved in transporting work.[81] The decline in numbers had already begun before 1523. In the Porters guild, there were forty–two new members in 1521, in 1522 there were twenty–two and in 1523 just sixteen.[82] Then the members list stops for nine years. In 1532 the records resume, and fifty–six guild members were registered a year later in 1533. After a longer interruption, the guild accepted eight new members.[83] A similar pattern of decline appears in the list of the Beer Carters guild. In 1524 it admitted only two new members, and similar to the Porters guild, there was then a sixteen–year–long pause; only in 1540 did twelve new members join.[84] When the Beer Carters and Porters guilds

---

76 Arbusow, 'Studien zur Geschichte der lettischen Bevölkerung Rigas', p. 92.
77 Böthführ, *Rathslinie*, no. 381, 415; Rīga, LVVA, 4038 f., 2 apr., 1159 l., fol. 2b.
78 Rīga, LVVA, 4038 f., 2 apr., 1087 l., fol. 61b.
79 Arbusow, *Die Einführung der Reformation*, pp. 210–15.
80 *The New Cambridge Modern History. The Reformation 1520–1559*, vol. 2, ed. by Geoffrey R. Elton (Cambridge: Cambridge University Press, 1990), p. 169.
81 Strenga, 'Turning Transport Workers into Latvians?', p. 75.
82 Arbusow, 'Studien zur Geschichte der lettischen Bevölkerung Rigas', p. 91; Strenga, 'Turning Transport Workers into Latvians?', p. 75.
83 Rīga, LVVA, 4038 f., 2 apr., 1159 l., fol. 63b; Arbusow, 'Zwei lettische Handschriften', p. 31.
84 Rīga, LVVA, 4038 f., 2 apr., 1089 l., fol. 5b; Arbusow, 'Studien zur Geschichte der lettischen Bevölkerung Rigas', p. 93.

resumed membership in the late 1530s and early 1540s, only Beer Carters and porters and their spouses could join their respective guilds.[85] After the Reformation the guilds never reached their previous strength.

During the decade after the Reformation, the Beer Carters and Porters did not halt their activities, but they experienced a crisis that resulted in radical transformations.[86] In 1535 the city council imposed new statutes on both guilds.[87] The Porters guild was transformed into the Servants' and Porters guild, its membership now limited to seventy men, losing its previous traditions and statutes.[88] Later in the sixteenth century, this guild was united with the Dockers guild, while the Beer Carters guild continued to exist independently.[89] Taking into account these dramatic changes, one could say that after the Reformation, the Beer Carters and Porters guilds ceased to exist in their previous form. By imposing the new statutes in 1535, the city council re-founded them as simple craft guilds.[90]

The Reformation's effect on the relations between elites and non–elites in these guilds can be described as a process of forgetting. The elites as patrons of the two guilds 'forgot themselves', forgot their commemorational and social obligations towards the non–elites, and 'forgot' their patronage.[91] They 'forgot' the dead and the social relations created for remembrance of the dead through renouncing the religious component of practices that had developed into merely social ones.[92] Through the 'forgetting of themselves,' the previous social bonds with groups and individuals were dismantled. If before the Reformation endowments and membership of the elites within the non–elite guilds guaranteed status and recognition for these groups, then the privileges were equally 'forgotten' after it. However, a new community was born during this process; the non-German (Latvian) Lutheran congregation, to which the members of the transport workers' brotherhoods belonged, was established in St Jacob's church between 1525 and 1527.[93]

Forgetting of these previous obligations developed over decades and resulted in deeper social and ethnic segregation in early modern Riga. *Memoria* and other liturgical rituals did not obliterate the social differences between the non–Germans and Germans or non–elites and elites, but the tasks of remembrance brought these groups closer together. Even if elite individuals, who became members of the guild and requested commemoration were not present

---

85 Arbusow, 'Studien zur Geschichte der lettischen Bevölkerung Rigas', p. 93.
86 Strenga, 'Turning Transport Workers into Latvians?', p. 75.
87 *Schragen der Gilden und Aemter*, no. 1, 13, pp. 233–35, 256–57.
88 *Schragen der Gilden und Aemter*, no. 1, pp. 233–35.
89 *Schragen der Gilden und Aemter*, no. 78, pp. 418–21.
90 Strenga, 'Turning Transport Workers into Latvians?', pp. 75–76; Strenga, 'Die Formierung der Letten als Ethnische Gemeinschaft zur Zeit der Reformation in Riga', pp. 89–91.
91 Gadi Algazi, '"Sich selbst vergessen" im späten Mittelalter. Denkfiguren und soziale Konfigurationen', in *Memoria als Kultur*, pp. 387–427, at p. 388.
92 Algazi, '"Sich selbst vergessen"', p. 402.
93 Strenga, 'Turning Transport Workers into Latvians?', pp. 74–77.

at all performances of that *memoria*, they were spiritually part of the groups. The Reformation removed the possibility of such social rapprochement, by stripping the poor and lower classes of the rights of the counter–gift. Prayers for the benefactor's soul were no longer needed, thus the charity itself emphasised the role of the donor, not the recipient, who before the Reformation had a more important role.

The separation of the elites and non–elites brought about by the Reformation was concluded by the establishment of the non–German (Latvian) parish in St Jacob's congregation, while St Peter's church hosted a German congregation.[94] Under these circumstances, the ethnicity, social status, and language played an even greater role than before the devotional spaces of the two groups were separated. After the Reformation the two groups had fewer opportunities for communication and social interaction. As I have argued elsewhere, the Reformation formed Latvians (non-Germans) as an ethnic community in Riga.[95]

The abolition of the liturgical *memoria* did not mean the end of the commemorative activities in the non–elite guilds. Although the elite members left both guilds as early as in 1522/23, their endowments remained, and the Beer Carters guild continued to use those resources to distribute alms, and organize funerals and communal meals. Yet, the Reformation was a blow to the guilds of the Beer Carter and Porters; their membership declined, and for a decade new members were not admitted. The Reformation and the end of the liturgical *memoria* changed the relationship between the rich merchants and poor transport workers. The elite 'forgot' their bonds with the non–elites. Both rich and poor no longer had opportunities for symbolic exchange of donations and prayers that had bonded them for at least three generations. The Beer Carters and Porters guilds and their members lost the prestige that they had accumulated during a long period of time.

Conclusion

The Reformation was not the end of *memoria*. The commemoration of the dead was abolished by the reformers in its liturgical form, but *memoria* continued to live on. It transformed because the institutions and communities needed to remember their past, and the Lutherans also needed to commemorate the Reformation and the reformers, first of all, Luther himself. In most cases we do not know what happened to the commemoration of the events that were closely bonded with the liturgical remembrance. For example, in

---

94 Arbusow, *Die Einführung der Reformation*, pp. 727–33; Pabst, *Die Typologisierbarkeit von Städtereformation und die Stadt Riga als Beispiel*, pp. 224, 225; Strenga, 'Turning Transport Workers into Latvians?', pp. 74–77; Strenga, 'Die Formierung der Letten als Ethnische Gemeinschaft zur Zeit der Reformation in Riga', pp. 89–91.

95 Strenga, 'Turning Transport Workers into Latvians?', pp. 74–77; Strenga, 'Die Formierung der Letten als Ethnische Gemeinschaft zur Zeit der Reformation in Riga', pp. 89–96.

Livonia the battle at Smolino (1502) in which the Livonian forces defeated Russians was commemorated during the feast of the Exaltation of the Holy Cross on 14 September; was the battle commemorated after the Reformation in forms other than just historiography?

It is evident that the Reformation had an impact on how groups remembered their past and sustained their identities. Although *memoria* greatly benefited the elites, many councillors in Riga and Reval sympathised with the reformers, even if that meant dismantling many memorial practices they and their families had maintained for generations. As a result they lost an effective instrument for the display and legitimation of their power and one that reinforced links with their past and their predecessors.

Similarly, as many city councillors of the Livonian cities supported the Reformation, numerous members of the elite Black Heads brotherhoods in Riga and Reval cut their ties with the Catholic cult and liturgical *memoria* with eminent ease, despite decades-long investment into the groups' commemoration. Moreover, as the example of the Black Heads in Riga, who took part in the iconoclasm in the city's churches, shows, 'the commissioners of images were the image destroyers'.[96] They smashed the altars, statues, and altarpieces commissioned by their predecessors in hope of their successors' prayers and remembrance. For the Black Heads, the brotherhoods of local unmarried and foreign merchants, groups in which members changed frequently, *memoria* was a tool of sustaining a feeling of continuity and common identity; however, they were amongst the first who joined the Reformation. The need for remembering predecessors also after the Reformation is manifested in the late sixteenth-century epitaph commissioned by Reval Black Heads that commemorated the brotherhood's members who had died during the Livonian war.

The Reformation brought about dramatic changes to the Beer Carters and Porters guilds. *Memoria* was degraded and then abolished, and so the urban elites no longer engaged with the guilds. *Memoria* had gained the Beer Carters and Porters guilds status within the city, and this was lost during the Reformation. By the time *memoria* was abolished in 1522–1524, the guilds lost the main attraction they held for the elites, their ability to commemorate the dead. After the Reformation beer carters and porters returned to their initial social positions in Riga's society, and the social status of their guilds – now strictly professional organizations – declined. The Reformation limited contacts between the German elites and non-German working poor. While the Reformation disrupted liturgical remembrance, the sources of the Beer Carters guild show that the tradition of non-liturgical *memoria* continued into the mid-1530s. For the guilds of the Beer Carter and Porters, *memoria* was even more important than for the elite guilds; therefore after the Reformation they still tried to maintain its non-liturgical forms. The end of liturgical *memoria*

---

96 Heimpel, 'Das Wesen des deutschen Spätmittelalters', p. 50.

marked the end of an age when the transport workers' guilds in Riga brought together rich and poor for common aims: shared prayers and commemoration. The non–elites were those who had benefited most by these bonds, and so the end of this close relationship was bound to be felt most sorely by them.

Conclusion

This book has aimed to demonstrate that *memoria* was a form of collective memory and a social practice. Although the two were not exclusive phenomena, *memoria* as a collective memory was orientated more towards the past, while as a social practice, it focused more on the present and future. Collective memory means a shared remembering of the past: it is fostered and not necessarily the truth about the past. Commemoration as an element of collective memory shapes identity, which is where it overlaps with social practice. As a social practice, *memoria* shaped reality in the present, made commitments to the future by obliging individuals and groups to commemorate, created bonds, and constituted groups. *Memoria* created reciprocity between the commemorated and the commemorators; it was a form of memorial gift giving in which material donations were exchanged for prayers and rituals.

Collective memory is here the most relevant place to begin. When this research project began, the intention was to map out the collective memory of medieval Livonia. However, it quickly became clear that there was no single tradition of collective memory in medieval Livonian society, and moreover, that in any medieval society, there were always multiple collective memories at play. Each social group in Livonia – the urban elite guilds, non–elite brotherhoods, cathedral chapters, monastic communities, and the Teutonic Order – had its own collective memory. There is only one exception that can be traced – the remembrance of the battle of Smolino (1502) that became, most likely, the first event commemorated in the whole of Livonia, and as a site of memory was shared by the Church of Riga and the Teutonic Order. In other cases, the memories of the past were group–based narratives, which differed both in form and content. *Memoria* had the same purpose in all groups – remembering the dead helped to remember the common past and to attain the salvation of souls – but *memoria* operates differently in different contexts; it has one purpose but different forms. Groups used different tools for the maintenance of *memoria*. Moreover, even where the narratives of different groups referred to the same historical events or epochs, these frequently contradicted one other.

Remembering the beginnings of the Christian faith in Livonia lies in the centre of identities for two groups in Livonia: the Church of Riga (bishops/archbishops and Riga cathedral chapter) and the Livonian branch of the Teutonic Order. Tombs of founders and leaders were crucial to the maintenance of identity and cultural memory. The Church of Riga possessed valuable assets, namely the tombs of the first three Livonian bishops, who brought Christianity to Livonia and shaped it as an ecclesiastical realm. The tombs of these bishops – Meinhard, Berthold, and Albert – in Riga cathedral's chancel were constant reminders of the Church of Riga's beginnings and helped to legitimise episcopal power. Meinhard and Berthold were most likely revered as saint bishops in the local tradition, and their remains added further sanctity to the cathedral. All three bishops were part of the collective memory of this community during the fifteenth and sixteenth centuries.

This cultural memory developed in the thirteenth century with the translation of Meinhard and Berthold from Üxküll to Riga and the composition of the Chronicle of Henry of Livonia, which later served as a source for the early history of the church in Livonia. The memory of the first bishops was supplemented by the remembrance of the fifteenth- and early sixteenth-century bishops, who were likewise buried in the cathedral chancel. The cathedral, and the chancel in particular, were places where the history of the Church of Riga was constantly remembered. This *memoria* was spatially bound to Riga cathedral and was performed by a small community: the archbishops and the cathedral canons.

The Teutonic Order in Livonia lacked the tombs of their thirteenth-century Masters, and its memorial tradition was not as closely bound to the remains of its leaders as was the case in the Church of Riga. Yet the Teutonic Order in Livonia had a memorial tradition that existed not only within the Livonian branch but was also shared with the Order as a whole. After their arrival in Livonia in the late 1230s, the Teutonic Order engaged in a military struggle against Livonian and Lithuanian pagans during which their brethren were killed. They were not forgotten; their memory was transformed into the cultural memory of the Teutonic Order.

This cultural memory was shaped by historical writings and also the Order's necrologies. The early fourteenth-century Livonian Rhymed Chronicle was not only a historical account of the Teutonic Order's participation in the Baltic crusades but also a text that created the *memoria* of the Livonian Masters and the brethren who were killed during the crusading period. The chronicle was one of the media that transmitted the information about those who had died in battle to the Order's bailiwicks further west, where the memory of these events was maintained. The Livonian Rhymed Chronicle was also used in the fifteenth century and was kept in the sacristies of the Order's Prussian castles.

The necrologies of the Order's bailiwicks in western Europe demonstrated the fact that the brethren killed in Livonia during the crusades were part of the Teutonic Order's collective memory. Numerous records in these necrologies commemorated the brethren and Masters killed in Livonia. Consequently, we know more how the brethren killed in Livonia were commemorated outside Livonia than we do about their commemoration within the Livonian branch. The battles in Livonia became realms of memory for the Teutonic Order. The battle at Durbe (1260) in which the Order suffered defeat, similarl to the later Tannenberg/Grunwald (1410), was the Teutonic Order's *lieu de mémoire*. The brethren killed at Durbe were commemorated by the Order in the Empire even two centuries after the battle. Livonia itself was also constructed as a realm of memory within the whole Order. With the help of chronicles and necrologies, the collective experiences of struggle against the Baltic pagans were communicated to those brethren of the Order who had never taken part in the crusade against non–believers and who lived centuries after that epochal age. These memories were used to sustain the identity of the Teutonic Order, and they were particularly important during the fifteenth century when the Order no longer primarily countered pagans.

The *memoria* and collective memory of the Teutonic Order's Livonian branch and the Church of Riga reached far into the past. It seems safe to say that in late medieval Livonia only the Teutonic Order's Livonian branch and the Church of Riga possessed the cultural memory that related back to their beginnings in the thirteenth century. *Memoria* of those who had died during this time period played a crucial role in the formation of cultural memory. Within the Church of Riga and the Teutonic Order, communicative memory was successfully translated into cultural memory during the thirteenth and fourteenth centuries through various media, including historical writing, necrologies, liturgical manuscripts, and grave slabs. The memorial traditions of both groups were similar to the memorial cultures of monastic communities, which were institutionalised and lasted for centuries. This continuity was possible because of the fixed and stable institutional structures they depended on and which altered comparatively little between the early thirteenth century and the Reformation. This cultural memory helped these groups to sustain identities until the Reformation.

The political *memoria* of the Teutonic Order's Livonian branch likewise sought to ensure institutional continuity and to present it to its subjects. The Teutonic Order's political *memoria* focused on the person of the Master. The Masters' *memoria* created a line of succession and provided legitimacy for the office. He was the only official to whom a burial place was granted in the branch's main chapel or church and for whom elaborate memorial services were enshrined in the Order's statutes; in the Masters' commemoration, that of all brethren was enfolded. The *memoria* of those Livonian Masters killed in battle dominated the historical and memorial texts that referred to the Order's experiences during the Baltic crusades. Also in the late Middle Ages, *memoria* of the Masters played an important role within the Order's memorial culture. As the foundation of Master Heidenreich Vincke von Overberg (1447) demonstrates, memoria of the Masters was not only retrospective but also prospective; Masters attempted to strengthen the legitimacy and positions of their successors. Yet, as the commemoration of the Livonian commander of the Order's forces Andreas von Steinberg demonstrates, memory of other Order's officials was also integrated into the collective memory of the Order and had numerous media: grave slabs, the historiographical texts, and information about their death circulated in the Order's documents.

The *memoria* of the Order's Masters was also projected outwards. In Livonia, as in Prussia, they were secular rulers on behalf of the Order, with Riga and Reval as its subjects. Reval's city council organised memorial services for deceased Livonian Masters in the city's churches and paid for their commemoration. Like the rituals that accompanied the Livonian Masters in life, such as entries into the city and oath–giving, his *memoria* in death marked the end of his role in what was essentially a political relationship.

The question of an individual's role within group *memoria* has been raised on several occasions in this book. *Memoria* was a group phenomenon, and all memorial efforts, including those fostering the commemoration of an individual, contributed to the collective *memoria*. According to Oexle, group *memoria* always referred to individuals, and in fact groups remembered their past by remembering individuals.[1] Individuals strengthened a group by founding their individual *memoria*, especially in cases where founders were office holders. Dietrich Nagel, a mid–fifteenth–century provost of the Riga cathedral chapter, created his individual *memoria* by using resources of the chapter. Nagel obliged his successors in office to foster his remembrance but at the same time also strengthened his predecessors' *memoria*, many of whom had died abroad. His individual commemorative efforts contributed to that of all provosts, past and future. Similar aims can be seen in *memoria* founded by the late medieval Livonian Masters. Heidenreich Vincke von Overberg created a memorial foundation for himself and for future Livonian Masters, but he also sought to commemorate all living and dead brothers. Vincke's individual *memoria* was sustained by the Order's resources and benefited the whole community. Similarly, city councillors in Riga and Reval fostered *memoria* of themselves and their families, in the hope both to gain individual benefits and to strengthen these institutions. *Memoria* revealed individual aspirations, yet this was only possible within the collective commitment of a group; individual *memoria* was integrated in the remembrance of a group.

The Cistercian nuns in Riga maintained other relationships as well based on mutual commemoration. In the mid–fifteenth century, they established a spiritual confraternity with the Birgittines in Mariendal, near Reval, with the mutual promise of prayers for the dead of both communities. This bond between the two religious communities survived the Reformation, when the Birgittines in the mid–sixteenth century recorded the name of a deceased Rigan Cistercian nun in their calendar. These communities supported each other by exchanging prayers for the dead; for example, the Birgittines needed to strengthen their position in the eastern Baltic region in the mid–fifteenth century and thus were looking for allies.

Memory was sustained not only by the communities themselves but also by networks of memory, created by involving other institutions and individuals outside them for remembering individuals and all the deceased of their

---

1 Oexle, 'Memoria als Kultur', p. 51; Oexle, 'Liturgische Memoria', p. 333.

communities. The Cistercian nuns in Riga, Dorpat, and Reval, as well as the Dominican friars in Reval, sustained close bonds with the Livonian nobility. Because few monasteries existed outside urban centres in Livonia, noblemen requested commemoration from the convents and friaries in the towns and cities. Many noblemen chose the Cistercian nuns as their commemorators because the majority of the nuns came from the nobility. The Dominican friaries similarly hosted *memoria* of the Livonian noble families. Yet, the Dominicans, as the Reval testaments show, were more closely bound to the townspeople. The friars in Reval were one of the main commemorators in the urban space.

The significance of *memoria* can be further seen in the relationship between the Teutonic Order and the Livonian Cistercians. The mid–fourteenth–century historical text – the Annals of Dünamünde – compiled by the Cistercians in Padis in the mid–fourteenth century, a few years after the destruction of the abbey's community during the St George's night uprising in 1343, represents the historical tradition of Dünamünde abbey and demonstrates the influence of the memorial tradition of the Teutonic Order on the collective memory of the monks. The history and the dead of the Teutonic Order dominate these Cistercian annals, which reflect the close relationship of the two groups that had developed during the thirteenth century. As the charter of the sale of Dünamünde abbey shows (1305), the relationship of the monks and knights was partially constituted by mutual remembrance. Although a historical text, the annals mirror the tradition of liturgical *memoria* practised in the Livonian Cistercian abbeys, in which the commemoration of the Teutonic knights most likely played an important role. The annals testify that the historical and memorial traditions of the two groups were so closely intertwined in some aspects that they are difficult to separate.

Memoria not only legitimised power but also served as a political tool during the conflicts. Livonia was exposed to the political and military struggles between the Teutonic Order, the archbishops of Riga, and the city of Riga. The Order aimed to establish control over the archbishopric, and *memoria* played an important role in this struggle. When the Order took over the cathedral chapter in 1451, it converted the cathedral chancel – where the archbishops were habitually buried – into the burial ground of its Masters. It was a political and a memorial conquest of a space where previously only the archbishops were buried. The planned burial and *memoria* of the Masters in the cathedral was intended to mark the incorporation of the Church of Riga into the Order. Yet, although Master Johann von Mengede Osthof was buried in the cathedral in 1469, this precipitated a new conflict between Archbishop Silvester Stodewescher and the Order. The dead Master was denied a grave slab and liturgical *memoria*. The denial of *memoria* exposed deep divisions between the Order and the archbishop. The Order fought for the Master's *memoria* but failed. As a result, Stodewescher's actions against the Master's *memoria* prevented the chapter's incorporation in the Order and also forced the Order to choose another location for the burial of its Masters.

Livonian politics were reflected in the *memoria* of the archbishops and the Riga cathedral chapter too. With its aspirations to increase the Order's power, the Livonian branch had pursued and persecuted those archbishops and canons that opposed them. The cathedral chapter and community of the Church of Riga in the late fifteenth century developed a memorial counter-narrative to that of the Teutonic Order. As the calendar of the Riga Missal demonstrates, the members of the cathedral community at the Holy Cross altar commemorated five fifteenth-century archbishops and canons who had suffered at the Order's hands. This *memoria* was politically motivated, and it expressed the chapter's aspirations for autonomy. In these conflicts, the past was instrumentalised and commemoration was used for political purposes, but the memories also further fuelled the conflicts and made the resolution of the conflicts difficult.

Although urban commemoration has the broadest range of surviving sources, it reflects only two types of memorial activities: liturgical *memoria* and non-liturgical *memoria* by associations, mainly during communal meals. These practices can be described as a communicative memory that almost never reaches more than eighty to one hundred years into the past. According to their fifteenth-century ordinance, during the communal meals the Reval Table Guild commemorated its foundation in 1363. Such references to the distant past and beginnings of the urban associations are, however, extremely rare: this is the only surviving example from late medieval Livonian cities that demonstrates a remembering that surpasses three to four generations.

The material from Riga and Reval shows that the memory of urban associations was focused on the recently dead and the recent past. This can be possibly explained by the fact that all late medieval guilds and brotherhoods in Riga and Reval were of the mid-fourteenth or early fifteenth-century foundation. Of the late medieval institutions of the Livonian cities, only the city councils were founded in the thirteenth century. It would further seem that the guilds and brotherhoods were only interested in the commemoration of the dead and events that were associated with their groups. When compared with the other groups analysed in this book, such as the Teutonic Order or the Church of Riga, the urban associations had a larger number of members to commemorate, and their numbers fluctuated more dynamically than in non-urban groups.

There was greater diversity in the urban *memoria* than in other environments. Not only did multiple institutions create remembrance, but individuals who possessed resources were also active in the creation of their own *memoria*, which in turn interacted with the group *memoria*. Numerous ecclesiastical institutions were also involved as commemorators. For example, a fifteenth-century merchant from Riga could have been commemorated by his family, by a foundation in a parish church, by the Great Guild, the Table Guild, the Black Heads brotherhood, the town council (if he had been a councillor), perhaps by the non-elite transport workers' guilds too, and also the parish churches, convents, friaries, and hospitals to which he had made donations. In a way it was a communal *memoria* because almost the whole community was involved in a commemoration of a one person.

Urban memorial culture was rich and enacted in the hands of many urban associations and commemorators. Every association possessed its own altar and had its own commemorative practices, but these commemorative traditions only met when they were coupled, as in the example of the Great Guilds and the Table Guilds. Communal memory of the dead, shared by most members of the community, was the memory of elites because only they could afford to sustain broad commemoration involving a large number of individuals – such as the poor – and institutions, such as churches, friaries, convents and monasteries, in their remembrance. This ability to command the field of memory was also a political tool that helped to legitimate their power and exclusivity.

The longevity of memory depended on the resources groups had at their disposal. Elite groups like the Black Heads could invest more in liturgical remembrance at brotherhood altars than the guilds of the transport workers. The merchant guilds and the town councils had more opportunities to sustain their *memoria* and collective memory in the long term than did the non–elite brotherhoods. In Riga, *memoria* of the non–German groups depended on the political support and resources of the elite; for example, the Beer Carters and Porters' guilds were only able to maintain their own altars and memorial chantries in the long term because of their elite members.

Memoria not only created and sustained collective memories, but constituted groups, their identities, and created relationships between groups and individuals.[2] The cases studied in this book demonstrate how a variety of groups used *memoria* for the sustaining of their identities and maintaining social bonds.

The brotherhoods of the Black Heads, groups of young unmarried or foreign merchants in Riga and Reval, were established in the early fifteenth century. From the earliest stages of their existence, even before they had their 'own' dead, they had already performed *memoria*. These brotherhoods were transitional groups in which membership did not last a lifetime but more likely for only a few years. For the Black Heads, *memoria* was crucial to maintain the group's long–term identity in circumstances when members constantly changed. Without commemoration of the dead and the past, maintenance of an identity would not have been possible.

In order to achieve these aims, the memorial activities of the Black Heads in Riga and Reval were intensive, especially during the brotherhood's drinking feasts. Because the Black Heads were not burghers and did not take part in urban politics, *memoria* served for their self–representation and helped to maintain social status. The Black Heads possessed extensive resources for

---

2 Oexle, 'Memoria als Kultur', p. 37; Oexle, 'Gegenwart der Lebenden', p. 75.

their commemorative and religious activities; they sustained several altars, employed numerous priests for the celebration of regular commemorative services, and commissioned valuable altarpieces.

While *memoria* helped to ensure continuity and identity within the brotherhoods of the Black Heads, *memoria* and religious activities within the non–elite Beer Carters' and Porters' guilds in Riga helped to establish these groups in the urban environment. Most members of these guilds were not professional transport workers but non–German artisans and servants; thus they had little in common with one another, and collective memorial activities played an important role in the formation of these guilds as communities. The events of the Reformation, when these guilds lost most of their members, support the hypothesis that religious activities and *memoria* were the main factors that attracted individuals to the Beer Carters' and Porters' guilds. Soon after the abandonment of liturgical *memoria*, the city council reorganised both brotherhoods, and they lost their previous status and recognition.

Memoria also played an important role in constituting and shaping the identities of the Riga and Reval Table Guilds. Alongside charity, *memoria* was the primary *raison d'être* of these charitable sub–groups within the Great Guilds. Although associated with the Great Guilds, the Table Guilds were independent in their social and commemorative activities; they kept name–lists of their own deceased members and commemorated them. The Table Guilds especially fostered the remembrance of those members who contributed to their charitable activities, and involved the urban poor in their *memoria*. It appears that these guilds fulfilled commemorative functions of the Great Guilds, and in the case of the Table Guild, *memoria* and charity were closely intertwined.

Several of the case studies in this book illustrate how *memoria* created and reflected relationships between groups and individuals. *Memoria* was involved in the relationship between elites and non–elites in late medieval Riga, as for example in the case of Beer Carters and Porters guilds. The town councillors, rich merchants, high–status clergymen, and their family members joined the non–elite guilds for the sake of *memoria*. These guilds of socially marginalised non–Germans welcomed members from other social classes, many from the economic and political elites, in order to attract additional prestige and resources. Some elite members – rich merchants and city councillors – made memorial foundations for these guilds and requested *memoria* from the Latvian and Livonian porters, beer carters, and artisans. Although elite members did not engage in all of the social activities organised by these guilds, a memorial exchange of resources and services did take place, similar to that between the early medieval monastic communities and their secular patrons. This kind of relationship between the transport workers guilds and the elite can also be found in other Hanseatic port towns.

Memoria played a central role in the unusual relationship between the Cistercian nuns of St Mary Magdalene and the guild of the Beer Carters in Riga.

This relationship began in 1495, when more than fifty nuns became members of the Beer Carter's guild, and continued during the early sixteenth century. The groups exchanged commemorational services based on this membership; the nuns had to pray for the deceased beer carters and the beer carters had to take part into the funerals of the nuns. They also exchanged payments in the form of membership fees and gifts for commemoration.

Memoria was essential for the legitimation of power and continuity of institutions; as Assmann famously put it, 'power requires origin'.[3] This kind of legitimising remembrance can be found in all institutions that exercised power. In the urban context, *memoria* helped the city councils to maintain their power, though it was performed not by the institution alone. *Ratsmemoria* combined institutional commemoration and family remembrance. It was organised by the councils, but the memorial efforts of the individual councillors and their families were integral to *Ratsmemoria*. In Riga and Reval, the city councils were small exclusive groups, which were selected from the members of the merchant Great Guilds. *Ratsmemoria* helped to maintain this exclusivity. Likewise, the institutional commemoration of their deceased predecessors legitimated power of living city councillors. The councils in the Livonian cities took care of *memoria* of individual councillors, controlled their memorial chantries, and when necessary, transformed them to maintain the memory. As the examples of the commemorative efforts of the Visch and Hunninghusen families in Riga and Reval demonstrate, *memoria* formed a bond between generations of city councillors. Investment into the memorial programmes increased the possibility that future generations of the councillors' families would be able to maintain a position in the city government. These families supported foundations made by their predecessors, and in doing so all displayed dynastic continuity. Political *memoria* was not only directed towards the council itself but towards the wider urban population, while regular memorial services in the city's churches fulfilled the function of self–representation.

Medieval *memoria* and charity were intertwined. *Memoria* enabled the elite to engage in gift exchange with the urban poor, through the making of material donations in return for prayers. The charity of elite groups, like the charitable Table Guilds in Riga and Reval, was aimed at self–legitimation and the fostering of their own commemoration. The Table Guilds distributed food and clothing in church bell towers, a logical environment in which prayers would be exchanged for the gifts received. In Riga elite members requested *memoria* from the Beer Carters' and Porters' guilds because within this exchange, the guild members were perceived as the 'poor'. The exchange of gifts and commemorative prayers was crucial for *memoria*; urban people and their institutions used it for the promotion of social and political aspirations.

Medieval *memoria* made the dead and absent present. By the help of *memoria*, the dead became part of the community of the living. The dead and

---

3 Assmann, *Cultural Memory and Early Civilization*, p. 54.

the absent became present when their names were evoked during liturgical commemoration as well as in non–liturgical practices, like communal meals. Alongside the performance of *memoria*, visual objects such as grave slabs and altarpieces made the dead depicted on them constantly present amongst the living. As the example of the Black Heads in Reval demonstrates, there was a meaningful interplay between the images of brotherhood members on the altarpiece of the Virgin Mary altar and the liturgical commemorations performed at the brotherhood's altar in the Dominican church. Such interplay of memorial media can rarely be studied closely since little has survived the iconoclasm of the Reformation. Yet that was the nature of *memoria*, to combine liturgical remembrance with different media of commemoration. In so many ways, *memoria* can be described as unending, a permanent process in which the new names of the dead were constantly added for commemoration with old ones being continually replaced and forgotten.

The developments over the period of the Reformation further highlight the relationship of urban groups to their own *memoria*. The urban elites of Riga and Reval eagerly supported the Reformation and were the first to abandon *memoria*, even though remembrance had been an instrument that had helped them to maintain power and exclusivity. Members of some elite groups, like the Black Heads in Riga, took part in the destruction of the associations' altars, where commemorations had taken place for decades. The Reformation and the dissolution of the liturgical *memoria* in the Livonian cities were radical and violent.

Despite the end of liturgical *memoria*, urban associations continued to commemorate their dead. Such continuity of memorial practices can be found in both elite and non–elite brotherhoods. The Black Heads in Reval in the 1560s commissioned an image commemorating the brethren who had died during the Livonian war; during the 1530s the Beer Carters brotherhood in Riga continued to spend its resources on activities – such as almsgiving and communal meals – which before the Reformation, had possessed a memorial character. After the Reformation *memoria* continued to exist but was transformed.

***

Memoria played a particular role in Livonia partly due to the unique characteristics of the region. Livonia was integrated into European Christendom relatively late, in a process that began in the late twelfth century and continued during the thirteenth. *Memoria* was brought to Livonia from western Europe alongside other ideas and practices, and it fulfilled the important social and political roles within Livonian society as in any other medieval society.

Memoria enabled Livonian groups to remember their past and to reach back to their origins. It helped them remember the past by commemorating individuals and their deeds but in the process also constituted groups and shaped identities. *Memoria* played an integral role in creating the social fabric of Livonian society, and it was essential for maintaining continuity of its institutions:

the guilds and brotherhoods, the Teutonic Order, the episcopal sees, and the cathedral chapters. There was also an important political dimension to *memoria*, which reflected, formed, and legitimated political relationships.

This book has argued that *memoria* was overwhelmingly a 'total social phenomenon' within late medieval Livonian society. Liturgical *memoria* was the most obvious form of *memoria*, but *memoria* was more than liturgy alone. Liturgical *memoria* interacted – and was intertwined – with a diversity of social practices, and the memorial image of the dead was carried by a wide range of media. Remembering the dead rendered them present. Finally, *memoria* was not only a process of recollecting and reaching back to the past but also one of validating the present and forging connections in the future. *Memoria* was at one and the same time retrospective, present, and prospective, though the future of *memoria* was influenced and transformed by the Reformation.

Place Name Equivalents

In this book I have used predominantly historical German place names because they have been extensively used in historiography.

Places (cities, towns, rivers, abbeys, castles, districts, bishoprics) in Southern Livonia

German	**Latvian**
Aa (Livonian)	Gauja
Ascheraden	Aizkraukle
Düna	Daugava
Dünamunde	Daugavgrīva
Dünaburg	Daugavpils
Goldingen	Kuldīga
Courland	Kurzeme
Hasenpoth	Aizpute
Kokenhusen	Koknese
Lemsal	Limbaži
Marienburg	Alūksne
Pilten	Piltene
Riga	Rīga
Ronneburg	Rauna
Roop	Straupe
Segewold	Sigulda
Selonia	Sēlija
Semigallia	Zemgale
Üxkull	Ikšķile
Warthe	Vārtāja
Wenden	Cēsis
Wolmar	Valmiera

Places (cities, towns, castles) in Northern Livonia

German	Estonian
Arensburg	Kuressaare
Dorpat	Tartu
Fellin	Viljandi
Harrien	Harju, Harjumaa
Karkhus	Karksi
Karusen	Karuse
Leal	Lihula
Mariendal	Pirita
Narva	Narva
Ösel	Saaremaa
Ösel–Wiek	Saare–Lääne
Padis	Padise
Reval	Tallinn
Valkena/Falkenau	Kärkna
Weissenstein	Paide
Wesenberg	Rakvere
Wierland	Viru, Virumaa

Places (cities, towns, abbeys, castles, districts, bishoprics) in Prussia

German	Modern–day name
Danzig	Gdańsk
Elbing	Elbląg
Königsberg	Kaliningrad
Marienburg	Malbork
Memel	Klaipėda
Thorn	Toruń

Bibliography

Archival sources

Berlin, Geheimen Staatsarchiv Preußischer Kulturbesitz (GStA PK)

GStA PK, XX. HA, OBA no. 16502, *Meister in Livland an Hochmeister betreffend seine Leistung zur Ausrichtung des Prokuratoramts*, 31 August 1474

GStA PK, XX. HA, OBA no. 16510, *Meister in Livland an Hochmeister betreffend seinen Vergleich mit dem Erzbischof von Riga*, 2 October 1474

GStA PK, XX. HA, OBA 16835, *Meister in Livland an Hochmeister betreffend den Tod des Erzbischiofs von Riga*, 12 October 1479

GStA PK, XX. HA, OBA 16989, *Meister in Livland an Hochmeister betreffend die Angelegenheit wegen d. Erzbistums Riga*, 16 December 1481

GStA PK, XX. HA, OF no. 281

Hamburg, Staatsarchiv der Freien und Hansestadt Hamburg (StAH)

StAH Coll. 612–2/6 Brüderschaft der Schwarzenhäupter aus Reval no. E 1, *Rechnungsbuch über Einnahmen und Ausgaben des Schawarzhäupteraltars in der Mönchskirche (sog. Altarbuch) (1403) 1418–1517*

StAH Coll. 612–2/6 Brüderschaft der Schwarzenhäupter aus Reval no. D 1, *Schafferbuch 1430–1527*

Linköping, Stifts- och Landsbiblioteket (LSL)

LSL manuskript H 33, *De Ordine Statutis Domus Teutonicus (Gesetze des livländischen Landmeisters Eberhard von Monheim)*

Ludwigsburg, Stadtarchiv Ludwigsburg (StAL)

StAL B 280 U 1, *Nekrolog und Anniversar des Deutschordenshauses Mergentheim aus der Mitte des 14. Jahrhunderts*

Marburg, Dokumentensammlung des Herder-Instituts (DSHI)

DSHI 120 Schwarzhäupter Riga no. 4, *Schafferrechungen 1417–1440*
DSHI 120 Schwarzhäupter Riga no. 5, *Das Buch der Oberkämmerer 1441–1523*
DSHI 120 Schwarzhäupter Riga no. 7, *Das Hauptbuch der Schwarzhäuptervikarie 1481– 1585*
DSHI 120 Schwarzhäupter Riga no. 8, *Das Hauptbuch der Schwarzhäuptervikarie 1481– 1585 II*
DSHI 120 Schwarzhäupter Riga no. 64, *Fastnachtschafferbuch 1413–1443*

Rīga, Latvijas Nacionālais arhīvs, Latvijas Valsts vēstures arhīvs (Latvian National Archive, Latvian State Historical Archives) (LVVA)

LVVA, f. 223, apr. 1, l. 369, *Die Grosse Gilde zu Riga, 'Bock der Breve' 1424–1538*
LVVA, f. 4038, 2 apr., l. 864, *Inventarium der Kirchengeräte von St. Jakob in Riga*
LVVA, f. 4038 f., apr.2, l. 1159 (l. 1089), *3 Bücher der Bierträger zu Riga. II – 1521–1524*
LVVA, f. 4038 f., apr. 2, l. 1087, *3 Bücher der Bierträger zu Riga. I –1462–1520*, actually *Straf– und Bruderbuch der Gilde der Lostrӓger zu Riga*
LVVA, f. 4038 f., apr. 2, l. 1089 (l. 1088), *3 Bücher der Bierträger zu Riga. III – 1461–1686*
LVVA, f. 7363, apr. 1, l. 367, *Das Vikarienbuch der Gilde der Lostrӓger zu Riga (c. 1450?)– 1523*

Rīga, Latvijas Universitātes Akadēmiskā Bibliotēka (University of Latvia Academic Library) (LUAB)

LUAB, R, Ms. 1, *Missale Rigense*, 15th c., Riga
LUAB, R, Ms. 61, *Liber privilegiorum Collegii Societatis Jesu Rigensis (Riga, saec. 16/17)*

Tallinn, Eesti Kunstimuuseum (Art Museum of Estonia), Niguliste Museum (EKM)

EKM j 18761, The Reval *Totentanz* by Bernt Notke (around 1468)
EKM j 18760, Altarpiece of the Virgin Mary of the brotherhood of the Black Heads in Reva (Tallinn)

Tallinn, Tallinna Linnaarhiiv (Tallinn City Archives) (TLA)

TLA f. 31, n. 1., s. 216, *Rechnungsbuch der Kirchenvormünder (Nicolaus Kirche)*
TLA, f. 191, n. 2, s. 1, *Mitgliederbuch der Tafelgilde nebst Satzungen und chronikalischen Nachrichten (Foliant C) (1364–1549)*
TLA, f. 191, n. 2, s. 2, *Memorialbuch der Tafelgilde (Foliant B) (96) (1416–1449)*
TLA f. 230, n. 1, Aa 7, *Denckelbuch der Stadt Reval 1415–1523*
TLA, f. 230, n. 1, Ad 32, *Städtische Kämmerei Rechnungen 1507–1533*
TLA f. 230, n. 1, s. Bk 3, *Dominikaner in Reval 1418–1579*

TLA, f 230, n. 1, s. BN 1, *Testamente*
TLA f. 230, n. 1, s. BN 1–III, *Testamente*
TLA, f. 230, n. 1, Cm 8, *Summa de arte predicatoria et al.*

Tartu, Rahvusarhiiv (National Archives of Estonia, former Eesti Ajalooarhiiv) (EAA)

EAA, f. 2069, n. 2, s. 128, *Testament von Herman Soye, vom 1. April 1470*

Uppsala, Uppsala universitetsbibliotek (Uppsala University Library) (UUB)

UUB C 436 *Breviarium*, 15th c., Riga,
UUB H 131 *Eynne schonne hysthorye von vunderlyken gescheffthen der herren tho Lyfflanth myth den Rüssen unde Tartaren*, c. 1508

Vilnius, Lietuvos mokslų akademijos Vrublevskių biblioteka (The Wroblewski Library of the Lithuanian Academy of Sciences) (LMAVB)

LMAVB RS F 22–96, *Psalterium Davidis*, 15th c., Riga

Wien, Deutschordenszentralarchiv (DOZA)

DOZA Hs. 427c, *Kalendarium, Nekrolog und Anniversar von Biesen*

Secondary literature and published sources

'Cronica episcoporum Rigensium', *Archiv für die Geschichte Liv–, Est– und Kurlands*, 5 (1846), 174–80
'Testamente Adeliger aus dem fünfzehnten und sechzehnten Jahrunderte', *Archiv für die Geschichte Liv–, Est– und Kurland*, 4 (1845), 209–24
Abert, Josef Friedrich, and Walter Deeters, eds., *Repertorium Germanicum*, vol. 6 (Berlin: Georg Bath, 1985)
Algazi, Gadi, '"Sich selbst vergessen" im späten Mittelalter. Denkfiguren und soziale Konfigurationen", in *Memoria als Kultur*, ed. by Otto Gerhard Oexle (Göttingen: Vandenhoeck & Ruprecht, 1995), pp. 387–427
———, 'Forget Memory: Some Critical Remarks on Memory, Forgetting and History', in *Damnatio in Memoria: Deformation und Gegenkonstruktionen von Geschichte*, ed. by Sebastian Scholz, Gerald Schwedler, and Kai–Michael Sprenger (Köln: Böhlau, 2014), pp. 25–34
Althoff, Gerd, 'Geschichtsbewußtsein durch Memorialüberlieferung', in *Hochmittelalterliches Geschichtsbewußtsein im Spiegel nichthistoriographischer Quellen*, ed. by Hans–Werner Goetz (Berlin: Akademie–Verlag, 1998), pp. 85–100

——, 'Zur Verschriftlichung von Memoria in Krisenzeiten', in *Memoria in der Gesellschaft des Mittelalters*, ed. by Dieter Geuenich and Otto Gerhard Oexle (Göttingen: Vandenhoeck & Ruprecht, 1994), pp. 56–73

——, *Adels- und Königsfamilien im Spiegel ihrer Memorialüberlieferung: Studien zum Totengedenken der Billunger und Ottonen: Bestandteil des Quellenwerkes, Societas et fraternitas* (München: Fink, 1984)

——, *Amicitiae und pacta: Bündnis, Einung, Politik und Gebetsgedenken im beginnenden 10. Jahrhundert* (Hannover: Hahn, 1992)

Alttoa, Kaur, 'Padise kloostri ehitusloo probleeme', in *Keskaja sild Padise ja Vantaa vahel = Keskiajan silta Padisen ja Vantaan välillä*, ed. by Erki Russow (Padise: Padise Vallavalitsus, 2012), pp. 63–80

Andreson, Krista, 'Research on Tallinn's Dance of Death and Mai Lumiste – Questions and Possibilities in the 20th Century', *Kunstiteaduslikke Uurimusi*, 22.3–4 (2013), 96–109

Angenendt, Arnold, 'Buße und liturgisches Gedenken', in *Gedächtnis, das Gemeinschaft stiftet*, ed. by Karl Schmid and Joachim Wollasch (München: Schnell und Steiner, 1985), pp. 39–50

——, 'Das Offertorium. In liturgischer Praxis und symbolischer Kommunikation', in *Zeichen – Rituale – Werte. Internationales Kolloquium des Sonderforschungsbereichs 496 an der Westfälischen Wilhelms-Universität Münster*, ed. by Gerd Althoff (Münster: Rhema, 2004), pp. 71–150

——, 'Theologie und Liturgie der mittelalterliche Toten-Memoria', in *Memoria, der geschichtliche Zeugniswert des liturgischen Gedenkens im Mittelalter*, ed. by Karl Schmid and Joachim Wollasch (München: Fink, 1984), pp. 79–199

——, *Heilige und Reliquien: die Geschichte ihres Kultes vom frühen Christentum bis zur Gegenwart* (München: Beck, 1997)

Angermann, Norbert, 'Die mittelalterliche Chronistik', in *Geschichte der deutschbaltischen Geschichtsschreibung*, ed. by Georg von Rauch (Köln: Böhlau, 1986), pp. 3–20

——, and Ilgvars Misāns, eds., *Wolter von Plettenberg und das mittelalterliche Livland* (Lüneburg: Verl. Nordostdt. Kulturwerk, 2001)

Arbusow, Leonid jun., 'Die handschriftliche Überlieferung des "Chronicon Livoniae" Heinrichs von Lettland', *Latvijas Universitātes Raksti. Acta Universitatis Latviensis*, 15 (1926), 189–341

——, 'Kirchliches Leben der Rigaschen Losträger im 15. Jahrhundert', *Latvijas Universitātes Raksti. Acta Universitatis Latviensis*, 6 (1923), 185–224

——, 'Studien zur Geschichte der lettischen Bevölkerung Rigas im Mittelalter und 16. Jahrhundert', *Latvijas Universitātes Raksti. Acta Universitatis Latviensis*, 1 (1921), 76–100

——, 'Zwei lettische Handschriften aus dem XVI und XVII Jahrhundert', *Latvijas Augstskolas Raksti. Acta Universitatis Latviensis*, 2 (1922), 19–57

——, and Albert Bauer, eds., *Heinrichs Livländische Chronik* (Hannover: Hahn, 1955)

——, *Die Beziehungen des Deutschen Ordens zum Ablasshandel seit dem 15. Jahrhundert* (Riga: Häcker, 1909)

——, *Die Einführung der Reformation in Liv-, Est- und Kurland* (Leipzig: M.Heinsius, 1921)

Arbusow, Leonid sen., 'Johannn von dem Broele gen. Plate im Deutschen Orden in Livland', *Jahrbuch für Genealogie, Heraldik und Sphragistik*, (1905/1906), 182–209

——, ed., *Livlands Geistlichkeit vom Ende des 12. bis ins 16. Jahrhundert* (Mitau: J. F. Steffenhagen und Sohn, 1913)

Arndt, Wilhelm, 'Neu entdeckte livländischen Chroniken', *Archiv für die Geschichte Liv-, Est- und Kurlands*, 4 (1845), 269–71

Arnold, Udo, 'Deutschordenshistoriographie im Deutschen Reich', in *Die Rolle der Ritterorden in der mittelalterlichen Kultur*, ed. by Zenon Hubert Nowak (Toruń: UMK, 1985), pp. 65–87

——, 'Die Deutschordensnekrologien von Alden Biesen und Mergentheim', in *Quellen kirchlicher Provenienz: neue Editionsvorhaben und aktuelle EDV-Projekte*, ed. by Helmut Flachenecker (Toruń: TNT, 2011), pp. 145–59

——, 'Die Entwicklung von Balleistrukturen des Deutschen Ordens zwischen Mittelrhein und Nordsee – Biesen, Koblenz and Utrecht', in *Adel, ridderorde en erfgoed in het land van Maas en Rijn: opstellen und Aufsätze zu Ehren von Udo Arnold*, by Udo Arnold, ed. by Jozef Mertens (Bilzen: Historisch Studiecentrum Alden Biesen, 2012), pp. 25–44

——, 'Edmund von Werth, priester van de duitse Orde en bisschop van Koerland', in *Leden van de Duitse Orde in de Balije Biesen* (Bilzen: Historisch Studiecentrum Alden Biesen, 1994), pp. 189–213

——, 'Livländische Reimchronik', in *Die deutsche Literatur des Mittelalters – Verfasserlexikon*, vol. 5, ed. by Kurt Ruh (Berlin: de Gruyter, 1985), cols. 855–62

——, ed., *800 Jahre Deutscher Orden: Ausstellung des Germanischen Nationalmuseums Nürnberg in Zusammenarbeit mit der Internationalen Historischen Kommission zur Erforschung des Deutschen Ordens*; (Gütersloh: Bertelsmann Lexikon-Verlag, 1990)

Assmann, Aleida, 'Canon and Archive', in *Cultural Memory Studies: An International and Interdisciplinary Handbook*, ed. by Astrid Erll and Ansgar Nünning (Berlin: de Gruyter, 2008), pp. 97–108.

——, 'Theories of Cultural Memory and the Concept of "Afterlife"', in *Afterlife of Events: Perspectives on Mnemohistory*, ed. by Marek Tamm (Basingstoke: Palgrave Macmillan, 2015), pp. 79–94

——, *Cultural Memory and Western Civilization: Functions, Media, Archives* (Cambridge: Cambridge University Press, 2011)

——, *Der lange Schatten der Vergangenheit: Erinnerungskultur und Geschichtspolitik* (München: Beck, 2006)

——, *Erinnerungsräume: Formen und Wandlungen des kulturellen Gedächtnisses* (München: Beck, 2006)

Assmann, Jan, 'Collective Memory and Cultural Identity', *New German Critique*, 65 (1995), 125–34

———, *Cultural Memory and Early Civilization: Writing, Remembrance, and Political Imagination* (Cambridge: Cambridge University Press, 2011)

———, *Das kulturelle Gedächtnis: Schrift, Erinnerung und politische Identität in frühen Hochkulturen* (München: Beck, 1992)

———, *Der Tod als Thema der Kulturtheorie: Todesbilder und Totenriten im Alten Ägypten* (Frankfurt am Main: Suhrkamp, 2000)

Autenrieth, Johanne, Dieter Geuenich, and Karl Schmid, eds, *Das Verbrüderungsbuch der Abtei Reichenau* (Hannover: Hahnsche Buchhandlung, 1979)

Babendererde, Cornell, *Sterben, Tod, Begräbnis und liturgisches Gedächtnis bei weltlichen Reichsfürsten des Spätmittelalters* (Ostfildern: Thorbecke, 2006)

Baranov, Alexander, 'Contra Multitudinem Ruthenorum Armatorum: The Russian–Livonian Battle of Lake Smolino (1502) Reconsidered', in *The Art of Siege Warfare and Military Architecture from the Classical World to the Middle Ages*, ed. by Michael Eisenberg, Rabei G. Khamisy, and Denys Pringle (Oxford: Oxbow Books, 2021), pp. 227–32

Barley, Nigel, *Dancing on the Grave: Encounters with Death* (London: John Murray, 1995)

Barron, Caroline M., and Clive Burgess, eds, *Memory and Commemoration in Medieval England: Proceedings of the 2008 Harlaxton Symposium* (Donington: Tyas, 2010)

Bartlett, Robert, *The Making of Europe: Conquest, Colonization, and Cultural Change, 950–1350* (London: Allen Lane, 1993)

Bassett, Steven R., *Death in Towns: Urban Responses to the Dying and the Dead, 100–1600* (Leicester: Leicester University Press, 1992)

Behrmann, Carolin, Horst Bredekamp, and Philipp Zitzlsperger, eds, *Grab, Kult, Memoria: Studien zur gesellschaftlichen Funktion von Erinnerung* (Köln: Böhlau, 2007)

Bender, Wolfang, 'Bernhard II. zur Lippe und die Mission in Livland', in *Lippe und Livland: mittelalterliche Herrschaftsbildung im Zeichen der Rose; Ergebnisse der Tagung 'Lippe und Livland', Detmold und Lemgo, 2006*, ed. by Jutta Prieur, Wolfgang Bender, and Gerhard Milting (Gütersloh: Verlag für Regionalgeschichte, 2008), pp. 147–68

Benninghoven, Friedrich, *Der Orden der Schwertbrüder: Fratres milicie Christi de Livonia* (Köln: Böhlau, 1965)

———, *Rigas Entstehung und der frühhansische Kaufmann* (Hamburg: Velmede, 1961)

Bergholde, Agnese, *Rīgas Doma viduslaiku arhitektūra un būvplastika eiropeisko analoģiju kontekstā: disertācija = Mittelalterliche Architektur und Bauplastik des Doms zu Riga im europäischen Vergleich* (Rīga: LMA Mākslas Vēstures Institūts, 2015)

Beuttel, Jan–Erik, 'Edmund von Werth', in *Die Bischöfe des Heiligen Römischen Reiches 1198 bis 1448: Ein biographisches Lexikon*, ed. by Erwin Gatz and Clemens Brodkorb (Berlin: Duncker & Humblot, 2001), pp. 313–14

Bietenholz, Peter G., and Thomas Brian Deutscher, eds, *Contemporaries of Erasmus: A Biographical Register of the Renaissance and Reformation*, vols. 1–2 (Toronto: University of Toronto Press, 1985–1986)

Bijsterveld, Arnoud-Jan, 'The Medieval Gift as Agent of Social Bonding and Political Power: A Comparative Approach', in *Medieval Transformations. Texts, Power, and Gifts in Context*, ed. by Esther Cohen and Mayke De Jong (Leiden: Brill, 2001), pp. 124–56

———, *Do ut Des: Gift Giving, Memoria, and Conflict Management in the Medieval Low Countries* (Hilversum: Verloren, 2007)

Binski, Paul, *Medieval Death: Ritual and Representation* (Ithaca, N.Y: Cornell University Press, 1996)

Biskup, Marian, ed., *Visitationen im Deutschen Orden im Mittelalter: 3 : 1528–1541 sowie Nachträge, Korrekturen und Ergänzungen, Orts- und Personenverzeichnis* (Marburg: Elwert, 2008)

Blese, Ernests, *Latviešu personu vārdu un uzvārdu studijas, I* (Rīga: Ansis Gulbis, 1929)

Bloch, Marc, 'From "Mémoire Collective, Tradition et Coutume : À Propos d'un Livre Récent"', in *The Collective Memory Reader*, ed. by Jeffrey K. Olick, Vered Vinitzky-Seroussi, and Daniel Levy (Oxford: Oxford University Press, 2011), pp. 150–55

———, *Mémoire collective, tradition et coutume. A propos d'un livre récent.* (Paris: La renaissance du livre, 1925)

Blümcke, Otto, 'Die S. Laurentius-Bruderschaft der Träger in Stettin', *Baltische Studien*, 35 (1885), 267–359

Boesch, Gottfried, ed., *Das Jahrzeitbuch der Deutschordenskommende Hitzkirch: aus dem Jahre 1432/33, mit dem Fragment A von 1399* (Stans: Josef von Matt, 1970)

Boockmann, Hartmut, 'Der Deutsche Orden in der Kommunikation zwischen Nord und Süd', in *Kommunikation und Mobilität im Mittelalter: Begegnungen zwischen dem Süden und der Mitte Europas (11.–14. Jahrhundert)*, ed. by Siegfried de Rachewiltz and Josef Riedmann (Sigmaringen: Thorbecke, 1995), pp. 179–89

———, 'Der Einzug des Erzbischofs Sylvester Stodewescher von Riga in sein Erzbistum im Jahre 1449', *Zeitschrift für Ostforschung*, 35 (1986), 1–17

———, 'Die Geschichtsschreibung des Deutschen Ordens. Gattungsfragen und "Gebrauchssituationen"', in *Geschichtsschreibung und Geschichtsbewusstsein im späten Mittelalter*, ed. by Hans Patze (Sigmaringen: Thorbecke, 1987), pp. 447–69

———, *Der Deutsche Orden: zwölf Kapitel aus seiner Geschichte* (München: Beck, 1994)

Borgolte, Michael, 'Das Grab in der Topographie der Erinnerung. Vom sozialen Gefüge des Totengedenkens im Christentum vor der Moderne', *Zeitschrift für Kirchengeschichte*, 111 (2000), 291–312

———, 'Die Stiftungsurkunden Heinrichs II. Eine Studie zum Handlungsspielraum des letzten Liudolfingers', in *Festschrift für Eduard Hlawitschka zum 65. Geburtstag*, ed. by Karl Schnith (Kallmünz: Lassleben, 1993), pp. 231–50

———, 'Memoria. Zwischenbilanz eines Mittelaltersprojekts', *Zeitschrift für Geschichtswissenschaft*, 46 (1998), 197–211

———, 'Stiftung, Staat und sozialer Wandel. Von der Gegenwart zum Mittelalter', in *Strukturwandel der Armenfürsorge und der Stiftungswirklichkeiten in Münster im Laufe der Jahrhunderte*, ed. by Franz-Josef Jakobi (Münster: Aschendorff, 2002), pp. 9–24

——, 'Stiftungen des Mittelalters im Spannungsfeld von Herrschaft und Genossenschaft', in *Memoria in der Gesellschaft des Mittelalters*, ed. by Dieter Geuenich and Otto Gerhard Oexle (Göttingen: Vandenhoeck & Ruprecht, 1994), pp. 267–85

——, *'Totale Geschichte' des Mittelalters? Das Beispiel der Stiftungen. Antrittsvorlesung, 2. Juni 1992.* (Berlin: Präsidentin der Humboldt–Universität, 1993)

——, 'Zur Lage der deutschen Memoria–Forschung', in *Memoria. Ricordare e dimenticare nella cultura del medioevo: Trento, 4–6 aprile 2002*, ed. by Michael Borgolte, Cosimo Damiano Fonseca, and Hubert Houben (Bologna: Il mulino, 2005), pp. 21–28

Böthführ, Heinrich J., *Die Rigische Rathslinie von 1226 bis 1876* (Riga: J. Deubner, 1877)

——, 'Einige Bemerkungen zu Sylvester Tegetmeier's Tagebuch', *Mittheilungen aus der livländischen Geschichte*, 13 (1881), 61–84

——, 'Jürgen Padel's und Caspar Padel's Tagebücher', *Mittheilungen aus dem Gebiete der geschichte Liv–, Est– und Kurlands*, 13 (1886), 291–404

Bourdieu, Pierre, 'The Forms of Capital', in *Handbook of Theory and Research for the Sociology of Education*, ed. by John G. Richardson (Westport: Greenwood Press, 1986), pp. 241–58

Bracker, Jörgen, Volker Henn, and Reiner Postel, eds, *Die Hanse: Lebenswirklichkeit und Mythos. Textband zur Hamburger Hanse–Ausstellung von 1989* (Lübeck: Schmidt–Römhild, 1998)

Brandt, Ahasver von, 'Die gesellschaftliche Struktur des spätmittelalterlichen Lübeck', in *Lübeck, Hanse, Nordeuropa: Gedächtnisschrift für Ahasver von Brandt*, ed. by Klaus Friedland and Rolf Sprandel (Köln: Böhlau, 1979), pp. 209–32

Brauns, Wilhelm, 'Livländische Reimchronik', in *Die deutsche Literatur des Mittelalters – Verfasserlexikon*, vol. 5, ed. by Wolfgang Stammler, Kurt Ruh, Burghart Wachinger, and Christine Stöllinger–Löser (Berlin: de Gruyter, 1955), cols. 956–67

Brenner, Elma, Mary Franklin–Brown, and Meredith Cohen, eds, *Memory and Commemoration in Medieval Culture* (London: Routledge, 2016)

Breviarium Rigense ([Paris]: [for Willem Corver (Amsterdam)], 1513)

Brodman, James, *Charity and Welfare: Hospitals and the Poor in Medieval Catalonia* (Philadelphia: University of Pennsylvania Press, 1998)

Brück, Thomas, 'Bemerkungen zur Kaufmannschaft Rigas in der ersten Hälfte des 15.Jahrhunderts unter besonderer Berücksichtigung der Schwarzhäupter zwischen 1413 und 1424', in *'Kopet uns werk by tyden': Beiträge zur hansischen und preußischen Geschichte; Festschrift für Walter Stark zum 75. Geburtstag*, ed. by Nils Jörn and Walter Stark (Schwerin: Helms, 1999), pp. 113–30

——, 'Die Tafelgilde der großen Gilde in Riga im 15. und 16. Jahrhundert', in *Buch und Bildung im Baltikum: Festschrift für Paul Kaegbein zum 80. Geburtstag*, ed. by Heinrich Bosse and Paul Kaegbein (Münster: LIT, 2005), pp. 59–88

——, 'Helewegh, Hermann', in *Encyclopedia of the Medieval Chronicle. 1. A–I*, ed. by Graeme Dunphy and Cristian Bratu (Leiden: Brill, 2010), p. 763

―――, 'Hermann Helewegh – Ratssekretär und Ratsherr in Riga im Spannungsfeld zwischen Stadt und Stadtherren im 15. Jahrhundert', in *Akteure und Gegner der Hanse: zur Prosopographie der Hansezeit*, ed. by Detlef Kattinger and Konrad Fritze (Weimar: Böhlau, 1998), pp. 145–63

―――, 'Konflikt und Rechtfertigung in der Geschichtsschreibung im Alt–Livlands Christoph Forstenau – Silvester Stodewescher – Hermann Helewegh', in *Geschichtsschreibung im mittelalterlichen Livland*, ed. by Matthias Thumser (Berlin Münster: LIT, 2011), pp. 87–132

―――, 'Riga in der ersten Hälfte des 15. Jahrhunderts. Das Verhältnis der Stadt zum Orden, zum Erzbischof und zur Hanse', in *Städtisches Leben im Baltikum zur Zeit der Hanse: zwölf Beiträge zum 12. Baltischen Seminar*, ed. by Norbert Angermann (München: Carl Schirren Gesellschaft, 2003), pp. 43–92

―――, 'Zwischen Autonomie und Konfrontation. Bemerkungen zur Politik des Rates von Riga in der ersten Hälfte des 15. Jahrhunderts', in *Riga und der Ostseeraum: von der Gründung 1201 bis in die frühe Neuzeit*, ed. by Ilgvars Misāns and Horst Wernicke (Marburg: Verlag Herder–Institut, 2005), pp. 144–68

Bruiningk, Hermann von, and Nikolaus Busch, eds, *Livländische Güterurkunden*, vols. 1–2, (Riga: Jonck & Poliewsky, Gulbis, 1908–1923)

―――, *Messe und kanonisches Stundengebet nach dem Brauche der Rigaschen Kirche im späteren Mittelalter* (Riga: Kymmel, 1904)

―――, 'Die ehemalige Andreaskapelle bei dem Schlosse des Deutschen Ordens zu Riga', in *Sitzungsberichten der Gesellschaft für Geschichte und Alterthumskunde der Ostseeprovinzen Russlands 1900* (Riga: W. F. Häcker, 1901), pp. 178–83

―――, 'Die Frage der Verehrung der ersten livländischen Bischöfe als Heilige', in *Sitzungsberichten der Gesellschaft für Geschichte und Alterthumskunde der Ostseeprovinzen Russlands für das Jahr 1902* (Riga: W. F. Häcker, 1903), pp. 3–35

Brundage, James A., 'Introduction: Henry of Livonia, The Writer and His Chronicle', in *Crusading and Chronicle Writing on the Medieval Baltic Frontier: A Companion to the Chronicle of Henry of Livonia*, ed. by Marek Tamm, Linda Kaljundi, and Carsten Selch Jensen (Farnham: Ashgate, 2011), pp. 1–22

―――, trans., *The Chronicle of Henry of Livonia* (New York: Columbia University Press, 2003)

Brünjes, Holger Stefan, *Die Deutschordenskomturei in Bremen: ein Beitrag zur Geschichte des Ordens in Livland* (Marburg: Elwert, 1997)

Bruns, Friedrich, 'Die ältesten lübischen Ratslinien', *Zeitschrift des Vereins für Lübeckische Geschichte und Altertumskunde*, 27 (1933), 31–99

Bueren, Truus van, 'Care for the Here and the Hereafter. A Multitude of Possibilities', in *Care for the Here and the Hereafter: Memoria, Art and Ritual in the Middle Ages*, ed. by Truus van Bueren and Andrea van Leerdam (Turnhout: Brepols, 2005), pp. 13–34

――― and Andrea van Leerdam, eds, *Care for the Here and the Hereafter: Memoria, Art and Ritual in the Middle Ages* (Turnhout: Brepols, 2005)

—— and Wilhelmina C. M. Wüstefeld, *Leven na de dood: gedenken in de late Middeleeuwen* (Turnhout: Brepols, 1999)

——, Kim Ragetli, and Arnoud-Jan Bijsterveld, 'Researching Medieval Memoria: Prospects and Possibilities. With an Introduction to Medieval Memoria Online (MeMO)', *Jaarboek voor Middeleeuwse Geschiedenis*, 14 (2011), 183–234

——, Paul Cockerham, Caroline Horch, Martine Meuwese, and Thomas Schilp, eds, *Reformations and Their Impact on the Culture of Memoria* (Turnhout: Brepols, 2016)

Bulmerincq, August von, ed., *Kämmerei-Register der Stadt Riga 1348–1361 und 1405–1474* (Leipzig: Duncker & Humblot, 1909)

——, ed., *Zwei Kämmerei-Register der Stadt Riga: ein Beitrag zur deutschen Wirtschaftsgeschichte* (Leipzig: Duncker & Humblot, 1902)

Bülow, Glenn M., 'Leineweber(innen). Handwerker zwischen Zunftausschluß, Verketzerung und Armutsspott', in *Randgruppen der spätmittelalterlichen Gesellschaft: ein Hand- und Studienbuch*, ed. by Bernd-Ulrich Hergemöller (Warendorf: Fahlbusch, 2001), pp. 198–218

Bunge, Friedrich Georg von, *Die Revaler Rathslinie* (Reval: Kluge, 1874)

Bunge, Friedrich Georg von, Leonid Arbusow sen., Hermann Hildebrand, Philipp Schwartz, August von Bulmerincq, Matthias Thumser, and others, eds, *Liv-, est- und kurländisches Urkundenbuch*, sect. 1, vols. 1–14; sect. 2, vols. 1–3 (Riga, Reval, Köln, 1853–2020)

Busch, Nicholaus, *Die Geschichte der Rigaer Stadtbibliothek und deren Bücher*, ed. by Leonid Arbusow (Riga: Rigaer Stadtvervaltung, 1937)

Butz, Eva-Maria, and Alfons Zettler, 'The Making of the Carolingian Libri Memoriales: Exploring or Constructing the Past?', in *Memory and Commemoration in Medieval Culture*, ed. by Elma Brenner, Mary Franklin-Brown, and Meredith Cohen (Farnham: Ashgate, 2013), pp. 79–92

Campe, Paul, 'Ein neuaufgefundenes Fragment der im Jahre 1786 zerstörten Umrahmung des Grabmals Bischof Meinhards im St. Marien-Dom zu Riga', *Latvijas Universitātes Raksti. Arhitektūras fakultātes sērija*, 1.5 (1932), 305–26

Carl, Horst, and Ute Planert, eds, *Militärische Erinnerungskulturen vom 14. bis zum 19. Jahrhundert: Träger – Medien – Deutungskonkurrenzen* (Göttingen: V & R Unipress, 2012)

Carruthers, Mary J., *The Book of Memory: A Study of Memory in Medieval Culture* (Cambridge: Cambridge University Press, 1990)

Caune, Andris, and Ieva Ose, *Latvijas viduslaiku mūra baznīcas* (Rīga: Latvijas vēstures institūta apgāds, 2010)

Caune, Māra, 'Rīgas pēdējais bruņotais konflikts ar Livonijas ordeni (1481–1491)', *Latvijas PSR Zinātņu akadēmijas vēstis*, 8 (1975), 36–45

——, 'Rīgas pilsētas un Livonijas ordeņa karš 1297.–1330. gadā', *Latvijas PSR Zinātņu Akadēmijas Vēstis*, 12 (1973), 63–74

——, *Rīgas pils – senā un mainīgā* (Rīga: Jumava, 2004)

——, *Rīgas pils* (Rīga: Zinātne, 2001)

Celmiņš, Andris, 'Rīgas arhibīskapa Mihaela Hildebranda apbedījums Doma pagalmā', in *Senā Rīga: pētījumi pilsētas arheoloģijā un vēsturē*, vol. 4, ed. by Andris Caune, Ieva Ose, and Andris Celmiņš (Rīga: Latvijas vēstures institūts, 2003), pp. 92–104

Chiffoleau, Jacques, *La comptabilité de l'au–delà: Les hommes, la mort et la religion dans la région d'Avignon à la fin du moyen âge (Vers 1320 – vers 1480)* (Rome: École française de Rome, 1980)

Christiansen, Eric, *The Northern Crusades: The Baltic and the Catholic Frontier 1100–1525* (London: Macmillan, 1980)

Cnattingius, Hans, *Studies in the Order of St. Bridget of Sweden: The Crisis in the 1420s*, vol. 1 (Stockholm: Almqvist & Wiksell, 1963)

Cowdrey, Herbert E. J., 'Legal Problems Raised by Agreements of Confraternity', in *Memoria, der geschichtliche Zeugniswert des liturgischen Gedenkens im Mittelalter*, ed. by Karl Schmid and Joachim Wollasch (München: Fink, 1984), pp. 233–54

Crumley, Carole L., 'Exploring Venues of Social Memory', in *Social Memory and History: Anthropological Perspectives*, ed. by Jacob Climo and Maria G. Cattell (Walnut Creek: AltaMira Press, 2002), pp. 39–52

Czaja, Roman, 'Das Patriziat in den livländischen und preußischen Städten. Eine vergleichende Analyse', in *Riga und der Ostseeraum: von der Gründung 1201 bis in die frühe Neuzeit*, ed. by Ilgvars Misāns and Horst Wernicke (Marburg: Verlag Herder-Institut, 2005), pp. 211–22

——, 'Patrician Guilds in Medieval Towns on the Baltic Coast', *Acta Poloniae Historica*, 92 (2005), 31–52

D'Avray, David L., *Medieval Religious Rationalities: A Weberian Analysis* (Cambridge: Cambridge University Press, 2010)

Daniell, Christopher, *Death and Burial in Medieval England, 1066–1550* (London: Routledge, 1997)

Derrik, Torsten, *Das Bruderbuch der Revaler Tafelgilde (1364–1549)* (Marburg: Tectum Verlag, 2000)

Dijn, Clemens Guido de, 'Altenbiesen vom mittelalterlichen Wallfahrtsort zur Residenz (1220–1794)', in *Alden Biesen: Acht Jahrhunderte einer Deutschordens–Landkommende im Rhein–Maas–Gebiet*, ed. by Johan Fleerackers, Udo Arnold, and Paul Rock (Marburg: Elwert, 1988), pp. 45–82

Doležalová, Lucie, ed., *The Making of Memory in the Middle Ages* (Leiden: Brill, 2010)

Donath, Matthias, 'Der Meißner Dom als Grablege', in *Die Grabmonumente im Dom zu Meißen*, ed. by Matthias Donath (Leipzig: Leipziger Universitäts Verlag, 2004), pp. 11–24

Donner, Gustav Adolf, *Kardinal Wilhelm von Sabina, Bischof von Modena 1222–1234: päpstlicher Legat in den nordischen Ländern (+ 1251)* (Helsingfors: Tilgmann, 1929)

Duffy, Eamon, *The Stripping of the Altars: Traditional Religion in England, c.1400–c.1580* (New Haven: Yale University Press, 1992)

Dünnebeil, Sonja, 'Die drei großen Kompanien als genossenschaftliche Verbindungen der Lübecker Oberschicht', in *Genossenschaftliche Strukturen in der Hanse*, ed. by Nils Jörn (Köln: Böhlau, 1999), pp. 205–22

———, 'Soziale Dynamik in spätmittelalterlichen Gruppen', in *Menschenbilder – Menschenbildner: Individuum und Gruppe im Blick des Historikers*, ed. by Ulf-Christian Ewert and Stephan Selzer (Berlin: de Gruyter, 2002), pp. 153–75

———, *Die Lübecker Zirkel-Gesellschaft: Formen der Selbstdarstellung einer städtischen Oberschicht* (Lübeck: Archiv der Hansestadt Lübeck, 1996)

Eckhart, Pia, and Marco Tomaszewski, eds, *Städtische Geschichtsschreibung in Spätmittelalter und Früher Neuzeit – Standortbestimmung und Perspektiven eines Forschungsfelds* (Göttingen: V&R unipress, 2019)

Ehrich, Susanne, *Die 'Apokalypse' Heinrichs von Hesler in Text und Bild: Traditionen und Themen volkssprachlicher Bibeldichtung und ihre Rezeption im Deutschen Orden* (Berlin: Erich Schmidt, 2010)

Eickels, Klaus van, 'Secure Base and Constraints of Mobility. The Rheno-Flemish Bailiwick of the Teutonic Knights between Regional Bonds and Service to the Grand Master in the Later Middle Ages', in *International Mobility in the Military Orders (Twelfth to Fifteenth Centuries): Travelling on Christ's Business*, ed. by Helen J. Nicholson and Jochen Burgtorf (Cardiff: University of Wales Press, 2006), pp. 167–72

Eihmane, Eva, 'Livonijas bīskapu delegācijas slepkavība 1428. gadā: zināmais un nezināmais', *Latvijas Vēstures Institūta Žurnāls*, 1 (2013), 29–59

———, *Rīgas arhibīskapa un Vācu ordeņa cīņas par varu viduslaiku Livonijā* (Rīga: LU Akadēmiskais Apgāds, 2012)

Eimer, Birgitta, *Gotland unter dem Deutschen Orden und die Komturei Schweden zu Årsta* (Innsbruck: Universitätsverlag Wagner, 1966)

Eimer, Gerhard, *Bernt Notke: Das Wirken eines niederdeutschen Künstlers im Ostseeraum* (Bonn: Kulturstiftung der Deutschen Vertriebenen, 1985)

Ekdahl, Sven, 'The Battle of Tannenberg–Grunwald–Žalgiris (1410) as Reflected in Twentieth-Century Monuments', in *The Military Orders. History and Heritage*, ed. by Victor Mallia-Milanes and Malcolm Barber (Aldershot: Ashgate, 2008), pp. 175–94

———, *Die Schlacht bei Tannenberg 1410. Einführung und Quellen*, vol. 1 (Berlin: Duncker & Humblot, 1982)

Elm, Kaspar, 'Christi cultores et novelle ecclesie plantatores. Der Anteil der Mönche, Kanoniker und Mendikanten an der Christianisierung der Liven und dem Aufbau der Kirche von Livland', in *Gli inizi del cristianesimo in Livonia–Lettonia: atti del Colloquio internazionale di storia ecclesiastica in occasione dell'VIII centenario della Chiesa in Livonia (1186–1986), Roma, 24–25 Giugno 1986*, ed. by Michele Maccarrone (Città del Vaticano: Libreria editrice Vaticana, 1989), pp. 132–45

———, 'Reform- und Observanzbestrebungen im spätmittelalterlichen Ordenswesen. Ein Überblick', in *Reformbemühungen und Observanzbestrebungen im spätmittelalterlichen Ordenswesen*, ed. by Kaspar Elm (Berlin: Duncker & Humblot, 1989), pp. 3–19

Elton, Geoffrey R., ed., *The New Cambridge Modern History. The Reformation 1520–1559*, vol. 2 (Cambridge: Cambridge University Press, 1990)

Erll, Astrid, and Ansgar Nünning, eds, *Cultural Memory Studies: An International and Interdisciplinary Handbook*, Cultural Memory Studies (Berlin: de Gruyter, 2008)

——, *Memory in Culture*, trans. by Sara B. Young (Basingstoke: Palgrave Macmillan, 2011)

Fehrmann, Antje, 'Grabmal und Totengedächtnis im westlichen Mittelalter', in *Sterben, Tod und Trauer in den Religionen und Kulturen der Welt*, ed. by Christoph Elsas (Hamburg: EB-Verlag, 2007), pp. 281–98

Feistner, Edith, Michael Neecke, and Gisela Vollmann-Profe, *Krieg im Visier: Bibelepik und Chronistik im Deutschen Orden als Modell korporativer Identitätsbildung*, Hermaea (Tübingen: Niemeyer, 2007)

Fenske, Lutz, and Klaus Militzer, eds, *Ritterbrüder im livländischen Zweig des Deutschen Ordens* (Köln: Böhlau, 1993)

Fentress, James, and Chris Wickham, *Social Memory* (Oxford: Blackwell, 1992)

Feser, Paul Ludwig, 'Bischof Berthold von Livland (1196–1198)', *Freiburger Geschichtsblätter*, 52 (1963), 101–28

Feuereisen, Arnold, 'Über das baltische Archivwesen', in *Arbeiten des ersten Baltischen Historikertages zu Riga 1908*, ed. by Bernhard A. Hollander (Riga: Löffler, 1909), pp. 249–73

Fey, Carola, ed., *Mittelalterliche Fürstenhöfe und ihre Erinnerungskulturen* (Göttingen: V und R Unipress, 2007)

Fischer, Mary, *'Di Himels Rote': The Idea of Christian Chivalry in the Chronicles of the Teutonic Order* (Göppingen: Kümmerle Verlag, 1991)

François, Etienne, and Hagen Schulze, eds, *Deutsche Erinnerungsorte*, vol. 1, (München: Beck, 2001)

Frank, Thomas, 'Bruderschaften, Memoria und Recht im spätmittelalterlichen Italien', in *Memoria. Ricordare e dimenticare nella cultura del medioevo: [Trento, 4–6 aprile 2002] = Memoria. Erinnern und Vergessen in der Kultur des Mittelalters*, ed. by Michael Borgolte, Cosimo Damiano Fonseca, and Hubert Houben (Berlin: Duncker & Humblot, 2005), pp. 327–46

——, *Studien zu italienischen Memorialzeugnissen des XI. und XII. Jahrhunderts* (Berlin: de Gruyter, 1991)

Freise, Eckhard, 'Kalendarische und annalistische Grundformen der Memoria', in *Memoria, der geschichtliche Zeugniswert des liturgischen Gedenkens im Mittelalter*, ed. by Karl Schmid and Joachim Wollasch (München: Fink, 1984), pp. 441–577

French, Katherine L., *The Good Women of the Parish: Gender and Religion after the Black Death* (Philadelphia: University of Pennsylvania Press, 2008)

Freytag, Hartmut, 'Der Lübeck–Revaler Totentanz. Text und Kommentar', in *Der Totentanz der Marienkirche in Lübeck und der Nikolaikirche in Reval (Tallinn): Edition, Kommentar, Interpretation, Rezeption*, ed. by Hartmut Freytag (Köln: Böhlau, 1993), pp. 127–342

——, 'Literatur– und kulturhistorische Anmerkungen und Untersuchungen zum Lübecker und Revaler Totentanz', in *Der Totentanz der Marienkirche in Lübeck und der Nikolaikirche in Reval (Tallinn): Edition, Kommentar, Interpretation, Rezeption*, ed. by Hartmut Freytag (Köln: Böhlau, 1993), pp. 13–58

Galvin, Michael, 'Credit and Parochial Charity in Fifteenth-Century Bruges', *Journal of Medieval History*, 28.2 (2002), 131–54

Ganz, David, 'Giving to God in the Mass: The Experience of the Offertory', in *The Languages of Gift in the Early Middle Ages*, ed. by Wendy Davies and Paul Fouracre (Cambridge: Cambridge University Press, 2010), pp. 18–32

Gardner, Julian, *The Tomb and the Tiara: Curial Tomb Sculpture in Rome and Avignon in the Later Middle Ages* (Oxford: Oxford University Press, 1992)

Gąssowska, Maja, 'Cysterki w Rewalu (Tallinie) w XIII–XV wieku', in *Przestrzeń klasztoru, przestrzeń kultury*, ed. by Joanna Pietrzak Thebault and Łukasz Cybulski (Warszawa: UKSW, 2017), pp. 35–49

——, 'Die Zisterzienser im mittelalterlichen Livland', in *Die Kirche im mittelalterlichen Livland*, ed. by Radosław Biskup, Johannes Götz, and Andrzej Radzimiński (Toruń: UMK, 2019), pp. 159–82

——, 'Klasztory żeńskie w średniowiecznym Rewalu (Tallinie)', in *Aktywność publiczna kobiet na ziemiach polskich. Wybrane zagadnienia*, ed. by Tomasz Pudłocki and Katarzyna Sierakowska (Warszawa: Neriton, 2013), pp. 11–18

——, 'Kto i kiedy zainicjował fundację klasztoru cysterek w Dorpacie?', *Studia z Dziejów Średniowiecza*, 25 (2022), 75–95

——, 'Portret cysterek rewalskich "we wnętrzu"', in *Ambona. Teksty o kulturze średniowiecza ofiarowane Stanisławowi Bylinie*, ed. by Krzysztof Bracha and Wojciech Brojer (Warszawa: IH PAN, 2016), pp. 109–25

Gatz, Erwin, and Clemens Brodkorb, eds, *Die Bischöfe des Heiligen Römischen Reiches 1198 bis 1448: Ein biographisches Lexikon* (Berlin: Duncker & Humblot, 2001)

Geary, Patrick J., *Living with the Dead in the Middle Ages* (Ithaca: Cornell University Press, 1994)

——, *Phantoms of Remembrance: Memory and Oblivion at the End of the First Millennium* (Princeton: Princeton University Press, 1994)

Geremek, Bronisław, 'The Marginal Man', in *Medieval Callings*, ed. by Jacques Le Goff, trans. by Lydia G. Cochrane (Chicago: University of Chicago Press, 1990), pp. 346–73

——, *Poverty: A History*, trans. by Agnieszka Kolakowska (Oxford: Blackwell, 1994)

Gerhards, Guntis, 'Traumas un ievainojumi Rīgas 13.–18. gadsimta iedzīvotājiem', in *Senā Rīga: pētījumi pilsētas arheoloģijā un vēsturē*, vol. 7, ed. by Ieva Ose (Rīga: Latvijas vēstures institūta apgāds, 2012), 128–48

Gertsman, Elina, 'The Dance of Death in Reval (Tallinn): The Preacher and His Audience', *Gesta*, 42.2 (2003), 143–59

——, and Elina Räsänen, 'Locating the Body in Medieval Reval', in *Locating the Middle Ages: The Spaces and Places of Medieval Culture*, ed. by Julian Weiss and Sarah Salih (London: King's College London, 2012), pp. 137–58

——, *The Dance of Death in the Middle Ages: Image, Text, Performance* (Turnhout: Brepols, 2010)

Geuenich, Dieter, 'Von der Adelsforschung zur Memoriaforschung', in *Pro remedio et salute anime peragemus: Totengedenken am Frauenstift Essen im Mittelalter*, ed. by Thomas Schilp (Essen: Klartext, 2008), pp. 9–18

Glauert, Mario, 'Die Bindung des Domkapitels von Riga an die Regel des Deutschen Ordens', in *Die Domkapitel des Deutschen Ordens in Preußen und Livland*, ed. by Radosław Biskup and Mario Glauert (Münster: Aschendorff, 2004), pp. 269–316

Goetz, Hans-Werner, *Geschichtsschreibung und Geschichtsbewußtsein im hohen Mittelalter* (Berlin: Akademie-Verlag, 1999)

Gordon, Bruce, and Peter Marshall, eds, *The Place of the Dead: Death and Remembrance in Late Medieval and Early Modern Europe* (Cambridge: Cambridge University Press, 2000)

Graf, Klaus, 'Fürstliche Erinnerungskultur. Eine Skizze zum neuen Modell des Gedenkens in Deutschland im 15. und 16. Jahrhundert', in *Les princes et l'histoire du XIVe au XVIIIe siècle: actes du colloque organisé par l'Université de Versailles – Saint-Quentin et l'Institut Historique Allemand, Paris/Versailles, 13–16 mars 1996*, ed. by Chantal Grell, Werner Paravicini, and Jürgen Voss (Bonn: Bouvier, 1998), pp. 1–11

———, 'Schlachtgedenken im Spätmittelalter. Riten und Medien der Präsentation kollektiver Identität', in *Feste und Feiern im Mittelalter: Paderborner Symposion des Mediävistenverbandes*, ed. by Detlef Altenburg (Sigmaringen: Thorbecke, 1991), pp. 63–70

Grassmann, Antjekathrin, 'Zwischen Nächstenliebe und Geschäft. Zum sozialen Wirken des Lübecker Kaufmanns', in *Der Lübecker Kaufmann: Aspekte seiner Lebens- und Arbeitswelt vom Mittelalter bis zum 19. Jahrhundert*, ed. by Gerhard Gerkens and Antjekathrin Grassmann (Lübeck: Museum für Kunst und Kulturgeschichte, 1993), pp. 97–102

Graus, František, *Lebendige Vergangenheit. Überlieferung im Mittelalter und in den Vorstellungen vom Mittelalter* (Köln: Böhlau, 1975)

Grautoff, Ferdinand-Heinrich, ed., 'Chronik des Kanzlers Albrecht von Bardewik vom Jahre 1298 bis 1301. Ein Fragment', in *Die lübeckischen Chroniken in niederdeutscher Sprache*, vol. 1 (Hamburg: Perthes und Besser, 1829), 411–28

Greiffenhagen, Otto, ed., *Tallinna kodanikkuderaamat 1409–1624 = Das Revaler Bürgerbuch 1409–1624* (Tallinn: Tallinna Eesti Kirjastus Ühisus, 1932)

Grewolls, Antje, *Die Kapellen der norddeutschen Kirchen im Mittelalter: Architektur und Funktion* (Kiel: Ludwig, 1999)

Groebner, Valentin, 'Mobile Werte, informelle Ökonomie. Zur "Kultur" der Armut in der spätmittelalterlichen Stadt', in *Armut im Mittelalter*, ed. by Otto Gerhard Oexle (Ostfildern: Thorbecke, 2004), pp. 165–88

Haak, Arvi, 'Problems in Defining Ethnic Identity in Medieval Towns of Estonia on the Basis of Archaeological Sources', in *Today I Am Not the One I Was Yesterday: Archaeology, Identity, and Change*, ed. by Arvi Haak (Tartu: University of Tartu, 2015), pp. 13–27

Hägglund, Anna-Stina, *Birgittine Landscapes: Three Monasteries in Their Local and Regional Environment across the Baltic Sea Region c. 1410–1530* (Åbo: Åbo Akademis förlag, 2022)

Hahn (Allik), Kadri–Rutt, 'Revaler Testamente aus dem 15. Jahrhundert. Das Testament des Revaler Bürgers Gerd Satzem (1491)', *Zeitschrift für Ostmitteleuropaforschung*, 46.2 (1997), 178–204

Hahn, Kadri–Rutt, *Revaler Testamente im 15. und 16. Jahrhundert* (Berlin: LIT, 2015)

——, Matthias Thumser, and Eberhard Winkler, eds, *Estnisches Mittelalter: Sprache – Gesellschaft – Kirche* (Berlin: LIT, 2015)

Halbwachs, Maurice, *La mémoire collective* (Paris: Presses universitaires de France, 1950)

——, *La topographie légendaire des Évangiles en Terre Sainte: étude de mémoire collective* (Paris: Presses universitaires de France, 1941)

——, *Les cadres sociaux de la mémoire* (Paris: Félix Alcan, 1925)

——, *On Collective Memory*, trans. by Lewis A. Coser, The Heritage of Sociology (Chicago: University of Chicago Press, 1992)

——, *The Collective Memory*, trans. by Francis J. Ditter, jr. and Vida Yazdi Ditter (New York: Harper & Row, 1980)

Hall, Edward, *The Vnion of the Two Noble and Illustre Famelies of Lancastre [and] Yorke, [...]* (London: Richard Grafton, 1550)

Heckert, Uwe, 'Die Ratskapelle als religiöses und politisches Zentrum der Ratsherrschaft in deutschen Städten des späten Mittelalters' (unpublished PhD Thesis, University of Bielefeld, 1997)

Heckmann, Dieter, ed., *Revaler Urkunden und Briefe von 1273 bis 1510* (Köln: Böhlau, 1995)

Heilskov, Mads Vedel, 'The Commemoration of the Lay Elite in the Late Medieval Danish Realm, c. 1340–1536: Rituals, Community and Social Order' (unpublished PhD thesis, University of Aberdeen, 2018)

Heimpel, Hermann, 'Das Wesen des deutschen Spätmittelalters', *Archiv für Kulturgeschichte*, 35 (1954), 29–51

Hellmann, Manfred, 'Bemerkungen zur sozialgeschichtlichen Erforschung des Deutschen Ordens', *Historisches Jahrbuch*, 80 (1961), 126–42

——, 'Der Deutsche Orden und die Stadt Riga', in *Stadt und Orden. Das Verhältnis des Deutschen Ordens zu den Städten in Livland, Preußen und im Deutschen Reich*, ed. by Udo Arnold (Marburg: Elwert, 1993), pp. 1–33

——, 'Die Anfänge christlicher Mission in den baltischen Ländern', in *Studien über die Anfänge der Mission in Livland*, ed. by Manfred Hellmann (Sigmaringen: Thorbecke, 1989), pp. 7–38

——, 'Gilden, Zünfte und Ämter in den livländischen Städten unter besonderer Berücksichtigung der "Undeutschen"', in *Festschrift für Berent Schwineköper. Zu seinem siebzigsten Geburtstag*, ed. by Helmut Maurer and Hans Patze (Sigmaringen: Thorbecke, 1982), pp. 327–35

——, 'Meinhard von Riga', in *Neue Deutsche Biographie*, vol. 16, ed. by Fritz Wagner (Berlin: Duncker & Humblot, 1990), p. 655

Henderson, John, 'Religious Confraternities and Death in Early Renaissance Florence', in *Florence and Italy: Renaissance Studies in Honour of Nicolai Rubinstein*, ed. by Peter Denley and Caroline Elam (London: Westfield College, University of London, Committee for Medieval Studies, 1988), pp. 383–94

Herweg, Mathias, 'Weibliches Mäzenatentum zwischen dynastischer Bestimmung, politischem Kalkül und höfischer Memoria', *Zeitschrift für Literaturwissenschaft und Linguistik*, 40.3 (2010), 9–34

Herzog, Markwart, and Cecilie Hollberg, eds, *Seelenheil und irdischer Besitz: Testamente als Quellen für den Umgang mit den 'letzten Dingen'* (Konstanz: UVK Verlagsgesellschaft, 2007)

Hill, Thomas, '"es für mich sehr nützlich ist, mir die Armen Christi zu Freunden zu machen". Voraussetzungen und Motive der Anlage von Zisterzienserklöstern in Dänemark', in *Zisterzienser: Norm, Kultur, Reform – 900 Jahre Zisterzienser*, ed. by Ulrich Knefelkamp (Berlin: Springer, 2001), pp. 65–90

Höhlbaum, Konstantin, 'Beiträge zur Quellenkunde Alt-Livlands', *Verhandlungen der Gelehrten Estnischen Gesellschaft zu Dorpat*, 7 (1873), 21–77

——— , 'Die Annalen von Dünamünde', *Neues Archiv der Gesellschaft für ältere deutsche Geschichtskunde*, 8 (1883), 612–15

Horch, Caroline, *Der Memorialgedanke und das Spektrum seiner Funktionen in der bildenden Kunst des Mittelalters* (Königstein im Taunus: Langewiesche, 2001)

Hucker, Bernd Ulrich, 'Der Zisterzienserabt Bertold, Bischof von Livland, und der erste Livlandkreuzzug', in *Die Anfänge christlicher Mission in den baltischen Ländern*, ed. by Manfred Hellmann (Sigmaringen: Thorbecke, 1989), pp. 39–64

Hugener, Rainer, *Buchführung für die Ewigkeit. Totengedenken, Verschriftlichung und Traditionsbildung im Spätmittelalter* (Zürich: Chronos Verlag, 2014)

Huijbers, Anne, *Zealots for Souls: Dominican Narratives of Self-Understanding during Observant Reforms, c. 1388–1517* (Berlin: de Gruyter, 2018)

Jähnig, Bernhart, 'Albert von Bekeshovede (Buxhöveden)', in *Die Bischöfe des Heiligen Römischen Reiches 1198 bis 1448: Ein biographisches Lexikon*, ed. by Erwin Gatz and Clemens Brodkorb (Berlin: Duncker & Humblot, 2001), pp. 645–47

——— , 'Bernhard zur Lippe', in *Die Bischöfe des Heiligen Römischen Reiches 1198 bis 1448: Ein biographisches Lexikon*, ed. by Erwin Gatz and Clemens Brodkorb (Berlin: Duncker & Humblot, 2001), pp. 727–28

——— , 'Bertholt Schulte', in *Die Bischöfe des Heiligen Römischen Reiches 1198 bis 1448: Ein biographisches Lexikon*, ed. by Erwin Gatz and Clemens Brodkorb (Berlin: Duncker & Humblot, 2001), pp. 644–45

——— , 'Der Kampf des Deutschen Ordens um die Schutzherrschaft über die livländischen Bistümer', in *Ritterorden und Kirche im Mittelalter*, ed. by Zenon Hubert Nowak (Toruń: UMK, 1997), pp. 97–111

——— , 'Die Verfassung der Domkapitel der Kirchenprovinz Riga. Ein Überblick', in *Kirchengeschichtliche Probleme des Preussenlandes aus Mittelalter und früher Neuzeit*, ed. by Arnold Bartetzky and Bernhart Jähnig (Marburg: Elwert, 2001), pp. 53–72

——, 'Dietrich (Theoderich) von Treiden', in *Die Bischöfe des Heiligen Römischen Reiches 1198 bis 1448: Ein biographisches Lexikon*, ed. by Erwin Gatz and Clemens Brodkorb (Berlin: Duncker & Humblot, 2001), pp. 144–45

——, 'Erzbistum Riga', in *Die Bistümer des Heiligen Römischen Reiches von ihren Anfängen bis zur Säkularisation*, ed. by Erwin Gatz (Freiburg im Breisgau: Herder, 2003), pp. 623–30

——, 'Henning Scharpenberg', in *Die Bischöfe des Heiligen Römischen Reiches 1198 bis 1448: Ein biographisches Lexikon*, ed. by Erwin Gatz and Clemens Brodkorb (Berlin: Duncker & Humblot, 2001), p. 657

——, 'Johannes, Graf von Schwerin', in *Die Bischöfe des Heiligen Römischen Reiches 1198 bis 1448: Ein biographisches Lexikon*, ed. by Erwin Gatz and Clemens Brodkorb (Berlin: Duncker & Humblot, 2001), p. 650

——, 'Zisterzienser und Ritterorden zwischen geistlicher und weltlicher Macht in Livland und Preußen zu Beginn der Missionszeit', in *Die Ritterorden zwischen geistlicher und weltlicher Macht im Mittelalter*, ed. by Zenon Hubert Nowak (Toruń: UMK, 1990), pp. 71–86

——, *Verfassung und Verwaltung des Deutschen Ordens und seiner Herrschaft in Livland* (Berlin: LIT, 2011)

Jahnke, Carsten, 'Bernd Pal, ein Kaufmann des 15. Jahrhunderts. Eine biographische Skizze', *Vana Tallinn*, 15 (2004), 158–76

——, 'Hansische Kaufleute und deren Religiosität außerhalb ihrer Heimat', *Zapiski historyczne*, 84 (2019), 7–41

——, 'Lübeck's Confraternities', in *A Companion to Medieval Lübeck*, ed. by Carsten Jahnke (Leiden: Brill, 2019), pp. 372–97

——, 'The Corpus Christi Guild in Lübeck', in *Guilds, Towns, and Cultural Transmission in the North, 1300–1500*, ed. by Lars Bisgaard, Lars Boje Mortensen, and Tom Pettitt (Odense: University Press of Southern Denmark, 2013), pp. 203–28

——, *Gott gebe, dass wir alle selig werden mögen: die Mitgliederverzeichnisse der Heilig-Leichnams-, St. Antonius- und St. Leonhards-Bruderschaft zur Burg in Lübeck sowie das Bruderschaftsbuch der Heilig Leichnams- und St. Mauritiusbruderschaft der Weydelude zu St. Katharinen* (Göttingen: V&R unipress, 2022), p. 387

Jakobsen, Johnny Grandjean Gøgsig, 'Friars Preachers in Frontier Provinces of Medieval Europe', in *Medieval East Central Europe in a Comparative Perspective: From Frontier Zones to Lands in Focus*, ed. by Gerhard Jaritz and Katalin Szende (London: Routledge, 2016), pp. 123–36

——, 'The Dominicans and the Reformation in Northern Europe', in *The Dissolution of Monasteries: The Case of Denmark in a Regional Perspective*, ed. by Per Seesko, Louise Nyholm Kallestrup, and Lars Bisgaard (Odense: University Press of Southern Denmark, 2019), pp. 75–103

Jamroziak, Emilia, 'Making and Breaking the Bonds: Yorkshire Cistercians and Their Neighbours', in *Perspectives for an Architecture of Solitude: Essays on Cistercians, Art and Architecture in Honour of Peter Fergusson*, ed. by Terryl Nancy Kinder (Turnhout: Brepols, 2004), pp. 63–70

——, *Rievaulx Abbey and Its Social Context, 1132–1300: Memory, Locality, and Networks* (Turnhout: Brepols, 2005)

Jaritz, Gerhard, '"Young, Rich, and Beautiful." The Visualization of Male Beauty in the Late Middle Ages', in *The Man of Many Devices, Who Wandered Full Many Ways: Festschrift in Honor of János M. Bak*, ed. by Balázs Nagy (Budapest: Central European University Press, 1999), pp. 61–77

——, 'Poverty Constructions and Material Culture', in *The Sign Languages of Poverty: International Round Table-Discussion, Krems an Der Donau, October 10 and 11, 2005*, ed. by Gerhard Jaritz (Wien: Verlag der Österreichischen Akademie der Wissenschaften, 2007), pp. 7–18

——, 'Seelenheil und Sachkultur. Gedanken zur Beziehung Mensch–Objekt im späten Mittelalter', in *Europäische Sachkultur des Mittelalters*, ed. by Manfred Mayrhofer (Wien: Verlag der Österreichische Akademie der Wissenschaften, 1980), pp. 57–82

——, 'Seelgerätstiftungen als Indikator der Entwicklung materieller Kultur im Mittelalter', in *Materielle Kultur und religiöse Stiftung im Spätmittelalter: Internationales Round-Table-Gespräch, Krems an der Donau, 26. September 1988*, ed. by Gerhard Jaritz (Wien: Verlag der Österreichischen Akademie der Wissenschaften, 1997), pp. 13–36

Jensen, Carsten Selch, 'The Nature of the Early Missionary Activities and Crusades in Livonia, 1185–1201', in *Medieval Spirituality in Scandinavia and Europe: A Collection of Essays in Honour of Tore Nyberg*, ed. by Lars Bisgaard (Odense: Odense University Press, 2001), pp. 121–37

Johansen, Paul, 'Die Bedeutung der Hanse für Livland', *Hansische Geschichtsblätter*, 65/66 (1940), 1–55

——, and Heinz von zur Mühlen, *Deutsch und Undeutsch im mittelalterlichen und frühneuzeitlichen Reval* (Köln: Böhlau, 1973)

——, *Ein Kalenderfragment aus dem Sankt Brigittenkloster zu Tallinn für den Mai und den Juni 1474–1544* (Pirita: Pirita Kaunistamise Selts, 1939)

Jóźwiak, Sławomir, and Janusz Trupinda, 'Pogrzeby, pochówki i sposoby upamiętnienia braci Zakonu Niemieckiego w średniowiecznych Prusach. Kilka uwag w kontekście funkcjonowania kaplicy św. Anny', in *Kaplica św. Anny na Zamku Wysokim w Malborku: dzieje, wystrój, konserwacja*, ed. by Janusz Hochleitner and Mariusz Mierzwiński (Malbork: Muzeum Zamkowe, 2016), pp. 27–36

——, and ——, *Organizacja życia na zamku krzyżackim w Malborku w czasach Wielkich Mistrzów: (1309–1457)* (Malbork: Muzeum Zamkowe, 2011)

Kaczmarek, Michał, 'Die schlesischen Klöster und ihr Beitrag zur Memorialkultur', in *Schlesische Erinnerungsorte: Gedächtnis und Identität einer mitteleuropäischen Region*, ed. by Marek Czapliński, Hans-Joachim Hahn, and Tobias Weger (Görlitz: Neisse Verlag, 2005), pp. 29–58

Kala, Tiina, 'Das Dominikanerkloster von Reval/Tallinn und die lutherische Reformation', in *Die Stadt im europäischen Nordosten: Kulturbeziehungen von der Ausbreitung des Lübischen Rechts bis zur Aufklärung*, ed. by Robert Schweitzer and Waltraud Basman-Bühner (Helsinki: Aue-Stiftung, 2001), pp. 83–93

——, 'Gab es eine "Nationale Frage" in mittelalterlichen Reval?', *Forschungen zur baltischen Geschichte*, 7 (2012), 11–34

——, ed., *Mittelalterliche Handschriften in den Sammlungen des Stadtarchivs Tallinn und des Estnischen Historischen Museums: Katalog* (Tallinn: Tallinna Linnaarhiiv, 2007)

——, *Euroopa kirjakultuur hiliskeskaegsetes õppetekstides: Tallinna dominiiklase David Sliperi taskuraamat* (Tallinn: Linnarhiiv, 2001)

——, Juhan Kreem, and Anu Mänd, 'Die Bruderschaft der Schwarzenhäupter im Mittelalter', in *Tallinna Mustpead : Mustpeade vennaskonna ajaloost ja varadest = Die Revaler Schwarzenhäupter. Geschichte und Schätze der Bruderschaft der Schwarzenhäupter*, ed. by Urmas Oolup and Juhan Kreem (Tallinn: Tallinna Linnarhiiv, 1999), pp. 61–66

Kaljundi, Linda, *The Baltic Crusades and the Culture of Memory: Studies on Historical Representation, Rituals, and Recollection of the Past* (Helsinki: University of Helsinki, 2016)

Kansteiner, Wulf, 'Finding Meaning in Memory. A Methodological Critique of Collective Memory Studies', *History and Theory*, 41.2 (2002), 179–97

Kaplinski, Küllike, 'Über die Einwohnerzahl und die Sozialstruktur Tallinns von 1369–1399', *Jahrbuch für Geschichte des Feudalismus*, 3 (1979), 111–39

Kersken, Norbert, 'Städtische Freiheit und die nichtdeutsche Bevölkerung. Livland und Oberlausitz im Vergleich', *Zeitschrift für Ostmitteleuropa-Forschung*, 57.1 (2008), 4–22

Kivimäe, Jüri, 'Das Scharmützel hinter dem Jerusalemer Berg Anno 1560', in *Tallinna Mustpead : Mustpeade vennaskonna ajaloost ja varadest = Die Revaler Schwarzenhäupter. Geschichte und Schätze der Bruderschaft der Schwarzenhäupter*, ed. by Urmas Oolup and Juhan Kreem (Tallinn: Tallinna Linnarhiiv, 1999), pp. 67–83

Klosterberg, Brigitte, *Zur Ehre Gottes und zum Wohl der Familie: Kölner Testamente von Laien und Klerikern im Spätmittelalter* (Köln: Janus, 1995)

Kołodziejczak, Piotr, 'Pious Gifts in Late Medieval Stockholm in the Context of Baltic Towns' (unpublished PhD Thesis, Uniwersytet Mikołaja Kopernika w Toruniu, 2023)

Knopken, Andreas, *In epistolam ad Romanos Andreae Knopken Costerinensis interpretatio, Rigae apud Liuonios praelecta* [...] ([Nürnberg: Johann Petreius, 1524])

——, *Vēstules romiešiem skaidrojums, ko kistrinietis Andreass Knopkens ir priekšlasījis livoniešiem Rīgā, kur viņš ir draudzes gans ; 24 tēzes disputam 1522. gadā sv. Pētera baznīcā*, trans. by Kaspars Bankovskis (Rīga: Profesora Roberta Feldmaņa fonds, 2017)

Koselleck, Reinhart, 'Erfahrungswandel und Methodenwechsel. Eine historisch-anthropologische Skizze', in *Zeitschichten: Studien zur Historik*, by Reinhart Koselleck (Frankfurt am Main: Suhrkamp, 2000), pp. 27–77

Koslofsky, Craig, 'From Presence to Remembrance. The Transformation of Memory in the German Reformation', in *The Work of Memory: New Directions in the Study of German Society and Culture*, ed. by Alon Confino and Peter Fritzsche (Chicago: University of Illinois Press, 2002), pp. 25–38

——, *The Reformation of the Dead: Death and Ritual in Early Modern Germany, 1450–1700* (Basingstoke: Macmillan Press, 2000)

Kreem, Juhan, 'Crusading Traditions and Chivalric Ideals: The Mentality of the Teutonic Order in Livonia at the Beginning of the Sixteenth Century', *Crusades*, 12 (2013), 233–50

——, 'Der Deutsche Orden und die Reformation in Livland', in *The Military Orders and the Reformation: Choices, State Building, and the Weight of Tradition*, ed. by Johannes A. Mol, Klaus Militzer, and Helen J. Nicholson (Hilversum: Verloren, 2006), pp. 43–58

——, 'Livland als Endstation? Mobilität nach Livland, in Livland und aus Livland', in *Akkon – Venedig – Marienburg: Mobilität und Immobilität im Deutschen Orden*, ed. by Hubert Houben (Ilmtal-Weinstraße: VDG, 2022), pp. 159–70

——, 'Mobility of the Livonian Teutonic Knights', in *Making Livonia : Actors and Networks in the Medieval and Early Modern Baltic Sea Region*, ed. by Anu Mänd and Marek Tamm (London: Routledge, 2020), pp. 158–69

——, *The Town and Its Lord: Reval and the Teutonic Order (in the Fifteenth Century)* (Tallinn: Kirjastus Ilo, 2002)

——, 'The Archives of the Teutonic Order in Livonia: Past and Present', in *Entre Deus e o Rei. O Mundo Das Ordens Militares*, ed. by Isabel Cristina Ferreira Fernandes (Município de Palmela: GEsOS, 2018), p. 57–65

——, and Kersti Markus, 'Kes asutas Pirita kloostri?', *Kunstiteaduslikke Uurmusi*, 4 (2007), 60–74

Kroeger, Gert, *Erzbischof Silvester Stodewescher und sein Kampf mit dem Orden um die Herrschaft über Riga* (Riga: Kymmels Buchhandlung, 1930)

Kroos, Renate, 'Grabbräuche–Grabbilder', in *Memoria, der geschichtliche Zeugniswert des liturgischen Gedenkens im Mittelalter*, ed. by Karl Schmid and Joachim Wollasch (München: Fink, 1984), pp. 285–353

Kubicki, Rafał, 'Cistercian Nuns of Zarnowitz (Żarnowiec) and the Teutonic Order in the Years 1309-1454', *Ordines Militares Colloquia Torunensia Historica. Yearbook for the Study of the Military Orders*, 25 (2020), 363–83

Kugler, Hartmut, 'Die "Livländische Reimchronik" des 13. Jahrhunderts', *Latvijas Zinātņu Akadēmijas Vēstis*, 9 (1993), 22–29

——, 'Über die "Livländische Reimchronik". Text, Gedächtnis und Topographie', *Jahrbuch der Brüder Grimm–Gesellschaft*, 2 (1992), 85–104

Kwiatkowski, Stefan, 'Verlorene Schlachten und Gefallene in der geistigen Tradition des Deutschen Ordens', *Ordines Militares Colloquia Torunensia Historica. Yearbook for the Study of the Military Orders*, 16 (2011), 141–57

Lampe, Karl H., 'Ein Anniversarienkalender des Deutschen Hauses zu Ulm', *Ulm und Oberschwaben*, 37 (1964), 154–81

Lange, Klaus, 'Sakralarchitektur und Memoria. Das Essener Münster als Ort der Erinnerung', in *Pro remedio et salute anime peragemus: Totengedenken am Frauenstift Essen im Mittelalter*, ed. by Thomas Schilp (Essen: Klartext, 2008), pp. 59–78

Lazda-Cazers, Rasma, 'Landscape as Other in the Livländische Reimchronik', *Amsterdamer Beiträge zur älteren Germanistik*, 65 (2009), 183–209

Le Goff, Jacques, 'Licit and Illicit Trades in the Medieval West', in *Time, Work, and Culture in the Middle Ages*, ed. by Jacques Le Goff, trans. by Arthur Godlhammer (Chicago: University of Chicago Press, 1980), pp. 58–70

——, *La naissance du purgatoire* (Paris: Gallimard, 1981)

Leimus, Ivar, Rein Loodus, Marta Männisalu, and Mariann Raisma, *Tallinna Suurgild ja gildimaja* (Tallinn: Eesti Ajaloomuuseum, 2011)

Lemmens, Leonhard, *Die Franziskanerkustodie Livland und Preußen* (Düsseldorf: Schwann, 1912)

Lenz, Wilhelm, 'Undeutsch. Bemerkungen zu einem besonderen Begriff der baltischen Geschichte', in *Aus der Geschichte Alt-Livlands: Festschrift für Heinz von zur Mühlen zum 90. Geburtstag*, ed. by Bernhart Jähnig and Heinz von zur Mühlen (Münster: LIT, 2004), pp. 169–84

Levāns, Andris, 'Die lebendigen Toten. Memoria in der Kanzlei der Erzbischöfe von Riga im Spätmittelalter', in *Kollektivität und Individualität: der Mensch im östlichen Europa: Festschrift für Prof. Dr. Norbert Angermann zum 65. Geburtstag*, ed. by Karsten Brüggemann, Thomas M. Bohn, and Konrad Maier (Hamburg: Kovač, 2001), pp. 3–35

——, 'Politiskās organizācijas modeļi viduslaiku Livonijā, 13.–16. gadsimts: manifestācijas un leģitimācijas formas', in *Latvieši un Latvija: Valstiskums Latvijā un Latvijas valsts – izcīnītā un zaudētā*, vol. 2, ed. by Tālavs Jundzis and Guntis Zemītis (Rīga: Latvijas Zinātņu akadēmija, 2013), 52–76

——, 'War Riga eine "heilige" Stadt im Mittelalter. Religiosität, Pilger und der urbane Raum. Riga in der Wahrnehmung des europäischen Stadtbürgertums', in *Starptautiska konference Hanza vakar – Hanza rīt, Rīga, 1998. g. 8.–13. jūnijs = International Conference Hansa Yesterday – Hansa Tomorrow, Riga, June 8–13, 1998*, ed. by Ojārs Spārītis (Riga: Izdevniecība Vārds, 2001), pp. 53–81

——, and Gustavs Strenga, 'Medieval Manuscripts in the Riga Jesuit College Book Collection: Manuscripts of the Riga St. Mary Magdalene Cistercian Nunnery and Their Tradition', in *Catalogue of the Riga Jesuit College Book Collection (1583–1621). History and Reconstruction of the Collection*, ed. by Gustavs Strenga and Andris Levāns (Riga: Latvijas Nacionālā bibliotēka, 2021), pp. 166–87

Löffler, Anette, 'Die Rolle der Liturgie im Leben der Ordensbrüder: Norm und Wirklichkeit', in *Das Leben im Ordenshaus: Vorträge der Tagung der Internationalen Historischen Kommission zur Erforschung des Deutschen Ordens in Tallinn 2014*, ed. by Juhan Kreem (Ilmtal-Weinstraße: VDG, 2019), pp. 1–20

Löffler, Heinz, *Die Grabsteine, Grabmäler und Epitaphien in den Kirchen Alt–Livlands vom 13.–18. Jahrhundert* (Riga: Löffler, 1929)

Löffler, Peter, *Studien zum Totenbrauchtum in den Gilden, Bruderschaften und Nachbarschaften Westfalens vom Ende des 15. bis zum Ende des 19. Jahrhunderts* (Münster: Regensberg, 1975)

Loit, Mari, 'Keskaegsest surmakultuurist ja hauatähistest reformatsioonieelse Tallinna kirikustes ja kloostrites', *Vana Tallinn*, 17 (21) (2006), 15–190

Lückerath, Carl August, 'Durben', in *Lexikon des Mittelalters*, vol. 3 (München: LexMA-Verlag, 1986), 1471–72

Lusiardi, Ralf, 'Die Lebenden und die Toten. Spätmittelalterliche Memoria zwischen Vergegenwärtigung und Vergessen', *Annali dell'Istituto storico italo–germanico in Trento*, 27 (2001), 671–90

——, *Stiftung und städtische Gesellschaft: religiöse und soziale Aspekte des Stiftungsverhaltens im spätmittelalterlichen Stralsund* (Berlin: Akademie-Verlag, 2000)

Luther, Martin, *Den Auszerwelten lieben Freunden gottis, allen Christen zu Righe, Reuell vnd Tarbthe ynn Lieffland* [...] ([Wittemberg: Hans Lufft, 1523])

Lutrell, Anthony, 'The Spiritual Life of the Hospitallers of Rhodes', in *Die Spiritualität der Ritterorden im Mittelalter*, ed. by Zenon Hubert Nowak (Toruń: UMK, 1993), pp. 75–96

Machilek, Franz, 'Böhmens Landespatrone im Mittelalter', in *Wenzel: Protagonist der böhmischen Erinnerungskultur*, ed. by Stefan Samerski (Paderborn: Schöningh, 2018), pp. 27–98

Mäesalu, Mihkel, 'Historical Memory as the Cause of Conflict in Medieval Livonia', *Vestnik of Saint Petersburg University. History*, 64.3 (2019), 1014–30

Mahling, Madlena, *Ad rem publicam et ad ignem: das mittelalterliche Schriftgut des Rigaer Rats und sein Fortbestand in der Neuzeit* (Marburg: Verlag Herder-Institut, 2015)

Maier, Wilhelm, Wolfang Schmid, and Michael Viktor Schwarz, eds, *Grabmäler: Tendenzen der Forschung an Beispielen aus Mittelalter und früher Neuzeit* (Berlin: Gebrüder Mann, 2000)

Mänd, Anu, 'Church Art, Commemoration of the Dead and the Saints' Cult. Constructing Individual and Corporate Memoria in Late Medieval Tallinn', *Acta Historica Tallinnensia*, 16 (2011), 3–30

——, 'Frauen, Memoria und Sakralräume im spätmittelalterlichen Livland', *Forschungen zur baltischen Geschichte*, 8 (2013), 11–39

——, 'Geselligkeit und soziale Karriere in den Revaler Gilden und der Schwarzhäupterbruderschaft', in *Vereinskultur und Zivilgesellschaft in Nordosteuropa: regionale Spezifik und europäische Zusammenhänge = Associational culture and civil society in North Eastern Europe*, ed. by Jörg Hackmann (Wien: Böhlau, 2008), pp. 39–76

——, 'Hospitals and Tables for the Poor in Medieval Livonia', *Mitteilungen des Instituts für Österreichische Geschichtsforschung*, 115.3–4 (2007), 234–70

——, 'Memoria and Sacral Art in Late Medieval Livonia: The Gender Perspective', in *Images and Objects in Ritual Practices in Medieval and Early Modern Northern and Central Europe*, ed. by Krista Kodres and Anu Mänd (Newcastle upon Tyne: Cambridge Scholars, 2013), pp. 239–73

——, 'Rome, Rostock and a Remote Region: Art Commissions and Networks of Livonian Bishops', in *Networking in Late Medieval Central Europe : Friends, Families, Foes*, ed. by Beata. Możejko, Leslie Carr-Riegel, and Anna Paulina Orłowska (London: Routledge, 2023), pp. 107–24

——, 'Saints' Cults in Medieval Livonia', in *The Clash of Cultures on the Medieval Baltic Frontier*, ed. by Alan V. Murray (Farnham: Ashgate, 2009), pp. 191–223

——, 'Table Guilds and Urban Space: Charitable, Devotional, and Ritual Practices in Late Medieval Tallinn', in *Space, Place, and Motion: Locating Confraternities in the Late Medieval and Early Modern City*, ed. by Diana Bullen Presciutti (Leiden: Brill, 2017), pp. 21–46

——, 'The Altarpiece of the Virgin Mary of the Brotherhood of the Black Heads in Tallinn: Dating, Donors, and the Double Intercession', *Acta Historiae Artium Balticae*, 2 (2007), 35–53

——, 'Über den Marienaltar der Revaler Schwarzenhäupter und seine Ikonographie', in *Die Kunstbeziehungen Estlands mit den Niederlanden in den 15.–17. Jahrhunderten. Der Marienaltar des Meisters der Lucialegende, 500 Jahre in Tallinn*, ed. by Tiina Abel (Tallinn: Eesti Kunstimuuseum, 2000)

——, 'Vicarius, Canonicus et Episcopus: Three Late Medieval Grave Slabs from Tartu and Tallinn', *Baltic Journal of Art History*, 7 (2014), 11–30

——, 'Visuelle Memoria: die Grabplatten der livländischen Ordensmeister und Gebietiger', *Forschungen zur baltischen Geschichte*, 15 (2020), 59–92

——, 'Women Shaping Sacred Space: Case Studies from Early 16th Century Lübeck and Tallinn', in *Hansische Identitäten*, ed. by Kerstin Petermann, Anja Rasche, and Gerhard Weilandt (Petersberg: Michael Imhof Verlag, 2018), pp. 83–91

——, and Anneli Randla, 'Sacred Space and Corporate Identity. The Black Heads' Chapels in the Mendicant Churches of Tallinn and Riga', *Baltic Journal of Art History*, 4 (2012), 43–80

——, and Anti Selart, 'Livonia – a Region without Local Saints?', in *Symbolic Identity and the Cultural Memory of Saints*, ed. by Nils Holger Petersen, Anu Mänd, Sebastián Salvadó, and Tracey R. Sands (Newcastle upon Tyne: Cambridge Scholars Publishing, 2018), pp. 91–122

——, and Marek Tamm, eds, *Making Livonia : Actors and Networks in the Medieval and Early Modern Baltic Sea Region* (London: Routledge, 2020)

——, *Urban Carnival: Festive Culture in the Hanseatic Cities of the Eastern Baltic, 1350–1550* (Turnhout: Brepols, 2005)

Markus, Kersti, 'Misjonär või mõisnik? Tsistertslaste roll 13. sajandi Eestis', *Acta Historica Tallinnensia*, 14 (2009), 3–30

———, 'The Pirita Convent in Tallinn. A Powerful Visual Symbol for the Self-Consciousness of the Birgittine Order', *Kungl. Vitterhets Historie Och Antikvitets Akademien. Konferenser*, 82 (2013), 95–110

Maschke, Erich, 'Die Unterschichten der mittelalterlichen Städte Deutschlands', in *Gesellschaftliche Unterschichten in den südwestdeutschen Städten*, ed. by Erich Maschke and Jürgen Sydow (Stuttgart: Kohlhammer, 1967), pp. 1–74

Mauss, Marcel, *The Gift : The Form and Reason for Exchange in Archaic Societies*, trans. by W.D. Halls (London: Routledge, 2002)

McLaughlin, Megan, *Consorting with Saints: Prayer for the Dead in Early Medieval France* (Ithaca: Cornell University Press, 1994)

McLuhan, Marshall, *Understanding Media: The Extensions of Man* (New York: Routledge, 2008)

Megill, Allan, *Historical Knowledge, Historical Error: A Contemporary Guide to Practice* (Chicago: University of Chicago Press, 2007)

Mentzel-Reuters, Arno, 'Heinrich von Hesler – von Thüringen nach Preußen. Facetten deutschsprachiger Bibeldichtung 1250–1350', in *Der Deutsche Orden und Thüringen: Aspekte einer 800-jährigen Geschichte*, ed. by Thomas T. Müller (Petersberg: Imhof, 2014), pp. 43–74

———, 'Leseprogramme und individuelle Lektüre im Deutschen Orden', in *Neue Studien zur Literatur im Deutschen Orden*, ed. by Bernhart Jähnig and Arno Mentzel-Reuters (Stuttgart: Hirzel, 2014), pp. 9–58

———, *Arma spiritualia: Bibliotheken, Bücher und Bildung im Deutschen Orden* (Wiesbaden: Harrassowitz, 2003)

Mettig, Constantin, 'Bücher der Rigaschen Bierträgergilde', in *Sitzungsberichten der Gesellschaft für Geschichte und Alterthumskunde der Ostseeprovinzen Russlands für das Jahr 1890* (Riga: W. F. Häcker, 1891), pp. 120–25

———, 'Die ältesten Bücher der Losträgergilde in Riga', in *Sitzungsberichten der Gesellschaft für Geschichte und Alterthumskunde der Ostseeprovinzen Russlands für das Jahr 1900* (Riga: W. F. Häcker, 1901), pp. 120–35

———, 'Die Gilde der Losträger und die mit ihr verwandten Aemter in Riga', in *Sitzungsberichten der Gesellschaft für Geschichte und Alterthumskunde der Ostseeprovinzen Russlands für das Jahr 1902* (Riga: W. F. Häcker, 1903), pp. 56–69

Michalski, Sergiusz, '"Hölzer wurden zu Menschen" Die reformatorischen Bilderstürme in den baltischen Landen zwischen 1524 und 1526', in *Die baltischen Lande im Zeitalter der Reformation und Konfessionalisierung. Teil 4.*, ed. by Matthias Asche, Werner Buchholz, and Anton Schindling (Münster: Aschendorff, 2012), pp. 147–63

———, 'Bildersturm im Ostseeraum', in *Macht und Ohnmacht der Bilder: reformatorischer Bildersturm im Kontext der europäischen Geschichte*, ed. by Peter Blickle, Andre Holenstein, Heinrich Richard Schmidt, and Franz-Josef Sladeczek (München: Oldenbourg, 2002), pp. 223–38

———, 'Die protestantischen Bilderstürme. Versuch einer Übersicht', in *Bilder und Bildersturm im Spätmittelalter und in der frühen Neuzeit*, ed. by Robert W. Scribner (Wiesbaden: Harrassowitz, 1990), pp. 69–124

Militzer, Klaus, 'Die Einbindung des Deutschen Ordens in die süddeutsche Adelswelt', in *Ritterorden und Region – politische, soziale und wirtschaftliche Verbindungen im Mittelalter*, ed. by Zenon Hubert Nowak (Toruń: UMK, 1995), pp. 141–60

———, 'Die Finanzierung der Erhebung Sylvester Stodeweschers zum Erzbischof von Riga', in *Zentrale und Region: gesammelte Beiträge zur Geschichte des Deutschen Ordens in Preussen, Livland und im Deutschen Reich, aus den Jahren 1968 bis 2008*, by Klaus Militzer (Weimar: VDG, 2015), pp. 113–29

———, 'Recruitment of Brethren for the Teutonic Order in Livonia, 1237–1562', in *The Military Orders. Fighting for the Faith and Caring for the Sick*, ed. by Malcolm Barber (Aldershot: Variorum, 1994), pp. 270–77

———, 'Rheinländer im mittelalterlichen Livland', *Rheinische Vierteljahrsblätter*, 61 (1997), 79–95

———, *Die Geschichte des Deutschen Ordens* (Stuttgart: Kohlhammer, 2012)

———, *Von Akkon zur Marienburg: Verfassung, Verwaltung und Sozialstruktur des Deutschen Ordens 1190–1309* (Marburg: Elwert, 1999)

Misāns, Ilgvars, 'The Western Model and the Autochthons: The Livs and Would-Be Latvians in Medieval Livonia', in *Das mittelalterliche Livland und sein historisches Erbe = Medieval Livonia and Its Historical Legacy*, ed. by Ilgvars Misāns, Andris Levāns, and Gustavs Strenga (Marburg: Verlag Herder-Institut, 2022), pp. 83–104

———, and Horst Wernicke, eds, *Riga und der Ostseeraum: von der Gründung 1201 bis in die frühe Neuzeit* (Marburg: Verlag Herder-Institut, 2005)

Moeglin, Jean-Marie, 'Hat das Mittelalter europäische lieux de mémoire erzeugt?', *Jahrbuch für Europäische Geschichte*, 3 (2002), 17–38

Mohr, Robert, 'Die Tischlesung im Deutschen Orden. Eine institutionsspezifische Lehrform', *Das Mittelalter*, 17.1 (2012), 76–84

Mol, Johannes A., 'Nederlandse ridderbroeders van de Duitse orde in Lijfland. Herkomst, afkomst en carrieres', *Bijdragen en Mededelingen betreffende de Geschiedenis der Nederlanden*, 111 (1999), 1–29

———, 'The "Hospice of the German Nobility". Changes in the Admission Policy of the Teutonic Knights in the Fifteenth Century', in *Mendicants, Military Orders, and Regionalism in Medieval Europe*, ed. by Jürgen Sarnowsky (Aldershot: Ashgate, 1999), pp. 115–30

———, 'The Knight Brothers from the Low Countries in the Conflict between the Westphalians and the Rhinelanders in the Livonian Branch of the Teutonic Order', *Ordines Militares Colloquia Torunensia Historica. Yearbook for the Study of the Military Orders*, 20 (2015), 123–44

Morton, Nicholas, *The Teutonic Knights in the Holy Land, 1190–1291* (Woodbridge: Boydell & Brewer, 2009)

Mugurēvičs, Ēvalds, ed., *Vartberges Hermaņa Livonijas hronika. Hermanni de Wartberge Chronicon Livoniae*, ed. & trans. by Ēvalds Mugurēvičs (Rīga: Latvijas Vēstures institūta apgāds, 2005)

Mühlen, Heinz von zur, 'Das Stadtbürgertum', in *Sozialgeschichte der baltischen Deutschen*, ed. by Wilfried Schlau (Köln: Wissenschaft und Politik, 2000), pp. 63–108

────── ──────, 'Zur Frühgeschichte der Revaler Gilden', in *Reval: Handel und Wandel vom 13. bis zum 20. Jahrhundert*, ed. by Norbert Angermann and Wilhelm Lenz (Lüneburg: Verlag Nordostdt. Kulturwerk, 1997), pp. 15–42

Murawski, Klaus Eberhard, *Zwischen Tannenberg und Thorn : die Geschichte des Deutschen Ordens unter dem Hochmeister Konrad von Erlichshausen 1441–1449* (Göttingen: Musterschmidt, 1953)

Murray, Alan V., 'The Structure, Genre and Intended Audience of the Livonian Rhymed Chronicle', in *Crusade and Conversion on the Baltic Frontier, 1150–1500*, ed. by Alan V. Murray (Aldershot: Ashgate, 2001), pp. 235–51

──────, ed., *Crusade and Conversion on the Baltic Frontier, 1150–1500* (Aldershot: Ashgate, 2001)

Napiersky, Jakob Gottlieb Leonhard, ed., *Die Erbebücher der Stadt Riga, 1384–1579* (Riga: Kymmel, 1888)

──────, ed., *Die Libri redituum der Stadt Riga* (Leipzig: Duncker & Humblot, 1881)

Naum, Magdalena, 'Multi-Ethnicity and Material Exchanges in Late Medieval Tallinn', *European Journal of Archaeology*, 17.4 (2014), 656–77

Neecke, Michael, *Literarische Strategien narrativer Identitätsbildung: eine Untersuchung der frühen Chroniken des Deutschen Ordens* (Frankfurt: Lang, 2008)

Neidiger, Bernhard, 'Die Reformbewegungen der Bettelorden im 15. Jahrhundert', in *Württembergisches Klosterbuch: Klöster, Stifte und Ordensgemeinschaften von den Anfängen bis in die Gegenwart*, ed. by Wolfgang Zimmermann (Ostfildern: Thorbecke, 2003), pp. 77–90

Neiske, Franz, 'Die Ordnung der Memoria. Formen necrologischer Tradition im mittelalterlichen Klosterverband', in *Institution und Charisma: Festschrift für Gert Melville zum 65. Geburtstag*, ed. by Franz J. Felten, Annette Kehnel, and Stefan Weinfurter (Köln: Böhlau, 2009), pp. 127–37

──────, 'Funktion und Praxis der Schriftlichkeit im klösterlichen Totengedenken', in *Viva vox und ratio scripta: mündliche und schriftliche Kommunikationsformen im Mönchtum des Mittelalters*, ed. by Clemens M. Kasper and Klaus Schreiner (Münster: LIT, 1997), pp. 97–118

──────, 'Gebetsgedenken und päpstlicher Ablaß. Zur liturgischen Memoria französischer Könige und Grafen im Spätmittelalter', in *Memoria in der Gesellschaft des Mittelalters*, ed. by Dieter Geuenich and Otto Gerhard Oexle (Göttingen: Vandenhoeck & Ruprecht, 1994), pp. 178–206

──────, 'Vision und Totengedenken', *Frühmittelalterliche Studien*, 20 (1986), 137–85

Neitmann, Klaus, 'Die Auswahl von Residenzorten. Methodische Bemerkungen zur spätmittelalterlichen geistlichen Residenzbildung', in *Spätmittelalterliche Residenzbildung in geistlichen Territorien Mittel- und Nordostdeutschlands*, ed. by Klaus Neitmann and Heinz-Dieter Heimann (Berlin: Lukas-Verlag, 2010), pp. 41–90

―――, 'Ludwig von Münster', in *Die Bischöfe des Heiligen Römischen Reiches 1198 bis 1448: Ein biographisches Lexikon*, ed. by Erwin Gatz and Clemens Brodkorb (Berlin: Duncker & Humblot, 2001), p. 640

―――, 'Riga und Wenden als Residenzen des livländischen Landmeisters im 15. Jahrhundert', in *Stadt und Orden. Das Verhältnis des Deutschen Ordens zu den Städten in Livland, Preußen und im Deutschen Reich*, ed. by Udo Arnold (Marburg: Elwert, 1993), pp. 59–93

―――, 'Um die Einheit Livlands. Der Griff des Ordenshochmeisters Bernd von der Borch nach dem Erzstift Riga', in *Deutsche im Nordosten Europas*, ed. by Hans Rothe (Köln: Böhlau, 1991), pp. 109–37

―――, 'Was ist eine Residenz? Methodische Übelegungen zur Erforschung der spätmittelalterlichen Residenzenbildung', in *Vorträge und Forschungen zur Residenzenfrage: Hans Patze zum 70. Geburtstag*, ed. by Peter Johanek and Hans Patze (Sigmaringen: Thorbecke, 1990), pp. 11–44

―――, *Der Hochmeister des Deutschen Ordens in Preussen: ein Residenzherrscher unterwegs: Untersuchungen zu den Hochmeisteritineraren im 14. und 15. Jahrhundert* (Köln: Böhlau, 1990)

Neitmann, Sonja, *Von der Grafschaft Mark nach Livland: Ritterbrüder aus Westfalen im livländischen Deutschen Orden* (Köln: Böhlau, 1993)

Neumann, Wilhelm, *Der Dom zu St. Marien in Riga: Baugeschichte und Baubeschreibung* (Riga: G. Löffler, 1912)

Nicholas, David, *The Later Medieval City 1300–1500* (London: Longman, 1997)

Nicholson, Helen J., 'Memory and the Military Orders: An Overview', in *Entre Deus e o Rei. O Mundo das Ordens Militares. Between God and the King. The World of the Military Orders*, ed. by Isabel Cristina Ferreira Fernandes (Palmela: Municipio de Palmela/GEsOS, 2018), pp. 17–28

Niitemaa, Vilho, *Die undeutsche Frage in der Politik der livländischen Städte im Mittelalter* (Helsinki: Uudenmaan Kirjapaino Osakeyhtio, 1949)

Noodt, Birgit, *Religion und Familie in der Hansestadt Lübeck anhand der Bürgertestamente des 14. Jahrhunderts* (Lübeck: Schmidt-Römhild, 2000)

Nora, Pierre, 'Between Memory and History. Les Lieux de Mémoire', *Representations*, 26 (1989), 7–24

―――, and Lawrence D. Kritzman, eds, *Realms of Memory: The Construction of the French Past*, 3 vols, trans. by Arthur Goldhammer (New York: Columbia University Press, 1996)

Nottbeck, Eugen von, and Wilhelm Neumann, *Geschichte und Kunstdenkmäler der Stadt Reval* (Reval: Kluge, 1904)

―――, *Die alten Schragen der grossen Gilde zu Reval* (Reval: Emil Prahm, 1885)

Nyberg, Tore, *Birgittinische Klostergründungen des Mittelalters* ([Lund]: Gleerup, 1965)

O'Connor, Kevin C., *The House of Hemp and Butter: A History of Old Riga* (Ithaca: Cornell University Press, 2019)

Oexle, Otto Gerhard, 'Adel, Memoria und kulturelles Gedächtnis. Bemerkungen zur Memorial-Kapelle der Fugger in Augsburg', in *Les princes et l'histoire du XIVe au XVIIIe siècle: actes du colloque organisé par l'Université de Versailles – Saint-Quentin et l'Institut Historique Allemand, Paris/Versailles, 13–16 mars 1996*, ed. by Chantal Grell, Werner Paravicini, and Jürgen Voss (Bonn: Bouvier, 1998), pp. 339–57

———, 'Armut und Armenfürsorge um 1200. Ein Beitrag zum Verständnis der Freiwilligen Armut bei Elisabeth von Thüringen', in *Sankt Elisabeth, Fürstin, Dienerin, Heilige: Aufsätze, Dokumentation, Katalog* (Sigmaringen: Thorbecke, 1981), pp. 78–100

———, 'Das Ende Der Memoria', in *Reformations and Their Impact on the Culture of Memoria*, ed. by Truus van Bueren, Paul Cockerham, Caroline Horch, Martine Meuwese, and Thomas Schilp (Turnhout: Brepols, 2016), pp. 315–30

———, 'Die Gegenwart der Lebenden und der Toten. Gedanken über Memoria', in *Gedächtnis, das Gemeinschaft stiftet*, ed. by Karl Schmid and Joachim Wollasch (München: Schnell und Steiner, 1985), pp. 74–107

———, 'Die Gegenwart der Toten', in *Death in the Middle Ages*, ed. by Herman Braet and Werner Verbeke (Leuven: Leuven University Press, 1983), pp. 19–77

———, 'Die Memoria der Reformation', in *Die Wirklichkeit und das Wissen: Mittelalterforschung – Historische Kulturwissenschaft – Geschichte und Theorie der historischen Erkenntnis*, ed. by Bernhard Jussen, Andrea von Hülsen-Esch, and Frank Rexroth (Göttingen: Vandenhoeck & Ruprecht, 2011), pp. 187–242

———, 'Die mittelalterlichen Gilden. Ihre Selbstdeutung und ihr Beitrag zur Formung sozialer Strukturen', in *Soziale Ordnungen im Selbstverständnis des Mittelalters*, ed. by Albert Zimmermann (Berlin: de Gruyter, 1979), pp. 203–26

———, 'Liturgische Memoria und historische Erinnerung. Zur Frage nach dem Gruppenbewußtsein und dem Wissen der eigenen Geschichte in den mittelalterlichen Gilden', in *Tradition als historische Kraft: interdisziplinäre Forschungen zur Geschichte des früheren Mittelalters*, ed. by Norbert Kamp and Joachim Wollasch (Berlin: de Gruyter, 1982), pp. 323–40

———, 'Mahl und Spende im mittelalterlichen Totenkult', *Frühmittelalterliche Studien*, 18 (1984), 401–20

———, 'Memoria als Kultur', in *Memoria als Kultur*, ed. by Otto Gerhard Oexle (Göttingen: Vandenhoeck & Ruprecht, 1995), pp. 9–78

———, 'Memoria in der Gesellschaft und Kultur des Mittelalters', in *Modernes Mittelalter: neue Bilder einer populären Epoche*, ed. by Joachim Heinzle (Frankfurt am Main: Insel-Verlag, 1994), pp. 297–323

———, 'Memoria und Memorialbild', in *Memoria, der geschichtliche Zeugniswert des liturgischen Gedenkens im Mittelalter*, ed. by Karl Schmid and Joachim Wollasch (München: Fink, 1984), pp. 384–440

———, 'Memoria und Memoriaüberlieferung im frühen Mittelalter', *Frühmittelalterliche Studien*, 10 (1976), 70–95

——, 'Soziale Gruppen in der Ständegesellschaft. Lebensformen des Mittelalters und ihre historischen Wirkungen', in *Die Repräsentation der Gruppen: Texte – Bilder – Objekte*, ed. by Otto Gerhard Oexle and Andrea von Hülsen–Esch (Göttingen: Vandenhoeck und Ruprecht, 1998), pp. 9–44

——, ed., *Memoria als Kultur* (Göttingen: Vandenhoeck & Ruprecht, 1995)

Ohler, Norbert, 'Zur Seligkeit und zum Troste meiner Seele. Lübecker unterwegs zu mittelalterlichen Wallfahrtsstätten', *Zeitschrift des Vereins für Lübeckische Geschichte und Altertumskunde*, 63 (1983), 83–103

Ohly, Friedrich, 'Bemerkungen eines Philologen zur Memoria', in *Memoria, der geschichtliche Zeugniswert des liturgischen Gedenkens im Mittelalter*, ed. by Karl Schmid and Joachim Wollasch (München: Fink, 1984), pp. 9–68

Olick, Jeffrey K., '"Collective Memory": A Memoir and Prospect', *Memory Studies*, 1 (2008), 23–30

——, 'Collective Memory. The Two Cultures', *Sociological Theory*, 17.3 (1999), 333–48

——, and Joyce Robbins, 'Social Memory Studies: From "Collective Memory" to the Historical Sociology of Mnemonic Practices', *Annual Review of Sociology*, 24 (1998), 105–40

Oolup, Urmas, 'Über das Stadtarchiv Tallinn (Reval) in Estland und seine Bestände', *Archivalische Zeitschrift*, 87.1 (2005), 165–84

Ose, Ieva, 'Mittelalterliche Klöster in Riga im 13.–16. Jahrhundert', in *Lübecker Kolloquium zur Stadtarchäologie im Hanseraum IX: die Klöster*, ed. by Manfred Gläser and Manfred Schneider (Lübeck: Schmidt–Römhild Verlag, 2014), pp. 509–20

Pabst, Martin, *Die Typologisierbarkeit von Städtereformation und die Stadt Riga als Beispiel* (Frankfurt am Main: Peter Lang, 2015)

Pac, Grzegorz, 'Frauen und Memoria in der Dynastie der Piasten im 11. und 12. Jahrhundert. Drei Beispiele', *Zeitschrift für Ostmitteleuropa–Forschung*, 60.2 (2011), 163–85

Paravicini, Werner, Rimvydas Petrauskas, and Grischa Vercamer, eds, *Tannenberg – Grunwald – Žalgiris 1410 : Krieg und Frieden im Späten Mittelalter* (Wiesbaden: Harrassowitz, 2012)

Päsler, Ralf G., *Deutschsprachige Sachliteratur im Preußenland bis 1500: Untersuchungen zu ihrer Überlieferung* (Köln: Böhlau, 2003)

Perlbach, Max, 'Deutsch–Ordens Necrologe', *Forschungen zur deutschen Geschichte*, 17 (1877), 357–71

——, ed., *Die Statuten des Deutschen Ordens. Nach den ältesten Handschriften* (Halle: Niemeyer, 1890)

Plakans, Andrejs, *A Concise History of the Baltic States* (Cambridge: Cambridge University Press, 2011)

Plästerer, Artur, ed., *Das Revaler Pergament–Rentenbuch 1382–1518* (Reval: Revaler Estnische Verlagsgenossenschaft Tallinn Eesti Kirjastus Ühisus, 1930)

Plate, Frauke, 'Biddet vor dat geslecht. Memoria und Repräsentation im mittelalterlichen Hamburg', in *Gemeinschaft und Geschichtsbilder im Hanseraum*, ed. by Thomas Hill and Dietrich W. Poeck (Frankfurt am Main: Lang, 2000), pp. 61–100

Poeck, Dietrich W., '"…bidde vor uns." Zu Fürbitte und Totengedenken im mittelalterlichen Bremen', *Bremisches Jahrbuch*, 72 (1993), 16–33

——, 'Biddet got vor enne. Zum Totengedenken in Soest', in *Soest. Die Welt der Bürger, Politik, Gesellschaft und Kultur im spätmittelalterlichen Soest*, vol. 2, ed. by Heinz-Dieter Heimann (Soest: Westfälische Verlag Buchhandlung Mocker und Jahn, 1996), 915–36

——, 'Der Dom als Ort der Erinnerung', in *Der Dom als Anfang: 1225 Jahre Bistum und Stadt Osnabrück*, ed. by Hermann Queckenstedt and Franz-Josef Bode (Osnabrück: Dom-Buchhanlung Osnabrück, 2005), pp. 301–26

——, 'Klöster und Bürger. Eine Fallstudie zu Lübeck (1225–1531)', in *Starptautiska konference Hanza vakar – Hanza rīt, Rīga, 1998. g. 8.–13. jūnijs = International Conference Hansa Yesterday – Hansa Tomorrow, Riga, June 8–13, 1998*, ed. by Ojārs Spārītis (Riga: Izdevniecība Vārds, 2001), pp. 423–52

——, 'Rat und Memoria', in *Memoria in der Gesellschaft des Mittelalters*, ed. by Dieter Geuenich and Otto Gerhard Oexle (Göttingen: Vandenhoeck & Ruprecht, 1994), pp. 286–335

——, 'Sühne durch Gedenken. Das Recht der Opfer', in *Die Legitimität der Erinnerung und die Geschichtswissenschaft*, ed. by Clemens Wischermann (Stuttgart: Steiner, 1996), pp. 113–36

——, 'Totengedenken in Hansestädten', in *Vinculum societatis: Joachim Wollasch zum 60. Geburtstag*, ed. by Franz Neiske, Dietrich W. Poeck, and Mechthild Sandmann (Sigmaringendorf: Regio–Verlag Glock und Lutz, 1991), pp. 175–232

——, 'Zahl, Tag und Stuhl. Zur Semiotik der Ratswahl', *Frühmittelalterliche Studien*, 33 (1999), 396–427

——, *Rituale der Ratswahl: Zeichen und Zeremoniell der Ratssetzung in Europa (12.–18. Jahrhundert)* (Köln: Böhlau, 2003)

Poelchau, Lore, 'Bernhards von Lippe Lebensende (1224) und seine Darstellung im „Lippiflorium". Ergänzende Interpretationen', *Zeitschrift für Ostforschung*, 51 (2002), 253–58

——, 'Das Zisterzienserkloster Dünamünde', in *Benediktiner, Zisterzienser*, ed. by Christof Römer (Berlin: Lukas–Verlag, 1999), pp. 172–83

——, 'Die Geschichte des Zisterzienserklosters Dünamünde bei Riga (1205–1305)', *Studien und Mitteilungen zur Geschichte des Benediktiner Ordens und seiner Zweige*, 115 (2004), 65–199

Põltsam-Jürjo, Inna, 'Die autochthone Bevölkerung', in *Das Baltikum: Geschichte einer europäischen Region. Band 1. Von der Vor- und Frühgeschichte bis zum Ende des Mittelalters*, ed. by Karsten Brüggemann, Detlef Henning, Konrad Maier, and Ralph Tuchtenhagen (Stuttgart: Hiersemann Verlag, 2018), pp. 341–75

———, 'Die Städte: Alltag, soziale Schichten, Handel und Gewerbe', in *Das Baltikum: Geschichte einer europäischen Region. Band 1. Von der Vor– und Frühgeschichte bis zum Ende des Mittelalters*, ed. by Karsten Brüggemann, Detlef Henning, Konrad Maier, and Ralph Tuchtenhagen (Stuttgart: Hiersemann Verlag, 2018), pp. 296–340

———, 'Lihula isepäised nunnad', *Läänemaa Muuseumi toimetised*, 18 (2015), 175–194

Prānis, Guntars, *Missale Rigense Livonijas garīgajā kultūrā: gregoriskie dziedājumi viduslaiku Rīgā* (Rīga: Neputns, 2018)

Queckenstedt, Hermann, *Die Armen und die Toten: Sozialfürsorge und Totengedenken im spätmittelalterlich–frühneuzeitlichen Osnabrück* (Osnabrück: Universitätsverlag Rasch, 1997)

Rader, Olaf B., 'Legitimationsgenerator Grab. Zur politischen Instrumentalisierung von Begräbnislagen', in *Grab – Kult – Memoria: Studien zur gesellschaftlichen Funktion von Erinnerung; Horst Bredekamp zum 60. Geburtstag am 29. April 2007*, ed. by Carolin Behrmann and Horst Bredekamp (Köln: Böhlau, 2007), pp. 7–20

Rajamaa, Ruth, 'Pirita kloostri asutamine ja ülesehitamine 1407–1436 Rootsi allikate valguses', *Kunstiteaduslikke Uurimusi*, 4 (2007), 75–92

———, *Katkenud laul: Pirita klooster 1407–1607*, ed. by Andres Adamson (Tallinn: Argo, 2018)

Rebane, Siiri, 'Geschichte des Dominikanerklosters in Tartu (Dorpat)', in *Estnische Kirchengeschichte im vorigen Jahrtausend*, ed. by Riho Altnurme (Kiel: Friedrich Wittig Verlag, 2001), pp. 55–60

Reidna, Ravo, *The Altar of Holy Mary of the Tallinn Brotherhood of the Blackheads* (Tallinn: Eesti Kunstimuuseum, 1995)

Reincke, Heinrich, 'Bevölkerungsprobleme der Hansestädte', *Hansische Geschichtsblätter*, 70 (1951), 1–33

———, 'Bevölkerungsverluste der Hansestädte durch den Schwarzen Tod 1349/50', *Hansische Geschichtsblätter*, 72 (1954), 88–90

Rexroth, Frank, 'Armut und Memoria im spätmittelalterlichen London', in *Memoria in der Gesellschaft des Mittelalters*, ed. by Dieter Geuenich and Otto Gerhard Oexle (Göttingen: Vandenhoeck & Ruprecht, 1994), pp. 336–60

———, *Deviance and Power in Late Medieval London*, trans. by Pamela E. Selwyn (Cambridge: Cambridge University Press, 2007)

Richard, Olivier, '"Fromme Klauseln" – "profane Klauseln". Eine sinnvolle Unterscheidung?', in *Seelenheil und irdischer Besitz: Testamente als Quellen für den Umgang mit den 'letzten Dingen'*, ed. by Markwart Herzog and Cecilie Hollberg (Konstanz: UVK–Verl.–Ges, 2007), pp. 69–78

———, 'Von der Distinktion zur Integration. Die Repräsentation des Regensburger Patriziats im Spätmittelalter', in *Repräsentationen der mittelalterlichen Stadt*, ed. by Jörg Oberste (Regensburg: Schnell Steiner, 2008), pp. 213–28

———, *Mémoires bourgeoises: 'memoria' et identité urbaine à Ratisbonne à la fin du Moyen Age* (Rennes: Presses universitaires de Rennes, 2009)

Riethmüller, Marianne, *to troste miner sele: Aspekte spätmittelalterlicher Frömmigkeit im Spiegel Hamburger Testamente (1310–1400)* (Hamburg: Verein für Hamburgische Geschichte, 1994)

Ritscher, Alfred, *Reval an der Schwelle zur Neuzeit. Teil I. Vom Vorabend der Reformation bis zum Tode Wolters von Plettenberg (1510–1535)* (Bonn: Kulturstiftung d. dt. Vertriebenen, 1998)

Robijn, Vincent, 'Brothers in Life and Death. The "Schepenmemorie" of Kampen (1311– c. 1580)', in *Trade, Diplomacy and Cultural Exchange : Continuity and Change in the North Sea Area and the Baltic, c. 1350–1750*, ed. by Hanno Brand (Hilversum: Uitgeverij Verloren, 2005), pp. 171–85

Rooch, Alarich, *Stifterbilder in Flandern und Brabant : stadtbürgerliche Selbstdarstellung in der sakralen Malerei des 15. Jahrhunderts* (Essen: Die Blaue Eule, 1988)

Rösener, Werner, ed., *Adelige und bürgerliche Erinnerungskulturen des Spätmittelalters und der Frühen Neuzeit* (Göttingen: Vandenhoeck & Ruprecht, 2001)

Rosser, Gervase, 'Finding Oneself in a Medieval Fraternity. Individual and Collective Identities in the English Guilds', in *Mittelalterliche Bruderschaften in Europäischen Städten: Funktionen, Formen, Akteure = Medieval Confraternities in European Towns: Functions, Forms, Protagonists*, ed. by Monika Escher-Apsner (Frankfurt am Main: Peter Lang, 2009), pp. 29–46

———, 'Going to the Fraternity Feast. Commensality and Social Relations in Late Medieval England', *Journal of British Studies*, 33.4 (1994), 430–46

Rößner, Regina, 'Zur Memoria Lübecker Kaufleute im Mittelalter', in *Beiträge zur Sozialgeschichte Lübecker Oberschichten im Spätmittelalter*, ed. by Harm von Seggern and Gerhard Fouquet (Kiel: Selbstverlag des Historischen Seminars, Kiel, 2005), pp. 75–84

Rößner, Renée, 'Hansische Geschichtsbilder. Das Brügger Kontor', in *Gemeinschaft und Geschichtsbilder im Hanseraum*, ed. by Thomas Hill and Dietrich W. Poeck (Frankfurt am Main: Lang, 2000), pp. 27–44

———, *Hansische Memoria in Flandern: Alltagsleben und Totengedenken der Osterlinge in Brügge und Antwerpen (13. bis 16. Jahrhundert)* (Frankfurt am Main: Lang, 2001)

Rubin, Miri, *Charity and Community in Medieval Cambridge* (Cambridge: Cambridge University Press, 1987)

———, *Corpus Christi: The Eucharist in Late Medieval Culture* (Cambridge: Cambridge University Press, 1991)

Ruf, Susanne, 'Memoria im Luthertum? Sachzeugnisse des individuellen Totengedenkens in thüringischen Kirchen vom 16. bis zum 20. Jahrhundert', in *Reformations and their impact on the culture of memoria*, ed. by Truus van Bueren, Paul Cockerham, Caroline Horch, Martine Meuwese, and Thomas Schilp (Turnhout: Brepols, 2016), pp. 141–70

Russow, Erki, 'Die Klöster in der Stadt Reval (Tallinn)', in *Lübecker Kolloquium zur Stadtarchäologie im Hanseraum, IX: Klöster*, ed. by Manfred Gläser (Lübeck: Schmidt-Römhild, 2014), pp. 531–43

———, ed., *Keskaja sild Padise ja Vantaa vahel = Keskiajan silta Padisen ja Vantaan välillä* (Padise: Padise Vallavalitsus, 2012)

Rüther, Stefanie, 'Strategien der Erinnerung. Zur Repräsentation der Lübecker Ratsherren', in *Gemeinschaft und Geschichtsbilder im Hanseraum*, ed. by Thomas Hill and Dietrich W. Poeck (Frankfurt am Main: Lang, 2000), pp. 101–23

———, 'Wo die Schwestern, die Armen und die Waisen wohnen. Zur Konstruktion einer sakralen Topographie Lübecks im 15. und 16. Jahrhundert', in *Topographien des Sakralen: Religion und Raumordnung in der Vormoderne*, ed. by Susanne Rau and Gerd Schwerhoff (München: Dölling und Galitz, 2008), pp. 330–47

———, *Prestige und Herrschaft: zur Repräsentation der Lübecker Ratsherren in Mittelalter und Früher Neuzeit* (Köln: Böhlau, 2003)

Sarnowsky, Jürgen, 'Buchbesitz, Bibliotheken und Schriftkultur im mittelalterlichen Preußen', in *Mittelalterliche Kultur und Literatur im Deutschordensstaat in Preussen: Leben und Nachleben*, ed. by Jarosław Wenta, Sieglinde Hartmann, and Gisela Vollmann-Profe (Toruń: UMK, 2008), pp. 291–308

———, 'Das Vermächtnis des Meisters in den geistlichen Ritterorden', in *Herrscher- und Fürstentestamente im westeuropäischen Mittelalter*, ed. by Brigitte Kasten (Köln: Böhlau, 2008), pp. 635–49

———, 'Der Tod des Großmeisters der Johanniter', in *Die Spiritualität der Ritterorden im Mittelalter*, ed. by Zenon Hubert Nowak (Toruń: UMK, 1993), pp. 205–16

Sauer, Christine, *Fundatio und memoria: Stifter und Klostergründer im Bild: 1100 bis 1350* (Göttingen: Vandenhoeck & Ruprecht, 1993)

Saul, Nigel, *Death, Art, and Memory in Medieval England: The Cobham Family and Their Monuments, 1300–1500* (Oxford: Oxford University Press, 2001)

Scheller, Benjamin, *Memoria an der Zeitenwende: die Stiftungen Jakob Fuggers des Reichen vor und während der Reformation (c. 1505–1555)* (Berlin: Akademie-Verlag, 2004)

Schewe, Dieter, *Geschichte der sozialen und privaten Versicherung im Mittelalter in den Gilden Europas* (Berlin: Duncker und Humblot, 2000)

Schich, Winfried, 'Zur Diskriminierung der wendischen Minderheit im späten Mittelalter: die Ausbildung des "Wendenparagraphen" in den Zunftstatuten nordostdeutscher Städte', *Europa Regional*, 10.2 (2002), 57–61

Schiemann, Theodor, ed., *Regesten verlorener Urkunden aus dem alten livländischen Ordensarchiv* (Mitau: Behre, 1873)

Schiferl, Ellen, 'Italian Confraternity Art Contracts. Group Consciousness and Corporate Patronage, 1400–1525', in *Crossing the Boundaries : Christian Piety and the Arts in Italian Medieval and Renaissance Confraternities*, ed. by Konrad Eisenbichler (Kalamazoo: Western Michigan University, 1991), pp. 121–40

Schilp, Thomas, 'Totengedenken des Mittelalters und kulturelles Gedächtnis. Überlegungen zur Perspektive der Memorialforschung für das Frauenstift Essen', in *Pro remedio et salute anime peragemus: Totengedenken am Frauenstift Essen im Mittelalter*, ed. by Thomas Schilp (Essen: Klartext, 2008), pp. 19–38

———, and Caroline Horch, eds, *Memoria, Erinnerungskultur, Historismus: zum Gedenken an Otto Gerhard Oexle (28. August 1939 – 16. Mai 2016)* (Turnhout: Brepols, 2019)

———, *Stadtgesellschaft und Memoria: die Ausrichtung auf das Jenseits und ihre sozialen Implikationen*, ed. by Arnoud–Jan Bijsterveld, Meta Niederkorn–Bruck, and Annemarie Staufer (Turnhout: Brepols, 2023)

Schmale, Franz–Josef, *Funktion und Formen mittelalterlicher Geschichtsschreibung: eine Einführung* (Darmstadt: Wissenschaftliche Buchgesellschaft Darmstadt, 1985)

Schmid, Karl, 'Das liturgische Gebetsgedenken in seiner historischen Relevanz am Beispiel der Verbrüderungsbewegung des frühen Mittelalters', in *Gebetsgedenken und adliges Selbstverständnis im Mittelalter*, by Karl Schmid, ed. by Gerd Althoff and Dieter Geuenich (Sigmaringen: J. Thorbecke, 1983), pp. 620–44

———, 'Mönchtum und Verbrüderung', in *Monastische Reformen im 9. und 10. Jahrhundert*, ed. by Raymund Kottje and Helmut Maurer (Sigmaringen: Thorbecke, 1989), pp. 117–46

———, 'Personenforschung und Namenforschung am Beispiel der Klostergemeinschaft von Fulda', *Frühmittelalterliche Studien*, 5 (1971), 235–67

———, 'Stiftungen für das Seelenheil', in *Gedächtnis, das Gemeinschaft stiftet*, ed. by Karl Schmid and Joachim Wollasch (München: Schnell und Steiner, 1985), pp. 51–73

———, and Joachim Wollasch, 'Die Gemeinschaft der Lebenden und Verstorbenen in Zeugnissen des Mittelalters', *Frühmittelalterliche Studien*, 1 (1967), 365–405

———, and ———, 'Societas et Fraternitas. Begründung eines kommentierten Quellenwerkes zur Erforschung der Personen und Personengruppen des Mittelalters', *Frühmittelalterliche Studien*, 9 (1975), 1–48

———, and ———, eds, *Memoria: der geschichtliche Zeugniswert des liturgischen Gedenkens im Mittelalter* (München: Fink, 1984)

———, and ———, eds, *Gedächtnis, das Gemeinschaft stiftet* (München: Schnell und Steiner, 1985)

Schmidt, Patrick, *Wandelbare Traditionen – tradierter Wandel: zünftische Erinnerungskulturen in der Frühen Neuzeit* (Köln: Böhlau, 2009)

Schmidt, Wolfgang, 'Die Zisterzienser im Baltikum und in Finnland', *Finska kyrkohistoriska samfundets årsskrift*, 29/30 (1939/1940), 1–286

Schmitt, Jean–Claude, *Ghosts in the Middle Ages: The Living and the Dead in Medieval Society*, trans. by Teresa Lavender Fagan (Chicago: University of Chicago Press, 1998)

Schneidmüller, Bernd, 'Europäische Erinnerungsorte im Mittelalter', *Jahrbuch für Europäische Geschichte*, 3 (2002), 39–58

Scholz, Sebastian, Gerald Schwedler, and Kai–Michael Sprenger, eds, *Damnatio in memoria: Deformation und Gegenkonstruktionen in der Geschichte* (Köln: Böhlau, 2014)

Schubert, Ernst, '"Hausarme Leute", "starke Bettler". Einschränkungen und Umformungen des Almosengedankens um 1400 und um 1500', in *Armut im Mittelalter*, ed. by Otto Gerhard Oexle (Ostfildern: Thorbecke, 2004), pp. 283–348

Schulz, Knut, 'Gewerbliche Strukturen des Hanseraumes unter besonderer Berücksichtigung der baltischen Städte (Riga, Reval) im Spätmittelalter', in *Von der Geschichte zur Gegenwart und Zukunft: Mittelständische Wirtschaft, Handwerk und Kultur im baltischen Raum*, ed. by Burghart Schmidt (Hamburg: DOBU, 2006), pp. 84–108

Schwartz, Barry, *Abraham Lincoln and the Forge of National Memory* (Chicago: University of Chicago Press, 2000)

Schwarz, Jörg, 'Zwischen Kaiser und Papst. Der Rigaer Erzbistumsstreit 1480–1483', *Zeitschrift für Historische Forschung*, 34.3 (2007), 373–401

Schwarz, Michael Viktor, 'Kathedralen verstehen. St. Veit in Prag als räumlich organisiertes Medienensemble', in *Virtuelle Räume: Raumwahrnehmung und Raumvorstellung im Mittelalter*, ed. by Elisabeth Vavra (Berlin: Akademie-Verlag, 2005), pp. 47–68

Schwedler, Gerald, and Sebastian Scholz, eds, *Creative Selection between Emending and Forming Medieval Memory* (Berlin: de Gruyter, 2022)

——, ed., *A Cultural History of Memory in the Middle Ages*, vol. 2 (London: Bloomsbury Academic, 2020)

——, *Vergessen, Verändern, Verschweigen und damnatio memoriae im frühen Mittelalter* (Köln: Böhlau, 2020)

Seidel, Kerstin, *Freunde und Verwandte: Soziale Beziehungen in einer spätmittelalterlichen Stadt* (Frankfurt am Main: Campus Verlag, 2009)

Selart, Anti, 'Die Bettelmönche im Ostseeraum zur Zeit des Erzbischofs Albert Suerbeer von Riga (Mitte des 13. Jahrhunderts)', *Zeitschrift für Ostmitteleuropa-Forschung*, 56.4 (2007), 475–99

——, 'Meinhard, Berthold, Bernhard – kein Heiliger für Livland', ed. by Hanne Lovise Aannestad, Christoph Stiegemann, Martin Kroker, and Wolfgang Walter (Petersberg: Michael Imhof Verlag, 2013), pp. 434–40

——, 'Non-German Literacy in Medieval Livonia', in *Uses of the Written Word in Medieval Towns: Medieval Urban Literacy II*, ed. by Marco Mostert and Anna Adamska (Turnhout: Brepols, 2014), pp. 37–63

——, 'Switching the Tracks. Baltic Crusades against Russia in the Fifteenth Century', in *The Crusade in the Fifteenth Century. Converging and Competing Cultures*, ed. by Norman Housley (London: Routledge, 2016), pp. 90–106

——, ed., *Baltic Crusades and Societal Innovation in Medieval Livonia, 1200–1350* (Leiden: Brill, 2022)

——, ed., *Eesti ajalugu II. Eesti keskaeg* (Tartu: Tartu Ülikool, 2012)

Selzer, Stephan, *Artushöfe im Ostseeraum: ritterlich-höfische Kultur in den Städten des Preussenlandes im 14. und 15. Jahrhundert* (Frankfurt am Main: Lang, 1996)

Signori, Gabriela, '"Family Traditions". Moral Economy and Memorial "Gift Exchange" in the Urban World of the Late Fifteenth–Century', in *Negotiating the Gift. Pre-Modern Figuration of Exchange*, ed. by Gadi Algazi, Valentin Groebner, and Bernhard Jussen (Göttingen: Vandenhoeck & Ruprecht, 2003), pp. 285–318

Silber, Ilana F., 'Gift–Giving in the Great Traditions: The Case of Donations to Monasteries in the Medieval West', *European Journal of Sociology / Archives Européennes de Sociologie*, 36.2 (1995), 209–43

Siliņa, Māra, 'Ikonographie und Typologie der gotischen Memorialplastik in Lettland', in *Gotik im Baltikum: acht Beiträge zum 6. Baltischen Seminar 1994*, ed. by Uwe Albrecht (Lüneburg: Carl–Schirren–Gesellschaft, 2004), pp. 143–66

Simon–Muscheid, Katharina, 'Sozialer Abstieg im Mittelalter', in *The Sign Languages of Poverty: International Round Table–Discussion, Krems an Der Donau, October 10 and 11, 2005*, ed. by Gerhard Jaritz (Wien: Verlag der Österreichischen Akademie der Wissenschaften, 2007), pp. 95–117

——, 'Zunft–Trinkstuben und Bruderschaften. "Soziale Orte" und Beziegungs netz im spätmittelalterlichen Basel', in *Geschlechtergesellschaften, Zunft–Trinkstuben und Bruderschaften in spätmittelalterlichen und frühneuzeitlichen Städten*, ed. by Gerhard Fouquet, Matthias Steinbrink, and Gabriel Zeilinger (Stuttgart: Thorbecke, 2003), pp. 147–62

——, *Basler Handwerkzünfte im Spätmittelalter: zunftinterne Strukturen und innerstädtische Konflikte* (Bern: Lang, 1988)

Skibiński, Szczęsny, *Kaplica na Zamku Wysokim w Malborku* (Poznań: Wydawnictwo Naukowe UAM, 1982)

Smith, Jerry Christopher, and William L. Urban, eds, *The Livonian Rhymed Chronicle* (Chicago: Lithuanian Research and Studies Center, 2001)

Soneji, Devesh, *Unfinished Gestures: Devadāsīs, Memory, and Modernity in South India* (Chicago: University of Chicago Press, 2012)

Speer, Christian, *Frömmigkeit und Politik: städtische Eliten in Görlitz zwischen 1300 und 1550* (Berlin: Akademie–Verlag, 2011)

Spieß, Karl–Heinz, 'Liturgische Memoria und Herrschaftsrepräsentation im nichtfürstlichen Hochadel des Spätmittelalters', in *Adelige und bürgerliche Erinnerungskulturen des Spätmittelalters und der Frühen Neuzeit*, ed. by Werner Rösener (Göttingen: Vandenhoeck & Ruprecht, 2001), pp. 97–123

Spliet, Herbert, 'Die Schwarzhäupter in ihrem Verhältnis zur deutschen kolonialen Ständegeschichte in Livland', *Zeitschrift für Ostforschung*, 3 (1954), 233–47

——, *Geschichte des rigischen Neuen Hauses, des später sogen. König Artus Hofes, des heutigen Schwarzhäupterhauses zu Riga* (Riga: Plates, 1934)

Stackelberg, Otto Magnus von, *Genealogisches Handbuch der estländischen Ritterschaft*, vol. 1 (Görlitz: Starke, 1931)

Stanford, Charlotte A., *Commemorating the Dead in Late Medieval Strasbourg: The Cathedral's Book of Donors and Its Use (1320–1521)* (Farnham: Ashgate, 2011)

Stavenhagen, Oskar, and Leonid Arbusow, eds, *Akten und Rezesse der livländischen Ständetage*, vols. 1–3 (Riga: Deubner, 1907–1923)

———, *Genealogisches Handbuch der kurländischen Ritterschaft*, vol. 1 (Görlitz: Starke, 1939)

Steindorff, Ludwig, *Memoria in Altrussland: Untersuchungen zu den Formen christlicher Totensorge* (Stuttgart: Steiner, 1994)

Šterns, Indriķis, 'Latvieši un krievi viduslaiku Rīgā', *Latvijas Vēstures Institūta Žurnāls*, 2 (1996), 22–54

———, *Latvijas vēsture: 1180–1290. Krustakari* (Rīga: Latvijas vēstures institūta apgāds, 2002)

———, *Latvijas vēsture: 1290–1500* (Riga: Daugava, 1997)

Stieda, Wilhelm, and Constantin Mettig, eds, *Schragen der Gilden und Aemter der Stadt Riga bis 1621* (Riga: Häcker, 1896)

Strehlke, Ernst Gottfried Wilhelm, ed., 'Die Annalen und das Necrologium von Ronneburg', in *Hermanni de Wartberge Chronicon livoniae* (Leipzig: Hirzel, 1863), pp. 142–48

———, ed., 'Die Chronik von Dünamünde', in *Hermanni de Wartberge Chronicon Livoniae* (Leipzig: Hirzel, 1863), pp. 131–34

Strenga, Gustavs, 'Distorted Memories and Power: Patrons of the Teutonic Order in the Fifteenth Century Prayer of the Livonian Branch', *Journal of Baltic Studies*, 50.2 (2019), 143–161

———, 'Donations, Discipline and Commemoration: Creating Group Identity in the Transport Workers Guilds of Mid Fifteenth–Century Riga', *Journal of Medieval History*, 48.1 (2022), 103–28

———, '"Bidden vor myner sele." The Dominicans as Intercessors Between Townspeople and God in Late Medieval Reval', *Annual of Medieval Studies at CEU*, 13 (2007), 111–32

———, 'Bonding with "Friends" and Allies. The Teutonic Order's Confraternity and Networking Strategies of the Livonian Master Wolter von Plettenberg', *Letonica*, 36 (2017), 136–60

———, 'Cistercian Networks of Memory: Commemoration as a Form of Institutional Bonding in Livonia and beyond during the Late Middle Ages', in *Making Livonia : Actors and Networks in the Medieval and Early Modern Baltic Sea Region*, ed. by Anu Mänd and Marek Tamm (London: Routledge, 2020), pp. 212–31

———, 'Die Formierung der Letten als ethnische Gemeinschaft zur Zeit der Reformation in Riga', in *Reformation und Ethnizität. Sorben, Letten und Esten im 16. und 17. Jahrhundert*, ed. by Madlena Mahling, Susanne Hose, and Friedrich Pollack (Bautzen: Domowina–Verlag, 2019), pp. 77–97

———, 'Distance, Presence, Absence and Memoria: Commemoration of Deceased Livonian Merchants Outside Their Native Cities during the Late Middle Ages', *Hansische Geschichtsblätter*, 136 (2018), 63–92

———, and Andris Levāns, 'Gradual Formation and Dramatic Transformation. Mendicant and Cistercian Book Collections in Late Medieval and Post-Reformation Riga', in *The Baltic Battle of Books: Formation and Relocation of European Libraries in the Confessional Age (c.1500-c.1650) and Their Afterlife*, ed. by Jonas Nordin, Gustavs Strenga, and Peter Sjökvist (Leiden: Brill, 2023), pp. 37-61

———, 'Remembering the common past: Livonia as a lieu de mémoire of the Teutonic Order in the Empire', in *Livland – eine Region am Ende der Welt? Forschungen zum Verhältnis zwischen Zentrum und Peripherie im späten Mittelalter = Livonia – a region at the end of the world? Studies on the relations between centre and periphery in the later Middle Ages*, ed. by Anti Selart and Matthias Thumser (Köln: Böhlau, 2017), pp. 347-70

———, 'Stāsts par Livoniju ārpus Livonijas? Vecākā Livonijas Atskaņu hronika kā Vācu ordeņa vēsturiskais teksts', in *Grāmata Latvijai ārpus Latvijas: kolektīvā monogrāfija*, ed. by Viesturs Zanders (Rīga: Latvijas Nacionālā bibliotēka, 2021), pp. 27-54

———, 'Turning Transport Workers into Latvians? The Ethnicity and Transport Workers' Guilds in Riga before and after the Reformation', *Journal of Baltic Studies*, 52.1 (2021), 61-83

Tabora, Laine, 'Fifteenth–Century Manuscripts: The Liturgical and Musical Testimonies from the Cistercian Nunnery in Riga', in *The Baltic Battle of Books: Formation and Relocation of European Libraries in the Confessional Age (c.1500-c.1650) and Their Afterlife*, ed. by Jonas Nordin, Peter Sjökvist, and Gustavs Strenga (Leiden: Brill, 2023), 13-36

———, 'Psalterium Davidis of the Cistercian Nunnery of Riga (LMAVB RS F 22–96) and Its Liturgical Calendar', *Analecta Cisterciensia*, 71 (2021), 119-69

Tamm, Jaan, *Eesti keskaegsed kloostrid. Medieval Monasteries of Estonia* (Tallinn: Eesti Entsüklopeediakirjastus, 2002)

Tamm, Marek, 'Communicating Crusade. Livonian Mission and the Cistercian Network in the Thirteenth Century', *Ajolooline Ajakiri*, 3.4 (2009), 341-72

———, 'How to Justify a Crusade? The Conquest of Livonia and New Crusade Rhetoric in the Early Thirteenth Century', *Journal of Medieval History*, 39.4 (2013), 431-55

———, 'Inventing Livonia. The Name and Fame of a New Christian Colony on the Medieval Baltic Frontier', *Zeitschrift für Ostmitteleuropa-Forschung*, 60 (2011), 186-209

———, 'The Livonian Crusade in Cistercian Stories of the Early Thirteenth Century', in *Crusading on the Edge: Ideas and Practice of Crusading in Iberia and the Baltic Region, 1100–1500*, ed. by Torben Kjersgaard Nielsen and Iben Fonnesberg-Schmidt (Turnhout: Brepols, 2016), pp. 365-89

———, 'When Did the Dominicans Arrive in Tallinn?', *Tuna. Ajalookultuuri ajakiri*, 4 (2009), 35-45

———, and Alessandro Arcangeli, eds, *A Cultural History of Memory in the Early Modern Age* (London: Bloomsbury, 2020)

———, Linda Kaljundi, and Carsten Selch Jensen, eds, *Crusading and Chronicle Writing on the Medieval Baltic Frontier: A Companion to the Chronicle of Henry of Livonia* (Farnham: Ashgate, 2011)

Thome, Markus, 'Das Bischofsgrabmal und die Visualisierung liturgischer Gemeinschaft. Die Mainzer Kathedrale als Gedächtnisraum', in *Tomb – Memory – Space: Concepts of Representation in Premodern Christian and Islamic Art*, ed. by Francine Giese, Anna Pawlak, and Markus Thome (Berlin: de Gruyter, 2018), pp. 222–49

Thumser, Antje, 'Livländische Amtsträgerreihen des Mittelalters. Kleine Meisterchronik – Rigaer Bischofschronik – Series episcoporum Curoniae', in *Geschichtsschreibung im mittelalterlichen Livland*, ed. by Matthias Thumser (Berlin: LIT, 2011), pp. 201–54

Thumser, Matthias, 'Antirussische Propaganda in der ‚Schönen Historie von wunderbaren Geschäften der Herren zu Livland mit den Russen und Tataren', in *Geschichtsschreibung im mittelalterlichen Livland*, ed. by Matthias Thumser (Berlin: LIT, 2011), pp. 133–53

———, 'Geschichte schreiben als Anklage. Der Weißensteiner Rezeß (1478) und der Konflikt um das Erzstift Riga', *Jahrbuch für die Geschichte Mittel- und Ostdeutschlands*, 51 (2005), 63–75

———, 'Medieval Livonia: Structures of a European Historical Region', in *Das mittelalterliche Livland und sein historisches Erbe = Medieval Livonia and Its Historical Legacy*, ed. by Ilgvars Misāns, Andris Levāns, and Gustavs Strenga (Marburg: Verlag Herder–Institut, 2022), pp. 11–23

Toomaspoeg, Kristjan, '"Confratres, procuratores, negociorum gestores et factores eorum." Storia dei "familiares" dei Cavalieri Teutonici in Sicilia (1197–1492)', *Sacra militia*, 1 (2001), 151–65

———, 'Der Deutsche Orden als Grund- und Kirchenherr in Italien', in *Die Ritterorden als Träger der Herrschaft: Territorien, Grundbesitz und Kirche*, ed. by Roman Czaja and Jürgen Sarnowsky (Toruń: UMK, 2007), pp. 187–201

Transéhe–Roseneck, Astaf von, *Genealogisches Handbuch der livländischen Ritterschaft*, vol. 1 (Görlitz: Starke, 1930)

Trio, Paul, 'The Social Positioning of Late Medieval Confraternities in Urbanized Flanders: From Integration to Segregation', in *Mittelalterliche Bruderschaften in Europäischen Städten : Funktionen, Formen, Akteure = Medieval Confraternities in European Towns : Functions, Forms, Protagonists*, ed. by Monika Escher–Apsner (Frankfurt am Main: Peter Lang, 2009), pp. 99–110

———, 'Confraternities as Such, and as a Template for Guilds in the Low Countries during the Medieval and the Early Modern Period', in *A Companion to Medieval and Early Modern Confraternities*, ed. by Konrad Eisenbichler (Leiden: Brill, 2019), pp. 23–44

Tumler, Marian, *Der Deutsche Orden im Werden, Wachsen und Wirken bis 1400* (Wien: Panorama, 1955)

Urban, William L., *The Baltic Crusade* (Chicago: Lithuanian Research and Studies Center, 1994)

———, *The Teutonic Knights: A Military History* (London: Greenhill Books, 2003)

———, 'The Diplomacy of the Teutonic Knights at the Curia', *Journal of Baltic Studies*, 9.2 (1978), 116–28

Vaivada, Vacys, ed., *1260 metų Durbės mūšis: šaltiniai ir istoriniai tyrimai = The battle of Durbe, 1260: sources and historical research* (Klaipėda: Klaipėdos Universiteto Baltijos regiono istorijos ir archeologijos institutas, 2011)

Valdez del Alamo, Elizabeth, and Carol Stamatis Pendergast, eds, *Memory and the Medieval Tomb* (Aldershot: Ashgate, 2000)

Valk, Heiki, 'Die ethnischen Identitäten der undeutschen Landbevölkerung Estands vom 13. bis zum 16. Jahrhundert. Ergebnisse der Archäologie', in *Estnisches Mittelalter: Sprache – Gesellschaft – Kirche*, ed. by Kadri-Rutt Hahn, Matthias Thumser, and Eberhard Winkler (Berlin: LIT, 2015), pp. 55–92

Vavra, Elisabeth, 'Kunstwerke als religiöse Stiftung. Überlegungen zum Stifterbild in der deutschen Tafelmalerei des Spätmittelalters', in *Artistes, artisans et production artistique au Moyen Âge. 2: Commande et travail*, ed. by Xavier Barral i Altet (Paris: Picard, 1987), pp. 257–72

Vogelsang, Reinhard, ed., *Kämmereibuch der Stadt Reval: 1432–1463* (Köln: Böhlau, 1976)

———, ed., *Kämmereibuch der Stadt Reval: 1463–1507* (Köln: Böhlau, 1983)

Walther-Wittenheim, Gertrud von, *Die Dominikaner in Livland im Mittelalter: Die Natio Livoniae* (Roma: Institutum historicum FF Praedicatorum, 1938)

Warda, Susanne, *Memento mori: Bild und Text in Totentänzen des Spätmittelalters und der frühen Neuzeit* (Köln: Böhlau, 2011)

Wenta, Jarosław, 'Über die ältesten preußischen Annalen', *Preussenland*, 32 (1994), 1–15

Wiersing, Erhard, 'Ein Mensch im Wandel seiner Rollen. Zur Darstellung mittelalterlicher Personalität am Beispiel des Edelherrn Bernhard II. zur Lippe', in *Lippe und Livland: mittelalterliche Herrschaftsbildung im Zeichen der Rose; Ergebnisse der Tagung 'Lippe und Livland', Detmold und Lemgo, 2006*, ed. by Jutta Prieur, Wolfgang Bender, and Gerhard Milting (Gütersloh: Verlag für Regionalgeschichte, 2008), pp. 17–32

Wittram, Reinhard, 'Die Reformation in Livland', in *Baltische Kirchengeschichte*, ed. by Reinhard Wittram (Göttingen: Vandenhoeck & Ruprecht, 1956), pp. 35–55

———, *Baltische Geschichte : die Ostseelande Livland, Estland, Kurland 1180–1918* (Darmstadt: Wissenschaftliche Buchgesellschaft, 1973)

Wolfs, Servatius Petrus, 'Dominikanische Observanzbestrebungen. Die Congregatio Hollandiae (1464–1517)', in *Reformbemühungen und Observanzbestrebungen im spätmittelalterlichen Ordenswesen*, ed. by Kaspar Elm (Berlin: Duncker und Humblot, 1989), pp. 273–92

Wollasch, Joachim, 'Die mittelalterliche Lebensform der Verbrüderung', in *Memoria, der geschichtliche Zeugniswert des liturgischen Gedenkens im Mittelalter*, ed. by Karl Schmid and Joachim Wollasch (München: Fink, 1984), pp. 215–32

———, 'Gemeinschaftsbewußtsein und soziale Leistung im Mittelalter', *Frühmittelalterliche Studien*, 9 (1975), 268–86

———, 'Toten- und Armensorge', in *Gedächtnis, das Gemeinschaft stiftet*, ed. by Karl Schmid and Joachim Wollasch (München: Schnell und Steiner, 1985), pp. 9–38

Wyss, Arthur, ed., *Hessisches Urkundenbuch*, sect. 1, vol. 3. (Leipzig: Hirzel, 1899)

Yates, Frances A., *The Art of Memory* (Chicago: University of Chicago Press, 1966)

Youmans, Nicholas W., 'Between Commemoration and Living Memory: Symbolic Acts of the Teutonic Knights in Light of Cultural Theory', *Ordines Militares Colloquia Torunensia Historica. Yearbook for the Study of the Military Orders*, 26 (2021), 285–313

Zajic, Andreas, 'Jahrtag und Grabdenkmal. Spätmittelalterliche Stiftungen und die Realien der Memoria', in *Freund Hein? Tod und Ritual in der Geschichte*, ed. by Wolfgang Hameter, Meta Niederkorn-Bruck, and Martin Scheutz (Innsbruck: Studien-Verlag, 2007), pp. 82–99

Zerbe, Doreen, *Reformation der Memoria: Denkmale in der Stadtkirche Wittenberg als Zeugnisse lutherischer Memorialkultur im 16. Jahrhundert* (Leipzig: Evangelische Verlagsanstalt, 2013)

Ziesemer, Walther, ed., *Das grosse Ämterbuch des deutschen Ordens* (Danzig: Kafemann, 1921)

———, ed., *Das Marienburger Ämterbuch* (Danzig: A. W. Kafemann, 1916)

Zirnis, Gunārs, *Pētera baznīca* (Rīga: Zinātne, 1984)

Index

Adventus 92, 95
Albert Suerbeer, archbishop of Riga 50
Albert von Buxhoeveden, bishop of Riga 39, 44–46, 50, 52, 97, 107, 256
Albrecht von Hohenzollern, Grand Master 241
Alden Biesen
    bailiwick of 57, 59
    commandery of 60, 68, 72
    necrology of 57–59, 60–66, 69, 127–28
Alms, almsgiving 28, 81–82, 96, 99, 160–70, 193, 195, 208–09, 229, 232, 249–250, 252, 264
Altars 27, 41, 47, 50, 52, 86, 89, 90, 94, 96, 98, 106–07, 110–11, 119, 137–38, 141, 153, 158–59, 164, 172, 174–87, 189–92, 194–98, 207, 210–11, 213–14, 216, 225, 228–30, 233–237, 240, 243–48, 253, 260–62, 264
Anagni 135
Andreas Knopken, priest and a reformer 239–40, 247, 249–50
Andreas von Steinberg, commander of the Teutonic Order's forces 89–91, 101, 257
Andreas Westfalen, Master of the Livonian branch 59
Annals of Dünamunde 65, 103, 114–15, 121, 123–25, 127–28, 131, 259
Anniversaries 80–81, 108, 137, 141–42, 145, 148, 163, 210
Annuity rent 88, 105, 159–60, 177, 186, 190, 229
Anonymous brethren 61–62, 80, 128
Arthur's Courts (Prussia) 171, 173

Ascheraden (Aizkraukle) 59, 89–91, 101

Beer 165, 200–01, 203, 209–10, 212, 217, 220, 231
Bernard of Clairvaux 126
Bernhard von der Borch, Master of the Livonian branch 136–37, 139, 141
Bernhard von Lippe, abbot of Dünamunde abbey, bishop of Selonia 121,126
Bernt Notke, artist 151–53, 189
Berthold Schulte, bishop of Üxkull 44, 121
Bruges 169, 179, 181
Bruno, Master of the Livonian branch 126–127
Burkhard von Hornhausen, Master of the Livonian branch 58, 61, 65, 69

Calendars 115–16, 119–20, 137, 139–41, 258, 260,
Chantries 82–83, 85–89, 95, 97–101, 105–06, 111, 159–60, 174–78, 181, 184–86, 190, 192, 194–96, 207, 210–15, 217, 221, 224–25, 228–34, 237, 245, 247–49
Choirboys 185, 228, 231
Chronicle of Henry of Livonia 36, 45, 256
Chronicle of Hermann Wartberge 59, 61, 65, 90, 101, 126–28
Church of Riga 38, 43–53, 97, 101–02, 121, 133–41, 144–50, 241, 255-57, 259-60
Circle Company, *see* Lübeck; Circle Company
Cisse von dem Rutenberg, Master of the Livonian branch 88

Cistercian annals 65, 125, 128–29, 259
Cistercians 106, 114–15, 117–18, 120–23, 125, 128–31, 259
Communal meals 28, 92, 157, 198, 213, 216, 219–20, 231, 236, 249–50, 252, 260, 264
Confraternity of prayer 115, 131
Council of Basel 96
Couronians 35

Dance of Death (*Totentanz*)
    Lübeck 151, 153
    Reval 151, 152, 153
Danzig (Gdańsk) 78, 81, 139, 162
Detmar Roper, dean of the Riga cathedral chapter 148
Dietrich Nagel, provost of the cathedral chapter of Riga 95–102, 258
Dominicans 104, 107–08, 110–12, 130, 174–76, 190, 196
    Master General 176
    Provincial of the Danish province 175–76
Donations 77, 81–82, 99, 105, 107–09, 112–13, 123, 151, 159, 164, 166, 175, 177–78, 184, 186, 193, 195, 210–17, 228, 230, 232–34, 236, 243–44, 252, 255, 261, 263
Dorpat (Tartu) 38–39, 41, 104, 106, 111, 162, 171, 191, 199–200, 244, 249, 259
    Cistercian convent of St Catherine 103, 105, 106, 107
    Dominican friary 104, 107
Drinking feast (*Drunke*) 119, 157, 172, 182–183, 198, 205, 209–10, 212, 213, 217, 227, 231, 249, 261
Drunke, see Drinking feast
Düna (Daugava) river 35, 39, 143
Dünamunde (Daugavgrīva)
    Cistercian abbey of 103, 114, 120, 121–23, 125, 129–31, 259
    Cistercian abbey of, abbot 121, 126, 129
    Cistercian abbey of, chapel of St Catherine 129

Durbe (Durben), battle of 53, 61–67, 72, 126, 256–57

Edmund von Werth, bishop of Courland 60, 73
Eilard, Danish captain of Reval 126
Enea Silvio Piccolomini, *see* Pius II
Ernest von Ratzenburg, Master of the Livonian branch 59, 69, 126, 128
Estonians 35, 40, 199
Eucharist 96, 163

Fellin (Viljandi) 104, 134, 142, 162
    city councillor 192
Foundation (*Stiftung*) 20, 28, 34, 78, 82, 83, 84, 85, 87–89, 95, 97–102, 110, 113, 155, 176, 177, 179, 184–85, 190, 193, 195–96, 198, 211, 215, 227–30, 240, 257, 260, 262,
Founding bishops 52, 97, 101, 107, 120, 133–34, 139, 144, 255–56
Franciscans 104, 106, 108, 118, 131, 157, 172, 174–78, 190, 193, 198, 212, 216, 240, 245
    Custodian 118
Friedrich III, Emperor 136
Funerals 50, 77, 80–81, 94, 98, 118, 131, 136, 158–159, 163, 166, 177, 183–84, 186, 192, 209–11, 214, 217–21, 236, 249, 252, 263
    Bier 98, 107, 164, 183–184, 192, 220
    Funeral masses 218
    Funeral procession 219

Gebietiger, high-ranking officials of the Teutonic Order 79, 84, 87
Georg Holland, provost of the Riga cathedral chapter 89, 137, 139, 141, 148
Gerhard von Katzenelnbogen, Master of the Livonian branch 59
Gift-giving 25, 26, 28, 33, 92, 113–14, 167, 255
Gifts 26, 28, 92, 99, 100, 108, 113, 114, 144, 160, 162, 164, 165, 167, 169, 171, 214, 215, 230, 234, 252

Gotland 117
Gravediggers 184, 210
Grave slabs 27, 32, 41–42, 44, 46, 50–52, 60, 72, 75, 78–79, 89–91, 101, 108, 141, 143, 146–49, 177, 178, 183–84, 186–87, 230, 257, 259, 264

Hanover 96
Hanse 34, 40, 153, 154–56, 162, 167, 170–73, 178, 188–90, 193–94, 197, 199, 202, 221–22, 224, 236, 241, 262
Heidenreich Vincke von Overberg, Master of the Livonian branch 80, 82–88, 94, 101, 257–58
Heinrich von Böckenförde alias Schüngel, Master of the Livonian branch 94
Henning Scharpenberg, archbishop of Riga 52, 85, 97, 111, 136–37, 139, 141, 144
Hermann von Balk, Master of the Livonian branch 58

Iconoclasm 41, 243, 247–48, 253, 264

Jakob Knopken, cathedral canon of Riga 239, 249
Jasper Linde, dean of the cathedral chapter and archbishop of Riga 52, 225
Jasper Noteken, of the cathedral chapter of Riga 225
Johann Bugenhagen, reformer 239
Johann Kerssenbrugge alias Osenbrugge, physician of the Teutonic Order in Livonia 82, 85–88
Johann von Mengede (Osthoff), Master of the Livonian branch 52–53, 94, 136, 143–49, 259
Johann von Wallenrode, archbishop of Riga 144
Johannes Ambundi, archbishop of Riga 50, 137, 139, 141
Johannes II, archbishop of Riga 134

Johannes von Lune, archbishop of Riga 52
Johannes von Vechta, archbishop of Riga 50, 134
Johannn Freitag von Loringhoven, Master of the Livonian branch 94, 149
John XXII, pope 122, 125

Karkhus (Karksi) 139
Karl Ulfsson, Swedish nobleman 61, 65
Kokenhusen (Koknese) 139
  castle of 136, 139
Konrad von Erlichshausen, Grand Master 80, 94
Konrad von Jungingen, Grand Master 81

Last wills 20, 26, 33, 41, 77, 82, 102, 107, 108, 109, 169, 178, 192, 193, 196, 221, 244, 259
Latgalians 35, 199
Latvians 35, 40, 119, 199, 201–02, 252
Leipzig 96
Liturgical commemoration 47, 67, 90, 128, 130–31, 165, 171, 190, 192, 210, 216–17, 264
  Anniversaries 80–81, 108, 137, 141–42, 145, 148, 163, 210
  Memorial masses 84, 86, 89, 94, 98, 100, 106, 110, 118, 129, 137, 158–59, 163–64, 166, 167, 179, 181–86, 209–12, 215, 217–18, 229, 233
  Vigils 76–77, 80, 84, 94, 100, 106–08, 110, 118, 157–59, 163–64, 167, 176–77, 182–86, 209–10, 213, 215, 217–18, 227, 230–33
Liturgical vessels 27, 157, 175, 177, 195, 228
Liturgical vestments 174–75, 195
Liturgy 25–26, 44, 83, 131, 147, 178, 186, 242, 265
Liva, lake 135

Livonian aristocracy 20, 103, 104, 105, 107, 110, 111, 116, 130, 225, 241, 259,
  noblemen 20, 54, 105–07, 110–12, 116, 226, 259
Livonian Rhymed Chronicle 36, 58–59, 65–73, 126–28, 256
Livonian war 241, 243, 264
Livs 35, 40, 45, 119, 199, 201
Lordly entry, *see adventus*
Lübeck 53–54, 98, 107–08, 151, 153, 173, 175, 178, 181, 194, 212, 222, 224, 245
  Circle Company 156–57, 162, 175
  City councillors 151, 156, 162, 186–187
Ludolf Grove, bishop of Ösel 97
Ludwig von Erlichshausen, Grand Master 93

Marienburg, Livonia (Alūksne) 125
Marienburg, Prussia (Malbork) 70–71, 81
  castle of the Teutonic Order 71, 78, 80–81
    chapel of St Anne 72, 81, 142–143
Mariendal (Pirita)
  Birgittine convent of 104, 106, 111, 115–17, 120, 131, 193
  nuns 106, 115–17, 120, 131, 244, 258,
  superior 115
Marienfeld, Cistercian abbey of 121
Martin Luther, reformer 239–40
Meinhard, bishop of Üxküll 35, 44–52, 97, 135, 256 (including tomb)
Memoriaforschung 24–25, 27, 30–31
Michael Hildebrand, archbishop of Riga 52, 187, 230, 241
Morimond, Cistercian abbey of 121, 122
Mourning 17, 25, 29, 80–81, 84, 92, 118–19, 151, 209

Necrologies 26–27, 42, 46, 57–59, 61, 63, 65–69, 72–73, 75, 77, 79–80, 90, 101, 120, 126–28, 131, 256–57

Necrology of Alden Biesen 57–59, 60–66, 69, 127–28
Necrology of Bern 58, 65–67
Necrology of Hitzkirch 57, 65–67
Necrology of Mergentheim 57, 59, 61, 64–66, 69, 126, 128
Nikolaus Sachow, bishop of Lübeck 98
Non-Germans 36, 156, 199–208, 213, 233, 236, 247, 249, 251–53, 261–62
  exclusion 202–04, 213

Ösel-Wiek, bishopric of 38
Otto von Lauterberg (Lutterberg), Master of the Livonian branch 58–59

Padis (Padise), Cistercian abbey of 103, 106, 114–15, 120, 122, 125, 129–31, 259,
Palls 98, 118, 131, 157–58, 164, 177, 183–84, 195, 210, 213–14, 219, 231
Papal curia 39, 45–46, 125, 134–35, 139, 143, 222
Pelplin, Cistercian abbey of 123
Pilgrimage 194
Pius II, pope 97
Poor 19, 28, 34, 54, 81, 108–09, 151, 158, 160–63, 167–71, 191, 193–95, 198–99, 206–09, 219, 222, 229, 231, 234, 236–37, 243, 246, 249, 252–54, 261–62
Poor tables 161, 166–67, 169
Pope 47, 97, 122, 125, 135, 137, 143–44, 151, 153
Poverty 77–78, 109, 159, 170, 206, 237
Prussia 38, 56, 62–63, 66, 68, 70–71, 73, 77–79, 81, 90, 93, 118, 123, 133–135, 142–143, 171, 173, 256, 258
Purgatory 18, 29, 95–96, 239

Ratsmemoria 167, 169, 171, 186–187, 190, 193–194, 197–198, 230, 243, 263

Reformation 19–20, 29, 41, 50, 81, 94, 107, 110, 112, 117, 120, 131, 149, 158, 165, 170, 174, 176, 179, 186–87, 196, 201, 203–04, 211, 216, 219, 223, 226, 232, 239–41, 243–45, 247–53, 257–58, 262, 264–65
Reichenau, abbey of 113
Requiem masses, *see* Liturgical commemoration, Memorial masses
Reval (Tallinn) 19, 38–41, 92–95, 101, 103–08, 112, 115–18, 126, 130, 151–59, 161–67, 170–71, 173, 177, 179, 186–88, 192, 196–97, 199–200, 243–44, 249, 258–60
   Bishop of 38, 136, 162
   Black Heads, brotherhood of the 40, 154–56, 171–77, 179–83, 186, 197–98, 216, 244, 246–47, 253, 260–61, 264
      members 172–74, 180, 183, 186, 198, 246, 253, 261, 264
   Burghers 110, 180, 261
   Cistercian convent of St Michael 103, 105–07, 131, 259
      abbess 117–18
   City council 84, 94–95, 110, 112, 151, 153–56, 169, 187–92, 196–98, 243–44, 258, 260, 263
      city councillors 156, 161–62, 166, 168–69, 180, 186, 188–92, 196–98, 243, 253, 258, 263
      city councillors' pews in the churches 175, 189–90, 198
      Ratsmemoria 167, 169, 171, 186–87, 190, 197–98, 243, 263
   Dominican friary of St Catherine 40, 104–05, 107–10, 112, 175–76, 243
      church 94, 108, 110–12, 158, 172, 174–75, 179, 189–90, 196–98, 246, 264
         Altarpiece of the Virgin Mary 174, 179–82, 246–48, 264
      chantries 110, 130, 175, 190, 196, 246
      the Passion altarpiece 197
   friars 105, 107–08, 109–12, 130, 175, 190, 196, 259
   prior 111, 190
   reform 107, 109, 112, 175–76
   Great guild 40, 153–54, 156–61, 163, 165, 168–73, 179–80, 188, 197–98, 261–63
   Holy Spirit 94, 158–60, 164, 170, 189, 191–92, 240,
   Belfry 164, 170–71
   hospital 244
   Reformation 93–94, 107, 110, 112, 165, 170, 174, 176, 179, 187, 196, 239–40, 243–44, 247, 253, 264
   St Nicholas church 94, 107, 151, 153–54, 158–159, 175, 189, 240, 244
   Table guild 154, 157, 159–71, 196, 198, 244, 260–63
Rhineland 26, 54–55, 80
Riga 19, 38–41, 43–46, 48, 50, 52, 75, 82–86, 88–89, 92–102 *passim*, 103–07, 110–12, 115–20, 122–23, 125, 127, 131, 133–37, 139, 142–45, 148–50, 154–76 *passim*, 178, 180–86, 187–90, 192–94, 197–98, 199–237 *passim*, 239–54 *passim*, 255–264
   Archbishop of 19, 38, 41, 43–44, 46, 50, 52–53, 85–86, 97–98, 100–102, 111, 123, 133–37, 241–42, 255–56, 259–60
   vassals 105–06, 110
   Beer Carters, guild of the 118–20, 131, 200–201, 203–10, 213–17, 219, 221–28, 230–34, 236–37, 247–53, 262–63
      foundations 230, 262
      memorial donations 213–15, 217, 230, 232–33, 236, 252, 263
   Bishop of 38–39, 44–48

Black Heads, brotherhood of the 39, 154, 156, 171–78, 180–86, 197–98, 205, 211, 224, 234, 244–47, 249, 253, 260–62, 264
castle of the Teutonic Order 39, 122, 142–43, 149
    chapel of St Andrew 143–44
Cathedral 39, 44–48, 50, 52–53, 86, 95–102, 111, 133–39, 141, 143, 145–50, 189, 192–93, 212, 224, 240, 256, 259–60
    altar of Holy Cross 50, 137–38, 141, 260
    tomb of bishop Meinhard 44–50, 52, 135, 255–56
Cathedral chapter 43–44, 53, 75, 96, 98–102, 133–36, 139, 141, 144–50, 224, 255, 258–60
    dean of 44, 145, 148, 225
    provost of 44, 95, 97, 99–100, 102, 148, 225
Church of Riga *see* Church of Riga
Cistercian convent of St Mary Magdalene 39, 83–86, 88, 103, 105–06, 115–20, 131, 193, 240, 261
    abbess 117–19
    nuns 82–84, 105–06, 115–20, 131, 193–94, 205, 219, 225, 258–59, 262–63
City council 41, 188–90, 192–95, 197–98, 203, 221, 223, 229–30, 233–34, 240, 243, 251, 260–63
    city clerks 192
    city councillors 93, 118, 120, 168, 188–90, 192–95,223–27, 229–30, 232–33, 236–37, 240, 243, 249–50, 253, 258, 260, 262–63
    city councillors' pews in the churches 189–90, 197–98, 233–34
    Ratsmemoria 187, 190, 193–94, 197–98, 230, 243, 263
Corpus Christi guild 212, 222
Dockers guild 203, 209–210, 251
Dominican friary 39, 104, 107, 110–12, 193, 195

Dominican friary of St John 107
    friars 107, 111–12, 193–94, 240
    prior 110–11
Franciscan friary of St Catherine 39, 104, 175–76, 193,224
    church 172, 174, 176–78, 182, 184, 190, 212
        Black Heads chapel 177
        stained glass windows 177, 184
    friars 212, 240, 193–94, 212, 240
Great guild 39, 154–58, 160–61, 163, 165, 168, 177, 180, 183, 188, 197–98, 202, 226, 260–63
Hospital in *Ellerrbroke* 193
Hospital of St George 193
Hospital of St John 193
Porters
    guild of the 184, 200–01, 203–07, 209–30, 232–37, 240, 247, 249–53, 261–63
    foundations 211, 215–16, 228–30, 262
    memorial donations 210, 212–17, 228, 232–33, 236, 252, 263
priests 98–100, 105–06, 120, 156, 167, 176–77, 184–85, 190, 194–95, 209–12, 217, 223–27, 229, 231, 233–34, 240, 243, 245, 247–50, 262
Reformation 112, 158, 186, 201, 203–04, 211, 223, 226, 239–41, 244–45, 247–53, 264
St Jacob's (James) church 39, 119, 158, 189, 192–93, 210, 225, 230, 236, 240, 245, 248, 251–52
St Peter's church 39, 96, 158, 161, 164, 167–68, 176, 178, 182–86, 189–90, 192–96, 198, 209–13, 217, 224, 228–30, 233–37, 240, 245, 247–50, 252
    Beer Carters guild's altar 210, 224–25, 230, 235–37, 247–48

belfry 161, 164, 168, 195
Black Heads altar 172, 183–86, 234, 245–46
chantries 176, 185–86, 190, 194–95, 210–13, 217, 228, 230, 233–34, 237, 245, 248
Porters guild's altar 210–11, 213, 228–29, 233–35, 237, 247
priests 167, 176, 184–85, 190, 209, 211, 212, 217, 224, 229, 231, 240, 245
Table guild 154, 157, 159–70, 176, 193, 197–98, 260–63
Transport worker's guilds 199-237 *passim*, 247-52, 254, 260–62
Riga Missal, also *Missale Rigense* 137–38, 140–41, 150, 260
Roma (Gotland), Cistercian abbey of 117
Rome 38, 96–97, 100, 134–35, 176, 224
Ronneburg (Rauna) 77, 123, 125
Rostock 96, 168
Russian–Livonian war 241–43, 253

Saule, battle of 38, 53
Semigallians 35–36, 38, 59, 127, 199
Siegfried Lander von Spanheim, Master of the Livonian branch 82, 87–88
Silvester Stodewescher, archbishop of Riga 43, 50, 52, 97, 100, 135–37, 139–40, 144, 146–50, 230, 234, 259
Simon von der Borch, bishop of Reval 136–37
Sixtus IV, pope 137
Smolino, battle at 241–42, 253, 255
St George's night uprising 125, 131, 156, 259
Stefan Grube, archbishop of Riga 52, 137, 139
Sword Brethren, Order of 38, 53–54, 133

Testaments, *see* Last wills

Teutonic Order 19, 32, 36, 38, 41–43, 52–68, 70–73, 75–80, 82, 85–87, 89–90, 92–93, 95, 97, 101, 105, 115–17, 120–23, 125–31, 133–36, 142, 144–45, 147–50, 156, 162, 171, 185, 192, 241–42, 255–57, 259–60, 265
brethren 38, 54, 55–70, 72, 75–78, 80, 84–85, 87, 101, 111, 126–28, 131, 142, 146, 256–57
funerals 77, 80–81, 94
Grand Master 58–59, 71–72, 76, 78, 80–81, 84, 93–95, 97, 101, 116, 136, 142–44, 241
Livonian branch 32, 38, 41, 43, 54–60, 63, 67–69, 72–73, 75–77, 79–82, 84–89, 92, 101, 115, 123, 125–129, 131, 135, 137, 144–47, 149–50, 241, 243, 255–57, 260
commander of the branch's military forces (*Landmarschall*) 89–90, 257
Master of the Livonian branch 38, 52, 58–61, 65–66, 69, 73, 75–77, 79–89, 92–95, 101, 106, 119, 126–29, 134, 136–37, 141–50, 241–42, 256–59
Prussian branch 56, 60, 76, 93, 123, 241
Theoderic von Treiden, abbot of Dünamunde abbey, bishop of Estonia 121
Torches 184, 210, 219

Urban V, pope 47, 135
Üxkull (Ikšķile) 35, 44–46, 256

Vadstena, Birgittine abbey of 116
Valkena / Falkenau (Kärkna)
Cistercian abbey of 103, 106, 120, 129
abbot of 129
Vigils 76–77, 80, 84, 94, 100, 106–08, 110, 118, 157–59, 163–64, 167,

176–77, 182–86, 209–10, 213, 215, 217–18, 227, 230–33

Wenden (Cēsis) 87–88, 127, 149–50
   castle of the Teutonic Order 142, 149–150
Westphalia 36, 54–55, 80, 112, 121, 144, 220, 244

Wilhelm (Willekin) von Nindorf, Master of the Livonian branch 59, 69, 126–28
Wolmar (Valmiera) 145
Wolter von Plettenberg, Master of the Livonian branch 93, 119, 134, 149, 241